Psychology

An Introduction   Fourth Edition

Psychology

An Introduction   Fourth Edition

Jerome Kagan
Harvard University

Ernest Havemann

Harcourt Brace Jovanovich, Inc.

New York ▪ San Diego ▪ Chicago ▪ San Francisco ▪ Atlanta ▪ London ▪ Sydney ▪ Toronto

Acknowledgments and copyrights for textual material and for illustrations begin on page 587, which constitutes a continuation of the copyright page.

ISBN: 0-15-572625-0

Library of Congress Catalog Card Number: 79-90430

Printed in the United States of America

Figure illustrations by Azora Graphics, Inc.

Cover illustration by Mona Mark

Preface

Users of previous editions of *Psychology: An Introduction* will find that this fourth edition is in many ways a brand-new book. From the past it retains its basic approach, striving for brevity and equal attention to scientific rigor and students' needs for clarity and relevance. But the order in which topics are presented has been shifted, and individual chapters have been reorganized and substantially rewritten—in many cases almost in toto.

Many of the changes, of course, were dictated by new developments in research and theory, for the book can now draw on scores of important studies that were not available when the third edition was published. Much of the revision, however, is a response to two serious problems that have been reported to us by instructors in all kinds of colleges and universities.

The first is the problem of classroom and study time. *Psychology: An Introduction* has always been a short book, designed for one-semester or one-quarter classes where instructors are hard-pressed to do justice to all the materials traditionally regarded as essential to the introductory course. Nevertheless, many instructors have found it im-possible to cover the entire book. A survey of users of the previous edition, in both two-year and four-year schools, showed that about 70 percent omitted at least one chapter (not counting the Statistical Appendix) and sometimes more. They regretted the omissions but felt they had no alternative. Time simply ran out on them.

One reason is that the science has been expanding in exponential fashion. Many of the topics that concern psychologists today were unexplored only a few years ago, and much of their present knowledge was undiscovered. Thus instructors have far more to teach but no more time to teach it, and often actually less time than in the past. They (and the textbook writers who try to help them) face the difficult task of establishing priorities—deciding that this topic is so important that it absolutely must be presented; this one, regrettably, will have to wait.

The second problem is that enrollment in the introductory course has expanded more rapidly than the number of students who plan to make psychology a career. For many of today's students, the introductory course will be their only exposure to psychology. Instructors tell us that they feel a great sense of obligation to these students—an obligation best fulfilled by concentrating on information that is most useful in understanding everyday human behavior, with a minimum of the finer details and specialized vocabulary that psychologists use in their own thinking and research. At the same time, instructors do not want to neglect the needs of their prospective majors and graduate students. Today's typical instructor (if there is such a thing, and if our reports from the pluralistic world of the classroom are at all representative) strives to make the course interesting, useful, relevant—and yet scientifically sound and rigorous, a firm foundation on which future study can solidly rest.

*   *   *

This new edition represents our attempt to deal head-on with the two problems. The new treatment of how the brain, the rest of the nervous system, and the glands control human behavior is perhaps the best example. In the previous edition these materials were covered midway through the book. Numerous instructors asked us to move the chapter to the beginning, on the ground that it is impossible to understand human psychology without first knowing something about the biological structures on which it is based. But an almost equal number reported that this was a topic they omitted entirely —partly because of time pressures, partly because many students found the details and terminology difficult and irrelevant.

Should the biological basis of psychology be stressed or omitted? Here is an especially urgent example of the need for establishing priorities. Our solution is this: We have indeed moved our discussion of the mysteries and marvels of the brain and body (and the limits and breathtaking opportunities they create for human behavior) to become Chapter 2. But the chapter itself is brief and written in very basic terms, confined to the kind of general information that is absolutely essential for an understanding and appreciation of the human organ-

ism. Additional details are presented in a chapter postscript, which instructors may or may not assign depending on the available time and their own view of the priorities.

The device of a brief and general chapter, with additional details presented in a chapter postscript, has also been used in Chapter 7 on the senses— another topic that many instructors have felt compelled to omit in the past. On the matter of intelligence and testing, which has become Chapter 6, the device has been adopted for a somewhat different reason. Many instructors have concluded that the construction and standardization of tests do not concern the majority of students and are more properly and more easily taught in an advanced course. Therefore the chapter now concentrates on the nature of intelligence and the pros and cons of intelligence testing, with the science of test construction presented in an optional postscript.

A number of new topics suggested by instructors, as being of both scientific importance and practical value to students, have been added to the book. Prominent among them is a discussion in Chapter 10 of the manner in which people have been sex typed or socialized into acting masculine or feminine. There is also a greatly enlarged section on human sexual attitudes and behavior (Chapter 9). Since some users will not consider these topics of high priority in the introductory course, however, they are presented as chapter postscripts—as are a number of other matters that instructors may or may not wish to include.

*   *   *

Those familiar with the previous edition will find many other changes in organization and presentation—all designed to aid instructors in establishing priorities and to provide greater flexibility in presenting the maximum amount of important information within the time limits of the course. In one major change, the materials on learning and memory have been reorganized and rewritten in an effort to make clear to students at the very start, before any details of classical and operant conditioning are presented, why these topics are essential to an understanding of human behavior. The relevance of learning experiments to real-life concerns is further apparent from recent findings about learned helplessness and medical applications of biofeedback (both now covered in considerably expanded form in Chapter 3).

Devoting a separate Chapter 4 to memory has enabled us to present a full discussion of the levels-of-processing theory, a major new development in psychology's understanding of how long-term memories are established. Since deep processing now appears to be the key to the successful learning and remembering of most kinds of information of greatest human concern, it has made obsolete many of the topics formerly of concern in the management of learning. Thus our discussion of efficiency in learning, which was a full chapter in the previous edition, has been condensed to eliminate materials that are no longer regarded as important and to present only those that continue to have the greatest practical value to students. This discussion is now a postscript to Chapter 4.

Also new in this edition is a series of boxed inserts, scattered throughout, called *Psychology and Society*. These boxes attempt to show how psychological findings pertain to some of today's social issues—for example, the relevance of split-brain experiments to the goals and confusions of our society (page 55) and of our knowledge of learned helplessness to failure of the educational system (page 116).

*   *   *

To make room for these additions and the new psychological findings of the last four years, without substantially affecting the length of the book, we have attempted throughout to simplify and condense wherever possible—though without eliminating anything that is essential to basic scientific knowledge. In this effort we have had invaluable help from two types of reviewers cited in the list of acknowledgments. The introductory-course instructors have advised us on classroom needs— what is vitally important to students, what is extraneous or unnecessarily detailed. The specialists in each of the fields covered in the book have advised us on scientific basics and accuracy.

The two groups of consultants have not only helped but indeed forced us to rethink our own priorities. Spurred by one set of reviewers, we have constantly asked ourselves: Is this really essential to students? Is it the kind of information that will actually get off the printed page and into the minds of the students? Does it deserve some of those precious and all-too-brief moments of time? Spurred by the other set of reviewers, we have asked: Is this a topic that can be explained adequately within the limitations of space? Is it sound and scientific or is it mere "pop psychology"? Does the discussion reflect today's thinking among specialists in the field? Is it accurate? These are the questions. The book itself will reveal how well we have been able to answer them.

In addition to our reviewers, we are especially indebted to Everett M. Sims, who was our constant advisor and edited the manuscript with skill and creativity.

Jerome Kagan
Ernest Havemann

Acknowledgments

Classroom consultants

The following people, who have been teaching the introductory course, provided us with many helpful suggestions on priorities, content, organization, and presentation:

Leonore Loeb Adler, The College of Staten Island, CUNY
Mary J. Allen, California State College
J. R. Arneson, South Dakota School of Mines & Technology
Heesoon Aust, Centralia College
Vergie Lee Behrens, Scottsdale Community College
Otto A. Berliner, SUNY, Alfred State College
James Bickley, Pasadena City College
Jack Blakemore, Monterey Peninsula College
Sue Bowen, Cleveland State Community College
James Brandt, Minot State College
Myron Brender, Kingsborough Community College, CUNY
James A. Briley, Jefferson State Junior College
Thomas Brothen, University of Minnesota
Dean Brysen, South Dakota School of Mines & Technology
Patrick Butler, San Jose City College
Susie C. Campbell, Davidson County Community College
W. John Cannon, Columbia Union College
Michael Ceddia, Massachusetts Bay Community College

Parnell W. Cephus, Jefferson State Junior College
Louis G. Cesaratto, Ulster County Community College
Carol E. Chandler, McHenry County College
Garvin Chastain, Boise State University
William Coggan, Massasoit Community College
David Stewart-Cohen, California State College
Francis B. Colavita, University of Pittsburgh
Betty T. Conover, Miami-Dade Community College
Alice M. Crichlow, Massasoit Community College
Anne Louise Dailey, Community College of Allegheny County
Anne G. English, University of Toledo
Elliot E. Entin, Ohio University
Paul E. Finn, Saint Anselm's College
Bess Fleckman, Miami-Dade Community College, North Campus
B. L. Garrett, DePauw University
Robert Gibson, Centralia College
Jon Gosser, Delta College
Mary Hamilton, Highline Community College
Judith Roes Hammerle, Adrian College
Gordon Hammerle, Adrian College
James M. Hammond, Columbia Union College
Francis J. Hanrahan, Hudson Valley Community College
W. Bruce Haslam, Weber State College
Roy K. Heintz, California State University, Long Beach
Judy Hensley, Otero Junior College
Faunie Hewlett, Cleveland State Community College
Annette Hiedemann, West Virginia Wesleyan College
Robert R. Higgins, Oakland Community College
John E. Hoffman, East Los Angeles College

Richard D. Honey, Transylvania University
Philip Howard, Enterprise State Junior College
Michael Hughmanick, West Valley College
Morton Isaacs, Rochester Institute of Technology
Charles W. Johnson, University of Evansville
James L. Johnston, Madison Area Technical College
Richard Kellogg, SUNY, Agricultural & Technical College
Kenneth A. Koenigshofer, Chaffey College
Charlton R. Lee, Cypress College
Edward E. Leech, Cleveland State Community College
Tim Lehmann, Valencia Community College
Diane Leroi, College of San Mateo
Harold List, Massachusetts Bay Community College
Cameron Marshman, Rio Hondo College
William A. Marzano, Illinois Valley Community College
Ann B. McNeer, Polk Community College
Douglas Miller, Miami University
Donald H. Millikan, San Diego Mesa College
Elizabeth Morelli, Henry Ford Community College
C. Thomas Musgrave, Weber State College
Dennis L. Nagi, Hudson Valley Community College
Edward F. O'Day, San Diego State University
Dan E. Perkins, Richland College
F. A. Perry, Jr., Erie Community College
David W. Prull, Community College of the Finger Lakes
David L. Quinby, Youngstown State University
Bob Rainey, Florida Junior College
Robert L. Ramlet, Elgin Community College
Mary Renfer, Mt. View College
O. L. Riner, Gulf Coast Community College
Carol Roberts, San Diego Mesa College
John C. Roehr, Hudson Valley Community College
Steve Rosengarten, Middlesex County College
Frank M. Rosenkrans, III, Eastern Washington University
Joel Rosevelt, Golden West College
Douglas A. Ross, Indiana University of Pennsylvania
Alva Sachs, College of San Mateo
Ganus Scarborough Jr., Jefferson State Junior College
Gary Schaumberg, Cerritos College
Jerome Seidman, Montclair State College
Michael B. Sewall, Mohawk Valley Community College
Ruth B. Shapiro, John Jay College
Jack P. Shilkret, Ann Arundel Community College
Charlotte Simon, Montgomery College
Lora S. Simon, Holyoke Community College
Ronald E. Siry, University of Cincinnati
David Skinner, Valencia Community College
Joseph L. Slosser, Chemereta Community College

Leo V. Soriano, Winona State University
Donovan Swanson, El Camino College
Jerome D. Tietz, Santa Barbara City College
William K. Trinkaus, South Connecticut State College
Luis Vazquez, Cleveland State College
Jerry L. Vogt, Stanford University School of Medicine
Albert C. Widhalm, Kankakee Community College
Michael Witmer, Skagit Valley College
Sherman Yen, Essex Community College

Reviewers

We have also had the benefit of advice from scholars who provided us with critiques of individual chapters. Some of the following reviewed the third edition chapters and provided us with suggestions for additional new materials. Some reviewed preliminary drafts of the new chapters, and some did both. The authors, of course, take full responsibility for any defects that may nonetheless appear.

John Altrocchi, University of Nevada
Allen E. Bergin, Brigham Young University
Ellen S. Berscheid, University of Minnesota
Thomas J. Bouchard, Jr., University of Minnesota
Eve V. Clark, Stanford University
Herbert H. Clark, Stanford University
Charles Clifton, University of Massachusetts
W. Andrew Collins, University of Minnesota
Kenneth J. Gergen, Swarthmore College
Julian Hochberg, Columbia University
Lloyd Kaufman, New York University
Walter Kintsch, University of Colorado
Eleanor E. Maccoby, Stanford University
Allan F. Mirsky, Boston University Medical Center
Barry Schwartz, Swarthmore College
Dan Slobin, University of California at Berkeley
Donald G. Stein, Clark University
Elliot S. Valenstein, University of Michigan

We also thank Joel Havemann, Ruth Havemann, Joan Lawson, Doris Simpson, Mark Szpack, and members of our publisher's staff, who performed the near miracle of swiftly turning manuscript pages into what we hope users will agree is a most attractive book.

Contents

Part one
What is psychology?

Part two
How we learn
and remember

Chapter three
The basics of learning
89

Chapter four
Memory
and how to improve it
129

Part three
Language, thinking, intelligence

Chapter five
Language and cognition
171

Chapter six
Intelligence:
the problem of defining and measuring it
207

Part four
Knowing what
goes on in the world:
the senses and perception

Part five
Emotions and motives

Part six
Human personality: normal and abnormal

Chapter eleven
Anxiety, stress, and coping
405

Chapter twelve
Personality and psychotherapy
441

Part seven
Growing up and living with other people

Chapter thirteen
Developmental psychology: from infant to adult
475

Chapter fourteen
Social psychology
513

Part one
What is
psychology?

More than any other subject you are ever likely to study, psychology is about you. It attempts to answer the kinds of questions you have doubtless asked about yourself—questions that also must have puzzled your ancestors for countless generations.

Here you are, starting to read this book. Strangely, you are very much like all people all over the world—yet there is no one exactly like you. You are a unique individual, with your own special abilities and weaknesses, your own personality, your own likes and dislikes, your own feelings of joy or depression or fear.

Were you born that way or did you get that way (and if so, how)? Are you the master of your fate or a helpless pawn of your environment? Can you change if you want to?

What about humanity in general? Are we human beings just another form of animal life, closely related to the beasts of the jungle and especially to the apes? Or do we possess some special quality that lifts us above all other living creatures? What accounts for the differences within the human species? Why are some people so quick to learn, others so slow? Why are some people generally cheerful, others generally glum; some hot-tempered, others easy going? Why are some people driven to become world leaders, others content to listen to music and contemplate the beauties of nature? Why do some people appear to be perfectly "normal" while others behave in ways that are labeled strange or neurotic or even "crazy"?

Until very recently people who tried to grapple with such questions had to rely on personal opinion and guesswork. Now psychology approaches the questions through the rigorous methods of scientific inquiry. Psychologists do not pretend to have all the answers—for human behavior is so complex that it may forever defy any full analysis. But they do have some of the answers and clues to many others, and they are making new discoveries almost every day.

Psychology explores what has happened to you not just since the day you were born but even earlier—for it is true that the very moment of conception established that you would become more or less the person you are. Psychologists have shown that all of us are influenced in many important ways by the traits we inherited from our ancestors—not only in such matters as skin color and body build but also in ability to learn and in tendencies to be calm or highly emotional, outgoing or introverted, sexually active or sexually passive.

But psychology also knows that heredity is not the entire story, perhaps not even the most important part. You were not destined at birth to become, in the words of the children's rhyme, "doctor, lawyer, beggarman, thief"—or anything else. From the moment of birth you began to learn to live with your own particular inherited traits, to make the most of them (or perhaps not), to modify and change some of them, and to get along with your fellow human beings. The learning process, which is far more complicated and far-reaching than you have probably ever imagined, is one of psychology's chief concerns. So is the related matter of how you have developed from a helpless baby to what you are today—and indeed of how people develop throughout their lifetimes, in middle age and old age.

If a single phrase can be said to summarize this relatively new science, that phrase might be: *psychology is the study of what makes you tick.* When you finish this course you will know more about this important matter than anybody in the world did a hundred years ago—even the most famous scholars, thinkers, and philosophers.

Chapter 1 of the book discusses "The Aims and Methods of Psychology," including its study of the way heredity operates and helps determine our lives. Chapter 2, "Body and Brain: The Physical Underpinning of Psychology," describes the biological equipment that sets limits on human behavior—but also makes possible the variety and richness of our lives.

Outline

Chapter one

The aims and methods of psychology

Have you read the introduction to this section of the book on pages 2–3? If not, you will find it helpful to turn back and look at it now before starting the chapter. The book is divided into seven parts, each preceded by an introduction that serves as a guide to what will be found in the section. These introductory discussions will tell you what to expect—and how each part of the book relates to the entire field of psychology and the study of human behavior.

Did you wake up this morning to the sound of an alarm clock? If so, you had your day's first experience with the subject matter of psychology. In prescientific days, no one knew how we hear sounds or even how to define a sound. Scholars used to argue endlessly over the question: If a tree falls in a lonely forest, where there is no one to listen, does it make a sound? (Since psychologists now know that a sound is ripples of vibration in the air—which may or may not strike a human eardrum and thus produce the sensation of hearing—the question has been solved.)

Were you hungry when you woke? If so, that was your second experience with the subject matter of this book. Only in recent years have psychologists and biologists acquired any solid knowledge of the reasons we become hungry and thirsty.

Has anything happened in the course of the day to make you happy, angry, or anxious—and, if so, did you notice such physical signs of emotion as a pounding heart or butterflies in the stomach? (Psychology has much to say about emotions and the way brain and body combine to produce them.) Did you give any thought to your ambitions for the future? (Motives such as ambition—and thinking itself—are prominent topics in psychology.) Did you use your vocal cords to speak? (Language is a complex human achievement about which psychology has made many fascinating discoveries.) Did you interact with other human beings, with happy or embarrassing results? (Social relationships are also a prime field of inquiry.)

At the moment, as you read this book, you are engaged in the process of learning. (Some of psychology's most important findings deal with how we learn, remember, and sometimes fail to remember.) And so it will go the rest of the day. Up to and including the moment you fall asleep (as you do because of chemical changes in the brain and body), you will be constantly engaged in activities that are the concern of psychologists and of this book.

From superstition to science

The study of human behavior, presumably, dates back to the very origins of the human race. We can assume, from what we know about some of the primitive tribes that still live today in isolation from modern civilization, that our early ancestors were so awed by human experience that they could explain it only in terms of the supernatural. They looked not within themselves but out into the vague realm of the occult. They decided that they sometimes were blessed by "good spirits" that brought them health and luck in the hunt, and sometimes were plagued by "evil spirits" that brought sickness and misfortune. Our ancestors probably considered themselves at the mercy of such outside influences rather than responsible for their own behavior. It must have been a long time, for example, before anybody suspected that sexual intercourse had anything to do with the birth of a baby nine months later.

By the time of the ancient Greeks, the study of human behavior had turned inward to speculation about the relationship between body and mind, which was thought to be a part of the soul. The science of mathematics was reaching great heights, and the Greek philosophers marveled that the human mind could create the world of mathematics—a world that was strictly imaginary and theoretical, yet much more logical and "pure" than the real world of eating, sleeping, physical illness, and death. The Greek physicians, who had learned a great deal about the human body, sought physical

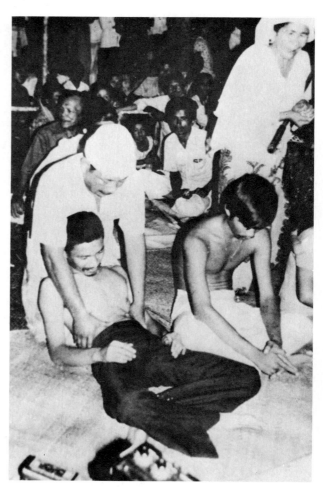

A Malaysian "physician" practices medicine not with antibiotics but by putting his patient into a trance believed to help drive sickness away.

In Sri Lanka, an island nation off the tip of India, an oracle foretells from lines in the palm what fate has in store.

explanations of behavior. Why were some people so melancholy? Doubtless, the physicians decided, because of an excess of black bile in their systems. Why were others so optimistic, happy, and warm-hearted? Doubtless because of a rich flow of blood.

The Greeks, though they were looking in the right direction, were handicapped by a lack of scientific methods and instruments. And they did not entirely abandon the idea that human behavior is dictated by forces beyond human control. Their oracles, notably the Delphic Oracle, brought them messages from the gods, predicting what fate had in store for them.

Indeed all societies seem to have had soothsayers and witch doctors to whom they looked for guidance. We still have them today. Almost every city has its fortune tellers, who profess to read the future in tea leaves, the lines of the palm, or the turn of a card. Astrology is a popular hobby. There are some people who will not make a move without first consulting their horoscopes to learn whether this is a good or bad day for a Pisces (or Libra or Taurus) to start a new venture, take a trip, or go to a party.

Psychology takes a totally different approach. It does not believe that our behavior is determined in any way by the position of the stars at our birth. True, most psychologists hold that our lives are in some ways predetermined at birth—but by workings of heredity that have a scientific explanation, not by the mysterious influence of some star billions of miles away. Psychologists do not seek the revelations of oracles. They are not content to describe human behavior as some past philosopher, however brilliant, may have imagined it to be. They do not necessarily accept the adages of previous generations, no matter how commonsensical those adages may seem. (Many of the adages, as a

A modern-day American fortune teller sets up shop outside a busy parking lot.

matter of fact, are mutually contradictory. Which is true: "A bird in the hand is worth two in the bush" or "Nothing ventured, nothing gained"?)

Psychology and other sciences

Psychology—which can be defined as *the systematic study of behavior and all the factors that influence behavior*—takes the scientific approach. It is skeptical and demands proof. It is based on controlled experiments and on observations made with the greatest possible precision and objectivity (meaning freedom from personal prejudices or preconceived notions).

Psychology is a relatively new science, founded only a little more than a century ago. Its existence would have been impossible without the spirit of disciplined inquiry that produced the older physical sciences, such as physics and chemistry. Indeed many of its findings rest on the work of other sciences. We could not know how our senses of hearing and vision operate were it not for the physicists' knowledge of sound waves and light waves, about which the ancient Greeks could only speculate. Chemistry has helped identify the substances that flash messages through our nervous system (from sense organs to brain and from brain to muscles) and the glandular secretions that flow through our blood stream and play an important role in our emotions. Physiology has provided the basis for understanding the glands and the nervous system—especially the intricate workings of the brain.

The lines that separate the various sciences are vague and somewhat arbitrary. Indeed human knowledge is a single great entity—a united, mass effort to comprehend our universe and our relationship to it. Thus many psychologists, as they try to fathom the secrets of behavior, do research that is scarcely distinguishable from the work of their colleagues in the older sciences. They analyze the physical nature of our world, to determine its effect on our sense organs. They look for new chemicals that may influence the operation of our nervous system and our emotions. They seek further information about the structure and functioning of our body and brain. They are interested in physics, chemistry, physiology, medicine, neurosurgery, and any other field of human knowledge that may contribute to our understanding of why we behave as we do.

Most psychologists, however, deal more directly with human behavior. For example, a group of psychologists might become interested in whether the use of marijuana affects the ability to drive an automobile. Instead of seeking opinions from law enforcement officials, proponents of legalizing marijuana, and opponents of marijuana use (all of whom would have their own prejudices), the psychologists would seek to find out for themselves. They might round up some willing subjects and test them on a machine that simulates actual driving conditions—once before using marijuana and again afterward. Do students who make all A's in college do better in their jobs after college than C students? Psychologists might find some all-A and some all-C students, keep track of them, and note how well they do in their later lives.

The goals of psychology

In the study of behavior and the factors that influence it, psychology has two goals: *1) to understand behavior* and *2) to predict behavior*. Indeed understanding and predicting are the goals of all sciences. Chemists, for example, have sought from the beginning to understand why wood burns and gold does not—and to be able to predict what will happen when a chemical substance is subjected to flame or combined with another chemical in a test tube. Psychologists seek, among other things, to understand why individuals behave as they do in a classroom or in social situations—and to predict what would happen if certain changes were made in the school or social environment.

Most scientists seek not only to understand and predict events but to control them as well. Chemists want to be able to control the substances they deal with so that they can produce new chemicals to serve useful new purposes, such as the various synthetics now used in clothing and automobiles.

"To your mental health."

Drawing by Fradan; © 1976
The New Yorker Magazine, Inc.

To a certain extent, psychologists too look for ways of controlling human behavior. This is especially true of those who devote their careers to helping people overcome mental and emotional problems. They want to control the behavior of the people who consult them by trying to relieve an unreasonable fear of going out in public, an inability to establish satisfactory sexual relationships, or alcohol addiction.

But dealing with human beings is far different from mixing chemicals in a test tube. The possibility of controlling human behavior raises thorny questions of moral and social policy, as is discussed in the box on Psychology and Society on page 10. Therefore psychologists have mixed feelings about whether control of behavior should or should not be considered a third goal of the science. Some psychologists have argued that human behavior is always under some kind of control—by the ways in which parents rear their children, the school system, the rewards and punishments provided in the business world, and the nation's laws—and that it would be better to have the control exercised in a scientific fashion by scientists dedicated to improv-

Control of human behavior: the ethical issues

Somewhere at this very moment, we can safely assume, a Ms. X is paying her first visit to the office of a psychologist who conducts a private practice for troubled people. She may be seeking help for any one of numerous problems. Perhaps she is bothered by a speech defect such as stuttering. Perhaps she is afraid to get on an elevator. Perhaps she is so beset by anxieties and inability to concentrate on her work that she fears she is about to have what is commonly called a "nervous breakdown."

Ms. X's visit to the psychologist does not pose any issues of ethics or social policy. She *wants* help. She wants her behavior to change in ways that will make her more comfortable and self-fulfilled. The psychologist, in trying to change her behavior, is performing a service that will be of unquestioned value to her—and that will benefit society as a whole by making her a happier and more effective member.

But there are other situations where the use of psychological knowledge to control human behavior raises grave questions. Suppose a mother and father arrive at the psychologist's office with their 16-year-old son, who has shown tendencies toward homosexuality. The parents want the boy's behavior changed, to redirect him along heterosexual lines. The psychologist knows some techniques that have been used to eliminate homosexual preferences. Though these techniques are not always successful, they sometimes work and might do so in this instance. However, on talking privately to the son, the psychologist learns that the boy is perfectly content with his present feelings and behavior. He does not want to change.

What should the psychologist do? What are the psychologist's moral obligations to the boy, the parents, and society as a whole?

Similar complications may arise in the administration of public institutions. The technique called behavior modification, based on psychology's study of the learning process, has been found extremely effective in mental hospitals and homes for retarded children. By manipulating such rewards as candy and television privileges, psychologists can induce the residents of these institutions to keep themselves clean and neatly dressed and display orderly eating habits. Behavior modification makes it possible to improve living conditions and to run the institutions more efficiently.

In the case of the mentally disturbed or retarded, behavior modification does not ordinarily pose any ethical questions. Presumably it benefits both patients and society. But what about using such techniques in prisons? They may succeed in making inmates more docile and easier to deal with—but what are the long-term effects on the ability of prisoners, once they finish their terms, to function as independent, self-reliant members of society, responsible for their own behavior?

The questions raised by psychology's discovery of techniques that can be used to control behavior are moral rather than scientific. They are outside the realm of psychology, depending instead on individual and community attitudes on what is ethical and what is unethical. Psychologists can only seek knowledge—then let society decide how, if at all, their findings should be applied. They are in somewhat the same position as the physicists whose search for truth led to the discovery of nuclear fission—which society can use to create either useful energy or destruction.

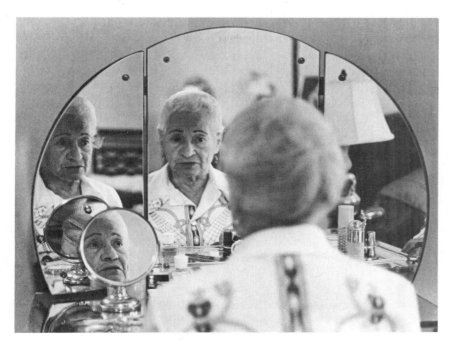

The mirrors reflect some of the many faces of human personality—an aspect of psychology that will be discussed in Chapters 11 and 12.

ing the human condition (1).* Most psychologists, however, shun the awful responsibility—and the dangers of abuse—inherent in any wide-scale efforts to manipulate human behavior.

What psychologists do

Because human behavior takes so many forms, the interests of psychologists range far and wide. One indication of the scope of their activities is the table of contents of this book. Some psychologists specialize in the study of how the human body and brain help determine behavior, which is the topic of

*The numbers in parentheses, which you will find throughout the book, are keyed to a chapter-by-chapter list of references (beginning on page 587) to the scientific publications that are the sources of information. This method of referring to sources is designed to prevent interruptions to the flow of the text and make the book easier to read and study.

Chapter 2. Others explore learning (Chapter 3), memory (Chapter 4), language and thinking (Chapter 5), and human intelligence (Chapter 6). And so on through the rest of the book, including the way we perceive the world, our emotions and motives, and the many-sided field of human personality, including distortions that result in abnormal behavior. Developmental psychologists study the ways in which infants grow physically and psychologically into adults. Social psychologists explore the ways in which our behavior is influenced by relationships with other people (the topic of the final chapter).

Many psychologists are concerned only with *pure science*—that is, knowledge for the sake of knowledge. They seek this knowledge in any way they can, using methods that will be described a little later. They often study the behavior not only of human beings but also of other living creatures.

With the help of a marriage counselor, this wife and husband seek to improve their relationship.

Indeed one flourishing branch of the science is *comparative psychology,* which is the study of lower organisms to discover similarities and differences between human beings and other animals. (*Organism* means any living creature.) Comparative psychologists can perform many experiments with lower organisms that it would be clearly unethical to attempt with human beings. One example is the removal of parts of the brain, a procedure that has shed considerable light on the influence of various brain structures on behavior. Another is the study of the effect of punishment on learning, which has produced results with important implications for human conduct.

Other psychologists are chiefly interested in *applied science*—the use of psychological knowledge to carry on society's everyday tasks, tackle its problems, and improve the quality of life. Applications of psychology have changed our world more than most people realize. Moreover, applied psychologists have produced a great deal of new knowledge that might never have been discovered in an experimental laboratory sealed off from society.

Clinical psychology and counseling

The largest single group of psychologists in the United States are engaged in applying their knowledge to help people solve the various problems that trouble so many in our society from time to time—everything from deciding on a suitable line of work to coping with crippling anxieties and sexual maladjustments. Of all professionally trained psychologists in the nation, nearly half are in this particular field of applied psychology (2).

Some members of this group practice *counseling,* which is assistance to people who need guidance on such temporary problems as difficulties in school

1-1

The first psychoanalyst's couch
It was in this room, on this couch, that psychoanalysis began. The photograph was made in the office of Sigmund Freud about 1895.

or choice of a vocation. In their search for the best solution, counselors often administer tests that have been developed by psychology, for everything from general intelligence to aptitude for specific tasks. One of psychology's most important findings, as you will see in Chapter 6, is that people are usually very good at doing some things but only mediocre to poor at others—and one secret of success, in both school and jobs, is to take advantage of your own particular strengths. Psychological counselors attempt to discover and encourage these strengths.

Some counselors specialize in helping married couples overcome difficulties that are caused not by deep-seated personality problems but by poor communication or inability to agree on financial or recreational priorities. These marriage counselors sometimes work with individual couples, sometimes with groups.

Clinical psychology is the diagnosis and treatment of psychological disorders of a more pervasive nature—all the symptoms that are popularly labeled "neurotic." Clinical psychologists, like marriage counselors, sometimes work with individuals, sometimes with groups. They use the technique called *psychotherapy*—or treatment through discussing problems, trying to get at the root of them, and modifying attitudes, emotional responses, and behavior.

In the early days of the science, psychologists had only a minor interest in psychotherapy. Those who did eventually begin to try to help people suffering from behavior disturbances usually adopted the theories and methods of Sigmund Freud—the famous Austrian physician and neurologist who developed the treatment called *psychoanalysis,* in which patients lay on a couch (see Figure 1-1) and let their thoughts roam as they talked

1-2

The psychoanalyst's couch updated: a modern encounter group

A new and currently popular form of treatment for personality disorders—or of attempts to strive for greater self-expression—is the encounter group.

about themselves and what was troubling them.

Today there are many forms of psychotherapy, most of them devised not by physicians but by clinical psychologists. Among them are encounter groups (see Figure 1-2), behavior modification, transactional therapy, and many others. Indeed clinical psychologists are constantly developing new techniques of psychotherapy as they try to cope with the special problems of the individuals they are trying to help. (They prefer to call these people clients rather than patients.)

The relative merits of the various techniques are a matter of debate. Some psychologists believe that the effectiveness of psychotherapy depends on the specific form of treatment. Others believe that the type of therapy is relatively unimportant. They feel that what actually counts is the relationship between the therapist and the client—that is, the sense of kinship, respect, and trust that the client has toward the therapist. This issue, and the evidence on both sides, will be discussed in Chapter 12.

Community and environmental psychology

In attempting to apply psychological findings to improve the quality of life, some psychologists have taken a different approach. Instead of concentrating on the individual, they have decided to look at the social environment in which individual problems arise. Do children have trouble adjusting to the school curriculum and taking advantage of its opportunities? Then perhaps we should change the way we operate our schools. Do adults have trouble getting along in the community? Then perhaps we should change the way the community operates. Those who take this approach are called *community psychologists,* or sometimes specialists in *community mental health.*

Other members of the profession share today's widespread interest in ecological problems, such as smog, water pollution, noise, and the overcrowding of urban areas. They seek to determine how these byproducts of our industrial society (see Figure 1-3) affect not only our physical health but

1-3 Some concerns of environmental psychologists

What are the effects on human behavior of such industrial byproducts as accumulations of waste, water pollution, the noise of airplanes, and air pollution? Environmental psychologists study these phenomena (as the man in the white jacket is measuring air quality) and their influence on physical and mental health.

also our psychological well-being. This branch of the science is called *environmental psychology,* and its ultimate aim is to balance the needs of an industrial society (for fuel, energy, transportation, and housing) against the maintenance of an environment that preserves the balance of nature and enables humanity and other organisms to continue to thrive.

Psychology in schools and industry

Many psychologists work in schools, not only as counselors to individual pupils but also in evaluating teaching methods, the organization of the curriculum, and textbooks and educational films. These *school psychologists* rely heavily on psychology's findings about the principles of learning. In some colleges they have developed a special course in the applied psychology of learning intended to help students do better in their classes.

Industrial psychologists, who work in business and manufacturing organizations, have discovered many facts about worker fatigue, working hours, rest periods, and employee morale. They help select and train employees, sometimes with training devices they have devised to help people learn specific skills. They also design equipment and machinery that are efficient and easy to operate because they fit the actual size, strength, and capabilities of the people who use them.

Public opinion surveys

Another area in which psychologists are active is the study of public opinion, as typified by the well-known Gallup Poll. Scientific methods of sampling and analysis have made it possible to show how all

"That's the worst set of opinions I've heard in my entire life."

Drawing by Weber; © 1975
The New Yorker Maagazine, Inc.

the people in the United States are divided on any controversial issue, within a few percentage points of possible error, by polling a mere 1,500 or so. (The techniques are discussed in the Appendix on Psychological Statistics.)

Public opinion surveys are a valuable contribution to the democratic process because they provide an accurate picture of how citizens actually feel about such issues as taxation, defense expenditures, foreign policy, abortion, and laws regulating sexual conduct and the use of drugs. Before such information was available, there was no accurate way to gauge public opinion—and often small but vociferous minorities, by waging intense publicity campaigns, were able to convince politicians that they represented the majority view. Now many Congressmen and other political leaders base their votes on the will of the majority (which is often unorganized and silent) as expressed in the polls.

Some well-known, though less important, uses of public opinion surveys include predictions of election results and the Nielsen ratings of the popularity of television shows. Business firms use surveys to measure public response to new products and to sales and advertising campaigns.

The woman above is applying some of the techniques of psychology in a shopping center survey of opinion.

The methods of psychology

In any science, the methods of investigation depend largely on the subject matter. Chemistry, dealing with substances that can be seen, felt, tasted, and manipulated, uses very direct methods. The chemist can simply put two substances together in a test tube, see what happens, and measure and analyze the result. Astronomy has to use more indirect methods. It cannot in any way manipulate the stars and planets. It must be content to observe them through telescopes or through the eyes of cameras and television equipment sent on space capsules to Venus and Mars.

Because behavior takes such a wide variety of forms, psychologists have had to improvise. No single method can be applied to all the activities that interest the science. Therefore psychologists

have had to adopt a number of different ways of studying their subject matter—and they are constantly seeking new ways. The most prominent methods of study now in use are described in this section of the chapter.

Observation

In many cases, psychologists do what astronomers do—that is, observe events pertinent to the science, such as the actual behavior of people in various kinds of social situations. To what extent, for example, is the way we behave toward other people dictated by how wealthy or important we think they are? One clue was found in a study in which psychologists observed how motorists behaved toward another driver who was slow to start and held up traffic when the light changed from red to green. If the offending driver was in an old rattletrap, it was found that the motorist behind was quick to honk in protest. If the slow-moving driver was in a shiny new luxury car, other motorists were much more patient (3).

In a sense all human beings constantly use the technique of observation. Everybody observes the behavior of other people and draws some conclusions from this behavior. If we note that a woman student rarely speaks up in class and blushes easily in social situations, we conclude that she is shy, and we treat her accordingly. (We may try to put her at ease, or, if we feel so inclined, we may enjoy embarrassing her and making her squirm.) Psychologists make their observations in a more disci-

plined fashion. They try to describe behavior objectively and exactly, and they are loath to jump to conclusions about the motives behind it.

In studying behavior through observation, psychologists usually try to remain aloof from what is going on in order to avoid influencing events in any way. They practice what is called *naturalistic observation,* in which they try to be as inconspicuous and anonymous as possible, lest their very presence affect the behavior they are studying. Sometimes they even arrange to be unseen, as illustrated in Figure 1-4. Some of our most valuable knowledge about the behavior of infants and the way they develop has come from observers who used this method. The famous Masters and Johnson findings on sexual response were obtained in part in this manner (4).

At other times, psychologists engage in *partici-*

1-4

An invisible observer studies child behavior

Unseen behind a one-way mirror, an investigator uses the method of naturalistic observation to study a child at play. To the observer outside the room, the wall panel looks like a sheet of clear glass. To the child inside, it looks like a mirror.

1-5 A Kinsey interview

Alfred Kinsey conducts one of the nearly 8,000 interviews on which he based his monumental book *Sexual Behavior in the Human Female.*

pant observation. They take an active part in a social situation—sometimes deliberately play-acting to see how other people behave toward someone who seems unusually withdrawn or hostile. Or they may participate in an encounter group to study their own as well as other people's reactions.

Interviews and case histories

Another way to discover how people behave and feel is to ask them—and therefore psychologists often use the *interview method,* questioning subjects in depth about their life experiences. Perhaps the best-known studies made through interviews were those of Alfred Kinsey, who became interested in human sexual behavior when some of his students

at Indiana University asked him for advice. When he went to the university library for information, he found many books of opinion about sexual behavior but almost none that shed any light on the kind and frequency of sexual experiences men and women actually had in real life. So Kinsey determined to find out, and the only possible way seemed to be to interview as many men and women as he could and ask them about their sexual feelings and experiences from childhood on, as he is shown doing in Figure 1-5. His well-known reports on male and female sexual behavior were the result (5, 6). Kinsey's findings are discussed in Chapter 9.

A special application of the interview method is the *case history,* in which many years of a person's life are reconstructed to show how various behavior patterns have developed. Case histories are particularly useful in revealing the origins of abnormal behavior. Indeed some forms of psychotherapy rely on building up a long and detailed case history as an aid to understanding and correcting the client's problems.

Questionnaires

Closely related to the interview is the *questionnaire,* which is especially useful in gathering information quickly from large numbers of people. A questionnaire is a set of written questions that can be answered easily, usually with a checkmark. To produce accurate results, a questionnaire must be worded with extreme care. Indeed the creation of a reliable questionnaire is a fine art, for the slightest change in the way the questions are worded may completely distort the results.

Questionnaires and interviews are sometimes challenged on the ground that people may not respond truthfully. Kinsey's work, for example, has been attacked by some critics who doubt that people would be honest about their sexual behavior. But experienced investigators have many ways of spotting people who are lying or exaggerating. Perhaps interviews and questionnaires do not always reveal the complete truth. When carefully planned and conducted, however, they can be extremely useful. They are the basis of surveys of public opinion and many other psychological applications and investigations.

Tests and measurements

Among the oldest tools of psychology are the tests it has developed for many human characteristics, abilities, and achievements. You have probably taken a number of such tests—for example, the Scholastic Aptitude Tests or SAT, which are a form of intelligence test, or examinations that showed your elementary and high-school teachers how your progress in reading or mathematics compared with the national average. When applying for a job you may be asked to take tests that psychologists have devised for ability at specific tasks, ranging from clerical work to being an astronaut. If you have occasion to visit a clinical psychologist, you may be tested for various personality traits.

The construction of truly scientific tests—which actually measure what they are supposed to measure and do so accurately and consistently—is much more difficult than is commonly supposed. Many of the so-called psychological tests in newspapers and magazines, which claim to tell you how happy, self-fulfilled, or neurotic you are, or how good you are likely to be as a husband, wife, or parent, have no value at all. They are simply parlor games dreamed up out of thin air by some nonpsychologist—and any score you may make on them, good or bad, is not to be taken seriously. Even psychology's best tests have weaknesses despite all

Could psychological testing have channeled these men's lives into different channels? They are the assassins of, from left, John Kennedy, Robert Kennedy, and Martin Luther King, Jr.

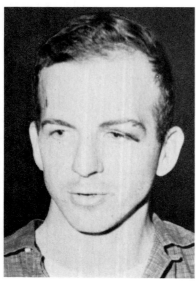

the scientific knowledge and effort that have gone into them. But they also have their uses, and the search goes on constantly for new and better versions.

Besides trying to develop tests of psychological traits, psychologists are also interested in the measurement of any and all physical characteristics that may have a bearing on behavior. They have spent considerable time measuring and studying the bodily processes that take place during such emotional states as fear and anger—including changes in heart rate, blood pressure, breathing, and the electrical conductivity of the skin due to activity of the sweat glands. (The "lie detector" and instruments that analyze stress patterns in the voice—see Figure 1-6—are sometimes useful though highly controversial applications of this kind of psychological measurement.) Psychologists also measure changes in the chemical composition of the blood stream, which are related not only to emotions but also to such psychological phenomena as hunger, thirst, and sleep. They examine various other chemicals that are essential to the operation of the brain and therefore play an important role in depression and mental illness.

Measurements, individual differences, and the normal curve

Psychology's tests and measurements have been particularly helpful in adding to our knowledge of individual differences. They have shown that every person is indeed unique and that all kinds of physical and psychological traits, from height and muscular strength to intelligence and emotional sensitivity, vary over a wide range from small to large, low to high, and weak to strong.

In studying what tests and measurements show about individual differences, the science relies

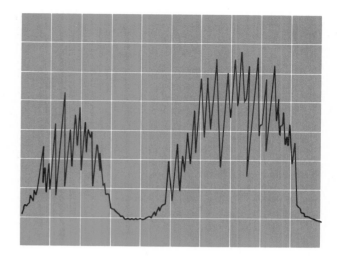

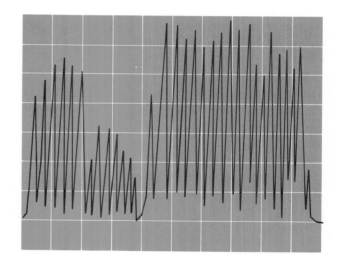

1-6

Two voices: is one telling a lie?

These are tracings from a voice stress analyzer, a device discussed in the text. The top one is of a normal voice, with irregular waves produced by a slight trembling of the vocal cords that occurs under ordinary conditions. The bottom one is the voice of a person who is under stress and suppressing the normal tremors. This person may be telling a lie—or may be tense or anxious for some other reason (7). The difference in the two voices would not be readily apparent to the ear.

1-7

Individual differences in IQ

The graph was obtained by testing the IQs of a large number of people in the United States. Note how many people scored right around the average of 100. (A total of 46.5 percent showed IQs between 90 and 109.) Note also how the number falls off rapidly from the midpoint to the lower and upper extremes. Fewer than 1 percent of all people showed IQs under 60 and only 1.33 percent were at 140 or over (8).

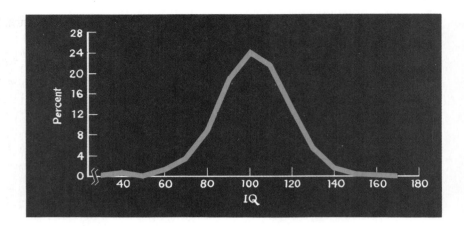

heavily on mathematical techniques known as *psychological statistics*. One of the most important contributions of psychological statistics has been the discovery that almost all events in nature follow a similar pattern. No matter what is measured, from the size of leaves in a forest to scores on an intelligence test, the measurements range from very small (or low) to very large (or high). But most of the measurements cluster around the average, and the number found at each point in the range goes down steadily as distance up or down from the average increases. This fact is readily apparent from the graph in Figure 1-7, which shows how IQs as measured by intelligence tests range from below 40 to above 160—but with the majority falling close to the average of 100, and only a very few at the extreme low or high levels.

The graph line in Figure 1-7 is so typical of the results generally found in all tests and measurements that it is known as the *normal curve of distribution*. The message of the curve is that in almost all measurable traits, physical and psychological, most people are average or close to it, some are a fair distance above or below, and a few are very far above or below. Those who are about average

have a lot of company. Those who are far removed from the average—in intelligence the geniuses and the mentally retarded, in height the seven-footers and the four-footers—are rare.

The curve of normal distribution helps explain a great deal about behavior, including the general similarities displayed by most people and the wide deviations shown by a few others. The curve applies to performance in school. (Most students have to do an average amount of struggling; some can make A's without turning a hair; some cannot handle the work at all.) It applies to musical talent, athletic skill, writing ability, and interest or lack of interest in sex.

The method of correlation

One question that has interested psychologists almost from the beginning of the science is this: Do children resemble their parents in intelligence? This is a question that has many implications for study of the part played in human behavior by heredity and environment—which, as will be seen a little later, is one of the basic issues in psychology. How would you try to go about answering it?

A person totally untrained in the methods of science might jump to conclusions based on personal experience: "No, obviously not. My neighbors the Smiths are both smart people—they went to college and have good jobs—but their two kids are having a terrible time in school." Or, "Certainly. My neighbors the Joneses are geniuses and their two daughters are the smartest kids in their school."

A more sophisticated approach would be to look at a much larger sample of children and parents than provided by just the Smiths or the Joneses—and to give both generations intelligence tests rather than to rely on one's own impression of how smart they seemed to be. This would be a good start toward a scientific answer. But the results would be difficult to interpret, because the tests will show all kinds of contradictions. One mother and father, both with IQs of 120, turn out to have an only child whose IQ is also 120—but another couple just like this one has an only child with an IQ of 90. One mother at 95 and father at 85 have an only child with an IQ of 90—but a similar couple has a child at 125. Even in the same family the tests would sometimes show three children with IQs as far apart as 85, 115, and 135. Without some method of analyzing and interpreting the test results, any scientific answer to the question would still be elusive.

In this type of situation, psychologists apply another statistical tool called *correlation*. This is a mathematical method used to examine two different measurements (such as the IQs of parents and the IQs of their children)—and to determine, from what would otherwise seem hopelessly jumbled numbers, what relationship if any actually exists between the two. The method, which is explained in the statistical appendix, boils down the figures into a *coefficient of correlation* ranging from 0.00 (no relationship at all) to 1.00 (a one-to-one or absolutely perfect relationship). In the case of parents and children, studies made by giving tests to many people and statistically analyzing the results have determined that the coefficient of correlation between IQs is .46 (9). This indicates a fairly high though by no means perfect relationship.

Correlations between various forms of human characteristics and behavior rarely reach the level of 1.00. Even such physical traits as height and weight, which would logically seem to go together in almost perfect proportion, do not approach that figure. Nor does the correlation between height in early childhood and in adulthood. (For males the coefficient between height at two and at eighteen is .60.) Between some traits there is a zero correlation, or no relationship at all—as between IQ and pitch discrimination, which is one aspect of musical talent.

The method of correlation has provided a great deal of psychological knowledge that would not otherwise be available. For example, it has given developmental psychologists many clues about the relationship of childhood behavior to behavior in later life. Do children who are passive at the ages of six to ten tend to be withdrawn in adulthood? The correlation is around .28 for males, .48 for females. Do children who are prone to displays of anger tend to exhibit disorganized behavior as adults? The correlation is about .42 for males, only about .12 for females (10).

One word of caution is in order. Correlations reveal the existence and extent of relationships, but they do not necessarily indicate cause and effect. Unless carefully interpreted, they can be misleading. There is a high correlation between the number of permanent teeth in children and their ability to answer increasingly difficult questions on intelligence tests. But this does not mean that having more teeth causes increased mental ability. The correlation is high because increasing age accounts for both the new teeth and the mental development.

The ultimate method: experimentation

There is one other method of investigation so important and productive that it deserves a separate section of the chapter. This is the *experiment*—in which the psychologist makes a careful and rigidly controlled examination of cause and effect. The experimenter sets up one set of conditions and determines what kind of behavior takes place under those conditions. Then the conditions are changed—and the effect of the changes, if any, is measured.

The experimental method has many applications. For example, social psychologists have been interested in this question: Does a man's height have anything to do with what other people think of him? One early clue came from observations of the way height seems to influence election results. It was found that in presidential elections the taller of the two candidates (who thus far have always been men) has consistently been the winner (11). But more direct information has been provided by psychologists who designed and conducted experiments. These experimenters could hardly arrange to change a man's height, to see how people behaved toward him before and after. But they found some ingenious ways of getting around this problem.

Two experiments on being tall or short

One experiment was conducted on a college campus by bringing in a man, who was a stranger to the students, and having him visit a number of classrooms. Sometimes the stranger was introduced as a student, sometimes as a lecturer, and other times as a full professor. After the man departed, students in the various classes were asked to estimate his height. As is shown in Figure 1-8, the estimates turned out to depend on the position the students thought the man occupied. When he was introduced as a student, the average estimate was 5 feet 10 inches. When he was introduced as a full professor, the average estimate jumped to over 6 feet (12).

The experiment seems to indicate that we tend to associate being tall with being important. If a man occupies a position of high esteem, we assume that he is above average in height. We might conclude that for men tall is beautiful, so to speak—that tall men enjoy more esteem and popularity. But hold on. Do people actually *like* tall men better (and are we who are less tall therefore at a social disadvantage)? Another group of psychologists tried a different kind of experiment. They made nine photographs of young men, pasted them on sheets of paper, and added some fictitious biographical information at the bottom, giving age (21 or 22), college class (junior or senior), and height. They deliberately arranged the height figures to make three of the men seem average, three shorter than average, and three taller. Then they asked 100 college women to look at the sheets and rate the nine men on such questions as "How attractive do you think this person is?" and "How much do you think you would like this person?"

Did the tall men (those described as being from 6 feet 2 inches to 6 feet 4) come off better? Not at all. It turned out that the 100 women, by and large, thought that the medium men (5 feet 9 to 11) were the most attractive, the ones they would expect to

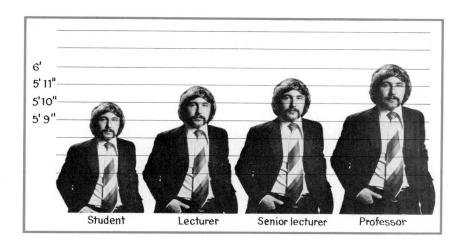

1-8

How can the same man seem so different?

Our estimates of a man's height, as was discovered in an experiment described in the text, seem to depend on how important he is. The photographs and scale of height show how the size of a stranger seemed to increase depending on whether he was believed to be a student, full professor, or something in between.

like the best, and also the ones they would prefer as dates.

The same nine photos were also shown to 100 college men. These male subjects gave virtually identical ratings of attractiveness to the photos of the tall, average, and short men. On the question of how much they would expect to like the people in the photos, they gave the highest rating of all to the short men and the lowest to the tall men (13).

From the two experiments just cited, along with studies of voter preferences, we can draw these conclusions: People in general seem to consider a man's height to be related to his leadership ability. We may tend to vote for the taller candidate and may think that people in positions of power (like the campus stranger introduced as a full professor) tend to be tall. But height does not have very much influence on our social relationships. When it comes to choosing friends, we prefer men of medium height (which is probably just as well because the great majority of men, in accordance with the normal curve of distribution, fall in the medium range).

Thus does the experimental method—with one

experiment leading to another and the results constantly being enlarged and refined—lead to knowledge of behavior that would otherwise never be explored. Most of the findings reported in this book were obtained through the experimental method.

Independent and dependent variables in experiments

Every psychological experiment is an attempt to discover whether behavior changes when conditions change. Both the possible behavior changes and the changes in conditions are called *variables.* Some variables are set up and controlled by the experimenter—like the labeling of the photographs with the fictitious biographical data that made the men seem short, medium, or tall. Such a change in conditions is called an *independent variable,* because it is manipulated by the experimenter and in no way dependent on anything the subject does or does not do. Any change in the subject's behavior—such as a different reaction to photos of men believed to be of different heights—is called a *de-*

pendent variable. The experimenter arranges to change the independent variable, then measures any change in the dependent variable.

In most human situations, there are many variables. In making our own judgments of how attractive we find new acquaintances and how much we think we would like them, we are likely to consider not only their height but also their facial features, the way they are dressed, their posture, the way they talk, and many other factors. But the experimenter usually wants to study only one independent variable—and therefore attempts to hold all other variables constant. In the experiment with the allegedly tall, medium, and short men, photographs were used instead of personal meetings to avoid any possible influence of dress, posture, and voice. The photographs were carefully selected so that there were no real differences in attractiveness among the faces. The only independent variable that could affect the results, so far as is known, was the height of the men as given in the fictitious biographical data.

Experimental and control groups

Another important aspect of the experimental method can best be explained by looking at a somewhat different kind of experiment. Let us suppose that a group of psychologists have developed a new method for teaching reading in the lower grades of school and want to test its effectiveness. They try out the new method on a group of children, then test the children to see how well they have learned to read. They get the average score for the group, which shows that the children have indeed made some progress. But, by itself, the score does not mean much. The question arises: How good a score would the children have made even without the new teaching method?

The problem can be solved by studying two groups of children instead of just one. One group is taught by the new method; this is called the *experimental group*. The other continues to study with the old method; this is the *control group*. At the end of the experiment, both groups are tested for reading skill and the results are compared. If the experimental group gets a better average score, this finding demonstrates that the new method is effective.

An experiment of this sort was conducted recently with a teaching method called computer-assisted learning, in which pupils respond to instructions presented through a computer, answer questions, and are guided step by step to building additional skills on those they already possess. An experimental group of pupils received this kind of computer-assisted learning in addition to their usual classroom work. A control group received the classroom instruction only. At the end of the third grade, both groups took the same test for achievement in reading, with results shown in Figure 1-9. A comparison of the test scores of the two groups clearly indicates that the computer-assisted instruction was helpful.

Having both an experimental group and a control group is essential in many psychological experiments. The two groups have to be chosen with great care. The results shown in Figure 1-9 would be meaningless if the experimental group was made up of pupils who were good at reading to begin with, while the control group was made up of poor readers. Thus psychologists try to make sure that their experimental and control groups are similar in all important respects. In experiments on learning, they select two groups that are approximately equal in such matters as average age, years of school completed, grades, and IQs. Often it is also important to match the two groups in respect to sex, race, and social background.

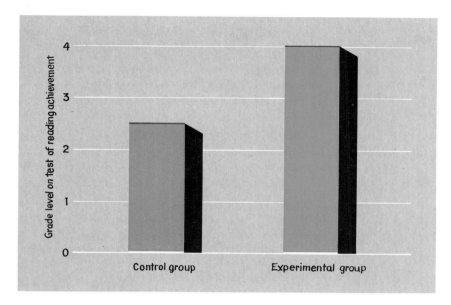

1-9

A two-group experiment

In the experiment on computer-assisted learning described in the text, the experimental group scored at the fourth-grade level in reading, the control group at only around the 2.5-grade level (14).

Single-blind and double-blind experiments

In trying to measure the effects of marijuana on driving ability, psychologists would divide their subjects into an experimental group that was under the influence of the drug and a control group that was not. But a further precaution would be necessary—for the subjects' performance might be affected by their knowledge that they had taken the drug and their expectations of how it might affect them. To avoid this possibility, it would be important to keep the subjects from knowing whether they had received the drug. This could be done by giving half the subjects an injection of the drug's active ingredient, THC, and the other half an injection of a salt solution that would have no effect, without telling them which was which. This experimental method, in which subjects cannot know whether they belong to the experimental group or the control group, is called the *single-blind technique*.

There is the further danger that the experimenter's own ratings of the subjects' performance might be affected by knowing which of them had taken the drug and which had not. To make the experiment foolproof, the drug or salt solution would have to be injected by a third party, so that even the experimenter would have no way of knowing which subjects had received which kind of injection. This method, in which neither the subject nor the experimenter knows who is in the experimental group and who is in the control group, is called the *double-blind technique*. It is particularly valuable in studying the effects of drugs, including the tranquilizers and antidepressants used to treat mental disturbances. It is also used in any other experiment where knowledge of the conditions might affect the judgment of the experimenter as well as the performance of the subjects.

Psychological versus nonscientific methods

As developed and refined over the years, and with the checks provided by such methods as use of a control group and the double-blind technique, the experiment is psychology's most powerful tool. For one thing, an experiment can be repeated by another experimenter at another time and in another place, ruling out the possibility that the results were accidental or influenced by the first experimenter's personality or preconceived notions of what would happen. (In this connection, a word frequently found in psychological literature is *replicate;* to replicate an experiment is to perform it again in the same manner and obtain the same results.) When facts have been established by the experimental method and verified time and again by other experimenters with other subjects, we can have great faith in their validity.

The precautions that psychologists take when conducting experiments—and indeed when using any of the other methods described earlier—help explain why their findings often go counter to what most people assume about human behavior. With-

out the use of scientific methods, it is difficult to reach valid conclusions. Behavior takes so many forms, and is influenced by so many factors, that the nonscientist is almost bound to make numerous mistakes of observation and interpretation and to form opinions based on faulty or insufficient evidence.

People who read a public opinion poll showing how the majority of Americans feel about an issue such as welfare policies or capital punishment sometimes exclaim: "This can't be true. Everybody I know thinks just the opposite." What they ignore is the fact, well established by social psychologists, that people who move in the same circles usually have similar opinions—which may be totally different from those of most other Americans. Many people who have never studied psychology would agree that punishment is an effective way of making children behave better, that you can judge another person's motives by that person's behavior, and that the higher you set your goals the more you are likely to accomplish. All these notions, when examined scientifically, have turned out to be false.

Schools of psychological thought

Like other sciences, psychology seeks through its various methods of investigation to discover the general principles that govern its subject matter. It constantly searches for basic laws of behavior—akin to the chemist's law that combining an acid with an alkali will invariably and inevitably produce a salt. In the study of behavior, however, such immutable laws are difficult to find. Even in the field of learning, where psychology has produced perhaps its most solid findings, few if any laws have

been established beyond any shadow of doubt. Even less is known about the general laws that govern emotional behavior, motives, and the human personality. Indeed we do not know at this point whether such laws even exist.

Thus psychologists must often rely on devising theories of behavior to give meaningful organization to their discoveries and to guide their future exploration. Theories are not laws but educated guesses that provide a plausible explanation for findings the science has made in the past and that, if accurate, will be borne out by future findings. It should be noted that other sciences must also rely in many cases on theories—to cite one well-known example, the theory of evolution, which cannot be proved but is merely a plausible explanation of what has been learned about the organisms that inhabit our planet.

Theories have played an important part in the progress of psychology. You will find many of them mentioned in this book—for example, past and present theories of how our nervous system operates to enable us to see colors and of how our brain and body join in producing our emotions. The current theories, on these and other topics, may eventually be proved faulty—but even so they are the best available guidelines, based on the best available evidence, to the scientific interpretation of behavior.

Thus the subject matter of psychology and of the introductory course takes two forms. One is the facts about behavior that have been discovered by applying the various methods of the science, from objective observation to controlled experimentation. The other is the theories that have been suggested to explain the findings. About the facts there can be no argument (except when, as sometimes happens, different investigators perform the same experiment and come up with different results). On matters of theory, however, there is often ample room for debate and sometimes heated controversy. Like all other human beings, psychologists display wide individual differences. They approach the science with many different viewpoints—for example, varying attitudes toward the basic quality of human nature (is it good or is it evil?) and what aspects of behavior are most significant. Therefore the science has from the beginning been divided into schools of thought that differ in their approach and in their theories of behavior.

From introspection to behaviorism

The first psychologists were chiefly interested in studying human consciousness. Indeed a textbook written by the most prominent of the early American psychologists, William James, began with the words: "Psychology is the study of mental life."

To make this study of "mental life," the early psychologists used as their tool the practice of *introspection,* or looking inward. They tried to analyze, as carefully and objectively as possible, the processes of their minds. They also asked their subjects to make this same kind of analysis. Among the interests of the early psychologists, as James defined them, were feelings, desires, thoughts, reasonings, and decisions—as well as people's struggles to attain their goals or to become reconciled to failure.

Before long, however, some doubts began to arise. Is introspection really a scientific method? Or is it merely another name for philosophizing about the human condition? One person who came to the second of these conclusions—and thereby started a revolution in psychology—was John Watson, who about the year 1913 founded the movement known as *behaviorism.* Watson declared that "mental life" was something that cannot be seen or measured and thus cannot be studied scientifically. Instead of trying to examine any such vague thing as "mental life" or consciousness, he concluded, psychologists should concentrate on actions that are plainly visible. In other words, he wanted the science to study what people *do,* not what they think.

Watson did not believe in anything like "free will," or the ability to control one's own destiny. Instead he believed that everything we do is predetermined by our past experiences. He considered all human behavior to be a series of events in which a *stimulus,* that is, an event in the environ-

James

Watson

ment, produces a *response,* that is, an observable muscular movement or some physiological reaction, such as increased heart rate or glandular secretion, that can also be observed and measured with the proper instruments. (For example, shining a bright light into the eye is a stimulus that causes an immediate response in which the pupil of the eye contracts; a loud and unexpected noise is a stimulus that usually causes the response of muscular contraction, or jumping, and increased heart rate.) Watson believed that through *conditioning,* a type of learning that will be discussed in Chapter 3, almost any kind of stimulus could be made to produce almost any kind of response. Indeed he once said that he could take any dozen babies at birth and, by conditioning them in various ways, turn them into anything he wished—doctor, lawyer, beggar, or thief.

Even the existence of a human mind was doubted by Watson. He conceded that human beings had thoughts, but he believed that these were simply a form of talking to oneself, by making tiny movements of the vocal cords. He also conceded that people have what they call feelings, but he believed that these were only some form of conditioned response to a stimulus in the environment. Behaviorism as Watson conceived it is sometimes known as *stimulus-response psychology,* or S-R psychology for short. The S-R psychologists emphasize study of the stimuli that produce behavioral responses, the rewards and punishments that help establish and maintain these responses, and the modification of behavior through changes in the patterns of rewards and punishments.

Behaviorism and B. F. Skinner

Watson was the most influential of American psychologists for many years, and he continues to have many followers. One famous modern leader of the behaviorist school is B. F. Skinner, who ranks

Skinner

Freud

as another of the most prominent American psychologists of the past half-century. Skinner has been chiefly interested in the learning process and has revised and expanded Watson's ideas into a theory of learning that continues to influence much psychological thinking. He has made many important contributions to our knowledge of how patterns of rewards and punishments produce and modify connections between a stimulus and a response and thus help control the organism's behavior—often in the most complex ways.

Skinner's best-known book is *Beyond Freedom and Dignity,* published in 1971 (15). Here he argues that people possess neither of the two attributes mentioned in his title. To Skinner, people are not responsible for their conduct; they are neither to blame for their failures nor deserving of credit for their achievements. They are simply the creatures of their environment. Their behavior depends on the kinds of learning to which they have been subjected, particularly which of their actions have been

rewarded. A "social engineer" aware of all the principles of learning could mold people into any form desired, whether for good or for evil.

Behaviorism shaped the course of psychology for many years and continues to have a strong influence. But its basic approach has always been controversial—and the controversy has been intensified by Skinner's belief that we have no real freedom of choice or responsibility for our own actions. Other schools of psychological thought are now moving in very different directions.

The cognitive school

One of the prominent new schools is *cognitive psychology.* As the name implies, cognitive psychology rejects Watson's contention that there is no such thing as a human mind (or that the mind, at most, is unimportant). Instead, the cognitive psychologists believe that mental processes play a central part in human behavior. They maintain that behavior cannot possibly be explained in full by conditioning and stimulus-response connections—and that our minds are much more than a mere reflection of the stimuli we have encountered. They tend to think of the mind as a sort of "mental executive" that actively makes comparisons and decisions, thus processing the information it receives into new forms and categories. It discovers meanings and uses old knowledge to find new principles that aid in constructive thinking and in the discovery of ways to solve problems.

The cognitive psychologists think of mental activity and behavior in general as a pattern and a unity. They regard learning, for example, as a series of very complex but closely related activities that can be described, in the aggregate, as *information processing*. Steps in this processing include seeing and hearing, the organization of what we see and hear into perceptual patterns (for example, perceiving a girl or a boy rather than a collection of arms, legs, and body), and storing what we have seen or heard in memory—then drawing on the stored information to make judgments and decide on appropriate behavior.

The humanistic school

Another school of thought that has attracted many followers is *humanistic psychology*, which stresses what it considers the unique quality of the human spirit. Humanistic psychologists take the view that we human beings are totally different from other organisms. We are distinguished by the fact that we have values and goals; we seek to express ourselves, to grow, to fulfill ourselves, and to find peace and happiness. Our thoughts and aspirations, which Watson considered inappropriate for study, appear to the humanistic psychologists to be the most important of all aspects of behavior.

The humanistic psychologists take a broad and very hopeful view of the true quality of human nature, its accomplishments, and its potentialities. They believe that human beings are strongly motivated to realize their possibilities for creativity, dignity, and self-worth. The techniques of psychotherapy used by humanistic psychologists are built around the assumption that people will always grow in a constructive way if their environment permits them to do so.

In general, humanistic psychologists are not particularly interested in studying specific aspects of behavior. They regard attempts to analyze the human experience by breaking it down into fragments, such as individual responses to individual stimuli, as futile and in fact a matter of "disrespect" for the unique quality of the human spirit (16). Thus the humanistic psychologists are in some ways more oriented toward philosophy, literature, and religion than toward the investigative methods of the sciences. Many humanistic psychologists have been associated with efforts to expand consciousness and achieve unity of mind and body through encounter groups, sensitivity training, and other kinds of mental and physical "reaching out."

Other approaches

A school of thought related in many ways to the humanistic movement is *existential psychology*, which also emphasizes the quality of the human spirit. The existential psychologists, in direct contrast to B. F. Skinner, believe strongly in the importance of free will. They maintain that the events in our lives do not control our destinies—for what really counts is our own attitude toward the events, which we are free to choose for ourselves. We are all responsible for our own behavior, since we can make our own decisions and thus control our own attitudes and thoughts and rise above even the

"Hadn't you best drop in?"

Drawing by Fradan; © 1973
The New Yorker Magazine, Inc.

see the book by Rollo May cited in the list of recommended readings at the end of the chapter.)

Many other psychologists have been influenced in various ways by the approach developed by Sigmund Freud. A number of clinical psychologists use methods based on his techniques—and even psychologists who are skeptical of the value of psychoanalysis in therapy accept some of his ideas about personality and the way it is formed. Particularly influential has been his idea that behavior is often influenced by *unconscious processes,* especially motives of which we are unaware. Freud's views on personality and his psychotherapy will be discussed in detail in Chapter 12.

There are a number of other schools of thought, for the science has moved in many directions during its hundred-year history. Psychologists have had many different interests, have conducted their studies in different ways, and have reached conclusions that are sometimes in sharp disagreement. All the approaches have contributed to our fund of knowledge and have raised provocative questions about human behavior and human nature. Today's students of psychology, without necessarily agreeing or disagreeing with any of the schools of thought, can profit greatly from the findings and theories of all of them.

most adverse events in our environment. The techniques of psychotherapy used by existential psychologists are designed to create a sense of identity and self-determination that fosters commitment and love. (If you want to learn more about the existential approach, which is difficult to summarize,

The issue of heredity versus environment

One basic issue to which psychologists have devoted much attention cuts across the various schools of thought. This is the question: To what extent is human behavior determined by factors present at birth, and to what extent is it molded by experience and learning? Or, to put this another way: How much do our personalities and actions

depend on heredity and how much do they depend on environment (which is the sum total of all the influences exerted from the moment of birth by our families, society as a whole, and the physical circumstances of our lives)?

A few hundred years ago, in the fifteenth and sixteenth centuries, many leading thinkers of the

Western world believed that heredity was the more influential factor. It was generally accepted that every human being was born with strong predispositions toward certain kinds of behavior. One baby inherited the tendency to be happy, another to be melancholy. One baby was born to be a leader, another to be a timid follower, another to be a troublemaker or even a criminal. This emphasis on heredity, it will be noted, constitutes a fatalistic view of human behavior. If the future of the individual human being is laid down at birth, then we can hardly expect to improve our personalities or our abilities. There is not much point in parents' trying to find better ways of bringing up their children or in the schools' attempting to find better ways of educating them.

A groundswell toward the opposite viewpoint was largely the work of John Locke, the seventeenth-century philosopher, who popularized the idea that the mind of the human baby is a *tabula rasa,* Latin for "blank tablet," On this blank tablet, Locke argued, anything at all can be written through experience and learning. In other words, heredity is unimportant. The child becomes whatever the environment dictates.

Locke's idea greatly influenced other philosophers who helped create the energetic intellectual climate in which psychology was born as a science. It was attractive to many of the early psychologists, who grew up in this atmosphere, and it remains a strong influence to this day. The belief that environment is the all-important factor is of course basic to the behaviorist school of thought. It is also central to much of the thinking of the humanistic and existential psychologists—who believe in general that the evils that have plagued humanity (jealousy, emotional conflicts, crime, even war) are the result of the wrong kind of social environment.

Other psychologists, however, continue to believe that heredity plays a dominant role in many forms of behavior—ranging from such a basic abili-

But in a way, we're *underprivileged, too. For example, I've never seen a rat, a pigeon or a cockroach.*

ty as learning to all the characteristics that make up personality, including tendencies to emotional and mental disturbances. The debate over the relative importance of heredity and environment is often called the *nature-nurture* argument, and it will be referred to often by that term throughout the book.

The key to heredity: chromosomes and genes

The study of heredity is known as *genetics*. The aspect of heredity of most interest to psychologists is called *behavior genetics,* which concerns the inheritance of traits that are of prime importance in influencing an organism's conduct—such as the glands and especially the nervous system. To understand behavior genetics and the issue of nature versus nurture, one must first know something about the mechanics of heredity, which explain how life is carried on from one generation to the next. A new life begins, of course, when the egg cell produced by the mother is penetrated and fertilized by the sperm cell of the father, as shown in Figure 1-10. The two join into a single cell—and this single cell eventually grows into a human baby. It does so by a process of division; the single cell splits and becomes two living cells, then each of these in turn splits to make four, and so on.

Thus the original fertilized egg cell must somehow contain the whole key of life. Something inside it must direct the entire development from single cell to the baby at birth (whose body contains about 200 billion cells organized into the various specialized parts of the body) and beyond that from infant to fully matured adult. Something in it

must also determine the inherited characteristics of the individual to be born—the color of the eyes, the facial features, the potential size, possibly the psychological characteristics.

This "something" is the *chromosomes*—the tiny structures shown in Figure 1-11 as seen under a powerful microscope. The original fertilized cell contains forty-six chromosomes. When the cell splits, the chromosomes also divide. Thus each cell of the newborn baby as well as of the fully grown human body contains exactly the same forty-six chromosomes that were present in the fertilized egg with which life began. The chromosomes are the key to the development of the human being and are the carriers of heredity.

Each chromosome, though tiny in itself, is com-

1-10 The moment of conception

The large round object is a human egg cell. At this moment it is being fertilized by a male sperm cell that has worked its way deep inside and can no longer be seen. Other sperm cells, with small heads and long tails, are also attempting to pierce the egg but have arrived too late.

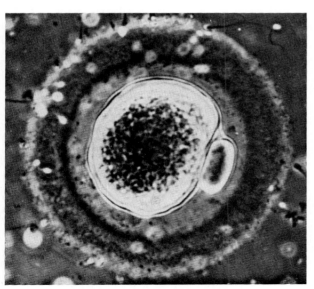

1-11 The human chromosomes

When enlarged 750 times, the human chromosomes look like this. These are from a man's skin cell, broken down and spread out into a single layer under the microscope. The labels point out the X- and Y-chromosomes, which determine sex, as will be explained later in the chapter.

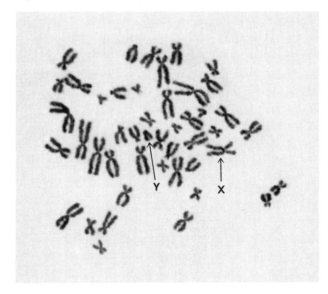

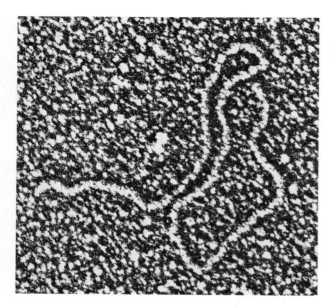

1-12 A single gene

The first gene ever isolated and photographed under high magnification was this twisted strand taken from one of the bacteria frequently found in the human intestinal tract. It is fifty-five millionths of an inch long (17).

posed of hundreds of even smaller structures called *genes*, each of which is a molecule of a complex chemical called DNA (deoxyribonucleic acid). Recently scientists managed to extract a single gene from a chromosome of one of the lower organisms and, through a microscope, take the photograph of it shown in Figure 1-12.

Human genes have not yet been isolated, examined, or counted. But it is believed that there are at least 20,000 of them in each human cell and perhaps as many as 125,000. Each gene is believed to be responsible—sometimes by itself but more often in combination with other genes—for some particular phase of development. The genes direct the process by which some cells of the body grow into skin and others grow into nerves or muscles and also the process by which cells become grouped into organs such as the heart, the stomach, and the liver. They control such characteristics as the color of the eyes and the length of the bones.

Our heredity depends on those many thousands of genes, organized into our forty-six chromosomes. It is the particular kinds of genes present in the original fertilized egg that make us develop into human beings and into the individual human being that each of us is.

Where we get our genes

In the living cell, the forty-six chromosomes are not arranged as in Figure 1-11, where they were deliberately separated and spread out to pose for their microscopic portrait. Instead they are arranged in twenty-three pairs. In each pair the two chromosomes are similar in structure and function and are composed of genes of similar structure and function. For purposes of exposition, we can think of them as pairs A_1–A_2, B_1–B_2, C_1–C_2, D_1–D_2, and so on.

In growth, the twenty-three pairs of chromosomes with their matched genes duplicate themselves exactly, so that each new cell also has pairs A_1–A_2, B_1–B_2, C_1–C_2, D_1–D_2, and so on. But the cells of reproduction—the mother's egg cell and the sperm cell of the father—are formed in very different fashion. Here the pairs split up. Half of each pair goes into one egg or sperm cell, the other half into another cell. Thus each egg or sperm cell has only twenty-three chromosomes, not twenty-three pairs.

When two cells of reproduction are formed by this process, it is a matter of chance whether cell 1 will receive A_1, or A_2, B_1 or B_2, C_1 or C_2, and so on. Cell 1 may receive A_1, B_2, and C_1, in which case

These twin sisters are married to twin brothers—a double exception to the rule that all human beings are unique individuals.

cell 2 will receive A_2, B_1, and C_2. Or cell 1 may receive A_2, B_2, and C_1, in which case cell 2 will receive A_1, B_1, and C_2. This random splitting of the twenty-three pairs can itself result in 8,388,608 different possible reproductive cells with different combinations of the two halves of the original pairs. Moreover, the splitting has a further complication. Sometimes A_1, in breaking away from A_2, leaves some of its own genes behind and pulls away some of the A_2 genes. Any one of the twenty-three chromosomes can and often does behave in this way, with anywhere from one to several hundred genes from its paired chromosomes. All in all, there are many billions of possible combinations of the original pairs of chromosomes and genes

An egg cell containing one of these combinations of the chromosomes and genes present in the mother is fertilized by a sperm cell containing one of the combinations of the chromosomes and genes present in the father. The chromosomes and genes pair up, and life begins for another unique human being. Never before, unless by a chance so mathematically remote as to be almost impossible, did the same combination of genes ever exist. Never again is it likely to be repeated.

The one exception to the fact that each human being is unique is in the case of identical twins. Here a single egg cell, fertilized by a single sperm cell, develops into two individuals. They have the same chromosomes and genes in the same combination, and they tend to be very much alike in every basic respect.

Being born male or female

One of the twenty-three pairs of chromosomes present in the fertilized egg cell plays a particularly significant role in development: it determines whether the fertilized egg will develop into a girl or a boy. In Figure 1-11 you will note that two chromosomes are pointed out by arrows. One of them, as the caption states, is called an X-chromosome, the other a Y-chromosome. Despite their different appearances, they constitute a pair—the only exception to the rule that paired chromosomes are similar in structure. You will also note that the chromosomes in Figure 1-11 are from a cell taken from a male. The X-Y pairing always produces a male. When there is an X-X pair, the result is always a female.

This, then, is how sex is determined. When the mother's X-X pair of chromosomes splits to form an egg cell, the result is always a cell containing an X-chromosome. When the father's X-Y pair splits to form two sperm cells, however, the X-chromosome goes to one of the cells, the Y-chromosome to the other. If the sperm cell with the X-chromosome fertilizes the egg, the result is an X-X pairing and a girl. If the sperm cell with the Y-chromosome fertilizes the egg, the result is an X-Y pairing and a boy.

Effects of heredity: the case for nature

People are born, live their lives, and die. But the chromosomes and the genes are passed on from generation to generation, from parent to child. All of us carry around, in every cell of our bodies, the genes that have influenced human development and behavior since the appearance of humans on earth. They guarantee that we will grow up in the image of our ancestors rather than into apes or fish. Yet the particular combination of genes that each of us carries is unique, coming from a grandfather here, a great-grandmother there, and so on back through countless individuals in countless generations.

There can be no question that the inherited structure of the human body and brain sets some limits on human behavior. Because of the way our brains operate, we cannot possibly make complex mathematical calculations as fast as a computer. Because of the way our nervous systems and glands cooperate, we cannot possibly live our lives without experiencing emotions—which, though they often exhilarate us, may also plunge us into fear or despair and make us incapable of performing with the computer's cold accuracy. Our sense organs, which are part of the nervous system, are incapable of detecting certain kinds of light waves that are visible even to the lowly bee or high-pitched sounds that are clearly audible to a dog. The structure of our bodies makes it impossible for us to live under water like a fish or fly like a bird. Heredity has provided us with our own kind of physical equipment—and we have to live our lives within its bounds. To this extent, at least, the nature side of the nature-nurture controversy is clearly correct.

Over the years it has been established that the genes also influence certain kinds of psychological traits. For example, the severe form of mental disturbance called *schizophrenia,* which occurs in only about one person in a hundred, is much more common among people who have a parent or a brother or sister who suffers from the disturbance. This fact cannot be attributed entirely to the environmental effect of living around someone who is schizophrenic. A study of children reared away from their own families in foster homes has shown that of fifty children of normal mothers not one developed schizophrenia, but of forty-seven children born to schizophrenic mothers, five became schizophrenic (18). There is some evidence that heredity also plays a part in determining whether individuals will be *extroverted,* that is, inclined to be sociable and outgoing, or *introverted,* that is, inclined to be withdrawn and preoccupied with them-

Does intelligence run in families? It does in this New York family, where all six children have IQs at the genius level.

selves (19). Inherited differences in the structure and functioning of the nervous system and the glands of the body (20) appear to influence emotional and sexual behavior.

On the matter of intelligence, it was mentioned earlier that there is a correlation of .46 between the IQs of children and parents. The IQs of brothers and sisters also tend to resemble one another to about the same degree, and the IQs of identical twins are remarkably alike. All these facts would

indicate that hereditary factors are at work. It has also been found that genetic defects are responsible for some forms of mental retardation.

Effects of environment: the case for nurture

However, there is also considerable evidence to support the nurture side of the argument. For example, it has been found that not all the people who may inherit a tendency toward schizophrenia actually develop the disorder. Presumably the factor that determines which will fall prey and which will escape is environment. Statistical studies have shown that schizophrenia is most common among people living in the slum or near-slum areas of big cities (21), where they are likely to experience poverty and frustration. The disorder is less likely to occur among people who live in more favorable circumstances.

It is also known that intelligence is affected by nurture—for a baby's mental capacity, regardless of what its genes decree, has been found to flourish in a stimulating environment and to be stunted by an unfavorable environment. Studies of the IQs of children who were unrelated by blood but were adopted into the same home, and therefore grew up in the same kind of environment, have shown correlations as high as .40 (22). This is an impressive figure, since the correlation for a group of unrelated children chosen at random would be zero.

All in all, a great deal of scientific evidence has accumulated since the days when the nature-nurture argument began. The evidence has led most of today's psychologists to take a position somewhere between the two extremes. Very few would agree with the old philosophers that heredity alone determines our fate. On the other hand, few would claim as did Locke that the human baby is a *tabula rasa* entirely free from hereditary influences. The general view today is that we human beings are shaped by both nature *and* nurture. For many important psychological traits, as well as for our physical characteristics, heredity sets tendencies and limitations. But then environment takes over to encourage or discourage the development and operation of our inborn traits.

The debate today is mostly over the relative importance of nature and nurture—the question of not whether but how much each of them influences such individual aspects of behavior and personality as the way we perceive and interpret the world around us, our intelligence and ability to learn from experience, our emotional behavior, and our reactions (normal or abnormal) to frustrations and stress. The debate continues to be important because it bears on the fundamental question of to what extent our lives are preordained at birth and to what extent we are masters of our own fate. Chapter 2 will discuss the kinds of brains and bodies that heredity has given us—which are the basis of all study of human behavior.

Summary

1 Psychology is the *systematic study of behavior and all the factors that influence behavior*.
2 Psychology is closely related to other sciences—especially physics (which explains the nature of the light and sound waves to which our sense organs respond), chemistry (which has helped identify the substances that activate our nervous system and the glandular secretions that play a role in emotions), and physiology (which studies the structure and functioning of the brain and body).
3 The goals of psychology are: 1) *to understand behavior* and 2) *to predict behavior*.
4 Many psychologists are concerned only with *pure science*—or knowledge for the sake of knowledge. Others are chiefly interested in *applied science*—or the use of psychological findings to improve the quality of life.
5 Fields of applied psychology include:
   a *Psychological counseling*—assistance to people who need guidance on such temporary problems as school difficulties, choice of a vocation, or marriage conflicts.
   b *Clinical psychology*—the diagnosis of more deep-seated psychological problems and the treatment of such problems through *psychotherapy*.

c *Community psychology*—the study of ways to improve the social environment to prevent maladjustments.

d *Environmental psychology*—the study of such ecological problems as smog, water pollution, noise, and overcrowding.

e *School psychology*—the application of psychological findings to teaching methods and the school curriculum.

f *Industrial psychology*, which includes the selection and training of employees and the study of working hours, fatigue, and employee morale.

g *Public opinion surveys*.

6 The methods of psychology include *naturalistic observation, participant observation, interviews, case histories, questionnaires, tests* and *measurements,* and *experiments*.

7 The results of tests and measurements are analyzed through mathematical techniques called *psychological statistics*.

8 One contribution of psychological statistics is the finding that almost all physical traits (like height) and psychological characteristics (like intelligence) follow the *normal curve of distribution*—with most measurements clustering around the average and only a few falling at the lowest or highest extremes.

9 *Correlation* is a statistical tool used to determine how much relationship if any exists between two different measurements—such as the IQs of parents and the IQs of their children.

10 In an experiment, the experimenter controls the *independent variable,* which is set up independently of anything the subject does or does not do, and then studies the *dependent variable,* which is a change in the subject's behavior resulting from a change in the independent variable.

11 Experiments often use both an *experimental group,* whose behavior is studied under new conditions, and a *control group,* who are not placed under the new conditions.

12 In a *single-blind* experiment, the subjects do not know whether they belong to the experimental group or the control group. In a *double-blind* experiment, neither the subjects nor the experimenter know.

13 An experiment is *replicated* when it is performed again in the same manner by another experimenter who obtains the same results—thus ruling out the possibility that the original results were accidental or influenced in some way by the first experimenter.

14 The first psychologists were chiefly interested in studying human consciousness through *introspection,* or looking inward at mental processes.

15 The school of *behaviorism,* a rebellion against introspective studies, was founded by John Watson, who declared that "mental life" cannot be seen or measured

and therefore cannot be studied scientifically. Watson believed that psychologists should study what people do, not what they think.

16 Watson's behaviorism is sometimes called *stimulus-response psychology* because it emphasizes the stimuli that produce behavioral responses, the rewards and punishments that help establish and maintain these responses, and the modification of behavior through changes in the patterns of rewards and punishments.

17 A modern leader of the behaviorist school is B. F. Skinner, who has revised and expanded Watson's ideas into theories that continue to influence much psychological thinking.

18 An entirely different approach is taken by the new *cognitive* school of psychology, which believes that mental processes play a central part in human behavior and regards learning not as the establishment of stimulus-response connections but as an active form of *information processing*.

19 The *humanistic school* stresses what it considers the unique quality of the human spirit. It holds that human beings are unique because they have values and goals; they seek to express and fulfill themselves and to find peace and happiness.

20 Other schools of thought include *existential psychology* and followers of Sigmund Freud's theory of *psychoanalysis*.

21 A basic issue that cuts across the various schools of thought is *nature-nurture*—the question of to what extent human behavior is determined by heredity and to what extent it is molded by environment.

22 *Behavior genetics* is the study of how human beings (and other organisms) inherit characteristics that influence their conduct.

23 The mechanisms of human heredity are the twenty-three pairs of *chromosomes,* forty-six in all, found in the fertilized egg cell and repeated through the process of division in every cell of the body that grows from the egg.

24 Each chromosome is made up of a large number of *genes,* which are composed of a chemical called *DNA.* The genes direct the growth of cells into parts of the body and also account for the individual differences we inherit.

25 Being female or male is determined by the *X-chromosome* and the *Y-chromosome.* An X-X pairing in the egg cell creates a female. An X-Y pairing creates a male.

Important terms

applied science
behavior genetics
behaviorism
case history
chromosome
clinical psychology
cognitive psychology
community psychology
comparative psychology
conditioning
control group
correlation
counseling
dependent variable
double-blind
environment
environmental psychology

existential psychology
experiment
experimental group
extroverted
gene
heredity
humanistic psychology
independent variable
industrial psychology
information processing
interviews
introspection
introverted
measurements
naturalistic observation
nature-nurture

normal curve of distribution
participant observation
psychoanalysis
psychological statistics
psychotherapy
public opinion survey
pure science
questionnaire
replication
school psychology
single-blind
stimulus-response
   psychology
tests
X-chromosome
Y-chromosome

Recommended readings

Boring, E. G. *History of experimental psychology,* 2d ed. New York: Appleton-Century-Crofts, 1950.

Chaplin, J. P., and Krawiec, T. C. *Systems and theories of psychology,* 3d ed. New York: Holt, Rinehart & Winston, 1974.

Chein, I. *Science of behavior and the image of man.* New York: Basic Books, 1972.

Evans, R. I. *The making of psychology: discussions with creative contributors.* New York: Knopf, 1976.

Hall, C. S., and Lindzey, G. *Theories of personality,* 3d ed. New York: Wiley, 1978.

May, R. *Psychology and the human dilemma.* Princeton, N.J.: Van Nos Reinhold 1967.

Meyers, L. S., and Grossen, N. E. *Behavioral research: theory, procedure, and design,* 2d ed. San Francisco: Freeman, 1978.

Murphy, G., and Kovach, J. K. *Historical introduction to modern psychology,* 3d ed. New York: Harcourt Brace Jovanovich, 1972.

Rogers, C. *Freedom to learn: a view of what education might become.* Columbus, Ohio: Merrill, 1969.

Watson, R. I. *The great psychologists: from Aristotle to Freud.* Philadelphia: Lippincott, 1978.

Wood, G. *Fundamentals of psychological research,* 2d ed. Boston: Little, Brown, 1977.

Woods, P. J., ed. *Career opportunities for psychologists: expanding and emerging areas.* Washington, D.C.: American Psychological Association, 1976.

Outline

Chapter two

Body and brain: the physical underpinning of psychology

You spend the evening at the movies, have a snack, and go to bed. Almost immediately, you drop off to sleep. There may be some sounds in the room, but you do not hear them. A breeze may be blowing across your face, but you do not feel it. To all intents and purposes, you are in a state of suspended animation—"dead to the world."

Nonetheless, a great deal is going on inside you. You continue to breathe—or else, deprived of oxygen, the cells of your body and brain would die. Your heart pumps blood, carrying oxygen and nourishment to the cells. The muscles of your alimentary canal make slow, rhythmic movements, helping digest the food you ate. If the room is cold, your cells begin to burn up food faster to produce more heat and help keep your body at its ideal inner temperature. The blood vessels in your skin constrict to keep the heat from being lost. If the room is warm, your cells begin to burn less food and produce less heat. Blood flows to the skin. You perspire so that evaporation can help cool you. Even in your state of suspended animation, you are somehow working hard to stay alive and healthy.

Suddenly there are shouts of "Fire!" You wake up in panic. In an instant, your body is mobilized for action. Your heart pounds. You breathe fast, as if panting for air. The muscles of your digestive system shut down—and the muscles of movement, in your arms and legs, grow tense and ready to spring to work. Your thoughts race to find a solution. You are immediately capable of doing almost anything required for your escape. You may, in fact, perform some almost unbelievable feats. You may manage to open a window that was stuck fast, or kick open a strongly bolted door, then run faster and farther than you would ever have dreamed possible.

This imaginary incident demonstrates something of great importance in human behavior. Obviously you have inside you a highly efficient system that regulates and coordinates all your activities. Even when you are asleep, it is alert to the temperature of your body and the presence of food in your stomach. It keeps your lungs and heart at work and controls the activity of your blood vessels and sweat glands. In situations of danger it mobilizes your body for action. It enables you to recognize danger signals, analyze the problem, and take appropriate steps.

Even in sheer physical makeup, your body is so complicated that it would seem to defy any attempt to keep it working properly. All the organs—heart, stomach, kidneys, liver, and others—perform different functions. You have your "five senses" (actually seven of them, as will be seen in Chapter 7) and

hundreds of bones moved by hundreds of muscles. This whole apparatus has to be fueled, fed, watered, kept clean, and constantly repaired. It is even more complex than a giant factory. You have to wonder: Who is in charge?

The answer is that your body and your behavior are under a very capable "management." In charge at all times, whether you are awake or asleep, in ordinary situations or in danger, are two remarkable supervisors—first and foremost your nervous system (especially your brain), second a set of glands that also help control and coordinate, sometimes on their own and sometimes on command from the nervous system. To understand your behavior, you must first know something about this managerial setup.

The brain and its "beautiful interrelationships"

The physical structures that make up the managerial system are the biological basis for all human behavior—and thus for the study of psychology. The way they are constructed and designed to function helps account for everything that will be discussed in this book—from learning and the use of language to emotional experiences and social relationships. Of course the structure of our brains and bodies sets some limits beyond which none of us can go. How we act and feel at any given moment depends on the messages that are racing through the brain, the work of brain chemicals that help transmit the messages, activity in the rest of the nervous system, and the influence of the glands. In a sense we are prisoners of our physical heritage. But the marvels of physiology—especially

nature's most elegant accomplishment, the human brain—provide us with a breathtaking range of experiences and opportunities. If human behavior is complex and endlessly fascinating, it is because our bodies and brains are themselves intricate and awesome creations.

The secret of being human: the cerebral cortex

In sheer physical appearance, your brain is not one of nature's most beautiful inventions. Seen from above, as if the top of your head were transparent, it looks as shown in Figure 2-1—a mass of pinkish tissue, with folds and creases like a crumpled piece

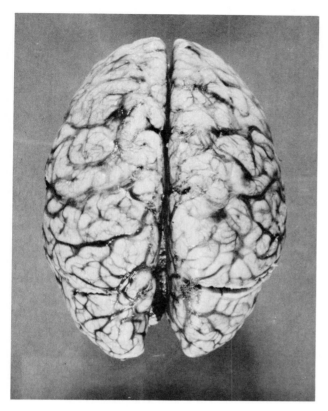

2-1 A topside view of the brain

The photograph shows the human brain as seen from above, displaying the elaborate folds and creases described in the text. Note especially the vertical line, resembling a narrow ditch, running down the middle from the top of the photo (which is the front of the brain) to the bottom. This is a deep fissure that divides this top part of the brain into two separate halves, or *hemispheres,* as discussed in the text.

of heavy cloth. This is the part of the brain that is chiefly responsible for your remembering and your thinking—the activities that make you far more intelligent than other animals. It is called the *cerebral cortex,* and nature has made it larger in human beings than in any other species. Indeed it is really too large to fit comfortably into the human head,

for it measures about 1.5 square feet (.14 square meter) in area. All the convolutions you see in the figure—the intricate foldings and refoldings—are needed to squeeze it into the skull. What you see in the photograph is only about a third of the cerebral cortex. All the rest is hidden in the creases.

The cortex is the surface—like the thick wrinkled skin of a prune—of the human brain's largest single structure, the *cerebrum,* which lies massively atop all the other parts of the brain. As the figure shows, the cortex and the cerebrum are split down the middle into a left half, or hemisphere, and a right hemisphere. Thus in a sense we have two brains doing our thinking—a fact raising some interesting questions that will be discussed later.

Beneath the cerebrum, and totally hidden by its bulk when the brain is viewed from above, lie many other structures all with their own roles to play in behavior. Now that your brain is fully grown and developed, it weighs in all about three pounds (1.4 kilograms). Thus in size as well as appearance, it is hardly impressive—making up only 2 percent or less of the average person's total weight.

Yet the human brain is one of nature's most elaborate and miraculous accomplishments. Within those three pounds of tissue are about 10 billion separate nerve cells, or *neurons,* all connnected and interconnected in the most complex fashion. Each of these fiberlike cells may receive messages from thousands of other neurons, then pass its own messages along to thousands more. The total number of possible connections and pathways is so great that it totally defies imagination (1).

The brain's neurons start their pattern of activity long before birth and are constantly at work, humming with their complicated messages, throughout life. They never stop, even when you are asleep. Even when you are sitting quietly, not performing any muscular activity, the brain cells that make up only about 2 percent of your body consume fully 20

*"I'm afraid we can't expect much of Holloway.
He left his brain to Johns Hopkins."*

Drawing by Fradan; © 1977
The New Yorker Magazine, Inc.

percent of all the oxygen you take in. They burn up far more than their share of the body's energy.

The brain's many functions

The brain uses a lot of energy because it does a lot of work. It accomplishes many tasks and displays "many beautiful interrelationships" (2). Its chief functions are these:

1 To interpret what is going on in the environment

All the information picked up by our sense organs is eventually transmitted, by way of the brain's many pathways, to the cerebral cortex. As Figure 2-2 shows, the cortex has specialized areas that receive the sensory messages for vision and hearing, also a long strip that receives messages of bodily sensations from the feet (at the top) to the head (at the bottom). In these specialized areas the messages are analyzed and interpreted. The brain decides which messages are important and what they mean. The sounds of speech—which are of particular im-

portance because language plays such a large role in human behavior—have an area of their own especially concerned with understanding the meaning of words and sentences.

2 To control our muscular movements

The messages from our sense organs often call for us to take appropriate action—and the cortex has another specialized strip, as shown in Figure 2-2, that controls bodily movements from feet to head. There is also an area for speaking that moves the vocal cords and muscles associated with them in a way that produces meaningful sounds.

3 To store our memories

Out of the information received from the sense organs, the brain also creates our memories of what has happened to us—and thus helps us learn from experience as will be explained in Chapter 4. How and where memories are stored is not known. Presumably this is the job of the unspecialized areas of the cortex, which are the uncolored portions of Figure 2-2, and of other parts of the brain that will be discussed later.

4 To do our planning

The unspecialized areas of the cortex also appear to be responsible for the fact that the brain "plans for the future, thinks, and reasons creatively" (4)—in other words, for all the cognitive processes that raise us far above the level of other organisms. The brain is the seat of human consciousness—our awareness of ourselves and what is going on in the world, our ability to think about our past and imagine our future. Though we take consciousness for granted, it is a strange and wonderful thing. We sometimes say, after making some kind of glaring mistake, "I think I'm losing my mind"—as if the human brain were like a house that somehow knows when it is falling down.

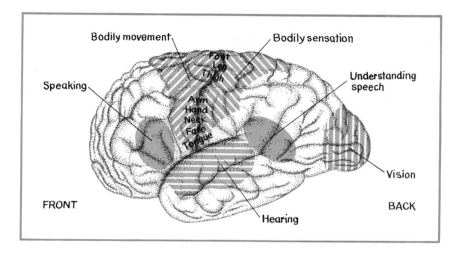

2-2
Some parts of the brain with special functions

On this drawing of the cerebral cortex as it would be seen from the left side of the body, the colored areas represent parts that are known to perform some of the special jobs described in the text (3).

5 To produce our emotions

Even with our superior cognitive abilities, our lives would be flat and barren without the deeply moving experiences we call emotions. True, the emotions of fear and danger are often upsetting and sometimes destructive. But they play an important part in the way we cope with the world and meet its crises. And there are other emotions that greatly enrich our lives—love, the joy of accomplishment, the spiritual glow we experience when we are in the presence of beauty and truth.

Emotions are also the product of our brains. They are particularly dependent on one part of the brain, lying well below the cerebral cortex, called the *hypothalamus*, and some of the circuits of which it is a part. The hypothalamus is the brain's most important link with the endocrine glands—which, as will be explained later, are active in fear, anger, and other emotions. Indeed the pituitary gland, which is the master gland of the body, is attached to the hypothalamus. Thus the hypothalamus, along with other parts of the brain, delivers messages that help produce the "stirred-up" bodily

processes that accompany emotion. The actual feelings we experience are another aspect of the human consciousness for which the cerebral cortex is responsible. In one way or another, it is the brain that accounts for our vivid appreciation of life's pleasures and our sorrow over its tragedies.

6 To manage our physical well-being

Some organisms manage to live their lives, feed themselves, and reproduce without the help of any nervous system at all. An example is the one-celled paramecium, which you may have seen under a microscope in a biology laboratory. Its entire single-celled "body" is somehow sensitive to heat and light and capable of initiating its own movements.

Animals a little higher in the evolutionary scale have specialized nerve cells but no brains. In the tiny sea creature called the coral, for example, there is simply a scattered network of nerve fibers with no central management. The neurons and the various parts of the body work together much like a loose federation of states, each preserving considerable independence. This haphazard arrangement is enough to serve the coral's needs—but it would be totally incapable of running the human body.

In discussing how the human body is maintained in a condition of well-being and efficiency, the key word is *homeostasis*—meaning a state of stability in such matters as internal temperature and chemical balance, with a proper supply of oxygen, water, and all the various other substances that the cells require. The air we breathe, the water we drink, and the food we eat are like the raw materials required to keep a factory busy. We need a central management to order them, make sure they arrive on time, distribute them where they are needed, and see that they are processed properly.

The hypothalamus, besides being a center for emotional behavior, plays a role in homeostasis by helping signal when the body needs more food or water and by regulating states of wakefulness and sleep. Another part of the brain acts like a highly accurate thermostat, turning on the instant the temperature inside the body gets a little too low and off again when the temperature gets a shade too high. One brain structure is responsible for coordinating such vital bodily processes as breathing and the heart beat, another for controlling bodily balance and keeping us right side up. (These structures are named and further discussed in the Postscript starting on page 69.)

The brain's miniature sense organs and glands

One reason the brain is so versatile is that its nerve cells are of many different kinds, with their own specialized functions. Depending on how finely one cares to make the differentiations, there are at least 100 types and perhaps as many as 500 (5). This is far more than other organs of the body possess. The liver, for example, has no more than two different kinds of cells.

The primary job of most brain cells is transmitting messages. They receive information from other neurons, process it in various ways, and pass it along through the brain's many billions of possible channels. Others, however, perform different tasks. The hypothalamus, for example, has some cells that operate very much like sense organs—serving as its "eyes" and "ears" to observe changes in the blood stream and thus detect when the body needs more food or water. Other brain cells operate like sense organs sensitive to changes in the body's internal temperature.

The brain also has neurons that operate like miniature glands, producing complicated chemicals called *hormones* (named after the Greek word meaning "activators" or "exciters"). These hormones are released into the blood stream and travel through the body, stimulating many kinds of physical activity. One such hormone, produced by the hypothalamus, acts directly on the pituitary gland, spurring the pituitary in turn to release a hormone that affects other glands (6). Thus the hypothalamus has two methods of control over the endocrine glands—not only by sending messages over the nerve fibers connecting it to the pituitary, but also by producing its own chemical stimulants.

The brain's ability to produce hormones, discovered only a few years ago, is now one of the most exciting fields of scientific investigation. One recent discovery, which may lead to great advances in our knowledge of behavior, is that the brain even manufactures hormonelike chemicals that are similar in structure and effect to the powerful pain-killer morphine (7). These chemicals may help explain the mystery of acupuncture, or the sticking of needles into nerves in various parts of the body, a technique that has been widely used by

Does acupuncture work? If so, its success probably results from spurring the brain to produce hormones resembling morphine.

studies along this line may shed considerable light on mental disturbances, emotional well-being and upset, and addiction to heroin—which, like morphine, is a derivative of the poppy plant. And the brain may produce other hormonelike substances, not yet discovered, that will also be found to have profound influences on behavior.

Chinese physicians to reduce pain and promote the cure of physical ailments. Applying needles in this way, it has been found, seems to increase production of the brain's own brand of morphine (8). Moreover, these newly discovered chemicals seem to affect parts of the brain associated not only with sensations of pain but with emotions and mood.

Psychiatrists in the Netherlands have reported that treatment with a substance derived from these brain chemicals has produced striking and long-lasting improvement in some patients suffering from the mental illness called schizophrenia (9). Further

Left brain and right brain

As was noted earlier, the topmost and most characteristically human part of the brain—the cerebrum and cerebral cortex—is divided into two hemispheres. Most of the nerve fibers connecting the brain with all the various parts of the body, either directly or through the spinal cord, cross from one side to the other. This means that the left hemisphere ordinarily receives sensory messages from and controls movement in the right side of the body. The right hemisphere deals with the left side of the body. Thus, if like most people you write with your right hand, it is your left hemisphere that directs the movements. The left hemisphere also controls the use of language—speaking and understanding the speech of others. Thus in most people the left hemisphere is the dominant one—the one we most often use and rely on.

Though we really have two brains—one for language and the right side of the body, the other for the left side of the body—we are not ordinarily aware of this dual thinking mechanism inside us. One reason is that the two hemispheres cooperate very closely. They have numerous interconnections, especially through a structure called the *corpus callosum* that resembles a thick telephone cable between the two hemispheres. Thus each half of the cerebrum and cerebral cortex ordinarily knows exactly what is going on in the other half.

What would happen if the corpus callosum were

missing and the two halves of the brain lacked this important channel of intercommunication? We do not have to guess the answer. We know—because surgeons sometimes cut the corpus callosum for medical reasons. (The surgery is performed as a last resort to relieve patients suffering from one type of epilepsy, a condition in which abnormal patterns of brain activity sometimes cause crippling seizures.) The operation has been found to produce some strange results. Patients may exhibit little change in intelligence, personality, and general behavior—yet careful testing reveals that in some ways they act as if they possess two separate brains functioning independently.

One of the most striking demonstrations of this fact has been obtained by using the photographs shown in Figures 2-3 and 2-4. The composite photo in Figure 2-3 is shown to "split-brain" subjects—as those with a severed corpus callosum are known—in such a manner that the right side of the photo is transmitted to the left hemisphere. The left half of the photo is transmitted to the right hemisphere. When split-brain subjects are asked to say whose photo they see, they answer that it is the child

2-3

Whose face is this? Can you pick it out of the "lineup" shown below?

If you saw this composite face and were asked to match it against the eight faces shown in Figure 2-4, you would have no trouble. But if you had a split brain your answer would be very different, as explained in the text.

2-4

The "lineup" of faces for comparison

These are the eight faces to be matched against the composite photo in Figure 2-3. Your own whole brain will see at a glance that No. 2 is the right half of the Figure 2-3 photo and No. 7 is the left half.

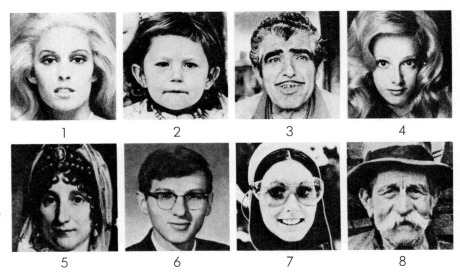

whose full photograph is No. 2 in Figure 2-3. But if they are asked to *point* to whose photo is shown, they select No. 7, the young woman with the large glasses (10).

Why should this be? Why should these subjects *say* so confidently that the photo is No. 2—yet *point* with equal confidence to No. 7? To find the reason, we must look to another split-brain experiment.

Left for logic, right for hunches

This other experiment is illustrated in Figure 2-5. The results show that the left brain of the split-brain subject did not seem to have much conception of form or spatial relationships. It produced only separate details of the model drawings, without putting them together into a whole. The right brain seemed to have a much better idea of the total pattern of the model drawings—but it had only a shaky grasp of many of the details. Neither brain,

working separately, could reproduce the model drawings with much accuracy. Try reproducing the cross and cube yourself, using your left hand if you are normally right-handed, your right hand if you are left-handed. You will find that your own intact brain, with the hemispheres cooperating through the corpus callosum, enables you to do a fairly good job even with the hand that you do not ordinarily use in this way.

The split-brain experiments indicate that the two hemispheres may operate in different ways and perform different functions. Such a difference in functioning would not be surprising, for the two hemispheres are not exactly alike even in structure. Numerous asymmetries—or differences in the sizes of various areas—have been found. These variations, with some areas substantially larger on the left side and others on the right, have been observed even in unborn babies, an indication that they are inborn rather than acquired as the result of experience and learning (12).

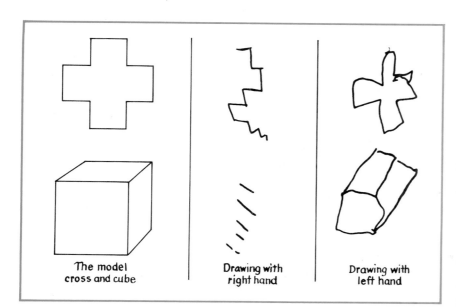

| The model cross and cube | Drawing with right hand | Drawing with left hand |

2-5

Drawings by a split-brain subject: the right brain does better

When a split-brain patient was asked to reproduce the drawings at the left, he could create only parts of the figures with his right hand, controlled by his left brain. He did better at reproducing the drawings as a whole with his left hand, controlled by the right brain—though he was still far from perfect (11).

A number of psychologists have concluded that the left hemisphere is specialized to deal with individual items of information, considered one by one in logical sequence—especially in the kind of thinking that we call reasoning, or arriving step by step at logical conclusions. It seems to be particularly adept at language, where sounds are put together in logical order into words, then words into sentences. The right hemisphere appears to specialize in considering things as a whole, taking account of many different items all at once. Thus the right hemisphere excels in processing many kinds of visual information, especially of form and space, and music and other sounds not related to language. It may also be the intuitive half of the brain. Albert Einstein, in making such great discoveries as the theory of relativity, apparently used this ability of the right half of his brain to view "the big picture" of things. He reported that he managed to do his most creative work by disregarding logic, letting his mind wander, and doing his thinking not in orderly language but in patterns of spatial relationships and hunches that could not be put into language at all. Einstein's experiences—and what has been learned in general about the differences between the right brain and the left brain—raise some profound questions about human life and civilization that are discussed in the box on Psychology and Society on page 55.

Knowledge about the left brain and right brain, however, is as yet very incomplete, and some of the findings are contradictory. One group of investigators, for example, found evidence of different functioning of the two hemispheres in the normal subject, with an intact corpus callosum, shown in Figure 2-6. When the subject was trying to master the toy shown in the photo (a spatial task), measurements of the electrical activity of his brain indicated his right hemisphere was doing most of the work. When he switched to writing a letter (lan-

2-6 A normal subject tackles a spatial task. What do his brain waves show?
This subject, a graduate student, has been fitted with a skull cap that holds electrodes against various parts of his skull. The electrodes are hooked up to an *electroencephalograph,* or *EEG* for short, that records the electrical activity (or brain waves) occurring beneath them. For what the waves showed when the subject was trying to perform a delicate feat of judging space and movement to get a steel ball through a labyrinth, see the text.

guage), the waves showed more activity in the left hemisphere (15). But other investigators, using somewhat different spatial and language tasks, have found little if any variation in brain waves on the two sides (16). One problem is the difficulty of interpreting what patterns of electrical activity can actually tell us about the functioning of the brain.

Is the right brain neglected?

In terms of the brain's two hemispheres and their different functions, the United States and other modern industrialized nations are strictly left-brain societies. Our schools emphasize reading, writing, mathematics, and science. Our most esteemed leaders—in industry, the professions, and government—are those who excel at the ability to focus sharply on the facts, analyze them, reason about them logically, and express their conclusions in convincing language.

Even our definition of intelligence has this same basis. Most intelligence tests require subjects to read written questions or follow spoken instructions. Most of the test questions measure the ability to remember facts, draw logical inferences, and manipulate words and mathematical symbols. It is these skills—all ordinarily residing in the left hemisphere—that determine whether a person's IQ is high, low, or average.

Because of our emphasis on left-hemisphere functions, some members of our society have a difficult time. Some children, for example, suffer from a condition of the nervous system called *dyslexia* that makes it very hard for them to read. They are seriously handicapped at getting along in society even though they sometimes have superior abilities of other kinds—drawing, for example. Had they been born into a society without a written language, some of them might be considered unusually talented because of their skill at manipulat-

ing form and space—while many of us who find it easy to read might be held in very low regard in such a society because we lack those talents (13).

Robert Ornstein is one of a number of psychologists who are concerned that our educational system and society as a whole have been unduly one-sided in training and valuing only "half our minds." Ornstein suggests that overemphasis on the left hemisphere, which tends to think about separate items of information in isolation from the big picture, may account for many of today's social problems. He points out that our society has made many brilliant technological advances—but often these individual advances have produced grave dislocations. Knowledge of atomic energy has led to an arms race and the threat of nuclear destruction. Advances in medicine have lengthened individual life expectancy but have also created overpopulation and the danger of famine.

As a result of our "preoccupation with isolated facts," says Ornstein, we have created many social problems "whose solutions depend upon our ability to grasp the relationship of parts to wholes. . . . The problem is not that technology is leading us to destruction, but that technical progress has outstripped our perspective and judgment." Perhaps it is time to "reinstate a balance"—and use the long-neglected talents of our right brains to gain an intuitive understanding of the grand pattern of human life and society (14).

How neurons speak to one another: synapses and neurotransmitters

Your brain performs its many functions by exchanging messages among its 10 billion neurons, through all the untold billions of possible pathways. These messages take the form of nervous impulses that are like tiny electical charges, each barely strong enough to jiggle the needle of the most sensitive recording device. If every neuron in the brain fired off its impulse at the same moment, the entire amount of electricity produced would be just about enough to power a small transistor radio. Yet these tiny impulses somehow account for all the brain's accomplishments.

Neurons in general resemble the drawing in Figure 2-7. The *dendrites* at the far left are the neuron's "receivers." When they are properly stimulated, they set off the nervous impulse, which travels the fiberlike length of the neuron to the other end, shown at the right in Figure 2-7. The *cell body,* which contains the chromosomes and genes that caused it to grow into a nerve cell in the first place, performs the work of metabolism.* Moreover, the surface of the cell body is dotted with numerous *receptor sites* that are also capable of responding to stimulation, like the dendrites, and setting off nervous impulses. The impulses travel along the *axon* to the axon's *end branches.* These are the neuron's "senders," which deliver its message.

Some neurons have their end branches in glands or muscles, which their impulses stimulate into action. Most neurons, however, particularly in the brain, have end branches that connect with other neurons. Their job is to pass messages along by acting on these other neurons.

---

*Metabolism is the process of converting the body's food supplies into new living cellular material, also of burning up food and cellular material to provide energy.

To understand how neurons speak to one another, it must first be noted that the nervous impulse can travel only the length of the neuron that produces it—from dendrites or cell-body receptor sites, along the axon, to the end branches of the axon. There it stops. It can go no farther. It can, however, influence other neurons.

The key to the transmission of messages is the *synapse.* This is a junction point where a sender of one neuron is separated by only a microscopic distance from a receiver of another neuron. At the synapse, where the two neurons almost touch, the first neuron can influence the second neuron in various ways. Sometimes the electrical charge arriving at the synapse is enough in itself to produce an effect. Usually, however, the action is chemical. The senders of the axon contain small amounts of chemical substances called *neurotransmitters.* When the neuron fires, a burst of these substances is released at the synapse (17). The chemicals flow across the tiny gap between the two neurons and act on the second neuron.

Different neurons produce different kinds of neurotransmitters. To date, six kinds have been identified (18). Some of the neurotransmitters act as stimulants; they urge the second neuron to fire off its own nervous impulse. Others, however, have the opposite effect; they tell the second neuron to refrain from action. They act to *inhibit* any activity in the second neuron.

To fire or not to fire?

Will the second neuron fire—or will it not? On this question, it must be pointed out again that the neuron has synapses with as many as several thousand others whose axon end branches are in close contact with its dendrites or cell-body recep-

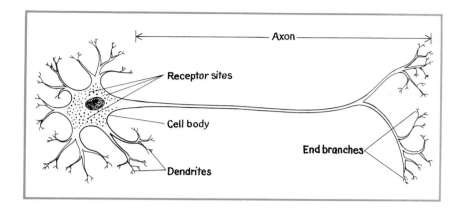

2-7

A more or less typical neuron

A typical neuron is a fiber-shaped cell with *dendrites* at one end, an *axon* at the other end, and a *cell body* somewhere in between, with *receptor sites* on its surface. The functions of the various structures are explained in the text.

tor sites. At any given instant, the neuron may be receiving messages from a few, many, or all of these axons. Some of the messages are delivered by neurotransmitters that stimulate it into action, others by neurotransmitters that inhibit it from firing. Moreover, the neuron itself responds in different ways depending on where the message arrives. Some of its receptor sites are like switches that signal "on." Stimulation at these points tends to make the neuron fire. Other receptor sites are like "off" switches. Stimulation at these points tends to inhibit the neuron from firing (19).

Thus whether the neuron fires or not depends on the whole pattern of messages it receives. Ordinarily it will not fire in response to a single message arriving at one of its many dendrites or on its cell body. Instead the firing process requires multiple stimulation—a whole group of messages arriving at once or in quick succession from the other neurons with which it has synaptic contact. Moreover, the messages that represent signals to fire must outweigh the messages that inhibit it from firing.

In the brain, with all its multiple interconnections, activity goes on constantly at many thousands of synapses all at the same time. Each neuron in the network is receiving messages from hundreds or thousands of other neurons. The nervous impulses it receives may have no effect at all. They may be too few in number or too far apart in time to make it fire. Or the incoming messages urging it to fire may be canceled out by messages that inhibit firing. So the messages it receives may not get through at all. On the other hand, the messages may make it fire anywhere from just once to many times in rapid succession—and in turn influence all the many other neurons with which its own axons form connections.

At each of these new synapses, the process is repeated. The message may get through or not. It may inhibit other neurons or it may cause them to fire—again just a single time or many times in quick succession. Thus once a message gets started through the brain, its possible pathways are virtually unlimited. One neuron's impulses may stimulate a few or many other neurons into action. The new impulses may travel in any one of many directions or in a number of directions at once. They may be few or many, slow or rapid. And at each new switching point the process is repeated, introducing thousands of possible new pathways. Small wonder that the human nervous system is capable of so many accomplishments—and that the possibility of "brain control," though a favorite topic of some science fiction writers, strikes many psychologists as highly dubious (see box on Psychology and Society on page 60). By comparison with the brain, the nation's telephone network is just a child's toy.

Neurotransmitters, mental problems, and drugs

The neurotransmitters will be mentioned frequently throughout the book, for they play a part in many forms of human behavior. Anything that affects the amount and effectiveness of neurotransmitters in the brain cells is likely to have a profound influence on our thinking and our moods. Many forms of mental illness seem to depend on abnormalities of brain chemistry. Some of the most bizarre symptoms—for example, those of the serious disturb-ance called schizophrenia—can be relieved through the use of medications that change the amount and activity of the neurotransmitters.

Feelings of depression, ranging from mild to crippling, appear to go along with low levels in the brain of a neurotransmitter called *noradrenalin* (which is also a powerful hormone produced by the adrenal glands, as will be seen a little later). These low levels of noradrenalin, it has been found, can be produced by intense or prolonged stress, either physical or emotional (26). The feelings of depression can often be treated successfully with medication that raises the level of noradrenalin in the brain and its effectiveness at the synapses (27).

All the substances commonly thought of as "drugs"—from marijuana to heroin—exert their mind-altering influences by acting on the brain's neurotransmitters. So, in a less spectacular way, do alcohol, nicotine, and the caffeine in coffee. So do the tranquilizers, sleeping pills, and pepper-uppers often prescribed by physicians. Thus neurotransmitters are a key to many aspects of human personality and attempts to alter it.

Members of a teenage drug group offer mutual help in kicking the drug habit—in other words, in no longer tampering with the brain's neuro-transmitters.

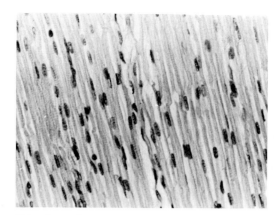

Striped muscle

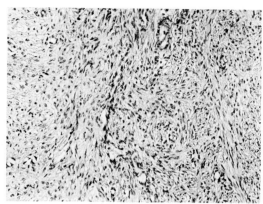

Smooth muscle

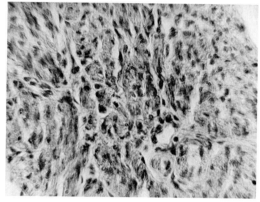

Heart muscle

2-8
Three kinds of muscles
for three different jobs

These are muscle cells of the human body as photographed through a high-powered microscope. For their functions and relations to the autonomic nervous system (ANS), see the text.

The autonomic nervous system

In controlling bodily processes, the brain has an effective assistant in the form of the *autonomic nervous system,* or ANS for short. The word *autonomic* means independent or self-sufficient—and in many ways the autonomic nervous system operates on its own, as its name suggests, without much if any conscious control. Even if we try, we cannot ordinarily command our glands to become more active—but the ANS, which sends its outgoing nervous messages to the various glands of the body, can do the job. The ANS also connects with some muscles over which we ordinarily have no conscious control. Note that we have three different kinds of muscles in our bodies:

1 The muscles of movement, such as those in our arms and legs. Because of their appearance under the microscope (see Figure 2-8) these

Brain control: Can a "Big Brother" manipulate our thoughts?

Many experiments with animals have shown that behavior can be greatly influenced by electrical stimulation through electrodes planted in the brain, or by surgery that destroys some of the brain tissue. When a particular small area of the hypothalamus is destroyed, animals stay awake until they die of exhaustion. When another part of the hypothalamus is destroyed, animals spend most of their time sleeping (20). Similar effects can be produced by chemical stimulation, using substances that resemble the brain's neurotransmitters. Thus injecting one kind of chemical into the hypothalamus will make an animal stop eating, even if it is very hungry. A different chemical makes the animal eat, even if it is already gorged with food (21).

We know that chemical stimulation can also change human behavior. Various drugs that influence brain activity (notably tranquilizers and stimulants such as amphetamines) affect human perception, thinking, and moods—as will be explained in detail in a section on altered states of consciousness in Chapter 8. Surgery has pronounced effects on human behavior, as in the case of split-brain patients with a severed corpus callosum.

All these facts raise the question of how subject we human beings might be to "brain control." Manipulation of human behavior through brain control, if it is possible, might serve to improve the quality of life. For example, some writers have suggested that what the world needs is a drug that will turn off humanity's aggressive impulses and therefore end crime and war. On the other hand, a dictatorial Big Brother might use some super-tranquilizer to keep everyone too placid to complain about the most brutal oppression and poverty.

Some psychologists believe that a considerable amount of brain control is indeed possible. Others reject the possibility—largely on the ground that the workings of the brain are so complex as to defy understanding, much less deliberate manipulation. Neuropsychologist Elliot Valenstein, a prominent member of this school of thought, has pointed out that an electrode in any given part of an animal's brain does not always produce the same response; nor does a drug always produce one specific ef-

---

are called *striped muscles*. They obey our conscious commands and move where and when we decide we want them to move.

2 The muscles of the stomach and intestines, other internal organs, and blood vessels (which they expand or constrict, thus regulating the body's flow of blood). Because of their very different appearance, readily seen in Figure

2-8, these are known as *smooth muscles*.
3 The *heart muscles*, which are of a type found nowhere else in the body—specially designed to work tirelessly throughout a lifetime of beating and pumping blood.

The smooth muscles and heart muscles usually do their work without any conscious commands.

fect. He believes that the circuits regulating behavior are so widespread, and the possible pathways so numerous, that the brain will probably always elude any attempts at control (22).

Certainly the brain seems to perform its myriad functions in many different ways. When necessary, it seems to call on its multiple connections and pathways to establish new routes of activity. To use the technical term, the brain exhibits considerable *plasticity,* especially in early life. Thus a woman born without one of the chief communications channels between parts of her brain showed no sign of its absence (23). A man born with several important parts of his brain missing or stunted had a normal personality and intelligence and in fact led his class in school (24). People have even managed to function satisfactorily after their brains had been seriously damaged in accidents suffered when they were adults (25).

The most valuable thing we know about the brain, indeed, is this: In a normal human being, with an intact and undamaged brain and with no artificial stimulation by electrodes or drugs, the brain acts as a unit. All its structures and circuits work as an entity to integrate behavior—and, most important, as the instrument through which behavior is modified by learning. We know that the pathways of learning somehow laid down in the brain are the real controllers of most of our behavior. They influence how we will interpret and respond to the stimuli that reach our senses. They influence what we find pleasant and what we find unpleasant. They determine what we find psychologically stressful and what we react to emotionally. They, even more than real physical needs, determine our habits of sleep, hunger, thirst, and sexual behavior.

Thus a Big Brother can probably accomplish more through manipulation of the educational system and other sources of information than through electrodes, drugs, or any other form of brain control. Dictators may hope that someday brain control will become a reality—but in the meantime they rely on decreeing what is taught in the schools and printed in newspapers. Censorship has been the most effective form of brain control to date—and may forever remain so.

We cannot order our stomachs to digest food. We cannot order the muscles of the blood vessels to channel a strong flow of blood to the stomach to aid digestion—or to redirect the flow of blood toward the striped muscles when we have to do physical work. We cannot make our hearts pump faster or slower. But the ANS can do all these things—and does so constantly, even when we are asleep or in a deep coma caused by an anesthetic or brain injury.

The system's little brains

The autonomic nervous system is made up of a number of centers called *ganglia.* These are like

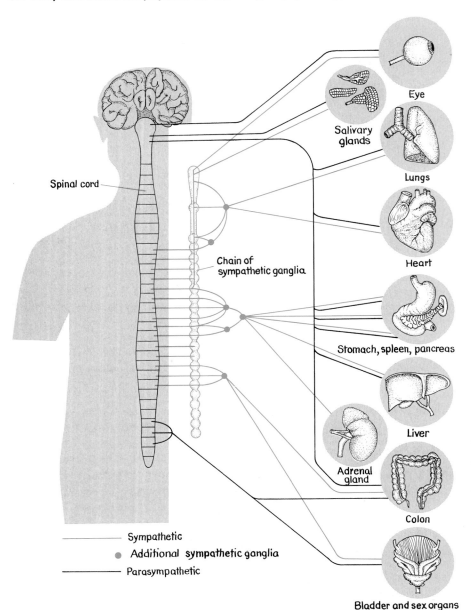

Spinal cord

Chain of
sympathetic ganglia

Eye

Salivary
glands

Lungs

Heart

Stomach, spleen, pancreas

Liver

Adrenal
gland

Colon

Bladder and sex organs

——— Sympathetic
● Additional sympathetic ganglia
——— Parasympathetic

2-9
Autonomic nervous system
The long chain of ganglia of the *sympathetic division* extends down the side of the spinal cord, to which it makes many connections. (There is a similar chain on the other side of the body.) The *parasympathetic division* has small ganglia near the glands and smooth muscles that both divisions help control, though in different ways (28).

small brains scattered through the body. They consist of masses of nerve cells packed together and connected with one another—just as in the brain itself but on a much smaller scale. Some of these neurons, as you can see in Figure 2-9, have long fibers over which they send commands to the glands, smooth muscles, and heart muscles. Others are connected to the brain and the spinal cord—which means that the ANS, though independent in many ways, does take some orders from above. In the case of being wakened by shouts of "Fire," your ears send a message to your brain, which then sends an emergency command to the ANS, which in turn springs into action through its various connections with the glands and muscles.

Running the ordinary business of living: the job of the parasympathetic division

As you can see in Figure 2-9, there are two divisions of the ANS, differing in both structure and function. One of them, the *parasympathetic division*, connects with the stem of the brain and the lower part of the spinal cord. It is made up of a number of widely scattered ganglia, most of which lie near the glands or muscles to which it delivers its messages. Because it is so loosely constructed, it tends to act in piecemeal fashion, delivering its orders to one or several parts of the body but not necessarily to all at once.

In general, the parasympathetic division seems to play its most important role during those frequent periods when no danger threatens and the body can relax and go about the ordinary business of living. It tends to slow down the work of the heart and lungs. It aids digestion by stimulating our salivary glands, producing wavelike motions of the

Joy is the most glorious of the emotions controlled by the ANS.

muscles of the stomach and intestines, and encouraging the stomach to produce digestive acid and the liver to produce the digestive fluid called bile. It also brings about elimination of the body's waste products from the intestines and bladder. At times, however, the parasympathetic division abandons these usual tasks and helps mobilize the body for emergency action. When it does this— operating in ways that are not yet understood—it seems to assist and supplement the work of the other part of the autonomic system, the sympathetic division.

Meeting emergencies: the job of the sympathetic division

The *sympathetic division* is shown in Figure 2-9 as a long chain of ganglia extending down the side of the spinal cord. There is a similar chain, not shown, on the other side of the cord. All the many ganglia of the sympathetic division are elaborately interconnected. Note that many of the nerve fibers going out from the chains of ganglia meet again in additional ganglia in other parts of the body, where they again form complicated interconnections with nerve cells that finally carry commands to the glands and smooth muscles. For this reason the sympathetic division, unlike the parasympathetic, tends to function as a unit.

When the sympathetic division springs into action, as when you experience fear or anger, it does many things all at once. Most notably, it commands the adrenal glands to squirt their powerful stimulants into the blood stream. By acting on the adrenal glands, liver, and pancreas, it increases the level of blood sugar, thus raising the rate of metabolism and providing additional energy. It causes the spleen, a glandlike organ in which red corpuscles are stored, to release more of these

The child's wide eyes are one of the bodily signs of strong emotion.

corpuscles into the blood stream, thus enabling the blood to carry more oxygen to the body's tissues. It changes the size of the blood vessels, enlarging those of the heart and striped muscles and constricting those of the smooth muscles of the stomach and intestines. It makes us breathe harder. It enlarges the pupils of the eyes, which are controlled by smooth muscles, and slows the activity of the salivary glands. ("Wide eyes" and a dry mouth are characteristic of strong emotion.) It also activates the sweat glands and contracts the muscles at the base of the hairs on the body, causing the hair to rise on animals and producing goose flesh in human beings. In general, the changes prepare the body for emergency action—such as fighting or running away.

The glands and their effect on behavior

Since the brain, autonomic nervous system, and glands all work together in managing the human organism and coordinating its activities, it has been impossible to discuss the first two without also referring to the third. But the work performed by the glands deserves further explanation—for the ways in which these little parts of the body operate have a significant influence on many aspects of our behavior. They control our growth from infant to adult, set our energy level, and have profound effects on our emotions and sexual activities.

The glands are specialized anatomical structures that perform a number of functions that are both useful and in some cases essential to keeping us alive. There are numerous glands in the body. One group merely produces substances that aid the bodily processes in routine ways. The sweat glands, for example, produce perspiration that helps cool the body. The salivary glands deliver fluids that mix with food in the mouth and aid the digestive process. The tear glands keep the surfaces of the eyeballs clean and moist. All these processes are important to our physiological well being but of only minor psychological interest.

There is another group of glands, however, that have a pronounced effect on bodily activities directly related to behavior. All the members of this group have a common characteristic. They have no ducts for the delivery of the substances they produce (like the passages through which the sweat glands deliver perspiration to the skin and the salivary glands deliver fluids to the mouth). Instead they discharge their products directly into the blood stream. For this reason, they are sometimes called the *ductless glands*. They are also known as *endocrine glands*, meaning glands of internal secretion.

The substances produced by the endocrine glands, as was mentioned earlier, are called hormones, meaning activators. These are complicated chemicals that trigger and control various kinds of bodily activities. Because they travel through the blood stream to all parts of the body, they have a widespread effect on many such activities and thus on the way we behave.

The master gland: the pituitary

The most important of all the ductless or endocrine glands is the *pituitary*. This little bundle of tissue, about the size of a pea, is buried deep inside the skull, attached to the hypothalamus at the bottom of the brain. Despite its small size, it produces a number of hormones that have profound effects.

In the early years of life, one of the hormones manufactured by the pituitary controls our growth,

2-10 Effects of the pituitary gland:
normal and abnormal

A man of normal height (television interviewer David Frost) entertains two guests with abnormalities of the pituitary gland—overactivity (at the left) and underactivity.

from infant to adult. If anything goes wrong, the results may be as illustrated in Figure 2-10. When the gland does not produce enough of the growth hormone, development is arrested and the child becomes a dwarf. When the gland produces too much of the growth hormone, the child becomes a giant.

At the time of puberty, beginning anywhere from the age of eleven to fifteen, the pituitary secretes another hormone that activates the sex glands—which then take over and change the child into a fully developed man or woman. Indeed one of the main functions of the pituitary is to produce hormones that speed up or slow down the activity of the other endocrine glands. It is the master gland, helping direct and control the others.

The energy glands: thyroid and adrenals

Two glands—both controlled in part by instructions delivered to them by the pituitary's hormones—play a vital role in regulating the general level of bodily activity. They determine the amount of energy we have available at any given moment to carry on our daily affairs and to meet emergencies.

The *thyroid* is a double-lobed mass of tissue lying at the sides of the windpipe. It produces a hormone that controls the rate of *metabolism,* the neverending process by which the cells of the body either burn up food to provide energy or else convert food into new living cellular matter. It is this thyroid hormone that makes the cells burn food faster to keep body temperature normal in a cold room—or that slows down the metabolic process in a warm room.

If the thyroid is not working properly, the results may be drastic. When the gland fails to produce enough of its hormone, the metabolic process is chronically slow. A person with an underactive thyroid tends to be sluggish and to tire easily (although these symptoms can be relieved by taking regular doses of thyroid substances extracted from animals). An overactive thyroid makes a person constantly "keyed up"—excitable and likely to have trouble sleeping.

The *adrenals* are a pair of endocrine glands lying atop the body's two kidneys. They are among the most important of all the glands. An athlete in the midst of competition or a student working at top speed to finish a term paper will often say, "I've got the adrenalin flowing." *Adrenalin* is one of the hormones secreted by the adrenal glands—a powerful stimulant that works on the heart muscles, raises the blood pressure, and prods the liver into releasing increased quantities of sugar into the blood stream, thus providing additional energy. Adrenalin also acts to relax the muscles of the digestive system, tense the muscles of movement, shift the flow of blood away from the digestive organs and toward the muscles, and serve as a clotting agent that makes the blood coagulate more quickly when exposed to air, as in the case of injury.

The adrenal glands also secrete a hormone called *noradrenalin*, another stimulant with effects on the body that are generally similar though different in a few respects. What the athlete in the midst of competition should really say, to be scientifically accurate, is "I've got the *nor*adrenalin flowing"—for noradrenalin is the hormone that

Running for their lives from an explosion, these people have adrenal glands secreting their hormones at top speed.

predominates in situations of intense physical effort, and especially in aggressive or angry behavior. Adrenalin, though the term is commonly used to describe both of the adrenal glands' stimulants, is actually secreted in greater quantities in situations of fear, as when you wake up to a shout of "Fire." Animals such as rabbits, which survive by being quick to show fear and run away, tend to have large amounts of adrenalin in their blood streams. Lions, which survive by fighting and killing their prey, have greater amounts of noradrenalin (29).

In addition to the stimulants adrenalin and noradrenalin, the adrenal glands produce a number of hormones that are essential to bodily health. Among other things, these hormones maintain a suitable salt balance and help regulate the body's supplies of food and energy. It is well established that changes in the way the adrenals operate, when they are overburdened by physical or psychological stress, can trigger many kinds of physical ailments, including stomach ulcers and heart disease—as will be explained in a discussion of psychosomatic illnesses in Chapter 11.

The sex glands

The sex glands are the female *ovaries* and the male *testes*. They are the glands of reproduction, producing the egg and sperm cells that unite to form new life—and carry along a heritage of the human genes that were described in Chapter 1. But they are also endocrine glands, secreting hormones into the blood stream that influence bodily development and behavior.

The ovaries produce large amounts of a hormone called *estrogen*, which, at puberty, brings about the bodily changes known as secondary sex characteristics— for example, the development of the breasts. Estrogen also controls many of the complex bodily processes that take place during menstruation and pregnancy. The testes produce large amounts of hormones called *androgens*, which bring about such secondary male characteristics as the growth of facial hair and change of voice and also play a part in male sexual arousal.

The female glands also produce small amounts of the male hormones, and the male glands produce small amounts of the female hormone. But the female blood stream ordinarily contains a large preponderance of estrogen, the male blood stream a preponderance of androgens. This raises a provocative question: Are the two sexes destined from birth, because of their glandular equipment, to behave in drastically different fashion? The question cannot be answered with a simple yes or no. It will be discussed in detail in Chapter 10, under the general topic of how men and women behave in our society.

The glands as an integrating system

As a group, the endocrine glands constitute an elaborate and efficient system that helps integrate many bodily activities. To a considerable extent, the endocrine system can operate independently. A hormone from one gland—especially from the pituitary—can spur another gland into action. But the operation also depends on the fact that the glands are connected with the nervous system.

Nerves ending in the glands carry messages from the brain and the autonomic nervous system that make the glands spring into action (or sometimes slow down). The relationship works both ways, for the glands influence the excitability of the brain and the rest of the nervous system and help create emotional experiences that influence our thinking. But overall, the glands serve mostly as a group of highly capable second-level supervisors and superintendents helping manage bodily activi-ties and behavior—with a certain amount of inde-pendence but subject to orders from above.

(Summary begins on page 80.)

Postscript

The nervous impulse and how it is transmitted

The nervous impulse is so foreign to anything else in our experience that it is difficult to comprehend at first. As has been said, it is a tiny charge of electrici-ty that passes down the length of the neuron fiber. But it does not travel like the electricity in the wires of a house. For one thing, it is much slower. House-hold electricity travels at the speed of light, 186,000 miles (299,338 kilometers) a second. The electric charge in the neuron travels only about 3 to 300 feet (slightly less than 1 meter to 91 meters) a second.

The charge can be compared to the glowing band of fire that travels along a lighted fuse, except that no combustion takes place in the neuron. What actually happens is that there is an exchange of chemical particles from inside and outside the nerve fiber, creating different electrical potentials between the neuron and the surrounding tissue.

Once the nervous impulse created by this change in electrical potentials has passed down the length of the fiber, the neuron quickly returns to its normal state and is ready to fire off another impulse.

How neurons give their all—or nothing at all

The neuron ordinarily operates on what is called the *all or none* principle. That is to say, if it fires at all it fires as hard as it can given its physiological condition at the moment (which, in complex ways, can be altered by the messages it is receiving from other neurons). All stimuli of sufficient power set off the same kind of impulse—as strong as the neuron is capable of producing at that moment.

After the neuron has fired, it requires a brief re-covery period before it can fire again. This recovery period has two phases. During the first phase the neuron is incapable of responding at all. During the second phase it is still incapable of responding to all the stimuli that would ordinarily make it fire, but it can respond if the stimuli are powerful enough. The lengths of these recovery periods vary. Some neurons recover very slowly and can fire only a few times per second. A few recover so swiftly that they can fire as often as 1,000 times a second when sufficiently stimulated. Most are in between, with a maximum firing rate of several hundred times a second.

Figure 2-11 shows the actual sequence of nervous impulses fired off by a neuron over a period of several tenths of a second, under three different kinds of stimulation. These tracings of the neuron's activity demonstrate that stronger stimulation makes the neuron fire more often but not with greater strength.

Turning beeps into meaning

Those little jolts of electricity shown in Figure 2-11 represent the basic activity that goes on inside the

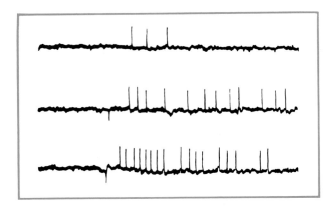

2-11 A neuron's messages:
all alike but in different patterns

These are tracings from an electrode that was placed on the neuron of a rat. Each upward movement of the lines shows a separate impulse. The neuron was from the rat's tongue, and the stimulus was salt solution in varying strengths. The response of the neuron to the weakest salt solution is shown in the top line. In the center line the stimulus was ten times stronger and in the bottom line a hundred times stronger. Note that the neuron's responses to these different intensities of stimulation varied only in rate and pattern, not in the strength of its individual impulses (30).

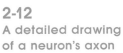

2-12
A detailed drawing
of a neuron's axon

The special functions of the *myelin sheath* and the *nodes* are discussed in the text. The drawing is of a motor neuron ending in a muscle (31).

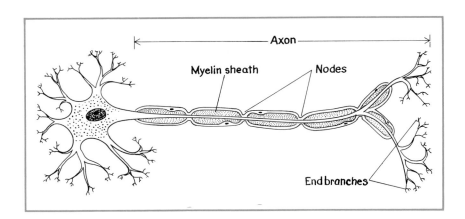

nervous system, in human beings as well as other animals. Each neuron ordinarily produces only one kind of impulse, its own little unvarying "beep." Yet somehow these monotonous beeps—by the rate at which they are produced, the patterns they form, and the way they are routed through the brain—manage to perform all the miracles of human cognition and consciousness. They tell us what our eyes see and our ears hear. They enable us to learn and to think. They direct our glands and internal organs to function in harmony. They direct our muscles to perform such intricate and delicate feats as driving an automobile or playing a violin.

More about the neuron

On page 57 you saw a drawing of a more or less typical neuron, showing its most important parts. Some additional details are illustrated in Figure 2-12.

The *myelin sheath* shown in the figure is a whitish coating that protects the axons of many but not all neurons. In neurons that have the myelin sheath, the nervous impulse travels faster than in other neurons. Transmission is further improved by the *nodes,* which are constrictions of the sheath acting as little relay stations that give the impulse a boost.

Figure 2-13 shows the dendrites of a neuron in full detail, so that the *dendritic spines* can be seen. These spines are the dendrite's receptor sites, which form synapses with the axons of other neurons. The dendritic spines seem to play an important part in learning. All the neurons of the brain are present at birth. The number never increases. Yet the brain quadruples in weight from birth to adulthood. Some of the added weight comes from the growth of supporting tissue. But the increased weight is also caused by the fact that the neurons grow and develop new dendrites and dendritic spines much as a young tree develops new branches. Experiments have shown that animals raised in an enriched environment, containing numerous toys and visual stimuli, develop heavier brains than animals raised in ordinary bare cages (33)—and that the neurons of their brains have more dendrites and spines (34). The neuron shown in Figure 2-13, with its heavy supply of dendritic

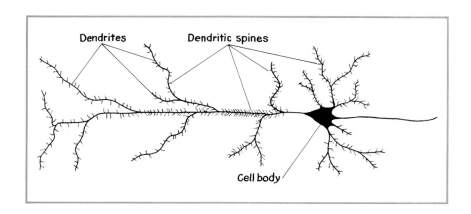

2-13
**A detailed drawing
of a neuron's dendrites**
Each of the *dendritic spines* shown here is a "receiver" as described in the text. The drawing is of a neuron in the cerebral cortex of a rat. (32).

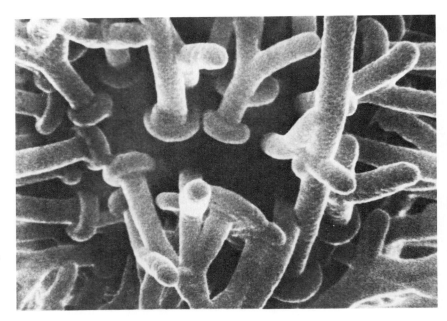

2-14

The synaptic knobs

This photograph, made at a magnification of about 2,000 times life size, was the first ever made of the synaptic knobs. It shows some of the synaptic connections of a snail (35).

spines, is from the brain of an animal raised in an environment that encouraged learning.

The synaptic knobs

Figure 2-14 is a photograph of another important part of the neuron—the little swellings called *synaptic knobs* found at the very tips of the end branches of the axon. It is these knobs that form synapses with other neurons at their dendritic spines or cell-body receptor sites. An enlarged drawing of a synapse is shown in Figure 2-15.

In the first neuron, the neurotransmitter is produced in the cell body and delivered down the length of the fiber to the *synaptic vesicles,* where it is

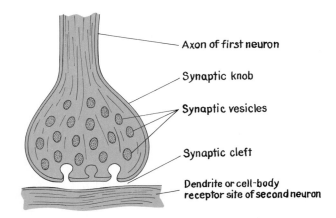

Axon of first neuron

Synaptic knob

Synaptic vesicles

Synaptic cleft

Dendrite or cell-body receptor site of second neuron

2-15 Where neuron meets neuron: the synapse

The axon of the first neuron ends in a synaptic knob, separated from the second neuron by only a tiny gap called the *synaptic cleft.* What happens at the cleft is described in the text.

stored until called upon. When the neuron fires, the nervous impulse reaching the synaptic knob causes the vesicles to release their transmitter chemicals. These neurotransmitters flow across the *synaptic cleft* and act on the second neuron—either helping stimulate this second neuron to fire off its own impulse or inhibiting activity. One of the neurotransmitters produced by nerve cells, incidentally, is noradrenalin—the same substance as the hormone that is secreted by the adrenal glands.

The first neuron, of course, has other synaptic knobs that form similar synapses elsewhere. And the second neuron has many other receptor sites that receive messages from many other neurons. Whether the second neuron fires depends not only on what goes on at this one synapse but also on neurotransmitters that may be reaching it simultaneously at its other receptor sites.

An overview of the nervous system

The neurons that make up the human nervous system, as has been said, are of between 100 and 500 different kinds, each with its own special function. They also differ greatly in size. Some of them are more than three feet (about one meter) long. For example, the motor neurons that enable you to wiggle your toes extend all the way from the lower part of the spinal cord to the muscles of the toes. Other neurons, especially in the brain, are only the smallest fraction of an inch in length. To understand the structure of the nervous system, however, we can think of neurons as falling into three classes.

1 *Afferent neurons.* These are the neurons of the senses. The word afferent is derived from the Latin words *ad,* which means "to" or "toward," and *ferre,* which means "to bear" or "to carry." The afferent neurons carry messages toward the central nervous system—from our eyes, ears, and other sense organs.

2 *Efferent neurons.* These carry messages *from* the central nervous system. Their axons end in either muscles or glands. Their impulses make the muscles contract or direct the activity of the glands.

3 *Connecting neurons.* These are communications neurons that carry messages between other neurons. They are stimulated only by the axon of another neuron. They do not end in muscle or gland tissue but only in synapses where they stimulate or inhibit other neurons. Most of these connecting neurons, though not all, are found in the brain and spinal cord.

A simple example of how the three kinds of neurons work together is illustrated in Figure 2-16, which shows how stroking a baby's hand produces the reflex action of grasping movements. As seen in the drawing, the nervous impulses that produce the reflex begin with the stimulation of an afferent neuron, which in turn stimulates a connecting neuron, which in turn stimulates an efferent neuron—whose impulses cause the muscle to contract.

The peripheral and central systems

The neuron fibers of the human nervous system extend to all parts of the body, as shown in Figure 2-17. The outlying neurons comprise what is called the *peripheral nervous system,* a network that extends to the fingertips, feet, and eyes and ears.

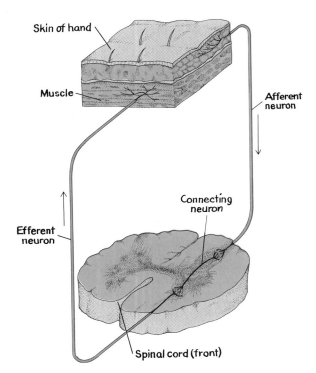

2-16 Afferent to connecting to efferent

Stroking the palm of a baby's hand stimulates an afferent neuron whose axon ends inside the spinal cord at a synapse with a connecting neuron. This connecting neuron, in turn, ends at a synapse with an efferent neuron whose axon ends in a muscle. Afferent neuron stimulates connecting neuron which stimulates efferent neuron—thus causing the reflex action of grasping movements. Note that the afferent neuron enters the spinal cord from the back, and the efferent neuron leaves from the front. This is always the case.

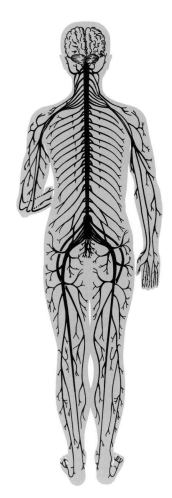

2-17 The human nervous system

Like the tributaries that form a river, individual neuron fibers at all the far reaches of the body join together to form small *nerves,* which is the name for bundles of neuron fibers. The small nerves join with others to form larger nerves, at last becoming the very large ones that join with the central nervous system—the brain and the spinal cord. Twelve *cranial nerves,* in pairs going to the left and right sides of the head, connect directly with the brain. There are also thirty-one pairs of large *spinal nerves,* connected with the spinal cord at the spaces between the bones of the spine.

All the neurons of the peripheral system eventually connect to the *central nervous system*—made up of the spinal cord, a sort of master cable to the brain, and the brain itself. The afferent neurons of the peripheral system carry messages which, when they reach the brain, account for our vision, hearing, and feelings of touch or of pain. The efferent neurons, originating in the brain or spinal cord, deliver their impulses in an outward direction and thus control the glands, organs, and muscles as far away as the fingers and toes.

The central nervous system roughly resembles a huge telephone exchange. The peripheral system is like the wires carrying messages to and from the central exchange, extending to the far reaches of the town it serves.

Some special brain structures and their functions

The main section of the chapter described some of the brain's most important features. As was stated, however, there are a number of other structures that play a part in carrying out the various functions of the brain that were discussed on pages 48–50. These structures, and the jobs they help perform, will now be described. While reading about them, refer to Figure 2-18, which shows their positions.

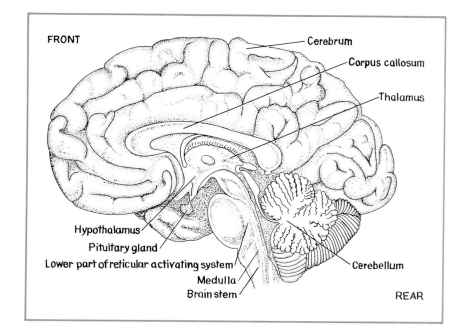

FRONT

Cerebrum
Corpus callosum
Thalamus
Hypothalamus
Pituitary gland
Lower part of reticular activating system
Medulla
Brain stem
Cerebellum
REAR

2-18
A sectional view of the brain
Individual parts of the human brain are shown here as they would be seen if the brain were divided down the middle from front to back (36). The functions of the various structures are described in the text.

Processing sensory information: the thalamus and reticular activating system

The brain structure called the *thalamus* has been aptly described as an "information processing center" (37). Messages from the various sense organs eventually arrive at the thalamus, where they are organized and sent on upward to the cerebral cortex. The thalamus also acts as a relay station for nervous impulses traveling in the opposite direction, especially some of the messages from the cerebral cortex calling for motor activity.

One part of the thalamus belongs to a network of brain circuits called the *reticular activating system,* which is related in a strange way to the processing of sensory information. The network gets its name from the fact that it appears under a microscope as a crisscrossed (or reticulated) pattern of nerve fibers. As shown in Figure 2-18, it extends downward to the bottom part, or stem, of the brain, where brain and spinal cord join together.

Nerve pathways carrying messages from the sense organs to the highest parts of the brain have side branches that enter the circuits in the reticular activating system. These side branches stimulate the system to send impulses of its own in an upward direction, thus arousing the top part of the brain to a general state of alertness and activity. For lack of such arousal, an animal in which the reticular activating system has been destroyed may remain permanently unconscious. Conversely, a sleeping animal can be awakened immediately by electrical stimulation of the reticular activating system (38).

Controlling muscular movements: the cerebellum

Of special importance in regulating the body's movements is the *cerebellum,* which is attached to the back of the brain stem. The cerebellum has

The cerebellum controls the intricate muscular movements of the musician.

The muscular coordination and balance of these dancers are also by courtesy of the cerebellum.

many connections with the parts of the cerebral cortex that initiate muscular activity. Its role is to coordinate all the various finely regulated muscular movements of which we are capable, such as typing and playing a flute. If the cerebellum is damaged, movements become jerky—and it requires great effort and concentration to perform even what was once such an automatic activity as walking. Victims of damage to the cerebellum also have difficulty speaking, which requires well-coordinated movements of the muscles of the vocal cords, windpipe, and mouth.

The cerebellum also controls body balance; it is the part of the brain that keeps us right side up. Like the cerebrum, the cerebellum is divided into two

lobes, or hemispheres. The left and right lobes are connected by the *pons,* which gets its name from the Latin word for bridge. The neurons of the pons serve as a bridge or cable that transmits messages between the two hemispheres of the cerebellum, just as the corpus callosum serves to exchange information between the two hemispheres of the cerebrum.

Storing memories: the hippocampus

A brain structure that plays a significant part in memory is the *hippocampus*. Psychologists have not established just how the hippocampus functions, but there is considerable evidence that it is essential to the establishment of long-lasting memories. For example, a case has been reported of a twenty-nine-year-old man whose hippocampus was surgically severed for medical reasons. He retained all his old memories but apparently could not establish any new ones. He could not learn the address of the new house to which his family had moved. He read the same magazines over and over again, and worked the same jigsaw puzzles, without ever realizing that he had seen them before (39).

It has been found that long-term consumption of alcohol by animals decreases the number of synaptic connections of the hippocampus—a fact that may explain the memory failures of human alcoholics (40). There are also indications that deterioration of nerve cells in the hippocampus may account for the loss of memory in very old people (41)—although some investigators doubt that aging in itself has much significant effect so long as people remain mentally active and continue using their brain cells (42).

Controlling emotions: the limbic system

The hippocampus is a part of the brain's *limbic system,* a network that also includes parts of the hypothalamus and is of special importance in emotional behavior (43) because of its connection with the autonomic nervous system and the pituitary gland.

In lower mammals, the limbic system appears to contain the programing that directs the instinctive patterns in which they feed, mate, fight, and escape from danger. Laboratory experiments have shown that surgery or electrical stimulation at various parts of the limbic system can cause animals to behave in ways that appear unusually docile or unusually aggressive, as illustrated in Figure 2-19.

This man has or will have a faulty memory—for alcohol damages a brain structure (hippocampus) that plays an important part in remembering.

We cannot be sure, of course, whether the behavior shown in Figure 2-19 represents genuine docility and rage or simply some other kind of change in the operation of the brain, as was discussed in the box on Psychology and Society on pages 60–61. One school of thought holds that abnormalities in the limbic system may account for the fact that some people are easily provoked into violent rages and physical violence. But other scientists disagree.

2-19 The limbic system and aggression

The photographs show the effect of electrical stimulation of the brain through electrodes planted in or around the limbic system of the cat. At left, under stimulation at one particular spot, the cat calmly ignores its traditional prey, the rat. At right, stimulation at another spot makes the cat assume a hostile posture toward a laboratory assistant with whom it is ordinarily on friendly terms.

In displays of emoton—perhaps aggression in particular—the brain structure of special importance is the limbic system.

Managing our physical well-being: the medulla

A brain structure responsible for coordinating a number of essential bodily processes, including breathing and the beating of the heart, is the *medulla*. The medulla is of vital importance in keeping us alive. It is also a major relay station, containing neurons that transmit messages between the spinal cord and the upper parts of the brain.

Summary

1 Our physical structures—brain and body—are the biological basis for all human behavior. How we act and feel at any given moment depends on the messages racing through the brain, the brain chemicals that help transmit the messages, activity in the rest of the nervous system, and the influence of the glands.

2 The human *brain* weighs about three pounds (1.4 kilograms) and contains about 10 billion *nerve cells* (or *neurons*).

3 The topmost and largest part of the brain is the *cerebrum,* covered by the *cerebral cortex.* The cerebrum and its cortex are split down the middle into a *left hemisphere* and a *right hemisphere.*

4 The cerebral cortex, larger in human beings than in any other species, is the part of the brain responsible for thinking and remembering.

5 The six functions of the brain are to:
   a receive messages from the sense organs and analyze and interpret them.
   b control muscular movements.
   c store memories.
   d provide for human consciousness and planning.
   e work with the endocrine glands to produce emotions.
   f manage our physical well-being by maintaining *homeostasis*—or a state of stability in internal temperature and chemical balance.

6 The *hypothalamus* is an important brain center for emotional behavior and plays a part in homeostasis.

7 The primary job of most brain cells is transmitting messages. Other brain cells act as sense organs sensitive to changes in body temperature and blood chemistry, thus detecting when the body needs more food or water. Other cells act as glands that secrete chemicals into the blood stream and thus stimulate many kinds of bodily activity.

8 The right hemisphere of the brain deals with the left side of the body. The left hemisphere controls the right side of the body and the use of language; in most people it is the dominant hemisphere.

9 The two hemispheres are in constant communication through the *corpus callosum,* a thick cable of interconnecting neurons.

10 Experiments with patients whose corpus callosum has been cut—split-brain patients—indicate that the left hemisphere specializes in individual items of information, logic, and reasoning, while the right hemisphere specializes in information about form, space, music, and entire patterns and is the intuitive half of the brain.

11 Each neuron in the nervous system is a fiberlike cell with receivers called *dendrites* at one end and senders called *axon end branches* at the other. Stimulation of the neuron at its dendrites—or at *receptor sites* on its cell body—sets off a nervous impulse that travels the length of the fiber to the axon end branches, where the impulse activates other neurons, muscles, or glands.

12 The key to the transmission of nervous messages is the *synapse,* a junction point where a sender of one neuron is separated by only a microscopic distance from a receiver of another neuron.

13 The sending neuron stimulates the receiving neuron electrically at times—but usually by releasing chemical *neurotransmitters* that flow across the tiny gap of the synapse.

14 Anything that affects the amount and effectiveness of neurotransmitters in the brain is likely to have a great effect on thinking and moods. Mind-altering drugs like marijuana and heroin act on the neurotransmitters; so do medications used to treat mental illnesses and depression.

15 The *autonomic nervous system* exercises a more or less independent control over the *glands,* the *heart muscles,* and the *smooth muscles* of the body's organs and blood vessels. It helps regulate breathing, heart rate, blood pressure, and digestion. In times of emergency it works in conjunction with the endocrine glands to mobilize the body's resources for drastic action.

16 The autonomic nervous system is composed of two parts: a) the *parasympathetic division,* which is most active under ordinary circumstances; and b) the *sympathetic division,* which tends to be active in emergencies.

17 The *endocrine glands,* or *ductless glands,* influence behavior by secreting chemicals called *hormones* (or activators) into the blood stream. The most important endocrine glands are:

a the *pituitary,* a master gland whose hormones control growth, cause sexual development at puberty, and regulate other glands.

b the *thyroid,* which regulates metabolism and affects the body's activity level.

c *adrenal* glands, which secrete the powerful stimulants *adrenalin* and *noradrenalin* as well as a number of other hormones essential to health and activity.

d the female *ovaries*, which secrete the hormone *estrogen* (responsible for the development of secondary sex characteristics at puberty and for bodily processes during menstruation and pregnancy).

e the male *testes*, which secrete hormones called *androgens* (responsible for secondary sex characteristics and sexual arousal).

Postscript

18 The nervous impulse is a tiny charge of electricity that travels down the nerve fiber at 3 to 300 feet (slightly less than 1 meter to 91 meters) a second.

19 A neuron ordinarily fires on the *all or none* principle—if it fires at all, it fires as hard as it can. Most neurons have a maximum firing rate of several hundred times a second.

20 Since each neuron usually produces only its own little unvarying beep, the miracles of human consciousness and cognition are determined by the rate at which the impulses are produced, the patterns they form, and the way they are routed through the brain.

21 *Afferent neurons* carry impulses from the sense organs to the brain. *Efferent neurons* carry messages from the brain to the glands and muscles. *Connecting neurons* are the middlemen between other neurons.

22 The *peripheral nervous system* is made up of the outlying neurons throughout the body. The *central nervous system* is made up of the brain and spinal cord.

23 Some special brain structures and their functions are the following:

a The *thalamus* is a relay and processing center for messages from the sense organs and for motor commands from the cerebral cortex to the peripheral nervous system.

b The *reticular activating system* helps keep the top part of the brain in a state of arousal and activity.

c The *cerebellum* controls body balance and the coordination of complicated muscular movements.

d The *hippocampus* appears to be essential to the establishment of long-lasting memories.

e The *limbic system* helps regulate emotional behavior.

f The *medulla* is responsible for a number of essential bodily processes including breathing and heart beat; it is also a relay station between the spinal cord and the upper parts of the brain.

Important terms

adrenalin	ductless glands	noradrenalin
adrenals	endocrine gland	ovaries
androgens	estrogen	parasympathetic division
autonomic nervous system	ganglia	pituitary
axon	homeostasis	receptor site
axon end branch	hormone	right hemisphere
brain	hypothalamus	spinal cord
cerebral cortex	left hemisphere	sympathetic division
cerebrum	metabolism	synapse
corpus callosum	neuron	testes
dendrite	neurotransmitter	thyroid

Postscript

afferent neuron	hippocampus	pons
all or none principle	limbic system	reticular activating
central nervous system	medulla	system
cerebellum	myelin sheath	synaptic cleft
connecting neuron	nodes	synaptic knobs
dendritic spines	peripheral nervous	synaptic vesicles
efferent neuron	system	thalamus

Recommended readings

Cooper, J. R., Bloom, F. E., and Roth, R. H. *The biochemical basis of neuropharmacology,* 3d ed. New York: Oxford University Press, 1978.

Eccles, J. C. *The understanding of the brain,* 2d ed. New York: McGraw-Hill, 1977.

Gazzaniga, M. S. *The bisected brain.* New York: Appleton-Century-Crofts, 1970.

Lewin, R. *The nervous system.* Garden City, N.Y.: Anchor Books, Doubleday, 1974.

Luria, A. R. *The working brain.* New York: Basic Books, 1973.

Ornstein, R. E. *The psychology of consciousness,* 2d ed. New York: Harcourt Brace Jovanovich, 1977.

Valenstein, E. S. *Brain control.* New York: Wiley, 1973.

Part two
How we learn and remember

One of the remarkable things about humanity is its great diversity. No human being, not even an identical twin, has ever been exactly like any other. Each of us is *unique,* unlike anyone who ever lived before or ever will again. Why?

Only a small part of the answer can be found in the workings of heredity described in Chapter 1. True, heredity does account for some of the wide range of individual differences. We are born with varying capacities in intelligence and physical strength—not to mention all the differences in size, body build, skin color, and facial features that distinguish each of us from all others. But in general all human babies are pretty much alike, whether born into a more or less average American family or in a European palace or a thatched hut on a Pacific island.

All babies possess the biological equipment that was discussed in Chapter 2—the same kinds of glands that help determine emotions and reactions to stress, the same kinds of nervous systems, including a brain capable of serving in a multitude of ways as "the supreme organ of integration." Presumably babies have always been built this way, ever since the beginnings of human life. An infant born today in a civilized part of the world will grow up to behave far differently from the way our ancestors behaved back in the wilds—but not because of any revolutionary changes in the structure of body or brain.

The chief reason we differ from our ancestors and from each other is *learning,* which shapes and changes us almost from the moment we are born. Most of what we think and do as adults is the result of learning. Some of us have learned to fix automobiles, others to perform brain surgery. Some of us have learned to fear snakes and others to keep them as pets, some to like school and some to hate it, some to welcome new experiences and others to shun them. Some of us have learned to be friendly, others to be suspicious. Inherited differences merely place limits on what each of us can do and probably push us toward certain kinds of emotional behavior. Learning does all the rest.

Few of today's psychologists agree with John Watson's theory that, by carefully controlling learning, he could turn a newborn baby into anything he wished—doctor, lawyer, beggar, or thief (page 30). One reason is that there is now considerable evidence, unknown in Watson's day, about the importance of inborn abilities and inherited influences on personality traits. But the chief reason is that the learning process has been found to be so complex, varying so greatly with the slightest differences in human experience, that it would seem to defy any attempt at total control.

Psychologists agree that learning is all-pervasive in our lives and in the science itself. Indeed almost everything discussed in this course is at least partly the result of learning—including, as you will see later in the book, our perceptions of the world around us, our motives and emotions, our personalities, and our relations with other people.

First must come a discussion of the learning process itself, in all its rich and varied aspects. Thus this section near the start of the book contains two chapters on the subject:

Chapter 3, "The Basics of Learning," deals chiefly with the simple form of learning known as *conditioning,* which is displayed by lower animals as well as human beings—yet, though it is by no means a unique part of human existence, has many long-lasting effects on our behavior.

Chapter 4, "Memory and How to Improve It," deals with how we acquire more complicated knowledge—such as the contents of this course—by committing it to that remarkable storehouse called human *memory,* then later somehow managing to call on the information when we need it. The chapter also contains a postscript on how you can use psychology's findings on memory and learning to help you study more easily and efficiently.

Outline

Chapter three
The basics of learning

When you were born, you were one of the most unlikely, helpless, pathetic, and incompetent creatures that nature ever invented. Unlike furred animals, you had no protection against cold. Unlike a newborn horse, you could not use your legs to move around and search for food. In fact you could hardly move at all in any useful way. Your chances of survival, had someone not immediately taken care of you, were zero.

Even a spider, when it first pops out of its egg, is much better prepared to cope with life. The spider, indeed, is born with all the equipment it ever needs. The built-in wiring of its nervous system contains all the blueprints for spinning a web to provide food, moisture, and shelter. The spider can get along, mate, and live to a ripe old age just by behaving as its inborn instincts direct it to behave. It does not need to learn anything.

Higher animals depend less on instincts, more on the ability to learn. As you know if you have watched trained animals perform, some amazing tricks can be taught to parrots, dogs, bears, lions, and dolphins. Under the guidance of psychologists, chimpanzees have learned to use language, at least after a fashion. This ability to learn, increasing at each step of the scale from lowest to highest forms of life, reaches its peak in human beings. Newborn babies may have less talent for survival than newborn spiders, but their capacity to perform in later life is infinitely greater and their individual behavior infinitely more varied. Spiders are limited to living in the same kind of web that the species has been weaving since time immemorial. Human beings build huts, pyramids, igloos, farmhouses, and high-rise apartments.

The change from helpless infant to self-sufficient and highly individual adult is partly a matter of what is called *maturation*. The baby's physical and nervous equipment need time to reach full efficiency. Babies cannot walk, talk, or show the full

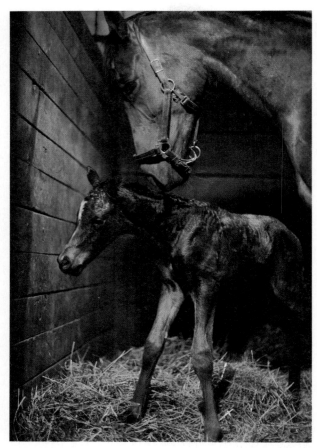

In ability to move around and cope with the world, this minutes-old foal far outstrips a human newborn.

human capacity for learning and thinking until the equipment is ready. This process of maturation, which will be discussed in detail in Chapter 13 on development, proceeds in orderly fashion throughout the early years of life, sometimes steadily and sometimes with dramatic leaps forward. At about the age of eight to ten months, for example, babies show a sudden and startling improvement in the ability to remember what has happened to them. This increased ability is not something they learned and has nothing to do with the experiences they have had. It is simply a particularly impressive case of maturation.

Most of the change from infant to adult, however, does result from learning—and learning does depend on experience. Indeed learning is often defined as *a lasting change in behavior produced by experience*. Many different kinds of experience can produce learning. They include not only what has actually happened to us (like a burn that teaches us quickly to avoid touching a flame) but also what we have observed (such as the behavior of other people, which we may imitate or decide to avoid). We even learn from our own thoughts—as when Einstein discovered that the formula for atomic energy is $E=mc^2$, an idea that he could not possibly have acquired from sheer experience or observation because it had never been expressed before.

Classical conditioning

Psychologists have been interested in learning ever since the science began. They have studied learning in fish, birds, and mammals ranging from mice to monkeys. They have studied babies, children, and adults—mentally gifted and mentally retarded, normal and psychotic. They have discovered a great many facts about learning—including, as you will find in the next chapter, a number of practical ways in which you can go about learning the contents of a book such as this one with greater ease and efficiency. But many aspects of learning are still surrounded by mystery and controversy. Psychologists are not even fully agreed—or sure in their own minds—about what happens in the simple form of learning that leads us to avoid flame after suffering a burn.

These chapters on learning are presented only as a general summary of findings about which most but not all psychologists would agree. To become acquainted with everything that is known and all the various ways in which different psychologists interpret the findings, you would have to start with the recommended readings listed at the end of the chapter, take advanced courses—and then spend a lifetime of concentrated study. (Many people have done just that—and have found their lives endlessly fascinating and rewarding.) With this warning that there is more to be learned about learning than the introductory course can ever hope to convey—or than has as yet even been discovered—let us start with one of the simplest and most universal forms of learning: *classical conditioning,* a process that accounts for many things that you do without knowing why.

Learning unreasonable fears, unreasonable preferences

Let us say that you suffer from a strange reluctance to be in any kind of small, enclosed place. It frightens you to step into an elevator or a closet. You breathe faster; you feel a sinking sensation in your stomach; your hands tremble. You know that this fear, which is called *claustrophobia,* makes no sense. But you cannot help it. You are frightened without knowing why.

Unreasonable fears of this kind trouble many people. Some are afraid of being in open spaces, as on a broad prairie or on a lake (*agoraphobia*). Some are afraid of heights (*acrophobia*); it frightens them to look out the window of a tall building or climb to the top of a football stadium. Some are thrown into mild panic by hearing a telephone ring, or driving past a cemetery, or even getting into an automobile.

Such fears are certainly not inborn. There are only two events that make newborn babies show

signs of fear—1) a sudden loud noise, or 2) an actual fall, when the body's support is suddenly removed. Thus other fears must somehow be learned—though usually we have no idea when or how.

Similarly, most of us have some equally unreasonable prejudices in favor of certain things, especially certain kinds of people. We may be instantly attracted to a man who has a mustache or a man who is bald, or to small women or women who are tall and broad-shouldered. We may feel unexplained warmth toward a certain tone of voice or the way a person walks or gestures or the way a

The old-time comedians knew how to frighten viewers suffering from even mild acrophobia.

person dresses. We know that these matters have nothing to do with what the person is really like, yet we find ourselves irresistibly drawn. Again we must somehow have learned this reaction, though again we do not know how.

In many cases the fears or preferences are the result of classical conditioning, which can best be explained by discussing the work of Ivan Pavlov, a Russian scientist who performed the most famous experiment in the history of psychology.

Pavlov and the drooling dogs

Pavlov made his experiment—indeed a whole series of experiments—in the early years of this century. His subjects were dogs, such as the one shown in the photograph. His experimental apparatus was the simple but effective device illustrated in Figure 3-1.

Pavlov's concern was the type of behavior called a *reflex,* exhibited by all organisms that possess a nervous system. The infant's grasping reflex, which operates through a simple nerve connection in the spinal cord, was described on page 73. In similar fashion, we automatically pull our hands away by reflex action if we touch a hot coffee pot. If a bright light strikes our eyes, our pupils automatically become smaller.

In a more complex way, the bodily changes associated with emotions are reflex responses. When a baby hears a sudden loud noise or feels the support for its body removed, for example, these stimuli automatically trigger the nervous system, which goes into action to produce the physical activities characteristic of fear. All the various kinds of reflex responses are forms of behavior that take place without any conscious effort. Our nervous system is just naturally wired in such a way that we

Pavlov (at right, foreground), assistants, and subject.

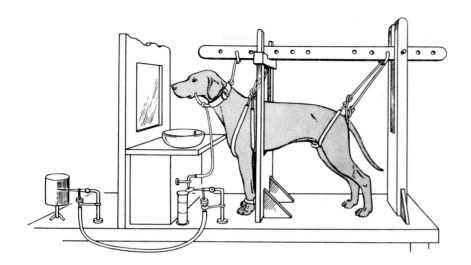

3-1
Pavlov's dog

A tube attached to the dog's salivary gland collects any saliva secreted by the gland, and the number of drops from the tube is recorded on a revolving drum outside the chamber. The experimenter can watch the dog through a one-way mirror and can deliver food to the dog's feed pan by remote control. Thus there is nothing in the chamber to distract the dog's attention except the food, when it is delivered, and any other stimulus that the experimenter wishes to present, such as the sound of a metronome. For the discoveries Pavlov made with this apparatus, see the text (1).

exhibit the reflexes in response to certain kinds of stimuli.

Reflex responses are built in, not learned. The question that interested Pavlov was this: Can they be modified by learning?

He set about answering the question by investigating the salivary reflex—which results in secretions by the salivary glands of the mouth when food is presented. He strapped a dog into the harness shown in Figure 3-1 and then introduced a sound, such as the beat of a metronome. The dog made a few restless movements, but there was no flow of saliva. This was what Pavlov had expected. The stimulus for reflex action of the salivary glands is the presence of food in the mouth—not the sound of a metronome, which is a neutral stimulus that has no effect one way or the other. When food was delivered and the dog took it into its mouth, saliva of course flowed in quantity.

Now Pavlov set about trying to connect the neutral stimulus of the sound with the reflex action of the salivary glands. While the metronome was clicking he delivered food to the dog, setting off the salivary reflex. After a time he did the same thing

again—sounded the metronome and delivered food. After he had done this many times, he tried something new. He sounded the metronome but did not deliver any food. Saliva flowed anyway. The sound alone was a sufficient stimulus to produce the salivary response (2). The dog had learned—through the form of learning now called classical conditioning—to exhibit the salivary reflex in response to a totally new kind of stimulus.

Learning to fear Santa Claus

How Pavlov's drooling dogs relate to more complicated forms of human behavior was demonstrated in another famous experiment performed by John Watson, the founder of behaviorism (pages 29–30). Watson's subject was an 11-month-old boy named Albert. His experiment was an attempt to establish whether the reflex response of fear produced in infants by a loud noise could be conditioned to take place in response to other and previously neutral stimuli.

At the start Albert had no fear of a white rat. But every time he touched the animal, a loud noise was sounded. After a number of pairings of animal and sound, Albert began to cry when he saw the rat. He also showed strong signs of fear toward some other furry objects, including a dog and a fur coat, and a suspicious attitude toward a bearded mask of Santa Claus (3). If the fear persisted, Albert may have come to be afraid of sidewalk Santa Clauses at Christmas—without ever knowing why. Unfortunately no information is available about Albert's future life because Watson lost touch with him—a fact that raises some questions of scientific ethics as discussed in the box on Psychology and Society on page 95.

The Albert experiment, despite its unsatisfactory conclusion, casts considerable light on the unexplained fears we often display as adults. In many cases they are simply conditioned responses, learned in childhood through some long-forgotten pairing of stimuli—indeed through an experience that may not even have impressed us very much at the time. Similarly, the experiment helps explain many of our unreasonable preferences. A liking for people of a certain type may go back to a childhood experience in which a person with that kind of face or body build or mannerisms elicited reflex responses of warmth and pleasure.

Conditioning comas and asthma attacks

Other experiments have shown that many kinds of bodily reactions can be conditioned to occur in response to previously neutral stimuli. Would you believe, for example, that a mere injection of salt solution, which has no effect on the body, could make animals lose consciousness and go into a coma? Or that human beings, prone to asthma attacks because of an allergy to dust or pollen, could suffer an attack when exposed to a harmless substance to which they had no allergy at all?

Such things can in fact be made to happen. In one experiment, rats were put into a coma with a heavy dose of insulin, producing the drastic reaction known as insulin shock. The drug was administered with a hypodermic needle while a bright light was shining. The association of needle, light, and coma resulted in a spectacular kind of conditioning. The same kind of light was turned on, the same needle was used to inject a harmless shot of salt water—and the animals went into a coma characteristic of insulin shock (7).

In an experiment on asthma, people allergic to certain kinds of dust or pollen were exposed to these substances—and responded with their usual symptoms of allergy—at the same time as other neutral and harmless substances were also presented. Eventually these neutral substances alone were enough to cause asthma attacks. In some cases, even a picture of the previously neutral substance was enough to produce an attack (8).

Conditioning, physical upsets, and treatment

The experiments on coma and asthma indicate the ways in which classical conditioning can produce some of the strange physical symptoms that may bother us as adults. An asthma sufferer may have been conditioned—not in the laboratory but by some real-life experience—to have an attack when walking into a particular room or seeing a particular person or even looking at a certain kind of picture on a television screen. Events that occur in our lives, unimportant in themselves but associated with past experiences, may make us have headaches or become sick to our stomachs. We may suddenly and inexplicably show all the symptoms of having a cold, heart palpitation, high blood pressure, dizziness, cramps, or loss of muscular control.

Another experiment points to a way in which the unfortunate effects of conditioning—whether physical symptoms or unreasonable fears—can be

Psychology and Society

The question of scientific ethics

Put yourself for a moment in the shoes of John Watson—a psychologist with a chance to perform an experiment in conditioning a fear reaction in 11-month-old Albert. Would you do it? Or would you worry about the possibility of doing long-term harm to the child? What if the fear actually did generalize to Santa Claus, thus depriving Albert of a childhood pleasure? What if he felt uncomfortable all his life around white animals, white rugs, and white-haired people?

The Albert experiment was performed at a time when psychology, in its early excitement over obtaining the first scientific understanding of human behavior, was inclined to ignore such questions. Now the science is much more concerned about the risks to its subjects. The great majority of today's psychologists would never undertake such an experiment. Any who did would be very careful to make sure that Albert's conditioned fear was promptly eliminated through further learning—a precautionary measure that Watson omitted (4).

The question of ethics has been the subject of much soul-searching among psychologists. Some methods of studying behavior seem to be clearly unacceptable. For example, no psychologist would consider urging a brain operation just for the sake of studying its effects. But in other cases, the line is difficult to draw. Are psychologists ever justified in deceiving their subjects—such as by telling them they are administering electric shocks to another person, when in fact the other person is a confederate who is only pretending to be shocked? Some psychologists defend the use of little white lies when necessary to achieve important findings (5). Others consider experiments that rely on deception to be "confidence games" that the science should scorn (6). There has been debate even over the propriety of using the technique of naturalistic observation (pages 17–19) to study people going about their usual activities—a technique that some feel may often be an invasion of privacy.

The American Psychological Association, to which most practitioners of the science belong, has drawn up a set of guidelines to ethical experimentation—and is prepared to expel any member who clearly violates them. But there are many borderline cases that psychologists can decide only by weighing any possible harm to their subjects against the value to humanity of the knowledge they may discover. This is a problem that will probably always plague a science that deals with human beings.

counteracted. The subject was a 3-year-old boy named Peter, who had a strange fear of rabbits. Though the origin of the fear was not known, presumably it was developed through classical conditioning in much the same way as Albert's fear of rats and beards. Could it be eliminated? A psy-

chologist approached the problem by gradually associating rabbits with a pleasant event—eating —instead of with fear responses. While Peter was enjoying a meal, a caged rabbit was brought within sight but at a safe distance. On subsequent days, again while Peter was eating, the rabbit was moved closer and closer. Eventually the fear disappeared—to the point where Peter petted the rabbit and let it nibble his fingers (9).

This kind of treatment, as you will find later in the book, is now one of the standard tools that psychotherapists use to treat physical and psychological symptoms that result from early conditioning. How the original conditioning occurred need not be known. The symptoms can often be eliminated through a reconditioning process that establishes different associations.

The elements of classical conditioning

With these facts in mind about the far-reaching effects that classical conditioning can have on our lives, let us now return to Pavlov's experiment and discuss this type of learning in more detail. To understand the process we must first consider its five basic elements, using the terms that Pavlov himself used to describe them.

1 The food used in the experiment was the *unconditioned stimulus*—the stimulus that naturally and automatically produces the salivary response, without any learning.
2 The sound of the metronome was the *conditioned stimulus*—neutral at the start but eventually producing a similar response.
3 Pairing the unconditioned stimulus of food with the sound was *reinforcement*—the key to conditioning.
4 The reflex action of the salivary glands when food was placed in the dog's mouth was the *unconditioned response*—the response that is built into the wiring of the nervous system and takes place automatically, without any kind of learning.
5 The response of the glands to the sound of the metronome was the *conditioned response*—resulting from some kind of change in the dog's nervous system produced by pairing the condi-

tioned stimulus with the unconditioned stimulus and therefore with the salivary response.

These elements are common to all cases of classical conditioning. In Watson's Albert experiment, the unconditioned stimulus was the loud noise; the conditioned stimulus was the rat; the unconditioned response was the automatic display of fear toward the noise; the conditioned response was the learned display of fear toward the rat.

Reinforcement, extinction, and spontaneous recovery

Once Pavlov had established the conditioned salivary response, he wanted to find out how long and under what circumstances it would persist. When he merely kept sounding the metronome without ever again presenting food—in other words, when he removed the reinforcement—he found that in a very short time the flow of saliva in response to the sound began to decrease, and soon it stopped altogether as shown in Figure 3-2. In Pavlov's terminology, this disappearance of the conditioned response is called *extinction*. But when Pavlov occasionally followed the sound with food—thus providing reinforcement not every time but sometimes—he could make the conditioned response continue indefinitely.

Pavlov also tried another approach. He withheld reinforcement and let the conditioned response undergo extinction, then gave the dog a rest away from the experimental apparatus, and later tried again to see if there would be any response to the metronome. Under these circumstances, the conditioned response that had seemed to be extinguished took place all over again. He called this *spontaneous recovery*—a phenomenon that may account for real-life situations in which unreasonable fears or preferences, learned originally through conditioning, suddenly crop up again after seeming to have vanished.

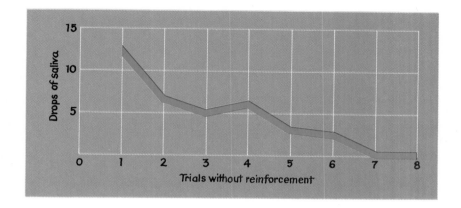

3-2
The conditioned reflex:
going, going, gone
The graph shows what happened to Pavlov's dog when the conditioned stimulus of sound was no longer accompanied by the unconditioned stimulus of food. The conditioned salivary response, very strong at first, gradually grew weaker. By the seventh time the metronome was sounded, the conditioned response had disappeared. Extinction of the response was complete.

Stimulus generalization and discrimination

In Pavlov's experiments, it must be noted, there was nothing magic about the sound produced by the metronome. Indeed he later used many other kinds of stimuli—and found that he could just as easily condition the salivary response to the sound of a bell or to a flash of light as to the metronome. He also discovered that a dog conditioned to the sound of a bell would also salivate to the sound of a different bell or of a buzzer. This phenomenon is called *stimulus generalization*—meaning that once an organism has learned to make a response to a particular stimulus, it tends to display this behavior toward similar stimuli as well. Stimulus generalization explains why little Albert feared not only rats but also a bearded man.

After Pavlov had established the principle of stimulus generalization in the dog, he went on to demonstrate its opposite, which is called *stimulus discrimination*. He continued to reinforce salivation to the bell by presenting food. But, when he sounded a different bell or a buzzer, he omitted the food. Soon the dog learned to salivate only to the sound of the original bell, not to the other sounds. The dog had learned to discriminate between the stimulus of the bell and the other stimuli. If the experiment is carried far enough, it can be shown that a dog is capable of quite delicate stimulus discrimination. It can learn to respond to the tone of middle C, yet not to respond to tones that are only a little higher or a little lower.

Learning to be neurotic

Pavlov also discovered that, by manipulating the problem of stimulus discrimination, he could condition a dog to behave as if it had become seriously neurotic. First he conditioned the dog to discriminate between a circle and an ellipse projected on a screen. Then he gradually changed the shape of the ellipse so that it looked more and more like a circle. Even when the difference in appearance was very slight, the dog still made the discrimination successfully. But when the difference became too small for the dog to recognize and discrimination became impossible, the dog acted strangely disturbed.

A number of dogs were placed in this situation, and the effects were always drastic. They became restless, destructive, or apathetic—sometimes all of these things. They developed muscle tremors and tics (10). This part of the Pavlov experiments suggests that human neuroses may also result from problems and difficulties that occur in classical conditioning. This possibility will be explored later in the chapter in connection with the phenomenon known as *learned helplessness*, which has been found to have profound effects on human behavior. First, however, must come a discussion of another kind of conditioning that is also a basic form of learning.

Operant conditioning

Classical conditioning, as has been seen, changes reflex behavior that, in the absence of any learning, would occur only in response to specific stimuli—like salivation to the presence of food. But reflexes are not the only form of behavior. For example, if a rat is placed in a cage, it exhibits many forms of behavior that seem to be spontaneous and self-generated, not mere predetermined responses to any kind of stimulus. The rat may sniff at the cage, stand up to get a better look, scratch itself, wash itself, and touch various parts of the cage. Similarly, babies in their cribs display many spontaneous actions. They move their arms and legs, try to turn over or grasp a blanket or the bars of the crib, turn their heads and eyes to look at various objects, and make sounds with their vocal cords.

Such actions are not reflexes set off by some outside stimulus. The actions are initiated by the rat or the baby; it is the organism itself that puts them in motion. Instead of having something in the environment produce a response, we have here just the opposite. The rat or the baby is acting on the environment. It might be said that the organism is "operating" on the world around it—and often bringing about some kind of change in the environment. Hence this type of activity is called *operant behavior*.

Like inborn reflexes, operant behavior can also be modified through learning. One way is through a form of learning that, since it resembles classical conditioning in a number of respects, is called *operant conditioning*.

B. F. Skinner and his magic box

The classic demonstration of operant conditioning was performed by B. F. Skinner, mentioned on pages 30–31, through the use of the special kind of cage shown in Figure 3-3. When Skinner first placed a rat in the cage, it engaged in many kinds of spontaneous operant behavior. Eventually, besides doing other things, it pressed the bar. A pellet of food automatically dropped into the feeding cup beneath the bar. Still no learning took place. In human terms, we might say that the animal did not "notice" any connection between the food and the

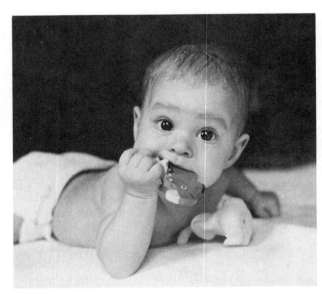

An infant demonstrates some operant behavior.

3-3
Learning in the Skinner box
With this simple but ingenious invention, a box in which pressure on the bar automatically releases a pellet of food or a drop of water, B. F. Skinner demonstrated many of the rules of operant behavior. For what happens to a rat in the box, see the text.

bar but continued its random movements as before. Eventually it pressed the bar again, and another pellet dropped. This time the animal "noticed" what had happened and an association was formed between the act of pressing the bar and the reward of food. The rat now began pressing the bar as fast as it could eat one pellet and get back to the bar to release another (11).

To put this another way, the rat in the cage (now famous as the "Skinner box") operated on the cage in various ways. One particular kind of operant behavior, pressing the bar, had a rewarding result; it produced food. Therefore the rat repeated that behavior. Using the same language that is applied to classical conditioning, we say that the presentation of the food was a reinforcement of the bar-pressing behavior. The rule in operant conditioning is that operant behavior that is reinforced tends to be repeated—while operant behavior that is not reinforced tends to be abandoned.

Some principles of operant conditioning

The Skinner box prompted a host of new studies of learning. It was found that operant conditioning followed many of the laws laid down by Pavlov for classical conditioning. Conditioned operant behavior, like the conditioned reflex response, was subject to *extinction*. If the rat was no longer rewarded with food for pressing the bar, it eventually stopped pressing. *Spontaneous recovery* also occurred. After a rest away from the Skinner box, the rat started pressing again.

Experiments with pigeons, which are especially good subjects in their own version of the Skinner box, clearly showed *stimulus generalization*. Once a pigeon had learned to obtain food by pecking at a white button, it would also peck at a red or green button. But if only the operant behavior toward the white button was reinforced, the pigeon displayed *stimulus discrimination*. In that case the pigeon learned to peck only at the white button and ignore the red and green ones.

Shaping behavior

Psychologists interested in operant conditioning have developed a method of teaching animals many complicated and unusual forms of behavior, a process called *shaping*. Figure 3-4 illustrates one way this process can be used with a pigeon. The bird is led step by step, through reinforcement by food as it approaches closer and closer, to exhibit a form of behavior that it might never have hit upon spontaneously. Pigeons shaped in this manner have become excellent quality control inspectors in manufacturing plants—watching drug capsules roll by on a conveyor belt and signaling when a defective one appears (12). Shaping is also the technique used to teach the many spectacular tricks performed by trained animals ranging from parrots to elephants.

3-4 Shaping a pigeon's behavior

How can a pigeon be taught to peck at that little black dot in the middle of the white circle on the wall of its cage? When first placed in the box, the bird merely looks about at random (A). When it faces the white circle (B), it receives the reinforcing stimulus of food in the tray below (C). Step by step, the pigeon is first rewarded for looking at the circle (D), then not until it approaches the circle (E), then not until it pecks at the circle (F). The next step, not illustrated here, is to withhold reward until the pigeon pecks at the dot.

Skinner (left), assistants, and one of his favorite subjects.

An example of shaping: an elephant that walks a tightrope.

The basic idea of shaping has been applied to complex forms of human learning through *programed learning* and teaching machines, another of Skinner's contributions. The contents of a classroom course are broken down into a series of very small steps. At each step a single new term or new idea is introduced or material that has been covered previously is reviewed. When programed learning is offered in printed form, as shown in Figure 3-5, students ordinarily fill in a blank or a series of blanks at each step. They can then uncover the correct answer—which, if they have matched it, provides reinforcement by saying in effect, "Yes, you're right. Good. Now go on." Teaching machines also present programed learning one step at a time, sometimes mechanically and sometimes through a computer, with the student making responses by pressing keys (see Figure 3-6) or using a light pen or typewriter-style keyboard.

Learning to be superstitious

Do you have a "lucky" sweater that you always wear to exams because it helps you get good grades? Do you win more tennis matches if you wear the same pair of socks and carefully pull on the right one before the left one? Do you avoid stepping on sidewalk cracks to prevent disaster?

If so, you are probably exhibiting the effects of operant conditioning—and have more in common with Skinner's pigeons than you might suspect. Pigeons, too, sometimes learn to be superstitious. Skinner showed this by retooling one of his boxes so that it delivered food from time to time without any rhyme or reason, and regardless of what the pigeon in the box did or did not do. The birds developed some strange and unusual habits. A bird that happened to be flapping its wings when the food appeared might continue to flap inces-

3-5

A programed psychology book

These are four frames on classical conditioning from a programed textbook that B. F. Skinner helped develop. After filling in the blanks, students look at the correct answers (at right, in color) to make sure they are right before going on to the next step (13).

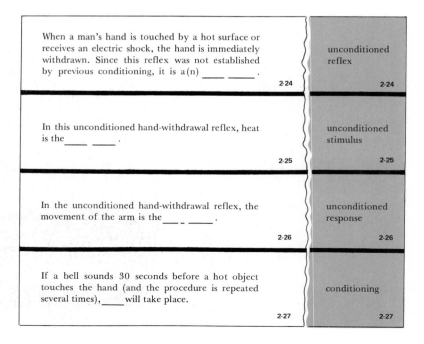

When a man's hand is touched by a hot surface or receives an electric shock, the hand is immediately withdrawn. Since this reflex was not established by previous conditioning, it is a(n) ____ ____ . 2-24	unconditioned reflex 2-24
In this unconditioned hand-withdrawal reflex, heat is the ____ ____ . 2-25	unconditioned stimulus 2-25
In the unconditioned hand-withdrawal reflex, the movement of the arm is the ___ _ ____ . 2-26	unconditioned response 2-26
If a bell sounds 30 seconds before a hot object touches the hand (and the procedure is repeated several times), ____ will take place. 2-27	conditioning 2-27

3-6
Learning with the help
of a teaching machine
The machine asks the pupil to distinguish between a toy and a non-toy, and the pupil responds by pressing the correct key.

santly, as if it "believed" that this produced food. Some pigeons learned to crane their necks, or to peck at a blank wall, or to keep moving in circles.

This kind of superstition, it has been suggested, often influences the behavior of animals in the wild (14). Animals engage in all kinds of random behavior, and their actions can be operantly conditioned very quickly through reinforcement. Nature provides many kinds of reinforcement that occur independently of anything the animal does—for example, rain that falls when the animal is thirsty, fruit that drops off a tree when it is hungry. If the environment just happens to provide food immediately after the animal has scratched an ear, the animal may acquire a lasting superstition that makes it scratch its ear regularly. Conversely, if an animal is scratching an ear just before being struck by a falling tree branch, it may behave afterwards as if it had decided that scratching means bad luck.

Many human superstitions, not only our own individual quirks but those common to many people, probably originated in the same manner. One widely held superstition may have been started by a boy who walked under a ladder and promptly fell into a mud puddle. Another may have been started by a girl who found a clover with an extra leaf, then promptly found a penny.

Some facts about reinforcement

The term reinforcement, as you will have noticed, keeps cropping up in these discussions of operant conditioning. Indeed it lies at the very core of the process and has therefore been the subject of a great deal of research. With animals, it is easy to provide reinforcement. Food and water constitute an obvious kind of reward; experimenters in operant conditioning call them *primary reinforcers*. But

Affection is one of the most powerful reinforcers.

is shown in Figure 3-8. The same thing holds true for young children. It is almost impossible to teach a 4-year-old to stay out of the street, for example, if the child is not rewarded for doing so (or punished for not doing so) until the father comes home in the evening (16). For adults, however, immediate rein-

3-7 The chimp and the poker chip
Why is the chimp dropping the chip into the slot? The reason is that the chip was used as a secondary reinforcer in a learning experiment—and now, when placed in a vending machine, produces a primary reinforcement by making food drop into the tray.

human beings seldom do any learning in order to receive food or water. Instead, they usually seem to learn for less tangible rewards such as praise or acceptance. Indeed even animal trainers often use the reward of affection rather than anything so elementary as food. Such rewards are called *secondary reinforcers*, and it has been assumed that they have gained their value through some kind of conditioning process that linked them originally with primary reinforcers. A simple example of secondary reinforcement is illustrated in Figure 3-7.

The effects of the time at which reinforcement is provided have been studied in great detail. In most animal experiments, it has been found, immediate reinforcement produces the most rapid learning. Any delay reduces the amount of learning, and too long a delay usually produces no learning at all, as

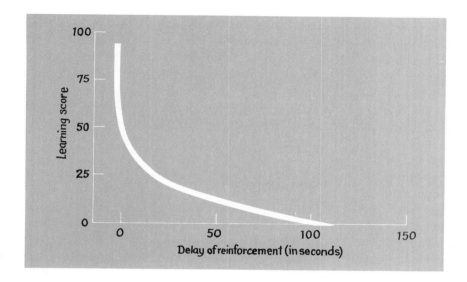

3-8
Oops . . . the reinforcement came too late
The steep drop in the curve shows how rapidly learning fell in an experiment in which reinforcement—food presented when rats pressed the bar in a Skinner box—was delayed for intervals ranging from a few seconds to about two minutes. Note that there was no learning at all when reinforcement was delayed for slightly more than 100 seconds (15).

forcement is not so important. They can associate behavior engaged in at one time with a reward that comes much later—as for example a grade given at the end of a course.

Experimenters have also studied the effects of *constant reinforcement* (reward for each performance) as compared with *partial reinforcement* (reward on some occasions but not on others). In general, learning takes place more rapidly with constant reinforcement—but the behavior is more persistent (that is, more resistant to extinction) after partial reinforcement (17). This finding has many applications to real-life situations. For example, parents who want their children to acquire a lasting tendency to work hard in school and get good grades will probably accomplish more with partial than with constant reinforcement. The trick is not to offer reinforcement for every good grade, but rather to bestow praise and affection (and possibly material rewards as well) a little more sparingly.

The long-lasting effects of partial reinforcement may also create problems in bringing up children. Suppose a little girl starts having temper tantrums whenever she asks for something and it is denied. Her parents try to ignore her behavior—but every once in a while, just to quiet her down, they give in and let her have what she wants. What they have done is set up a situation where the operant behavior of temper tantrums (the very thing they would like to eliminate) produces the reward of candy, or whatever it is the girl wants, on a schedule of partial reinforcement (the very thing most likely to make the behavior resist extinction and occur over and over again).

Applications of operant conditioning: a look at behavior modification

Animal trainers who want their dolphins to jump through hoops and parents who want their children to stop throwing temper tantrums have something in common: Both are trying to mold behavior. Indeed all of us are constantly trying to influence behavior—our own actions as well as those of the people around us (18). We try to lose weight, quit smoking, get higher grades, perform better on the job, be more cheerful, generous, and thoughtful. We try to influence other people to give us better grades or a raise, show us more appreciation and respect, stop doing things that annoy us. In so doing we often practice what psychologists call *behavior modification,* based largely on operant conditioning and the use of secondary reinforcement.

As psychologists use the term, behavior modification means any deliberate program designed to influence and change behavior through learning. The assumption is that behavior is controlled to a considerable degree by its consequences. If a certain type of behavior "works"—that is, if it results in some tangible reward or praise or even just feelings of self-esteem—it is likely to be learned and repeated. If it does not produce satisfactory results, it will be abandoned. This of course is a basic principle of operant conditioning, as was explained on page 99.

Experiments in behavior modification have produced some dramatic results. One of the first attempts was made with a 3-year-old girl in a nursery school. She was too shy and withdrawn to take part in any of the group activities. Instead she tried to hide by staying on the floor, motionless or crawling. How could she be led to get up, start moving around, and join the other children? The secret turned out to be very simple. As long as she was on the floor, her teachers ignored her. As soon as she got up on her feet, they flattered her with attention. Given this reinforcement, she quickly became an active member of the group (19).

The same kind of behavior modification—ignoring undesirable actions, rewarding and reinforcing desirable actions—has since been successful in many situations. It has been used to help other withdrawn children become more sociable and to produce normal conversation from children who refused to talk. In schools it has proved effective with pupils who disrupted their classes and had

fallen behind in achievement (20). Children who seemed well on the road to becoming delinquents have been led to cooperate with their family, take care of their room, and become less hostile and aggressive (21). Adults have learned to eliminate stuttering and unreasonable fears—and to some extent such problems as sexual impotence or frigidity and insomnia (22).

Token economies

One special kind of behavior modification, in which the reinforcement is a sort of make-believe cash payment for desirable behavior, is called a *token economy.* It is widely used in mental hospitals, where it was originated as an attempt to improve the general atmosphere and the daily lives of patients. For dressing properly, eating in an acceptable manner, and working at useful jobs, patients are rewarded with tokens that they can use like money to "buy" such privileges as movies, rental of radios or television sets, cigarettes, candy, and opportunities for privacy. These token economies have produced some remarkable changes in behavior, as can be seen in Figure 3-9.

Token economies have also been used successfully in schools, particularly to help retarded or emotionally disturbed children and those with learning problems (24). In one interesting experiment, a psychologist used actual cash instead of tokens in dealing over a period of years with a group of about 400 teenage boys who had done so badly in school that they were considered "uneducable." To get them interested in learning, he paid them small sums of money for any accomplishments. This seemed to get the boys going, to such an extent that later he could reward them successfully simply by permitting them to study favorite subjects. On the average the boys managed to cover between two and three years of schoolwork in a single year, and even their scores on

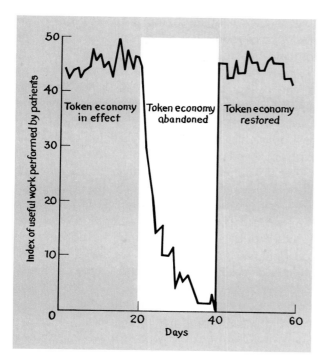

3-9 Behavior modification revolutionizes a hospital
Under a token economy, patients worked actively at useful jobs and helped run the hospital (line in colored area at left). From the twentieth to fortieth days of the experiment, the token economy was abandoned and the patients quickly went back to their old passive ways (line in center area). As soon as the token economy was put back in effect, they again pitched in as shown by the line in colored area at right (23).

intelligence tests improved substantially. Apparently they began to actually enjoy learning (25)—a development that could hardly have been predicted from their previous behavior.

Conditioning, biofeedback, and medicine

Another attempt to apply the principles of conditioning—in this case to the field of medicine—has added a new word to the English language. The word is *biofeedback,* which did not appear in dictionaries published even a few years ago but is now widely used. Newspapers, magazines, and television programs have acclaimed biofeedback as a revolutionary new tool capable of curing everything from headaches to high blood pressure, crippled muscles, and epilepsy.

Attempts have been made to apply biofeedback to all the various bodily activities over which we ordinarily have no conscious control—notably those produced by the autonomic nervous system (as was explained in Chapter 2), including heart rate, blood pressure, and the movements of the stomach muscles. Perhaps one reason we cannot control these activities is that we are not ordinarily aware of them; we do not know how fast our

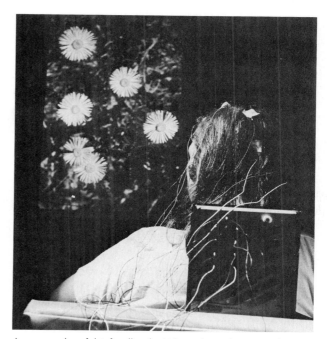

An example of biofeedback: When the subject produces a certain kind of brain wave, the picture of a flower appears.

hearts are beating, whether our blood pressure is high or low, or whether our alimentary canals are busy digesting food. Nor are we aware of many other bodily events—for example, rigidity of the muscles of the forehead and neck (which appears to be the cause of tension headaches), spasms of blood vessels in the head (migraine headaches), or patterns of brain waves (which may be related to epilepsy and also, in another form, to feelings of relaxation, peace of mind, and happiness).

Biofeedback procedures attempt to establish control over these activities by providing a moment-to-moment reading of what is going on in the body. With headache patients, for example, electrodes are attached to the muscles of the forehead and neck and connected to a device that clicks rapidly when the muscles are tense, more slowly when they begin to relax. Given this knowledge of what is going on, patients may learn to control the activity of the muscles. Similarly, through devices that monitor and report the temperature of the hands, migraine sufferers may learn to direct the flow of blood to the outer parts of the body and away from the blood vessels in the head that cause the problem. Some studies have reported consider-

able success with these methods (26). But other studies have found that patients showed no significant improvement (27).

Similarly conflicting results have been reported for the use of biofeedback in treating other ailments. One reason may be that people show wide individual differences in the ability to learn to control bodily activities, just as they differ in other kinds of physical skills. Another is that it is always difficult to evaluate medical treatment because ailments often improve or disappear with the passage of time—and may get better even if the physician merely prescribes a placebo (a sugar pill that has no effect at all on the body) that the patient feels confident will help (28).

Biofeedback is being studied by many psychologists and by researchers in numerous hospitals and medical schools (29). So far the results are not nearly so spectacular as the publicity suggests. But it is a promising field in which serious researchers have only scratched the surface. Certainly the technique has shown that at least some people can establish considerable control over bodily activities once believed to operate totally outside conscious influence.

Operant escape, punishment, and learned helplessness

Another finding made in studies of operant conditioning has many implications for real-life behavior. This is the fact that operant conditioning can be established with two very different kinds of reinforcement. The first, which has already been described, is providing such rewards as food, praise,

or valuable tokens. This is called *positive reinforcement*. The other is removing something that the organism finds unpleasant, such as an electric shock or a painfully loud noise. This is called *negative reinforcement*.

When negative reinforcement is used in the laboratory, animals usually learn very quickly how to get away from it. This has best been demonstrated with dogs as subjects and electric shock as the negative reinforcer in the device called a hurdle box that has two compartments separated by a barrier. The barrier is high enough to discourage the animal, but low enough for the animal to jump over when there is a real incentive. One of the compartments it separates has a wire mesh floor through which a shock can be administered; the other does not.

When the dog is placed in the wired compartment and the electricity turned on, the animal quickly learns to jump across the hurdle to the other side. This behavior is called *operant escape*. If some kind of warning is given, such as a light turned on or off a few seconds before the shock is administered, the animal will quickly learn to jump the hurdle when the light changes and thus miss the shock entirely. This behavior is called *operant avoidance*.

Escape and avoidance in human behavior

A great deal of everyday human behavior seems to represent some learned form of operant escape and avoidance. For example, a young boy finds the presence of a stranger in his home distasteful—a negative reinforcer from which he desires to escape. He may make a series of random movements and eventually hide his head in his mother's lap, thus shutting out the sight and sound of the stranger. Having once discovered this kind of escape from one particular kind of negative reinforcement, he may generalize the behavior to other situations—and conceivably turn into the kind of adult who stays away from social functions and remains as inconspicuous as possible in the most inconspicuous kind of job.

Many defenses against events that arouse unpleasant anxiety appear to be forms of operant escape and avoidance. You may have noticed that many people who are made anxious by criticism

Experience—as with this hot stove—can be a harsh but effective teacher.

become overapologetic. This may very well be a form of conditioned operant behavior that in some way served as a successful escape from anxiety in the past—perhaps with a mother who stopped criticizing and instead showed affection when her child apologized.

Punishment: does it deserve its popularity?

The discussion of operant escape and avoidance leads us to a topic of great importance—the widespread use of punishment to eliminate undesirable behavior by providing unpleasant consequences. Most people and indeed society as a whole seem to believe in the effectiveness of punishment. Babies are punished by a slap on the hand if they seem about to knock over a lamp or by a slap on the bottom if they cry too much. Older children are punished if they are "sassy," get into fights or the cookie jar, or make poor grades at school. The punishment comes in a wide range of severity—from a firm "No!" to a harsh spanking.

In elementary school, teachers punish pupils by keeping them after hours, by making them write essays on the evils of laziness, and by sending them to the principal's office for a stern lecture. In college, poor grades are in themselves a form of punishment and being flunked out is the ultimate. Employers punish workers by bawling them out or firing them. Society as a whole levies fines or prison sentences on people who drive too fast or without a license, create a public nuisance, or do any of hundreds of other things prohibited by law. There is considerable public support for the death sentence for crimes such as murder. The popular belief is that punishment or the threat of punishment stops bad behavior and leads to good behavior.

Students of marriage have found that even in this theoretically close and loving relationship both partners often use punishment in an attempt to change each other's behavior. Note this case: A husband is annoyed because his wife is often in a bad mood and has the habit of swearing at the children when they misbehave. In an effort to change her behavior, he throws a tantrum and yells at her, or storms out of the house for the evening, or stops doing household chores. The wife, in turn, is annoyed because the husband always leaves the den in a mess—with newspapers, magazines, and books scattered over the floor and on top of the television set. In an effort to change *his* behavior, *she* throws out his magazines, stops talking to him, and rejects his sexual approaches (30). Both are saying, in effect, "Yes, I'm punishing you by being as unpleasant as I can—and I'll keep it up until you change your ways."

The question is: Does punishment really work? In the case of the sour-tempered wife and the messy husband, it did not. They wound up taking their problems to a marriage counselor. But the question cannot always be answered with a simple yes or no. It is surrounded by many complications, all bearing on our attempts to get along in society and with our fellow human beings.

Punishment works with animals

Because ethical considerations limit experiments with human beings, most laboratory studies of punishment have used animals as subjects. In general, punishment often results in rapid and long-lasting learning by animals (31). As might be expected from what was said earlier about delayed reinforcement, the punishment is most effective if administered as soon as possible after the behavior that the experimenter wants to eliminate (32).

The punishment is most effective of all when combined with reward—that is, when the "wrong" behavior is punished and the "right" behavior is rewarded. This can be shown by placing a rat in a simple T-shaped maze where the animal starts at

Threats and punishments: Do they work as well as society seems to believe?

the bottom of the T and has the choice, at the top, of turning either right or left. The rat will learn the "correct" turn very quickly if rewarded with food when it turns right and punished with shock when it turns left. A real-life demonstration of the same principle is provided by the housebreaking of a young puppy, which, as countless dog owners have discovered, is best accomplished by punishing the animal immediately with a slap with a rolled-up newspaper when it wets the rug but showing that the same act is praiseworthy when performed outdoors.

But does punishment work with people?

In at least some cases, punishment also helps babies and small children to learn. Sometimes, indeed, its use is unavoidable. A slap on the hand when a child reaches toward a forbidden object may be the only way to prevent damage, as when the object is a fragile lamp, or even serious injury, as when the object is a sharp knife.

With older children and adults, however, the effectiveness of punishment is not at all clear. One reason is that it is impossible to say how any given individual feels about any particular kind of supposedly punishing treatment. If that statement strikes you as peculiar, consider this situation: A mother and father make it a regular practice, when their children misbehave, to raise a great fuss. They yell at the children, call them to task, bawl them out, threaten them with everything from being sent to bed without supper to a thorough spanking. They believe that this punishment will make the children mend their ways. The children, however, may view the situation in an entirely different light. Let us say that their parents ordinarily ignore them, displaying very few signs of interest or affection. Thus, to the

"If I never TRY nothin' . . . how am I gonna find out what I can get away with?"

"Dennis the Menace" used courtesy of Hank Ketcham and © 1976 by Field Newspaper Syndicate, T.M.®

children, the intended punishment is actually a form of attention that they crave. It constitutes a positive reinforcer that they are likely to seek again and again—not an unpleasant, negative reinforcer to be escaped from or avoided. Even a spanking may be regarded by a child as more of a positive reinforcer than a negative one.

Psychologists are well aware that punishment often achieves exactly the opposite of its intended effect. It often creates a vicious circle within the family: The child misbehaves, the parent punishes, and the punishment leads to further misbehavior (33). Punishment may also have far-reaching side effects. Studies of children who received drastic verbal or physical punishment have shown that they tend to acquire a dislike for the people who punish them, for example, their parents or teachers (34). They often become aggressive and punishing toward other children—and as adults are often cruel to their own offspring.

The sad case of the helpless dogs

Even with animals, punishment may produce unfortunate results. This was demonstrated in an experiment in which a dog was strapped into the kind of harness used by Pavlov. The dog then received a series of sixty-four electrical shocks, each lasting five seconds, delivered at random intervals. There was no way the dog could avoid the shocks or escape from them before the five seconds were up. Next day the dog was placed in a hurdle box. From time to time the light inside the box was dimmed, and a few seconds later a shock was administered through the floor of the compartment in which the dog had been placed. The animal could avoid the shock altogether by jumping over the hurdle into the other compartment when the warning light was dimmed, or it could escape the shock by jumping after the electricity was turned on. If the dog did not jump into the other compartment, the shock continued—this time for a full fifty seconds.

The results of the experiment, shown in Figure 3-10, were dramatic. A number of dogs were used in the experiment. All had ten trials in the hurdle box during which they could learn to avoid or escape the shock. But the amount of learning that took place was small. Most of the animals simply accepted the shock for the full fifty seconds, making no attempt to leap over the hurdle. They behaved in totally different fashion from a control group of dogs that had not previously received inescapable shocks. In accordance with what was said earlier about operant escape and avoidance, these "normal" dogs learned very quickly to leap the hurdle in time to avoid the shock or to escape in a hurry once the shock had begun.

How are we to account for the failure of the experimental dogs to learn—for their passive acceptance of a severe and long-lasting shock? The experimenters attribute it to what they have called

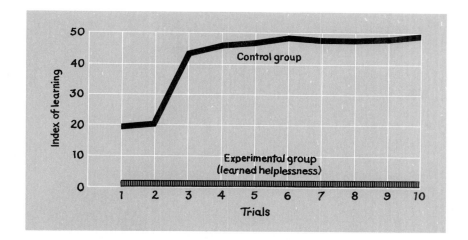

3-10
**Results of an experiment
in learned helplessness**
The rapid rise in the solid line shows
how quickly normal dogs learned how
to cope with an electric shock delivered
in a hurdle box, as explained in the
text. The shaded line shows the very
different behavior of animals that had
acquired learned helplessness—and
therefore seemed incapable of learning
how to do anything about the shock.

learned helplessness. While in the Pavlov harness the dogs had learned that nothing they could do had any effect on whether they received a shock or for how long. In human terms they had no expectation that they could do anything about the shock, even when moved to the hurdle box, and therefore no incentive to try to escape (35).

Learned helplessness in human beings

Human beings as well as animals, it has been shown, can be led to acquire learned helplessness through simple laboratory procedures. In one experiment, for example, college volunteers were subjected to punishment in the form of a loud and unpleasant noise. They were told that they could stop the noise by learning how to manipulate some control devices—but actually these devices had no effect. Later, when placed in another situation where it would have been easy to move a control lever and turn off the noise, the subjects made no effort and simply put up with the punishment until the experimenter called a halt (36).

The experiments on learned helplessness suggest that attempts to change human behavior through punishment are fraught with danger. Many parents who believe in the old adage "Spare the rod and spoil the child" are quick to punish almost any kind of behavior of which they disapprove. Often they do so with the same degree of verbal or physical intensity regardless of how major or minor the child's transgressions may be. Some parents seem to operate by whim. Depending on their moods, they may at times severely punish exactly the same behavior that they ignore at other times.

Children who are continually bawled out or spanked—especially if the punishment is inconsistent—may very well acquire learned helplessness. They may decide that they have no control over when, how, or why they are punished. They may give up trying to learn what their parents are trying to teach them, in which case the attempts to punish them into learning the difference between good behavior and bad become self-defeating. Such children may even become what the experimental dogs would have to be called in human terms—that is, seriously neurotic. The same unfortunate results may occur when elementary school teachers who are unsympathetic to the slow learners in their classes constantly berate them for their stupidity.

Do the sulllen faces indicate that reprimands are producing learned helplessness?

Helplessness as the result of failure

The original experiment on learned helplessness, performed with the dogs in the Pavlov harness in the late 1960s, opened up a new line of psychological investigation in which many important developments have been occurring. Punishment, it has been found, is not the only possible cause of learned helplessness. An even more common cause is failure—at any of the tasks we face throughout life, in the classroom or in the outside world.

In laboratory experiments, many of the symptoms of a temporary kind of learned helplessness have been produced by giving students problems that they were told could be solved but that were in fact impossible (37). In real-life situations, children have been found to display learned helplessness as a result of failure in a school assignment, such as mathematics (38). They may then fail at other subjects and take a pessimistic attitude toward their general abilities and prospects for the future. (For a discussion of the serious social problem caused by learned helplessness in the schools, see the box on Psychology and Society on page 116.) Adults may acquire similar feelings because of failure to find or hold a job or to establish satisfactory social relationships.

These findings are of great practical importance to all of us because failure is an inevitable part of life in our modern society. We cannot always succeed at everything. In college, only a few students get all A's and only one is at the top of the class. Not all would-be athletes make the team, and only one is chosen most valuable player. In the world of jobs, a dozen people may be competing for a promotion that only one of them can get. In our social relations not all of us can be voted most popular on campus (or in the neighborhood or at the office). Even if we have many friends who like us, there will always be others who ignore us or view us with distaste.

Thus all of us experience failure of one kind or another at one time or another. If the failure produces learned helplessness, we may become as passive and psychologically crippled as the dogs in the Pavlov harness. We may become victims of a deep depression—a "blue funk"—that a psychiatrist would classify as highly neurotic or even psychotic (45). But, though everyone experiences failure, not everybody suffers these drastic consequences. One of the great contributions of studies of learned helplessness has been to offer some clues as to when, how, and why this unhappy result is likely to occur—a matter that deserves discussion here even though it digresses from simple conditioning.

When failure occurs, who's to blame?

One finding is that, to understand any symptoms of helplessness you yourself may display, you have to ask yourself this question: When you fail, where do you place the blame?

Suppose you are in love—but the object of your affections rejects you. It makes a great deal of difference whether you blame yourself, blame him (her), or blame men (women) in general. Blaming yourself usually results in a serious loss of self-esteem and is closely associated with lack of confidence in the future (46) and sometimes serious depression (47). The particular way in which you blame yourself is also important. If you make a

sweeping condemnation—"I am unattractive to men (women)"—your symptoms of helplessness are likely to generalize to all future contacts with the opposite sex and indeed to your entire approach to life. If you limit your self-criticism to the particular situation—"I just happen to be unattractive to this one person"—your helplessness is less likely to become generalized. It tends to apply only to the particular situation.

If you blame the other party or the other sex in general—thus attributing your failure to outside factors—you preserve your self-esteem. But this does not necessarily exempt you from the symptoms of helplessness. Again it appears that if you make a sweeping condemnation—of all men (or all women)—your helplessness is likely to generalize and handicap you in other situations. If you blame

"I thought it was me, but maybe the school is no darn good."

Drawing by Addams; © 1974 The New Yorker Magazine, Inc.

Psychology and Society

Do pupils fail–or do the schools?

Educators have known for a long time that there is something seriously wrong with the American school system. Numerous large-scale studies have shown that elementary and secondary schools turn out many students who are not adequately prepared either to go on to college or to hold any but the most unskilled jobs (39). Despite all their years in the classroom, they have not mastered such basic skills as reading and arithmetic.

What has gone wrong? Many theories have been proposed. Some people blame television, for providing spoon-fed entertainment that makes children passive and discourages reading. Some blame lack of discipline in the home, resulting in unruly pupils who disrupt the classroom and refuse to do the work of learning. Some blame the schools themselves, for paying more attention to frills than to the ABCs. There is probably some truth to all these theories—but the recent studies of learned helplessness suggest another and more general explanation.

Of all the children who start school, those most likely to wind up without an adequate education come from low-income homes. Even by the sixth grade, it has been found, the average child from a low-income home is two years behind the average child from a middle-income home in scholastic achievement. By the eighth grade, the gap has grown to three years. Children from low-income homes are much more likely to drop out before finishing high school and much less likely to go to college even if they finish high school and have the ability to go on (40).

Why should this be? Does the answer lie in inherited intelligence? Or discipline in the home? Or the inferior quality of schools in low-income neighborhoods? Perhaps all these factors have some effect. But a well-known and influential government study called the Coleman Report, prepared by a sociologist, found very little relation between pupils' achievement and such facilities as modern buildings, libraries, and laboratories, or between achievement and salaries paid teachers or the presence or absence of guidance counselors. What really determines achievement, the Coleman Report found, is the attitude pupils have about themselves and their environment.

If pupils have what the report called a good

one particular person—"He (she) is overly competitive and rejecting"—there is less likelihood that the incident will affect other relationships (48).

Any form of learned helplessness can cause serious problems. One group of investigators has cited the example of an accountant who is fired from his job. If his symptoms do not generalize to other situations, he may continue to be a good husband and father and to function well in social situations. But the symptoms may cripple him nonetheless. He cannot get started on preparing his own income tax return; he cannot bring himself to try for a new job in accounting. If the helplessness becomes generalized, his entire life may be affected. He may become sexually impotent, neglect his children, and avoid any social contacts (49).

"self-concept" (meaning confidence in their own abilities) and a sense of control over the environment (that is, a belief that they can control their destinies through their own efforts, rather than being helpless pawns of other people and the world in general), then they are likely to do well in school. The psychological atmosphere of the school also plays a part. Pupils do best if they are surrounded by other children who come from families that encourage learning and who are themselves ambitious to do well (41).

The Coleman Report was prepared before psychologists began studying learned helplessness—but its findings are totally in accord with the new psychological developments. A bad self-concept and a sense of lack of control over the environment are characteristic of learned helplessness. Moreover, they have been found much more prevalent among the members of low-income families. When sociologists try to divide our society into social classes, ranging from lower-lower to upper-upper, they often use years of education and annual income as their guidelines—but an even more accurate indication is the degree to which people believe that they have power or access to power in the society and have control over their own and their children's lives (42). Low-income people generally lack these feelings of power and control—and so do their children (43).

The school system as it now operates appears to be helping establish a vicious circle. Its failure to provide adequate education for so many young people is likely to result in large numbers forced to spend their adulthood in marginal jobs or on public assistance—and at a poverty level that probably destines their own children to repeat the cycle. One of the most pressing social problems of our day, therefore, revolves around the questions: Why are the schools failing? How can the failure be remedied? As a start toward answering the questions, psychologists have been experimenting with teaching techniques based on recognition of the fact that low-income children are often ill at ease in school and especially vulnerable to any criticism—but sometimes show great improvement when a long-term program of encouragement provides positive reinforcement in the form of praise and other rewards for their efforts (44).

Therapy—and self-therapy—for helplessness

Though most of us suffer at times from learned helplessness—when failure makes us question our own abilities and call ourselves incompetent, lazy, unattractive, and just generally good for nothing—these pessimistic attitudes fortunately do not usually last very long. We have trouble with math but overcome it by working a little harder—or make up for our lack of mathematical talent by doing well in another subject. Though one person of the opposite sex rejects us, we soon find someone else who likes us a great deal. After being fired, we find another job at which we are more efficient and happier. We feel much better about ourselves and the world.

When we do this, we provide our own very effective therapy—for we are doing exactly what a therapist would try to do if our problems were so severe that we had to seek help. The best treatment for learned helplessness, it has been found, is to provide its victims with evidence that they do have the ability to succeed (50). Sometimes they have set their goals impossibly high and have to be taught to be more realistic. Sometimes they have to work at developing their skills, as for example at the job they want or in conducting their social relationships. But in general, by providing situations in which they can and do succeed, a therapist can demonstrate that they are more competent at more things than they ever realized while so down on themselves. This new confidence in their abilities generalizes to other situations (51), and they begin to feel a growing faith in controlling their own futures.

The cognitive view of learning

At one time psychology's study of learning was confined almost entirely to classical and operant conditioning—and indeed much of the work, like the influential experiments by Pavlov and Skinner and the first experiment on learned helplessness, was performed with animals as subjects. But many psychologists began to question whether conditioning, particularly as exhibited by animals, could account for all the things that human beings learn in a lifetime. The rise of the cognitive school of psychology (which was described on pages 31–32) was based in large part on the fact that we human beings remember things that happened to us even though we made no response at the time and received no apparent reinforcement. How, in terms of simple conditioning, can we explain how we know what we had for lunch yesterday, what was in an item read in last week's newspaper, a joke heard last year on television, the name of a movie seen five years ago? How, without assuming that cognitive processes play a part in learning, can we account for Einstein's discovery of $E = mc^2$?

Perhaps the best way to understand the cognitive theory is to examine some aspects of learning that led to its formulation—and some of the important differences in attitudes toward human conduct in general between members of the cognitive school and behaviorists like Skinner and Watson.

The behaviorists, the cognitive psychologists, and nature-nurture

One of the points of debate between the two schools concerns our old friend, the issue of nature versus nurture. The behaviorists tend to think not only of learning but of human behavior in general in terms of conditioning, produced by events in the environment. They maintain that we are all pretty much the creatures of our environment. Classical conditioning produced by outside influences has stamped certain kinds of reflex responses into us. Operant conditioning has led us to repeat actions that have been rewarded by our environment in the past and to refrain from actions that have been unsuccessful or have been punished. From the behaviorist viewpoint, we can study and understand human behavior without assuming that there is any such thing as a human mind—or that our conscious thoughts, whatever these may be, make any real difference in how we act.

In the case of animals, conditioning has most

certainly been demonstrated to explain behavior that might otherwise seem complicated and mysterious. For example, if you had watched an experiment once performed with a rat, you would probably have been thoroughly baffled. The animal was placed in a Skinner box that happened to be painted white but was standard, ordinary, and harmless in every respect. Yet the animal immediately showed signs of intense fear and tried frantically to escape. Why? Rats do not usually act that way in a Skinner box. Was this one strange in some way? In human terms, was it neurotic? Not at all. In a previous stage of the experiment, the animal while in the white box had received an electric shock from which it could escape only by learning to open a partition and flee into a black cage alongside. It had been conditioned to show fear when it was shocked; it continued to fear the white compartment though the shock was no longer present (52).

In behaviorist terms, human actions usually have an equally simple explanation. An analogy has been drawn between human beings going about their daily lives and a rat in a simple T-maze. In the case of the rat, we can accurately predict its behavior if we know in which arm of the T it has previously been rewarded with food and in which arm it has been punished by a shock. Human beings have had more complex experiences, and their environment constitutes a much more elaborate kind of maze. But we could also predict their behavior fairly well if we knew which of their responses had been rewarded in the past and which had been punished, and in what way and to what extent (53).

Cognitive psychologists, by and large, do not question the importance of classical and operant conditioning. But they believe that there are also other forms of learning—and that, at least in the case of human beings, these other forms play a more significant part. Moreover, they do not believe that the organism is merely a creature of its environment. True, they concede, our experiences do influence and change us—but we also take an active part in shaping and changing our own environment. For example, some of us behave in such a friendly fashion that we create a warm and approving atmosphere wherever we happen to be. Others "are problem-prone individuals who, through their aversive conduct, predictably breed negative social climates wherever they go." In other words, some of us ask for and get a friendly and rewarding environment. Others ask for and get rejection and failure. To a large extent, we control our own rewards and punishments—not the least of which are feelings of self-satisfaction and self-esteem, or, on the other hand, of self-blame and guilt (54).

Why you can't teach even a young dog every new trick

John Watson thought he could condition a newborn baby to be anything he wished. Indeed the strict behaviorists have assumed that any behavior of which an organism is capable can be conditioned to any kind of outside stimulus. But this has been found not to be true. The best evidence comes from a husband-and-wife team of psychologists who became professional animal trainers, applying their knowledge of shaping to raccoons, cockatoos, reindeer, pigs, chickens, and whales. They began on the assumption that they could teach almost any animal to do almost anything. Some 6,000 animals of thirty-eight different species later, they were forced to admit that they were wrong.

The animals' learning, they found, was limited by what is called *species-specific behavior*. Chickens have an inborn tendency to scratch for their food, pigs to root for it, raccoons to wash it. Thus the two psychologist-animal-trainers never were able to teach raccoons to pick up two coins and drop them into a piggy bank. The animals insisted on going through their natural washing motions by rubbing the coins together, dipping them into the bank, then rubbing them together again. The pigs insisted on rooting, the chickens on scratching (55).

One experiment of special interest, because it bears on the relationship of species-specific behavior to evolutionary survival, was performed in this manner: A rat was permitted to drink some sweet-flavored water while a bright light was flashed and a noise was sounded. Later the rat was made sick to its stomach through X-ray irradiation. Under these circumstances, what did the rat learn? It turned out that the animal learned to avoid sweet-tasting water. It did not learn to avoid the light or the noise (56). But if the negative reinforcement in this situation is an electric shock, rather than sickness, the animal will learn to avoid the flashing light and the sound as well as the food itself.

Presumably rats have a species-specific tendency to associate taste—but not other kinds of stimuli—with feelings of being sick. Indeed variations of the experiment have shown that a rat that gets sick after eating a certain kind of food does not avoid the dish from which the food was eaten, nor foods similar in appearance or texture—but only foods with that particular taste (57). This characteristic of rats and some other animals, which is known as "bait shyness," has obvious advantages in keeping them alive under ordinary circumstances where illness means that food was poisonous. It also offers another indication, of course, that not all responses can become associated with all stimuli.

Bait shyness may have a sort of human counterpart in some of the phobias mentioned earlier in the chapter. Phobias usually center around matters that have presented real dangers during human history—such as heights and open spaces, as was stated, or darkness and certain kinds of insects and animals. People seldom acquire troublesome fears of lawn mowers, power tools, or bathtubs, though today these things are potentially much more dangerous than darkness or open spaces (58). Our tendency to shun some objects and events, though not others, may be a form of species-specific human behavior. Certainly our use of language is species-specific behavior, dictated by the structure and dynamics of the human brain, that greatly enhances our range of learning.

Learning without reinforcement

The cognitive theory of learning also rests on an impressive accumulation of evidence that learning can and often does take place without any reinforcement at all. This fact was first discovered in an experiment performed about a half-century ago. At the time, the results were considered puzzling and their implications were not realized—but the experiment remains the best and simplest demonstration of nonreinforced learning.

The experimenter used a maze and three groups of rats. Group 1 always found food at the end of the maze—an obvious and immediate reinforcement. Group 2 never found food at the end of the maze; the rats in this group were simply placed in the maze and permitted to move around in any way they chose. Group 3 was treated the same way as Group 2 for the first ten days, receiving no reinforcement. After the tenth day, however, Group 3 always found food at the end of the maze.

How the three groups performed, as measured by the number of errors they made by going into blind alleys of the maze, is illustrated in Figure 3-11. The rats in Group 1 learned rapidly, improving every day right from the beginning. The rats in Group 2, never reinforced, displayed little learning.

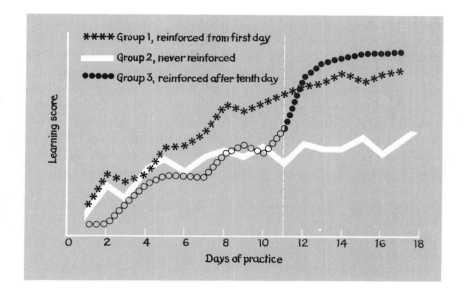

3-11
Learning a maze: with and without reinforcement
The graph shows the progress at learning a maze made by three groups of rats under different conditions of reinforcement. For the meaning of these results, see the text (59).

But the important line in the graph shows what happened to Group 3. For the first ten days this group also showed little learning. But as soon as a reward was provided at the end of the maze, on the eleventh day, they immediately began running the maze like veterans. Even in just wandering about the maze for ten days, without any reinforcement, they apparently had learned a great deal about the correct path. As soon as a reward was provided, they began to demonstrate this knowledge.

Acquiring knowledge in this way is called *latent learning,* meaning learning that takes place but lies latent and unused until there is some reason to use it. You can probably recall many instances in your own life when you learned something although you received no reinforcement at the time. Some common examples are these: A friend drives you to the nearby town of Smithville. You have no intention of ever returning to Smithville. You make no effort to learn the route. Still, if the occasion ever arises when you yourself have to drive to Smithville, you find that you remember the way, at least to some extent. Or, wandering through a business district, you see a window full of typewriters. At the moment you have no interest in typewriters. But later, when you decide to buy one, you find that you remember the location of the shop.

Do we learn a response—or a goal?

Cognitive psychologists cite another indication that learning must be more than the establishment of a mere stimulus-response or S-R connection: Even in simple operant conditioning experiments, an animal learns more than performing one simple type of response or activity. Thus, in a Skinner box, a rat may learn to press the bar with its right paw to produce food. But if its right paw is immobilized, it will manage to press the bar anyway, using its left paw. If both paws are immobilized, it will use its nose or its body (60). Similarly, rats that have learned to run through a maze to get food will take the same path even if the maze is flooded and they have to swim (61).

For a simple human analogy, consider the case of children who learn to pick up their toys at the end of a play period for the reward of pleasing their parents. What they seem to have learned, as one psychologist has pointed out, is "not a particular set of muscle movements, but the goal to be achieved." In other circumstances, they use different movements, or they pick up clothing instead of toys; they "perform the response in different but functionally equivalent ways" (62). Thus some psychologists believe that the core of learning is some kind of cognitive process that results in the acquisition of motives to behave in certain ways under certain conditions (63).

Other psychologists think that cognitive learning is based on expectancy (64). They would say that a rat in a Skinner box presses the bar or a pigeon pecks at the disc because the animal has learned to expect that this action will produce food (65). Similarly, we human beings take an aspirin when we have a headache because we have learned to expect that the aspirin will give us relief.

Learning as information-processing

Cognitive psychologists, whether they stress motivation or expectancy, regard learning as a highly active and complex process in which the mind constantly examines the information that our sense organs bring us about the environment. Out of all the information that bombards us, the mind selects and pays attention to what seems important; it compares this information with what we already know from previous experience; it weighs and judges the information and makes decisions about what ac-

tion to take. By forming meaningful associations between the new information and the old, it often stores the new information in memory—and when this happens we have learned something (66).

To cognitive psychologists, learning is only one element in a closely related series of mental processes (67) that will be discussed later in the book—notably memory (Chapter 4), the use of language (Chapter 5), thinking (Chapter 6), and perception (Chapter 8). The idea that all these elements and others play a part in how we view our environment and learn from it is known as the *information-processing theory*.

Learning through observation

Cognitive psychologists believe that the most common and useful form of learning, especially among human beings, is *learning through observation* (or, as some psychologists prefer, *learning through modeling* or *learning by imitation*). All three terms refer to the process through which we learn new behavior by observing the behavior of others.

Many experiments have demonstrated that even lower animals learn by observation and imitation. For example, one cat was taught in a Skinner box that it could obtain food by pressing the bar when a light went on. Another cat, which had been watching, was then placed in the box. This second cat began very quickly to press the bar when the light went on. Through observation, it had learned much faster than the first cat (68).

One dramatic demonstration of observation learning in human beings was recorded on film by Albert Bandura. In his experiment, children watched a movie showing an adult striking a large doll with a hammer. When the children then had an opportunity to play with the doll themselves, they showed remarkably similar behavior. The photo-

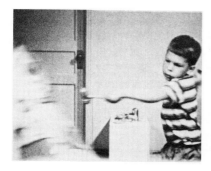

3-12 See aggression, learn aggression

Why are the boy and girl at the left acting so aggressively toward the toy? And why does their aggressive behavior take such remarkably similar form? The answer is reminiscent of the old saying, "Monkey see; monkey do." The children were imitating the behavior of a model—the woman at the right, who had behaved in exactly this fashion in a movie they had observed.

graphs of this experiment, some of which are shown in Figure 3-12, have greatly influenced psychologists' attitudes toward observation learning. (They have also raised some serious questions about the effect of the violence shown in the movies and on television.)

Cognitive theorists do not, however, think of observation learning as merely an automatic and unthinking imitation of what one has seen. Rather they believe that we begin in early childhood, and continue throughout our lives, to observe what goes on around us and to store up the information that this observation provides. We observe what other people seem to value, how they go about getting what they value, their behavior in general, and the results of their behavior. At the same time we make judgments. We may or may not decide to value what they value. We may imitate their behavior, adopt some but not all of it, or reject it entirely. As Bandura has written, learning by observation is "actively judgmental and constructive rather than a mechanical copying" (69).

An example of learning through observation?

Summary

1 Learning is *a lasting change in behavior produced by experience.*

2 One of the simplest and most universal forms of learning concerns the *reflex,* which is an inborn and built-in response to a stimulus.

3 Through learning, a reflex response can become attached to a stimulus that did not originally cause the response. The process was demonstrated when Pavlov taught a dog to respond to a sound with the salivary reflex originally caused only by the presence of food in the mouth. This type of learning is called *classical conditioning.*

4 In classical conditioning, the stimulus that naturally sets off the reflex (in Pavlov's experiment, the food) is called the *unconditioned stimulus.* The previously neutral stimulus to which the reflex becomes attached (the sound) is called the *conditioned stimulus.*

5 The original reflex response (in Pavlov's experiment, salivation) is called the *unconditioned response.* The response to the conditioned stimulus is the *conditioned response.*

6 The pairing of the unconditioned stimulus and the conditioned stimulus is called *reinforcement.* When reinforcement is no longer provided (in Pavlov's experiment, if food no longer accompanies the sound), the conditioned response tends to disappear—a process called *extinction.* After a rest period, however, the conditioned response may reappear—a process called *spontaneous recovery.*

7 When a response has been conditioned to one stimulus, it is also likely to be aroused by similar stimuli—a process called *stimulus generalization.* Through further conditioning, however, the organism can learn to respond to one particular conditioned stimulus but not to other stimuli that closely resemble it—a process known as *stimulus discrimination.*

8 Classical conditioning by past events accounts for many of the unreasonable fears and preferences displayed by human adults—also for such strange physical symptoms as unexplained headaches or nausea.

9 Another type of learning, demonstrated by Skinner, concerns *operant behavior*—the random or exploratory activities in which organisms engage, not in reflex response to a stimulus but as a self-generated way of "operating" on the world around them.

10 Skinner showed that a rat in a cage containing a bar would eventually press the bar as part of its operant behavior—and would learn to keep pressing if rewarded with food. This form of learning is called *operant conditioning.*

11 In operant conditioning, the *reinforcement* is the reward (in Skinner's experiment, the food). The rule is that operant behavior that is reinforced by a reward tends to

be repeated, while operant behavior that is not reinforced tends to take place only at random intervals or is abandoned.

12 Like classical conditioning, operant conditioning also *displays extinction, spontaneous recovery, stimulus generalization,* and *stimulus discrimination.*

13 Using operant conditioning, animals can be taught to perform complex tasks by rewarding them for the successful completion of each step that leads to the desired behavior. This process is called *shaping.* One application of the shaping technique to human behavior is *programed learning,* often presented through *teaching machines.*

14 Rewards that the organism finds basically satisfying, such as food and water, are *primary reinforcers.* The less tangible rewards for which human beings often learn, such as praise or acceptance, are *secondary reinforcers.*

15 Operant learning usually takes place fastest with *constant reinforcement,* or reward for each performance. It is usually more resistant to extinction, however, with *partial reinforcement,* or reward on some occasions but not on others.

16 The use of rewards to influence human activities—for example, persuading a withdrawn nursery school child to become more sociable—is called *behavior modification.*

17 A special form of behavior modification, widely used in mental hospitals, uses the reinforcement of tokens that can be spent like money for goods and privileges. This method is called a *token economy.*

18 Attempts to use operant conditioning to relieve physical ailments employ the technique called *biofeedback*—through devices that provide the subject with moment-by-moment readings of such bodily activities as muscle tension and blood flow.

19 In *operant escape,* an organism learns through operant conditioning to get away from an unpleasant or *negative reinforcement,* such as an electric shock. In *operant avoidance,* the organism learns to prevent the negative reinforcement by taking some kind of action before it occurs.

20 Punishment, often used as a negative reinforcement, can help produce rapid learning in lower animals but is of questionable value in human behavior.

21 One result of punishment, in both animals and human beings, may be *learned helplessness*—a tendency to believe that events cannot be controlled and to give up trying to learn.

22 Learned helplessness can be caused not only by punishment but also by failure. The effects depend partly on whether victims blame themselves or blame outside factors.

23 Learned helplessness may apply only to one kind of performance or situation. Or it may become generalized and affect the victim's entire approach to life.

24 Therapists try to treat learned helplessness, which can make its victims seriously

neurotic, by persuading them that they have more ability to succeed than they realize.

25 The ability of organisms to learn is limited by *species-specific behavior*—or acting in ways dictated by their inherited characteristics.

26 *Latent learning* is learning that takes place without reinforcement and lies latent and unused until there is a reason to use it.

27 Cognitive psychologists think of learning not as simple stimulus-response connections but as the acquisition of *motivation* to behave in certain ways to attain certain goals—or of an *expectancy* that a certain form of behavior will produce a predictable result.

28 Most cognitive psychologists also accept the *information-processing theory,* which holds that learning is one element in a closely related series of mental processes including memory, language, thinking, and perception.

29 The cognitive view holds that the most common and useful form of learning, especially among human beings, is *learning through observation* (also called *learning through modeling* or *learning by imitation*).

Important terms

behavior modification
biofeedback
classical conditioning
conditioned response
conditioned stimulus
constant reinforcement
extinction
information processing
latent learning
learned helplessness
learning through observation
  (or modeling or imitation)
negative reinforcement
operant avoidance
operant behavior
operant conditioning
operant escape

partial reinforcement
positive reinforcement
primary reinforcer
programed learning
reflex
reinforcement
secondary reinforcer
shaping
species-specific behavior
spontaneous recovery
stimulus discrimination
stimulus generalization
teaching machine
token economy
unconditioned response
unconditioned stimulus

Recommended readings

Hilgard, E. R., and Bower, G. H. *Theories of learning,* 4th ed. New York: Appleton-Century-Crofts, 1975.

Kintsch, W. *Memory and cognition,* 2d ed. New York: Wiley, 1977.

Pavlov, I. P. *Conditioned reflexes.* New York: Oxford University Press, 1927.

Seligman, M. E. P. *Helplessness.* San Francisco: Freeman, 1975.

Seligman, M. E. P., and Hager, J. L., eds. *Biological boundaries of learning.* New York: Appleton-Century-Crofts, 1972.

Skinner, B. F. *The behavior of organisms.* New York: Appleton-Century-Crofts, 1938.

Solso, R. L., ed. *Contemporary issues in cognitive psychology: the Loyola symposium.* New York: Halsted Press, 1973.

Wickelgren, W. A. *Learning and memory.* Englewood Cliffs, N. J.: Prentice-Hall, 1977.

Outline

Chapter four

Memory and how to improve it

(with a postscript on how to study)

Long ago you learned the name of your first-grade teacher. Do you still remember it? If not, can you remember what the teacher looked like? And could you perhaps recall the name if something happened to "jog your memory"?

Human memory is tricky and often exasperating. If you stop for a moment and try to recall some of the events of your lifetime, you will find a whole flood of memories pouring into your thoughts—many of them trivial and of absolutely no value. Even if you cannot remember your first-grade teacher's name, you will doubtless remember the names and faces of some early classmates who moved away long ago and whom you never saw again. You may recall the color and feel of an old childhood sweater, what you ate at a long-ago birthday party, or an insulting remark that the child next door made in a moment of anger— memories that are of no possible use to you now.

Yet you surely have had the experience of failing to remember something that you very much wanted to retain. You forgot the birthday of someone important to you. You forgot an appointment. You forgot some of the multiplication tables and had trouble figuring out your budget. Or you sat down to take a final exam and found that your mind had gone blank.

We grow as human beings, as was explained in Chapter 3, because we learn. But what we learn is of no use to us unless we remember it. Why do we remember some things and forget others? Is there any way we can improve our ability to remember?

To the first of these questions, psychology has discovered many interesting and valuable clues. To the second question, it has found that the answer is definitely yes. There is no magic formula, and it turns out that how well we remember is closely related to how well we learn in the first place. But on this dual problem of how to improve efficiency at learning and memory, psychology has some very practical suggestions. These will be discussed later in the chapter. First must come an explanation of how memory operates—sometimes pleasing us, sometimes disappointing us.

The three kinds of memory

The memory process—which is in fact a series of processes—can best be understood by starting with an example. Suppose a college woman is driving across the country to her campus. She expected to arrive at about five o'clock in St. Louis, where some friends had invited her to have the evening meal and spend the night. As she nears the city, however, her automobile develops engine trouble. A mechanic at a roadside garage tells her the repairs will take an hour or two. So she goes to a phone booth to call her friends and explain that she will be late.

In the phone book she finds her friends' number, which is 317–1962. But at that moment there is a loud squeal of brakes out on the highway. Startled, she glances toward the road and sees that there has been a near collision. Turning back to the phone, she finds that she has completely forgotten the number. Indeed it seems that the number never registered at all in her memory. She looks it up again and this time starts repeating it to herself: *three, one, seven, one, nine, six, two*—as she turns from the book and drops a coin into the phone. She dials the number correctly but gets a busy signal.

The young woman's experiences in a phone booth tell a great deal about human memory, as explained in the text.

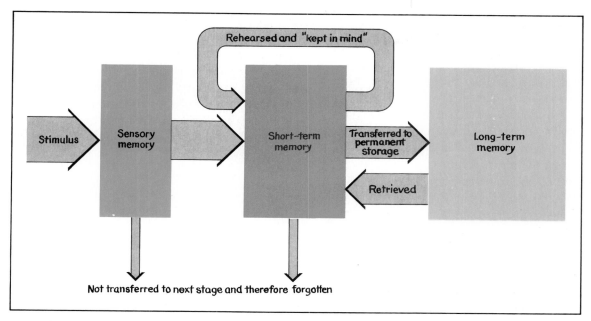

4-1 How the three-part theory views memory

The theory that there are three different kinds of memory systems or processes holds that they operate as shown here. Stimuli from the outside world register briefly in the sensory memory; some are promptly lost but others are transferred to short-term memory. There again some are lost, but others are rehearsed and "kept in mind" long enough to be transferred to permanent storage in long-term memory, from which they can later be retrieved. The three systems are described in further detail in the text (1).

By the time she has fished the coin out of the return slot, dropped it back into the phone, and waited for a dial tone, she finds that she has forgotten the number again. She remembered it longer this time—but not long enough.

So she looks the number up again. This time, while repeating it to herself, she notices that it is exactly the same as her birth date, for she was born on March 17, or 3/17, in 1962. Now she remembers the number no matter how many times she gets a busy signal and has to try again. In fact she may remember it the rest of her life.

As this example suggests, memories may persist over a time span that varies over an extremely wide range, from a mere fraction of a second to a lifetime. This fact has led to the theory that there are three different systems or processes of memory. Though not all psychologists accept the theory, it offers a convenient framework for discussing how memory operates. The following pages will describe the three types of memory as the theory views them. To follow the description, it will be helpful to refer to Figure 4-1 while reading the pages.

Sensory memory: gone in a second

Everything that impinges on our sense organs seems to be remembered for at least a brief instant, but sometimes no longer. Thus the young woman in the phone booth remembered the numbers 317–1962 after she had stopped looking at them in the directory. But the squeal of brakes on the highway knocked the numbers right out of her head, so to speak. She forgot them completely.

The three-part theory of memory holds that this type of remembering is *sensory memory,* which contains just the lingering traces of information sent to the brain by the sense organs. The information in sensory memory begins to deteriorate rapidly—within a few tenths of a second—and ordinarily has disappeared completely by the end of a full second (2) unless it is transferred to the next of the three memory systems.

Short-term memory: a half minute at best

The second of the three systems is *short-term memory,* into which some but not all of the information about the environment that arrives in the sensory memory is transferred. In the case of the college woman at the telephone, her second look at the phone book resulted in the transfer of the number 317–1962 to short-term memory. There it remained long enough for her to dial once—but, when she tried to dial again after getting a busy signal, it had already disappeared.

Unless some further processing takes place within short-term memory, information held there deteriorates as is shown in Figure 4-2 and seems to be forgotten completely within about thirty seconds (4). So much information is lost in this way that one psychologist has described short-term memory as a "leaky bucket" (5). However, this is not entirely a disadvantage. For example, a bank teller remem-

bers only briefly that he is cashing a customer's pay check for $150.89. By the time the next customer steps up to the window, the figure $150.89 has already vanished from his memory. This is just as well—for he would be totally confused by the end of the day if he recalled every transaction starting with the first one of the morning.

The same thing happens when we add a column of figures such as

$$37$$
$$49$$
$$65$$
$$\underline{22}$$

We say to ourselves (adding the right-hand digits from the top down) 16, 21, 23. Then we write down the 3 and start over on the left-hand numbers, 5, 9, 15, 17; thus we get the answer 173. All the intermediary numbers that flash through our consciousness—the 16, 21, 23, 5, 9, and 15—disappear almost as rapidly as they are formed. If they did not, we would find it almost impossible to add the columns. The numbers would get hopelessly confused.

Indeed it appears that much of the forgetting we do from short-term memory is intentional (6). We have no need to remember the information. We do not want to remember it—and it would only get in our way, for the capacity of the short-term memory is quite small in terms of amount of information as well as time span. On the average, it holds seven items—exactly the number of digits in a phone number—although for some people the limit is only five and for others it is as much as nine (7). When short-term memory is full to capacity with its five to nine items, new information can be added only by dropping some of the old. Therefore we often throw out the old items deliberately. We do so by manipulating the processes that go on in short-term memory, which will now be described.

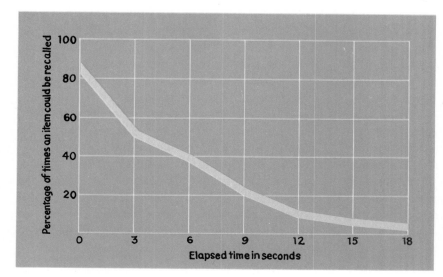

4-2
The brief lifespan
of short-term memory

In a study of the duration of short-term memory, experimenters spoke a group of letters and a number, such as KRG 297. Subjects were asked to begin immediately to count aloud, going backward by threes beginning with the number (297, 294, 291, etc.). At various intervals, a light was flashed informing them to stop counting and try to recall the letters. Under these circumstances, which kept them too busy counting to rehearse or do any other kind of processing of their memory for the letters, their recall dropped rapidly as shown by the graph line (3).

Processes in short-term memory

A number of information-processing activities seem to take place in short-term memory (8). First, there must be some kind of *scanning* of the information briefly held in sensory memory. From the constant flow of sights, sounds, and other messages from the sense organs, some particular items must be selected as worthy of attention. (This scanning and selection process is closely related to the psychological phenomenon of perception and will be discussed more fully in Chapter 8.)

If the information selected for attention is to be held for any length of time, some sort of *rehearsal system* must also be set up. That is, the information must be deliberately kept in mind and prevented from slipping out of the "leaky bucket." Through rehearsal, information can be kept in short-term memory as long as desired—though the amount of information that can be kept alive, as has been stated, is quite small.

To help with further processing, the information held in short-term memory is often transformed in some way that makes it as simple and easy to handle as possible. This process is called *encoding* —for it resembles the manner in which a business machine can take complicated facts (such as a customer's name and address, past-due balance, and new purchases) and code them into a series of holes on a punch card. When the information in short-term memory is language or numbers, the encoding is usually done in acoustical terms—that is, the information is encoded into sounds (9).

Finally, if the information is to be remembered more or less permanently, it must be passed along and stored in the next of the memory systems, which is *long-term memory*. This process, called *transfer of information*, seems to take place somewhat as follows. The new information, held in short-term memory and kept alive through rehearsal, is associated with any relevant pieces of information that already exist in long-term memory. Comparisons are made and relationships sought. When the transfer process is successful, the new information is more or less permanently fitted into long-term memory, like a new item dropped into the appropriate bin in a warehouse.

This transfer of information may require additional encoding and recoding. Its efficiency also depends to a great extent on *organization*. Materials that are themselves well organized, as for example a self-contained two-line poem, are more easily transferred to long-term memory than a meaningless string of digits. The transfer process can also be helped by any kind of organization the learner can impose on the materials (10).

Long-term memory: for as long as we live

In the case of the woman in the phone booth, the transfer of the numbers into lasting memory included all the processes just described. Visual images of the numbers in the directory arrived in sensory memory. These images were scanned, encoded into sounds, and held in short-term memory through rehearsal. While rehearsing the numbers, the woman managed to impose an organization on them by noting that they were the same as her birth date. With the help of this organization, the new information was readily associated with old information and the transfer to long-term memory became easy and effective.

How long is long? As you surely have discovered to your sorrow at times, not always as long as we would wish. We often forget things we would like to remember—for reasons that will be discussed later. But many long-term memories persist for a lifetime. As for how much information we can store in long-term memory, there is really no way of knowing. Certainly the capacity is very large.

Most people have the meanings of tens of thou-sands of words stored in memory. Some have vocabularies that run into the hundreds of thousands. With the help of these words we build all kinds of facts and assumptions. One psychologist has estimated that the number must be in the tens of millions or more. Nonetheless, this psychologist believes that the human capacity to learn and remember has definite limits (partly because we have only a certain number of hours to devote to learning) and that these limits have some important implications—as will be seen in the box on Psychology and Society on page 136. Other psychologists believe that most of us have never even begun to test the limits of our memory capacity—that we use only a fraction of our abilities.

How the storehouse operates: the memory trace

Every time we store a new piece of information in long-term memory, we are somehow changed. We can do something—recall a new fact or engage in a new kind of behavior—that we could not do before. Obviously something has happened inside us. But what?

Psychologists do not know for sure. They must confine themselves to saying that a *memory trace* has been established. They can only speculate as to what this memory trace is, how it gets created, and why it sometimes persists and results in long-lasting memories and sometimes vanishes and results in forgetting.

The memory trace surely represents a change in the nervous system. Sometimes the change seems to take place inside the spinal cord. At least experiments with animals have shown that simple reflexes can be conditioned through the spinal cord when it has been disconnected from the brain (12). More often, however, the change appears to take place in the brain, especially in the highest part, or cortex, of the brain. It probably occurs at the switching points, or synapses. When we learn, we route nervous impulses over a particular pathway, passing through a number of synapses in a particular pattern. The various kinds of nervous activity that take place along this pathway presumably have a lasting effect that makes it possible to reactivate the pattern on future occasions—thus enabling us to remember what we have learned.

Memory and the neurotransmitters

Establishment of the memory trace seems to depend in part on the brain's neurotransmitters (described on pages 56–58). Studies of lower animals indicate that when one neuron stimulates another neuron to fire, by releasing its neurotransmitters into the synapse between them, these chemicals produce a lasting change in the efficiency of the synapse (13). The second neuron becomes more likely to fire again in the future—and this makes it easier for nervous impulses to travel the same pathway again.

In the case of human beings, it has been observed that drugs that influence the way brain cells produce their neurotransmitters have some pronounced effects on memory. Investigators have found that human subjects often show an increased ability to store information in long-term memory after they have received even small doses of a drug that increases the brain's active supply of the neurotransmitter called acetylcholine (14). Indeed almost any drugs that stimulate the chemical activity of the brain tend to improve the establishment of memories. These drugs include caffeine, nicotine, and amphetamines (15)—provided they are taken in small doses that provide stimulation without causing arousal that is so intense as to cause con-

Do the coffee and cigarette help this student memorize?

fusion. Conversely, drugs that slow down the brain's chemical activity interfere with learning. This is true of alcohol (16), tranquilizers (17), and even mild doses of such anesthetics as ether or laughing gas (18).

Forming new synapses

The establishment of memory traces also appears to depend at times on the formation of new synapses—resulting in new connections between neurons that did not previously influence one another (19). The formation of new synapses presumably can continue throughout life. It is especially apparent in the development of the brain from birth,

Planning our lives within the limits of memory: one psychologist's view

We are what we are today largely because of what we have learned, what we have remembered, and what we have forgotten. All of us will be very different people five or ten years from now—because of what we have learned, remembered, and forgotten in the meantime. Our children, as they grow into adulthood, will lead lives determined mostly by what they have learned (from us, from their schools, and from what they have observed in our society) and how well they have remembered it.

How can we best use psychology's findings about memory when we plan our own futures—and when, as parents, we help mold the lives of our children? How can society use the findings to create an educational system that will do the best possible job of preparing students to live useful and rewarding lives? (Should elementary-school students learn the names of all the capital cities of Europe? Should high-school students learn a foreign language?)

One provocative though controversial view comes from Wayne A. Wickelgren, a psychologist at the University of Oregon. Wickelgren believes that the human capacity to learn and remember, though very large, has definite limits. Moreover, he believes that most of us operate most of the time at fairly close to capacity. We learn and remember about as much as the workings of our nervous systems permit. We would all be happier if we recognized our limitations and took a more charitable view of our own accomplishments and those of other people. The schools would do a better job if they recognized that students cannot learn everything all at once.

Wickelgren believes that *what* we learn—in school or in our life experiences—is far more important than *how much* we learn. In the educational

when it weighs only about 11 ounces, to adulthood, when it weighs about 3 pounds. All the neurons of the brain are present at birth; the number never increases. But the neurons increase in size and develop new dendrites (making possible new synaptic connections) much as a young tree develops new branches.

The effect of learning on the brain has been demonstrated by experiments in which young animals have been raised under conditions offering different kinds of opportunities to learn. For example, one group of rats was brought up in ordinary cages, another in an environment enriched by various kinds of visual stimuli and toys. Examination after death showed that the animals from the enriched environments had heavier brains (20). Encouraging animals to learn has also been found to result in an increased number of dendrites in the brain, indicating that more new synapses were formed (21). The brains of animals from enriched environments have also been found to contain more neurotransmitter chemicals (22)—another in-system "emphasis should be on the quality rather than the amount of knowledge that students are required to learn." The schools should concentrate on information that "we can use to achieve some important goal"—such as the general principles that provide "insight and understanding" of our universe, our society, and the workings of the human organism: "It is of far less general value to know the superficial physical characteristics of various plants and animals than to know about nutrition, disease, first aid, the anatomy and physiology of the human body, and the general principles of living systems." Wickelgren concedes that learning a foreign language may provide some personal, social, and intellectual satisfactions—but questions whether this is as valuable in the early school years as acquiring a broader understanding of human experience.

In planning our own lives, Wickelgren suggests,

we should recognize that acquiring a great deal of knowledge in any one field—whether it be the history of ancient Greece or the works of Shakespeare or chess or playing tennis—means that we will learn and remember less about other topics. Moreover, there has to be a trade-off between time spent studying and time spent doing: "Some people who know more than others have accomplished less as a direct result of their learning."

Recognizing the limitations of memory, Wickelgren believes, can also help us understand and sympathize with other people: "It is unreasonable to tell a coworker or friend in a five-minute period ten things you want that person to do and expect him or her to remember it all without mistakes. . . . One source of friction in personal relations and of inefficiency in job performance could be eliminated if we remembered that the capacity for learning and memory is limited" (11).

dication that the establishment of memory traces may depend on both the formation of new synapses and greater chemical activity and efficiency at the synapses.

The continuing mystery of the memory trace

But how and why synaptic changes take place remains a mystery. Some investigators have suggested that they may depend on a chemical called RNA, similar to the DNA that makes up the genes

and serves as the carrier of heredity (as was explained on pages 34–36). These investigators point out that in every cell of the body, including the nerve cells, the DNA manufactures various forms of RNA that act as its "messengers," controlling the growth and functioning of the cell. Their theory is that learning changes the amount and type of RNA produced in nerve cells (23) and that the RNA then operates to establish new synapses or change the efficiency of existing synapses. But the evidence linking RNA to learning has been seriously challenged (24)—and, even if true, it would not shed much light on the mystery of the memory trace. You may have heard the suggestion that some day we might all be able to become mathematical geniuses instantly by taking RNA extracted from the brain of an Einstein—but this is a notion that few psychologists take seriously.

All in all, the establishment of long-term memories—all those tens of millions of them that we may accumulate in a lifetime—is another example of how the human organism operates in marvelous ways that may never be completely understood.

Despite what has been discovered about the relationships among learning, the neurotransmitters, and the synapses, we cannot even be sure whether any specific memory trace represents a change in a specific pattern or part of the brain or a more generalized change affecting widespread parts of the nervous system (25). The process is far too complex to offer much hope of quick and easy results from any kind of "learning pill." We will just have to reconcile ourselves to the fact that laying down long-term memories usually requires the kind of work that will be described later in the chapter.

Why we forget

Memory cannot be discussed without also discussing forgetting. They are opposite sides of the same coin. We learn something—that is, we store some piece of information in our memory. Sometimes this information persists and we can call on it whenever we need it. We say that we remember. Sometimes the information seems to disappear—and we say that we have forgotten. Why do we remember some things and forget others?

How remembering and forgetting are measured

Attempts to investigate the twin processes of remembering and forgetting pose many difficulties. There is no way psychologists can examine the nervous system to see what kinds of changes have been laid down in it by learning and how well these changes persist. They can only devise tests to determine how much is remembered and how much is forgotten. Unfortunately, these tests can never make a direct measure of memory. All they can

measure is how well people *perform* on the tests—and their performance may not be an entirely accurate indication of how much they remember.

To explain why this should be true, let us say that two girls in elementary school are taking the same arithmetic course. They listen to the same explanations by their teacher and study the same textbooks. Now one day the teacher gives a written examination. Girl A gets 90. Girl B gets 70. The logical conclusion is that girl A learned her arithmetic very well and remembered it and that girl B either learned it poorly or quickly forgot it.

The truth, however, is that we do not really know. All we can say for sure is that girl A *performed* much better on the examination than did girl B. It may very well be that girl B had learned addition, subtraction, and the multiplication tables backward and forward and did badly on the examination because these subjects were so old hat to her that she was bored when asked to show how well she could perform.

Performance on tests of memory can be adversely affected not only by poor motivation but also by anxiety, distractions, and many other factors. Thus tests of remembering and forgetting must always be viewed with reservations. But psychologists, in their effort to do the best they can, have adopted three standard methods of measurement.

Recall

One way to prove you have learned the Gettysburg Address is to recite it—which means to demonstrate that you can *recall* it, that you can bring it out intact from wherever it is stored in your memory. In school, a common use of recall is in the essay type of examination. When teachers ask "What is classical conditioning?" they are asking you to recall and write down what you have learned.

Recognition

Often we cannot recall what we have learned, at least not completely, but we can prove that we remember something about it by being able to recognize it. For example, you may not be able to recall the Gettysburg Address. But if someone asked you what begins with the words "Fourscore and seven years ago," you might immediately recognize the speech, thus demonstrating that you certainly remember something about it.

Multiple-choice examinations are a test of recognition; you are asked to choose the right answer from among several possible answers and thus prove that you recognize it. Because recognition is easier than recall, many students would rather take a multiple-choice test than an essay examination.

Relearning

The most sensitive method of measuring memory is one that is seldom used. This is the method of *relearning,* which is accurate but cumbersome. All of us once learned the Gettysburg Address, or, if not that, then some other well-known piece of writing (anything from a nursery rhyme to Hamlet's soliloquy). We may not be able to recite these pieces now; so we would fail the recall test. We might recognize them if we saw or heard them again. This would prove that we remember something but would not be a very precise measure of how much. If we set about relearning them, however, the length of time this took us would serve as a highly accurate measure.

Theories of forgetting

Relearning was the measurement used in one of psychology's earliest and most famous studies of forgetting, made by a nineteenth-century German named Hermann Ebbinghaus. For his experiments, Ebbinghaus invented the nonsense syllable. He learned lists of such syllables and then measured how long it took him to relearn the lists to perfection after various intervals. He came up with the *curve of*

"*I can't remember the last time I treated a case of amnesia, and I can't even remember if I ever did treat one.*"

4-3

Ebbinghaus' famous curve of forgetting

Ebbinghaus memorized lists of thirteen nonsense syllables similar to those shown here, then measured how much he could remember after various intervals. After twenty minutes, he remembered only 58 percent and after about an hour only 44 percent. After the initial sharp dip, however, the curve flattened out. After one day he remembered about 34 percent and after two days about 28 percent. Although the graph line does not extend that far, he recalled 21 percent after a month (26).

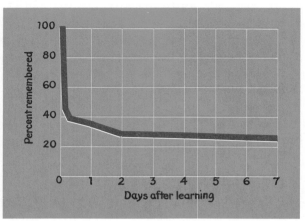

forgetting shown in Figure 4-3. The curve does not always apply, because we learn some things so thoroughly that we never forget them. However, it tells a great deal about the forgetting of such varied kinds of learning as motor skills, poems we have memorized, and college courses we have taken. Its message is this: *When we learn something new, often we quickly forget much of it, but we remember at least some of it for a long time.*

As to why we forget, the answer is not yet fully known—and indeed may never be known for sure. But there are a number of theories worth considering. In fact all the theories may be correct at least in part, for forgetting may be such a complex process that it takes place in different ways under different circumstances.

Theory 1: fading of the memory trace

One of the oldest theories of forgetting assumes that the memory trace, whatever its physical nature, is subject to decay—that it begins to fade as time goes on and sometimes disappears entirely. The theory regards the memory trace as resembling the marks of a pencil on a piece of paper, or a path

worn into a plot of grass. It can be kept functioning through use, as a pencil mark can be emphasized by tracing and retracing and a pathway can be kept clear by continuing to walk over it. But without use, the memory trace may vanish, as a pencil mark fades with time and a pathway becomes overgrown when abandoned.

Many of today's memory theorists continue to believe that the memory trace has some physical quality that changes with the passage of time, thus reducing the likelihood that it can be retraced or reactivated. Indeed they think of it as having two qualities. The first is its *strength*—meaning how likely it is to "pop into mind." This quality, the strength of the memory trace, is at its peak immediately after learning and declines with the passage of time. The second quality is *resistance to extinction*, meaning how well the trace can manage to survive and become immune to fading or decay (27).

Establishing resistance to extinction is believed to take a certain amount of time. It requires what memory theorists call *consolidation*, a period during which the trace undergoes a process that might be compared with the hardening or "setting" of a newly laid sidewalk. (During the consolidation

The woman's pathway through the forest: Does it resemble the memory trace?

period, whatever changes are produced at the synapses by learning may somehow become more permanent, or perhaps new synapses may have time to form.) The consolidation process takes place most rapidly in the first minutes after learning —but it continues, though at a gradually slowing rate, as long as the memory trace exists. Thus, though the memory trace may decrease in strength with the passage of time, it becomes more and more resistant to extinction as the years go by.

The idea that time affects both the strength and resistance of the memory trace is based in part on studies of people who have suffered amnesia, or loss of memory, because of head injuries. This type of amnesia often takes a very strange form. Patients may be unable to remember anything that happened in the past five years yet have a normal memory for events that happened earlier. As they begin to get over the effects of their injuries, their

memories return on a predictable time schedule. First they recover their memory for events that are five years old, then for four-year-old events, and so on until their recovery is complete (28). It would appear that the older their memory traces, the more resistant the traces were to temporary disruption by injury.

Theory 2: failure in retrieval

Other psychologists take a different view. They believe that the memory trace, once it has been established as part of long-term memory, probably persists for as long as we live. But information held in memory is of no use to us unless it remains not only stored but available. To remember it, we must be able to find it and call upon it when needed—a process called *retrieval*. If we cannot call upon it, we say we have forgotten it. Thus forgetting may be not a failure in memory, but rather a failure in retrieval. As one psychologist has put it: "In this respect memory is like a huge warehouse in which all sorts of things are stored but which is less than perfectly organized, so that it is not always easy to find a given item upon demand" (29).

Some evidence that forgetting may be a failure in retrieval was provided by the experiment illustrated in Figure 4-4. The *A* drawing, containing only a few meager details, was typical of the drawings produced by the subjects on their first attempt. But then the subjects went through a process designed to improve their retrieval. They were asked to look again at the blank screen on which the photo had been flashed, to concentrate as hard as possible on what they had seen, and to say out loud any words that came to mind, regardless of whether the words had any apparent connection with the photograph. That is to say, they were asked to free-associate to their memory of the picture—to blurt out any associations that occurred to them. The first twelve words they came up with were put on index

4-4
Improved retrieval = less forgetting

The photograph was flashed on a screen for a tenth of a second and a college man was asked to reproduce what he had seen. He could remember no more than the few details he put into his drawing A. But after the experimenter helped his retrieval process as described in the text, the student produced the much more detailed drawing B.

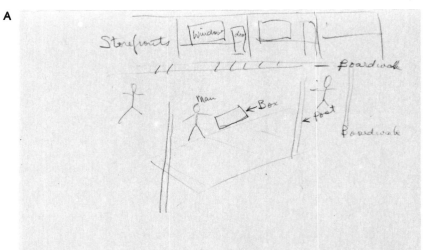

A

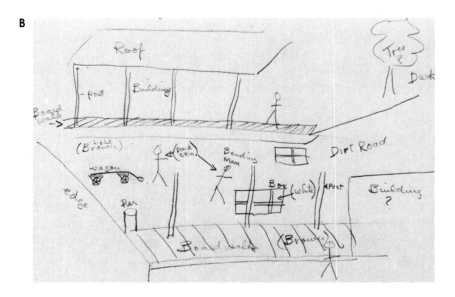

B

cards, and these words were used to evoke some further free associations. Then the subjects were asked to try to draw the picture again. This time, as can be seen from drawing *B* in Figure 4-4, they came much closer to the original, putting in many details that they had been unable to remember while making their first drawing. On the average, their memory of the photo improved by about 44 percent (30).

The behavior of subjects under hypnosis also suggests that many memory traces may be present but simply not retrievable under ordinary circumstances. In the hypnotized state, people sometimes are able to talk in great detail about long-ago events of their childhood—incidents that they had no idea they remembered at all. The same phenomenon has been observed during brain operations performed to relieve epilepsy, under a local anesthetic that leaves the patients conscious and able to report their thoughts. When certain parts of the brain are stimulated with a mild electrical current, these patients may report vivid memories of bygone events. They seem to be actually listening to a piece of music they once heard or to a tele-phone conversation they once took part in, almost as if a tape recording of the incident were being played (31).

Theory 3: interference

Another possible explanation for forgetting is that our ability to remember any given piece of information is interfered with by other information stored in memory. This theory holds that our memory for what we learn today is often adversely affected by what we have learned in the past and also by what we will learn in the future. The various pieces of information compete for attention and survival—and not all of them can prevail.

When old information causes us to forget new information, this process is called *proactive interference*. The phenomenon of proactive interference can be demonstrated very strikingly through simple laboratory procedures, such as asking subjects to try to learn and remember several lists of words. The results of one such experiment are illustrated in Figure 4-5. Note the steady decline in the ability to

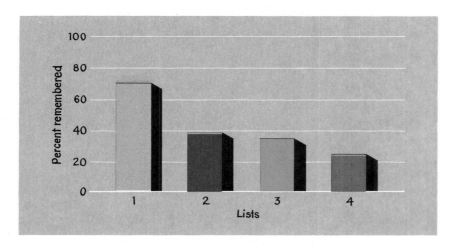

4-5

How the old interferes with the new

The subjects learned a list of paired adjectives. Two days after learning, they were tested for their recall of list 1 and asked to learn list 2. After a similar interval they were tested on list 2 and learned list 3. Two days later they were tested on list 3 and learned list 4. Finally, after another two-day interval, they were tested on list 4 and the experiment ended. The steady decline in the height of the bars shows how learning list 1 interfered with memory for list 2, how learning lists 1 and 2 interfered with memory for list 3, and so on (32).

remember new materials caused by more and more proactive interference from prior learning.

Proactive interference is greatest when we try to learn new materials that are similar to old materials already stored in memory—as was the case with the word lists used in the Figure 4-5 experiment. Proactive interference is less troublesome when the new materials are substantially different from the old. In one experiment, for example, it was found that subjects had trouble remembering a list of the names of fruits that they tried to learn after previously learning lists of vegetables—but they had less trouble if they had previously learned lists of flowers, and least of all if they had previously learned lists of professions, which are totally dissimilar to fruits (33).

In proactive interference, old information gets in the way of remembering new information. The opposite situation—when new information causes us to forget old information—is called *retroactive interference*. This phenomenon has also been demonstrated through simple laboratory procedures, as in the experiment illustrated in Figure 4-6. Note that again similarity between old and new materials was found to play an important part. When subjects learned a new list of words with the same meaning as the words in the old list (synonyms), there was more retroactive interference than when the new list contained such very different materials as nonsense syllables or numbers.

Perhaps the most interesting—and consoling—fact about retroactive interference is that it has a greater effect on unimportant materials that are not worth remembering anyway (like lists of words learned in a laboratory) than on important and meaningful materials. Retroactive interference often makes us forget the specific details of what we have learned, especially if the details are not essential. It is not nearly so likely to make us forget the basic meaning of what we have learned. Thus you will probably forget some of the things you have learned in this course as a result of retroactive

4-6

How the new interferes with the old

The bars show the results of an experiment in which subjects were asked to learn a list of adjectives, then were tested ten minutes later to find how many of the adjectives they could remember. During the ten minutes some subjects were kept busy at various new learning tasks—such as learning synonyms for the adjectives or their opposites—and some were just permitted to do nothing. The fact that the subjects who worked at new learning tasks recalled fewer of the adjectives than the "do nothing" group demonstrates the effect of retroactive interference. The more similar the new learning was to the old, the greater was the amount of retroactive interference (34).

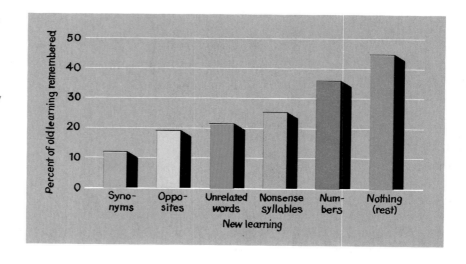

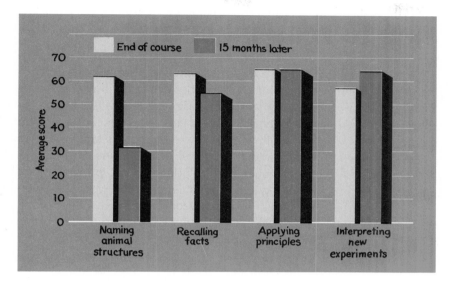

What college students forget — and what they remember

The scores represented by the bars of different colors were obtained by testing college students on their knowledge of zoology—first immediately after they had finished a course, then fifteen months later. By the time of the second test the students had forgotten about half the terminology they had learned for animal structures and many specific facts. But they still knew the principles as well as ever and could apply them to new situations. On the matter of interpreting experiments that they had never heard of before, they were actually better than at the end of the course. This improvement was probably due to the greater general knowledge and maturity acquired in an additional year of college (35).

interference from the things you learn in future courses and from your life experiences. You may not remember the exact meaning of such terms as *classical conditioning* and *reinforcement.* But you will probably always remember the general principles of learning and of how memory operates. One study that demonstrates this fact about college students and what they remember is illustrated in Figure 4-7.

Theory 4: motivated forgetting

The fact that we seem to forget some things deliberately has already been mentioned in connection with the processes that take place in short-term memory. Many theorists believe that at times we also forget information stored in long-term memory simply because we want to forget it. For example, we forget the name of a person we dislike, or we

forget the problems we had at a certain stage of life and look back to that period as a time when we were ideally happy. People who gamble are notoriously prone to remember the times they won and to forget the times they lost, often building up a totally false impression of how well they have done over the years.

Motivated forgetting has been widely studied by psychoanalysts, who have found it often plays a part in certain forms of abnormal or neurotic behavior. It is less important in the lives of more or less normal people. Indeed most of us are troubled by persistent memories of embarrassing and painful events that we would gladly forget if only we could. Perhaps the best way to summarize the facts about motivated forgetting is to say that it does seem to occur at times—but less often than most of us would wish. It accounts for only a small part of our forgetting.

Levels of processing as the key to remembering

The four theories of why we forget, all of which may be correct at least in part and at times, offer some valuable hints on how we can avoid the handicap and embarrassment of forgetting. The motivation theory suggests that we are more likely to remember when we want to remember. The other theories indicate that we will be most efficient at remembering if we can manage to store information in such a way that the memory traces will not fade away with the passage of time, that the information can be retrieved when we want it, and that it will remain more or less intact despite interference from previous and future learning.

All these matters depend on the ways in which we go about storing information in long-term memory. Thus the key to remembering lies in two related questions: What is the nature of the processing that creates our store of knowledge? How can we do the processing more effectively—and learn and remember to greater advantage?

One clue to processing: the "tip of the tongue" phenomenon

One important study of how information is processed into memory was based on a commonplace occurrence. You are trying to think of something—somebody's name, a word you want to use in a letter or term paper, a fact that you need to answer an exam question. You are sure you know it. You have it "on the tip of the tongue." But, at the moment, you cannot quite bring it to mind.

This "tip of the tongue phenomenon" was investigated by asking university students to try to recall, from hearing the definitions, such words as *sampan*, *sextant*, *nepotism*, and *ambergris*—all being fairly

unusual words that they probably once had an opportunity to learn but would not have had many occasions to use. As was expected, it turned out that often they could not remember the word but felt that they had it "on the tip of the tongue." What exactly did this mean? It was found that the students could often—indeed in 57 percent of the cases—guess the first letter of the word they were seeking. They also seemed to have considerable recall for the last letter of the word. Often they thought of words that had a similar sound. When trying to remember *sampan,* for example, they thought of such words as *Saipan, Siam, Cheyenne,* and *sarong,* and even such made-up words as *sanching* and *sympoon.* Moreover, as is shown in

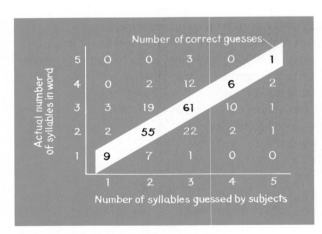

4-8 "I can't remember the word— but I do know how long it is"

Students who had a word on "the tip of the tongue" but could not quite recall it, in the experiment described in the text, were asked to guess how many syllables it had. As shown by the figures in the white band, their guesses were more right than wrong unless the word had more than three syllables.

This conversation pit at a California university serves as an aid to deep processing in many ways.

Figure 4-8, they usually knew how many syllables were in the word—at least if the number of syllables, as in the great majority of everyday English words, was no more than three. There was even some indication that they knew which syllable the accent was on. Most important of all, they often thought of words with a similar meaning. For example, in the case of *sampan*, which is defined as a small Chinese boat, they thought of *barge, houseboat,* and *junk* (36).

The experiment demonstrates that the way words are encoded and stored in memory takes place on a number of different levels. One level is the way they look in writing—such visual characteristics as the letters with which they begin and end. Their auditory characteristics are also taken into account. We encode and store information about the way words sound when spoken and how many syllables they have. We also encode and store the meaning. We associate the words with other words that mean more or less the same thing. Thus the

processing we do when we add to our memory store takes many forms, ranging from the most superficial (appearance and sound) to the deepest and most significant (the meaning of the new information and how it relates to what we already know).

Learning and levels of processing

The "tip of the tongue" experiment and other findings have led to what is known as the *levels-of-processing theory of memory* (37). This theory, to which many psychologists now subscribe, holds that how well we remember new information depends on the kind of cognitive processing we do when we learn it—that is, how many characteristics of the new information we become aware of, how thoroughly we analyze the information, and how well we relate it to other information already stored in memory. The deeper, richer, and more elaborate our analysis, the more likely we are to establish a long-lasting memory that will resist interference or any of the other causes of forgetting (38).

The levels-of-processing theory states, in effect, that how well we remember depends on how well we learn in the first place. In studying a page such as this one, for example, merely reading and re-reading the words is not the best technique. What really matters is analyzing what is on the page as thoroughly and deeply as possible. As one psychologist has written:

> The critical thing for most of the material you learn in school is to understand it, which means encoding it in a way that makes it distinctive from unrelated material and related to all the things it ought to be related to in order for you to use it. . . . The time you spend thinking about material you are reading and relating it to previously stored material is about the most useful thing you can do in learning any new subject matter (39).

Moral for learners: take your time

Learning effectively depends more on the cognitive processing we do than on the amount of time we spend (40). Thus even a small amount of time spent at deep processing is more effective than a great deal of time devoted to merely rehearsing what is on a page more or less verbatim—which, as many experiments have shown, does not help much in either acquiring information or remembering it (41). But effective processing usually requires deliberate effort—we have to work at it—and a certain amount of time. Indeed the more time we spend the more likely we are to remember, provided of course that we use it for deep processing rather than for rehearsing superficial characteristics.

Thus there are no short cuts in learning. For example, nothing is gained through "speed reading," which is the popular name for techniques that are supposed to enable you to read a printed page much faster while still comprehending everything the words mean. In fact studies have shown that the faster you read the less you are likely to understand or remember (42). There are certain advantages, of course, in saving time through the rapid scanning of materials that you do not need to remember, or when you are glancing through a long and complicated article or book in which there are only a few specific pieces of information that you want to seek out and concentrate on. But in general any increase in reading speed, beyond your normal rate, saves time only at the expense of remembering. The kind of deep processing that results in long-lasting memory, like the sinking of a deep foundation that will solidly support a skyscraper, simply cannot be rushed.

Memory for "the products of comprehension"

The levels-of-processing theorists have made some important discoveries not only about how we store new information but also about what it is that we store. What we put into memory, they have found, is usually not an exact carbon copy of what we have read nor a tape transcription of what we have heard. Instead we remember the results of our processing, whatever forms these may have taken. To put this another way, we remember not the stimulus itself—the printed page or a lecture or conversation—but the meanings and relationships we have found in the stimulus. As one study has put it, we remember "not what was out there" but what we ourselves "*did* during encoding" (43)—the way in which we processed the information into some kind of meaning.

A useful analogy comes from another study that also concluded our memories are not for the stimulus itself but for "the products of comprehension." When we read or listen to something, the analogy goes, we do not usually try to remember the material word-for-word. Instead we take mental notes—like the brief reminders you might jot down in your notebook while listening to a lecture. It is these notes, not the actual words we read or heard, that we store in some appropriate "pigeonhole in memory" until we need them. While stored in that pigeonhole, the notes may become smudged. Some of them may even get lost. Thus, when we try to retrieve the information, we find that it is incomplete—only a sketchy reminder of what we actually read or heard. All we can do is "fetch the notes from their pigeonhole and from this fragmentary information reconstruct what . . . was in the original message"—or rather what we now have come to believe was in it (44).

With the brief and sometimes smudged or incomplete notes, we do the best we can. We try to make sense out of them. We fill in the missing details— sometimes accurately and sometimes not. Thus a great deal of what we think we remember never really happened to us or appeared on a page that we read—or, if it did, it was different in many respects from the way we remember it. Memory, as one scholar has said, is often "unreliable, given to invention, and even dangerous" (45). Nonetheless, for all practical purposes it usually serves us well—especially on essential meanings and general principles that we have encoded at the deepest levels of processing.

If you ever happen to watch the movie *Gigi* on a late night television show, pay particular attention to the song *I Remember It Well,* sung as a duet by Hermione Gingold and Maurice Chevalier. (Or you may hear a recording taken from the movie sound track.) In the song, Gingold and Chevalier play an elderly couple recalling their first meeting. She insists that they had dinner at eight, that he was late, and that she wore a gown of gold. He insists that they dined at nine, that he was on time, and that she wore blue. They disagree totally on the details—and there is no way of knowing which if either of them is right. But they are in full agreement on what really counts—which is that the meeting led to a lifetime of happy affection. The song tells a lot about memory, forgetting, and especially levels of processing.

A caution on memory theory

For the sake of completeness and accuracy, one other fact must be mentioned here about levels of processing. Many theorists now believe that the three memory systems mentioned earlier in the chapter—sensory, short-term, and long-term—do not exist as separate entities. They maintain that there is in fact just one kind of memory trace—and that how long this trace lasts, whether for a moment or for a lifetime, depends on the level of processing that created it. If the processing is done at a superficial level (like a mere glance at a number in a telephone directory), the trace tends to have only a very short life. If the processing is done at a deep level (like making a connection between the phone number and date of birth), the trace tends to last for a long time (46).

If you plan a career in psychology, this question of the basic nature of memory and the memory trace will be one of your concerns, for it promises to be a major topic of future research and debate. For all practical purposes, however, both the three-part theory of memory and the levels-of-processing theory are helpful in understanding how memories become established, sometimes persist, and sometimes are forgotten. Even if it eventually turns out that there is only a single kind of memory trace, the idea of three memory systems is still a convenient tool for thinking about this important aspect of behavior. In the context of this chapter, the concepts of sensory, short-term, and long-term memory—and the chart on page 131 that illustrates their relationships—provide a helpful guide for your own deep processing of the facts about memory so that you will remember them for a long time.

The importance of finding meaning and organization

The deep processing that creates long-lasting memories is essentially an attempt to analyze information in order to discover 1) its *meaning*, and 2) some kind of *organization* that makes the new information hang together and become firmly associated with what we already know. These two elements are closely related. When we fully understand new materials, this discovery of the deep and underlying meaning helps us organize them and relate them to other facts in our memory store. At the same time, organizing them into a logical pattern and fitting them into appropriate relationships with what we already know helps further clarify their meaning.

Thus the key to the kind of learning that produces lasting results is to conduct a search for both meaning and organization. The key will open the door to more effective learning and better memory for almost anything—from how to plan a diet or keep a budget to the skills required on a new job or the contents of a college course.

How meaning helps

Because meaning plays such a big part, some things are just naturally easier to learn and remember than others. If the materials themselves make sense—that is, if they are intrinsically meaningful—we have a good head start on our deep processing. Thus it is much easier to remember lists of actual three-letter words (such as SIT, HAT, BIN, COW) than lists of three-letter nonsense syllables. In fact it is easier to remember lists of nonsense syllables that resemble real words than syllables that are truly nonsensical. One experimenter found that subjects were about 50 percent better at remembering lists of syllables such as DOZ, SOF, LIF, and RUF, all of which remind most people of actual words, than lists of totally unfamiliar syllables like ZOJ, JYQ, GIW, and VAF (47).

In another experiment, subjects were asked to learn and remember 200 items or words that were in four different forms: lists of nonsense syllables, lists of random digits, passages of prose writing, and passages of poetry. The results of the experiment are illustrated in Figure 4-9. Note how much better the subjects remembered the prose or poetry than the nonsense syllables or the nonsense arrangements of digits. Poetry—which has both meaning and a kind of internal logic and organization provided by the cadence and rhymes—proved the easiest of all to remember.

Rule is far better than rote

Both meaning and organization help account for the fact that we usually remember longer if we learn by rule or logic (that is, trying to understand the underlying principles) than if we learn by rote (or simply trying to memorize materials by repeating them mechanically, without any regard to what they mean). A simple classroom experiment that demonstrates this fact is illustrated in Figure 4-10.

In the class shown in the left-hand photo, the students learned by rote. By simply repeating the numbers over and over, they managed to get them into memory after a fashion. But this superficial

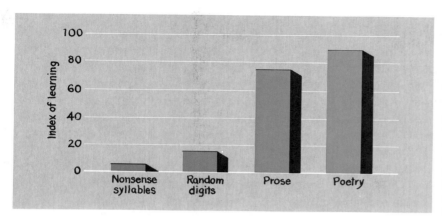

4-9
**Meaningful materials:
so much easier to remember**
The height of the bars shows how little
the subjects in one experiment could
remember of meaningless lists of nonsense syllables or random digits—and
how much they remembered of more
meaningful materials that were of
equal length (48).

4-10 A classroom demonstration of rule versus rote

In this experiment, the instructor is asking two different classes to try to learn and remember the
numbers she has written on the blackboard, which are the same in both cases. In the class at
left, however, she suggests that the numbers can be most easily remembered in groups of
three, as she has arranged them. In the class at right, she explains that the digits are not in
random order but fall into a definite and logical pattern in both lines. She does not say what the
pattern is, leaving the students to find out for themselves. (Most of them did find the pattern,
and this had an important effect on how well they learned and remembered the numbers as
described in the text. Try it yourself before you read the explanation in the footnote on page
152.)

level of processing produced only very short-lived
memory. When they were tested three weeks later,
not one of them remembered the numbers correctly. Most members of the class in the right-hand

photo, alerted to the fact that the numbers could be
learned by finding a logical rule, managed to do
their processing at a deeper level—and this class
remembered the numbers much better after three

weeks had passed (49). If you try the experiment yourself as suggested in the caption beneath the photos, or on some of your friends, you will probably get the same convincing results.

Most college courses readily lend themselves to learning by rule rather than by rote. They have patterns of meaning and organization, built around underlying principles, and are presented by instructors and in textbooks in ways designed to help you find, understand, and analyze the patterns. In this book, for example, the basic meaning of each chapter is given in the summary at the end. The headlines at the beginning of each new section (and also listed in the outline at the start of each chapter) provide a guide to the organization. The trick is to take advantage of the various guides to achieve a deep understanding of the materials. This requires some work, of course—but it takes no longer and is considerably more rewarding than trying to memorize the chapter by rote.

How categories help

Even when materials do not seem at first glance to have any deep meaning or pattern of their own, they can often be organized in a more easily remembered fashion by lumping similar items together in convenient pigeonholes—or, to use more scientific terminology, by trying to learn them by categories. This generally efficient way of learning can best be explained by citing an experiment that used word lists like the one shown on page 153. The words in the list do not seem to have much in

The blackboard figures are arranged in this logical pattern: The numbers following the first one, which is 5, are obtained by regularly adding 3-4-3-4-3-4-3-4 to the preceding number. Thus 5 is followed by 8 (5 plus 3); 8 is followed by 12 (8 plus 4); 12 by 15 (12 plus 3); and 15 by 19 (15 plus 4). Number 26 at the end of the first line is followed by 29 (26 plus 3) to start the second line, and 29 is then followed by 33 (29 plus 4) and so on.

common, unless you happen to notice that they all name things that come out of the ground. They do not fall into any kind of obvious pattern—and you might think that, if you wanted to commit them to memory, you would have to learn them by rote. This is the way the experimenter's control group went about trying to memorize them—painfully and, as will be seen in a moment, without much lasting success.

Another group of subjects, however, got some help. To these subjects, the words on the list were presented in the manner shown in Figure 4-11. The subjects were helped to see that all the words fell into the general category of minerals, that this category could be broken down into the subcategories of metals and stones, and that these subcategories could again be divided into three different kinds of metals (rare, common, and alloys) and two different kinds of stones (precious stones and stones used in masonry).

The control group and the experimental group were both asked to try to learn four lists, containing 112 words in all, within four trials. The difference in the amounts learned by the two groups proved striking. As Figure 4-12 shows, the subjects who had been helped to organize the words into categories proved far superior. Indeed they remembered all 112 words perfectly on the third and fourth trials—a level never even approached by the subjects who tried to learn the words by rote (50).

Categories and clustering

Organizing materials into categories is one form of what memory students call *clustering*—that is, the lumping together of materials that have some sort of affinity. Materials stored in memory in clusters—either by categories, in terms of meaningfulness or logic, or in some other way—tend to hang together in a tightly bound group that resists the erosion of forgetting.

Is there any easy way to learn these words?

Slate	Emerald	Diamond	Steel	Sapphire	Brass
Bronze	Gold	Lead	Limestone	Aluminum	Ruby
Iron	Granite	Marble	Platinum	Silver	Copper

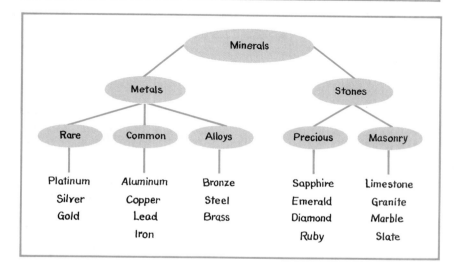

4-11

The words as organized into categories

This is how the words shown above were presented to the experimental group in the learning study described in the text. Question: Did the categories make learning easier, and if so by how much? For the answer, see the text and Figure 4-12.

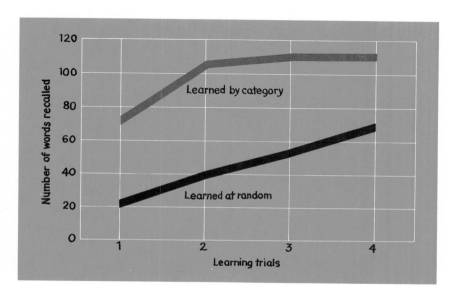

4-12

Did the categories make a difference? Yes, indeed.

The colored line shows how rapidly the experimental subjects were able to learn as a result of seeing words arranged in categories as in Figure 4-11. Subjects who tried to memorize the words by rote (black line) did not do nearly so well.

Clustering also aids retrieval. Within each tightly bound and cohesive cluster there may be many individual items of information. In the search of memory that goes on during retrieval, we have a much better chance of hitting on one of many items than on any single item—just as we have a much better chance of making a hit when we throw a dart at a whole board covered with balloons than when we aim at a single balloon. And when we manage to find this one item, we can pull the whole cluster of information out with it.

An example might be this: You are taking an essay examination and are asked to define the term *stimulus generalization*. At first the meaning of the term eludes you. You seem to have forgotten it. But then the term suggests the category of learning principles; this suggests the subcategory of classical conditioning—and out pour all the facts you have clustered under that heading, including the meaning of *stimulus generalization*.

Made-up stories and imagery as an aid to clustering

In establishing clusters of information, a number of tricks can be effective. One method, useful in remembering any kind of list, is to make up a story about the items on the list. Let us say, for example, that you are going to a supermarket to buy the following ten items, listed in the order you would find them along the route you ordinarily take through the aisles:

1 milk	6 coffee
2 matches	7 cigarettes
3 apples	8 light bulbs
4 bread	9 paper towels
5 steak	10 garbage bags

One way you can be almost sure of remembering everything in proper order is to make up a story like the one presented in Figure 4-13. The method is

4-13 Remembering a supermarket shopping list

The ten shopping items mentioned in the text can easily be remembered in order by making up this story: I am delivering *milk* to a kitchen where I find a small boy playing with *matches*. I try to distract the child by giving him an *apple*. His mother rushes in, thinks I am trying to lure the child away, and hits me with a loaf of *bread*. Then, recognizing me, she puts a piece of *steak* on my bruised eye and offers me a cup of *coffee*. As I light a *cigarette* to go with the coffee, the kitchen *light bulb* burns out. I replace it, using a *paper towel* to protect my hand, and throw the old bulb into the *garbage bag* (51).

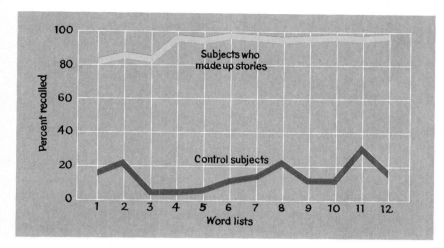

4-14

How well do made-up stories work? Extremely well.

The graph lines show the results of an experiment in which one group of students was asked to make up stories to help them remember a dozen lists of words, while a control group was merely asked to try to memorize the lists. When tested later, the subjects who made up stories remembered the lists almost perfectly. The other subjects had forgotten most of the words (53).

especially effective if you picture the story as actually happening, as in the drawings. Many studies have shown that such use of imagery, or mental pictures of events, is a great aid in remembering and retrieving (52). As for how well made-up stories work, particularly with the help of imagery, see the convincing experimental results illustrated in Figure 4-14.

Mnemonic devices

Closely related to the trick of making up stories about word lists are the various learning techniques called *mnemonic devices,* after the Greek word for memory. Like the term itself, these devices probably date back to the ancient Greeks (54). Among the well-known ones are the jingle that begins "Thirty days hath September" (for remembering how many days there are in each month), the sentence "Every good boy does fine" (for remembering the notes in music), and "I left port" (for remembering the difference between the port, or left side of a ship, and the starboard, or right side).

A somewhat more complicated mnemonic sys-

tem, for remembering things like a shopping list or chores to be done during the day, has been used in a number of psychological experiments and found extremely helpful. You begin by memorizing this jingle:

One is a bun; two is a shoe;
Three is a tree; four is a door;
Five is a hive; six is sticks;
Seven is heaven; eight is a gate;
Nine is wine; ten is a hen.

To use this device to help remember the supermarket shopping list mentioned earlier, the trick is to form some kind of mental image connecting the items on the list (milk, matches, etc.) with the words in the jingle rhyming with the numbers (bun-one, shoe-two, etc.). The way such images might be formed is illustrated in Figure 4-15. Forming images around the words in the jingle usually takes only a few seconds and has been found to result in almost perfect recall (56).

Similar systems, more elaborate in that they can provide memory hooks for as many as 100 items, are the secret of the "memory experts" who perform such seemingly incredible feats as quickly

4-15 Using "one is a bun" to remember the shopping list

The drawings show one set of images that might be built on the "one is a bun" device to help remember the same shopping list that was presented on page 154. If you spend a few moments studying and thinking about the drawings, thus getting the images into your own memory, you will probably be surprised to find how long you can remember the list—probably days and even weeks from now. You will remember it even longer if you think up a set of images of your own (55).

learning long lists of objects or of people's names. For learning things that do not hang together through any organization or logic of their own, mnemonic devices are unquestionably useful. One reason is that they take advantage of the well-established value of imagery. Another is that they provide a ready-made framework into which the new information can be clustered.

(*Summary begins on page 162.*)

Postscript

How to study

All the devices that have just been discussed—mnemonic systems, made-up stories, and imagery—are useful in learning and remembering things that you would otherwise have to learn by rote. With practice, you can apply them to schoolwork that requires you to memorize facts that have little or no intrinsic meaning or organization of their own. For example, imagery has been found very useful in learning the vocabulary of a foreign language (57). If you are studying Spanish, for example, it might help you remember that *jabon* (pronounced ha-bone) means *soap* if you note that the Spanish word contains the sound of "bone"—and form a mental image of a soupbone being scrubbed by a bar of soap.

Most college courses, however, do not require crutches of this kind. They lend themselves readily to learning by rule—understanding the meaning of information and organizing it into a natural, "sense-making" entity, with the new items clustered together and related to information already held in memory. How well you remember them depends on how deeply you process the new information. And psychology has some valuable advice on the kinds of study methods most likely to help you.

The value of recitation

Suppose you have six hours to devote to learning this chapter and that reading through the chapter carefully—not speed reading but taking your time

to understand as you go along—takes two hours. What should you do? Read the chapter three times?

To spend the six hours reading sounds logical, but actually it is the worst possible way to approach the task. You will learn and remember much better if you cut down the amount of reading and spend the rest of the time reciting what you have learned. Indeed you might find it best to spend *most* of your time in recitation. As Figure 4-16 shows, it has been found that in at least some forms of learning the most efficient method is to spend as much as 80 percent of study time in recitation.

Why is recitation such a valuable tool? There are several reasons. In the first place, it helps motivate you—for just knowing that you are about to try to recite what you are reading stimulates the desire to learn. It also provides immediate feedback, telling you how much you remember and on what points you are still shaky.* Since you do not attempt to recite what was on the page verbatim, you are encouraged to do the kind of deep processing that will help you understand and organize the information. You have to think about the materials and find meanings and associations. Moreover, since reci-

---

*Immediate feedback is one reason for the effectiveness of teaching machines and programed learning, which were described on pages 102–03. In that case the feedback takes the form of telling students whether they are right or wrong—and thus whether they have grasped the meaning or must try again.

4-16
Recitation: it beats reading hands down

The bars show the results of an experiment in which students of various ages, from elementary school to college, studied nonsense syllables in different ways. The total amount of study time was the same for all subjects. Some subjects, however, spent the entire time reading the syllables, while others spent 20 to 80 percent of the time reciting. When tested immediately afterwards and again four hours later, it was found that their ability to remember the syllables went up in direct proportion to how much time they had spent in recitation (58).

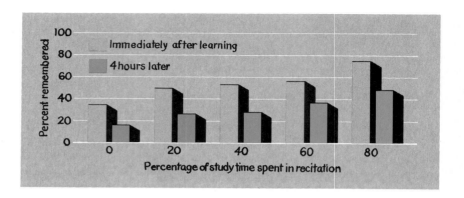

tation gives you practice in retrieval (59), it helps you store the materials in such a way that you can readily call on them. For all these reasons, recitation is the most valuable of all study techniques.

The SQ3R system of studying: a method that works

Recitation lies at the heart of a method of studying that has produced excellent results for students who have tried it. This is the so-called SQ3R system (60), which holds that the most efficient way to study is to follow five steps that can readily be remembered by their first initials (SQRRR):

1 Survey

Study the outline at the beginning of the chapter (if there is one, as in this book) and then glance through the chapter to get a general idea of how much attention is devoted to each point in the outline.

A young pupil seeks some feedback on her performance.

2 Question

Look through the chapter again, asking yourself questions that the headings suggest. Let the topics whet your curiosity.

3 Read

Now read the chapter straight through, without taking notes.

4 Recite

You have surveyed the chapter, asked some questions about it, and read it. Now see how much of the chapter you can recite, either to yourself or to a friend.

5 Review

Go through the chapter again, making another survey of its topics and noting how much of it you were able to recite and what points you left out. This review will show you where you must devote further study. After making this additional study, you will probably want to repeat steps 4 and 5—that is, recite again the gist and meaning of what you have learned, then make another review that will show if you need still further study.

Going through the five SQ3R steps, and repeating whichever ones are indicated as often as necessary, is an exercise in deep processing that leads to understanding, lasting associations, and memory. It is a method that works.

Learning to learn

What you remember of this chapter many years from now may turn out to be associated in a strange way with some of the fairy tales of your childhood—for, like them, it has a happy ending. You can expect to get better and better at learning and remembering as time goes on. This is because all of us, in our college courses and from our life experiences, acquire something even more valuable than facts and general principles. We learn how to learn.

One need not be an Einstein. Even the monkey shown in Figure 4-17 learned to learn. Asked to perform a long series of learning tasks that were similar in general but different in detail, it got better

4-17

What is this monkey learning?

All the monkey seems to be learning is that it will find food under one of the two objects in front of it but not under the other. When the photo was taken, the food was always under a funnel and never under a cylinder, regardless of which was on the left or right. At other times, the food was under a circle but not a rectangle, a cube but not a sphere, a black object but not a white object, and so on. At first the monkey had trouble learning where to find the food. But after the experiment had gone on long enough—with several hundred pairs of objects—it turned out that the monkey had learned to learn. When a new pair of objects was presented, the monkey mastered the problem on the very first trial. Whether or not it found the food under the first object it examined, it went almost unerringly to the correct object the next time the pair was presented (61).

and better as the series went on. It acquired what is called a *learning set* that helped it approach the task successfully. In an experiment with human beings, using a similar but more difficult series of problems, the results were much the same. It was also found, as might be expected, that college students were quicker to develop effective learning sets than fifth-graders. In turn the fifth-graders were quicker than preschool children (62).

The ability to learn to learn, which develops constantly as we grow older and more experienced, helps explain what would otherwise be a rather baffling fact about schoolwork. Insofar as can be measured, children entering high school have matured to the point where they seem to possess all the neurological equipment that makes learning possible. Their innate ability to learn will not increase very much if at all. They are already just

These older graduates, contrary to popular belief, may have found college easier than when they were younger.

about as smart, to use the popular term, as they will ever be. Yet everybody knows that high-school seniors can learn things that would be beyond high-school freshmen—and college students can go a long step farther. People who go back to college when they are in their 40s or older, as many do nowadays, are often surprised to find how much easier the work seems than it did when they were younger.

Transfer of learning

The fact that we learn to learn depends largely on the principle of *transfer of learning*—that is, the ability to apply what has been learned in one situation to situations that are in some way similar. A simple example is this: Learning to use the handlebars of a tricycle when we are very young helps us later on to learn to use the steering wheel of an automobile. Similarly, though in a more complex way, everything you learn in a course such as this will probably help you later on to understand other courses and to deal with situations outside the classroom.

One form of learning easily transferred to new situations consists of the attitudes and strategies we develop as we learn. It has been found that one of the most valuable things high-school students can be taught in any specific course, such as history or science, is how to outline and summarize the course, interpret the tables and charts provided in their books or by their teachers, and use the appropriate reference works—all of which improve their performance not only in that course but in others (63). Similarly, if you adopt the SQ3R system of studying explained in this chapter, you will probably find it of great help in learning the contents of any courses you take in the future, even those totally different from psychology.

Almost any kind of learning is likely to produce a

certain amount of transfer. The more we know, the easier it is to learn and remember something new. As we go through school and college, we acquire a bigger vocabulary, more mathematical symbols and rules, more knowledge of the general principles of science, human behavior, and the working of our society. All this helps us to understand the new information we encounter, organize it, and associate it with facts already in our memory store—in other words, to do the deep processing that enables us to remember and use it.

How learning builds on learning

Psychologists have known for a long time that the greatest aid to learning is the possession of prior knowledge—that learning builds on learning. Indeed this all-important idea has never been explained more eloquently than by William James, even though James lived and wrote many years before the discovery of most of what is now known about the processes of learning and memory:

> *The more other facts a fact is associated with in the mind, the better possession of it our memory retains.* Each of its associates becomes a hook to which it hangs, a means to fish it up by when sunk beneath the surface. Together, they form a network of attachments by which it is woven into the entire tissue of our thought. The "secret of a good memory" is thus the secret of forming diverse and multiple associations with every fact we care to retain. . . . Most men have a good memory for facts connected with their own pursuits. The college athlete who remains a dunce at his books will astonish you by his knowledge of men's records in various feats and games, and will be a walking dictionary of sporting statistics. The reason is that he is constantly going over these things in his mind, and comparing and making series of them. They form for him not so many odd facts but a concept-system—so they stick. So the merchant remembers prices, the

politician other politicians' speeches and votes, with a copiousness which amazes outsiders, but which the amount of thinking they bestow on these subjects easily explains. The great memory for facts which a Darwin and a Spencer reveal in their books is not incompatible with the possession on their part of a brain with only a middling degree of physiological retentiveness [by which James means inborn ability for remembering]. Let a man early in life set himself the task of verifying such a theory as that of evolution, and facts will soon cluster and cling to him like grapes to their stem. Their relations to the theory will hold them fast; and the more of these the mind is able to discern, the greater the erudition will become (64).

A word on negative transfer and overlearning

James' graphic figure of speech about facts clustering "like grapes to their stem" summarizes a great deal of what has been said in this chapter, and it would be nice to stop right here. However, two more topics require brief explanation before the discussion of "Memory and how to improve it" can be considered complete.

You may have noticed an apparent inconsistency while you were reading the last few pages. The discussion of transfer of learning stated that what we already know is a great help in acquiring new knowledge. But earlier in the chapter it was stated that one cause of forgetting is proactive interference—when old memories compete with and sometimes disrupt new memories. Both statements, though they seem in conflict, are true. Previous knowledge does make it easier to learn and remember new information. In terms of the principle of transfer of learning, it results in *positive transfer*. But previous knowledge may also, at times, result in forgetting because of proactive interference—which can be described as *negative transfer*.

You can observe negative transfer in many everyday situations. Knowing how to steer a bicycle or an automobile will thoroughly confuse you the first time you try to operate the tiller of a boat, which has to be moved in the opposite direction. If you are used to hot water faucets that turn on to the left and off to the right, you may scald yourself the first time you are in a shower where the faucet turns the other way. In your college courses, some of the details of one period of history may get mixed up with the details of another. But have no fear. There is no such thing as learning or knowing too much. For every case in which negative transfer hinders you, there will be a hundred in which positive transfer helps.

The other topic is the *law of overlearning,* which states: Even after we have learned something, continuing to work at learning it tends to increase the length of time we will remember it. The law of overlearning explains why we never seem to forget such childhood jingles as "Twinkle, twinkle, little star," or the stories of Cinderella and Goldilocks and the three bears. Long after we knew these things by heart, we continued to listen to them over and over. We not only learned but overlearned.

The law of overlearning also explains why cramming for an examination, though it may result in a passing grade, is not a satisfactory way to learn the contents of a college course. By cramming, students may learn the subject well enough to get by on an examination, but they are likely to soon forget almost everything they learned. A little overlearning, on the other hand, is like the time spent thinking about new materials and trying to understand them. It is a good investment in your future ability to remember.

Summary

1 One widely accepted theory holds that there are three types of memory: a) *sensory,* b) *short-term,* and c) *long-term.*

2 *Sensory memory* is made up of the lingering traces of information sent to the brain by the senses. The information is forgotten within a second unless transferred to short-term memory.

3 *Short-term memory* engages in *scanning* of the sensory memory and chooses some items as worthy of attention. Short-term memory has a capacity of about seven items, which are forgotten within about thirty seconds unless further processing takes place.

4 Processes that may take place in short-term memory include *rehearsal* (to keep information in mind longer than thirty seconds), *encoding* of information (to make it simple and easy to handle), and *transfer of information* to long-term memory.

5 *Long-term memory* is a more or less permanent storehouse of information.

6 A *memory trace* is a change that takes place in the nervous system as a result of learning. The physical nature of the memory trace is not known—but it appears to depend on the activity of the brain's *neurotransmitters* and at times on the formation of new *synapses.*

7 Remembering cannot be measured directly but only by how well people *perform* on tests of memory. Three methods used by psychologists to test performance are: a) *recall,* b) *recognition,* and c) *relearning.*

8 When we learn something new, we often quickly forget much of what we have learned, but we remember at least some of it for a long time. The fact that we forget rapidly at first but more slowly later on is shown by the *curve of forgetting.*

9 There are four theories of why we forget, all of which may be true at least in part and at times: a) *fading of the memory trace,* b) *failure in retrieval* (which is the process by which information stored in long-term memory is found and used), c) *interference* from other information stored in memory, and d) *motivated forgetting,* or forgetting because we want to forget.

10 When old information causes us to forget new information, the process is called *proactive interference.* When new information causes us to forget old information, the process is called *retroactive interference.*

11 The *levels-of-processing theory* holds that how well we remember new information depends on how deeply we have processed it—that is, how many characteristics of the new information we become aware of, how thoroughly we analyze it, and how well we relate it to other information already stored in memory.

12 The key to deep processing is analyzing new information in order to discover a) its *meaning* and b) some kind of *organization* that makes the information hang together and become firmly associated with what we already know. Thus learning by rule is much more effective than learning by rote.

13 *Clustering* is a method of organizing materials by lumping together those that have some form of affinity. Effective ways of clustering include *categories, made-up stories,* and *imagery.*

14 *Mnemonic devices,* like the "Thirty days hath September" jingle, are useful in providing a memory framework for materials that cannot be organized in any logical way.

Postscript

15 *Recitation* is of great value in studying. It is better to spend as much as 80 percent of study time in an active attempt to recite than to spend the entire time rereading the material.

16 The very effective *SQ3R system* of studying is named for the five steps it recommends taking in order: *survey, question, read, recite,* and *review.*

17 *Positive transfer of learning* occurs when what has been learned in one situation can be applied to other situations that are in some way similar. One form of positive transfer is a *learning set.*

18 Positive transfer accounts for the fact that *learning builds on learning*—the more we know, the easier it usually is to learn.
19 *Negative transfer of learning* occurs at times when previous knowledge interferes with the learning of new information.
20 The *law of overlearning* states: even after we have learned something, continuing to work at learning it tends to increase the length of time we will remember it.

Important terms

categories	organization
clustering	proactive interference
consolidation	recall
curve of forgetting	recognition
encoding	rehearsal
imagery	relearning
levels of processing	retrieval
long-term memory	retroactive interference
made-up stories	scanning
memory trace	sensory memory
mnemonic devices	short-term memory
motivated forgetting	synapse
neurotransmitter	

Postscript

learning set	recitation
negative transfer	SQ3R system
overlearning	transfer of learning
positive transfer	

Recommended readings

Cermak, L. S., and Craik, F. I. M., eds. *Levels of processing and human memory*. Hillsdale, N. J.: Erlbaum, 1979.

Estes, W. K., ed. *Handbook of learning and cognitive processes,* Vol. 6. Hillsdale, N. J.: Erlbaum, 1979.

Hilgard, E. R., and Bower, G. H. *Theories of learning,* 4th ed. Englewood Cliffs, N. J.: Prentice-Hall, 1975.

Kintsch, W. *Memory and cognition*. New York: Wiley, 1977.

Lindsay, P. H., and Norman, D. A. *Human information processing: an introduction to psychology,* 2d ed. New York: Academic Press, 1977.

Nilsson, L. G., ed. *Memory problems and processes*. Hillsdale, N. J.: Erlbaum, 1979.

Norman, D. A. *Memory and attention: an introduction to human information processing,* 2d ed. New York: Wiley, 1976.

Tulving, E., and Donaldson, W., eds. *Organization of memory*. New York: Academic Press, 1972.

Wickelgren, W. A. *Learning and memory*. Englewood Cliffs, N. J.: Prentice-Hall, 1977.

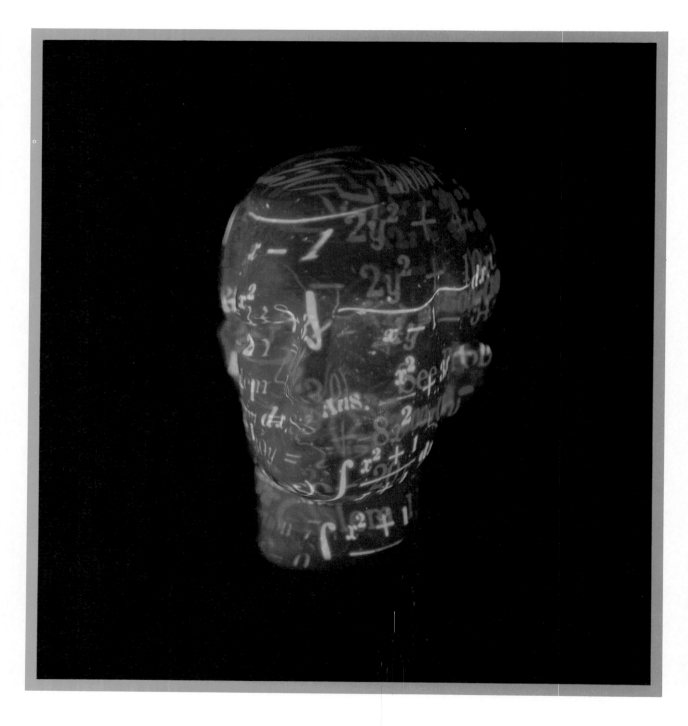

Part three
Language, thinking, intelligence

Of all the things you will ever learn and remember, in the ways described in the preceding section, which one do you suppose is the most important? The question may seem, at first glance, impossible to answer. Such subjects as algebra, chemistry, political science, and biology may enrich your understanding of the world—but you can live a reasonably successful life without knowing anything about them. Practical knowledge about mechanical matters may be useful, especially in this technological age—but you do not really need to know how a computer operates, how to repair an automobile, or even how to change a tire. Social skills are helpful—but you can get by, though you might find your life rather lonely, without learning very much about human relationships or how to get along with other people.

One skill, however, is absolutely essential. You cannot possibly survive, much less thrive, without learning how to use language.

Words are the key to human existence. From the beginning, people have used words to help one another find such basic essentials as food, shelter, and clothing. In our own highly industrialized society, words make possible the manufacture and distribution of such products as computers and automobiles. We use words to express our needs and our emotions, to find our mates and rear our families. In fact all our social relationships are based on an exchange of words with other people. As you go through a typical day, try to see how long you can go without speaking. You will have trouble getting through the first hour, much less the whole day.

In our left-brained society (as was described on page 55), language is the basis of almost all other learning. There are only a few exceptions. Without using words, you can learn to paint, enjoy music and dancing, or play one-on-one basketball, but not much else. The great bulk of what we learn and know takes the form of language. Humanity's accumulated knowledge, indeed, is stored in words printed on the pages of books—readily available to those who have learned to use language, forever a secret to those who have not.

Language is the most complex as well as the most basic of all human skills. Yet, oddly enough, it is also one of the easiest to learn. You picked it up without effort at a time when you were still too young and immature to learn most of the other skills required in our society. You could make yourself understood almost as soon as you could walk. Even severely retarded children, who have difficulty learning anything else, usually learn to use language, at least after a fashion.

In this new section of the book, Chapter 5, "Language and Cognition," discusses some of the marvels of communication—for example, how we English-speaking people manage to build the mere twenty-six letters of our alphabet into all the rich variety of meanings we express. It describes how we learn language, speak and listen to it (a more difficult task than you might suppose), and build our thinking around it. The topic of thinking leads naturally to a discussion of human intelligence, which is presented in Chapter 6, "Intelligence: The Problem of Defining and Measuring It." Just what is intelligence? (The answer, as you will see, is not nearly so clear to scientists as is popularly assumed.) How can intelligence be measured? (The answer is: in ways that are useful in many respects, but not nearly so accurate as all the talk about IQs of 101 or 107 or 119 might indicate.)

Outline

The function and structure of language 172

Chapter five

Language and cognition

Note the flags on this page. They are three of the signals used in an international system of communication among ships at sea. Each of them conveys a single, simple message—in two cases a request for a specific kind of help, in the other a specific warning.

Suppose that your language, which is your own communications system, worked the same way. For each idea that you wanted to express—everything from "Let's eat" to "Psychology is the science of behavior"—you would need a separate "flag" of some kind, in the form of a spoken or written word. How many flags or spoken words—each conveying only one simple message—would you need to convey everything that you now say in the course of an ordinary day? How long would it take just to tell a classmate that you would like to go along to a movie but have a history examination tomorrow and must study; also you have to do some laundry and return a book to the library; so all in all, though you appreciate the invitation and

I am disabled—
communicate with me.

I require
medical assistance.

You are running
into danger.

would like a rain check, you feel you must say no.

How long would it take to write a letter to a relative explaining what you have been studying in this psychology course? How many pages would the letter run, and how much postage would it cost?

The number of flags you would need, each conveying its own message, is almost beyond imagination. In fact, no matter how many flags you had, you would not be able to communicate more than a fraction of what you now do. Most of the thoughts you express in the course of an ordinary day take the form of sentences you have never used or heard before. You make the messages up on the spot. Your listeners, in most cases, have never before heard the same combination of words. If you were a ship captain, you would be constantly designing and sewing up new flags. Your listeners, never having seen the flags before, would not have the faintest idea what they meant.

The function and structure of language

Language is a brilliant invention that has been described as humanity's most distinctive and perhaps most complex achievement (1). It is a tool of immense versatility. We use it to express everything from our physical needs to our spiritual desires. We use it to tell one another how we think and feel and what we have learned about the world around us. Using language is a special human technique that permits us to exchange an unlimited number and variety of messages, from a child's simple request for a drink of water to the most complex philosophical theories.

In evolutionary terms, language gives humanity a tremendous advantage over all other organisms. People need not learn everything for themselves; they can share what they have learned. Moreover, written language makes available to us all the recorded learning of the past—the philosophies of the ancient Greeks, the mathematical systems of the ancient Arabs, the scientific discoveries of Galileo. Thanks to language, each of us knows more than any one person, starting from scratch, could discover in a thousand lifetimes. As one psy-

The sign recognizes the fact that people—except in their own language—are "as helpless as a baby who has not yet learned to talk."

chologist has said, language "makes life experiences cumulative . . . [and therefore] cultural evolution takes off at a rate that leaves biological evolution far behind" (2).

If you happen to be in a foreign country, not knowing a word of the native tongue and unable to find anyone who speaks English, you will soon appreciate the importance of language. You cannot ask or receive directions. You cannot order food, except by pointing. You cannot ask for a physician, except by making gestures of distress. If you do find a doctor, you cannot describe your symptoms. You are as helpless as a baby who has not yet learned to talk.

Language, being such an all-important part of human behavior, has always been one of psychology's central concerns. Many studies have been made of how and why we use language (its function), how we put sounds and words together to form such a marvelously useful signaling system (its structure), and the ways in which we send our own signals and understand those that other people send to us (the processes of producing and comprehending language). Psychologists have also been interested in the question of how in the world children ever manage to acquire mastery of such a complicated signaling system—so quickly and easily that they seem to know many of the rules and can convey their own messages as early as the age of two.

This chapter describes some of the fundamental psychological findings about language and also about cognition, or thinking, to which language is closely related. The way we think about the world and about ourselves, as you will see, helps determine the kind of language we use. Our thinking, in turn, is influenced by our language. Indeed much of the thinking we do would be impossible without the use of words and the ideas they represent. Language is a powerful help in finding meanings and relationships in the events of our lives. It is therefore

a key to the kind of deep processing by which we commit new information to long-term memory, as was described in the preceding chapter.

Language and communication

The origin of human language is lost in the mists of antiquity. But we can assume that its first purpose was to exchange messages of vital concern to survival—to enable people to communicate with one another about food supplies and how to obtain them, about danger and how to avoid it. Other animals, lower in the evolutionary scale, also manage to do this in one way or another. Bees that have found a new food supply, for example, go back to the hive and perform a dance; the nature and speed of this dance tell the other bees how to get to the food (3). Birds sing their characteristic songs to attract mates and discourage interlopers. Chimpanzees use sounds and gestures to warn their friends of danger and to threaten their enemies.

Communication is the basic function of language. Our utterances are designed, as one study has put it, "to inform listeners, warn them, order them to do something, question them about a fact, or thank them for a gift or act of kindness." We "intend to have some effect on our listeners"; we "want to convey certain ideas"; we expect our listeners to recognize our intentions and "act accordingly" (4). Written language, likewise, aims to communicate and in some way influence. Its purpose may be to inform (a textbook), to change an opinion (a newspaper editorial), to urge action (a letter to a Congressman), to present a demand (a letter requesting immediate payment of an overdue bill), or perhaps just to amuse (a mystery novel).

As these examples suggest, we now use language to convey a great deal more than simple messages about food and danger. But language

This dialogue illustrates the fact that the basic function of language is communication.

continues to be essentially a communications system—based on an agreement between those of us who speak the language that certain sounds used by all of us, strung together according to rules that all of us know, convey messages intended by the speaker and understood by the listener.

Language structure: the building blocks

The sounds and the way we put them together constitute the structure of language—and here the strange fact is that all the variety and richness of language rest on the simplest kind of foundation. All spoken language depends on the number of sounds that can be produced by the human vocal cords, and the number is quite limited. This may seem hard to believe, in view of the apparent complexity and variety of all the sentences that can be heard in the halls of the United Nations—English, French, Spanish, German, Russian, and all the languages of Asia and Africa—but it is true. No language contains more than eighty-five different basic sounds, and some contain as few as fifteen. English has about forty, or a few more depending on regional dialects.

The basic sounds, called *phonemes,* are the building blocks of language. In English, the phonemes include such sounds as the short *a* in *pat,* the long *a* in *pate,* the consonant *p* as in either *pat* or *pate,* the *ch* in *chip,* the *th* in *the,* and the *sh* in *shop.* Thus the word *pat* contains three phonemes. By changing any of the three, you can produce many different words. Changing the first phoneme will give you *bat, cat, chat,* and so on. Changing the second creates *pate, pet, pit, pout,* and others. A new sound at the end creates *pack, pad, pal, pan,* and more. If you play around with the word *pat* in this way, changing just one of the three phonemes at a time, you will find that you can produce more than thirty different words.

Units of meaning: the morphemes

By themselves, the phonemes usually have no meaning. (Although some meaningful sounds, like the article *a*, are made up of a single phoneme.) But they can be put together, in combinations of two or more, to form sounds that do have meaning. For example: we can start with the phoneme *t*, add the phoneme pronounced as *ee*, then add the phoneme *ch*, and arrive at a combination *teach*. The result is called a *morpheme*—a combination of phonemes that possesses meaning in and of itself. Like *teach*, many morphemes are words. Others are prefixes or suffixes, which can in turn be combined with other morphemes to form words. For example, we can combine the three morphemes *un* (a prefix), *teach* (a word in itself), and *able* (a suffix) to form the word *unteachable*. Or we can start with the same morpheme *teach*, add -*er* (meaning *one who*) and -*s* (to denote the plural), and form the word *teachers*. The plural -*s* is one of the most commonly used morphemes, as is -*ed* to indicate the past tense of a verb (*walked, talked*).

Some very long words represent a single morpheme—for example, *hippopotamus*. But most long words are combinations of morphemes and therefore of meanings. Note the following:

$$\overset{1\ \ 2}{\widehat{\text{pitiful}}}$$

$$\overset{1\ \ \ 2\ \ \ 3}{\widehat{\text{disjointed}}}$$

$$\overset{1\ 2\ \ \ \ 3\ \ \ \ \ 4}{\widehat{\text{insurmountable}}}$$

Or consider *antidisestablishmentarianism,* which you have probably heard cited as the longest word in the English language. This is a combination of no fewer than seven meaningful morphemes:

$$\overset{1\ 2\ \ \ \ \ 3\ \ \ \ \ \ \ 4\ 5\ 6\ \ 7}{\widehat{\text{antidisestablishmentarianism}}}$$

The building blocks of language, though simple, make possible a tremendous variety of expression. The forty English phonemes (which can be written using only the twenty-six letters of the alphabet) are combined in various ways to produce more than 100,000 morphemes. These are in turn combined with one another to produce the 600,000 or more words found in the largest dictionaries.

Grammatical structure

Words alone, however, are not enough to make language possible. True, we must understand and agree on what is called *semantics,* or the meaning of the morphemes and words in our language. But, in addition, we must know how to string the words together into meaningful sentences. Thus every language has two essential elements: 1) a vocabulary of meaningful sounds and words; and 2) a set of rules, called grammar, for combining the words into an almost infinite number of sentences that can be constructed to express an almost infinite variety of semantic meanings.

Vocabularies differ from one language to another, of course, and often very greatly. The English word *house* is *maison* in French and *casa* in Spanish, and in Chinese it is pronounced something like *ook*. Yet the rules of grammar, though they vary in detail, share some basic similarities in all languages—including the dead languages of the past as well as those spoken today. Presumably this is because people everywhere have the same abilities and limitations in processing language—that is, in producing and understanding sentences (5).

Even these ancient Hittite inscriptions follow the same rules of grammar we use today.

Syntax: Did John see Bill or Bill see John?

Among the most important rules of grammar are those called *syntax*, which relate to sentence structure. The rules of syntax regulate the manner in which nouns, verbs, adjectives, and adverbs are placed in proper order to form phrases—and how the phrases are combined in turn into sentences that convey a meaning readily understood by anyone else who speaks the language. Without these rules, language would be a jumble. For example, even very young children know the meaning of the individual names and words *Bill, quickly, who, the, down, was, street, saw, walking, John, a, sweater, his, in, yellow, friend.* But when presented in that order, the words do not convey any message. Rearranged according to the rules of syntax, they become the meaningful sentence:

John, who was walking quickly down the street, saw his friend Bill in a yellow sweater.

If that is the message you want to convey about John and Bill, you have to arrange the words in that order. Any change in the arrangement might convey an entirely different meaning, as for example:

John, who was in a yellow sweater, quickly saw his friend Bill walking down the street.

Bill saw his friend John, who was walking quickly down the street in a yellow sweater.

You will find that you can use the sixteen words to express several other meanings, simply by altering the syntactical structure.

The rules of syntax vary somewhat from language to language. Thus we place adjectives before nouns (*red house*), while the French place them after the nouns (*maison rouge*). But the pattern is always logical. The basic rule, as one student of language has said, is that "what belongs together mentally is placed close together syntactically" (6).

As will be noted later, we acquire a knowledge of syntax and other rules of grammar during early childhood. We may not be aware of all the rules either as children or as adults, but we follow them even if we cannot explain what they are—and they are the magic key to human communication (7).

Producing sentences and understanding them

The major function of language, as has been said, is communication. The structure consists of the sounds called phonemes, combined into meaningful morphemes and words, which are in turn strung together into meaningful sentences according to the rules of grammar and especially syntax. Thus a small number of sounds and an even smaller number of written letters, when used as the rules dictate, provide us with everything we need to exchange all the messages we will ever conceive of in our lifetime.

A marvelous tool indeed—but, as with all complicated devices, its use requires a great deal of skill and work. Producing language—speaking or writing new sentences created on the spot—is a process that requires thinking and planning. Understanding language is a process that also demands the most complex kind of mental activity.

Especially in the case of the spoken word, communication depends on close cooperation between speaker and listener. The speaker, having a purpose in mind, must carefully choose words and produce sentences that will "get the message across." The listener, in turn, must interpret the meaning and intention of the combination of sounds reaching the ear.

Suppose, for example, that you are in a room with a friend who is sitting near the window. You want the window opened wider. How, exactly, shall you phrase the suggestion? From all the possible words and syntactic arrangements available, you decide to say, "It's hot in here." Now your friend has to do some processing—for the words "It's hot in here" can be interpreted in a number of different ways. Your friend has to decide: Were you merely stating a fact? Do you mean that you want the window opened wider—or shut? Are you perhaps suggesting that both of you move to a different room? The possibilities have to be considered and accepted or rejected. Your friend will probably get the message, but not without working at it. For both speaker and listener, the use of language "makes full contact with our full cognitive abilities" (8).

The speaker's problem

One way to get some idea of the difficulty of producing language is to make a tape recording of some of your own utterances, especially when you are trying to explain something fairly complicated.

Hearing the tape afterward, you will probably be shocked at how tongue-tied you sound. Or listen carefully to someone else's conversation, paying attention not to the meaning but to the flow of words.

The spoken word is not nearly so smooth and fluent as is generally believed. As we talk, we often have to stop and think; our speech is full of long pauses, *and-uhs,* and *ers.* We make mistakes or fail to express ourselves clearly and have to amend our utterances with phrases like *I mean* or *that is to say.* Sometimes we stop in the middle of a sentence, leave it unfinished, and start all over. We make "slips of the tongue"—as was shown by one language scholar who, listening carefully to the utterances of the people around her, collected such amusing errors as these words that popped out in the middle of a marriage ceremony: *With this wing I thee red.* Or the case of a mother who wanted to say *David, feed the pooch* and actually said, *David, food the peach.* Or the person who apparently thought simultaneously of the adjectives *grizzly* and *ghastly,* so that the actual utterance came out *grastly* (9).

These errors in spoken language point to the problems we face when we produce sentences. We have to think of the meaning we want to convey—perhaps a message that will be several sentences long. Then we have to plan each sentence and each part of a sentence. We have to find the right words to flesh out the sentence and then put the words in their proper places. Finally we have to command all the muscles we use in speech to carry out the program we have planned—even as we are mentally racing ahead to what we want to say next (10).

Writing poses the same problems, though writers can correct their errors and have second thoughts before they put their language on public exhibition. Even the most experienced writers often start a sentence, cross the words out, and start over. After finishing the sentence they may go back and add new phrases or reword old ones. Many noted authors find that it takes a full day's work to produce, in final form, a page as long as this one.

The listener's problem

When you listen to someone speak, and try to interpret the meaning and intent, you face what is perhaps an even more difficult problem. All you have to go on is the sound waves that are produced by the speaker's voice and transmitted through the air to your ears. Ordinarily these waves meet with considerable competition from other sounds elsewhere in the vicinity. Other people are carrying on conversations in the same room. Footsteps thud against the floor. Noisy automobiles go by. A telephone rings. A door slams. A whistle blows. You may think you hear every word and every syllable uttered by the speaker—but in fact you do not. Many of the sounds are blotted out.

Even if you heard all the words, your ears could not immediately identify them. Many English words sound pretty much alike—for example *writer* and *rider, wave* and *waif.* Moreover, most of us are very careless about the way we pronounce words. We say not *I'm going to* but *I'm gonna,* not *Won't you?* but *Woncha?,* not *Give me* but *Gimme.* Regional accents further confuse matters. Bostonians say not *Harvard* but *Havad.* Many Southerners say not *whether* but *whethah.*

Two psychologists once made high-fidelity tape recordings of some everyday conversations, then cut up the tapes so that they could play back separate portions—anything from a single word to longer phrases. Listeners to these excerpts had a hard time recognizing what they heard. When they listened to a single word, they failed to identify it more than half the time. Even when they heard a phrase three words long, they missed it nearly 30 percent of the time (11). What this shows is that making sense out of the sound waves that strike our ears is as difficult as trying to read a page on which paint has been splattered, making it impossible to recognize many of the words.

Listening and active processing

How do we manage this seemingly impossible task? One clue comes from a study made with some doctored tape recordings of speech. A simple sentence was recorded just as it was spoken, for example:

It was found that the wheel was on the axle.

Then the phoneme *wh* was masked, as if by a cough, leaving the sound of (?)*eel*. Next some other words were spliced into the tape in place of *axle*. The experimenters now had four tapes in all, presenting these sounds:

It was found that the (?)eel was on the
$$\begin{cases} \text{axle.} \\ \text{shoe.} \\ \text{orange.} \\ \text{table.} \end{cases}$$

The last word, it turned out, made all the difference. Subjects who listened to the first tape were sure they heard a *wheel* was on the *axle*, but other subjects were equally sure a *heel* was on the *shoe*, a *peel* was on the *orange*, and a *meal* was on the *table* (12).

The interesting thing here is that the clue to the unintelligible sound (?)*eel* came after the sound

The United Nations interpreters in the foreground, as they translate the proceedings, have a special problem in active processing.

itself—indeed four words later. Somehow, in processing the sentence, the listeners managed to hold up judgment until they had the clue. Then they were absolutely sure they had heard a word that fit logically into the sentence. Evidence such as this has led many psychologists to take what is called the *active processing* view of speech comprehension. They believe that listeners carry out many mental processes all at the same time. They simultaneously try to recognize sounds, identify words, look for syntactic patterns, and search for semantic meaning. When sounds and words are in themselves vague or unintelligible—as so often happens in everyday speech—the processing for syntax and semantics makes order out of chaos (13). All this takes place so smoothly that we are not even aware of the mental work we do when listening or the handicaps we overcome.

How language is learned

Considering all the mental processing required to produce or understand language, it seems almost a miracle that children ever learn to use it. Yet learn they do—and very quickly. By the age of two, many are already speaking such sentences as "Baby drink milk." By the age of five, they understand the meaning of about 2,000 words (14). By about the age of six, they have learned virtually all the basic rules of grammar. They can string words together according to the rules to create meaningful new sentences of their own. And they understand the meaning of sentences they have never heard before.

Everything about the use of language must be learned except how to create the sounds, which is an inborn ability common to all normal children. Early in life, all babies begin to produce many sounds that resemble the phonemes of language—presumably because of movements of the muscles of the mouth, throat, and vocal cords associated with breathing, swallowing, and hiccuping. This "babbling" occurs spontaneously. It is not an attempt to imitate sounds that have been heard—as was demonstrated by observations of a deaf baby whose parents were deaf and mute. This baby never heard a sound, yet did the same kind of babbling as any other child (15).

Indeed it appears that children of all nationalities make the same sounds in their earliest babbling. It has been found, for example, that there are no differences among the babbling sounds of infants born to families that speak English, Russian, or Chinese (16). American infants have been observed to utter sounds that are not used by English-speaking adults but only by people who speak French or German (17). Soon, however, babies begin to concentrate on the sounds appropriate to their own language, which they hear from their parents and others around them. The other sounds, not used in English, disappear through disuse.

Sadly for those of us who try to learn foreign languages after we have grown up, these other sounds are eliminated quite thoroughly. Many of us who try to learn French or German are never able to pronounce some of the phonemes properly, even though we may have done so quite naturally when we were babies. This fact has an important bearing on one of the current debates over public policy in education, as explained in the box on Psychology and Society on page 182.

Can television replace mother?

As for how children learn all the many other things required for the use of language, psychologists have some clues and some theories—but as yet they have found no single and totally satisfactory explanation. About all that can be said for certain is that semantics and grammar can be learned only through exposure to language as used by other people, through a learning process whose dynamics are not yet fully understood.

What happens to a child who never hears the language of others has been demonstrated by the unfortunate case of a girl named Genie who spent most of the first thirteen years of her life shut up in a small room, isolated from human contact. When she was finally found by the Los Angeles police, she could not speak and in fact made no sounds at all except for a whimper. But it may never be too late to learn language. Taken first to a children's hospital and then to a foster home, Genie soon began to discover the meanings of words and to speak short sentences such as "Genie love Marilyn." Though still handicapped by her unnatural childhood, at last report she was continuing to make progress (21).

Mere exposure to the language of adults, however, does not appear to be enough. A case has been reported of a boy named Jim, the son of deaf parents who used only sign language. As deaf parents often do, they encouraged him to listen frequently to radio and television, to make up for their own inability to provide him with the sounds of speech. Although Jim had normal hearing and speech ability, he did not seem to profit much from his experiences with television. In his preschool years he knew only a few advertising jingles and some words he had probably picked up from playmates. He lagged far behind other children his age until arrangements were made for an adult from outside the home to engage him regularly in direct, two-way conversation (22). Similarly, it has been noted that children in the Netherlands who listen regularly to nearby German television stations do not ordinarily learn any German as a result (23).

Interaction between child and mother, or some other intimate caretaker, appears to be the crucial factor (24). The two seek to communicate. And somehow, as a result of this mutual effort, the child quickly acquires an understanding of the structure of language and a mastery of the processes of producing and understanding it. The first accomplishment of young babies is to speak a few meaningful words: *baby, mama, milk*. Soon afterward, within a few months, they begin to string words together: *baby walk, see mama*. The average length of their utterances increases as will be seen in Figure 5-1 on page 185. Some children learn more quickly than others—but all of them, if normal, show steady and consistent progress.

The child's struggle to convey meaning

From the beginning, children use speech in an attempt to send a message. They are not trying to copy adult grammar. They do not yet know how to string their words together in accordance with the rules of syntax. As one study stated, "The child is not reciting sentence types but is conveying meanings" (26).

At first, children seem to throw their words together haphazardly, and the adults around them may sometimes have trouble understanding the meaning. For example, a child of about two may say, "Put suitcase for?" when an adult would say, "What did you put it in the suitcase for?" Or the child may say, "Who dat . . . somebody pencil?" when an adult would say, "Whose pencils are they?" (27). Yet the meaning is there. Children are

How can we give equal education to children of families who do not speak "standard English"?

The United States, as a melting pot for people from all over the world and with many different language backgrounds, has always faced a serious educational problem. Today the problem centers mostly on the Spanish-speaking population. We have more than eleven million citizens of Spanish origin—including many children who have grown up in homes where only Spanish is spoken. These children—like their predecessors from homes where only Italian or German or Polish or Yiddish was spoken—often face serious difficulties in acquiring knowledge in English-speaking schools.

How can these children receive the American ideal of equal educational opportunity? One possible solution—urged by many Spanish-speaking parents—is to have them taught in Spanish by Spanish-speaking teachers. It has been suggested that this should be done throughout the early grades of elementary school. Later, English would be introduced and taught as a second language (as many English-speaking American children are now taught Spanish or French). Even after the children began to learn English, they would continue to devote as much time to Spanish and Latin-American history and culture as to United States history and English literature.

The suggestion has considerable appeal. It would preserve a cultural heritage—that is, fluency in the language of origin and familiarity with the traditions and customs of the Spanish-speaking world. Especially for children in the early grades, it would avoid the dislocations and handicaps of attending schools that use an unfamiliar language—and possibly the learned helplessness (pages 112–18) caused by failure.

But to function fully and efficiently as members of our English-speaking society, all children must eventually become adept at English. And psycho-

constantly struggling to express themselves as best they can, within the limits of their knowledge of semantics and grammar. When they want to say something but do not know the proper words or phrases, they make up their own way of expressing it. Note these examples of the speech of children at about the age of three:

By a child struggling to take off a sweater: *I wanta be it off*.

By a child who is trying to smooth down a piece of paper and has been urged by the mother to "make it nice and flat": *How would you flat it?*

By a child who is holding a piece of paper over a baby sister's head and plans to drop it: *I'm gonna fall this on her* (28).

If you are like most people, your first impulse is to laugh at such childish awkwardness. But, on second thought, might it not be more appropriate to marvel at the children's ingenuity?

Acquiring the rules of structure

Even at an early age, children acquire some of the rules of structure as practiced by the adults around logical findings raise some serious questions about the wisdom of delaying the process. As the text states, the ability to pronounce unused phonemes decreases with age. Most people who acquire a new language after childhood never manage to speak it without an accent (18). Indeed learning a new language at all becomes more difficult, for reasons that are not entirely understood. One study has cited the case of a professor from a foreign nation who visited the United States. Though he had spent many years studying English, he had great difficulty making himself understood—while his five-year-old child, with no previous instruction, picked up English so fast as to begin laughing at the father's mistakes (19).

Thus Spanish-speaking schools represent a trade-off, with certain advantages but also some dangers that would not be apparent without psychology's studies of language. The same findings apply to children from homes where American Indian languages are spoken, and also to black children whose parents speak what is sometimes called "Black English" as opposed to "standard English." Black English is almost a language of its own, with its own rules of pronunciation and grammar. Where standard English calls for the sentence *I asked John if he played basketball,* for example, Black English calls for *I asked John do he play basketball.* In the way it applies its rules, Black English is just as consistent as any other language (20). Indeed some linguists feel that it is more direct and expressive than standard English as spoken by many middle-class Americans. It does, however, create problems for children who, though fluent in Black English, must cope with schools—and later with a society—where a very different language is demanded. How can education be best tailored to such students?

them. Children of about the age of two, for example, are likely to say such things as *Gooses swimmed.* Even through the statement is not put correctly, it shows that they have learned something about structure. They have discovered that ordinarily a noun can be made plural by adding an *-s* and a verb can be turned into the past tense by adding an *-ed.* We can hardly blame them for the fact that our language is not always consistent and decrees that the plural of *goose* is *geese* and the past tense of *swim* is *swam.*

The way children learn the rules of structure shows a remarkable consistency. Whether they are fast learners or slow, and regardless of the size or nature of their vocabularies, they seem to acquire knowledge of the rules in a predictable order. In the study of the three children presented in Figure 5-1, for example, a careful record was kept of the age at which they showed an ability to use morphemes that have structural significance. The first such morpheme generally used was *-ing,* added to a verb to denote an action going on at the moment (in the phraseology of grammarians, the present progressive tense). One of the girls, trying to explain that her father was at work, said he was "making pennies."

Somewhat later came the addition of an -s to words to make them plural. And still later—again for all three children—the use of an -'s to indicate possession. They learned to use some of the articles (the, a, an) before they added an -ed to a verb to convey the past tense (29).

Learning the rules seems to proceed in much the same fashion the world over. With minor variations, the first two-word utterances of children are similar not only in function but in structure whether they are learning to speak English, Russian, or Samoan (30). Regardless of the language, children all seem to go about learning the rules in much the same way (31)—with the ultimate aim of using them to make sense.

Parents help—but children are fine pupils

Adults help children learn in a number of ways. They speak to children slowly, with many pauses (32). They use short sentences (33) and often repeat words or phrases to help the child understand. Their sentences, however, are well formed and readily understandable (34). All in all, by gearing their speech to the child's level of ability to follow and comprehend the words, they provide what have been called "language lessons in miniature" (35)—helping the child pick up not only meaning but structure (36).

As far as meaning is concerned, parents usually make a deliberate effort at clarity. Thus mothers have been found to repeat and clarify as in these utterances to a child: *Put the red truck in the box now. The red truck. No, the red truck. The red truck in the box* (37). Perhaps these repetitions also help children acquire knowledge of syntax by breaking utterances down into separate phrases, thus emphasizing how words are strung together into phrases and phrases into sentences. But such utterances serve only as models. They do not explain the rules, which children have to figure out for themselves.

On the matter of the grammatical rules, parents seldom provide feedback that would let children know whether their own utterances are put together properly or not. Indeed it has been found that mothers almost never correct or punish errors in syntax; they ignore mistakes of this kind although they usually correct children for speaking in a way that gets the facts wrong. Thus when one of the children in the study illustrated in Figure 5-1 said, *Mama isn't boy; he a girl*—a statement that was factually correct though grammatically all wrong—the mother replied approvingly, *That's right*. When another of the children said of a television program, *Walt Disney comes on Tuesday*—a statement grammatically correct but factually wrong—the mother was quick to point out the error with the firm comment, *No, he does not* (38).

Nonetheless, even without any direct guidance, children learn the rules quickly. They are much more likely to wind up using correct syntax, on which they have received no feedback, than always telling the truth, on which they have received a great deal.

Theories of language learning

At one time most psychologists believed that the manner in which language is learned could be explained fully in terms of operant conditioning. They thought that some of the sounds made by babies in their early babbling were reinforced by their parents' smiles, fondling, or other forms of approval. These sounds tended to be repeated. Other sounds, not appropriate to the language, were not reinforced and tended to disappear. The same process of reinforcement or lack of it, it was believed, accounted for the manner in which

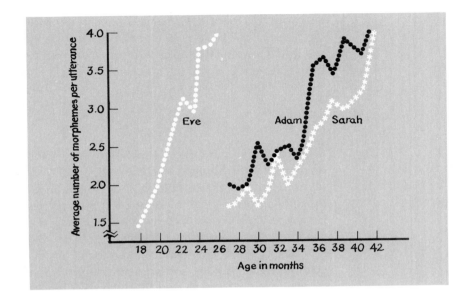

5-1

**Children's speech:
from simple to complex**

Charted here is the increasing complexity of the language spoken by three children whose utterances were carefully recorded over a period of months to determine the average number of morphemes they strung together in each burst of speech. The fastest progress was made by Eve, who was observed from the time she was 18 months old. Less quick to use longer strings of words were Adam and Sarah, both of whom were studied beginning at 27 months. Although the three children progressed at different rates, there were some remarkable similarities in their development, as is explained in the text (25).

babies started to string sounds together into meaningful sentences (39).

Later, some psychologists who became impressed by the importance of learning through observation proposed a different theory. They suggested that language was learned not through operant conditioning but through imitation of the way parents combined phonemes into meaningful morphemes, then strung morphemes together into meaningful words and sentences.

Both these theories may account at least in part for how language is learned, yet neither seems to offer a complete explanation. It is difficult to see how operant conditioning can lead children to acquire rules that will enable them to create new sentences of their own—especially since they may receive positive reinforcement in the form of approval for grammatically incorrect utterances (*Mama isn't boy; he a girl*) and negative reinforcement when their grammar is correct (*Walt Disney comes on Tuesday*). It is also difficult to see how

imitation can result in completely new and original sentences—and in fact there is evidence that children who do very little imitating learn language just as well as children who do a lot of it (40).

A totally different theory has been proposed by Noam Chomsky, a linguist at the Massachusetts Institute of Technology. Chomsky suggests that the human brain is wired in such a way that we are born with some kind of "innate mechanism" for learning and using language. This innate mechanism serves as what he calls an LAD, or language acquisition device, which enables us as children to do some rapid information processing on the language we hear from our elders. We quickly develop our own theories of how they are stringing words together to convey their meaning. Later we modify and expand these theories as we get more experience at communicating with others—and soon we are using the rules of grammar in such a sophisticated fashion that we can understand or express almost anything. The Chomsky theory

"WHAT'S THE BIG SURPRISE? ALL THE LATEST THEORIES OF LINGUISTICS SAY WE'RE BORN WITH THE INNATE CAPACITY FOR GENERATING SENTENCES."

holds that, in a sense, we cannot help learning language and using it the way we do. This is simply the way our brains operate (41).

It is impossible to prove or disprove the existence of Chomsky's LAD. But certainly our use of language depends more on the dynamics of the human brain than on anything else. It is true that we have some advantages over other animals even in the creation of sounds. The structure and muscles of our mouths, jaws, tongues, and air passages provide superior versatility in producing speech (42). But other mammals also possess vocal cords, which are the key factor, and even birds can make many of the sounds of human speech. As far as is known, however, human beings are the only organisms in which one particular part of the left half of the brain is larger than the corresponding part of the right half—and it has been found that the ability to speak and understand language depends primarily on this special area of the brain (43). It seems possible that the use of a complex and infin-itely varied language is a species-specific behavior dictated by our biological inheritance. Just as fish are born to swim and moles to burrow, we may be born to speak.

Can animals learn language?

One fascinating question is whether any other animals share the human talent for language. In an effort to find the answer, psychologists have made many attempts to teach language to other species. Until recently, the attempts always ended in failure. Experimenters who raised chimpanzees in their homes along with their own children found that the chimps rather readily learned such human habits as eating with a spoon and brushing their teeth—yet never learned to speak more than a few simple words (44). Even dolphins, which seemed promising subjects because their brains closely resemble

5-2 A chimpanzee "talks"

The chimpanzee named Washoe, asked to describe the object in her teacher's hand, makes her sign for the word "hat."

the human brain, proved unable to learn.

A few years ago, however, one group of investigators had a brilliant idea. Perhaps chimpanzees simply find it difficult to learn to use their vocal cords like human beings. Instead of trying to teach them to speak, why not try to teach them a sign language, such as used by the deaf? This experiment proved surprisingly successful. A chimpanzee named Washoe, shown in Figure 5-2, managed to learn an expressive vocabulary of more than 130 signs in a little more than four years of training. (Among the signs were *toothbrush, you, please, cat, enough, time,* and many others.) Moreover, Washoe learned to string the signs together into fairly complex sentences, such as *hurry gimme toothbrush* (45). She even made up a word of her own using the signs available to her—*water-bird* to describe a duck.

Another ingenious approach was made with a chimpanzee named Sarah, who was taught to communicate by using symbols for words in the form of pieces of plastic cut into various shapes. The plastic symbols have a metal backing and can be arranged on a magnetized board. In this manner Sarah has learned the meaning of numerous words and the use of sentences such as *Mary give apple Sarah* (46). Indeed she has demonstrated what may be at least some idea of syntax. Once she had learned the meaning of the words *take, dish,* and *red,* she obeyed a sentence of a type she had never seen before: *Sarah take red dish.* When her caretaker showed her two foods she liked, chocolate and a banana, she spontaneously created the sentence *Mary give Sarah banana chocolate*—which needs only an *and* between the two food names to be exactly the way a human child might ask for two things at once (47).

The newest development in the use of language by animals is illustrated in Figure 5-3. Here two chimpanzees, trained to communicate by using a

5-3
A two-way conversation between chimpanzees
Sherman, at left, complies with Austin's signalled request for bread, then licks his own fingers.

keyboard that flashes symbols on a projector, are actually conducting what seems for all the world a human conversation (48). This is the first known case of two-way communication by animals using symbols like the words in human language.

What do the animals have to tell us?

What these experiments with animals reveal about the use of language is still unclear. Because of the large amount of specialized training required to bring chimpanzees up to the level of normal three-year-old children, some psychologists question whether the experiments show that animals can use language in anything like the way human beings do (49). In particular, they question whether the animals have grasped any of the rules of syntax or have merely learned how to place symbols for words into ready-made structures provided by their

training (50). Chimpanzees do not create many new sentences, or long sentences, although children are constantly doing this.

Other observers have been more impressed. One view is that the experiments seem to show that human language is hardly "beyond the grasp of other species"—and the work to date has only begun to indicate how much chimpanzees may actually be capable of learning. Some interesting questions for the future are whether the Washoes and Sarahs will pass along their knowledge of language to their children—and, if so, whether the offspring will pick up language as effortlessly as human children do. Possibly it will be found that the ability to use language is not the unique species-specific attribute that Chomsky suggests but just one aspect of the general cognitive superiority we enjoy because of our larger and more complex brains (51).

Language, concepts, and cognition

Certainly language and cognition are closely related. We use language to communicate our ideas about our world and our relations to our physical and social environment. Thus our language reflects our thinking. But language, in turn, serves as a tool for thinking about the objects and events in our lives. Language helps us to find meanings and relationships, and to compare new experiences with old ones. It enables us to plan for future events that have not yet occurred. As one study has put it, human thinking "both affects and is affected by language" (52).

The interaction between language and thinking can perhaps best be understood by starting with the fact that only a few of the words we use are the

names of specific, one-of-a-kind objects—for example, the chemical elements oxygen and nitrogen. Most words, on the contrary, represent whole groups of objects, events, actions, and ideas. Even a simple word like *water* means not only the colorless fluid in the glass we hold in our hands but also any somewhat similar fluid anywhere, including the salty contents of the oceans and the raindrops that fall from the sky. The word *justice* represents many different abstract ideas held by people around the world at various times in history and embodied in various legal codes and practices.

Thus most words represent what are called *concepts*—which are notions of similarity. The concept of *water* is derived from our observation that the fluids in drinking glasses, oceans, and raindrops, though they look so different, are in fact similar. (If we know chemistry, we are aware that they are all H₂O.) The concept of *bigger* denotes a relationship that is shared by such diverse pairs of objects as fly-to-gnat, adult-to-child, and Texas-to-Delaware. *Justice* represents the shared similarities of many diverse attitudes and legal systems.

The use of concepts lends a tremendous variety and versatility to our processes of cognition. When we encounter a new object or experience, we do not have to deal with it as a unique event to which we bring no prior knowledge and which we must learn about from scratch. Usually we can fit it into an already-existing concept (53). A dog of a species we have never seen before is instantly recognizable as a dog—and we know how it is likely to behave. A strange new sculpture by a modern artist is immediately recognizable as a piece of art. Studying a book of this sort is greatly helped—indeed made possible—by the concepts represented by such words as *college, course, psychology, theory, experiment,* and many others.

Concepts with and without words

It is possible to acquire and use concepts as a tool of thinking without the help of language (54). Dogs appear to have a concept of *tree*—and, as you know if you have ever taken one out for an airing, will behave toward a new tree they have never seen before just as they behave toward more familiar trees. Many experiments have shown that various animals can learn concepts of triangles, as shown in Figure 5-4, and other general principles, such as recognizing the odd object in a group of three where two are alike and one is different. Babies who have not yet learned the words have concepts of the human face and animals.

Much human thinking, however, entails the use of complex concepts embedded within other concepts, in a way that would be difficult if not impossible without the use of language. What do you think of, for example, when you encounter the term *human being?* Perhaps you immediately think of some simple characteristics such as physical appearance (two arms and two legs) and what peo-

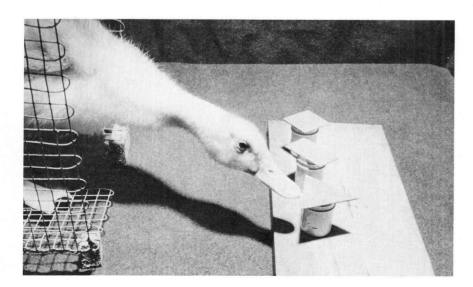

5-4
The duck can't say "triangle"—but knows one when it sees it
The duck has learned that food is always found beneath some kind of three-sided figure, never beneath a four-sided figure. Even if the size and exact shape of the figures are changed, the duck will look under the triangle. It must have some concept of triangularity—gained, as explained in the text, without the use of language.

ple do (work as teachers, students, law officials, teamsters). But you probably also have a much richer concept of *human being* as the highest (which is itself a concept) of all mammals (another concept)—a mammal being a particular kind of organism (still another concept) that produces (another) its young (another) inside (another) the body (another) of the mother (another), which nurses (another) the baby (another) after (another) birth (still another).

Without the help of language, it would be difficult to find any similarity between *human being* and *whale*—but we can think of them as related because we know that these two very dissimilar organisms are both mammals. What we have learned of history and geography, through the use of language, enables us to include in our concept of *human being* such diverse items as the ancient Egyptian pharaohs and the lamas of Tibet.

Concepts, categories, and memory

Concepts are a great help in acquiring new information, storing it in memory, and using it effectively. They are the key to organizing information into categories, which was described in the preceding chapter as one form of the deep processing that creates long-lasting memory. Note Figure 5-5, which is a condensed version of an illustration used in the preceding chapter to show how students learned and remembered a word list much more easily when the words were arranged in categories. You will see that all the words representing the categories and subcategories are terms for concepts. It was these concepts (*minerals, metals, stones,* etc.) that made it possible to organize the word list so effectively.

Language accounts to a great extent for the fact that learning builds on learning—or, in William James' words, that new items of information may "cluster and cling like grapes to a stem." It does so both by helping us acquire concepts and giving us specific words that help us think about specific details. It is difficult to imagine, for example, how a surgeon could be trained without all the words that medical science has developed over the years to describe the human body—some representing the general principles of how the body is put together and functions, others identifying specific anatomical structures with which a surgeon may be concerned. Effective surgery would probably be impossible without an "effective language" (55).

The relation between language and learning and memory is a two-way street. As one study stated, "Learning new words enables children to conquer new areas of knowledge, and these new areas enable them to learn new words, and so on" (56). This is one reason, unfortunately, that children from poorly educated families often have a difficult time in school, thus continuing a vicious circle that leads one generation after another to have trouble getting along. Children whose parents have very little formal education and use a limited vocabulary start school with a severe handicap. There are hundreds and perhaps thousands of words and concepts that they have never heard of but that are already familiar to children whose parents are better educated. They simply do not have the same kind of "effective language" that makes it easy to find similarities and relationships between the new information presented in school and their prior knowledge.

Language as a pair of eyeglasses for viewing the world: Does it distort our vision?

One of the interesting questions about language and cognition is this: As they interact, each affecting the other, which has the stronger influence? Is it

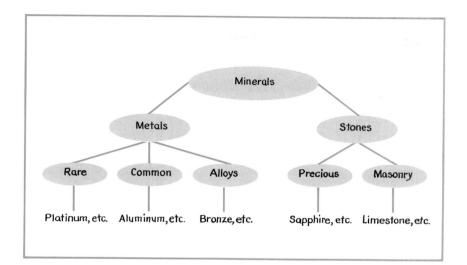

5-5
Concepts and learning by categories
You will recognize this list from Chapter 4, where it illustrated an experiment in committing information to long-term memory through the use of categories and subcategories. For its significance in the present chapter's discussion of concepts, see the text.

possible that our language restricts our cognitive abilities? Does it perhaps serve as a pair of faulty eyeglasses through which we get only a limited and sometimes distorted view of the world?

One prominent language student, Benjamin Whorf, suggested that people who use different languages have very different ways of looking at the world and different concepts about the similarities and relationships that it displays. In his study of many languages, Whorf found one group of American Indians who lump together with a single word things that fly—insects, airplanes, and even airplane pilots. He found other languages that do not have any devices for distinguishing the past, present, and future tenses of verbs (57). In Whorf's view, such differences are bound to affect the ways in which people who speak these languages conceive the world, organize it, and think about it.

This is an intriguing theory—and it seems to receive a certain amount of support from some of the matters discussed in the last few pages. The trained surgeon, with an "effective language" of anatomy, looks at and thinks about the human body dif-

ferently from the rest of us. Children who start school with impoverished vocabularies probably conceive of the world in more limited fashion than their more fortunate classmates. It would appear that cognitive processes can be influenced not only by the use of different languages but also by differences in the vocabularies of people who speak the same language.

Or do we design the eyeglasses to fit our vision?

There is a great deal of evidence, however, that language is usually tailored to human thinking, rather than vice versa. In all the many languages of the world, there are more basic similarities than differences. Certainly on the matter of the physical objects and everyday events found in the world, people everywhere seem to perceive them, find names for them, organize them into concepts and categories, and think about them in ways that are often very similar.

Some colors, for example, seem particularly striking—doubtless because of the way the sense organs of the eye and the process of perception operate (as will be explained in Chapters 7 and 8). And, though languages differ in the number of colors for which they have names, the names always refer to the colors that "hit the eye," not to all the many other hues and shades found in nature (58).* Similarly, most languages have terms for shapes that human perception seems to find compelling, such as squares and circles. They have terms indicating that people all over the world think in much the same fashion about the dimensions of objects (like the English *height* and *length*) and distance and direction (59).

One theory is that our concepts about the physical world are based on what is actually "out there" in nature, as viewed by human perception and cognition. Objects just naturally fall into groups (like birds and animals, vegetables and fruits). Human concepts and language reflect this fact (60). Our brains are wired to notice certain attributes of the objects and events we encounter, and we form concepts and categories based on family resemblances among these attributes.

Perhaps, as we observe the world, we develop a notion of a sort of ideal or *prototype* bird (or vegetable or fruit). Then we place other objects in this same category, or reject them, depending on how much family resemblance they have to the prototype. For many Americans, the prototype bird might be the robin—which is rather small, has two short legs and two wings, flies, sits in trees, and sings. Thus we have no trouble identifying as birds such similar creatures as thrushes and song sparrows. We might take a little longer to decide that a chicken is a bird, for it is a good deal larger than a

robin and does not fly or sit in trees.

Sometimes the boundary line between one category or family and another is extremely fuzzy. We may have trouble deciding whether a bat is a bird or an animal and whether a tomato is a vegetable or a fruit (61). This same kind of "fuzziness" in the way we form categories makes it difficult to classify a 16-year-old female as a girl or a woman, or rheumatism as a disease or something else. Our concepts and categories—and indeed our thinking in general—are not always so neat as we would like them to be. But perhaps this simply reflects the fact that our world is itself a rather messy place, not easy to describe in cut-and-dried terms.

How new thinking produces new language

Certainly language changes when people's thinking changes. Note, for example, all the new words that football has created while developing to its present highly technical level. There were no such terms in the English language, even a few years ago, as *cornerback*, *noseguard*, *reddog*, and *safety blitz*. All grew out of the need to find new terms for new concepts developed by inventive coaches.

When we need a new word, we coin it—or borrow it from another language. (Many everyday "English" words are borrowed—*goulash* from Hungarian, *whisky* from Gaelic, *sabotage* from French.) And as additions to the language become more and more widely used, we often shorten them to make them more convenient (62). Thus the original term *moving picture* has been condensed to *movie*, *gasoline* to *gas*, *telephone* to *phone*. Specialists in certain areas of knowledge, such as surgeons, coin or borrow their own vocabulary and often engage in their own form of shortening terms for simplicity and convenience.

All in all, though thinking may in some ways be molded and limited by language, as Whorf has

---

*The only colors for which any language in the world has basic terms are red, yellow, green, blue, brown, purple, pink, orange, black, white, and gray. Not all languages have words for all these colors; indeed some have words for only two colors.

pointed out, the human brain seems remarkably capable of adapting this useful tool to its own advantage. One study stated: "Apparently when people lack a word for a useful concept, they soon find one. . . . What this suggests is that language differences reflect the culture and not the reverse" (63). The moral for all of us is that we have in language a tool of virtually infinite possibilities—limited, for all practical purposes, only by how well we learn to handle it.

Thinking and problem solving

Thinking in general, like the formation of concepts, does not necessarily require the use of language. An artist working on a painting thinks in terms of mental images—a mind's-eye picture of what the details and final results should look like. Many musicians compose and orchestrate by manipulating sounds that they "hear" only inside themselves. (Beethoven wrote many of his greatest works after he became deaf and could not hear tones at all.) Mathematicians manipulate their own special symbols and formulas, and often think about their nonverbal conceptions of space and of intersecting planes.

Thinking, indeed, is very difficult to define. About the best we can do is call it *the mental manipulation of information,* including images, language, concepts, and the facts we have discovered about the way our universe operates.

Sometimes thinking is the mental manipulation of objects that are physically present in the environment—for example, the thinking of carpenters while working with tools and lumber to build a cabinet. Carpenters do not just move these objects about. They think about the uses and measurements of the objects in relation to the as yet unfinished products they are building. In other cases, thinking is entirely independent of physical objects. We can think about objects that are not present, about events that occurred in the distant past, or about abstract concepts (such as *justice*) that have no physical reality at all. Thinking is such a remarkable ability precisely because it can range so widely, in both space and time, and is so free from restrictions imposed by the immediate environment.

Though language is not essential, it is the basis of most thinking. Some time when you are engaged in thinking—about anything at all, from your plans for

The sculptor thinks not in language but in mental images.

your next meal to your ideas about politics or religion—stop yourself and try to examine what kind of process has been going on. Most likely you will find that you have been talking to yourself—thinking through the use of words, and especially words that represent concepts. This chapter is a compilation of the findings and ideas that numerous psychologists have expressed in their own words, summarized and presented here in the words of the authors of this book. When you think about the chapter, trying to do some processing of its meanings and relationships, you will use words. Certainly you cannot practice the SQ3R system of studying, by reciting what you have learned in the chapter, without calling on language.

Thinking by inference

One important kind of thinking with the help of language is demonstrated by this example: Someone says to you, "There is a bird in Brazil called a cariama. Does it have wings?" Almost immediately, you answer, "Yes." You do not know this from your own experience, for you have never seen a cariama. You have reached your answer through the useful form of thinking called *inference*—or drawing logical conclusions from facts already known. Though you were probably not aware of the individual steps, your thinking has taken this form:

1 A cariama is a bird. (As you were just told)
2 All birds have wings. (A fact that you have previously observed and stored in memory—a part of your concept of bird)
3 Therefore a cariama has wings. (Your inference)

The process of inference enables you to think about many matters without having any direct knowledge of the situation (64). At the end of a long day's drive, you feel confident that you will find a motel room if you push on another fifty miles

toward Denver because Denver is a big city and it has been your experience that all big cities have many motels on their outskirts. You may never have read *A Midsummer Night's Dream,* but you are confident it is in blank verse because you know it was written by Shakespeare and every other play you have read by Shakespeare was in blank verse.

All of us constantly make inferences. When we hear a sentence such as "John just pushed Bill into the water," we think of it in far richer terms than the mere string of words conveys. We automatically assume that John pushed with his hands, that Bill is now in the water, that Bill is wet, that Bill is either swimming or struggling, and so on (65).

Our inferences may sometimes be wrong. Suppose, for example, that the question about the Brazilian bird had been, "Does a cariama fly?"

5-6 A chimpanzee has an insight and solves a problem

The chimpanzee is in a cage with a bunch of bananas hanging high above its reach and with three boxes, none of which is high enough in itself to enable the chimp to climb up and reach the bananas. After looking the situation over for some time, it starts to pile one box atop another for additional height and thus manages to reach the bananas.

Again the process of inference would doubtless have led you to answer yes, on the premise that all birds fly. But there are a few birds that do not fly—and the cariama just might happen to be one of them.

Many of our conclusions, however, are correct and are therefore useful. Just as the rules of grammar enable us to generate sentences we have never spoken before and to understand sentences we have never heard before, so does the process of inference enable us to think about all kinds of matters we have never actually encountered. We can generalize about the new and unfamiliar from what we have observed about similar objects or events. Indeed most of what we know—or think we know—is based on inference rather than on direct observation.

Problem solving

Many years ago an experimenter put cats into a number of "puzzle boxes"—little cages from which the cats could escape only by lifting a latch or pulling a loop of string. Outside each box he placed food. The cats had a goal—namely, to get out of the box and get the food. But how? That was the problem.

It developed that the cats could solve the problem only through the method of *trial and error*. They made all kinds of movements. They stretched, bit, and scratched. Eventually, by chance, they stumbled onto the solution and made their escape (66).

The chimpanzee shown in Figure 5-6 is also faced with a problem. High above its head hangs a bunch of bananas. Its goal is to reach them. But how? The solution to the problem, as the chimp has just discovered, is to pile the boxes one atop another and climb up. In this case the animal caught on; it got the idea; the solution came in a flash of what is called *insight*.

Perhaps some trial and error took place, in the sense that the chimpanzee thought of other possible ways to solve the problem and discarded them as unworkable. If so, the trial and error took place inside the animal's head. It was all done by manipulating the boxes through whatever kind of thinking takes place in a chimpanzee.

Techniques of problem solving

We human beings are constantly faced with problems. Students must solve not only the theoretical problems in their mathematics courses but also many real-life problems. You have a certain number of dollars available for tuition, books, clothes, housing, food, and entertainment: How can you best allot the dollars to these expenses? If you are driving from California to New York, you have problems of a different sort: What highways will make the trip fastest? How can the trip best be broken up into how many days on the road? The

mechanic looking at an automobile that refuses to run must ask: What is wrong? How can I fix it?

In our attempts to solve problems, we sometimes are lucky enough to have a flash of insight, like the chimpanzee with the boxes. Sometimes we are reduced to using trial and error, like the cats in the puzzle box. More often, we think and think and think—drawing on the knowledge we have stored in memory and on the techniques, such as inference, that we have learned for manipulating information. Sometimes, after much mental work, we succeed. Sometimes we are baffled.

Efficiency at problem solving can be improved through practice, and we can learn to become better problem solvers just as we can learn anything else. Psychologists have found a number of interesting and effective techniques. But the art of problem solving is a whole field of its own that is too large to be covered adequately in an introductory textbook. Any brief discussion of the subject must be limited to pointing out some of the pitfalls that lie in wait for the would-be solver.

Pitfall 1: taking too much for granted

One of the common errors in problem solving is beautifully illustrated by the experiment shown in Figure 5-7, which you should try for yourself before going on to the next paragraph.

The problem presented in Figure 5-7 is really quite simple—yet few people manage to solve it. The answer is that you must turn over cards 1 and 3. If card 1 has a colored circle on the back, or if card 3 has a colored triangle on the back, then the statement you are asked to prove or disprove is false. But if card 1 has a black circle on the back, and card 3 has a black triangle on the back, then the statement is true.

Most people insist that the cards to turn over are

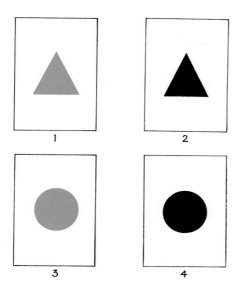

1   2

3   4

5-7
Can you solve this problem?
These four cards, which have symbols on both sides, lie on a table so that you can see them as shown here. You are told that each card has on one side a triangle, which may be either colored or black, and on the other side a circle, which also may be either colored or black. You are asked to prove or disprove this statement about them: *Every card that has a colored triangle on one side has a black circle on the other side.* How many cards—and which ones—would you have to turn over to find out whether the statement is true or false? For the answer, see the text (67).

1 and 4. But in fact card 4 has no bearing on the problem. Regardless of whether the triangle on the back is colored or black, this card cannot prove or disprove the statement. The reason people tend to fall into the error of picking this card seems to be that they take too much for granted in reading the problem. From the statement given in the experiment, *Every card that has a colored triangle on one side has a black circle on the other side,* they assume that it is also true that every card that has a black circle on one side must have a colored triangle on

the other side. But this has never been stated and is not part of the problem. The psychologist who devised the experiment has made many similar studies and has found that most people have this tendency to jump to unwarranted conclusions.

Pitfall 2: thinking what we would like to think

Closely allied to the error of taking too much for granted is another pitfall in problem solving: the fact that we sometimes tend to let our personal biases get in the way. We try hard—and sometimes against all the weight of evidence and logic—to find the answer we would like to find. The way our personality traits can affect problem solving has been demonstrated by an experiment in which each of the students in a psychology course received a piece of paper on which this question was written: "A man bought a horse for $60 and sold it for $70. Then he bought it back for $80 and sold it for $90. How much money did he make in the horse business?" The students were asked to check one of five possible answers: lost $10, broke even, made $10, made $20, or made $30. (Think about the problem for a moment and decide on your own answer.)

In the original experiment, it turned out that men students and women students reacted quite differently to the problem. As is shown in Figure 5-8, considerably more women than men checked "broke even." Considerably more men than women got the correct answer, which is "made $20." The psychologists who conducted the experiment concluded that the women tended to favor the "broke even" answer because they were more conservative and less aggressive than the men; they preferred to think of people as breaking even

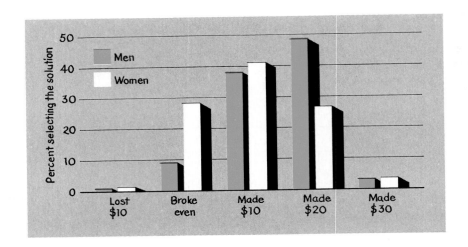

5-8

**The horse-trading problem:
men answer it one way,
women a different way**

The bars show the percentages of men
and women college students who selected the various possible answers to
the horse-trading problem described in
the text. Note how many more women
than men selected "broke even" and
how many more men than women selected "made $20."

in financial transactions rather than as taking risks
and winding up with a substantial profit (68).

It should be noted that this experiment was conducted in the 1960s, before much had been heard
about the women's liberation movement. You
might find it interesting to try the problem on some
friends of both sexes to see if the results are different in today's world.

Pitfall 3: persistence of set

Another tendency all of us share is to suffer from
what is called *persistence of set*. We develop our
own methods of approaching problems—and we
tend to use them even in situations where other
methods would be more appropriate. In other
words, we get into a rut. It is persistence of set that
makes it so difficult for most of us to solve brain-
teasers that require a fresh approach to familiar
situations. For example, there is the old puzzle
about the man who lived on the top floor of a nine-
story apartment building. Every morning, when he
went to work, he got on the elevator at the ninth

floor. But in the evening, returning home, he got off
at the eighth floor and walked up the remaining
flight. Why? A somewhat similar puzzle concerns
the man, bitter about life, who planned one last
grim joke on humanity. His body was found hanging, with his feet a good two feet from the floor, in
an otherwise empty closet. How did he manage to
hang himself? Only by a determined effort to avoid
persistence of set can we come to the answers.*

Pitfall 4: functional fixedness

A special form of set is called *functional fixedness*.
This is a tendency to think of objects as functioning
only in one certain way and to ignore their other
possible uses. A demonstration of how functional
fixedness can interfere with problem solving is illustrated in Figure 5-9. Test your own skills on the

*The man on the elevator was a midget who could reach only
as high as the button for the eighth floor. The man who hanged
himself stood on a cake of ice that had melted by the time his
body was discovered.

problem presented in this figure before going on to the next paragraph or turning the page to Figure 5-10, which shows the solution.

As can be seen in Figure 5-10, the key to solving the problem is to forget about the ordinary uses of a pair of pliers and to turn the pliers instead into a support for the flower stand. In an experiment in which subjects were asked to solve the problem by actually manipulating the objects, it was found that their attempts were hampered if they had to begin by using the pliers to loosen the wire. This seemed to serve as a reminder that the usual function of pliers is to loosen or tighten wires, turn bolts, or pull nails—not to serve as the legs of a flower stand. Subjects for whom the wooden bar was merely tied to the board and could be removed by simply untying a knot—and who therefore did not have to use the pliers to loosen a wire—were considerably more likely to find the solution (69).

In many real-life situations functional fixedness reduces our efficiency at solving problems. A nail file is for filing nails; we may overlook entirely the fact that it might help us tighten a screw and thus repair a broken lamp. A goldfish bowl is for fish; the first person who used one as a terrarium for growing house plants had to break some powerful old associations. Similarly, we have a tendency to think that things that perform the same functions should look alike. As old photographs show, the first automobiles strongly resembled buggies.

Creative thinking—and why it is so rare

Functional fixedness and persistence of set have certain advantages in helping us meet the routine problems of daily living. We are set to use many of the articles around us in certain ways—the soap and toothbrush in the bathroom, our clothing, the knives and forks on the table. These sets help us bathe, dress, and eat breakfast almost without thinking about what we are doing. We are set to start an automobile in the routine way, to stop at red lights and start at green lights, to step on the

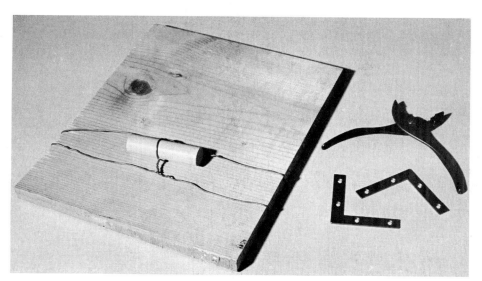

5-9
This doesn't look like a flower stand— but it can be
Could you arrange any or all of these objects so that the board will stand firmly on supports and can serve as a stand for a vase of flowers? This exercise in problem solving is particularly difficult when you have only a photograph and cannot actually manipulate the objects. But, with effort and luck, you may be able to visualize the solution before turning to Figure 5-10, which demonstrates how the job can be done. The first step, of course, is to use the pliers to loosen the wire and detach the wooden pin.

5-10
The solution to the flower-stand problem
The problem posed in Figure 5-9 can be solved only by using the pliers in an unusual way, as two "legs" for the stand. The metal joints go unused.

brake when something gets in our path. Sets are particularly valuable when we must react quickly, as when avoiding another automobile or a pedestrian, and do not have time to ponder all the possible answers to the problem.

On the other hand, persistence of set and functional fixedness help account for the fact that truly creative thinking is so rare. For example, early attempts to teach language to chimpanzees failed because the experimenters were set to think of language in terms of speech; it was not until this set was broken by the brilliant idea of using sign language that the attempts became more successful.

Studies of creative people have shown that they tend to have a number of traits in common that are not shared by most other people. Generally speaking, they were lone wolves in childhood. They either were spurned and rejected by other children or sought solitude themselves. If being different from other children caused them anxiety, they eventually overcame it. They grew up with no need to conform to the people and the ways of life around them. In fact creative people *want* to be different and original and to produce new things. They are not afraid

of having irrational or bizarre thoughts, are willing to examine even the most foolish-seeming ideas, and are not worried about success or failure. Many of them are aggressive and hostile, not at all the kind of people who win popularity contests (70).

Creativity of any kind—the invention of a new mechanical device such as the airplane, the discovery of a new scientific principle, the writing of a great and original poem or novel—demands superior intelligence. But of the people who have the required intelligence perhaps not even as many as 1 percent are in fact creative. Even more than intelligence, creativity demands the kind of personality that scorns the tried and true, does not get imprisoned by persistence of set, but on the contrary seeks out new and unusual ideas even in the face of failure and ridicule.

Tests of creativity

Many attempts have been made to devise tests that will spot creative people so that they may receive special treatment to encourage their talents. One such test is illustrated in Figure 5-11. If potentially creative people could be protected from pressures toward conformity—particularly in their early work in school—perhaps more of them would actually flourish. In trying to recognize and encourage creativity, however, there are many problems. For one thing, true creativity requires more than mere originality. Sheer novelty—or what might be called "offbeat" thinking—is not enough. Besides being new and unusual, a creative idea must also be *appropriate*. A new scientific theory must, like Einstein's theory of relativity, be in accord with the known facts. When we look at a painting or hear music we must have some perception of aptness, of a disciplined relationship to the world as we know it, if we are to consider the work of art esthetically pleasing and thus genuinely creative.

Do computers think?

One new approach to the study of human thinking—with possibilities that are just beginning to be explored—is based on the way computers have been programed to perform many of the accomplishments once believed to be the sole prerogative of human cognition. Computers already carry out many tasks of great complexity. In the business world, they make out payrolls, write payroll checks, keep track of immense inventories, and in some cases operate manufacturing plants with very little human help. They direct space ships to the moon. Along lighter lines, they play creditable games of checkers and chess—well enough, indeed, to beat most of us run-of-the-mill human players.

Computers capable of doing these things give the appearance—to those of us who are not electronics engineers—of being exceedingly complicated. They have myriads of electronic circuits and huge memory banks of information that has been fed in and stored in the form of magnetic traces.

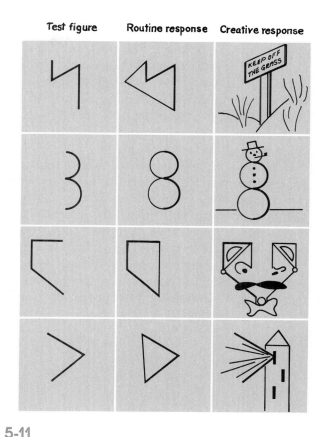

Test figure   Routine response   Creative response

5-11
A test of creativity
Subjects are asked to start with the simple lines in the left-hand column and turn them into any kind of drawing the lines suggest. Most subjects produce the kinds of drawings shown in the middle column. Very creative people come up with imaginative elaborations like those in the right-hand column (71).

The way they operate, however, is basically simple. They perform most of their miracles by routing electronic impulses through a series of what are essentially mere two-way switching points, where the impulse is directed one way or the other. Their efficiency depends largely on the fact that if you keep multiplying 2x2x2x2, you soon begin to reach some astronomical totals. Two multiplied by itself 15 times (or raised to the 15th power, as a mathematician would say) totals 32,768—and the next multiplication raises the figure to 65,536 and so on. Thus the number of possible pathways through a large computer, even with simple two-way switching points, runs into the millions.

Computers manage to "think"—or at least accomplish many of the same results as human thinking—through their serial processing of one simple step after another. This suggests the possibility that the human brain, with its synapses as switching points, may operate in similar fashion. Many computer experts have concluded that this is actually what happens. They believe that human thinking and problem solving are also based on simple processes, repeated one after another in a long string that can lead to the most complicated conclusions and decisions (72).

On the other hand, many machines duplicate other forms of human behavior in ways that bear no resemblance to the way we ourselves perform the acts. Perhaps the best example is the pitching machine used by baseball teams to throw the ball up to the plate for batting practice. The machine can toss fast balls and curves, high and low, but it does not imitate any of the processes that take place in the muscles of a human pitcher's back, shoulders, arms, and hands.

Computers already serve as valuable assistants to human thinking. Perhaps future work with them will help us understand and improve our own cognitive processes. But exactly what they have to tell us about human thinking—if anything—is not yet known.

Summary

1 Language is humanity's most distinctive and perhaps most complex achievement. Its chief function is *communication*—and it enables us to exchange an unlimited number and variety of messages and to pass knowledge along from one generation to the next.
2 The building blocks of language are the basic sounds called *phonemes*. English has about forty phonemes, and no language has more than eighty-five.
3 Phonemes are combined into meaningful sounds called *morphemes,* which may be words, prefixes, or suffixes. English has more than 100,000 morphemes, which are combined in turn to produce more than 600,000 words.
4 *Semantics* is the meaning of a language's morphemes and words.

5 Every language has two essential elements: a) a *vocabulary* (or set of sounds and words with meanings dictated by semantics) and b) a *grammar* (or set of rules for putting sounds and words together).

6 An important part of grammar is the rules of *syntax,* which govern sentence structure.

7 Speaking or writing is a complex mental activity that requires us to think of the meaning we want to convey, plan each sentence and each part of a sentence, find the right words to flesh out our thoughts, and put the words in their proper order.

8 When listening, we also carry out many mental processes. We simultaneously try to recognize sounds, identify words, look for syntactic patterns, and search for semantic meaning. All these activities are part of the *active processing* view of speech comprehension held by many psychologists.

9 In the early learning of language, interaction between child and mother (or some other intimate caretaker) appears to be the crucial factor.

10 Some theorists believe that language is learned through operant conditioning, others that it is acquired through learning by observation. Another theory is that the human brain contains a "language acquisition device" (LAD) that enables children to learn quickly.

11 Language contains only a few words that are names of specific one-of-a-kind objects (such as the elements oxygen and nitrogen).

12 Most words represent *concepts,* which are notions of similarity. Thus *water* is a concept that embraces not only the fluid that comes out of a faucet but any somewhat similar fluid anywhere, including raindrops and the salty contents of the ocean. The concept of *bigger* denotes a relationship shared by such diverse pairs of objects as fly-to-gnat and Texas-to-Delaware.

13 Concepts are extremely useful in acquiring new information, storing it in memory, and using it effectively. They are the key to forming categories and other forms of organization of information.

14 The language we use affects the way we look at the world—but, at the same time, the way we look at the world influences the language we use.

15 One way we form concepts is to develop a notion of a sort of ideal or *prototype* (of a bird, vegetable, etc.). Then we place other objects in this same category, or reject them, depending on how much family resemblance they have to the prototype.

16 Language is the basis of most *thinking,* which is the *mental manipulation of information*.

17 One important kind of thinking, conducted with the use of language, is *inference*—

or drawing logical conclusions from facts already known. We can generalize about the new and unfamiliar from what we have previously observed about similar objects or events.

18 Two methods of problem solving are *trial and error* and *insight*.

19 Pitfalls in problem solving include: a) taking too much for granted, b) thinking what we would like to think rather than what the facts dictate, c) persistence of set, and d) functional fixedness.

20 Persistence of set and functional fixedness help account for the fact that truly creative thinking is so rare.

21 Although creativity demands superior intelligence, probably fewer than 1 percent of people who have the required intelligence are in fact creative. Even more than intelligence, creativity demands the kind of personality that scorns the tried and true, does not get imprisoned by persistence of set, but seeks out new ideas even in the face of failure and ridicule.

22 Computers serve as a valuable aid to human thinking—but we do not yet know what similarities if any exist between the workings of computers and of the human brain.

Important terms

active processing
cognition
communication
concept
creative thinking
functional fixedness
grammar
inference
insight
morpheme

persistence of set
phoneme
problem solving
prototype
semantics
syntax
thinking
trial and error
vocabulary

Recommended readings

Brown, R. *A first language*. Cambridge, Mass.: Harvard University Press, 1973.

Chomsky, N. *Language and mind,* enl. ed. New York: Harcourt Brace Jovanovich, 1972.

Clark, H. H., and Clark, E. V. *Psychology and language*. New York: Harcourt Brace Jovanovich, 1977.

de Villiers, J. G., and de Villiers, P. A. *Language acquisition*. Cambridge, Mass.: Harvard University Press, 1978.

Newell, A., and Simon, H. A. *Human problem solving*. Englewood Cliffs, N. J.: Prentice-Hall, 1972.

Raphael, B. *The thinking computer*. San Francisco: Freeman, 1976.

Silverstein, A., ed. *Human communication: theoretical perspectives*. New York: Halstead, 1974.

Wickelgren, W. A. *How to solve problems*. San Francisco: Freeman, 1974.

Outline

Intelligence and resourcefulness 208

Intelligence tests: what they do and don't do 215

IQ and nature-nurture 226

Postscript

The science of test construction 234

Some other kinds of tests 236

Summary 238

Psychology and Society

Chapter six

Intelligence: the problem of defining and measuring it

(with a postscript on the science of test construction)

Of all those 600,000-odd words that are found in a complete English dictionary, as was mentioned in the previous chapter, some are used far more often than others. (The most common of all is *the,* which you call on almost every time you open your mouth or put pen to paper.) Among the frequently used words are adjectives describing the human attribute that is the subject of the present chapter. Note how often you hear comments like these:

That was a very *intelligent* remark.

What a *smart* child.

That's a *brilliant* idea.

I did a really *dumb* thing.

That wasn't very *bright* of you.

Ask a *stupid* question and you get a *stupid* answer.

Intelligence, or the lack of it, is one of the most widely discussed of all human characteristics. It is also a prime concern of psychologists, who have devoted a great deal of research to questions such as these: How can intelligence be defined, if at all, in scientific terms? To what extent is it an inborn trait; to what extent does it depend on environment? How well can it be measured? If an intelligence test shows that a person has an IQ of 108 (or 88 or 98 or 118), how much does this tell us about that person's chances for getting along in school—and, more important, for leading a happy and successful life?

Intelligence and resourcefulness

The word *intelligence* is batted around in conversation as if everyone agreed on its meaning. But psychologists who have spent a lifetime trying to pin down a definition are not so sure. In the early 1920s, seventeen eminent scholars were invited to express their ideas about intelligence in a symposium—and they came up with very close to seventeen different and distinct opinions (1). Among today's scholars there is probably no more agreement than there was in the past. Some have been forced to the vague conclusion that "intelligence is nothing more nor less than what standard intelligence tests measure" (2)—whatever that is.

The tests themselves are a matter of controversy. They are widely used by employers to judge job applicants and by educators to decide which students can profit from what kind of training. (The Scholastic Aptitude Tests that most colleges require for admission are one brand of intelligence test.) Many psychologists consider them to be the best measure ever devised—at least for the ability to perform well in school, and perhaps for useful talents in general. But other psychologists consider them seriously biased in favor of people from middle-class backgrounds. Some believe that the tests are "altogether worthless" (3). There is something to be said, as you will see later, on both sides of the argument.

A working definition of intelligence

Perhaps the most practical definition of intelligence has been proposed by David Wechsler, who has constructed a number of today's most widely used intelligence tests. Wechsler has said that *intelligence is the capacity to understand the world and the resourcefulness to cope with its challenges.* By this broad standard, you are intelligent if you know what is going on around you, can learn from experience—and can act in ways that will be successful under the circumstances. Your behavior, as Wechsler describes it, will have meaning and direction and will be rational and worthwhile (4).

Wechsler's definition is a useful guideline. One problem, however, is that different people living under different circumstances may disagree about the meaning of resourcefulness—and certainly about what constitutes worthwhile behavior. Attitudes toward intelligence have varied greatly from time to time and from place to place through world history. The ancient Greeks considered intelligence to mean talent for oratory. The Chinese, until the Communist revolution, judged it to mean mastery of the written word, which is a very different skill. (Many fluent conversationalists and eloquent speakers are poor writers—and many literary giants are tongue-tied in conversation or on the speaker's platform.) Some tribes in Africa measure intelligence in terms of hunting ability, many South Pacific islanders in terms of ability to navigate a boat (5).

There have been and still are places in the world where people who score high enough on today's American intelligence tests to be classified as geniuses would be considered hopelessly retarded because they are tone-deaf and cannot sing or play a musical instrument, or because they cannot run fast or hit a moving target with a spear. Even in our own nation, intelligent behavior can mean different things in academic circles, the business community, rural farm areas, and big-city ghettos. Wechsler concedes that use of the word *intelligence* represents a value judgment. That is to say, we call people intelligent when they have qualities that we ourselves—or our society as a whole, or the special part of society in which we live—consider resourceful and worthwhile.

Is intelligence one talent — or many?

In general, modern industrial societies place a high value on the qualities that were described earlier in the book as being the province of the left brain (pages 51–53). Our American culture as a whole, though not all parts of it, admires fluency in language and talent for mathematics and science. The most intelligent people, according to the consensus, are those who can analyze facts, reason about them logically, and express their conclusions in convincing words. These are the very qualities that are associated with doing well in our schools—and, as will be seen later, our tests of intelligence measure academic ability better than they measure anything else.

In talking about intelligence, we have to assume that it is in fact what most people agree that it is. But is it a single ability or a combination of several different abilities? Can you be highly intelligent in some respects but way below average in others?

One of the first attempts to find the answer to these important questions was made by L. L. Thurstone, who gave dozens of different tests to schoolchildren, measuring how well they performed at various tasks. He decided that intelligence is composed of seven distinct factors, which he called *primary mental abilities:*

1 *Verbal comprehension*—indicated by size of vocabulary, ability to read, and skill at understanding mixed-up sentences and the meaning of proverbs.

2 *Word fluency*—the ability to think of words quickly, as when making rhymes or solving word puzzles.
3 *Number*—the ability to solve arithmetic problems and to manipulate numbers.
4 *Space*—the ability to visualize spatial relationships, as in recognizing a design after it has been placed in a new context.
5 *Associative memory*—the ability to memorize quickly, as in learning a list of paired words.
6 *Perceptual speed*—indicated by the ability to grasp visual details quickly and to observe similarities and differences between designs and pictures.
7 *General reasoning*—skill at the kind of logical thinking that was described in Chapter 5.

Thurstone also noted, however, that a person who was above average on his tests for any one of these abilities was usually above average in all the others. He concluded, therefore, that intelligence is composed of the seven primary mental abilities plus some kind of *general factor* common to all (6).

Thurstone's "general factor" is a matter of dispute among psychologists. Newer investigations have shown that when enough tests of widely different kinds of learning and problem solving are devised and given to children, it turns out that some children do much better on some of the tests, others on different tests. Often there is so little relationship between scores on separate tests as to cast doubt on the existence of any general factor (7).

A new theory: 120 separate abilities

One group of investigators, headed by J. P. Guilford of the University of Southern California, has concluded on the basis of more elaborate testing that intelligence is probably made up of no less

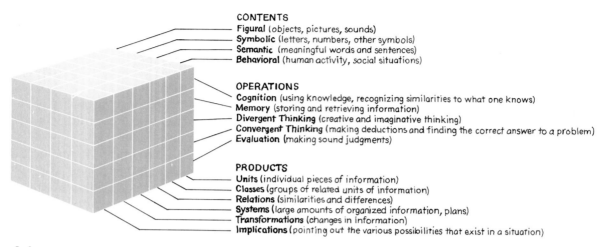

CONTENTS
— **Figural** (objects, pictures, sounds)
— **Symbolic** (letters, numbers, other symbols)
— **Semantic** (meaningful words and sentences)
— **Behavioral** (human activity, social situations)

OPERATIONS
— **Cognition** (using knowledge, recognizing similarities to what one knows)
— **Memory** (storing and retrieving information)
— **Divergent Thinking** (creative and imaginative thinking)
— **Convergent Thinking** (making deductions and finding the correct answer to a problem)
— **Evaluation** (making sound judgments)

PRODUCTS
— **Units** (individual pieces of information)
— **Classes** (groups of related units of information)
— **Relations** (similarities and differences)
— **Systems** (large amounts of organized information, plans)
— **Transformations** (changes in information)
— **Implications** (pointing out the various possibilities that exist in a situation)

6-1 The 120-factor theory of intelligence

The 120 different kinds of ability suggested by Guilford are represented by the small individual blocks contained in the cube. The theory maintains that each factor is the ability to perform one of five different types of mental *operations* on one of four different kinds of material, or *contents*, with the aim of coming up with one of six different kinds of end results, or *products*. Thus the total number of abilities that make up intelligence (or blocks in the cube) is 5 × 4 × 6, or 120. Followers of the theory measure the mental operation called "divergent thinking" by asking a question such as "How many uses can you think of for a brick?"—and noting how many different answers the individual can come up with and how imaginative the answers are. One test of the mental operation called "evaluation" is to present the four words *cat, cow, mule,* and *mare* and ask whether these are best categorized as: a) farm animals, b) four-legged animals, or c) domestic animals. The answer will be found at the bottom of page 212.

than 120 different kinds of ability. The 120-factor theory, illustrated in Figure 6-1, maintains that an individual may display a very high level of ability at some tasks, average ability at others, and low ability at still others. Guilford and his associates have devised finely differentiated tests for many of the 120 factors—and have found very little relationship between their subjects' scores on one test and their scores on many of the others (8).

Among other things, Guilford has found that people differ widely in their abilities to deal with different kinds of materials (or *contents,* as they are termed in Figure 6-1). For example, some people are very good at handling what he labels *semantic*

contents, or language and ideas. These people might be outstanding as writers or philosophers. Others excel at working with *symbolic contents,* such as numbers. These people might be most productive as mathematicians or accountants. Others do best with *figural contents,* such as specific objects. These people would seem best suited to become artists or master mechanics.

Some practical implications for choosing a job

The Guilford view of intelligence, if correct, has some important applications to a serious decision that everyone must make—and that is especially urgent during the college years. This is the choice of job and career. If intelligence is largely some general factor, then you could expect to be about equally good (or equally bad) at almost any kind of work. But if it is made up of many different abilities, as seems possible, then your choice of job is crucial to how well you will perform and how successful and happy you are likely to be.

Certainly many people find their lives miserable because they are trying to adjust to jobs that they find a constant struggle—where they have to work painfully hard, and run very fast, just to stay in place. You probably know some examples in your circle of friends and relatives. Such people are constantly worried about mistakes and failure. No matter how hard they try, they never manage to get on top of the work they have chosen. Yet the Guilford theory suggests that they might have found some other job easy, pleasant, and rewarding. Guilford's findings would seem to bear out the truth of the old saying that you should never try to be a success at

something you find difficult—for there are always other people who find it easy.

Fortunately the college years provide an opportunity to learn your strong points and weaknesses. If you find mathematics difficult, the Guilford theory would suggest that you quickly abandon any thought of being an engineer or working in a bank. Difficulty in English courses, especially composition, is a warning against attempts to find a career where fluency in language is important, such as journalism, teaching, the law, or politics. Conversely, the subjects you find easier and more interesting than others point to your best opportunities for a fruitful career. Many people, without ever having heard of Guilford's work, have found that the best thing that happened to them in college was discovering that they were unusually good at something they had never suspected.

Piaget's theory of intellectual development

Another view of intelligence comes from the Swiss psychologist Jean Piaget, who has spent more than a half-century observing the behavior of his own and other children as they grew from infancy through adolescence. We can learn a great deal about the nature of intelligence by examining how Piaget found it flowers in the growing child.

Piaget has concluded that mental growth is basically an increased ability to adapt to new situations and that this growth takes place because of two key processes that he calls *assimilation* and *accommodation*. Assimilation is the process of incorporating a new stimulus into one's existing cognitive view of the world. Accommodation is the process of changing one's cognitive view and behavior when new information dictates such a change.

As a simple example, consider a young boy who has a number of toys. To these familiar old toys we add a new one, a magnet. The boy's initial impulse

Piaget, with pipe and beret, studies children at play.

will be to assimilate the new toy into his existing knowledge of other toys; he may try to bang it like a hammer, throw it like a ball, or blow it like a horn. But once he learns that the magnet has a new and unprecedented quality—the power to attract iron— he accommodates his view of toys to include this previously unfamiliar fact. He now behaves on the revised assumption that some toys are not designed to bang, throw, or make noise with but to attract metal.

There is always tension, Piaget has concluded, between assimilation (which in essence represents the use of old ideas to meet new situations) and accommodation (which in essence is a change of old ideas to meet new situations). And it is the resolution of this tension that results in intellectual growth. Piaget believes that the growth takes place in a series of stages, in each of which the child thinks and behaves in quite different fashion than earlier. He maintains that the child grows intellectually not like a leaf, which simply gets larger every day, but like a caterpillar that is eventually transformed into a butterfly. The various stages and approximate ages at which they occur have been charted by Piaget as follows (9).

Sensorimotor stage (birth to age two)

During this stage most children have not yet learned to use symbols and language to represent the objects and events in their environment. According to Piaget, they know the world only in terms of their sensorimotor interactions with it—that

A child in Piaget's sensorimotor stage—operating on the toys in the environment and noting the results.

is, their own actions toward objects and the results of these actions. By the age of four to six months, children have started to operate on the environment. They will repeatedly kick at toys hanging over their cribs, apparently to make them swing and thus produce a change of stimulus that they find interesting. By the age of twelve months they act as if they know that objects are permanent and do not mysteriously disappear. If a toy is shown to them and then is hidden behind two pillows side by side in the crib, they know how to find it. They look first behind one of the pillows. If the toy is not there, they look behind the other.

Preoperational stage (two to seven)

In this stage the ability to use symbols begins to dominate the development of intellectual ability. As the use of language increases, children begin to attach new meanings to the stimuli in their environment and to use one stimulus to stand as a symbol for another. They may behave toward a doll as if it were a child and toward a stick as if it were a gun.

Although all three of the answers to the question posed in Figure 6-1 are correct, the best answer is (c) domestic animals. This makes the finest and neatest distinction between the four animals and other kinds of animals. "Farm animals" is not the best answer because a cat is often found elsewhere. "Four-legged animals" is not the best answer because almost all animals have four legs.

6-2 The puzzle of liquid and jars: it baffles a preschool child

The child points to both the squat jars to acknowledge that they contain an equal amount of liquid. But when the liquid is poured from one of these into a tall, thin jar, she thinks the tall jar contains more liquid. Not until she is around seven will she realize that the amount of liquid remains the same.

By the age of four concepts have become more elaborate, but they are still based largely on the evidence of the senses. Children can learn, for example, to select the middle-sized of three rubber balls. They have attained what Piaget has called an *intuitive understanding* that the middle-sized ball is bigger than the small one but smaller than the big one. But if three balls of very different size from the original three are then shown, they must learn to make the selection all over again (10). Until about the age of seven they are fooled by the puzzle illustrated in Figure 6-2. Apparently the height of the jar is such an outstanding characteristic that they cannot help equating height with the amount of liquid the jar contains.

Stage of concrete operations (seven to eleven)

For the typical American child, this begins some time between the ages of six and eight. For children who grow up in isolated, nonindustrial societies, it may begin somewhat later. At this stage children possess a set of rules, not previously available to them, that help them adapt to their environment. They now know, for example, that if A is as heavy as B, and B is as heavy as C, then A and C must be equal in weight. They also have acquired considerable sophistication in the use of concepts and categories. They realize, for example, that "all the pets that are dogs" plus "all the pets that are not dogs" go to make up a category called "all pets." They also realize that objects or attributes can belong to more than one concept; they know that animals can be tame or wild, furry or feathered.

Piaget has conducted many experiments demonstrating the intellectual conquests that children achieve in this stage of concrete operations. One of them is becoming aware that the amount of liquid does not change in the experiment that was shown in Figure 6-2. They have discovered the

In the stage of concrete operations, a child reasons logically and applies rules—especially to objects that can be seen and felt.

important principle of *conservation*—that is, the fact that such qualities as mass, number, weight, and volume remain constant regardless of changes in appearance. If asked why the tall jar and the short jar contain an equal amount, they may say, "Well, this one is taller, but this one is fatter." A little later their explanation may become more sophisticated: "If you poured the stuff from the tall jar into the other jar, then it would still be the same."

Thus children in the stage of concrete operations show an ability to reason logically about objects and to apply rules. But as Piaget's name for the stage implies, they seem to reason more effectively about objects that they can see or feel than about verbal statements. Suppose, for example, that children of this age are asked: "A is the same size as B, but B is smaller than C; which is bigger, A or C?" They may not be able to answer—for the question requires thinking about a sentence rather than about concrete objects.

Stage of formal operations (beginning at about ten or eleven)

In this stage children can reason not only about actual objects and events but about things that "might be." They can assume hypothetical conditions and make correct inferences about them. They are no longer merely preoccupied with what is real and concrete. Instead they are able to deal with the possible and the abstract—and they enjoy it. In Piaget's words, "Thought takes wings."

Adolescents can determine the logical validity of a statement such as this: "If X or Y leads to Z then it is false to assume that if Y does not occur Z will not occur." They can deal with hypothetical questions such as: "If all unicorns have yellow feet and I have yellow feet, am I a unicorn?" (They can examine the logic and quickly answer, "No.")

Children in the stage of formal operations are less likely to waste their time with trial and error techniques. Instead, they use abstract strategies. They examine their premises and beliefs systematically, searching for consistencies or inconsistencies. They approach problems with some definite plan, try to think of all the possible solutions, and re-examine their thinking to make sure that they have indeed exhausted all the possibilities. Moreover, their thinking is what might be called "self-conscious." They think about their thoughts and are curious to learn how these thoughts are organized and where they will lead.

Piaget and you

In one way or another, you have progressed through the four stages of intellectual development in the manner charted by Piaget. Your timing may have been on the fast side or the slow side, for there are considerable individual differences in the ages at which children move from one stage to the next. But the transformation from sensorimotor infant to adolescent capable of formal operations seems to take place in the same manner for most people—even children of different nationalities, and regardless of what kind of education they receive (11).

You have probably forgotten the details of how your own mental abilities were transformed, in Piaget's terms, from caterpillar to butterfly. But you may have the chance to observe the process in your own offspring or other children. One finding of importance to those who deal with children is that it appears impossible to speed up the process by trying to teach the reasoning skills appropriate to a more advanced period (12). It seems that children can understand only experiences and pieces of information that match what they already know about vocabulary, facts, and rules—or that are just a bit in advance of their existing information and cognitive skills. If a new experience or idea has no readily apparent connection with what they already know, they are not likely to learn much if anything about it. Indeed they may not even pay attention to it.

On the other hand, it appears likely that the progress of many children is retarded by learned helplessness acquired as the result of their home environment or failure and criticism in the early years of school, as was described in the box on Psychology and Society ("Do pupils fail—or do the schools?") on page 116. Children from low-income homes, in particular, may become so discouraged that they never take full advantage of the abilities they develop during the stage of formal operations. They may have a good deal more intelligence than they display or even realize. One reason is that their environment may lead them to make low scores on intelligence tests, which in turn leads both them and their teachers to have lower expectations for them, which leads to a further inhibition of their ability to display the skills measured by the tests. Hence the importance of taking a realistic look at intelligence tests, which is our next topic.

Intelligence tests: what they do and don't do

Intelligence tests began as a psychologist's solution to a problem faced by Paris schools at the beginning of the century. Many classrooms were crowded, and slow students were holding up the progress of the better ones. One solution, it seemed, would be to identify the children who lacked the mental capacity required by the standard curriculum and put them in a separate school of their own. But how could they be recognized?

A French psychologist named Alfred Binet who went to work on the problem realized that the task of identifying the poorer students could not safely be left to the teachers. There was too much danger that a teacher would show favoritism toward children who had pleasant personalities and would be too harsh on those who were troublemakers. There was also the question of whether a teacher could recognize children who appeared dull but in fact

Alfred Binet and his daughters.

could have done the work had they tried (13).

To avoid these pitfalls, Binet developed a test designed to measure potential ability at school tasks rather than performance in school—and to produce the same scores regardless of the personalities or prejudices of those who gave or took the test. Binet's test was first published in 1905, has been revised many times since, and is still widely used today. In fact all modern intelligence tests bear a considerable resemblance to Binet's original work.

In the United States, one of the best-known current versions of the original test is the *Stanford-Binet Intelligence Scale*. It can be given successfully even to children who are too young to have developed a wide range of language skills, using the simple kind of physical equipment shown in Figure 6-3. Older children and adults are asked questions that measure such things as vocabulary, memory span for sentences and numbers, and reasoning ability. Some of the test items used at various age levels are shown in Figure 6-4.

Mental age, chronological age, and IQ

The scoring method originally used by Binet as well as in the initial versions of the Stanford-Binet test was based on the concept of *mental age,* or MA for short. As children mature, they are able to pass more and more of the items on tests of this type. The testing of large numbers of children has shown exactly how many items the average child is able to pass at the age of six or seven or whatever the child's actual age happens to be. (To testers, actual age in years and months is known as *chronological age,* or CA for short.)

For the average child, mental age and chronological age are equal. But children who have less intelligence than average will not be able to pass all the items suitable to their age level and thus will show an MA that is lower than their CA. Those who have more intelligence than average will pass some of the items designed for older children and thus will show an MA that is higher than their CA.

The relationship between mental age and chronological age was the original basis for that well-known term intelligence quotient, or IQ. The average IQ was arbitrarily set at 100, a convenient figure, and the individual child's IQ was determined by the formula

$$IQ = \frac{MA}{CA} \times 100$$

As an example of how the formula is applied, take the case of a child whose mental age works out on the test to six years and eight months. To make the arithmetic easier, this mental age is converted into months; six years and eight months equal eighty

6-3 An examiner's bag of tricks for the Stanford-Binet test
Small children taking the Stanford-Binet Intelligence Scale are asked to perform various tasks with a paper doll and toys.

Two years old	On a large paper doll, points out the hair, mouth, feet, ear, nose, hands, and eyes.
	When shown a tower built of four blocks, builds one like it.
Four years old	Fills in the missing word when asked, "Brother is a boy; sister is a _____" and "In daytime it is light; at night it is _____."
	Answers correctly when asked, "Why do we have houses?" "Why do we have books?"
Nine years old	Answers correctly when examiner says, "In an old graveyard in Spain they have discovered a small skull which they believe to be that of Christopher Columbus when he was about ten years old. What is foolish about that?"
	Answers correctly when asked, "Tell me the name of a color that rhymes with head." "Tell me a number that rhymes with tree."
Adult	Can describe the difference between laziness and idleness, poverty and misery, character and reputation.
	Answers correctly when asked, "Which direction would you have to face so your right hand would be toward the north?"

6-4

Some Stanford-Binet test items
As shown by these examples, the questions asked very young children do not demand fluency in language. The questions increase in difficulty, particularly in matters of language and reasoning, at higher age levels.

months. If the child's chronological age is also eighty months, the formula works out as follows

$$IQ = \frac{80}{80} \times 100 = 1 \times 100 = 100$$

If the child is only six years old (seventy-two months) the formula becomes

$$IQ = \frac{80}{72} \times 100 = \frac{10}{9} \times 100 = 111$$

If the child's actual age is eight years (ninety-six months) the formula becomes

$$IQ = \frac{80}{96} \times 100 = \frac{10}{12} \times 100 = 83$$

The intelligence quotient can still be thought of in terms of its original meaning. The average IQ is 100; the ability to pass items above one's age level indicates an IQ of more than 100; the inability to pass all the items appropriate for one's age level results in an IQ of less than 100. In actual practice, the IQ of an individual taking the Stanford-Binet or other intelligence tests is now determined from tables that translate the individual's raw score on the test and chronological age into an IQ figure. The way IQs are distributed in the population, according to the Stanford-Binet test, is shown in Figure 6-5.

Some well-known intelligence tests: individual and group

The Stanford-Binet is only one of many tests now available. Even more widely used today are three devised by David Wechsler—the Wechsler Adult Intelligence Scale (or WAIS for short), another for children aged 7 to 16, and still another for children 4 to 6½. The distinguishing feature of the Wechsler tests is that they contain two separate kinds of items, called verbal and performance. The verbal items measure vocabulary, information, general

IQ	Classification	Percentage of people at each level
Over 139	Very superior	1
120-139	Superior	11
110-119	High average	18
90-109	Average	46
80-89	Low average	15
70-79	Borderline	6
Below 70	Mentally retarded	3

6-5 IQs, what they mean, and how many people are found at each level

Administering the Stanford-Binet to thousands of people has shown that one person in a hundred comes out with an IQ over 139 and can be classified as "very superior." (In popular terminology, this person is a "genius.") Three in a hundred come out with IQs under 70 and are classified as "mentally retarded." Almost half of all people have IQs in the "average" range of 90 to 109.

comprehension, memory span, arithmetic reasoning, and ability to detect similarities between concepts. The performance items measure ability at completing pictures, arranging pictures, working puzzles, substituting unfamiliar symbols for digits, and making designs with blocks (see Figure 6-6).

The subject's IQ can be calculated for the test as a whole or for the verbal items and the performance items considered separately. This feature is often an advantage in testing people who lack skill in the use of the English language. Such people may score much higher on the performance items than on the verbal items.

Both the Stanford-Binet and the Wechslers are *individual tests*, given to one person at a time by a trained examiner. The advantage of individual tests is that the examiner can readily detect if the results are being influenced by such factors as poor vision, temporary ill health, or lack of motivation. Their disadvantage, of course, is that they cannot con-

6-6 A performance item on a Wechsler test
With colored blocks of various patterns, the subject is asked to copy a design as one of the performance items in a Wechsler intelligence scale. The examiner notes how long the task takes as well as how accurately it is performed.

veniently be used for the testing of large numbers of people, such as all the pupils in a big school.

Available for large-scale testing of many people at the same time are a number of *group tests*—typically taking the form of printed questions, such as those shown in Figure 6-7, which are answered by making penciled notations. Among the widely used group tests is the *Armed Forces Qualification Test,* taken by applicants to the armed services. Another is the *Scholastic Aptitude Tests,* or SAT. The SAT is designed to produce an average score of 500 for high-school seniors, with about 68 percent of scores falling in the range of 400 to 599. Since the seniors who take the test are a highly selected

group, who have already proved their ability to get along in school, an SAT score of 500 represents an IQ of well over 100.

IQ and school achievement

All the standard intelligence tests do a good job of measuring whatever it is that they measure—which certainly includes language skills, reasoning ability, alertness, motivation, and memory for past experiences (15). If you take several of the tests, you will come out with a very similar IQ score on all of them. You will also get pretty much the same result if you take the same test on two different occasions, separated by a reasonable length of time.

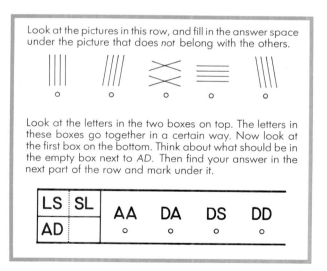

6-7 A group intelligence test for young children
These are sample items for second- and third-graders from the Otis-Lennon School Ability Test. Sample items demonstrate how the questions should be answered and are not counted in the actual scoring. The actual items in this test range from about as difficult as the sample items shown here to much more difficult. At this age level, the person administering the test reads the instructions to the children taking it. Older children and adults taking group tests read the instructions themselves, so that the tests can be given just by handing them out (14).

6-8

The relation of IQ
to achievement in school

These correlations between IQ and performance in specific school subjects or skills were found in a study that used the Stanford-Binet Scale to measure intelligence (17). Note that the correlation was greatest for reading comprehension and lowest for reading speed—a fact in keeping with the idea, expressed in Chapter 4, that the deep processing helpful in committing the contents of a printed page to long-term memory requires a certain amount of time.

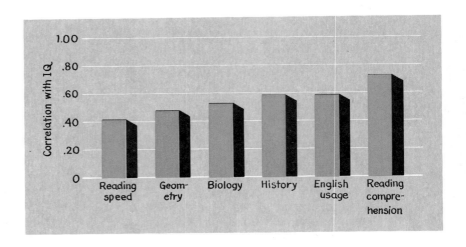

The tests provide the best available—and perhaps best possible—measure of how well a person will do in school. This is what Binet originally intended them to do, and it is still what they do best. Many studies have been made of the relation between IQ and school grades, with the results expressed in terms of correlation (pages 22–23). The studies have shown correlations ranging from .40 to .60 or even higher (16). Some forms of school achievement show a closer relationship than others, as is shown in Figure 6-8.

Students with low IQs usually have so much difficulty that they drop out of school before or immediately after the twelfth grade, leaving a group that is in general well above average to go on to college. A study made in the 1960s found that the average IQ of college freshmen was 115 (18). Those who went on to a doctoral degree averaged around 125 (19).

IQ and occupation

Though the IQ is a good predictor of success in school, there is some question as to how well it predicts other matters. What about jobs, for example? Does a high IQ mean you are destined for a high-level occupation, a low IQ for a low-level job?

One massive body of evidence bearing on these questions comes from a study of the many thousands of men who took the Army's group intelligence test during the Second World War. The results, some of which are illustrated in Figure 6-9, indicate that there is indeed a relation between IQ and occupation—but less than one might expect. The average IQ of such professional people as accountants and engineers was around 120, while the average for truck drivers and miners was below 100. But there was a wide range of IQs in every occupation. The IQs of accountants ranged from about 95 to over 140. The IQs of truck drivers showed a particularly wide range—all the way from under 40 to nearly 140. Some accountants had IQs lower than the average for truck drivers—and a number of truck drivers (and miners and mechanics as well) had IQs higher than the average for accountants, engineers, and teachers.

One reason for these findings undoubtedly lies in

the amount of education the men in the study had received. Of two people with equal IQs, the one able to go to college may become an accountant or engineer. The one unable for one reason or another to go to college or even complete high school may have to settle for a job of much lower prestige. In fact other studies have shown that education is the chief factor in determining occupational status (21). In general, college graduates have better jobs than high-school graduates, who in turn have better jobs than those who have not completed high school. The relation between IQ and job status, such as it is, seems to depend chiefly on the fact that people with higher IQs generally manage to acquire more education than others, barring such circumstances as illness or family financial problems. (There is a correlation of about .55 between IQ and years of school completed.)

Does IQ determine success?

One of the most important questions about IQ is the extent to which it relates not just to classroom grades or choice of occupation but to successful living. This is a difficult question to answer, for success is an elusive concept. It can hardly be defined in terms of income, for many people have little interest in making a lot of money. And other types of success—efficiency and pleasure in one's job, good human relations, happiness in general—are hard to measure. Thus the answer has never been definitely established and is a matter of considerable dispute among psychologists.

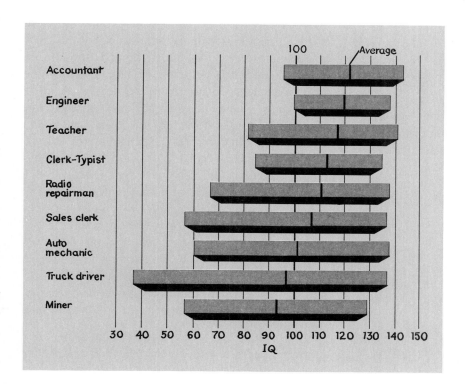

6-9
Jobs and IQs

The bars show the range of IQs of men in various occupations. Miners, for example, were found to have IQs of under 60 to nearly 130. The average IQ for each occupation is indicated by the vertical black lines inside the bar. For miners, the average was 93. For an interpretation of the figures, see the text (20).

In the first mass application of group intelligence tests, World War I recruits take an early version of the present Armed Forces Qualification Test.

Yes, says the Terman study

One study that has led many psychologists to consider a high IQ to be a great asset in achieving success of any kind was made with a group of 1,500 California schoolchildren who qualified as mentally gifted, with IQs of 140 or more putting them in the top 1 percent of the population. The study was begun in 1921 by Lewis M. Terman and continued by him and his associates for many years, as the children grew into adulthood and middle age.

As children, Terman's subjects were superior in many respects besides IQ. They were above average in height (by about an inch), weight, and appearance. They were better adjusted than average and showed superiority in social activity and leadership.

In later life, not all the gifted children lived up to their early promise. Some of them dropped out of school and wound up in routine occupations; some, even though they went to college, turned out to be vocational misfits and drifters. But these were the exceptions, and their records tended to show problems of emotional and social adjustment and low motivation toward achievement. On the whole the group was outstandingly successful. A large proportion went to college, achieved above-average and often brilliant records, and went on to make important contributions in fields ranging from medicine and law to literature and from business administration to government service. Many have earned the recognition of a listing in *Who's Who* or *American Men of Science*. The average level of accomplishment was far higher than could be expected of a group chosen at random. Terman's mentally gifted children also seemed to display a high level of physical and mental health, a death rate lower than average, and a lower divorce rate. One psychologist has expressed this view of the Terman study:

Findings such as these establish beyond a doubt that IQ tests measure characteristics that are obviously of considerable importance in our present technological society. To say that the kind of ability measured by intelligence tests is irrelevant or unimportant would be tantamount to repudiating civilization as we know it (22).

No, say other psychologists

There are, however, many dissenters. Terman's findings have been challenged on the ground that he made no allowance for the family background of his subjects or the possibility that they may have had better than average opportunities for education and career (23). And a number of investigators, after studying not just the mentally gifted but people in general, have reported finding little or no relationship between IQ and success outside the classroom. Studies have shown no significant correlations between the IQs of college students and their actual accomplishments in science, writing, music, the arts, speech and drama, or social leadership (24, 25). Grades in school, which are closely correlated with IQ, have been found to be unrelated to actual efficiency at such diverse jobs as bank teller, factory worker, or air traffic controller (26)—or even at scientific research (27).

Some scholars have concluded that IQ bears on success only to the extent that an IQ in the lower ranges may make it impossible for a person to complete high school, perform successfully in college, or qualify for certain demanding jobs. (If you turn back to Figure 6-9, you will note that none of the men in that study who was working as an accountant had an IQ under 95, and none of the engineers was below about 98.) For people in or above the 100–110 range, differences in IQ do not seem to have much effect on achievement in later life (28). Certainly success as measured in financial terms appears to depend mostly on other factors (29). And, in the words of one study, a person "can obtain a very high IQ score and still not behave very admirably in the real world" (30).

Are intelligence tests fair—or biased?

If IQ does not bear much relation to real-life success among people who are average or above, what is the reason? One possibility has been suggested by Guilford, who believes that a single IQ figure cannot possibly measure and express all the many differences in mental abilities that his 120-factor theory proposes. In Guilford's view, there is little point in discovering that a person has an IQ of 90 or 100 or 110, because that number can be only a rough average of many specific abilities in many specific areas. We may be geniuses in some respects and morons in others (to use the popular terminology). Our chances for success in occupation or in living may depend more on what special talents we possess—and how well we manage to discover and apply them—than on any average struck between our strong points and weaknesses.

The problem of aptitude versus achievement

Other critics question the very nature of intelligence testing on grounds that relate to the difference between what are called *aptitude tests* and what are known as *achievement tests*. In theory, all intelligence tests are aptitude tests, measuring a person's ability to learn a new skill or perform a new task. Some even bear that name—for example, the Scholastic Aptitude Tests, which attempt to measure a student's ability to learn the new materials of the college curriculum. Achievement tests have a different purpose; they attempt to measure how much the subjects have learned or accomplished at the time of taking the test. A final exam in college is an achievement test, measuring how much you have actually learned about the course. The Iowa and Stanford achievement tests, widely used in elementary and high schools, measure what pupils have learned about such classroom topics as reading and arithmetic—and how their present skills in these fields compare with those of students around the nation. In general, achievement tests measure how well the subjects have mastered some specific topic—usually a topic that has been studied only recently.

For some kinds of ability, it is possible to devise tests that measure actual aptitude, regardless of the subjects' present level of achievement in that field. There are tests of musical aptitude, for example, on which people can make high scores even if they have never tried to play a musical instrument and do not even know the notes of the scale. For such a broad and general concept as intelligence, however, it is impossible to devise a test that measures aptitude without any regard for achievement. Our scores on an intelligence test necessarily depend to a considerable extent on the vocabulary we have acquired, our knowledge of the rules of mathematics, and what we have learned about manipulating numbers and visual symbols.

If you look back at the items from the Stanford-Binet test shown in Figure 6-4, you will note that many of the questions are based on what the subjects have learned. To answer them correctly, the two-year-old must have learned the meaning of hair, mouth, and hands. The four-year-old must have acquired some fairly rich concepts of houses and books. The adult must have learned the points of the compass and the distinctions between such words as *laziness* and *idleness*.

Intelligence tests are aptitude tests in the sense that they attempt, insofar as possible, to measure the subjects' ability to use their existing knowledge in a novel way. Thus two-year-olds are asked to apply to a paper doll their knowledge about their own mouths and hair. Adults are asked to make a novel spatial orientation based on their knowledge of the compass. Moreover, in constructing intelligence tests an attempt is made to base all the questions on knowledge and skills that everyone

has had an equal chance to obtain. It is assumed that every two-year-old has had an opportunity to learn the meaning of *hair, mouth,* and *hands,* that every four-year-old knows the meaning of *houses* and *books,* and that every adult should have been exposed to information about the points of the compass. No questions are asked that can be answered only by a child who has had special training in summer camp about nature study, or only by an adult who has studied trigonometry or Spanish.

Nonetheless, there is a certain amount of bias in intelligence tests. In a nation containing as many diverse social and ethnic groups as the United States, not all people grow up with equal opportunities to learn the same kinds of basic knowledge. The tests favor those who have acquired the knowledge and language skills typical of the middle and upper-middle classes and fostered by a school system largely staffed by middle-class teachers. Thus the tests produce some uneven results. Children from middle-class and upper-class homes make higher scores in general than children from lower-class homes (31). City children tend to make higher scores than children from rural areas (32). Blacks and ethnic groups from other cultural backgrounds make lower average scores (33, 34, 35).

Can the tests be improved?

Some critics of intelligence tests would like to prohibit their use in the school system, as you will see in the box on Psychology and Society on page 225. Others are trying to revise the tests to remove their weaknesses and biases. For example, a panel of scholars appointed to study the Scholastic Aptitude Tests has recommended that these tests be enlarged and diversified. The panel wants the tests to include measurements of musical and artistic talent, athletic skills, mechanical skills, the ability to ex-

Should intelligence tests be banned?

A lawsuit that may some day reach the Supreme Court and become a landmark in legal history—as well as in psychology—is currently wending its way through the courts in California. It was filed by a group of psychologists against the state superintendent of schools, and its aim is to outlaw the use of intelligence tests for assigning pupils to special classes for slow learners.

The suit was filed on behalf of six pupils who, on the basis of intelligence tests given in the San Francisco schools, were placed in classes designed for the "educable mentally retarded" with IQs of 50–70. In these classes, of course, pupils receive only the kind and amount of education they are considered capable of absorbing—by no means the full range of instruction offered to other children.

The suit contends that the six children were wrongly deprived of equal educational opportunity. It attacks the validity of the tests on the grounds that they are biased against children who do not come from the same kinds of middle-class homes as their teachers and the people who construct the tests—and also that they measure only a limited range of special abilities, not such important matters as creativity and personality.

At the original trial, both sides presented expert witnesses—so many, indeed, that the trial lasted six months and produced 10,000 written pages of testimony. Some social scientists who appeared as witnesses attacked the use of intelligence tests, others called it valuable and even essential to the educational system—the only known method of discovering how much a child is capable of learning in school. It was argued, in fact, that the tests provide a safeguard against the erroneous assignment to classes for the retarded of pupils who have more ability than their teachers might otherwise realize.

The California case typifies a controversy that has been going on all over the nation. Other suits are planned—for example, in Chicago—by opponents of intelligence testing in the schools. And some states, because of the controversy, have voluntarily abandoned such testing. The issue is: Just exactly how accurate and how fair are the tests? Do they forever damage some students, by labeling them as incapable of progressing as far as they could if they had the chance? Or do the tests provide a realistic basis for recognizing and encouraging ability, especially among pupils who for one reason or another have not yet shown it in the classroom? And for preventing a small minority of students—only about 3 percent have IQs under 70—from holding up the progress of the rest?

The six pupils in the California case are blacks, as are the psychologists who are suing in their behalf (and, as it happens, as is the superintendent of schools who is the defendant). Thus one unspoken issue is whether intelligence tests, by the very nature of their questions, automatically discriminate against blacks and members of other minority groups—another important social issue that will be discussed in a later box on Psychology and Society.

press oneself in nonverbal ways, the ability to adapt to new situations, and many other factors not now taken into account (36).

One suggestion is that tests of IQ should be replaced by tests of "social competence," which would measure not only cognitive abilities but also physical health and well-being, degree of self-fulfillment, and motivation and emotional attitudes (37). On the matter of motives and emotions, the tests would try to determine such factors as self-image, learned helplessness, expectations of success, response to social approval, and creativity. The proponents of such tests believe that they would provide a better indication than IQ of the ability to cope with real-life situations as well as schoolwork.

IQ and nature-nurture

We come now to the question of whether intelligence is mostly inborn or mostly dependent on environment. In other words, we return once again to the nature-nurture issue. And in this case the issue is particularly heated, for it bears on a number of important social problems. If intelligence is largely determined by the genes and established at the moment of conception, then it would appear to be difficult to change intelligence through preschool and other programs designed to improve the environment in which children grow up. Moreover, since people tend to marry people of similar intelligence, our society may unwittingly be engaged in a selective breeding program that will eventually result in a sharp division—with one group blessed with high intelligence, another doomed to inferior status because of low intelligence.

Unfortunately, any discussion of these questions must be presented with reservations. As was said earlier, psychologists are not entirely agreed on the nature of intelligence. There is even greater question whether our present tests really measure intelligence or only such aspects of it as apply to schoolwork. All our information bearing on the nature-nurture issue comes of necessity from studies of IQs. Therefore we can talk only about the manner in which heredity and environment seem to affect IQ—ignoring entirely the matter of how well IQ reflects the total pattern of intelligence.

The influence of heredity

Does heredity influence IQ? Most psychologists would answer yes, chiefly because it is well established that the more closely related two people are—that is, the more similarity they have in genetic background—the more similar their IQ scores are likely to be. Correlations between the IQs of children and their parents, brothers and sisters, and even more distant relatives all indicate that IQ tends to "run in families."

The correlation between the IQs of children chosen at random would be zero. But the correlations between blood relatives, as can be seen in Figure 6-10, are fairly high. The midpoint or median figure found in various studies is over .45 for children and parents. For brothers and sisters, the figure is over .35 for those who for some reason were reared in different homes and nearly .50 for those brought up together. For identical twins, who have inherited exactly the same genes, the figures are even higher.

It seems only logical that our genes, which influence so many other aspects of our physical and

A college student helps conduct a Head Start program for young children.

psychological functioning, should also influence the way our nervous systems and brains operate and therefore our IQs. But to what extent? On this question there is much disagreement. One psychologist estimates that heredity accounts for fully 80 percent of the differences people display in IQ (39). But other psychologists consider this figure much too high. A number of studies have suggested that heredity may account for only about 30 to 40 percent of IQ differences. One investigator places the figure at zero (40).

The part played by environment

Does environment influence IQ? To this question, *all* psychologists would answer yes—though again the amount of influence is a matter of debate. The effect of environment is just as apparent as the effect of heredity in the correlations shown in Figure 6-10. Note that there is a positive correlation between the IQs of children who are not related in

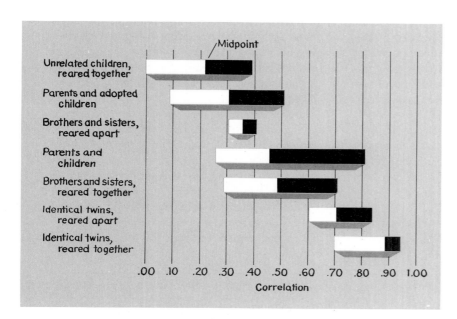

6-10
Family resemblances in IQ
The graph summarizes the results of more than fifty studies of comparisons in IQ between blood relatives—also people who, though not related, grew up in the same homes. The total length of each bar indicates the range of correlations found in the studies, which produced varying results. The break between the white and black portions of the bar shows the midpoint, or median finding (38).

Psychology and Society

Race and intelligence: the Jensen controversy

The question of whether heredity or environment has the greater effect on IQ has been argued most hotly over the issue of possible racial differences in intelligence. The controversy has centered around Arthur Jensen, a psychologist at the University of California, and an article he published in 1969. On the basis of his own estimate that heredity accounts for about 80 percent of differences in IQ—and the fact that blacks have been found to score an average of 10 to 15 points lower in IQ than whites— Jensen concluded that there is an innate, genetically determined difference in intelligence between blacks and whites (43).

To any of us as individuals, Jensen's conclusions are irrelevant. Both blacks and whites show a wide range of individual differences in IQ, and an individual's score is not affected by the average for the race or ethnic group to which that person belongs. But any large difference in average inborn ability might greatly affect attempts to improve performance through changes in the educational system or the establishment of programs like Head Start for preschool pupils. Moreover, Jensen's article—though it expressed only his considered opinion as an objective scientist—has stirred up a great deal of emotion. It has been widely approved by people who like to think that blacks are generally inferior to whites—and widely deplored by the enemies of racism.

Some psychologists agree with Jensen; they believe that the test results of blacks and whites clearly indicate a hereditary difference. The majority opinion, however, is that Jensen's conclusion is wrong.

Regardless of how well they feel IQ measures actual intelligence, most psychologists believe that blacks make a lower average score in IQ for the same reason that whites from rural areas or lower-class homes make a lower average score. That is, they have not in general had equal exposure to the kind of white middle-class culture on which intelligence tests are based. Worthy of special note in this regard is a study made of 130 black and interracial children who were adopted into white families that were above average in education, occupational status, and income. These children, who grew up in favorable environments, were found to have an average IQ of 106, which is higher than the national average. The authors of the study have reached this conclusion: If all black children grew up in such an environment, the average IQ of blacks would rise by 10 to 20 points—thus erasing all the difference now found between blacks and whites (44).

Jensen's famous 1969 article has inspired a great many responses, pro and con, based on research and analysis of race and intelligence. Indeed well over 100 other scholarly articles were published within the next five years alone (45). If you want to pursue the topic in greater detail, you will find the literature carefully reviewed and summarized in Race differences in intelligence, cited in the recommended readings at the end of the chapter.

any way yet for one reason or another happen to be brought up in the same home. There is an even higher correlation between the IQs of adopted children and of the foster parents who have brought them up and therefore helped shape their environment. Note also that the correlation for identical twins is considerably lower when they are brought up in two different homes rather than in the same household.

One way in which environment has clearly been shown to affect IQ is through severe deprivation that affects the development of a child's physical and nervous equipment. In a study made in South Africa, undernourished children were found to have IQs that averaged 20 points lower than the average for children who had received an adequate diet (41). Indeed malnutrition can jeopardize the mental development of children even before birth. In a study of families living at the poverty level in our own nation, one group of pregnant women continued to follow their own usual and inadequate diet. Another group of pregnant women received pills to supplement their diet and bring it up to normal nutritional standards. When the children these two groups of women bore were tested some years later, those of the diet-supplement mothers showed significantly higher IQs (42).

Environment also seems to affect IQ in some purely psychological ways. For one thing, growing up in a low-income home is less likely to provide exposure to the kinds of information that intelligence tests assume to be available to all children. In the important matter of vocabulary, for instance, low-income children are often handicapped—not only in getting along in school, as was discussed on pages 219–20, but also in taking intelligence tests. For another thing, home environments vary greatly in how much they offer children in the way of intellectual stimulation.

Whether environment or heredity is more impor-

tant has been the subject of much debate—especially over the issue of whether there are inborn racial differences in IQ, as is discussed in the box on Psychology and Society on page 228. The prevailing view among today's psychologists, however, is that the argument is futile (as on most nature-nurture issues). The majority would say that there is a constant interaction between heredity and environment—with heredity probably setting a top and bottom limit on an individual's IQ score, and the environment then determining where within this range the score will actually fall (46).

Intellectual stimulation, class differences, and large versus small families

On the matter of intellectual stimulation in the home, it has been found that middle-class mothers tend to spend more time than lower-class mothers talking to their young children, playing with them, and encouraging them to learn and to solve problems on their own (47). Thus they provide the kind of environment that might be expected to produce higher IQs—and this is exactly what happens. A number of studies have shown that the average IQs of children are significantly related to the social class of the home (48). Similarly, IQs are related to the educational level parents have attained; on this matter correlations ranging between .32 and .59 have been found (49).

The highest correlations of all between IQ and aspects of the environment were obtained by one investigator who ignored such indirect measures as social class and parents' education and instead made a direct attempt to measure the stimulation provided by the parents. This investigator drew up a scale on which parents were rated on such factors as how much encouragement and help they gave the child in using language and increasing vocabulary, how much motivation and reward they provided for intellectual accomplishment, and the opportunities for learning they provided in the home, including personal help, books, and other learning materials. The correlation between the parents' total scores on this scale and the children's IQs turned out to be .76 (50).

Even the number of children in the family has been found to influence IQ, perhaps because the number is related to differences in environment and level of intellectual stimulation. A large-scale study made in the Netherlands showed that average IQ declines as the number of children in the family goes up. IQ was also found to depend on order of birth, with the average declining steadily from first-born to last-born (51).

On the basis of the Netherlands studies, it has been suggested that parents who want to provide their offspring with the best possible intellectual environment should have two children and no more (52). The spacing of the two children—whether they are born close together or several years apart—does not seem to matter (53). Having an only child is dubious, for the Netherlands figures show that only children rank below other first-borns in average IQ. The reason may be that only children lack the mental stimulation that comes from interacting with and serving as teachers to others. The Netherlands study, incidentally, may offer a further explanation for the racial differences in IQ that were discussed in the box on Psychology and Society on page 228—for blacks have been much more likely than whites to grow up in large families (54).

The lucky orphans: a 28-point gain in IQ

As a final word on the effect of environment, we can turn to the dramatic results of a long-term study

Intellectual stimulation in the home shows a high correlation with the child's IQ.

of children who began life in the 1930s in an overcrowded, understaffed Iowa orphanage in which they had little opportunity for any kind of intellectual stimulation. Thirteen of the young orphans, with an average IQ of only 64 as shown by standard tests, were moved to a state home for retarded teenage girls and women. Here there was less crowding. And the older girls and women, despite their own mental handicaps, managed to provide an affectionate and homelike atmosphere for the young children. The home contributed toys and books, and there was great competition over which of the children could be helped to show the greatest progress in walking and talking.

With this personal attention and stimulation, even by people who were themselves retarded, the children made remarkable advances. Within about a year and a half their average IQ had risen by 28 points to 92 and they were considered ready for adoption into foster homes. A follow-up study many years later showed that they had been able to complete an average of twelve years of schooling. Most had held jobs successfully, and all of them were living at about the average level of occupation and income for their area of the nation.

The study also followed the careers of twelve other children who, for lack of opportunity to move elsewhere, had to remain in the overcrowded and unstimulating environment of the orphanage. These children, as it happened, actually began with a higher average IQ than the others, 87. But in the next two years the average declined by 26 points to 61. A follow-up when they were adults showed that they had completed an average of only four years of school. A third of them were still inmates of an institution. Only one of them worked at a job above the level of dishwasher or napkin-folder in a cafeteria (55).

The mystery of spontaneous changes in IQ

It is not surprising that drastic changes in environment, as in the study of the Iowa orphans, should produce changes in IQ. But another phenomenon is much more difficult to explain. This is the finding that children who remain in their own homes, and thus grow up in a relatively unchanging environment, may also show substantial changes in IQ over the years.

This puzzling fact comes from a study in which the progress of 140 girls and boys was carefully followed over a ten-year period, from the time they were two years old until they were twelve. Intelligence tests given every year indicated that about half the children showed just about the same IQ from one year to the next and indeed from the start of the ten-year period to the end. But for the other half there were changes upward or downward that in some cases reached striking proportions. In Figure 6-11, which illustrates some of the individual records from this study, note that one child's IQ rose from about 110 to 160, while another's dropped from about 140 to 110.

We have one clue to the reason for these results. This is the fact that the children who showed increases in IQ, as compared with those who showed declines, were found to be more independent, competitive, and likely to take the lead in conversation. They worked harder in school, showed a strong desire to master intellectual problems, and persisted at even the most difficult tasks. These are personality traits, as will be seen in Chapter 10, that our society has encouraged in boys, while at the same time urging girls to be dependent and passive and not to seem smarter than their brothers. And it is worthy of note that the study found boys more likely to show increases in IQ, girls more likely to show decreases.

One thing the study seems to demonstrate is that the IQ is by no means a constant and unchanging trait like a person's fingerprints. Parents and teachers often take a child's score on an intelligence test too seriously; they give up on the child who has made a low score and expect too much from the child who has made a high score. Second, it appears that intelligence tests as now designed measure achievement motivation as well as ability, for the strength of the child's desire for intellectual

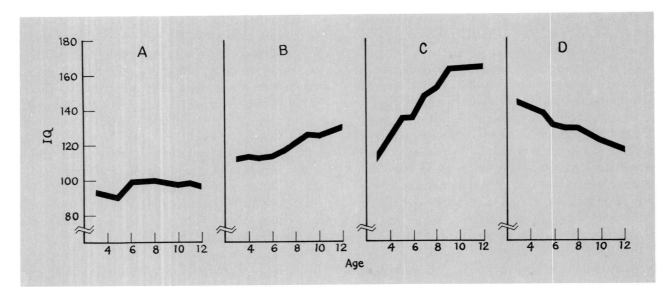

6-11 IQ from year to year: it may stay the same, rise, or fall

These graphs were obtained from annual tests of children's IQs as they grew up. About half the children showed nearly straight-line results as in *A*, with IQ remaining almost constant. Some showed substantial increases, such as the 20-point rise in *B*. A few showed very striking improvement, such as the 50-point rise in *C*. And some showed decreases of as much as 30 points, as in *D* (56).

achievement seems to be closely related to upward or downward changes in IQ. Parents who emphasize and reward intellectual accomplishment and independence and who provide a model of intellectual achievement are the most likely to find their children gaining in IQ over the years.

The study raises an interesting question: Can people improve their IQs through a deliberate effort toward better achievement? The answer is not known. But certainly some college students who make poor grades as freshmen suddenly begin making much better grades later. It may be that retesting of these students would show an increase in IQ.

Does intelligence decline with age?

Our ability to pass increasingly difficult items on intelligence tests, as was said in the earlier discussion of mental age and chronological age, grows rapidly throughout our childhood years. But what happens after we are fully mature? At what age does our intellectual ability reach its peak? Once the peak is attained, does our intelligence decline as we move to middle age and old age?

The best evidence bearing on these questions comes from a long-term study in which nearly a hundred men were tested as they moved from their late teens into their sixties. They began by taking a

Older people can still offer instruction and intellectual stimulation to the young.

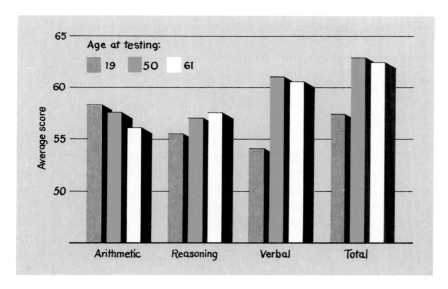

6-12

At what age are we smartest?

The bars show the raw scores (not IQ) for three of the skills measured by intelligence tests, as well as the total score, made by a group of college men as they grew older (57).

group intelligence test when they were college freshmen, with an average age of nineteen years. Later they took a similar test when they were fifty and finally when they were sixty-one. The results of the three tests are in Figure 6-12, page 233.

As the figure shows, scores on the arithmetic items in the test were highest at the age of nineteen and went down steadily thereafter. Scores on items measuring reasoning ability did just the opposite; they rose steadily and were highest at sixty-one. Scores on items measuring verbal ability were substantially higher at fifty than at nineteen but then declined slightly at sixty-one. The total score rose markedly from nineteen to fifty and afterward showed only a slight decline.

The results of this study are not entirely satis-factory, for two reasons. First, the group included no women—and the results therefore do not apply to both sexes except by inference. Second, since the men were chosen from the college population they had an above-average IQ—and presumably they led lives more favorable than average to continued intellectual stimulation and growth as they got older. However, the findings do offer a strong indication that intelligence—at least as measured by present tests—is by no means the monopoly of the young and that there is hardly any cause for despair over what will happen to our mental abilities as we grow old.

(Summary begins on page 238.)

Postscript

The science of test construction

Informal tests of human characteristics go back to the beginnings of history. Mythology and literature are full of stories about young men who had to slay a dragon to prove that they were brave enough to deserve the hand of the princess—or stories about people who had to answer riddles posed by wise men to prove that they were intelligent enough to become rulers. The ancient Chinese used tests to select people for governmental posts. The ancient Greeks made selections on the basis of tests they developed for both physical and mental skills (58).

Until very recently, however, tests were based largely on guesswork, and the results doubtless left a great deal to be desired. (Slaying a dragon does not necessarily make a man a good husband. Nor does answering a riddle necessarily indicate leadership ability.) Even today, a great many of the tests you find in newspapers and magazines have dubious value. If you want to take one of these popular tests for the fun of it, fine. But you cannot take seriously the claim that such tests will show how good a spouse or parent you are likely to be, or whether you are suffering from depression or in danger of becoming an alcoholic, or any of the other things they claim to tell you about yourself.

Constructing a test that will actually do a good job of measuring what it is supposed to measure is a science in itself—a difficult job to which many psychologists have devoted many years of study. The difficulties can best be explained by discussing the four strict requirements that a test must meet to qualify as scientifically sound.

Requirement 1: objectivity

A satisfactory test should be *objective*—that is, it should provide results that are not affected by the personal opinions or prejudices of the person who gives and grades it. The first intelligence test, as was mentioned earlier, was an attempt to obtain a more objective measure of a child's ability to profit from classes in school than could be provided by the opinion of the teacher, which might be colored by the child's personality, behavior in class, or family's position in the community.

Insofar as is possible, psychological tests are designed so that any qualified person can present them to the subject in the same manner and under the same testing conditions. A uniform method is provided for scoring the results. Thus the person taking the test should get the same score regardless of who administers and scores the test.

Requirement 2: reliability

To show why a test must also be *reliable,* an analogy can be drawn between a test and an oven thermometer. If the thermometer is reliable—that is,

if it gives the same reading every time for the same amount of heat—the cook can count on roasts and pies to come out of the oven in perfect shape for the table. On the other hand, if the thermometer is damaged and unreliable, it may give a reading of 300 degrees on one occasion and 400 degrees the next, even though the actual temperature is exactly the same. In this case the food is likely to be somewhat disappointing.

Just as a good thermometer must produce consistent temperature readings, a good test must produce consistent scores. One way of determining the reliability of a test is to compare the same person's score on all the odd-numbered items with the score on all the even-numbered items; these two scores should be similar. Or two versions of the test can be constructed and given to the same person on two different occasions. Again, the scores should be similar.

Requirement 3: validity

The most important requirement of all is *validity*. That is, a test must actually measure what it is intended to measure. There are a number of ways to determine this. Common sense is one of them; the items in the test must bear a meaningful relationship to the characteristic being measured. (The thought of trying to assess musical ability by asking questions on the rules of football does not make sense and must be rejected.) But common sense is not always enough. It would seem perfectly logical, for example, to assume that tests of finger dexterity would measure aptitude for being a dentist—yet one scientific study found that finger dexterity actually shows a negative correlation with the income of dentists (59).

A better way is to observe the behavior of people who have taken the test and determine whether they behave as their test scores predicted. Thus the validity of intelligence tests, as measures of academic ability, has been shown by the high correlations between IQ and school grades. A test of aptitude for dentistry could be proved valid or invalid by following the careers of people who took it—or, to save time, by determining the test scores of dentists who are already practicing and whose abilities and performance are already known.

Requirement 4: standardization

The final requirement of scientific testing can best be explained by imagining this situation: A psychologist has drawn up a 100-question test that can be given and scored objectively. It has proved reliable, and it seems to be a reasonable and valid measure of (let us say) aptitude for working with computers. Another psychologist decides to use the test and gives it to a college student, who answers 60 of the items correctly. What does this score of 60 tell the psychologist? By itself, not very much. The psychologist cannot know, after giving the test to a single person, whether a score of 60 indicates exceptional aptitude, very low aptitude, or something in between.

As this example indicates, the results of a test are generally not very useful unless they can be compared with the scores of other people. Thus most tests, before they are considered ready for use, are themselves tested by administering them to a large and representative sample of the population. Records are kept of how many people score at all the possible levels from highest to lowest. This process, called *standardization,* makes it possible to determine whether the score made by an individual is average, low, or high. Indeed the individual's ranking can be pinpointed precisely. We can say that the score falls (let us say) on the 71st *percentile*—that is, the individual has done better than 71 percent of all people, while 29 percent of all people make the same or a higher score.

Some other kinds of tests

All the accepted intelligence tests have been standardized on large samples of the population. They meet the requirements of objectivity and reliability and have proved valid for predicting academic success (although, as you have seen, their validity for doing anything else is in question). There are also many other kinds of tests, devised for special purposes, that have been constructed with the greatest possible regard for scientific accuracy.

Vocational aptitude tests

Some tests attempt to measure specific talents that would be useful at specific kinds of jobs. These are called *vocational aptitude tests* and are widely used in counseling people on choice of career.

Tests have been developed for all kinds of special skills, among them musical ability, dealing with details as required in clerical jobs, manual dexterity, and the motor coordination required to operate complicated machinery. These tests are often used by industry in selecting job applicants and by the military services in assigning people to specific tasks such as radio operator or astronaut.

Some vocational aptitude tests attempt to measure several different skills and arrive at a sort of aptitude profile that shows where the test-taker is strongest and weakest. One such test measures skill at spelling and grammar, dealing with numbers, clerical speed and accuracy, mechanical problems, and several types of thinking and reasoning (60). Those taking the test can be advised that they will probably do best in a job requiring the skills for which they score highest.

Interest tests

Also used in vocational guidance are *interest tests* —which attempt to measure how the subject feels about various activities. The tests try to establish whether the subject is interested in or bored by such activities as literature, music, the outdoors, mechanical equipment, art, science, social affairs, and all kinds of specific activities ranging from butterfly collecting to repairing a clock or making a speech. Tests of this type provide an indication of the sort of work in which subjects are likely to be happiest.

Personality tests

A great deal of time, energy, and ingenuity has gone into the creation of personality tests, which are potentially the most valuable of all. A test that could accurately distinguish between normal and neurotic personalities would enable clinical psychologists to find the people most in need of psychotherapy and perhaps lead to the discovery of new methods of treatment. It would make comparisons possible among people who have grown up in different environments and with different experiences and thus greatly add to the knowledge of developmental psychology. By spotting certain kinds of disturbed personalities, it could con-

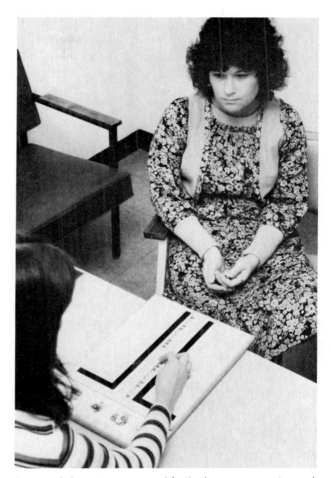

A manual dexterity test, scored for both accuracy and speed, can help pinpoint vocational ability.

ceivably prevent such tragedies as assassination attempts.

Personality tests will be discussed in detail in Chapter 12. Suffice it to say here that they present as many difficulties as opportunities. Indeed few psychological tests at present are entirely satisfactory. Tests of vocational aptitudes and interests, for example, usually show a much lower correlation with actual success on a job than intelligence tests show with school achievement. Nonetheless, the tests often offer valuable clues about an individual's personality, patterns of skills, and preferences for certain activities. They are often a helpful guide to clinical psychologists and vocational counselors.

Summary

1 Intelligence is the *capacity to understand the world and the resourcefulness to cope with its challenges.*

2 According to Thurstone, intelligence is composed of seven *primary mental abilities* (verbal comprehension, word fluency, number, space, associative memory, perceptual speed, and general reasoning) plus a general factor.

3 Guilford has suggested that intelligence is made up of no less than 120 different kinds of ability—and that a person may rank high in some of them but low in others. His theory suggests that success and happiness on a job depend largely on choosing work that suits your own particular strengths and weaknesses.

4 According to Piaget, intellectual development is basically an increased ability to adapt to new situations. The key processes in development are *assimilation* (incorporating a new stimulus into one's existing cognitive view of the world) and *accommodation* (changing one's cognitive view and behavior when new information dictates such a change).

5 Piaget has charted intellectual development through the following stages: a) *sensorimotor stage* (birth to age two), b) *preoperational stage* (two to seven), c) *stage of concrete operations* (seven to eleven), and d) *stage of formal operations* (beginning at about eleven or twelve).

6 Intelligence tests provide a measure of *intelligence quotient,* or IQ. The intelligence quotient gets its name from the fact that it was originally determined by comparing a child's *mental age* (as shown by the ability to pass test items that can be passed by the average child of various ages) with *chronological age* (or actual age).

7 The average IQ is 100, and almost half of all people score between 90 and 109.

8 An *individual test* is given by a trained examiner to one person at a time. Two widely used individual intelligence tests are the *Stanford-Binet Intelligence Scale* and the *Wechsler Adult Intelligence Scale.*

9 A *group test* can be given to many people at the same time. Two widely used group tests are the *Scholastic Aptitude Tests* (SAT) and *Armed Forces Qualification Test.*

10 All standard intelligence tests show a correlation of .40 to .60 with grades made in school.

11 Psychologists disagree about the extent to which IQ is related to success and happiness.

12 *Aptitude tests* measure a person's ability to learn a new skill or perform a new task. *Achievement tests* measure how much a person has learned or accomplished.

13 In theory, all intelligence tests are aptitude tests. They must depend to a considerable extent, however, on the subject's present level of knowledge about vocabulary, mathematics, and the manipulation of numbers and visual symbols.

14 Thus intelligence tests are biased to some extent in favor of people who have acquired the knowledge and language skills typical of the middle and upper-middle classes. Children from such homes make higher average scores than children from lower-class homes. City children make higher scores than rural children. Blacks and members of other ethnic cultures make lower average scores.

15 Studies of blood relatives and foster children have suggested that IQ is determined partly by heredity and partly by environment. Although Jensen has suggested that inheritance accounts for 80 percent, most psychologists believe that IQ depends on a constant interaction between heredity and environment—with the former setting a top and bottom limit, and the latter then determining where within that range the IQ will actually fall.

16 Even when children remain in the same home environment, their IQ may show spontaneous changes over the years—sometimes by as much as 50 points, upward or downward. The child's motivation for intellectual achievement seems to be closely related to these changes.

Postscript

17 To qualify as scientifically sound a test should be:
 a *Objective*—meaning that the subject will receive the same score regardless of who administers and scores the test.
 b *Reliable*—yielding similar scores when the same person is tested on different occasions.
 c *Valid*—found to actually measure what it is supposed to measure.

d *Standardized*—pretested on a large and representative sample so that an individual's score can be interpreted by comparison with the scores of other people.

18 *Vocational aptitude tests* measure ability to perform the special tasks required in specific jobs.

19 *Interest tests* measure how much an individual likes or dislikes various activities—thus providing a clue to what sort of job might be most congenial.

20 *Personality tests* attempt to measure all the many traits that make up personality and to distinguish between normal and neurotic patterns.

Important terms

accommodation
achievement test
aptitude test
assimilation
chronological age
(stage of) concrete operations
conservation
(stage of) formal operations

general factor
group test
individual test
intelligence
intelligence test
mental age
preoperational stage
primary mental abilities
sensorimotor stage

Postscript

interest test
objective
personality test
reliable

standardized
valid
vocational aptitude test

Recommended readings

Anastasia, A. *Psychological testing,* 4th ed. New York: Macmillan, 1976.

Buros, O. K., ed. *The mental measurements yearbook.* Highland Park, N. J.: Gryphon, published annually.

Butcher, H. J. *Human intelligence.* London: Methuen, 1970.

Cronbach, L. J. *Essentials of psychological testing,* 3d ed. New York: Harper & Row, 1970.

Loehlin, J. C., Lindzey, G., and Spuhler, J. N. *Race differences in intelligence.* San Francisco: Freeman, 1975.

Matarazzo, J. D., and Wechsler, D. *Wechsler's measurement and appraisal of adult intelligence,* 5th ed. New York: Oxford University Press, 1972.

Sattler, J. M. *The assessment of children's intelligence.* Philadelphia: Saunders, 1974.

Terman, L. M., and Oden, M. H. *The gifted child grows up.* Stanford: Stanford University Press, 1947.

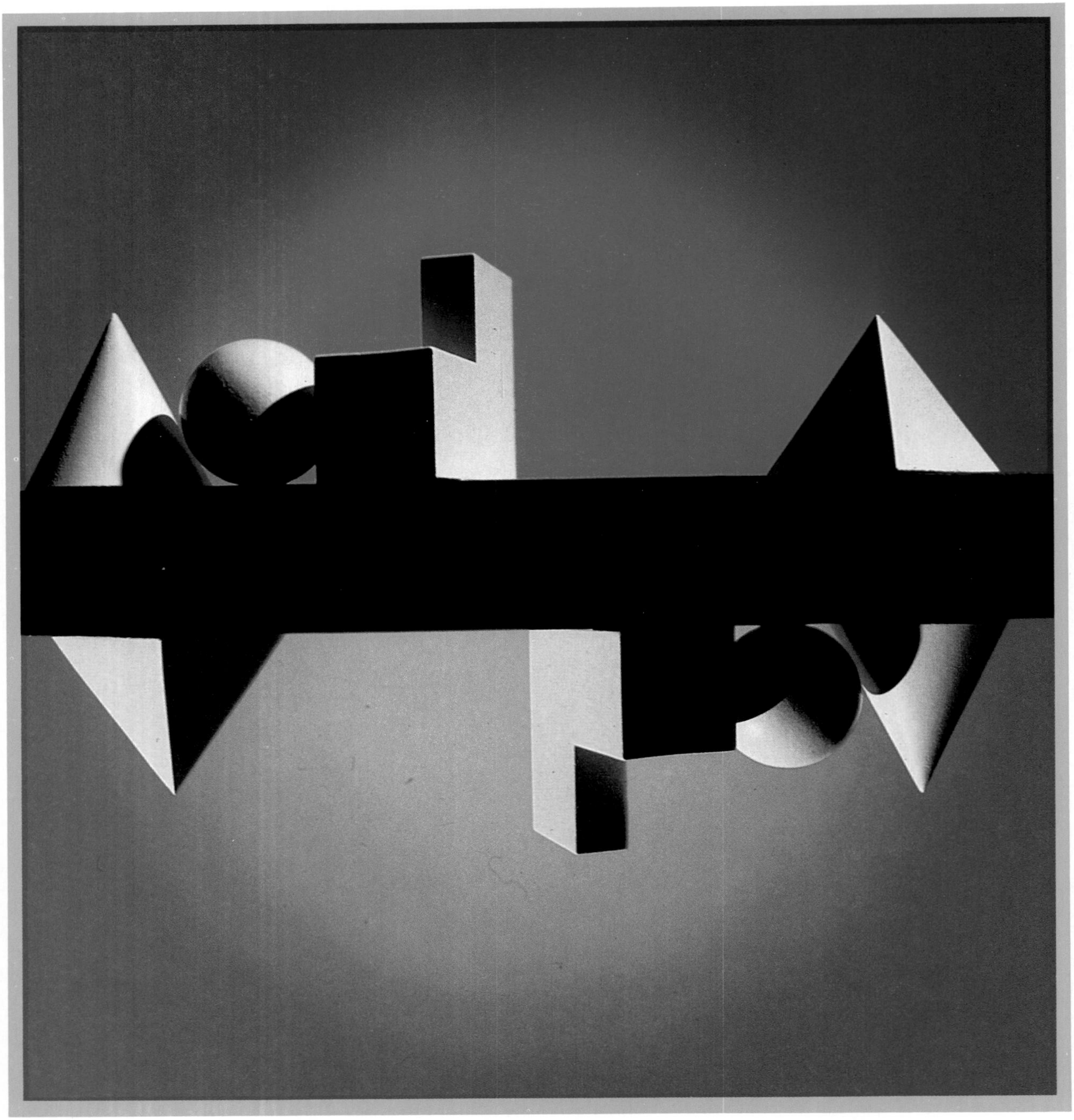

Part four
Knowing
what goes on
in the world:
the senses
and perception

Have you ever peered through a microscope at the tiny creature shown on this page? This is a paramecium—the simplest form of life because it has only a single cell. And it has a good deal to tell us about the marvels of human psychology.

The paramecium has no sense organs to bring it messages from the outside world. Instead, its entire "body" is sensitive in a general way to light, dark, heat, cold, and the presence of food. This is all it knows about the world. It has no idea that outside the stagnant water in which it lives there is a universe full of sights, sounds, tastes, and smells. It is unaware of such phenomena as the rising and setting of the sun, lightning and thunder, the fall of rain, the color and smell of a rose, the taste of salt.

Suppose the process of evolution had somehow gone awry and created human beings with all our present complexities of body and brain except for a

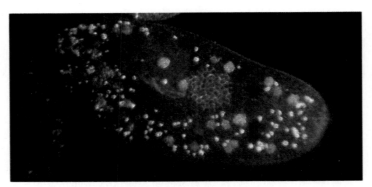

A paramecium, photographed under high magnification, in a drop of water.

paramecium-like absence of any sense organs. We would still be potentially capable of all the behavior that has been discussed in preceding chapters—learning, memory, the use of language, and thinking. But all these capabilities would never develop. Without the input provided by our senses, we would have nothing to learn or remember, nothing to talk or think about. We would be conspicuous examples of wasted ingenuity—like an expensive computer whose inventor forgot to provide any means of getting information into its elaborate circuits.

Thus the way the senses operate, which is the topic of Chapter 7, has been one of psychology's prime interests since its beginning as a science. Equally important is the manner in which our nervous system organizes and interprets the information provided by the senses through the process called perception, which is the topic of Chapter 8.

As you will see, your own behavior and thinking at this moment depend in part on the fact that your eyes are sensitive to the light waves reflected off this book. The process of perception enables you to recognize the light waves as a particular object that you know to be a textbook. A child, seeing the same light waves, might interpret them as something to mark up with a crayon or to use like a building block. A dog might perceive the book as something to gnaw on or carry to the back yard. A bookworm (the insect type, not the human) would perceive it as lunch.

The senses provide the information. Perception gives meaning to what we see, hear, feel, smell, and taste. Together, the senses and perception enable us to know what goes on in the environment and to use all our other psychological strengths to cope with the world.

Outline

Chapter seven

The senses: our source of information

H elen Keller, born in a small town in Alabama in 1880, is history's most famous example of human dependence on the sense organs. When she was nineteen months old, an illness left her blind and deaf. She was abruptly cut off from the world's sights and sounds. Her learning stopped. Her memory contained only the meager store of information a child acquires in the early months of life. She possessed a brain capable of learning and memory processing—but how could it operate in the darkness and silence that engulfed her?

In the following years, her mental development was at a virtual standstill. She knew nothing of other people except through the sense of touch. She could not communicate with them. They could not communicate with her. She knew nothing about how to feed herself, or dress, or act in any other way like a human being. Except for her eyes and

Helen Keller (left) at the age of 17, with her teacher Anne Sullivan.

ears, her physical structure remained intact, in both brain and body. But without the usual sensory input, she was helpless.

The story, of course, has a happy ending—proof that the human structure (or, as the humanistic psychologists would prefer, the human spirit) is strong and versatile enough to surmount even the most crippling adversity. When Keller was six, she came under the care of a remarkable teacher named Anne Sullivan, who herself had once been blind.

Keller was taught to use her sense of touch—through signals pressed into the palm of her hand—to acquire the knowledge ordinarily gained through eyes and ears. She soon achieved the gift of language. Eventually she became a *cum laude* college graduate, linguist, and author. But the message of the Helen Keller story is this: Although human psychological processes can make do in an emergency with the most meager sensory information, they do need some input from the senses.

How the senses operate

How do our sense organs bring us information about the world? As you sit reading this book, you are demonstrating the two basic principles.

First, there must be a *stimulus* from the environment—some form of energy impinging on the body. At the moment, the stimulus is the light waves reflected off your book. Turn off the light and darken the room, thus cutting off the light waves, and you can no longer see the book.

Second, there must be *receptors* in the nervous system that are sensitive to the stimulus. The receptors you are using now are light-sensitive nerve endings in your eyes. These receptors respond to the light waves and send nervous impulses to the brain, where they are translated into the conscious sensations of vision. Block off the receptors by closing your eyelids, and again you cannot see the book. You cannot see with your ears or your skin because they do not contain any receptors sensitive to light.

Each of the senses has its own special receptors, responsive to a particular kind of stimulus. The hearing receptors in the ears respond to the stimulus of sound waves. Receptors in the nose and

tongue respond to the chemical energy that produces smell and taste. Receptors in the skin respond to the stimuli of pressure and temperature.

The range and limits of the human senses

The receptors in the human eye are so sensitive that on a night when the air is clear but the moon and stars are obscured, a person sitting on a mountain can see a match struck fifty miles away. Our noses can detect the odor of artificial musk, a perfume base, in as weak a concentration as one part musk to thirty-two billion parts of air.

Even so, our senses are by no means perfect. Owls can see far better in the near-dark than we can. Hawks soaring high in the air can see mice that we would never be able to distinguish at such a distance. Bees can see ultraviolet light (the rays that produce sunburn), which we cannot see at all. Dogs and porpoises hear tones that go unheard by the human ear. (You can buy whistles that will call your dog without disturbing your neighbors.) The minnow, which has taste receptors all over its body,

A perfume tester works at the limits of the human sense of smell.

has a far sharper sense of taste than we do. Bloodhounds have a far superior sense of smell.

In some ways, the deficiencies of our sense organs are a blessing. The world is full of forms of energy that are of no special concern to us—all kinds of potential stimuli that would only confuse rather than inform us. For example, the light waves to which our eyes are sensitive are very similar to the waves of radio and television signals, cosmic rays, X-rays, and the electricity passing through the wires of our houses. It is perhaps just as well that our visual receptors do not respond to all these extraneous forms of energy.

The absolute threshold

You can make a simple test of your hearing that points to one of the important facts about the senses. Have a friend hold a watch somewhere in the vicinity of one of your ears, moving it closer and farther away. The watch is constantly ticking, sending out sound waves. But sound waves decrease in intensity as they travel through the air, and if the watch is too far away, you cannot hear it at all. As it is moved closer, eventually there comes a spot at which you can hear it quite clearly. At one distance the sound waves are too weak to make the receptors in your ear respond. A little closer the waves are strong enough. The receptors send signals to your brain, and you can hear the watch. This test is a crude measurement of the *absolute threshold* of hearing in that ear—in other words, the minimum amount of stimulus energy to which the receptors will respond. By comparing your threshold with that of other people, you can get a rough idea of whether your sense of hearing is average, sharper than average, or below average.

Many experiments have been performed to determine the absolute threshold for each of the senses. In a typical experiment on vision, a subject is placed in a dark room and brief flashes of light are presented, with the exact intensity of the light controlled down to the tiniest fraction. Some flashes are so weak in intensity that the subject never sees them. Other, stronger flashes are seen every time. In between, there is a sort of twilight zone of intensities at which the subject sometimes sees the flash and sometimes does not.

There are many reasons for this "sometimes" factor. The human body is constantly at work; the heart is beating, the lungs inhaling or exhaling air. Each cell of the body, including the sensory receptors, is being fed by the blood stream and is throwing off waste materials. All sorts of spontaneous nervous activity are constantly going on in the brain. Sometimes all these conditions work together to detect a weak stimulus. Sometimes they work against it. So the absolute threshold is not really absolute. It is arbitrarily considered to be the intensity at which the subject detects the stimulus half the time.

The difference threshold

The senses have another kind of threshold, which can also be demonstrated by flashes of light in a dark room. This time we change conditions by presenting two lights to the subject, side by side. We start with two lights of exactly equal intensity, and the subject, as we would expect, sees them as exactly the same. We show the two lights again, but this time we have increased the intensity of the right-hand light by a tiny fraction. If we continue the experiment long enough, keeping the left-hand light at the same intensity and varying the intensity of the right-hand light, eventually we will discover the smallest possible difference that our subject's eyes are capable of recognizing 50 percent of the time. This is the *difference threshold,* an important concept in sensory psychology.

The difference threshold—often called the *just noticeable difference,* or j.n.d. for short—is a measurement of our basic capacity to discriminate among different stimuli. Measurements have shown that if the left-hand light in our experiment has an intensity of 1, the right-hand light must have an intensity of 1.016 to be recognized as different. If the left-hand light is 10, the right-hand light must be 10.16. If the left-hand light is 100, the right-hand light must be 101.6. In other words, the difference in intensity between two lights must be 1.6 percent before it can be recognized. For sound, the just noticeable difference is about 10 percent.

This rule that the difference threshold is a fixed percentage of the original stimulus is called *Weber's Law,* in honor of the physiologist who discovered it more than a century ago. The law does not apply at very low intensities or at very high intensities, but it holds generally over a large part of the range of stimulation. In practical terms, it means this: The more sensory stimulation to which the human organism is being subjected, the more additional stimulation is required to produce a recognizable difference. In a room where there is no sound except the buzzing of a mosquito, you can hear a pin drop. On a noisy city street you can hear the honk of an automobile horn but may be completely unaware of a friend shouting to you from down the block. At an airport where jet planes are warming up, a small cannon could go off beside you without making you jump.

Sensory adaptation

At this moment, unless you happen to be sitting in a draft or in an unusually hot room, you almost surely are not conscious of feeling either hot or cold. And you probably feel the same all over. You are not conscious that your feet are cooler or warmer than your hands or that the skin on the calves of your legs is any cooler or warmer than the skin on the small of your back. Yet careful measurements of your skin temperature would probably show small but significant differences for your feet, which are encased in shoes; your uncovered hands; your calves; and the small of your back, covered by several layers of clothing and a belt.

Nor are you conscious of any special pressures against your skin. But wherever your clothing touches your skin, there certainly is pressure; and at some places the pressure is made so intense by a wristwatch band or by a belt that you may find marks on your skin tonight when you undress. Why do you not feel these stimuli? The answer lies in the principle of *sensory adaptation,* which means that after a time the sensory receptors adjust to a stimulus—they get used to it, so to speak—and stop responding.

In some ways this tendency of our senses to adapt to stimuli makes them less accurate than they would otherwise be. The human skin would make a poor thermostat for a heating system; what we want in a heating system is a thermostat that

"Alden, which of the five senses do you value most?"

Drawing by Saxon; © 1978 The New Yorker Magazine, Inc.

Because of the principle of sensory adaptation, some scientists define a stimulus as a *change in energy* capable of exciting the sense organs. Such a definition is not literally correct, because we never adapt completely to a pressure strong enough to cause severe pain, and we continue to feel uncomfortably warm in a 110-degree room no matter how long we stay there. But the definition is a useful reminder that our sensory apparatus is best equipped to inform us of changes in our environment—exactly the kind of information that is most valuable. Our brains cooperate in this search for change. Even when the sensory receptors continue to send messages, the brain often begins to ignore them, as if it had become bored with the information. Thus the brain cells too display a kind of sensory adaptation.

All the principles just mentioned—absolute threshold, difference threshold, and adaptation—apply to all the senses, though each responds to different stimuli and produces very different conscious sensations. It is popularly assumed that we are gifted with five senses—which we will now examine starting with *vision*, the most valuable, and proceeding to *hearing, taste, smell,* and the *skin senses.* After we have looked at these five, however, we will have to consider two more—*bodily movement* and *equilibrium*—to understand the full range of human sensory apparatus.

will invariably turn the heat on when the room temperature drops to 67 degrees and turn the heat off as soon as the temperature rises to 69 degrees. But in everyday living, sensory adaptation is generally an advantage. It would be distracting indeed if we were conscious all day of the pressure of every garment we wear and of every slight temperature change from one patch of our skin to another.

Vision

The most remarkable thing about our eyes is the vast number of conscious sensations they produce. You can concentrate your vision on a single black word on the white page of this book—or look out the window and see an entire landscape full of objects in what seems to be an infinite variety of shadings and hues. You can see a whole range of brightness from pure white through various grays to jet black, plus all the colors of the rainbow, in hues that run from vivid blue to muddy red. According to one estimate, our eyes are capable of distinguishing among 350,000 just noticeable differences in color and brightness—which means that the sense of vision has a tremendous scope.

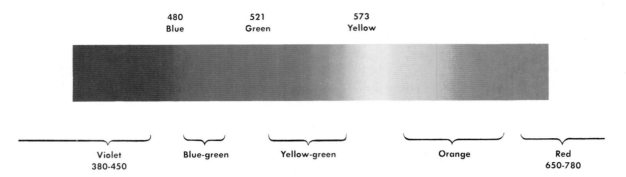

480
Blue

521
Green

573
Yellow

Violet
380-450

Blue-green

Yellow-green

Orange

Red
650-780

7-1 The hues of the spectrum

A spectrum of all the visible hues is obtained when a beam of white light passes through a prism. The white light is a mixture of all the wavelengths to which our eyes are sensitive—and the prism, bending each wavelength at a slightly different angle, separates the mixture into all its component parts. The numbers show the wavelengths of the hues in billionths of a meter.

The visual stimulus

The light waves that stimulate the eyes are a pulsating form of electromagnetic energy produced by many kinds of physical and chemical activity. In the daytime, waves strong enough to illuminate the entire landscape reach us from the burning fires and explosions of the sun. At night, light reaches us by reflection from the moon and, at much lower intensities, from the more distant suns that we call stars. We also create our own nighttime illumination by using electricity to heat the filaments in light bulbs. Most of the light waves we see do not reach our eyes directly but by reflection from objects in the environment.

Light waves travel at a speed of 186,000 miles (300,000 kilometers) a second, the fastest speed known and presumably the fastest possible. This is such great velocity that a light wave, if you could manage to reflect it around the world, would make the long journey and get back to you in less than one-seventh of a second.

All the many sensations that light waves create

depend on three basic differences in the form they take:

1 Variations in *wavelength,* which is the distance between the peaks of the waves. The wavelength determines *hue,* which is the scientific name for the sensation produced by light waves from colored objects. The longest wavelengths look red. The shortest wavelengths look violet. White light is a mixture of all the wavelengths. When a beam of white light is passed through a prism, the different wavelengths are separated and the result is a spectrum of all the hues, as shown in Figure 7-1. The same phenomenon can be seen in a rainbow, which occurs when sunlight is broken down into its component wavelengths as it passes through raindrops that act like prisms.

2 Variations in *intensity,* or the amount of energy the waves possess. These variations are the chief explanation for our sensations of brightness or dimness. A 100-watt light bulb produces light waves of greater intensity than does a 50-watt bulb—which is why it makes a room

look so much brighter. Our sensations, however, do not depend entirely on intensity. For some reason, our eyes are most sensitive under good illumination to the wavelengths at the middle of the color spectrum—and therefore greens and yellows look brighter than violets or reds of equal intensity.

3 Variations in *complexity,* or the purity of the light wave. If the light that strikes our eyes is composed almost entirely of a red wavelength, we see a very vivid hue. If the red is mixed with other wavelengths, thus increasing its complexity and making it less pure, what we see becomes what we call "duller," or "less red," or "muddier." These varying sensations are called degrees of *saturation.* An almost pure wavelength produces a sensation of high saturation. A mixture of greater complexity causes a sensation of reduced saturation. The effects of complexity (and also intensity) are illustrated in Figure 7-2.

The structure of the eye

The receptors for vision lie in a small patch of tissue at the back of each eyeball, called the *retina.* Each retina, if flattened out, would appear as an irregular ellipse with a total area of around three-fourths of a square inch (just under five square centimeters) —about the size of a quarter. These two little sensory surfaces bring us all the pictures we see, even of the vast areas of landscape visible through the window of a high-flying airplane.

This would be impossible unless the eye, in addition to its receptors, had some sort of equipment for bending light waves and focusing them on the retina, much as a fine camera takes a sharp photograph of a wide sweep of landscape by focusing the light waves on a small piece of film. The human eye, indeed, has much the same structure as a camera. If you have ever taken a photograph,

7-2 Brightness and saturation
All the little squares are of the same hue. The other two dimensions of light—brightness and saturation—are varied. The squares in the left-hand column are saturated (or pure) blue. Their brightness decreases from top to bottom. From left to right, the pure blue is diluted with more and more gray of equal brightness. In the right-hand column are the least saturated blues that can be distinguished from pure gray. The illustration is only an approximation of the two phenomena because it is impossible to reproduce light waves exactly in color printing.

especially with a camera that must be focused and set before each picture, you should feel right at home with the diagram of the eyeball in Figure 7-3.

The *iris* and *pupil* of the eye resemble the diaphragm at the front of a camera. When the smooth muscles of the iris open to maximum size, the pupil admits about seventeen times as much light as when it is contracted to its smallest size. The lens of the eye serves the same purpose as the lens of a camera but in a way that would not be possible with even the most carefully designed piece of

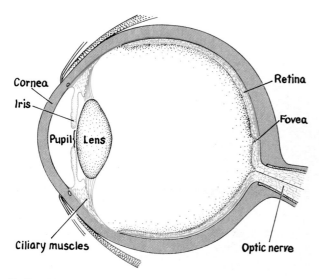

7-3 A cross section of the eye

Light waves first strike the *cornea*, a transparent bulge in the outer layer of the eyeball. The cornea serves as a sort of preliminary lens, gathering light waves from a much wider field of vision than would be possible if the eyeball merely had a perfectly flat window at the front. The light waves then pass through the *pupil,* which is an opening in the *iris,* a circular arrangement of smooth muscles (page 59) that contract and expand to make the opening smaller in bright light and larger in dim light. (When you look at your eyes in a mirror, the pupil is the dark, almost black circle at the center. The iris is the larger circle around it containing the pigments that determine eye color.) Behind the pupil lies the transparent *lens,* the shape of which is controlled by the *ciliary muscles.* The lens focuses the light rays on the *retina,* which contains the light-sensitive receptors of the eye. The receptors are most tightly packed in the *fovea,* where visual acuity is greatest. Messages from the receptors are transmitted to the brain by way of the *optic nerve,* which exits from the back of the eyeball, a little off center. Attached to the eyeball are muscles that enable us to look up, down, and sideways. The space inside the eyeball is filled with a transparent substance, as is the space between the cornea and the iris (1).

glass. The lens of a camera has to be moved forward and backward to focus on nearby or faraway objects. The lens of the eye remains stationary but changes shape. The action of the *ciliary muscles* makes the lens thinner to bring faraway objects into

focus and enables it to thicken to focus on nearby objects.

At the point where the optic nerve exits from the eyeball, there is a small gap in the retina, with no receptors for vision. The area is almost insensitive to light and is therefore known as the *blind spot.* We are never aware of this blind spot in ordinary life, but you can discover it by examining Figure 7-4.

The visual receptors

Any experienced photographer will tell you that the lens of an expensive camera is sharper than the lens of the human eye and that the camera diaphragm has a much wider range than the iris. But the retina is sensitive to very low intensities of light that would not register at all on photographic film, and it can function under very high intensities of light that would completely burn out photographic film. Most important of all, it responds continuously, without any winding from one frame to the next. At this instant you see these words on the page. If you raise your eyes slightly, you immediately see the wall of the room. If you shift your eyes again, you can look out the window and see the landscape— all in one continuous and uninterrupted series of visual sensations. In photographic terms, the retina is a highly versatile film capable of constantly renewing itself.

Packed into the small area of each retina are about 127,000,000 receptors of the kind shown in Figure 7-5. The great majority of the receptors are long and narrow, a fact that has given them the name *rods.* The rest, numbering about 7,000,000, are somewhat thicker and are tapered; these are called *cones.* The rods function chiefly under conditions of low illumination and send information to the brain about movement and about whites, grays, and blacks but not about color. The cones function in strong illumination and provide information not only about movement and brightness from

7-4
A demonstration of the blind spot

Hold the book at arm's length, close your right eye, and look at the helmet on the right. Now move the book slowly closer. When the image of the helmet at the left falls on the blind spot of your left eye, it will disappear. To demonstrate the blind spot of the right eye, repeat with the left eye closed and your gaze concentrated on the helmet at the left.

white to black but also about color. The cones are most numerous toward the middle of the retina. Indeed the area called the *fovea,* at the very center of the retina, contains only cones, packed together more tightly than anywhere else. This is where our vision is sharpest. When we read or do anything else that requires a very sharp image, we keep the object in the center of our field of vision so that its light waves fall on the fovea.

The manner in which light waves stimulate the receptors of the retina was discovered many years ago when physiologists managed to extract a substance known as *visual purple* from the rods. Visual purple is highly sensitive to light, which bleaches it at a rate depending on intensity and wavelength. Thus light waves striking the retina produce chemical changes in the visual purple, and these changes act to stimulate the neurons next in the pathway that carries messages from receptors to brain (2).

More recently, it has been found that the cones contain substances somewhat akin to visual purple. There are three kinds of cones. All three show chemical changes in response to a broad range of wavelengths—but one is most sensitive to the wavelengths in the yellow and red part of the color spectrum, another to the middle wavelengths of green, and the third to the wavelengths at the violet-blue end (3, 4).

The pattern theory of vision

Basically, the eye contains only four kinds of receptors—rods that operate to detect brightness, plus three types of cones that are most sensitive to red, green, and blue. How does this limited number of receptors manage to provide us with all the vast range of visual sensations we experience, including those 350,000 just noticeable differences in hue and brightness?

The answer appears to lie in the *pattern theory,* which holds that visual sensations are produced by

7-5 The retina's rods and cones
The shapes that give the names to the rods and cones can be seen clearly in this photograph of the retina of a mudpuppy, made with an electron microscope.

the total pattern of nervous impulses set off by the rods and cones, modified by some of the neurons in the pathway from eye to brain, and eventually delivered to the visual area of the cerebral cortex. There is no simple one-to-one relationship between visual receptor and visual sensation. We do not have some cones that respond only to special shades of orange, purple, or yellow-green. Instead, the light waves that fall on the retina stimulate some receptors to a high rate of activity, stimulate others to a lesser rate, and act on still others in a way that tends to inhibit or cancel out some of the retina's responses. The retina's entire pattern of activity determines the number and rate of nervous impulses delivered through the complex pathway of neurons that runs from the eye to the visual centers of the brain. And it is the highly varied pattern of these impulses that provides our highly varied sensations.

The pattern theory applies not only to vision but to all the senses. Apparently none of the senses has receptors specifically designed to respond to a single kind of stimulation, as Channel 2 on your television set is zeroed in on one station and one only. Instead, sensory receptors are what one investigator has called "broadly tuned" (5). They are like the cones that show a maximum response to green light waves—but also respond to some extent, and in one way or another, to waves of different length. A stimulus for any of the senses affects a great many broadly tuned receptors, resulting in many different patterns of nervous impulses arriving at the brain.

Vision in bright sunlight and in a dark theater

One valuable aspect of our visual equipment is that it can function under an extremely wide range of illumination. Note what happens when you walk through bright afternoon sunlight into a movie theater where there is hardly any light at all. At first the theater seems pitch-black, and you can hardly find your way down the aisle to an empty seat. But after a while, as your eyes get used to the dark, you can clearly see the aisle, the seats, and the faces of the people around you.

Full adjustment to dark conditions takes about an hour, by which time the eyes are about 100,000 times more sensitive to light than they were in the bright sunlight. Note that you do not see colors in a dimly lighted place such as a theater—nothing but shades of gray. This is because your vision then depends on the rods. The color-sensitive cones cannot function at such a low intensity of light.

Eye movements and scanning

Although the eyes can adjust to intensity, they seem in everyday experience to violate the general rule of adaptation discussed earlier in the chapter, which is that sensory receptors stop responding to a steady level of stimulation after a time. No matter how long you continue to stare fixedly at an object, your vision never goes blank.

Under laboratory conditions, however, it can be shown that the eyes are no exception to the rule. One investigator has invented a sort of miniature slide projector that can be attached to the eyeball, where it continues to throw its picture on the same receptors of the retina despite any eyelid blinks or eye movements by the subject. Under these circumstances, the receptors of the eye adapt and stop responding rather quickly (6). Indeed a small stimulus such as a fine line disappears within a few seconds (7).

One reason this never happens under ordinary circumstances is that the muscles controlling the eyeballs constantly make spontaneous movements —like tiny but very fast pendulum swings at the rate

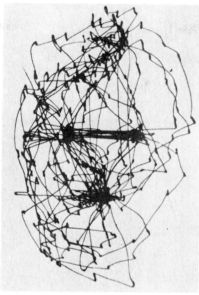

7-6
A pattern of eye movements
The pattern of lines was made by bouncing a light beam off the white of a man's eye as he looked at the photograph of the girl, thus recording his eye movements. Note how many movements took place and how they trace all the important elements of the photograph.

of 30 to 100 a minute. Another reason is that we continually shift our gaze, making voluntary movements of the eyeballs. This is especially obvious in reading, as you can observe for yourself. You gaze first at a word or two at the beginning of a line. Then your eyes jump to the next word or words, and so on until you have reached the end of the line, when they jump to the start of the next line.

Even when we think we are looking steadily at some stimulus such as a photograph, our eyes shift constantly, as is shown in Figure 7-6. We do not stare fixedly at an object, even when we think we are doing so. Instead we scan it, feature by feature. As our eyes make these scanning movements, they receive an impression of one part of the object, then another, then another, on and on until we have seen the whole as a succession of many different parts.

To prove for yourself the importance of this scanning and "putting together," try a little experi-

ment next time someone is driving you through the countryside. As the automobile approaches the top of a hill, close your eyes. When the car starts down the other side, open your eyes, take a quick look at the new landscape spread out in front of you, close them again—and discover how little your eyes have told you about that landscape. You may know that you saw some horses and cows—but how many? Were they moving or grazing? How many houses did you see? What color were they? Did the road ahead of you curve to the left or to the right?

You will probably be surprised to discover how few such questions you can answer. You thought you saw the landscape—but actually you saw very little of it. Our visual process does not operate like the taking of a snapshot, recorded on film in its entirety within a fraction of a second. Instead it is more like the creation of a mosaic, formed by the brain from a very rapid succession of fragmentary bits of information from the eyes.

Hearing

Our sense of hearing, in its own way, is just as versatile as vision. We can distinguish tones ranging from the lowest notes of a tuba to the highest notes of a shrill whistle, changing in loudness from the merest hint of a whisper to the most deafening clap of thunder, taking such diverse and varied forms as the tick of a watch, the human voice, and the blended richness of a hundred instruments in a symphony orchestra. Our world contains many kinds of sound stimuli—and our ears, like our eyes, have a remarkable capacity to respond to all the stimuli and tell them apart.

The stimulus for hearing

The stimulus for hearing is sound waves, traveling unseen through the atmosphere. The waves are little ripples of compression and expansion of the air, typically produced by the banging together of two objects or by the vibration of a piano string or the human vocal cords. The waves travel much more slowly than light, as is apparent from the fact that we see a lightning flash before we hear the thunder it creates. The speed of the waves depends on the density of the atmosphere. At sea level it is around 750 miles (1,200 kilometers) an hour, or 1,100 feet (335 meters) per second.

Although sound waves are an entirely different form of energy from light waves, they too exhibit three basic variations very similar to those that account for the different sensations produced by light. The three are:

1 Variations in *frequency,* or the number of waves per second. Frequency determines the hearing sensation of *pitch.* The notes of a tuba are low in frequency and therefore low in pitch. The tweet of a whistle is high in frequency and therefore sounds high-pitched.

2 Variations in *amplitude,* or strength—similar to the variations in intensity displayed by light waves. Amplitude determines the *loudness* we hear. A whisper is very weak in amplitude, a

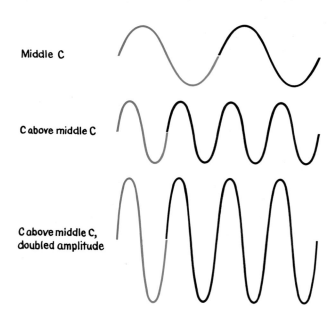

Middle C

C above middle C

C above middle C, doubled amplitude

7-7 Sound waves: frequency and amplitude
The wave at the top, for the pure tone of middle C, has a frequency of 256 ripples a second of compression and expansion. The wave in the middle, for a note an octave higher, ripples at twice that frequency, or 512 cycles a second. Sounding this same note with twice the force produces the wave at the bottom, which continues to have a frequency of 512 cycles a second but has double the amplitude, as indicated by the height of the wave. The colored portions of the waves show a single cycle of compression and expansion.

thunderclap very strong. How waves vary in amplitude (and also frequency) is illustrated in Figure 7-7.

3 Variations in *complexity,* or, again as in the case of light, the purity of the wave. Pure sound waves, traveling at a single frequency, are very rare. (About the closest thing to a pure tone is produced by a flute.) Most waves are composed of a number of different frequencies. When you strike middle C on a piano, for instance, the string as a whole vibrates at a frequency of 256 cycles per second, thus creating the pitch you hear. But the string also creates some secondary sounds. Each half vibrates separately, at a rate of 512 cycles a second. Each third of the string vibrates at 768 cycles, each quarter at 1,024 cycles, and so on. These secondary vibrations are called *overtones.* They have less amplitude than the basic wave of 256 cycles, but they change the pattern of the wave and create what is called the *timbre.* Each musical instrument has its characteristic timbre, or pattern of complexity. Thus the middle C of a piano sounds different from the middle C of a violin (whose complex wave is shown in Figure 7-8) or a trumpet.

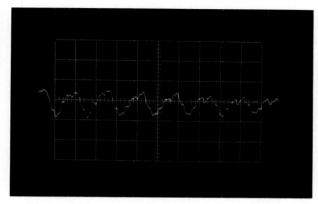

7-8 A complex sound wave
A sound wave from a violin string takes this pattern of complexity, which accounts for the characteristic timbre of the violin.

The structure of the ear

What you call your ear—the flap of tissue at the side of the head—is in fact the least important part of your hearing equipment. The working parts, including the receptors, lie hidden inside the skull.

The structure is shown in Figure 7-9. The *outer ear,* or visible portion, merely collects sound waves. The waves create vibrations of the *eardrum* that are passed along through the *middle ear,* an air-filled cavity containing three small bones that conduct and amplify the vibrations. The last of the three bones transmits the vibrations to the *cochlea,* a bony structure shaped like a snail's shell, which contains the *inner ear's* receptors for hearing.

The cochlea is filled with fluid, and stretched across it, dividing it more or less in half, is a piece of tissue called the *basilar membrane.* When the vibrations of sound reach the cochlea, they set up motions of the fluid inside, thus bending the basilar membrane. Lying on the membrane is the *organ of Corti,* a collection of the receptors for hearing.

How the hearing receptors work

Sound waves cause the entire basilar membrane to respond with complicated wavelike motions that travel along its length and breadth (8). These motions in turn activate the hearing receptors, which

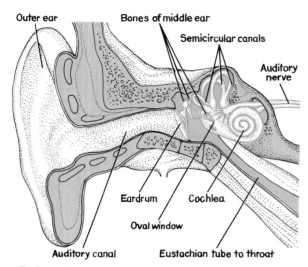

Outer ear
Bones of middle ear
Semicircular canals
Auditory nerve
Eardrum
Cochlea
Oval window
Auditory canal
Eustachian tube to throat

7-9 A diagram of the hearing apparatus

Sound waves enter the *outer ear*, pass through the *auditory canal*, and set up vibrations of the *eardrum*. The three bones of the middle ear transmit the vibrations to the *cochlea* through its *oval window*. The *auditory nerve* carries messages from the hearing receptors inside the cochlea to the brain. The *Eustachian* tube, traveling from middle ear to throat, keeps the air pressure inside the middle ear at the same level as outside. (When the tube is temporarily clogged, as sometimes happens when you have a cold or ride in an airplane or elevator, you can feel a difference in pressure against the eardrum.) The *semicircular canals* play no part in hearing but contain receptors for the *sense of equilibrium*, which keeps us right side up.

are shaped like very fine hairs resting on the membrane. When the floor beneath the receptors moves, the hair-shaped cells jiggle like little dancers—setting off nervous impulses that are sent to the brain and produce the sensations of sound.

The basilar membrane varies in width from one end to the other, somewhat like an elongated harp. Moreover, it is very flexible and easily moved in some places, more rigid and difficult to move in others. Thus different sounds—and especially different pitches of sound—cause its wavelike motions to take many different forms. At times the waves have their greatest effect on the hearing receptors in one area, at other times on the hearing receptors in other areas. Where the membrane is flexible, the dancing of the hair-shaped cells tends to stimulate other nearby cells. Where the membrane is stiffer, this is less likely to happen. Thus there are almost endless patterns of nervous activity that can be set up in the hearing receptors by different kinds and amplitudes of sounds. It appears that our sensations of pitch, loudness, and timbre depend on the particular receptors that are stimulated, the number of them, the rate of firing of nervous impulses sent to the brain, and especially the pattern of these impulses (9, 10). Hearing, like vision, seems to operate in accordance with the pattern theory rather than to depend on the sensitivity of individual receptors. Indeed the hearing receptors are even more broadly tuned than the rods and cones of the eye. All of them are capable of responding to almost any kind of movement of the part of the basilar membrane on which they rest.

The rest of the five senses

Most of the information we receive about the world comes through our eyes and ears. We do not ordinarily depend on the other senses except in an emergency, as in the case of Helen Keller after she lost the use of her eyes and ears. We do not rely on the sense of smell, as do many lower animals, to

help us track down the prey that will provide the next meal (or to signal the approach of an enemy). We do not use the sense of taste to learn which foods are poisonous, as do the animals that exhibit bait shyness as was discussed on pages 119–20. Indeed we sometimes deliberately develop an

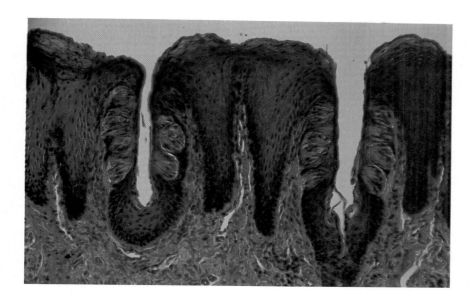

Human taste buds, photographed under high magnification.

acquired taste for foods that were repugnant the first time we tried them, like strong cheeses.

Nonetheless, the other senses do have their uses, even under ordinary circumstances. The skin senses, by flashing pain signals, helps us avoid injury. Taste and smell, though they may not bring us much essential information about the world, help us enjoy it.

Taste

Though we can recognize a great variety of foods, and either relish or reject them, our sense of taste is probably our simplest and least efficient. The flavor of food actually depends only in small part on our taste receptors. Much of the sensation is produced by other factors—warmth, cold, the consistency of the food, the mild pain caused by certain spices, and above all smell. The next time your nose is stuffed up by a cold, notice that your meals seem almost tasteless.

Unlike the receptors for vision and hearing, the taste receptors are more or less out in the open. If you examine your tongue in a mirror, you will notice that it is covered with little bumps, some very tiny, others a bit larger. Inside these bumps, a few of which are also found at the back of the mouth and in the throat, are the *taste buds,* which contain the receptors for the sense of taste. Each bump contains about 245 taste buds, and each taste bud contains about 20 receptors sensitive to chemical stimulation by food molecules. Food dissolved in saliva spreads over the tongue, enters small pores in the surface of the bumps, and sets off reactions in the receptors. These reactions trigger activity in adjacent neurons, which fire off nervous impulses toward the brain.

The taste receptors, as the pattern theory suggests, appear to be broadly tuned to respond to many kinds of chemical stimulation. But they seem to respond most vigorously to four basic taste qualities—some to stimuli that are sweet, others to stimuli that are sour, salty, or bitter. The receptors

A coffee tester depends on both the sense of taste and the sense of smell.

that are especially sensitive to sweetness are concentrated near the tip of the tongue, those most sensitive to sour stimuli at the sides toward the rear.

Some organisms seem to have a different sense of taste from the human kind. One species of butterfly, for example, has been found to have receptors sensitive to two different kinds of saltiness—both to the sodium contained in common table salt and to potassium (11). Cats do not seem to be sensitive to sweetness and show no fondness for candy. Dogs usually like candy, and horses seem to prefer a lump of sugar to anything else.

Smell

The receptors for the sense of smell, as shown in Figure 7-10, lie at the very top of the nasal passages leading from the nostrils to the throat. As we breathe normally, the flow of air from nostrils to throat takes a direct path, as the figure indicates, but a certain amount rises gently to touch the smell receptors. The receptors are sensitive only to gases and to substances that become dissolved in the moisture of the air much as sugar dissolves in water. The air contains molecules of various chemical substances—gases, liquids, and even solids dissolved in moisture—and the receptors are sensitive to some of them. Very little is known about how the molecules stimulate the receptors. Perhaps the molecules create a chemical reaction. Perhaps the receptors respond in some way to the shapes of the molecules—like locks activated by keys of a certain type.

The skin senses

The receptors for the skin senses are nerve endings scattered throughout the body, just under the sur-

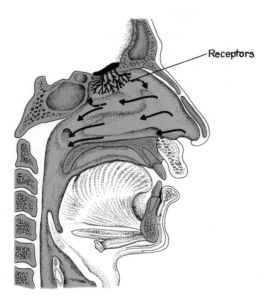

7-10 The nose and its receptors
This cross section of the human head shows the position of the receptors for the sense of smell, at the very top of the nasal passages. The arrows indicate how some of the air we breathe rises to touch the receptors.

face. They are sensitive to four basic types of stimulation—pressure, pain, cold, and warmth. As with the other senses, the sensation they produce appears to depend on the pattern of nervous impulses set off by a number of broadly tuned nerve endings. Indeed manipulation of the pattern can fool us into experiencing a sensation that is totally at odds with the actual stimulation. This has been demonstrated with the device illustrated in Figure 7-11. When cool water is passed through both coils, the device feels cool to the touch. When warm water is passed through both coils, it feels warm. But when one coil is warm and the other is cool, the device produces a sensation of heat—so great that anyone who grasps it immediately pulls

away. Somehow the pattern of nervous impulses set up by this kind of stimulation completely fools the sense of touch.

Nerve endings that contribute to the sensation of pain are found not only in the skin but also in our muscles and internal organs. Indeed some of the most excruciating pains come from muscle cramps or from distention of the intestines by gas. Yet the receptors in most of the internal organs do not respond to stimuli that would cause pain if applied to the skin. The intestines, for example, can be cut or even burned without arousing any sensation of pain.

It was recently discovered that there seem to be two different kinds of nerve fibers whose impulses, when they arrive at the upper part of the brain, result in sensations of pain. One kind is responsible

**7-11 When you touch
this harmless coil, watch out!**
This device can fool the skin senses in startling fashion. The colored and gray coils are completely separate and can be connected to different sources of water. The surprising result described in the text is obtained by running cool water through one coil and pleasantly warm water through the other.

for sharp, localized pain, such as the sensation produced when you cut a finger. The other is responsible for duller, more generalized pain, such as the sensations produced by a headache or stomachache (12).

Although pain seems to be one of the crosses we must bear, it actually serves a purpose. Without the warning given us by pain, we might hold our hands in a flame until the tissues were destroyed or cut off a finger while peeling an apple. Even the pain of headache, which cannot be attributed to any specific outside stimulus, is probably a warning that we have subjected ourselves to too much physical or psychological strain. By forcing us to slow down or even take a day off, the headache takes us away from a situation that, if continued, might cause some serious damage to the tissues of our bodies or to our mental stability.

The two forgotten senses

In addition to the five senses just described, there are two others that are generally ignored but equally important in enabling us to function. The reason they are not usually thought of as senses is that they bring us information not about the world but about ourselves. Without this information, however, we would be helpless. We would not be able to perform all the delicate body movements required to move through our daily lives. We would have trouble walking or even keeping our balance.

Bodily movement

To appreciate the first of these two forgotten senses, try this: Close your eyes. Now point your index finger up toward the ceiling, next down toward the floor, off toward the right, and finally off toward the left. Now stand up, still with your eyes closed, raise your left knee, and touch the knee with your right hand.

You had no trouble—did you? And what you did may not seem at all remarkable, for it is an accomplishment that you take for granted. But think about it. How did you know where your arm was to begin with, and how did you know when you had moved it so that your finger was pointing up, down, or to the sides? How did you know where your left knee was and how to move your right hand to touch it?

None of your five senses helped you do this. They had no way of telling you about the position of your arms and legs and could only verify the fact, through the pressure receptors of the skin, that you had actually succeeded in finding and touching your knee. You could never have done what you did without the *sense of bodily movement*, which keeps us constantly informed of the position and movement of our muscles and bones.

The receptors for the sense of bodily movement are nerve endings found in three parts of the body. The first are in the muscles, and they are stimulated when the muscles stretch. The second are in the tendons that connect the muscles to the bones; they are stimulated when the muscles contract, putting pressure on the tendons. The third, and apparently most important, are in the linings of the joints between the bones, and they are stimulated by movement of the joints.

Without these receptors, walking would be a

problem. We would have to keep constant watch with our eyes to help guide the motions of our legs and feet. Even with the help of our eyes we could never perform the rapid and closely coordinated movements required to dance or to play baseball.

Equilibrium

The second forgotten sense accounts for some other accomplishments that we take for granted. When we walk, we have no trouble staying erect rather than at an angle to the ground. When we lose our footing and start to fall, we catch our balance through reflex action, without even thinking about it. Standing in a closed elevator and unable to see any motion, we nonetheless know when we start to move and whether we are moving up or down, and we also know when we stop. If we sat blindfolded in a totally silent swivel chair, we

would know immediately when someone began to rotate the chair.

All these abilities depend on our *sense of equilibrium,* which operates through receptors found in the inner ear. If you look back at Figure 7-9, you will see that the cochlea, containing the hearing receptors, is only one part of the inner ear. The rest is made up of three *semicircular canals* that extend out from a passageway called the *vestibule.* The canals and vestibule are filled with fluid and equipped with hairlike receptors for the sense of equilibrium.

Because of the angles at which the three semicircular canals are arranged, movement of the head in any direction creates movement of the fluid in at least two of them, stimulating the receptors they contain. The receptors in the vestibule operate in a different fashion. They are matted together, and tiny pieces of stonelike crystal are embedded in the mattings. The little crystals are heavy enough to be pulled downward by the force of gravity, and

This stunt would be impossible without the human sense of equilibrium.

this downward pull creates a pressure that stimulates the receptors. Thus the receptors in the vestibule keep us aware of being upright even when we are not moving.

Between them, the receptors of the vestibule and of the canals constantly monitor the position of the head and any change in position, providing the messages needed to keep us in balance and oriented to the force of gravity. If we start to fall, information from these receptors enables us to regain our equilibrium quickly.

Perhaps the most dramatic evidence of how the sense of equilibrium operates is an old experiment performed with a lobster—chosen because its equivalent of the human inner ear is readily accessible when the lobster sheds its shell. For the stones that are the lobster's equivalent of the crystals in the human vestibule, the experimenters substituted iron filings. These worked just as well as the stones, and the lobster had no problem of equilibrium. But when a magnet was placed above the lobster, exerting a stronger upward force on the iron filings than the downward force of gravity, the lobster turned right over on its back.

(Summary begins on page 276.)

Postscript

Light waves, color vision, and the visual neurons

Light waves, as was said earlier, are very similar to waves of X-rays, radio and television waves, and electricity. All are forms of electromagnetic radiation, though the waves show an immense variation in length. As you will see in Figure 7-12, measurable electromagnetic waves can be as small as the gamma rays emitted by certain radioactive substances, which are only one 100,000,000,000,000th of a meter in length. At the other extreme, the waves of electricity are 100,000,000 meters long.

The visible spectrum of light waves ranges from about 370 billionths of a meter to about 750 billionths of a meter. Violet waves, which are the shortest, are just a little bit longer than the invisible ultraviolet rays that cause sunburn. Red waves, which are the longest, are just a little bit shorter than the invisible infrared waves produced by a heating lamp. The cones of the eye are capable of responding in one way or another to all the wave lengths in the visible spectrum, though some of the cones show the greatest response to the shorter waves of violet-blue, others to the longer waves of yellow and red, and still others to the green waves that lie in between.

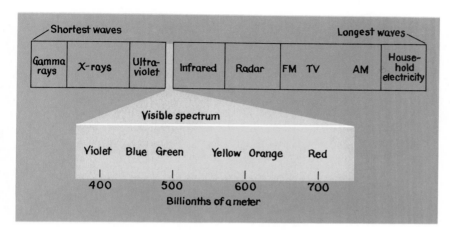

7-12
Electromagnetic radiation and the visible spectrum
Various forms of electromagnetic radiation range from gamma rays, the shortest waves, to ordinary alternating current electricity, the longest waves. The visible spectrum of light occupies only a small portion of the band.

Adding and subtracting colors

To understand more fully how the sense of vision operates, it helps to know what happens to our sensations when various wavelengths in the visual spectrum are mixed—and what happens is not at all what everyday experiences would indicate. For example, every schoolchild who owns a paint set knows that if you have no green, you can produce it by combining blue and yellow. But every schoolchild is wrong. Mixing blue and yellow paints does not *combine* the two colors. It does something very different.

This may sound startling, but there is a simple explanation. Blue paint looks blue because it absorbs most of the wavelengths found in the white light provided by sunshine or artificial illumination. It reflects only the waves in and around the violet-blue portion of the spectrum, including, since no paint is a pure blue, some of the green waves. Yellow paint absorbs most of the wavelengths of white light except those in and around the yellow part of the spectrum, again including some of the

green waves. When you put blue and yellow paint together, you get a mixture that absorbs all the wavelengths of the spectrum except the greenish ones that both the paints happen to reflect. But this is not combining light waves. It is more like subtracting them.

Adding light waves together cannot be done with paint, but only with special equipment. One way is to use color filters that permit only waves of a certain length to get through, like a fairly pure violet-blue and a fairly pure yellow. When two slide projectors are equipped with different filters, two wavelengths can be thrown on the same white screen and thus actually mixed. The results are as shown in Figure 7-13. Note that the combination of violet-blue and yellow light waves produces not green but a neutral gray.

The laws of color mixture—the true blending of light waves, not the mixture of paints—are summarized in Figure 7-14, where the visible spectrum is arranged in a circle. The combination of any two waves opposite each other in the circle produces gray—and such opposites are known as *comple-*

7-13

What happens when light waves are combined
The circles show what happens when two colors are projected through filters onto the same screen. In the case of combining violet-blue and yellow light waves, note that the result is far different from the result of mixing blue and yellow paints. Note also that the combination of red and green wavelengths produces yellow.

mentary colors because they cancel each other out. Two waves not opposite each other combine into the sensation of a hue somewhere between them in the circle.

Two famous old theories of color vision

What happens when colors are truly combined led to the formulation more than a century ago of a theory of color vision that occupies a justly famous place in psychological history. This is the *Young-Helmholtz theory,* which has held up remarkably well although it was proposed at a time when little was known about the chemistry of the visual receptors or the transmission of nervous impulses from retina to brain.

Young and Helmholtz held that all our sensations of hue were produced by just three types of color receptors: for red, green, and blue. The sensation of yellow, which had no receptor of its own, was produced by simultaneous stimulation of the red and green receptors, just as a yellow hue can be created by combining red and green light waves.

As was explained earlier, it is now known that the retina indeed contains three types of cones. To this extent, the Young-Helmholtz theory has proved correct. However, all three types are more broadly tuned than the theory suggested. Moreover, the type that responds to red wavelengths responds even more strongly to yellow.

Another early attempt to explain color vision was the *Hering theory,* also famous in psychological history. Hering suggested that the visual system

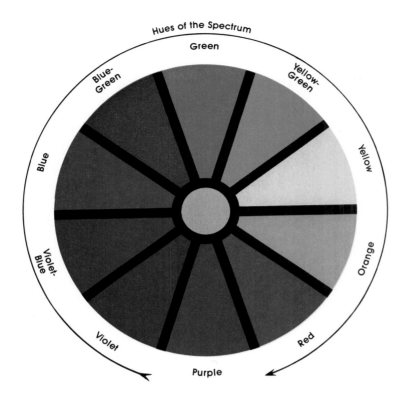

Hues of the Spectrum

Green

Blue-Green

Yellow-Green

Blue

Yellow

Violet-Blue

Orange

Violet

Red

Purple

A circular guide to the hues

The laws of color mixture can be summarized by bending the spectrum into an incomplete circle, as shown here, and filling the gap with purple—a color that does not exist as a light wave in its own right but is nonetheless seen as a distinct hue when the violet waves at the low end of the spectrum are combined with the red waves at the upper end. To find what hue a combination of any two wavelengths will produce, draw a line between them. If the line passes through the center of the circle, the result will look gray. If not, the result will be a hue midway between the wavelengths that are combined.

must somehow operate on the basis of nervous messages paired as black-white, red-green, and blue-yellow. This would account for the phenomenon of *afterimages,* which are demonstrated in Figure 7-15. (Experiment with the illustration, according to the instructions, before you go on to the next paragraph.)

What happens when you look at Figure 7-15 is this: By staring fixedly at the pattern of colors, you provide a prolonged stimulus to the receptors in the retina and the neurons that carry their messages to the brain. When the stimulus is then withdrawn (as you transfer your gaze to another part of the page) you see an afterimage that is in complementary hues to the original stimulus. If you follow the instructions carefully, this afterimage should be so vivid as to startle you—if not on the first try, at least

after you have made a few practice attempts.

Actually, although this is difficult to show except under laboratory conditions, there are two afterimages. Immediately after the stimulus is withdrawn you see a *positive afterimage,* in the same color as before. But this quickly vanishes and is replaced by a longer-lasting *negative afterimage,* in which the complementary colors appear.

Hering's theory of visual pairs suggests an explanation. Activity in the red-green pair, for example, would be stimulated in one direction by the greenish stripes in Figure 7-15. This activity would continue for an instant after the stimulus was removed, accounting for the positive afterimage. Then the complementary sensation would be produced as the red-green pair acted in the opposite direction as it returned to normal, so to speak.

7-15 The afterimage comes to modern art

This modern painting uses the principle of the afterimage to create a startling effect. To experience it, stare at the top rectangle for about half a minute, fixing your eyes on the white spot in the center. Then shift your eyes quickly to concentrate on the dark spot in the lower rectangle. The painting, *Flags*, is by Jasper Johns, 1965, and is from the artist's collection.

The new opponent-process theory

Scientists today have methods, unknown in the time of Young, Helmholtz, and Hering, of investigating the chemical activity in individual receptors of the retina and the impulses in individual neurons that carry messages from the retina toward the visual center of the brain. These new techniques indicate that, just as the Young-Helmholtz theory was substantially correct about the three types of receptors, the Hering theory was right about the neurons.

Between the receptors and the brain's visual area lies a complicated pathway of nerve fibers that process messages from the rods and cones and send them along upward. The pathway begins in the retina itself, which contains many interconnecting nerve cells, and includes a major processing and relay station in the thalamus. Among all these nerve cells there appear to be four kinds concerned with color vision, each behaving in a different way in response to different stimuli reaching the eye. One shows a burst of activity when the stimulus is red but is turned off by a green stimulus. Another shows a high rate of activity when the stimulus is green, a low rate when the stimulus is red. The third type is activated by blue and slowed down by yellow, the fourth type activated by yellow and slowed down by blue. There are also two other kinds of nerve cells that appear to be responsible for black-and-white vision and sensations of brightness. One is turned on by white or bright stimuli and turned off by black or dark stimuli. The other works in exactly the opposite fashion and is turned on by dark stimuli (13).

Because of these on-and-off pairings of activity in the neurons, the current explanation of vision is known as the *opponent-process* theory. It is of course a pattern theory. A visual stimulus sets up a pattern of chemical response in the rods and the three kinds of cones in the retina. This pattern in turn stimulates the neurons of the visual system into their own pattern of nervous activity, with the six opponent-process cells for red-green, blue-yellow, and bright-dark all behaving in different ways. It is this total pattern of nervous impulses, arriving at the visual centers of the brain, that determines what we see.

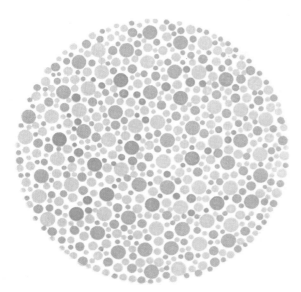 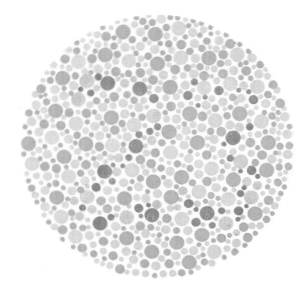

7-16

A test of color blindness

What numbers, if any, do you see in the circles? People with normal color vision see a 92 at the left and a 23 at the right. People with various types of color blindness see something different: only partial numbers or no numbers at all.

Color blindness

The opponent-process theory explains why we can see hues such as greenish-yellow but never experience a sensation such as greenish-red. The different nerve cells activated by green and yellow can operate at the same time—but the neurons for green and red are off for one of the two colors when they are on for the other. The theory also explains afterimages and color blindness, a visual deficiency that affects about 1.5 million Americans.

For a test of color blindness, look at the two circles in Figure 7-16 and note what numbers you see in them, if any. Then read the caption to determine what the test tells about your vision. If you yourself have passed the test, try showing it to some friends, especially male friends. You should soon come to someone who fails the test—and, when you do, you will have an experience that is worth going to some trouble to obtain. It seems almost unbelievable that you can clearly see one number, while someone else clearly sees another number or is absolutely sure that there is no number at all.

The reason for picking male friends for the test is that far more men than women suffer from color blindness. Only about one woman in a thousand is color blind, but about seven men in a hundred have some form of this visual defect. Total color blindness, in which the world is seen only in shades of gray, like a black-and-white photograph, is extremely rare—probably limited to only about 5,000 people in the entire United States. The most common form involves a difficulty in distinguishing between reds and greens. Less common is an inability to distinguish blues and yellows. These red-green and blue-yellow problems suggest an abnormality in some of the opponent-process nerve cells.

The retina's rich network of neurons

The retina, within its small area, is equipped not only to respond to light waves but also to start processing the information picked up by its receptors. Besides its rods and cones, it contains many millions of neurons that are connected and interconnected into an elaborate network. Some idea of the network's intricacy can be gained from Figure 7-17, though the diagram is only a simplified representation of the actual complexity.

The network acts as a sort of funnel between the retina's receptors and the optic nerve that carries messages from eyes to brain. The receptors, as was said earlier, number about 127,000,000. But there are only about 1,000,000 *ganglion cells* whose fibers make up the optic nerve. To channel information from the receptors into only 1/127th as many neuron fibers, the network must perform a good deal of processing and interpretation. It acts very much as if it were a little brain in its own right—picking up information from the rods and cones, condensing the information, and creating meaningful patterns of nervous impulses that are sent along to the cerebral cortex.

Variations in the network, sensitivity, and acuity

Although the network always exhibits the general form shown in Figure 7-17, it varies in structure at different parts of the retina. At the outer part of the retina, where rods predominate, a single ganglion

cell may be fed information from as many as several thousand receptors. Thus the outer part of the retina is most sensitive to low intensities of light, as you can observe for yourself by finding a very dim star in the skies at night. If you look directly at the star, so that its light waves fall at the center or fovea of the retina, it will disappear. But if you glance at it from the side, so that its waves fall on the outer part of the retina, you will see it again. One or more ganglion cells serving the outer part of the retina—and picking up messages from thousands of rods

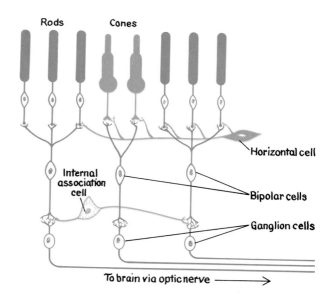

7-17 The retina's processing apparatus

This is a simplified diagram of the elaborate network through which activity in the rods and cones is funneled to the optic nerve leading to the brain. Activity in the receptors stimulates tiny neurons called *bipolar cells,* which connect to the *ganglion cells* of the optic nerve. Interconnection is provided by *horizontal cells* and *internal association cells.* The network is so constructed that some ganglion cells are affected by activity in only a few receptors, while others are fed information from several thousand receptors. The number of possible patterns of stimulation created in the optic nerve is almost beyond imagination.

—has gathered in enough stimulation through the network to fire off a message to the brain.

The greater sensitivity to light at the outer part of the retina, however, is accompanied by a considerable loss of sharpness of vision, or *acuity*. The message sent to the brain by the ganglion cell could have originated in the stimulation of any one of the thousands of receptors it serves. Therefore the exact spot at which the retina was stimulated and the exact nature of the stimulus cannot be specified (14).

At the fovea, the network takes a very different form. The ganglion cells serving the densely packed cones in this part of the retina get messages from only a few receptors. Moreover, each cone in the fovea activates several different ganglion cells, each of which compares the information coming from this and other cones and thus extracts different kinds of information from the different patterns of stimulation it receives. Thus acuity is greatest at the fovea. When you read or do anything else that requires a very sharp image, you automatically focus your eyes so that the light waves fall directly on the fovea. Because fewer receptors feed into each ganglion cell—and because each ganglion cell is stimulated in different ways by a number of receptors—the ganglion cells at the fovea can send along precise messages about the exact part of the retina that has been stimulated and by what kinds of object.

Sound waves, loudness, and locating sounds

Sound waves, the stimulus for hearing, are roughly analogous to the waves on water. When you throw a stone into a quiet pond, waves start to radiate out. It looks as if the water is moving away from the stone, forming circles of ever-increasing size. Actually, as you can tell if there are some leaves floating on the surface, this is not true. The leaves stay in the same spot and merely bob up and down.

What happens is this: When the stone hits the surface, it puts pressure on the water. The surface is pushed down, then rises again, and in so doing passes the pressure along to the adjoining water. The falling and rising motions continue outward in ever-widening circles, with the ripples getting smaller and smaller as the pressure of the stone's impact is absorbed.

So it is with sound waves in the air. When you hit a note on a piano, the string vibrates. As it moves, it compresses the air ahead of its movement, just as an accordion player compresses the air inside the instrument by pressing the ends together. As the piano string vibrates in the other direction, it expands the air behind it and creates a partial vacuum, just as the accordion player does by pulling the ends of the instrument apart. These alternations of compression and expansion are passed along through the air like the waves on the pond, growing weaker and weaker until at last they disappear. Sound waves do not blow past you like a gust of wind. The air may be perfectly motionless, like the pond water, except for the ripples of compression and expansion.

For this woman on a subway platform, the decibel level has risen too high for comfort.

Measurements of loudness

The human ear, in people whose hearing is sharpest, is capable of responding to sound waves ranging in frequency from about 20 cycles per second, the lowest pitch we can hear, to about 20,000, the highest. We are most sensitive, however, to the frequencies between 400 and 3,000, which is about the range of the human voice. Frequencies higher or lower than that do not sound as loud even when they have exactly the same amplitude. If we listen to waves of the same amplitude at 100, 1,000, and 10,000 per second, the middle wave sounds the loudest. The low note sounds the weakest, and the high note falls in between.

Though our hearing is least sensitive to the low frequencies, these are the very ones used by the foghorns on ships at sea. The reason is that sound waves of low frequency travel much farther than waves of high frequency. High-frequency waves are absorbed faster by the air through which they travel and by any objects that get in their way, while low-frequency waves travel on and on. The next time you hear a band playing in the distance—as when a parade is approaching or when you are driving toward a football stadium—notice that it is the tubas you hear rather than the flutes.

A familiar measure of amplitude is the *decibel*, and the decibel scale is shown in Figure 7-18. You will note, of course, that this is not an absolute scale. A clap of thunder at 120 decibels is far more than twice as loud as conversation at 60 decibels. But it is an ingenious scale (of the type mathematicians call logarithmic) that condenses the entire range of possible amplitudes of sound into meaningful numbers. Sound-sensitive devices that give readings expressed in decibels can be used to measure everything from the applause at television shows to the effectiveness of a sound-absorbent ceiling in reducing the noise level in a business

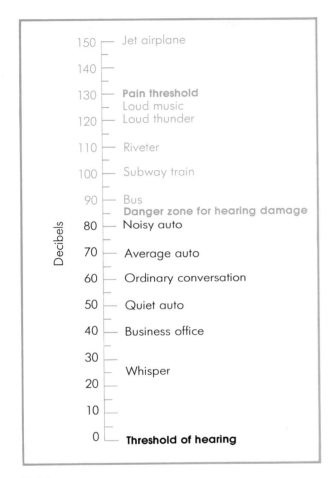

7-18 Decibel scale of loudness
The zero point on the decibel scale is set at the absolute threshold of hearing, and from there the readings go up to the neighborhood of 60 decibels for the sound of ordinary conversation, around 120 for a clap of thunder, and 150 for the noise of a jet airplane engine (15, 16).

office. An absolute scale of amplitude would have to use numbers going all the way up to 500,000, for the smallest amplitude we can hear is just about 1/500,000 as great as the largest amplitude.

How do you know where the sound comes from?

If someone sitting behind you coughs, you know immediately where the sound comes from; you may turn in that direction without even thinking. If you hear an automobile pass by, unseen, you can tell at once in which direction it is moving. Something about the sound waves and the manner in which they stimulate your hearing receptors tells you where they come from and in what direction they are moving.

A general explanation of how the ears determine the location of sounds has been provided by the device illustrated in Figure 7-19—a set of earphones that capture the sound waves at the left ear and transfer them to the right ear, while transferring the waves that would ordinarily reach the right ear to the left. If you were wearing this device, a car

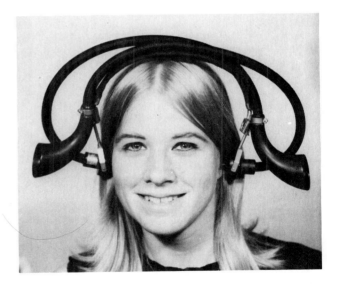

7-19 A device that fools the ears
The strange gadget is a pseudophone, which reverses the way sound waves strike the two ears. For what happens to a person who wears the device, see the text.

passing outside from your left to your right would sound as if it were moving in the opposite direction, from right to left.

The device demonstrates that our ability to determine the location of sounds depends on differences in the ways our two ears are stimulated. But the nature of the differences is not entirely understood. Presumably one clue is the fact that sound waves coming from the left strike the left ear a tiny fraction of a second before they strike the right ear. Moreover, the waves reaching the right ear have been slightly modified as they traveled around the head, with high-frequency waves being affected the most because they are more likely to be absorbed by any object that gets in their path. The waves at the right ear also have slightly less amplitude because they have traveled a little farther.

Another important clue seems to depend on the structure of the outer ear, which has an intricate shape that bounces sound waves around in complex ways much as the walls and furniture in a room affect the music coming from a stereo set. The two outer ears, receiving waves from different directions and of slightly different timing, reflect them toward the ear drum in different ways.

In one way or another, the receptors in the two ears receive a slightly different pattern of stimulation and send along slightly different patterns of nervous impulses toward the brain, which can usually make an instant judgment about the location of the sound. Even so, we are probably not so skillful at locating sounds as are animals with movable outer ears—like dogs and horses that prick their ears when curious about a noise.

Summary

1 The senses keep us informed about the world and provide the input essential to learning, memory, and other psychological processes.
2 The two requirements for sensation are (1) a *stimulus,* or form of energy impinging on the body, and (2) a *receptor,* or nerve ending capable of responding to that particular stimulus.
3 To activate a sensory receptor, a stimulus must be above the *absolute threshold,* or minimum amount of energy required to make the receptor respond. The absolute threshold is affected by *adaptation,* or tendency of all receptors to stop responding to a continued steady level of stimulation.
4 To be distinguished as different, two stimuli must vary by more than the *difference threshold,* also called *just noticeable difference,* or *j.n.d.* for short.
5 The stimulus for vision is light waves, a pulsating form of electromagnetic energy. Light waves vary in *wavelength, intensity,* and *complexity.* Wavelength determines *hue,* which is the term for the sensation produced by a colored object. Intensity determines *brightness* (though not entirely). Complexity determines *saturation,* or the sensation of a vivid or muddy hue. White light is a mixture of all the wavelengths, as can be demonstrated by passing it through a prism and obtaining a *spectrum* of the hues.

6 Light waves enter the eyeball through the *pupil,* which is an opening in the *iris.* They then pass through a transparent *lens,* which is changed in shape by the *ciliary muscles* to focus the waves sharply on the *retina* at the back of the eyeball. The retina contains the receptors for vision—nerve endings called *rods* and *cones.*

7 The rods function chiefly under low illumination and send information to the brain about movements and about whites, grays, and blacks but not about color. The rods contain *visual purple,* a chemical that is bleached by light.

8 The cones function in strong illumination and send information to the brain about not only movement and brightness but about color. The cones are most numerous at the *fovea,* or center of the retina, which is where vision is sharpest. There are three kinds of cones, containing chemical substances most sensitive to wavelengths of either blue-violet, green, or red and yellow.

9 The *pattern theory* holds that visual sensations are produced by the total pattern of nervous impulses set off by the rods and cones, modified by some of the neurons in the pathway from eye to brain, and eventually delivered to the visual area of the cerebral cortex. The theory maintains that all the senses operate in this fashion—with receptors that are broadly tuned rather than specifically designed to respond to a single type of stimulation.

10 When the eye is completely adjusted to dark conditions, its absolute threshold declines to the point where it can respond to a stimulus with only 1/100,000th of the intensity required in bright sunlight. At low intensities only the rods function, and color vision is absent. The cones have a much higher absolute threshold.

11 When we look at an object, our eyes make a series of scanning movements, focusing first on one part, then on another, then on still another. Our visual impressions resemble the creation of a mosaic, formed by the brain from a very rapid succession of these fragmentary bits of information from the eyes.

12 The stimulus for hearing is sound waves, which are ripples of expansion and compression of the air. Sound waves vary in *frequency, amplitude,* and *complexity.* The frequency determines our sensation of *pitch.* Amplitude determines *loudness* (though not entirely). Complexity determines *timbre.*

13 Sound waves are collected by the *outer ear,* or visible part. The waves create vibrations of the *eardrum,* which are then passed along by the three bones of the *middle ear* to the *cochlea* of the *inner ear.* In the cochlea, the vibrations set up complicated wavelike motions of the *basilar membrane.* These motions activate the hairlike receptors of hearing, which are in the *organ of Corti,* lying on the basilar membrane.

14 The receptors for taste lie mostly in the *taste buds* of the tongue. They are broadly tuned to respond to chemical stimulation—but there are four types especially sensitive to either sweet, sour, salty, or bitter.

15 The receptors for smell lie at the top of the nasal passage leading from the nostrils to the throat. They are sensitive to gases and to substances that become dissolved in the moisture of the air.

16 The receptors for the skin senses are nerve endings lying just beneath the surface. They account for our sensations of pressure, pain, cold, and warmth.

17 In addition to the so-called five senses just mentioned, there are two others. The *sense of bodily movement* keeps us informed of the position of our muscles and bones and is essential to such complex movements as walking. The receptors are nerve endings in the muscles, tendons, and joints. The *sense of equilibrium* keeps us in balance and oriented to the force of gravity. The receptors are hairlike nerve cells in the inner ear's *vestibule* and three *semicircular canals*.

Postscript

18 Light waves occupy a small portion of the range of electromagnetic radiation, which extends from gamma rays (the shortest) to household electricity (the longest). Violet waves are a little longer than the invisible ultraviolet waves that cause sunburn. Red waves are slightly shorter than the invisible infrared waves produced by a heating lamp.

19 Two famous old explanations of color vision are the *Young-Helmholtz theory* and the *Hering theory*. The generally accepted explanation today, combining elements of both old theories, is the *opponent-process theory*.

20 The opponent-process theory holds that the pathway of neurons from the visual receptors to the visual area of the brain contains six different types of neurons. One type shows a burst of activity when the receptors respond to a red stimulus but is lowered in activity when the receptors respond to a green stimulus. Another type does exactly the opposite. It is turned on by a green stimulus but turned off by a red stimulus. Another pair of neurons responds in opposite ways to a blue or yellow stimulus. Another responds in opposite ways to white (or brightness) and black (or darkness). The total pattern of nervous impulses—activated by the response of the rods and cones to a stimulus, then carried to the visual area of the brain over a pathway containing the six types of neurons—accounts for our visual sensations.

21 Processing of information picked up by the rods and cones begins in the retina, which contains an elaborate network of neurons. This network acts as a sort of funnel, channeling information from the 127,000,000 rods and cones into the mere 1,000,000 *ganglion cells* whose fibers make up the optic nerve.

22 The amplitude of sound waves is measured on a *decibel scale* of loudness.

23 Our ability to know which direction a sound comes from depends on the fact that the hearing receptors in the two ears receive a slightly different pattern of stimulation and send slightly different patterns of nervous impulses to the brain.

Important terms

absolute threshold
adaptation
amplitude
basilar membrane
blind spot
bodily movement
brightness
ciliary muscles
cochlea
complexity
cones
difference threshold
eardrum
equilibrium

fovea
frequency
hue
inner ear
intensity
iris
just noticeable difference
lens
middle ear
organ of Corti
outer ear
overtones
pattern theory

pitch
pupil
receptor
retina
rods
saturation
semicircular canals
stimulus
taste buds
timbre
vestibule
visual purple
wavelength

Postscript

afterimage (positive, negative)
complementary colors
decibel scale
ganglion cell

Hering theory
opponent-process theory
optic nerve
Young-Helmholtz theory

Recommended readings

Carterette, E. C., and Friedman, M. P., eds. *Handbook of perception,* Vol. IV *(Hearing)* and Vol. V *(Seeing).* New York: Academic Press, 1975 and 1978.

Hochberg, J. *Perception,* 2d ed. Englewood Cliffs, N.J.: Prentice-Hall, 1978.

Kaufman, L. *Perception: the world transformed.* New York: Oxford University Press, 1979.

Lindsay, P. H., and Norman, D. A. *Human information processing,* 2d ed. New York: Academic Press, 1977.

Ludel, J. *Introduction to sensory processes.* San Francisco: Freeman, 1978.

Outline

Chapter eight

Perception: the science of first impressions

As you sit reading the start of this new chapter, something truly remarkable is going on inside you. Though you are not aware of it, your central nervous system is being bombarded by an almost hopeless jumble of messages from the outside world. The rods and cones in your eyes are responding to a bewildering number of light waves of many kinds and intensities. They are stimulated by the white space on the page and by a host of little black lines, curves, squiggles, and dots that make up the letters and words. The nerve endings at the outer part of the retina receive light waves from the walls and furniture, perhaps the movement of other people in the room, a curtain blowing, a car visible through a window as it passes down the street.

Your ears are registering the presence of many sounds—perhaps the complicated waves of music from a radio, perhaps people talking in the room and the noise of traffic outside. Your nose may smell something cooking or the odor of fresh paint or of peanuts that someone is eating nearby. Your skin senses are telling your central nervous system about the pressure of your hands against the book, your body against your chair, perhaps a cool breeze blowing across your cheeks.

In terms of the stimuli reaching your sense organs at any given moment, the world is a baffling place, containing an endless variety of constantly shifting light and sound waves, odors, pressures, heat, and cold. Your own body adds to the confusion by sending its own messages to your brain—perhaps the information that you are getting hungry, thirsty, or sleepy, or that you are starting to get a headache. If you were an electronics engineer, how would you possibly go about designing a computer that could accept these inputs all at once and make any sense out of them?

Yet you yourself are having no trouble. The meaning of the various squiggles on the page leaps instantly into your consciousness. You are not bothered at all by the other light waves reaching your eyes or by the stimuli affecting your ears and skin senses—unless, of course, they become so intense as to distract you from the book.

It happens all the time. We take it for granted. Yet the way we manage to make sense out of the barrage of stimuli constantly supplied by the environment is one of the miracles of how we function as human beings. Somehow or other, out of all this stimulation of our sense organs, we manage to be aware almost instantly and without any conscious effort of what is important. We pay attention to some of it and disregard the rest. When reading we quickly grasp the meaning of the light waves that come to us from a printed page. When moving about in the world we immediately adjust to what is happening. If a car approaches we know without thinking how far away it is, how fast it is going, and what we must do to get out of its way. In the noisiest room we respond immediately to the call of our name. When someone talks to us our hearing receptors are under a rapid-fire onslaught of 600 to 720 sounds and pauses every minute—far too many to be remembered individually. Yet we have no trouble understanding what is said (1).

The marvels and mystery of perception

The key to these remarkable accomplishments is *perception*, which can be defined as *the process through which we become aware of our environment by selecting, organizing, and interpreting the evidence from our senses.* The world around us provides the evidence by stimulating our sense organs. The sense organs pass the messages along to the central nervous system. There the process of perception manages quickly and effortlessly to extract from all the miscellaneous and potentially confusing stimulation the information that is important to us (2).

Without our skills at perception we would be in deep trouble. Suppose you had to stop to think about and analyze every message your eyes send to your brain. That patch of blue light waves coming from somewhere up ahead—is it an automobile or something else? Is it moving? How fast and in what direction? Is it a threat or can you ignore it?

How fast could you read if you had to figure out each time that a vertical line with a little horizontal dash across it is a *t*, a vertical line with a curve an *h*, a partial circle with a horizontal line across it an *e*—and that a combination of *t*, *h*, and *e* means *the*?

But you do not have to stop to think. You perceive the automobile or the word *the* without even trying. Undoubtedly the process requires considerable work by the central nervous system, but the work takes place quickly and effortlessly. In fact in most cases you cannot help perceiving what you do, even if you make a deliberate effort, because perception is a process over which we have little conscious control.

Perception and survival

Our perceptions of the world are not always in accord with the facts. For example, you may have had the experience, when riding along a highway, of being sure you saw a dead dog at the side of the road—only to discover, as you got closer, that it was just a piece of rumpled cloth. Your perceptual process, in its effort to make sense out of the visual stimulation reaching your eyes, signaled *dog* when in fact there was no dog at all. Students of perception have shown that we can be fooled by many types of optical illusions, some of which are illustrated in Figure 8-1. Perceptual accuracy can also be affected during what are called altered states of consciousness (like those produced by hypnosis or drugs), as will be discussed in a chapter postscript.

Most of the time, however, your perceptions are in reasonable accord with the facts. They enable you to move about confidently, taking for granted that you know what is going on around you and will immediately become aware of any danger. Perception is one of the psychological abilities that have enabled the human race to survive. Had our ancestors not been able to recognize immediately the approach of an enemy—had they been forced to stop and analyze every nervous impulse from their eyes, then painstakingly piece together all these bits of information—they would never have lived through the prehistoric ages.

Perception of objects and people

The study of perception—or the attempt to unravel the mystery of how we arrive at all the quick and automatic first impressions that are so useful to us—was originally confined mostly to vision and hearing. Psychologists made many investigations of the kinds of light and sound waves that physical objects transmit to our senses and the manner in which we then process the sensory evidence into something meaningful. This line of inquiry continues and is significant for many aspects of our daily lives, as is explained in the box on Psychology and Society on page 284.

Recently the study of perception has taken on a new dimension—to include our first impressions not only of objects but also of people. Many psychologists are now interested in the manner in which, in all our social relationships, we size people up very quickly on the basis of their appearance, facial expressions, and gestures as well as their words. It has been found that we make immediate decisions about whether they are friendly or hostile and whether they are dominant or submissive toward

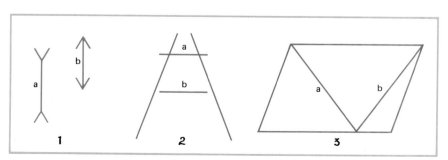

8-1
How good is your judgment of length?
Look at the three drawings carefully. In no. 1, which line is longer, *a* or *b*? In no. 2? In no. 3? After you have made your judgments, see the footnote on page 284 for the correct answers.

Psychology and Society

Perception, safety, and the motion picture industry

Perception is a field in which psychology offers many useful suggestions that can be applied to the everyday workings of society. Perhaps the most important is the prevention of accidents caused by some of the common errors that plague the workings of perception.

Airplane pilots, for example, were once the victims of what is called the *autokinetic illusion*—the fact that a spot of light, seen in darkness without any frame of reference, sometimes seems to move of its own accord. Pilots flying at night often had difficulty judging the position of a beacon light seen off in the distance or of another plane visible only by the lights on its wingtips and tail. Though the reasons for the autokinetic illusion are not completely understood, the problem was easily solved. You may have noted that beacons and the lights on airplanes now keep flashing on and off—thus greatly reducing the chance of error.

Automobile drivers sometimes encounter conditions that make it difficult to judge distance and speed or even to distinguish another vehicle from the background against which it is seen. Many automobile accidents occur at twilight, when visual perception is most subject to error. Ways of preventing such accidents are now a promising field of study.

Another perceptual illusion is the basis of the motion picture industry. This illusion is called *stroboscopic motion,* which is the apparent movement perceived when we look at a rapid succession of images that are actually stationary. The simplest form of such motion, called the *phi phenomenon,* is shown in the accompanying drawing, which represents two slits cut into a screen. When a light is flashed behind slit 1 and an instant later behind slit 2, the bar of light seems to move as indicated by the arrows. You have seen many advertising signs

us (4). We also form impressions of what emotions they are experiencing, their personality traits, and whether we find them attractive or unattractive (5).

Sometimes we even ascribe personality traits to people when all we have to go on is a photograph. This was demonstrated in an experiment in which subjects were asked to read a copy of a supposed conversation that could be interpreted in several

different ways. There was some question as to whether the first speaker was offering a bribe to the other person or simply being reassuring—or possibly even just being neutral and noncommittal, not saying anything of much importance. Along with a copy of the conversation the subjects received what they were told was a photograph of the first speaker. The kind of photograph that was shown to them was found to have a strong effect on their interpretation of the conversation. Looking at one kind of face they were prepared to believe the

In all the drawings in Figure 8-1, lines *a* and *b* are exactly the same length—though almost everyone perceives the *a* lines to be longer.

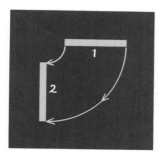

that seem to produce this kind of movement by means of stationary lights that flash on and off in rapid succession. In the movies stroboscopic motion is produced by a series of still photographs projected onto the screen. When you think you see a horse running full speed you actually get a brief glimpse of the horse at one point, then another glimpse when the horse has moved a little farther

along. Your perceptual processes fill in the gaps and you seem to see a continuous movement.

Animated cartoons are made by taking pictures of a series of drawings that have just the right amount of difference from one to the next—and are shown at just the right speed—to produce the illusion of smooth and constant motion. Many other effects in movies or on television—for example, a good part of *Star Wars*—stem from studies of how perception operates. Artists, fashion designers, and makeup experts are all skilled at creating perceptual illusions (3).

The study of perception is also useful in evaluating eyewitness accounts, such as reports of UFO sightings or courtroom testimony about crimes. Important here is the well-established fact, discussed later in the chapter, that two people looking at exactly the same event may perceive it in entirely different ways.

worst of the first speaker, at another kind to expect the best (6).

The study of how we perceive other people is still in its infancy, a promising field for psychologists of the future. It is of special importance because social relationships make up such a large part of our daily life. How we perceive others—and how they perceive us—affects our behavior in almost everything we do in school, on the job, in social gatherings, and in friendships and marriage. And our first impressions, as will be seen in Chapter 14 on Social

Psychology, have a strong and lasting effect on how we behave toward others.

The nature-nurture argument over perception

Like almost everything else in psychology, perception has been a battleground in the nature-nurture controversy. One side has argued that our inherited sensory and nervous equipment dictates our perceptions. Especially in the case of vision and hearing, the two senses that have been most widely studied and speculated about, this side has maintained that we respond as we were born to respond. Our eyes, for example, react to any given stimulus in a predetermined way. They send messages to the brain that create a predetermined impression. We see what our inherited nature makes us see when we look at that particular stimulus.

The nature theory is undoubtedly correct up to a point. Our nervous system is "wired" in a way that greatly affects our perceptions, as will be seen in a moment. But our perceptions also depend on many learned factors, such as previous experiences with various kinds of stimuli and our motives, emotional state, interests, and even personality in general.

The old nature-nurture argument is no longer an issue among most psychologists. They regard perception as resulting from a combination of the inherited wiring patterns of the human nervous system and many kinds of experience and learning. They look to both nature and nurture to explain how we form our first impressions by selecting, organizing, and interpreting the evidence of our senses.

The built-in wiring: the nervous system's feature detectors

One great advance in the study of perception was the discovery that the nervous systems of lower animals—and presumably of human beings as well—contain some specialized cells that seem to play an important part in reactions to the environment. The parts of the nervous system concerned with vision are apparently wired in such a way that they are quick to respond to movement and patterns. The parts concerned with hearing are wired in such a way that they are quick to respond to different pitches and to changes in pitch.

This finding was made by using delicate equip-

ment capable of measuring the activity of a single nerve cell. Tiny electrodes were planted on individual cells of monkeys or cats in the part of the brain to which the eyes send messages. The animals were placed in front of a screen on which various kinds of visual stimuli were flashed. It was found that some of the brain cells responded sharply to a vertical line on the screen but did not respond at all when the stimulus was a horizontal line (see Figure 8-2). Other cells responded to a horizontal line but not to a vertical line. Others responded to angles and still others to movement

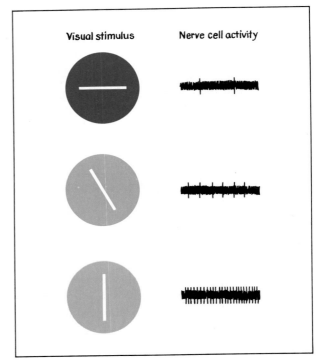

8-2 How a feature detector cell works

The spikes in the graph lines represent the activity of one of the feature detector cells in a cat's brain. In response to a horizontal line, the cell displays only its normal amount of spontaneous activity; to an oblique line, there is a small response; to a vertical line—the kind of feature to which this cell is specifically sensitive—there is a sharp burst of activity (7).

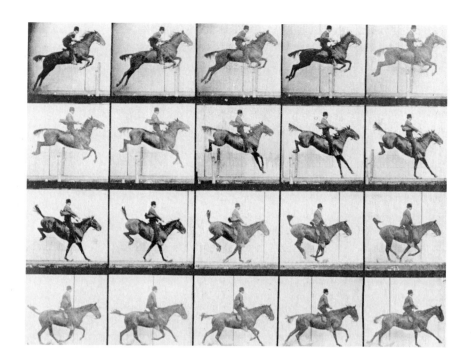

This famous old series of still photos—made a century ago with a battery of cameras whose shutters could be tripped in rapid succession—was the forerunner of today's motion pictures.

rather than to any spatial characteristic (8).

Similarly, it was found that the area of the brain to which the ears of animals send messages contains specialized cells that are activated only by low-pitched sounds, others by high-pitched sounds, still others only by a change in pitch (9).

Nerve cells of this kind, especially sensitive to particular events in the environment, are called *feature detectors*. In animals they have been found not only in the brain but also outside it in the pathway of nerve cells carrying messages to the brain from the receptors of the eyes and ears. Thus it would appear that some processing of the messages picked up by receptors in the eye, for example, goes on at each stage of the pathway of nerve cells from the retina to the visual center of the brain.

Even the retina itself has been found to contain cells that are especially sensitive to certain kinds of stimulation. For example X cells respond most actively to patterns of light. Others called Y cells respond to a change in the stimulus (10). But, to speak of our nervous equipment for a moment as if its units had minds of their own, we might say that an individual cell in the retina—stimulated only by the light that falls on its own tiny area—cannot possibly know whether the light is part of a vertical line, a horizontal line, or anything else. Nerve cells at the next step in the pathway to the brain, which receive messages from a number of individual receptors, can begin to get an idea. And at each subsequent step the processing continues and becomes more complete, until the knowledge is fully developed in the highest part of the brain.

We cannot know, of course, whether feature

detector cells in cats and monkeys actually have any effect on how these animals perceive the world. And we do not know for sure, because the experiments cannot be repeated with human subjects, whether our own nervous system has the same kinds of feature detectors. However, some indirect evidence (highly technical in nature) suggests that our nervous system is also wired in such a way that it can readily distinguish such features as horizontal and vertical lines (11), and that the wiring contains separate routes for patterns and for movements (12). This inborn ability to process patterns and movements separately is a great asset in the survival of the species—for there are many situations, especially in life under primitive conditions, where it is more important to respond to the movement of an object than to know exactly what the object is. The sudden approach of a wild animal means trouble whether it happens to be a tiger or a bear.

When the world changes, you know it

Certainly our sense organs and nervous system are highly efficient in making us instantly aware of movement or any other change in the environment. Movement itself is such a compelling stimulus that even very young babies follow any moving object with their eyes. When you yourself look at a pasture full of horses, you will find you are most aware of those that are running. An advertising sign that uses stroboscopic motion catches your eye more readily than a sign that remains stationary.

If a radio is playing softly in the background while you are reading, you are likely to ignore it—but you notice at once if the sound stops. You are instantly aware of the change if a light becomes brighter because of a sudden surge of electricity or dims because one of its filaments has burned out.

If you came across this young woman on a city street, would your attention be captured? Probably—because she is in such contrast to anything else you are likely to encounter.

Closely related to change in stimulation, and often equally as compelling, is *contrast*—for example, any sharp difference in the intensity of the light reflected by two objects in your field of vision. Even babies are attracted by contrast. If a black triangle is placed in the field of vision of babies only two days old, they will spend most of their time focusing on one of the triangle's sides or angles—

the places where there is the sharpest contrast between the black of the triangle and the light background (13). Babies also show an early interest in the human face, especially the face of the mother. What they notice particularly is the high degree of contrast between a light face and dark eyes or hairline, or between a dark face and the whites of the eyes and the teeth.

Contrast in *size* tends to leap to awareness. When you look at a chain of mountains, no single one of them stands out—but a single mountain rising from a level plain attracts you at once. A six-foot man stands out in a room full of smaller people because he is so tall—and commands attention in a group of seven-foot basketball players because he is so short. But size itself, aside from any contrasts, is also a factor in perception. In general you are more likely to be aware of a large object than of a small one. When you look at the front page of a newspaper, you notice the biggest headlines first. Similarly *intensity* has an effect. The brighter or louder the stimulus the more likely you are to pay attention to it. When you drive at night along a street where all the advertising signs are of equal size, the brightest sign is the most compelling.

All in all we perceive what is likely to be most important to us—movement and change, contrasts between stimuli, big objects, bright objects, loud noises. All this appears to depend on the ways in which our sense organs operate and our nervous system is wired—including, in all probability, the special role of feature detector cells. But perception also depends on many other factors, as we will now see.

Element no. 1 of perception: selection

The definition of perception given earlier in the chapter stated that we become aware of our environment by (1) selecting, (2) organizing, and (3) interpreting. Of these three elements *selecting* comes first—for, out of all the stimuli constantly bombarding our senses, we can perceive only a very few. We select and pay attention only to these few and ignore the rest. For a rough analogy, think of a man working as a forest ranger. Standing on a high observation tower, he looks out over a wide expanse of hills, valleys, trees, open spaces, and streams. As he scans this scene, he thinks he spots a plume of smoke. He raises his binoculars and focuses his eyes on this single aspect of the landscape. Only now, after selecting this one spot on which to concentrate, can he try to find some organization in the stimuli reaching his eyes (do they really represent a plume of smoke or something else?) and make an interpretation (if it is smoke is it coming from a cabin or is it the start of a forest fire?).

What we select and pay attention to is sometimes dictated by the nature of the stimuli reaching us and by our built-in tendencies. The discussion of wiring in the last few pages, in fact, was really about how our attention is captured in certain predetermined ways. We are especially likely to perceive movement, change, contrast, and so on because they compel us to pay attention, of their own accord. But selection can also be voluntary. (There is nothing inherently compeling, for example, about a hazy little blob on the landscape that a forest ranger may or may not find to be smoke.) Sometimes we do our selecting deliberately. Sometimes we do it more or less uncomsciously, because of our personality traits or how we happen to feel at the moment.

Three ways to read a page

On the matter of deliberate selection, one student of perception has pointed out that even reading a page like this one can be approached in different ways by different people. You are probably paying attention sentence by sentence because you want to learn what the words have to say. You perceive the meaning of the words. But suppose this were somebody else's book, from a course you were not interested in, and you had merely picked it up for lack of anything better to do. In that case you might just look at it casually, with no intention of reading it, and perceive it merely as a page of printed matter. If you were a proofreader at a publishing house, you would ignore the meaning of the page and concentrate your attention instead on perceiving any typographical errors (14). To emphasize this point, three typographical errors have been planted on the page. You probably did not perceive them. But if you go back and read the page again, directing your attention to misspellings, you will find them.

One of the best examples of how selection and attention are essential to perception occurs when driving an automobile. As you drive along a highway where the traffic is light, you are listening to the radio—to a football game or to a news broadcast that is about to give a weather report. But now you come to a busy intersection. The traffic lights are changing. You have to slow down, veer into another lane, watch out for a car that has moved into

your path. When all this activity ends, you find to your surprise that the score in the football game has changed or that the news is over and you have missed the weather report. While your attention was directed elsewhere the radio was on just as loud as before, but your perceptual processes missed it entirely.

Trying to do two things at once

It is difficult to pay attention to more than one event in the environment at a time, and selecting one event usually means losing perception of another. This has been demonstrated in the laboratory with earphones that deliver one spoken message to the right ear and a completely different one to the left ear. It has been found that subjects can pay attention to and understand either one of the two messages—but not both at once. Indeed subjects usually get very little information of any kind from the unattended ear. In one experiment, for example, they were asked to listen carefully to the message in the right ear and also to tap with a ruler any time they heard the word *the* in either ear. They caught most of the *the*'s heard by the right ear but only a few of those heard by the left ear (15).

For visual stimuli, the crucial importance of selection and attention has been most effectively shown by the experiment illustrated in Figure 8-3. When subjects looking at the mirror were asked to follow the boxing match, they could not say what had happened in the ball game. Those who directed their attention to the ball game did not know what had happened in the boxing match (16).

As these experiments indicate, selecting one stimulus interferes drastically with perception of another stimulus when both affect the same sense organ. It is somewhat easier to pay attention to two things at once when two different senses are being stimulated. You may have noticed, for example,

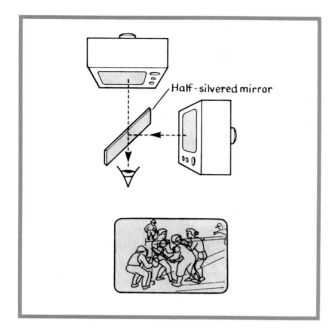

8-3 Boxing match or ball game?—it can't be both

In the experiment on selective perception discussed in the text, one television set showed a videotape of a boxing match, visible to subjects through a one-way mirror. Another set showed a tape of a baseball game, reflected off the mirror to the eyes of the subjects. Thus subjects saw two events occurring at the same time, as in the drawing at the bottom. For what they perceived, see the text.

that you can continue to read with fairly good comprehension while listening to a radio or a telephone conversation. Apparently the mental processes required for perception can operate more efficiently on two different kinds of sensory information than on two messages in the same sensory channel.

Why we select as we do

In our moment-to-moment responses to the environment what kinds of events are we likely to select and pay attention to? This is another way of asking: In all the varied sensory stimulation that constantly impinges on us, what are we most likely to perceive?

For one thing, we are likely to pay attention to events that interest us. This has been demonstrated in experiments with a device called a tachistoscope, which shows words or pictures for very brief exposure times—as small a fraction of a second as the experimenter desires. One experiment was performed with subjects who had a high level of interest in either religion, economics, politics, or the arts. It was found that most of them, looking at words flashed briefly by the tachistoscope, were more likely to recognize words relating to their special interest than other words. Subjects interested in religion were quick to perceive *sacred*. Those interested in economics were quick to perceive *income* (17).

Motivation also plays a part. Another tachistoscope experiment compared subjects known to be highly motivated for achievement with subjects who had low motivation for achievement. Both were tested on a succession of words including some that were closely related to achievement, such as *strive* and *perfect*. The subjects with high achievement motivation perceived these words more rapidly than did the other subjects (18).

Many other individual differences affect the selection process, including such factors as emotional state and personality traits. You can observe this yourself. When you are feeling out of sorts you are likely to pay attention to anything in the environment that is potentially irritating—a noise in the next room, a watchband that feels too tight, another person's frown. When you are feeling on top of the world you may be unusually aware that the sun is shining, everybody seems to be friendly to you, and there are a great many attractive people of the opposite sex walking around. As the old saying goes, a pessimist sees a glass that is half empty, an optimist a glass that is half full.

Element no. 2: organization

As you read this page you are a living demonstration of the part that organization plays in perception. You do not perceive the page as a jumble of light waves of varying intensity. Instead you organize the evidence that your eyes bring you into black letters and words seen against a white background. In fact you form an even more complex kind of organization—you probably perceive whole phrases made up of a number of words. The better you are at reading—in other words at organizing the visual stimuli from a printed page—the more information you can perceive at a single glance.

The way in which we organize the evidence of our senses was first studied by Wilhelm Wundt, who is generally credited with founding the science of psychology by establishing its first laboratory at the University of Leipzig in 1879. When Wundt tried to analyze the conscious experiences that occur when listening to a metronome, he noticed something peculiar. The metronome itself went on and on monotonously—click-click-click-click—with all the clicks equally loud and all the pauses between them of equal length. There was no pattern at all. Yet Wundt and his subjects always perceived the sounds in some kind of pattern. One person might perceive them in march time: *click*-click, *click*-click, *click*-click. Another might perceive them in waltz time: *click*-click-click, *click*-click-click, *click*-click-click. Others might perceive them in more complicated patterns: CLICK-click-*click*-click, CLICK-click-*click*-click.

Another experimental tool in the early study of visual organization was the checkerboard shown in Figure 8-4. This is a visual equivalent of the metronome, in that all the colored blocks are of equal size and are equally distant from one another. There is no pattern in the drawing. But if you keep looking at it as suggested in the caption, you are likely to perceive patterns, and these will change as you continue to look and shift your eyes from one point to another. You may perceive horizontal rows, vertical rows, or diagonals. Or you may perceive patterns in which the individual blocks seem to be arranged in pairs or in groups shaped like squares or rectangles.

Individual differences in organization

Our perceptual processes always seem to be trying to organize and make a pattern out of the evidence of our senses, even when no pattern exists. The pattern we find—like the way we select the events to which we pay attention—depends on many factors. Because of different learning experiences and personalities, any two of us may perceive entirely different patterns in exactly the same set of stimuli.

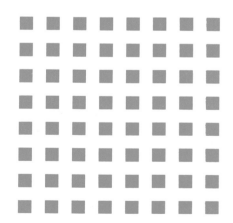

8-4 No pattern—or is there?
As you look at this collection of colored squares of uniform size and spacing, what do you see? Look at it closely for a time, letting your eyes shift from one part of it to another, and compare your perceptions with those described in the text.

One example of the effect of individual differences comes from an unusual experiment that was performed with an ordinary chess set. The pieces were set up on the board as they would appear if an actual match had been interrupted and frozen in time. Subjects were asked to look at the board for five seconds and then try to reproduce the arrangement of the pieces. To people with no experience at chess the task was hopeless. All they had perceived was a jumble of objects of different colors and shapes, spread around a board at random. Chess experts, however, did remarkably well. They had perceived a clear organization, resembling patterns of attack and defense they had often encountered before, and they had little trouble reproducing it. But when these same experts viewed a board on which the pieces had actually been placed in random positions, bearing no likeness to any situation they had ever experienced in a match, they were no better than anyone else at reproducing the arrangement (19).

Some general rules

There are however some general rules of organization that apply to all of us. Presumably they operate largely because of the way our nervous system is designed. The most important are the following.

Figure and ground

On this page you perceive letters and words of black, against a background of white. Thus you organize the visual stimuli reaching your eyes into *figure and ground*. Similarly you perceive a picture on the wall as a figure against a ground. This is also the way you perceive a chair, a person, or the moon in the sky. The figure hangs together, into a shape. The ground is a neutral and formless setting for the figure. What separates the two and sets the figure off from the ground is a clearly perceived dividing line called a *contour*.

Some interesting examples of how we organize visual stimuli into figure and ground are shown in Figure 8-5. In the upper drawing you can perceive a white figure—the goblet—against a colored ground. Or you can perceive two colored figures—the faces—against a white ground. But you cannot perceive both at once. In the bottom drawing you can perceive some strange colored figures against a white ground. Or you can perceive the white figure TIE against a colored ground.

8-5 The rule of figure and ground
When you first look at the top drawing you probably perceive a white goblet. In the bottom drawing you probably perceive some colored figures that look a little like pieces of a jigsaw puzzle. But you can also perceive something quite different in the two drawings, as explained in the text.

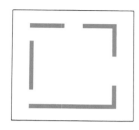

8-6

Some examples of closure
Though the figures are incomplete in one way or another, we perceive them at once for what they are.

Closure

We do not need a complete and uninterrupted contour to perceive a figure. If part of the contour is missing, our perceptual processes fill in the gaps. This rule of perception, called *closure*, is illustrated in Figure 8-6. The rule of closure also operates for sounds. A tape recording of a spoken message can be doctored so that many of the sounds are missing—consonants, vowels, syllables, or entire words. Yet if you heard this incomplete tape you would have no trouble perceiving the message.

Continuity

Closely related to closure is *continuity*, an example of which is shown in Figure 8-7. We tend to perceive continuous lines and patterns. The two lines at the left in Figure 8-7 have their own kind of continuity, but when they are put together as at the right, a different kind of continuity makes us perceive them quite differently. In looking at any kind of complex visual stimulus we are likely to perceive the kind of organization dictated by the most compelling kind of continuity.

Similarity and proximity

Two other rules are illustrated in Figure 8-8, which shows a standard checkerboard square and two slight variations. In the variation lettered *B* note how changing the color of some of the blocks to white makes a white cross fairly leap off the page. This is explained by the rule of *similarity*, which states that we tend to group stimuli that are alike.

8-7

Continuity in perception
At the left we clearly perceive two continuous lines that are combinations of straight and curved segments. When the two lines are put together as at the right, however, we find it difficult to perceive the original pattern. Instead we perceive a continuous wavy line running through another continuous line of straight horizontal and vertical segments.

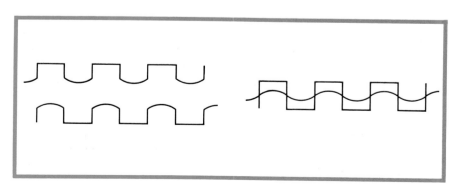

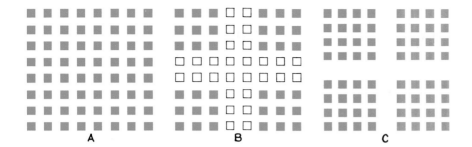

8-8

The effects of similarity and proximity

Drawing A is the same patternless checkerboard that was shown in Figure 8-4. Note what happens to your perception when some of the colored blocks are changed to white, as in B, or moved closer together, as in C.

The white blocks form a clump with a compelling organization.

In variation C note how moving some of the colored blocks closer together makes you perceive four squares. The fact that we tend to form a pattern of stimuli that are close together is the rule of *proximity*. This rule also operates for sounds. If we listen not to a steady metronome but to a device that varies the intervals between clicks, the patterns we hear depend on the timing. When we hear click-click . . . click-click (with the dots indicating a pause) we organize the sounds into pairs. When we hear click-click-click . . . click-click-click we perceive patterns of three. Even different sounds presented this way—such as click-buzz-ring . . . click-buzz-ring—are still perceived in groups of three.

Perception of distance and depth

In our three-dimensional world the ability to perceive distance and depth is essential. Merely to walk around without bumping into doors, furniture, trees, and other people, we must not only perceive these things as objects but have an immediate impression of how far away they are. Before we step off a bus onto the pavement we need to know how deep a drop there is. Fortunately we know without thinking. Exactly how we manage this is a mystery that fascinates psychologists who study perception.

Apparently the ability depends partly on inborn factors and partly on learning—though it is difficult to say where one leaves off and the other begins.

One important inborn factor has been demonstrated with the apparatus shown in Figure 8-9. This device, which its inventor termed a "visual cliff," is a piece of heavy glass suspended above the floor. Across the middle of the glass is a board covered with checkered cloth. On one side of the board the same kind of cloth is attached to the bottom of the glass, making this look like the solid, or shallow, side of the cliff. On the other side the cloth is laid on the floor, and to all appearances there is a drop at that side.

As the photograph shows, even a very young baby crawls without hesitation over the shallow-looking side but hesitates to crawl onto the deep side. Animals also show this tendency. A baby chick less than twenty-four hours old avoids the deep side. So do baby lambs and goats tested as soon as they are able to walk. This ability, shown before any kind of learning has presumably had time to take place, seems to be the secret of how even very young animals—particularly mountain goats born into an environment full of sharp and dangerous drops—manage to avoid falls.

Other factors that influence the perception of depth and distance are more difficult to classify as either inborn or learned. Indeed they are probably

8-9

A baby avoids a fall
on the visual cliff

At left a baby fearlessly crawls toward
its mother on the glass covering the
shallow-looking side of the visual cliff.
But at right the baby stops—seeming
afraid to cross the glass that covers
the apparently deep side (20).

a combination of the two (21). Some of the most
important are the following.

Eye muscle movements

When you look at a faraway object, then shift your
gaze to a nearby object, your eyeballs make small
movements. The muscles controlling their position
make the lines of vision from the two eyes converge
on the object. At the same time the muscles controlling the shape of the lenses operate to bring the
object into the sharpest possible focus. These
movements take place automatically and you are
not ordinarily aware of them. But you can feel them
if you deliberately shift your gaze from the farthest
object within view—preferably the distant horizon
as seen outdoors—and try to look at the tip of your
nose. The attempt will be unsuccessful, of course,
but it will demonstrate that eye movements do produce sensations. These sensations are probably
one clue to distance perception.

Binocular vision

Because your eyes are about 64 millimeters apart
(2½ inches), they receive different images—a fact
that you can demonstrate for yourself by looking at
some distant object while holding a finger twelve
inches or so in front of your nose. If you close first
your left eye and then your right, your finger seems
to move, because the image it casts on one eye is
in a noticeably different part of the visual field from
the image it casts on the other eye.

The different images received by the two eyes,
which are somehow put together by the brain,
greatly assist the perception of distance. This is the
secret of the three-dimensional camera—which
simultaneously takes two pictures through two different lenses and on two pieces of film that are
some distance apart like the human eyes. When
the two pieces of film are seen through a viewer
that presents one to the left eye and the other to the

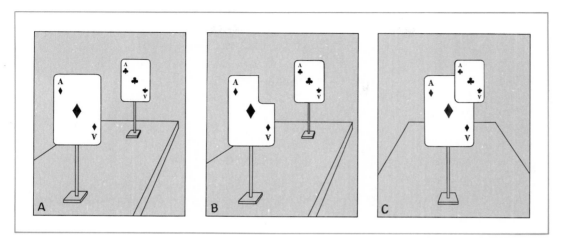

8-10 Fooling the eye with interposition

The drawings illustrate an experiment that shows how your perception of distance can be thrown off by manipulating the clue of interposition. Two ordinary playing cards are arranged as shown in A and are the only objects visible in an otherwise dark room. You perceive clearly that the ace of clubs is farther away. Now a corner is clipped from the ace of diamonds, as shown in B, and the stand holding this card is moved to the right. If you now look at the cards through one eye and see them as shown in C, you perceive a small ace of clubs, close by, and a larger ace of diamonds farther away (22).

right eye, the three-dimensional effect is vivid and unmistakable.

Interposition

Nearby objects interpose themselves between our eyes and more distant objects, blocking off part of the distant images. The manner in which *interposition* serves as a clue to distance—so important a clue that when manipulated in the laboratory it completely fools the eye—is illustrated in Figure 8-10.

Perspective

Artists learned many centuries ago that they could convey the impression of distance and three dimensions in a flat painting by following the rules of *perspective*, which all of us use in real life as a clue to distance.

Artists speak of two kinds of perspective. One,

linear perspective, refers to the visual phenomenon that parallel lines seem to draw closer together as they recede into the distance. A good example is railroad tracks or the edges of a highway seen on a level stretch of ground. *Aerial perspective* refers to the fact that distant objects, because they are seen through air that is usually somewhat hazy, appear less distinct and less brilliant in color than nearby objects. If you have lived within sighting distance of mountains or the skyscrapers of a large city, you may have noticed that the mountains or buildings seem much closer on days when the air is unusually clear.

Another factor in perspective is *gradient of texture,* which you can best observe by looking at a large expanse of lawn. The grass nearby can be seen so well that every blade is distinct, and therefore its texture looks quite coarse. Farther away, the individual blades seem to merge and the texture becomes much finer. This and the other aspects of

8-12 From circle to ball through shadowing
The two images are exactly alike except that some shadowing has been added to the one at right—which now resembles a three-dimensional ball as it would ordinarily be seen with light falling on it from above (23).

8-11 Perspective and distance perception
Serving as clues to distance in this single photograph are all three kinds of perspective—linear, aerial, and gradient of texture.

perspective as a clue to distance are illustrated in Figure 8-11.

Shadowing

One other clue to the perception of distance and depth is the pattern of light and shadow on the objects you see. Note in Figure 8-12 how the addition of *shadowing* turns what looks flat into something you clearly perceive as three-dimensional. In everyday experience, patterns of light and shadow are produced by natural or artificial illumination coming from overhead.

Perceptual constancy

As was said earlier, our perceptual processes are especially alert to change. But they also manage to find a remarkable amount of consistency in the environment. Thanks to a principle called *perceptual*

constancy we perceive a stable world even though the stimuli that reach our eyes are inconsistent and potentially confusing.

A stimulus such as an automobile, for example, may make many kinds of images on the receptors of your eyes. You may see it right in front of you or down the block, and from different angles. All these events constitute very different kinds of visual stimuli. But you perceive the automobile as constant and unchanging. You immediately know what it is and how big it is.

Size constancy

One important form of perceptual constancy, as the example of the automobile indicates, relates to *size*. Regardless of what kind of image falls on your eyes, you usually manage in some way to perceive the correct size of any object you view. For a demonstration follow the suggestions in Figure 8-13. As far as the receptors in your eyes are concerned, the two plates are just alike—yet what you perceive will be a small plate fairly close to you and a larger plate on the table. The salad plate looks small. The dinner plate looks big. You cannot perceive them any other way.

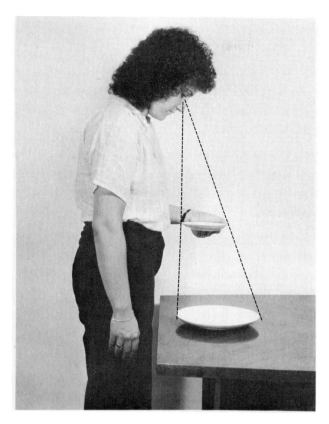

8-13 Salad plate or dinner plate?

For a clear demonstration of size constancy try the experiment illustrated in the photo. Put a dinner plate on the table. Then move a salad plate up and down until its image exactly blots out the dinner plate. Without changing the height at which you hold the salad plate, move it to one side. The images cast on your eyes by the two plates are exactly the same size—but what do you see?

The light post near the camera casts a much larger image on the eye than the buildings across the river—yet you have no trouble perceiving their actual size.

Or watch some friends approaching down a sidewalk. The images they cast on your eyes become larger at every step—yet you certainly do not perceive that they are growing taller. Such differences between what we actually see and what we perceive are illustrated in Figure 8-14, which shows

how a camera, lacking the gift of size constancy, records a distorted view of the world.

There is a close relationship between perceived size and the perception of distance. In part we perceive how big an object is by perceiving how far away it is. Thus we can look at an unfamiliar building off in the distance and know immediately that it is a skyscraper even though it casts a very small image on our eyes. When we are fooled about distance we may make mistakes in perception of size, as is shown in Figure 8-15.

Just as perceived size depends in part on perceived distance, so does perceived distance depend in part on perceived size. This is one way in which we judge the distance of such familiar objects as a person, or as a basketball being thrown down the court. But just how our brains manage to work out these relationships between size and distance is another of the mysteries that make the field of perception so fascinating to many psychologists.

Shape constancy

Have you ever had trouble recognizing the shape of a plate like the ones shown in Figure 8-13? Or of

8-14 What the eyes really see
This is how two people on a beach look to a camera held at close range. If you were holding the camera, your eyes would see much the same kinds of images—hands of different sizes, exaggerated torsos, undersized heads. But you would not be aware of the distortion. You would perceive the two people in proper size and perspective.

a door? Of course not. But, when you stop to think about it, the fact that you recognize them so easily is something of a miracle.

A plate is a circle only when you look straight down on it or hold it directly in front of your eyes. From any other angle it casts very different kinds of images on your eyes—all sorts of ovals and ellipses. A door is a rectangle only when you are right in front of it. The rest of the time—as you move around or as the door swings open and shut—it forms all kinds of images belonging to the family of trapezoids. Yet you perceive the plate and the door as retaining their proper shapes regardless of the true images that reach your eyes—a perceptual phenomenon called *shape constancy*.

Brightness and color constancy

For another small miracle consider the difference between a black shoe viewed against a sidewalk in bright sunlight and the same shoe lying on a snow-

bank in deep shade on a cloudy winter day. In either case the shoe looks black, its background white. But if you make some measurements with a photographer's light meter you will discover something strange. The shoe in sunlight reflects as much light as does the snow in the shade—perhaps even more. Why does the shoe always look black and the snow look white? The explanation is *brightness constancy*—or the fact that we continue to perceive constant impressions of blacks, grays, and whites regardless of the actual intensity of the light waves falling on our eyes. How and why brightness constancy operates is another mystery—though it appears to depend in part on the ratio of the intensity of light. The proportion between sunlit shoe and sidewalk is much the same as between cloudy-day shoe and snow (25). A similar phenomenon is *color constancy*—or the fact that we tend (to a certain extent though not always) to see a red coat as red and a blue carpet as blue regardless of changes in the light waves they reflect to our eyes under different lighting conditions.

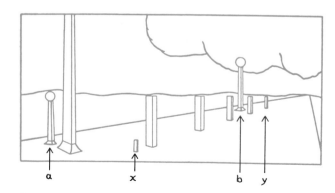

8-15 The case of the deceptive lampposts
There is no doubt in your mind—is there?—that lamppost *a* is much smaller than lamppost *b*. Or that the wooden block *x* is much smaller than *y*? But measure them with a ruler and you will find that the two posts and the two blocks are exactly the same size. The reason you perceive them as you do is that the drawing uses the principle of linear perspective to make the objects at the right appear to be farther away (24).

Element no. 3: interpretation

The final element in perception—interpreting the evidence of our senses—represents our constant attempt to find meaning in the environment. It is closely related to organization. Note the way we respond to the stimuli reaching our ears. When we listen to someone speak our own language, the rapid succession of sounds and pauses falls into a pattern of words and phrases. We readily grasp—or interpret—the meaning. In fact we often get ahead of the speaker and know what the next words will be. But when we listen to a foreign language we perceive only a meaningless jumble that we cannot interpret at all.

The same is true of visual stimuli, as has been demonstrated by an experiment that used the photographs shown in Figure 8-16. Some subjects looked at the top photograph of a normal, every-day scene, projected briefly on a screen. Then the screen went blank and an arrow pointed to the place where the bicycle had been, and the subjects were asked to recall what they had seen at that spot. Other subjects looked at the bottom photo-graph, made by cutting the scene into segments and rearranging them into a jumble. The bicycle was in exactly the same spot in both cases—but subjects who had viewed the normal scene were much better at recalling it than the other subjects. They had extracted a good deal more information from the normal scene, which fell into a more or less familiar pattern, than the other subjects extracted from the jumbled picture.

8-16 Organization and interpretation
In which of the photographs, unaltered or jumbled, does perception work more efficiently? The answer is in the text (26).

Perception and prototypes

The manner in which we arrive at our perceptions is now generally regarded as a form of information processing in which both short-term and long-term memory play a part. We seem to hold the evidence of our senses in short-term memory, then call on the information stored in long-term memory to help find some kind of organization and make an interpretation. Thus a more or less familiar pattern, which we can readily recognize by comparing it with memories of similar events, is easiest to interpret. Subjects who looked at the normal street scene in Figure 8-16 had many past experiences to call on. They could tell at a glance that they were looking across a street at a sidewalk, a gateway, and a building. They had an immediate impression of the details that are likely to be found in such a scene and even of the location of the various objects. The position of the bicycle was easy to recall.

One view held by many psychologists today is that we have stored in our memories a general, typical idea of stimuli we have often encountered. This is called a *prototype*—meaning a model of street scenes in general, of what bicycles look like, or of the human face. When we encounter a new stimulus we can identify it immediately because it resembles the prototype. Then we note the special features that distinguish this particular new event, making it similar to but different from all other events that also fit the prototype.

Let us say that a woman student new to the class sits in front of you today. At first you see only the back of her head, then she turns. You perceive without effort a human face that matches your prototype of faces in general. But this new face has some features of its own that make it different from all other faces you have ever seen. You note these special features and store a new and more specific pattern in long-term memory, from which you will recognize her when you see her again.

According to this view, perception is largely a matter of rapidly comparing what we see and hear with what we have seen and heard in the past. We match the present stimulus with some generalized prototype that we carry in our long-term memories, then against more specific and detailed patterns. We see a face in the distance (or very tiny on a

"Take your finger out of your ear and listen to me!"

photograph) and know at once what it is. But *who* is it? To find out, we have to compare the individual characteristics with the special patterns of the people we specifically remember. Is it Ms. A? No, not quite. Ms. B? Again no, not quite. Ms. C? Ah, yes, the details all match. All this testing—discarding A, discarding B, deciding on C—takes only a fraction of a second.

Of course the notions of prototypes and individual features, even if correct, do not fully explain how perception operates. In fact this kind of information processing—so complex and yet so rapid—may never be completely understood. Numerous theories have been proposed and later revised or discarded. The experiments cited in this chapter are only a few among many that psychologists have devised. And often it seems that each new discovery, though it may clarify one mystery, only creates another. For example it is obvious that nothing in our long-term memories—whether prototypes or patterns of individual features or any other kind of knowledge—affects our perceptions in all cases. Look back at Figure 8-1. You know now that lines *a* and *b* are of equal length in all the drawings—but you cannot possibly perceive them that way.

8-17
**A little perceptual magic:
now it's a man, now it's a rat**
For a startling demonstration of how
perception is affected by expectations,
cover both rows of drawings, then ask
a friend to watch while you uncover
the faces in the top row one at a time,
beginning at the left. The friend will
almost surely perceive the final drawing as the face of a man. Then try the
bottom row in similar fashion on another friend. This friend will almost
surely perceive the final drawing as a
rat. The psychologists who devised this
experiment found that 85 to 95 percent
of their subjects perceived the final
drawing as a man if they saw the other
human heads first, as a rat if they saw
the animals first—though of course the
final drawings are exactly alike (28).

Perceptual expectations

Past experiences, however, do have an effect on
perception in many instances. Experience has led
us to expect to find certain events happening in our
world in certain familiar ways. In a way perception
is a method of predicting the meaning of what we
are now seeing or hearing, then testing this prediction against the stimuli (27)—either to prove it correct or to revise it. We have a "mental set" toward
our environment. What we perceive and how we
interpret it depends to a considerable extent on this
set—in other words on our *perceptual expectations*.

Laboratory experiments have shown that manipulating people's expectations can greatly affect
their perceptions. Would you believe, for example,
that two people could look at exactly the same
drawing—yet that one would see a man and the
other would see a rat? To convince yourself, try the
demonstration illustrated in Figure 8-17. Then, for

added proof, experiment with Figure 8-18.

The drawings in these figures, of course, were
specially designed to show the effect of perceptual
expectations. The final drawing in each set was
deliberately made ambiguous, so that it looks both
like a man's face and a rat, or like a woman's
figure and a face. You can just as easily perceive
one as the other. But many of the sights we encounter in real life are also ambiguous—and the
way we perceive them is also likely to depend on
what we expect to see. An example would be the
new student sitting in front of you. You will probably
store enough information about the special features of her face to know her in the future. But you
will recognize her much more readily if you see her
again in the classroom, where you can predict that
she will be, than if you run into her in unexpected
circumstances—for example, if you should happen
to see her working in uniform as a part-time traffic
director.

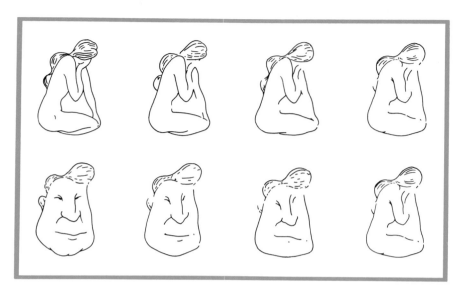

8-18

More magic: is it a figure or is it a face?

For another demonstration of perceptual expectations try these drawings on some friends, using the same procedure as in Figure 8-17. Though the final drawings in each row are exactly alike, your friends will almost surely perceive the figure of a woman in the top row, the face of a man in the bottom row (29).

Some influences on perceptual expectations—and some results

Many factors can influence our perceptual expectations—and thus our interpretations. For example, the effect of hunger has been demonstrated by an experiment that used three groups of subjects—one that had gone only an hour since eating, another four hours, and a third sixteen hours. All three were asked to describe pictures that they were told they would see dimly on a screen. Actually there were no real pictures, merely blurs or smudges. But the subjects, trying to make some kind of interpretation, showed some revealing differences. Those who had gone four hours without eating thought they saw more objects relating to food than did those who had gone merely an hour. Those who had gone sixteen hours without eating—and were thoroughly hungry—saw the most food-related objects of all (30).

In real-life situations the effect of perceptual expectations is often apparent in the way we interpret the behavior of other people. Suppose you have an elderly uncle who you have decided is cranky and critical. When you are around him, your perception of him is colored by the expectation that he will act in a disagreeable way. You are likely to notice his more acid remarks and may not even be aware that much of his conversation is as pleasant as that of anyone else. In fact you may interpret as sarcastic many remarks that would strike you as harmless or even good-natured if someone else said them in exactly the same words and tone. Similarly, when you are around someone you know likes you and from whom you expect warmth and acceptance, you may be totally unaware of a momentary outburst of anger or hostility. This is one reason husbands and wives often complain that they have trouble communicating with one another. They communicate their feelings, all right—but often the listener's expectations cause the message to be either ignored or misinterpreted.

(Summary begins on page 314.)

Perception and altered states of consciousness

The chapter has talked about perception as it occurs in everyday life, during the waking hours when our sense organs and brains are functioning normally. But some psychologists (and many nonpsychologists) believe that we may also extract information from the world around us without using our ordinary senses—a possibility that is discussed in the box on *Psychology and Society* on page 306. And there is no question at all that strange and unusual forms of perception take place when our brains are not working in the usual fashion and we are experiencing what are called *altered states of consciousness*.

A prime example of perception during an altered state is sleep. Our eyes are closed; we see nothing. Our sense of hearing is turned off to the point where it would take a loud shout to wake us. Yet in our dreams we perceive all kinds of things. We see scenes and people, some familiar and some unlike anything or anybody we have ever really seen in our lives. We hear ourselves talk and other people answer. All these sights and sounds, though nonexistent, may be as vivid as any of our real-life perceptions. Like the events we actually experience when awake, they can move us to intense feelings of love, pleasure, hostility, anger, and fear.

Sleep and dreams

Dreams presumably have always fascinated humanity, for they seem to free us from all limitations of space or time. Our early ancestors must have been baffled by dreams in which they seemed to move about in distant places and to talk to people long dead. The line between dream and reality must have been difficult to draw—and must have hinted at all sorts of mysteries of the human spirit and of a world beyond ordinary human understanding.

Dreams have often been regarded as portents of the future, for dreams sometimes come true. To a statistician, this fact is not surprising. There are more than four billion people in the world. The average adult, it has been found, dreams for nearly two hours a night (37). Thus there are bound to be numerous occasions when somebody dreams of the death of a friend and the friend actually does die soon afterward—or when a dream seems to accurately predict the receipt of an important letter, the result of a sports event, or a train wreck. Such coincidences are startling and memorable. The great majority of dreams that turn out to be mistaken go unnoticed.

305

Extrasensory perception: new frontier or human delusion?

Can we human beings perceive events through channels other than our eyes, ears, and the rest of the five senses? In other words, do we possess what is popularly known as ESP, short for *extrasensory perception*? Are there at least some of us who can read other people's minds, or know what an object is without looking at it, or perhaps even know in advance what is about to happen?

The idea that such things are possible is attractive to many people. Humanity has always been interested in trying to predict the future. The ancient Greeks had their Delphic oracle, whom they believed to utter predictions based on messages from the gods. Today's world is full of fortune tellers who read palms or tea leaves. Newspapers and magazines print horoscopes that forecast how the position of the stars will influence today's events in one way for Leos and in another way for Libras. The popular belief in mind reading was emphasized

when one of the nation's astronauts made a serious effort to transmit mental messages to the earth from his space capsule on its way to the moon.

Nothing that science has yet discovered can explain or even allow for the existence of ESP. But every possibility is worth examining—and thus some investigators have been engaged for many years in the field of *parapsychology*, or the study of ESP and other psychological events that seem to go beyond normal limits and to defy explanation in any normal scientific way. They have done research on three kinds of ESP that have been reported from time to time:

1 *Mental telepathy,* or what is commonly known as mind reading.
2 *Clairvoyance,* or the ability to perceive an object without using the ordinary senses—such as knowing what card will be turned up next from a shuffled deck.

Since the time of Sigmund Freud, a different kind of meaning has been attached to dreams. Freud believed that dreams were an expression of wishes prohibited by the dreamer's conscience. Forbidden sexual desires in particular, he thought, were likely to crop up—often in a hidden form in which the male sexual organ was symbolized by a snake, a tower, or an airplane, the female organ by a basket or a flower.

Many psychoanalysts and other therapists have followed Freud's lead; they try to analyze their patients' dreams in search of clues to hidden conflicts.

Although different therapists use different methods of interpreting dreams, enough successes have been reported to indicate that the content of a dream may indeed reflect the dreamer's unconscious wishes at times (38). An interesting sidelight is the fact that there seem to be some sex differences in dreams. One study found that American men tend to dream about such matters as achievement, hostility, and aggression. Women's dreams were found to be more emotional and friendly, often taking place in indoor settings and relating to home and family life (39). This may be due to the

3 *Precognition,* or the ability to perceive something that has not yet happened—such as how a pair of dice will turn up on the next roll.

The field of parapsychology is too complex and controversial to be covered adequately here. About all that can be said is that some researchers have reported finding subjects who seemed to display abilities at telepathy, clairvoyance, and precognition. These subjects were by no means 100 percent accurate, but they did seem to produce results that could not be accounted for by sheer luck (31, 32). Other researchers have reported telepathy experiments in which the dreams of "receivers" seemed to be influenced by the thoughts of "senders" who were some distance away, in one case by forty miles (33, 34).

A large majority of psychologists remain skeptical. Many of the experiments that seemed to demonstrate ESP have been attacked as poorly designed and lacking safeguards against cheating (35). The skeptics like to point out that attempts to apply ESP have been failures—like one well-known experiment at breaking the bank in Las Vegas (36). Indeed the critics say the economic system would collapse if even a few people could utilize ESP.

The controversy has some important implications for the future of society. If ESP actually exists—or is possible—then human abilities have some unexplored dimensions that may revolutionize human life and the future course of science. But if a belief in ESP is nothing more than wishful thinking and superstition, like the faith of the Greeks in their Delphic oracle, then the popular interest in it is a serious barrier to an understanding of human behavior. If you want to know more about the topic and judge for yourself the evidence pro and con, you can start with the books on ESP listed in the recommended readings.

different roles men and women have traditionally been taught to play in our society—a topic that will be discussed in Chapter 10.

Ordinary and paradoxical sleep

As for how sleep differs from the waking state of consciousness, some clues have been provided by studies of brain waves and muscle activity, measured by electrodes attached to people sleeping through the night in laboratories. The studies have shown quite clearly that sleep is by no means a state of suspended animation in which body and brain are shut down for a time. Sleep is not just a slowing down but a kind of activity in its own right. The brain continues to be highly active—though in a different way (40). Moreover it has been found that there are several different kinds of sleep.

Most of the night is spent in what is called *ordinary sleep.* As can be seen in Figure 8-19, the brain's activity during ordinary sleep differs considerably from the pattern during waking hours, and the muscles of the body are considerably more relaxed. Four stages of ordinary sleep, ranging from light to very deep, can be distinguished from

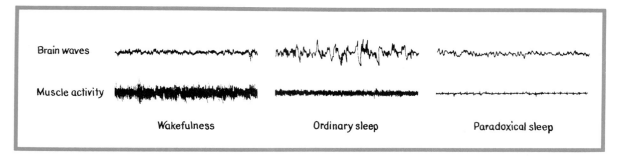

8-19 Brain and muscle activity during sleep

The tracings show typical patterns of brain waves and muscle activity during periods of wakefulness, ordinary sleep, and paradoxical (or REM) sleep. Note that during paradoxical sleep the brain waves resemble the pattern during wakefulness, but the muscles are most relaxed of all (41).

tracings of brain and muscle activity. We move back and forth among these four stages during the night. Most people have three periods of the deepest sleep, the first starting within an hour after dropping off, the last ending after about three or four hours.

About a quarter of the night is spent in *paradoxical sleep*—which gets its name from the fact, also shown in Figure 8-19, that the brain's activity is very similar to the waking state but the bodily muscles are almost totally relaxed. When subjects who are in paradoxical sleep are awakened, about 80 to 85 percent of them report that they have been dreaming (42). In fact during paradoxical sleep the eyes dart quickly about as if following a series of visual images. Thus this stage is also known as *REM sleep*—REM standing for the *rapid eye movements* that can be observed.

How much sleep do we need?

Young adults sleep an average of 7½ hours a night (43), but there are wide individual differences. Some people prefer to sleep as long as ten hours or more, others only a few hours. One woman was found to get along on 45 minutes of sleep a night (44). Why these differences exist is not known. One study concluded that they were related to personality. People who need a lot of sleep were found in general to be "worriers" who brooded over their personal problems and the state of the world, whereas those who got by on little sleep were energetic, efficient, hard-working, and self-satisfied (45). But other studies have failed to show any significant personality differences (46). Whatever your own sleeping habits, you are stuck with them. They cannot be comfortably changed. In one experiment some couples were asked to try to get along on less sleep by cutting down slowly—a half hour a week. None of them ever got below five hours a night and all of them eventually gave up the attempt (47).

Most people are occasionally troubled by insomnia, or the inability to fall asleep, and some people suffer from it chronically. In one large-scale survey 6 percent of adult men and 14 percent of women reported that they experienced insomnia often or fairly often (48)—an indication that perhaps 10 million or more adult Americans spend many nights tossing and turning before they drop off to sleep. Among the people most likely to experience insomnia are those suffering from depression (49) and those who have frequently used sleeping pills, which are occasionally helpful but can lead to chronic sleep disturbances if used too often (50).

Why do we sleep at all?

As you probably have observed for yourself, a sleepless night produces unpleasant aftereffects. Merely lying in bed and resting is no substitute for real sleep (51). In fact any lack of sleep below your natural requirements, whether from insomnia or other causes, is likely to make you feel logy, irritable, and generally below par. Yet you can go without sleep entirely for remarkably long periods without suffering any real damage. Volunteers have gone more than a week. Often they developed shaky hands and a lowered tolerance for pain. Some of them began to have hallucinations, but this was rare and never occurred before sixty sleepless hours. Their breathing, heart rate, blood pressure, and body temperature remained normal. They showed a minor loss of ability to perform some kinds of tasks but none at other kinds (52).

These facts raise the question: Why do we sleep at all? Part of the answer has been established in experiments showing that the brains of sleepy animals seem to contain a chemical that has been called the "sleep factor." When the substance is extracted and injected into wide-awake animals, they too become sleepy (53). But the nature of the chemical, and how and where it is produced, are as yet unknown. Body chemistry as well as brain chemistry may play a part. Some investigators have suggested that ordinary sleep serves to restore the body's chemical balance, while REM sleep restores the brain's ability to function (54)—perhaps by somehow renewing the chemical substances that serve as neurotransmitters (55).

Hypnosis

Like sleep in some ways, but totally unlike it in others, is the altered state of consciousness called *hypnosis*. This too produces some strange perceptions. At the hypnotist's suggestion, the subject may see a chair where none exists; if asked to walk around the room, the subject will carefully avoid this imaginary obstacle. Like dreams, hypnosis leaps across the normal limits of space and time. Therapists who use hypnosis sometimes persuade their subjects to regress in age and relive forgotten experiences that seem to have caused their psychological problems (56).

The nature of the hypnotic state is unknown; psychologists know only how to produce it, not what it is. The hypnotist may ask the subject to sit as relaxed as possible and stare fixedly at some small object, such as a key, the tip of a pencil, or a point of light. Meanwhile the hypnotist speaks in a quiet and repetitious monotone, suggesting that the subject is growing more and more relaxed, that the subject's eyes are tiring, and that the subject is becoming sleepy. Soon the subject seems to respond to the suggestions: The eyelids flutter and close; the body becomes limp; the head droops; apparently the subject is sound asleep (57).

There is no similarity, however, between the hypnotic state and real sleep. The brain waves show a different pattern. So do many measures of bodily activity. Moreover the subject remains fully conscious of the hypnotist's voice and responds to the hypnotist's suggestions. Indeed one characteristic of the hypnotic state is an intense and sharply focused attention to the hypnotist's words and the perceptions and events that are suggested (58).

Not everybody can be hypnotized. Perhaps as many as 10 percent show almost no response at all. Only about 25 percent enter the deeper stages of the hypnotic experience and only about 5 to 10 percent enter the very deepest stages (59). Those who are most susceptible tend to be normal, out-going people of the type who readily become im-aginatively involved in events—"carried away" by books or movies, for example. Many of them say they were rather severely punished in childhood, an experience that perhaps inclines them to obey the hypnotist's suggestions (60).

Meditation

Many Americans are currently seeking another kind of altered state of consciousness through the practice of *meditation,* which has long been a part of philosophies and religions in the Eastern world. Among the methods followed are Yoga, Zen, and Transcendental Meditation. Though these vary somewhat, they all have as their goal a frame of mind in which ordinary thought processes are sus-pended and the mind is opened to enhanced per-ceptions of beauty and truth and perhaps religious insights that defy any attempt to put them into words.

Methods of meditation usually have four features in common (61):

1 They are practiced in a quiet atmosphere, free from distractions.
2 The meditator assumes a comfortable position, but not one likely to lead to sleep.
3 The meditator tries to achieve deep relaxation and freedom from intruding thoughts by con-centrating on the breathing process (also, in Transcendental Meditation, by silently repeat-ing a word called a mantra, usually taken from the Hindu holy books).
4 The meditator tries to be as passive as possible, not thinking or worrying about anything.

After a time—perhaps twenty or thirty minutes—even consciousness of what the meditator has been concentrating on, breathing or the mantra, may disappear, leaving the mind in a sort of sus-pended state of nothingness (62). This is often ac-companied by feelings of floating on air, timeless-ness, expanded awareness, and deep joy (63).

Meditation has been found to change patterns of brain activity. In particular it increases the occur-rence of what are called alpha waves (64), which are associated with relaxation. The rate of breath-ing and consumption of oxygen by the body may decline by about 15 percent (65), indicating a very deep kind of relaxation. It has been found that people who practice meditation regularly are able to cut down or eliminate the use of cigarettes or drugs (66) and perhaps even free themselves from symptoms of high blood pressure (67). Some in-vestigators have reported that meditation seems to make people less tense, anxious, aggressive, and neurotic (68, 69)—although these findings have been challenged on the ground that people who meditate may be less tense and anxious to begin with (70).

You can try meditation yourself simply by sitting in a quiet room with your eyes closed, paying close but relaxed attention to your breathing in and out, and saying to yourself the word *one* after each breath. This has been found to produce many of the effects of more elaborate techniques, especially the decrease in oxygen consumption and bodily activity (71).

Drugs

The use of drugs to alter states of consciousness goes far back in history. It would appear that hu-manity has always been interested in finding sub-stances that relieve anxiety, produce feelings of contentment and happiness, and sometimes result in strange experiences that make the user perceive the world in distorted fashion, have hallucinations of imaginary sights and sounds, and perhaps at-tain a mystical religious sense of oneness with the universe.

Some of the mind-altering substances used today are so routine a part of our social scene that they are seldom even thought of as drugs. *Nicotine,* whose effects constitute the chief appeal of smoking, is a chemical that acts in several different ways—sometimes as a stimulant, sometimes as a sort of tranquilizer relieving feelings of anxiety. *Caffeine,* found in coffee and tea, is a powerful stimulant. *Alcohol* acts as a depressant to the activity of parts of the brain; it relieves inhibitions and encourages the talkativeness characteristic of cocktail parties. In large quantities alcohol sometimes releases feelings of hostility and aggressiveness (as in the barroom fight) and often interferes with motor coordination (causing the drunken person to stagger).

The substances ordinarily thought of as drugs include a number of substances whose use is il-legal, ranging from marijuana to heroin, as well as prescription drugs such as sleeping pills and stimulants when taken for "kicks" rather than on a physician's orders. The use of these drugs, though widely publicized in recent years, is less common than generally believed. As is shown in Figure 8-20, a recent survey showed that marijuana was the only one that had ever been tried by as many as half the people of roughly college age. For other drugs the figures ranged downward from 17 percent for stimulants to 4 percent for heroin. The number of young people who could be considered regular users—even to the extent of having taken the drug within the past month—was extremely small, no more than 5 percent for anything but marijuana and less than one-half of 1 percent for heroin.

All the mind-altering drugs create their effects by

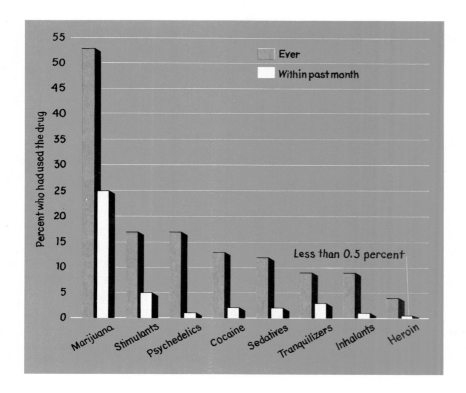

8-20

How many people use drugs? —fewer than you might think

A survey in the mid-1970s found these figures on drug use among people in the 18-to-25-year-old bracket. The gray bars show the percentages who had ever tried the drugs, the white bars those who had used them recently, or within the previous month. For people over 25 the figures were considerably lower; for example, only 13 percent had ever tried marijuana and only 2 percent had ever tried psychedelics. The term *inhalants* in the bar graph refers to the sniffing of airplane glue or the like. The other drugs are discussed in the text (72).

temporarily changing the activity of the brain—certainly by assisting or hindering in the transmission of messages at the brain's innumerable switching points, perhaps also by changing the circuits over which messages ordinarily flow. Almost invariably, their effects depend not only on the drug itself and the amount used but also on the frame of mind of the user and the circumstances in which the drug is used.

In one experiment, for example, a group of college women thought they were drinking vodka but in fact received nothing but tonic water. Another group thought they were drinking tonic water that in fact contained vodka. Those who expected to feel the effects of alcohol showed more signs of physical arousal, such as increased heart rate, than those who actually drank the vodka (73). The effects of various drugs have also been found to depend on whether the user is alone or in company and on how these companions behave. Discussions of the best-known drugs and their effects follow.

Marijuana

Despite its illegality, marijuana is easy to obtain in most parts of the nation and is by far the most widely used of all drugs except alcohol, caffeine, and nicotine. Indeed a 1978 report from the University of Michigan suggested that marijuana may be on its way to becoming "a permanent recreational drug," especially among younger people. The report was based on a survey of high-school seniors around the nation, which showed that a majority had experimented with marijuana and about 9 percent used it daily—and that large majorities believed the drug was not harmful and should be legalized (74).

Marijuana is the dried leaves and flowers of the hemp plant, usually smoked though sometimes swallowed. It probably should be classified as a psychedelic drug—one that produces enhanced perceptions and sometimes hallucinations of imaginary sights and sounds—because this is the effect of its active ingredient when taken in its pure and concentrated form. As marijuana is ordinarily used, however, the amount of the active ingredient that gets into the body and brain produces only a sort of intoxicating effect—feelings of well-being, friendliness, and often an unusually vivid perception of colors, music, and tastes. In the laboratory, the drug seems to reduce the span of short-term memory and the ability to make decisions rapidly (75). On simulated tests of driving ability, subjects make more errors in judging speed (76).

As to whether continued use of marijuana produces any harmful physical or psychological effects, a recent government study concluded that there is no solid evidence that it does—but on the other hand no proof that it does not (77). There are no indications that people who use marijuana become physically dependent on it, though there is some evidence that it may create a certain amount of psychological dependence (78). The often-expressed theory that it leads to the use of other and harder drugs appears to be false (79).

LSD and other psychedelic drugs

The best-known of the clearly psychedelic drugs is *LSD*, often called "acid." Users may stare at a simple object for minutes on end, finding it unbelievably fascinating because they say they experience a richness of color and texture unknown to normal consciousness. When they close their eyes, they are likely to see imaginary designs, scenes, and faces and hear imaginary conversations and music. On a "bad trip," as an unpleasant experience with LSD is known, they may imagine that their bodies are distorted or rotting, that they are surrounded by darkness and gloom, perhaps that they are dying (80).

A marijuana seller at a music festival.

Even the same person, using LSD with the same companions and under much the same circumstances, is likely to experience different effects on different occasions—sometimes pleasant, sometimes terrifying. Of the people who try LSD and similar drugs, only a very small number continue for very long—apparently because of the unpredictable effects and the fact that the perceptual distortions and hallucinations lose their novelty appeal (81). Similar drugs are *mescaline,* which comes from a cactus plant, and *psilocybin,* found in a Mexican mushroom.

Stimulants

Another group of drugs, classified as stimulants, affect self-perception more than perception of the outer world. By increasing the activity of the brain, especially the centers for arousal and wakefulness, they create a sense of energetic well-being. Chief among them are various compounds chemically labeled *amphetamines,* known by the slang terms of "uppers," "bennies," "meth," and "speed." Used for "kicks," or over long periods by truck drivers and athletes to mask fatigue, they are among the most dangerous of drugs. Many users build up a tolerance and must take ever-increasing amounts to achieve the same effect. The "high" they create may be accompanied by severe anxiety and irrational thinking that sometimes leads to violent behavior. The high is often followed by a deep depression in which the user becomes suicidal. Prolonged abuse of the drug has been found to produce brain damage (82).

Similar in effect to the amphetamines is *cocaine,* a drug extracted from the leaves of the South American coca plant. Usually sniffed into the nose and quickly absorbed by the membranes there, cocaine creates a powerful surge of confidence and contentment. Experiments with monkeys have shown that, once they have experienced the effects of cocaine, they will choose it even in preference to food if they can have one or the other but not both. One group of monkeys did so for eight full days, though they showed so much weight loss and evidence of starvation that the experiment had to be ended (83). The drug may also produce addiction and dangerous behavior among human users.

Sedatives

The drugs called *sedatives,* popularly known as "downers," include barbiturates and other such sleep-producing compounds as *Quaaludes* and *Seconals.* By slowing down brain activity, they produce feelings of relaxation and abandonment—in which, according to their intended use, the user can quickly and blissfully fall off to sleep. People who take them for kicks fight off the urge to sleep and try to maintain the pleasant feelings, which in many ways resemble those produced by alcohol.

Heroin

Considered so dangerous that its use even for medical purposes is prohibited in the United States is *heroin*. Like two similar but less potent drugs called *morphine* and *codeine,* it is a derivative of the poppy plant. All three drugs are narcotics, meaning that they cut off some of the brain circuits and produce lethargy and profound sleep. Their medical value is to relieve even the most intolerable pain. Used for kicks, heroin produces an immediate rush of pleasure and freedom from anxiety—a high in which users forget their problems and feel on top of the world.

People who use heroin often become addicted and need the drug desperately to avoid the painful withdrawal symptoms that occur when the effect wears off—shakes, cold sweats, and stomach convulsions. Moreover, they need more and more of the drug as time goes on, and the habit may eventually cost $150 a day or more. Some addicts can support the habit only by turning to crime, and in many communities large numbers of the people arrested for such offenses as burglary and prostitution are found to be users (84).

Angel dust

The strangest of all drugs used for kicks is *angel dust*—a compound that was developed in medical laboratories not as a stimulant or sedative but as an operating room anesthetic. Its real name is *phencyclidine,* and it has drastic and often unpredictable effects on the brain. Taken in any strength or amount, it can make users lose their muscular coordination, forget where they are, and have bizarre hallucinations. When this happens they act as if they were psychotic—or in popular language, insane—and indeed they are psychotic until the effect wears off. Cases have been reported in which people under the influence of angel dust did things they would ordinarily never have dreamed of doing—such as killing a good friend without even knowing or remembering it.

Summary

1 *Perception* is the process through which we become aware of our environment by selecting, organizing, and interpreting the evidence from our senses. The impression we receive as a result of this process is also called a perception.
2 Our perceptions of the world are usually—but not always—in accord with the facts. Among the exceptions are optical illusions and distortions during *altered states of consciousness* (like those produced by hypnosis or drugs).
3 Perception results in quick and automatic first impressions not only of the physical environment but also of the people we encounter.
4 Most psychologists believe that perception depends on both nature (the way our nervous system is wired) and nurture (including what we have learned from previous experience with various stimuli).
5 Among the important inborn influences on perception are nerve cells called *feature detectors,* found in the neural pathways from sense organs to brain and in the brain itself. In vision, some feature detectors respond sharply to patterns (such as a vertical line, a horizontal line, or an angle), others to movement.

6 Because of the wiring of the nervous system, we are especially likely to perceive movement, change, contrast, and stimuli that have substantial size or intensity.

7 *Selection* is a key element in perception, because we can perceive only a few of all the many stimuli that constantly bombard our senses. When we select and pay attention to one event, we usually lose perception of other stimuli.

8 The selection process depends on our interests, motivation, emotional state, personality, and other factors.

9 *Organization* is a key element because we have a strong tendency to perceive patterns even in stimuli that do not of themselves possess any pattern—such as the steady click of a metronome or a uniform mass of checkerboard squares.

10 Factors that influence organization include *figure and ground* (the tendency to perceive an object as a figure set off from a neutral ground by a dividing line called a *contour*), *closure, continuity, similarity,* and *proximity*.

11 In perceiving distance and depth, we utilize clues provided by *eye muscle movements, binocular vision, interposition, perspective,* and *shadowing*.

12 The organization process is also influenced by *perceptual constancy,* which is the tendency to perceive a stable world even though the stimuli that reach our eyes are inconsistent and potentially confusing. Perceptual constancy includes *size, shape, brightness,* and *color constancies*.

13 *Interpretation* is a key element in perception because we constantly attempt to find meaning in our environment. It is closely related to organization.

14 Many psychologists view perception as a form of information processing. We hold the evidence from our senses in short-term memory, then call on the information stored in long-term memory to help find some kind of organization and make an interpretation.

15 One view held by psychologists is that we have stored in our memories a general, typical idea of stimuli we have often encountered. This is called a *prototype,* meaning a model. When we encounter a new stimulus we can identify it immediately because it resembles the prototype. Then we note the special features that distinguish this particular new event—making it similar to but different from all other events that fit the prototype.

16 Our interpretations are influenced by *perceptual expectations,* which are a form of "mental set" toward the environment and the people we know.

Postscript

17 Some psychologists believe that we have a potential ability at *extrasensory perception* (ESP), or perceiving events through channels other than the five senses. ESP is one aspect of *parapsychology,* the study of psychological phenomena that seem to go beyond normal limits and to defy explanation in any normal scientific way.

18 Forms of ESP include *mental telepathy* (mind reading), *clairvoyance* (the ability to perceive an object without using the ordinary senses), and *precognition* (the ability to perceive something that has not yet happened).

19 *Altered states of consciousness,* in which brain activity and perception do not operate in the usual fashion, include *sleep, hypnosis,* and changes produced by *meditation* or *drugs.*

20 In *ordinary sleep,* which occurs through most of the night, brain waves show a different pattern from that of waking hours, and the muscles of the body are more relaxed. In *paradoxical sleep,* which occurs for about a quarter of the night, the brain's activity is very similar to the waking state but the bodily muscles are almost totally relaxed. Paradoxical sleep is also known as *REM sleep*—REM standing for the *rapid eye movements* that accompany it. Dreaming takes place during REM sleep.

21 Sleep appears to depend on brain chemistry and possibly body chemistry. Some psychologists believe that ordinary sleep restores the body's chemical balance, while REM sleep restores the brain's ability to function.

22 Drugs that produce altered states of consciousness include *stimulants* (caffeine, amphetamines, cocaine), *depressants* (alcohol), *psychedelic drugs* (marijuana, LSD), *sedatives* (barbiturates, Quaaludes, Seconals), and *narcotics* (heroin, morphine, codeine). Another drug sometimes used for "kicks" is *angel dust,* or *phencyclidine,* an anesthetic that has drastic and unpredictable effects on the brain.

Important terms

aerial perspective	feature detectors	phi phenomenon
autokinetic illusion	figure and ground	prototype
binocular vision	gradient of texture	proximity
brightness constancy	interposition	selection
closure	interpretation	shadowing
color constancy	linear perspective	shape constancy
continuity	organization	similarity
contour	perception	size constancy
contrast	perceptual constancy	stroboscopic motion
depth perception	perceptual expectation	visual cliff
distance perception	perspective	

Postscript

altered states of conscious-ness	narcotics
clairvoyance	ordinary sleep
depressants	paradoxical sleep
extrasensory perception (ESP)	parapsychology
hypnosis	precognition
insomnia	rapid eye movement (REM)
meditation	REM sleep
mental telepathy	sedatives
	stimulants

Recommended readings

Carterette, E. C., and Friedman, M. P., eds. *Handbook of perception,* Vol. VIII *(Space and object perception)* and Vol. IX *(Perceptual processing).* New York: Academic Press, 1978.

Cartwright, R. D. *A primer on sleep and dreaming.* Reading, Mass.: Addison-Wesley, 1978.

Dember, W. N., and Warm, J. S. *Psychology of perception,* 2d ed. New York: Holt, Rinehart & Winston, 1979.

Edmonston, W. E., Jr., ed. *Conceptual and investigative approaches to hypnosis and hypnotic phenomena.* Annals of the New York Academy of Sciences, Vol. 296, 1977.

Hochberg, J. *Perception,* 2d ed. Englewood Cliffs, N.J.: Prentice-Hall, 1978.

Kaufman, L. *Perception: the world transformed.* New York: Oxford University Press, 1979.

Lindsay, P. H., and Norman, D. A. *Human information processing,* 2d ed. New York: Academic Press, 1977.

Neisser, U. *Cognition and reality.* San Francisco: Freeman, 1976.

Ray, O. S. *Drugs, society, and human behavior,* 2d ed. St. Louis: Mosby, 1978.

On ESP:

Hansel, C. E. M. *ESP: a scientific evaluation.* New York: Scribners, 1966.

Rhine, J. B., and Brier, R., eds. *Parapsychology today.* New York: Citadel Press, 1968.

Tart, C. T. *Learning to use extrasensory perception.* Chicago: University of Chicago Press, 1976.

Part five
Emotions
and motives

Up to this point, the book has talked mostly about characteristics you have in common with all other members of the human race. You share with everyone else the kind of genes that produce our typically human body and brain and incline all of us to certain species-specific patterns of behavior. What psychologists have discovered about learning and memory applies to all of us. So does their knowledge about the use of language, the nature of human intelligence, and the operation of the senses and perception.

True, all these matters are subject to individual differences. All of us have our own physical characteristics, including unique facial features that distinguish us from other people. We display a wide range of ability to learn and remember. Our perceptions, as was discussed in Chapter 8, are affected by our individual expectations. But, by and large, we are far more alike than different in all these respects.

Psychology began, indeed, as an attempt to discover general laws that would explain human behavior—just as chemistry began as an attempt to discover general laws about the forms of matter that make up our Earth. But psychologists—and people who hope to use psychological knowledge to enrich their own lives—are concerned not just about universal rules of behavior but about the *individual*. This concern is most apparent among clinical psychologists, who devote their careers to helping individuals overcome their own special problems. It is also apparent in the professional (and popular) attention paid to differences in human personalities, normal and abnormal behavior, and social relationships.

This section of the book is a bridge between general laws and individual behavior. Chapter 9 discusses human emotions—which, as you will see, can be described in ways that apply to everyone and yet enrich or plague our lives in innumerable individual ways. Chapter 10 discusses motives—which, again, display a general pattern that takes a different form in each of us, making us all seek varied goals with varying degrees of intensity.

Emotions and motives are like the human face—always the same in general, yet never wholly alike. These two chapters will introduce you to psychology's findings about the many factors that create the infinite variety of human personality, which is the total pattern of psychological traits that makes each of us unique.

Outline

Emotions and the body: "stirred up" or "toned down" 324

Emotions and the brain 332

Individual differences in emotion 336

The drives and behavior 339

Stimulus needs as a driving force 345

Postscript

Sexual feelings and behavior 349

Summary 357

Psychology and Society

Chapter nine

Emotions and drives

(with a postscript on sexual feelings and behavior)

There is evidence all around us about the wide range of individual differences in emotional experiences and behavior. You doubtless know some people who cry at the movies and others who would not shed a tear at the funeral of their best friend. You know people who go into ecstasies when they receive a birthday card and others who would be unmoved by the gift of a diamond. You probably have terrible-tempered friends who are angry at the world from morning till night and sweet-tempered friends who never raise their voices no matter how badly the world treats them. You know fearful people who are terrified by thunderstorms and brave people who would not hesitate to fight off an armed robber. One student gets an attack of the butterflies when asked a simple question in a small class. Another stays calm while addressing an assembly of hundreds.

Such differences are easy to see but hard to explain. Indeed emotions are something of a mystery. Just what is an emotion? What happens to us when we are angry, afraid, joyous, or sad? Do we control our emotions—or do they control us?

These questions have always interested and often baffled psychologists. The science now has some of the answers, but emotions continue to present a fascinating and frustrating puzzle that is still surrounded by speculation and debate.

Emotions and the body: "stirred up" or "toned down"

One essential characteristic of emotions is that they are accompanied by bodily changes. The easiest cases to recognize are those in which the body is obviously "stirred up." We assume that people are emotional when their voices rise, when they blush or get pale, when their muscles grow tense or tremble. We know that we are ourselves emotional—even if we manage to conceal all outward signs—when we feel that we are inwardly shaking, or are "hot under the collar," or that our mouth is dry, our pulse racing, or our stomach "full of butterflies." But there are also quieter emotions in which the body seems to be "toned down." Such are the calm, peaceful, and contented feelings we experience when we enjoy a sun bath, a beautiful piece of music, or a cup of coffee after a satisfying meal. In these cases too, however, the body is affected in some manner.

The relationship between mind and body in emotion seems to work both ways. Think about something very pleasant, such as inheriting a million dollars from an unknown relative. Quite possibly you will soon *feel* pleasant. Think of something that angers you, such as a bad grade, a social snub, being blamed for someone else's mistake. Soon you may *feel* angry. Or try the opposite. Make a smile, hold it, and see if you do not begin to feel happy and have pleasant thoughts. Clench your fist, keep clenching it, and see if you do not begin to feel angry and have aggressive thoughts.

A psychologist once demonstrated this relationship through an experiment in which college students were led to manipulate their facial muscles without realizing that what they were doing had any relationship to emotions. They were told that the experiment was a study of the effect of muscle movements on perception. Electrodes were attached to the facial muscles to make this explanation seem plausible. The subjects were then asked to contract or relax their muscles in a way that at times resembled a smile and at other times resembled a frown. To a very considerable extent,

To be emotional usually means to be emotional all over. The obvious outward display shown here is accompanied by equally turbulent inner changes.

9-1 Displays of emotion in the cat
An angry or friendly cat shows many signs of a stirred-up bodily state. The angry cat (left) crouches and growls. Its hair stands on end and its ears are laid back and its eyes wide and staring. The friendly cat (right) arches its back, pricks its ears, narrows its eyes, and purrs (2).

the subjects reported feeling happy when the muscles were in a smiling position and angry when the muscles were in a frowning position—though they were not consciously aware of their own facial expressions (1).

Being emotional all over

The fact that emotion is accompanied by changes affecting many parts of the body is most apparent in the behavior of lower animals, such as the cat pictured in Figure 9-1. It is less obvious among human beings, for most of us have learned to hide many of the outward signs of emotion. But the changes can readily be measured with laboratory equipment like the device illustrated in Figure 9-2. This is an elaborate version of what is commonly called a lie detector, used in attempts to pick up emotional reactions caused by lying. The changes can also be shown by chemical analysis of the composition of the blood.

When we experience a strong emotion, such as fear, heartbeat may increase from the normal rate

9-2 A machine that measures emotions
This device produces continuous tracings of bodily processes that often change during emotion. The bands around the man's body measure his rate and depth of breathing. The sleeve around his upper arm measures blood pressure. Electrodes attached to his hand, not shown in the photo, measure what is called the galvanic skin reflex, or changes in the electrical activity of the skin caused by activity of the sweat glands.

of around 72 per minute to as high as 180. Blood pressure may also rise sharply, and blood is often diverted from the digestive organs to the muscles of movement and to the surface of the body, resulting in flushed cheeks and the sensation of warmth. The composition of the blood changes. The number of red corpuscles, which carry oxygen, increases markedly. Secretion of hormones by the endocrine glands produces changes in the level of blood sugar, the acidity of the blood, and the amount of adrenalin and noradrenalin (powerful stimulants secreted by the adrenal glands) in the blood stream.

The normal movements of the stomach and intestines, associated with the digestion and absorption of food, usually stop during anger and rage. In other emotional states they may show changes resulting in nausea or diarrhea (3). The body's metabolic rate tends to go up. Food in the blood stream and the body tissues themselves are burned off at a faster rate, creating additional energy. Breathing may change in rate, depth, and ratio between time spent breathing in and time spent breathing out. We may gasp or pant. The salivary glands may stop working, causing the feeling of dryness in the mouth often associated with fear and anger. The sweat glands, on the other hand, may become overactive, as shown by the dripping forehead that may accompany embarrassment or the "cold sweat" that sometimes accompanies fear. The muscles at the base of the hairs may contract and raise goose flesh. Finally, the pupils of the eyes may enlarge, causing the wide-eyed look that is characteristic of rage, excitement, and pain.

Emotions, the autonomic nervous system, and the glands

All these changes represent bodily activities controlled by the autonomic nervous system (described on pages 59–65) and the endocrine glands (pages 65–69), over which we ordinarily have little if any conscious control. And it is worthy of note that we do not seem to have much control over our emotions. They often seem to boil up of their own accord, and we feel them even if we manage to hide all outward signs. Even in situations where we have determined in advance to remain calm, we often find ourselves unaccountably angry, frightened, or anxious.

In the case of fear and anger, two of the most powerful emotions, the adrenal glands seem to be unusually active. In one study, a chemical analysis was made of the urine of players on a professional hockey team to determine how their adrenal glands functioned before and after a game. The players who took an active part in the game, fighting to win, showed about six times as much noradrenalin after the game as beforehand. But two injured players, who were unable to play and were worried about their future with the team, showed increased amounts of adrenalin. The coach sometimes showed more noradrenalin and sometimes more adrenalin, depending on how well his team had done (4).

Aside from detecting the presence of adrenalin in fear and noradrenalin in anger, however, psychologists have found it very difficult to match any particular bodily state with any particular emotional experience. The same person, on two separate occasions when reporting feelings of joyousness, may show a different pattern of bodily change each time. And a group of people who report feeling exactly the same emotion (say of joy or distress) may show a number of different patterns. Among

students anxious over an examination, for example, one may tend to perspire a great deal, another to show muscle tension, another to have a rapid pulse (5). Certainly bodily changes are an important element in emotion. But the changes have been described as "rather diffuse and global in character" (6). It is very hard to determine, through physiological measurement alone, what kind of emotion a person is experiencing.

The role of the facial muscles

A number of other bodily changes that often accompany emotion have nothing to do with the autonomic nervous system, the glands, or the visceral organs. Instead these changes represent activity of the striped muscles of movement (pages 58–59), over which we do ordinarily have conscious control. You probably have been aware of some of them—for example, muscular tension (as

The men are Montreal Canadiens watching Stanley Cup play from the sidelines. Are their emotions influenced more by adrenalin or noradrenalin?

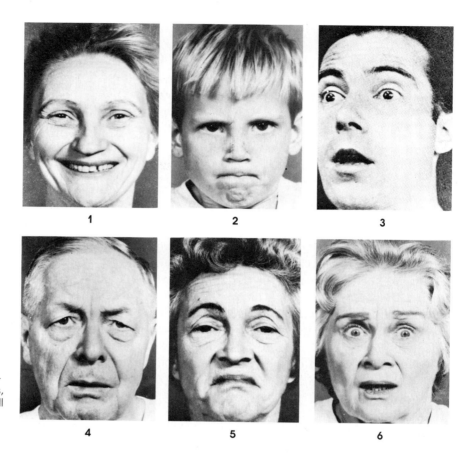

9-3

Facial expressions of emotion: can you identify them?

Try to match these faces with the emotions of anger, disgust, fear, happiness, sadness, and surprise. The answers will be found at the bottom of the page.

when the teeth are clenched in anger) or trembling (which occurs when two sets of muscles work against each other). Many people, when emotionally excited, have a tendency to blink their eyes or make nervous movements, such as brushing back their hair or drumming their fingers. Emotions are often expressed vocally (in laughter, snarls, moans, or screams) or in facial expressions (smiles, grimaces, and frowns).

One group of psychologists maintain that facial expressions are a key factor in emotional experience. They hold that every basic emotion is ac-

companied by a characteristic facial pattern that occurs automatically because of the manner in which our bodies and brains are programed by heredity (7). The various patterns, they believe, are the product of evolution, since an ability to communicate through facial expressions has considerable survival value. Especially for animals that do not have a spoken language, it is an advantage to be able to avert hostility through facial expressions of friendliness or submission. Expressions of fear can alert other members of the group to the presence of danger. Thus the process of natural selection favored the survival of individuals carrying genes programing their facial expressions (8).

The emotions being expressed in Figure 9-3 are: 1) happiness, 2) anger, 3) surprise, 4) sadness, 5) disgust, and 6) fear.

This theory is based in part on a study that used the photographs shown in Figure 9-3. These photos and several others were shown to subjects in a number of different societies, and the subjects were asked to try to identify the emotions being displayed (as you are asked in the caption accompanying the faces). There was remarkable agreement about the emotions—not only among subjects in the United States, Argentina, Brazil, China, and Japan but among members of isolated and underdeveloped societies in New Guinea (9). The study indicates that the facial expressions that accompany at least some emotions seem to be universal and unlearned, as if they were indeed genetically programed—set by nature rather than nurture.

Left brain, right brain, and facial expressions

A provocative finding about facial expressions was made in a recent experiment that used the three photographs shown in Figure 9-4. Before you read the next paragraph, look at the photos and try to determine your answer to the question posed in the caption.

If the three photos struck you as being alike yet somehow different, there is a reason. *A* is an undoctored photograph of the man. The other two are composites, made by splitting the original photo down the middle and flopping the two halves. In *B*, you see the man as he would appear if his entire face were like the right side. *C* shows the face as if it were made up of two left sides. If you found that *C* seemed to display the most intense emotion, you have considerable company. When the experimenters showed the three photographs—and similar ones of other people displaying various other emotions—they found that subjects tended to agree that the left-face composites gave the most intense impression (10).

The experiment may remind you of what was said earlier about the differences between the left brain and right brain (especially on pages 51–55). The left hemisphere of the brain, you will recall, seems to specialize in language, logic, and details. The right hemisphere seems to specialize in spatial relationships, form, and music, and in achieving intuitive understanding of "the big picture" instead of concentrating on details. There is also some evidence that the right hemisphere plays a dominant role in activating the muscles of the face (11)

A   B   C

 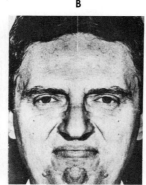 

9-4

Three expressions of emotion: Which is the strongest?

In all three photographs the man is expressing disgust. In which one, would you say, is his expression clearest and strongest? The way most people answer this question is explained in the text.

and in emotional reactions (12). Thus it seems possible, as the experiment with the composite photographs suggests, that expressions on the left side of our face give the best indication of the emotion we are experiencing. All this is still somewhat speculative—but it suggests that, if you want to know how other people really feel, you should concentrate on the expression on the left side of their face and ignore the right side. This is not as easy to do in the ordinary rapid flow of conversation and changes in facial expression as in a laboratory where photographs can be manipulated, but it may prove worth the effort.

The eyes as clues to emotion

Back in the sixteenth century a French poet wrote that the eyes are "windows of the soul." Modern psychology testifies that these words were more than a felicitous figure of speech. Studies have shown that one very sensitive measure of some emotions is the size of the pupil of the eye.

Pupil size is a good indication of even such a mild emotion as interest. One experiment that demonstrates this fact is illustrated in Figure 9-5. In general, it was found that subjects showed significant increases in pupil size when they looked at pictures they found interesting, but no increase when they looked at something they found unpleasant (13). In another experiment, male subjects looked at the two photographs shown in Figure 9-6, which you should examine before reading the next paragraph.

The only difference in the two photographs in Figure 9-6 is that the one at the left has been retouched to make the woman's pupils seem larger, the one at the right to make them seem smaller. Yet this slight difference made a considerable difference in the way subjects responded—and perhaps in the way you reacted. When the subjects

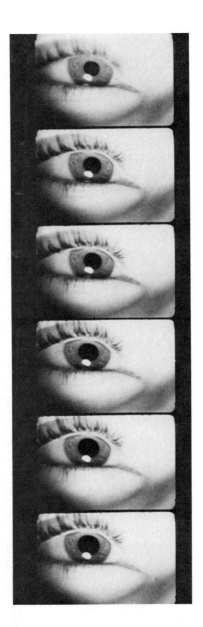

9-5 A photographic record of pupil response

This series of photographs, taken over a period of four seconds, show a man's eye as he looked at a picture of a woman's face. Note the rapid increase in pupil size from the normal, at top, to the bottom, where the diameter was about 30 percent greater.

An experiment in judging facial expressions

Take a careful look at these two photographs. In which of them does the woman appear to be more sympathetic? In which does she seem to be angrier? Or do you find no difference? For the opinions of subjects who took part in an experiment using the photos, see the text.

were asked in which photo the woman seemed to be more sympathetic (or warmer, happier, or more attractive), they tended to pick the face with the large pupils. When they were asked in which one she seemed angrier (or more unfriendly or more selfish) they tended to pick the one with the small pupils (14). Moreover, their own pupils grew wider when they looked at the photo with the large pupils than when they looked at the other.

One experimenter, who worked with mothers and babies in their homes, examined the effect of a drug that dilated her pupils on one visit, then a different drug that made her pupils artificially small on another visit. When the experimenter's pupils were large, she found that the babies smiled at her more often. The responses of the mothers were also affected. When her pupils were large, the mothers described her in such terms as "soft," "gentle," and "open." When her pupils were small, they found her "harsh," "brassy," and "cold" (15).

All in all, it appears that pupil size—which is controlled by the autonomic nervous system and the smooth muscles of the iris—not only reflects emotional states but serves as a clue that all of us use in assessing how other people feel. We may not even be conscious of the fact, but we seem to be somehow aware that large pupils indicate interest and therefore warmth and acceptance. Long before psychology began studying this matter, women used belladonna, a drug that dilates the pupils, as a standard part of their cosmetic equipment. They believed that putting drops of belladonna in their eyes made them more attractive—indeed the word *belladonna* means "beautiful lady." Perhaps they were right, though for reasons not understood at the time. Along similar lines, we speak warmly of children who are "wide-eyed" with wonder at Christmas—and we describe unfriendly and hostile people as being "sharp-eyed" or "gimlet-eyed."

It is interesting to note, however, that not everyone reacts more favorably to wide pupils under all circumstances. It has been found that male homo-sexuals tend to prefer photos of women with small pupils to photos of women with wide pupils. The same seems to be true of Don Juans—men who are more interested in sexual conquests than in forming close relationships with women (16).

Feedback theories of emotion (James-Lange and others)

The various changes that take place in the body, welling up without conscious control and often de-spite our determination to suppress them, have na-turally commanded the attention of psychology from its earliest days. They were the basis of the first important theory of emotions—which was pro-posed by William James (discussed on page 29 as one of the science's founding fathers) and repre-sented a radical change in thinking about emo-tional behavior. Common sense says that we cry because we are sad, strike out because we are angry, tremble and run because we are afraid. James made the suggestion—startling to the scien-tific world of his day and even now to someone who hears it for the first time—that things were exactly the opposite.

James said that emotion occurs in this fashion: Certain stimuli in the environment set off the psysio-logical changes. These changes in turn stimulate the various sensory nerves leading from the visceral organs and other parts of the body to the brain. It is these sensory messages from our aroused bodies that we then perceive as emotion. In other words, we do not cry because we are sad. On the con-trary, we feel sad because we are crying. Similarly, we do not tremble because we are afraid, but feel afraid because we are trembling (17).

This notion that the physiological changes come first and that the perceived emotion is a feedback from the changes was also proposed at about the same time by the Danish scientist Carl Lange. It persisted more or less unchallenged for many years as the *James-Lange theory of emotion*. The weak-ness of the theory is that it is so difficult to match any particular kind of bodily state (and whatever kind of feedback this might produce) with any par-ticular emotion.

A more recent theory has been proposed by psychologists impressed with the role of the facial muscles. They too believe that our feelings of emo-tion represent a feedback of bodily sensations—but not so much from the visceral organs as from the muscles of the face, which, as has been said, they believe are programed by nature to respond in certain definite ways to certain stimuli in the environment (18). Again the question is whether specific facial expressions can be matched with specific emotions. Proponents of the facial feed-back theory believe that the matching exists. Other psychologists are skeptical.

Emotions and the brain

Whether or not our feelings of emotion depend on feedback—either from the visceral organs, as the James-Lange theory presumed, or from the facial muscles—is just one of the many problems that continue to make emotions a topic of speculation and debate. But there is no doubt that emotions are accompanied by bodily changes of many kinds—ranging, as has been said, from pupil size to activity of the glands, digestive organs, and heart muscles, even the chemical composition of the blood. Nor is there any doubt that the activity of the brain changes—a fact that many psychologists now believe is the real key to emotional behavior.

Certainly emotions must be numbered among our most intense conscious experiences. Strong emotions—of the kind that made Oedipus gouge out his eyes, Juliet renounce her family for Romeo, and Hamlet kill his uncle the king—have been the chief subject of literature in all cultures throughout history. In our own day-to-day lives, our emotions frequently command our attention. When they boil up, we cannot ignore them. Our pleasant emotions (joy, love) have us "walking on air." Our unpleasant emotions (anger, fear, shame, disgust) fill us with despair. Emotions sometimes make it impossible for us to choose our words carefully, to concentrate on our work, or even to read or listen to music. They may make us, for the moment, totally irrational. A study of how people acted in emotional crises, such as being caught in a fire that threatened their life, found that about 15 percent became so panicky that they were unable to take any appropriate action. Another 70 percent showed at least some signs of disorganization (19).

The Cannon-Bard theory

The brain's activity was the basis of another famous theory of emotions—the *Cannon-Bard theory*. According to the Cannon-Bard view, certain stimuli in the environment cause the hypothalamus* to fire off patterns of nervous activity that have two simultaneous effects. One, the hypothalamus arouses

---

*Actually Cannon believed that the thalamus was the key. But it has since been found that the hypothalamus, with its close relationship to the autonomic nervous system and the pituitary gland, is the important structure.

the autonomic nervous system and thus triggers the various physiological changes associated with emotion. Two, at the same time the hypothalamus sends messages to the cerebral cortex that result in our feelings of emotion. Note that the Cannon-Bard theory attaches no importance to the feedback of bodily sensations, which is the basic element of the James-Lange theory. It considers the physiological changes to be a sort of side effect—useful in preparing the body to take appropriate action but not essential to our conscious experience of emotion.

At first glance, the Cannon-Bard and James-Lange theories seem totally at odds. It would appear that if one is right, the other must be wrong. But, as so often happens in the study of human behavior, what seems to be true is not necessarily true at all. Many psychologists now believe that both theories were partially correct but also partially wrong, in that neither was a full explanation.

The cognitive view of emotions

A number of psychologists, all leaning more or less to the cognitive school, have contributed to a new view of emotions. Their ideas are still being formulated and refined and at present differ in many respects, as you will see if you take an advanced course in emotional behavior. For our present purposes, however, their ideas can be put together into a sort of composite picture of the cognitive theory of emotion. The discussion that follows ignores some of the fine points that are at issue, and perhaps no single psychologist would agree with all the generalities—but it will serve as an introduction to this important area of research.

The cognitive view emphasizes the conscious experience of emotion—that is, the mental processes that account for our feelings of joy, anger, and fear.

Many factors contribute to this experience. One is information about events in the environment, delivered to the cortex or highest part of the brain from the sense organs. Another is the brain's storehouse of information about similar events in the past, which aids in appraising and interpreting the new stimuli. Another is patterns of nervous impulses in the hypothalamus and the rest of the brain's limbic system—which, acting through the autonomic nervous system and probably also directly on the pituitary gland, create the physiological changes of being stirred up or toned down. Still another is feedback from these physiological changes, delivered to the cortex via sensory neurons from the visceral organs and the muscles of the body and face. All these factors interact to produce the emotions we experience—and sometimes to initiate behavior that expresses our emotions, intensifies the pleasant ones, or helps us escape from the unpleasant ones.

Indeed some psychologists think of emotional experiences as another of the altered states of consciousness that were discussed on pages 305–14.

People who strike back with unaccustomed vigor in anger or panic in fear sometimes say afterward, "I wasn't myself" or "I must have been out of my mind." And certainly emotions, like other altered states, affect perception. To a joyous person, the world appears bright and cheerful. To a person caught up in distress and disgust, the world is full of gloom and disaster (20).

Cannon-Bard and its cognitive updating

The cognitive psychologists, you will have noted, agree with Cannon-Bard about the importance of the hypothalamus—but not with the theory that messages sent from the hypothalamus to the cortex account for our emotions. Though the exchange of messages between hypothalamus and cortex works in both directions, the new view holds that the cortex plays the commanding role by appraising events that occur in the environment. At any given moment, the information received by the cortex from the sense organs may be neutral in terms of emotional impact, in which case we make a

A blue mood, in which the whole world seems blue? Or is the slumping man just tired? Perhaps he himself has not yet made the appraisal.

As this family demonstrates, the same stimulus may be appraised by different people as calling for different emotions.

cognitive decision that no emotional reaction is called for. The information may set off patterns of nervous impulses, traveling from cortex to hypothalamus, that are associated with the emotions of interest. The sense organs may convey what the cognitive process decides is good information that calls for joy, or bad information calling for distress, anger, or fear.

The cognitive appraisal of the environment is often immediate and almost automatic (21)—something like the rapid first impression that occurs in perception. If we find a snake in our path, for example, everything seems to happen at once. Our hearts jump. We feel afraid. We leap back. All this seems to occur without any conscious decision making. At other times our appraisal is more complex and deliberate (22). An example is the "slow burn" we sometimes experience when we hear a remark, have no immediate reaction, then think about it, decide it was insulting, and get angry.

On some occasions the appraisal appears to follow rather than to precede physiological arousal. For some reason that we do not understand at the moment, our bodies become stirred up or toned down. Perhaps stimuli in the environment have affected the unconscious workings of our minds. Perhaps we have exhibited a conditioned reaction—as in Watson's famous experiment, described on pages 93–94, in which the child Albert's fear response was conditioned to furry animals and men with beards. At any rate, we experience some kind of change in the nature and level of our internal sensations, which we must then try to appraise and interpret (23). For example, a student sitting alone in a room at night may become aware of unusual bodily sensations and interpret them as feelings of loneliness. A student who has a similar pattern of sensations when a difficult examination is coming up may interpret them as anxiety. Another who has put in an unusually hard day's work may decide that they simply represent fatigue. Such cases of unexplained arousal are infrequent (24), but they do occur.

James-Lange and its cognitive updating

Just as the cognitive view accepts the Cannon-Bard theory in part, so does it agree with the James-Lange theory that bodily sensations are an essential aspect of emotion. Indeed it maintains that the brain and body work together in many ways during emotional experiences. For example, the student who interprets bodily sensations as representing anxiety over an examination may, as a result of this interpretation and labeling, experience additional activity of the autonomic nervous system, intensified physiological changes, and greater feedback—all of which add to the feeling of anxiety. On the other hand, attributing the feelings to fatigue may reduce the activity of the autonomic nervous system, dampen the physiological activity, and thus lessen the bodily feedback and the feelings being experienced.

The cognitive view maintains, however, that bodily states are not enough in themselves to account for all the very different emotions we experience. What really determines our feelings is our cognitive activity—our thinking about the stimulus that has produced the bodily changes and the entire environmental situation in which it occurs.

Individual differences in emotion

If someone asked you how many different kinds of emotions a human being can experience, how would you answer? Our language contains hundreds of words that describe emotional feelings—and your answer might depend on how many of these words you are familiar with, also how many of them you use to appraise and label your own feelings. The range of possibilities—and the intensity with which we experience all the various feelings, from mild to overwhelming—is almost limitless.

One psychologist has suggested that there are ten basic emotions, listed in Figure 9-7. Our other emotional experiences, according to this view, are combinations of two or more of these ten. The possible ways in which ten emotions can be combined, of course, runs into the thousands. If feelings of interest are considered to be emotions, as in this listing, then it appears that we experience some degree of emotional arousal during most or all of our waking hours (26). But the more spectacular feelings that most people think of as emotions (joy, anger, fear, and the like) occupy less of our time—by one estimate, probably under 10 percent for most of us (27).

Learning to be different

There are of course many individual differences in emotional experience. Some of these differences are the result of learning. Even simple classical conditioning, as was discussed in Chapter 3, can create unreasonable fears (as in the experiment in which 11-month-old Albert came to be afraid of dogs and other furry objects—pages 93–94) and unreasonable preferences. Because of this kind of childhood conditioning, some individuals have intense emotional reactions to objects or events in the environment that leave other people entirely unmoved. Moreover, the more complex cognitive processes that help determine emotional experience vary greatly from one person to another, mostly because of associations laid down in long-term memory through learning.

Behavior resulting from emotion also shows many individual differences. Some people have learned to suppress many of the outward signs of emotion. (Such people are often called "poker-faced.") Others are quick to display their feelings. (They are said to "wear their hearts on their

---

The ten basic emotions

anger	guilt
contempt	interest-excitement
disgust	joy
distress	shame
fear	surprise

Four important complex emotions

anxiety
(fear plus anger, distress, guilt, interest, or shame)

depression
(distress plus anger, contempt, fear, guilt, or shame)

hostility
(a combination of anger, contempt, and disgust)

love
(interest plus joy)

9-7 One psychological view
of the range of emotions
The fundamental human emotions, according to one investigator, are those listed at the top of the table. Other emotions that we frequently experience, notably those at the bottom, are combinations of some of the fundamental feelings (25).

sleeves.") Displays of emotion vary from culture to culture, obviously because of what these cultures have taught their members about appropriate behavior. When Navaho or Apache Indians are angry, they do not raise but lower their voices. When inhabitants of the Andaman Islands want to show joy at greeting a visiting relative, they sit down in the visitor's lap and weep (28).

Some inborn differences

On the other hand, some differences appear to be inborn. Studies of very young children, who have not yet had the opportunity to do much learning, have shown that some are much more inclined to smile than others, while some have a pronounced tendency to be irritable and to cry at the slightest provocation (29).

There is considerable evidence that one inborn difference affecting emotions is the sensitivity of the autonomic nervous system (ANS), which controls

Joy—as expressed here at a happy reunion—is one of the basic human emotions.

many of the bodily changes associated with emotion. It has been found, for example, that people differ widely in the way they respond to drugs that act directly on the ANS (30). Some of us seem to react to weaker stimulation of the ANS than others—and to react more rapidly and with greater intensity. Patterns of ANS activity also vary. In the same kind of emotional situation, one person may consistently show a rapid heartbeat, while another may show only a small change in heart rate but a pronounced increase in skin temperature (31). Differences of this kind can be observed even in children. Two-year-olds who are chronically anxious, timid, and shy have been found to have a heart rate that is unusually high but generally stable. Two-year-olds who are less fearful usually have a heart rate that is low and subject to considerably more variation (32).

There are also wide differences in the size and activity of the endocrine glands that play such an important part in emotion. A normal thyroid gland may weigh anywhere from 8 to 50 grams, the testes from 10 to 45 grams, the ovaries from 2 to 10 grams. The output of human adrenal glands under similar conditions has been found to vary from 7 to 20 grams, of pituitary glands from 250 to 1,100 milligrams (33). Presumably a person with large and active endocrine glands displays different physiological changes—and therefore has different emotional experiences—from a person with smaller or less active glands.

Certainly any abnormality of the glands or nervous system can have a drastic effect on emotional experience. One demonstration comes from a study of people who had suffered injuries to the spinal cord and had lost all bodily sensations below the point of damage. These people reported that their emotions were considerably less intense after the injury than before. The higher up the spine the damage had occurred, and thus the less feedback of bodily sensations they retained, the greater was the loss of emotional intensity (34).

Emotional stress—for better and for worse

Because the emotions are associated with so many physiological changes, often of a highly stirred-up nature, they put the body under considerable stress. They can be physically exhausting, as is evident from the washed-out feeling that often follows an outburst of anger or a serious scare. Wear and tear on the body are caused by pleasant as well as unpleasant emotions. As one investigator has stated, "A painful blow and a passionate kiss can be equally stressful" (35).

Up to a point, emotional stress is an unavoidable and even desirable aspect of life. Some of our most glorious moments arise from the tension and excitement of joy and love. The milder emotion of interest adds zest and meaning to our work, our recreation, and our social relationships. Without our emotions and their accompanying stress, our lives would be drab and colorless.

Even fear is useful. It helps us avoid or escape from situations that threaten our well-being and sometimes our lives. It makes us drive more carefully and plan more constructively for the future. Unless fear becomes so intense as to create panic, it can help us perform better in many situations. Many combat pilots, for example, have reported that mild fear made them more efficient. In one study, a third of the pilots said that even strong fear was helpful rather than disorganizing (36).

When the wear and tear of emotional stress persist too intensely and for too long a time, however, they can create disastrous effects. The topic of stress—and its relation to adjustment, coping, and abnormal psychology—will be discussed in Chapter 11.

The drives and behavior

Besides emotions, there is another group of psychological conditions that are accompanied by psysiological changes and have a pronounced effect on behavior. For example, as you know from experience, a state of hunger can make you jumpy, jittery, and unable to concentrate. The urge to find food, when the body lacks it, can be just as strong as the tendency to run away in fear or strike back in anger. In the famous case of a party of pioneers stranded by an 1846 blizzard in the Donner Pass, the urge overrode all moral and esthetic scruples and turned some of them into cannibals.

There is no clear dividing line between emotions and such states as hunger. Both depend on bodily activities. Both may produce strong sensations. Both may trigger behavior, sometimes of the most explosive kind. Yet there is a difference. In ordinary conversation, we would never think of referring to hunger as an emotion. Psychologists acknowledge a scientific difference by distinguishing between emotions and what they call *drives*.

The drives center on the process of homeostasis, or the maintenance of bodily stability. It is one of the brain's functions, as was explained in Chapter 2, to preserve homeostasis by making sure our bodies have a constant supply of all the substances our cells require to perform efficiently. When our bodies lack any of these substances, we experience a drive—which can be defined as *a pattern of brain activity resulting from physiological imbalances that threaten homeostasis.* Among the drives are *hunger* (caused by the lack of food), *thirst* (lack of water, which makes up two-thirds of our bodies), and *breathing* (the need for oxygen). The breathing drive goes unnoticed most of the time, but people who are drowning or being suffocated will fight as hard for air as they would fight for food when starving.

The pattern of brain activity that constitutes a drive makes us seek whatever our bodies need to maintain homeostasis. By so doing—for example, by finding food—we restore the physiological balance, change the pattern of brain activity, and thus satisfy the drive.

The signals for hunger

How do we know when we are hungry? Common-sense observation tells us we have hunger pangs that occur in the stomach, which feels empty and overactive and sometimes actually growls for food. This common-sense explanation is partially true. There are nerve fibers that carry messages to the brain from the stomach (37), and also from the mouth, throat, and intestines. But these messages do not seem essential. Experiments have shown that rats continue to show signs of hunger even if all the sensory neurons leading from the stomach to the brain are cut (38)—indeed even if the animal's entire stomach is removed (39). There have also been cases in which the human stomach has been removed for medical reasons, without any pronounced effect on the desire for food (40).

More important than sensations from the stomach, it now appears, are hunger messages originating in that previously unsuspected organ the liver. It is the liver that does the chief job of receiving food supplies after they have been absorbed into the blood stream from the intestines, then converting these foods into chemicals that provide energy for the cells of the body and brain. Apparently the liver is alert to any deficiencies in the body's food supplies and signals the brain when such deficiencies occur (41).

The role of the hypothalamus

Within the brain, the hypothalamus plays an important part in sensations of hunger. At one time, indeed, it was believed that the hypothalamus had two areas that acted as an on switch and an off switch for the hunger drive. This belief arose from experiments with animals. It was found that when an electrode is implanted in one part of the hypothalamus, and electrical stimulation is applied, an animal will start eating. If this same area is surgically destroyed, the animal loses virtually all interest in food (42). When an animal is stimulated through an electrode implanted in another part of the hypothalamus, it immediately stops eating. If this area is destroyed, the animal eats voraciously and becomes grossly fat (43).

These experiments, however, do not tell the whole story. For one thing, a rat stimulated in what might seem to be the on switch of the hypothalamus does not necessarily eat. If no food is present, the animal will do something else. It may drink water or gnaw on wood (44), as if the stimulation merely produced some kind of general arousal. Moreover, animals can be made to start eating by electrical stimulation of brain areas outside the hypothalamus (45)—or sometimes even by just pinching a rat's tail (46).

It appears now that the hunger drive depends on brain patterns that are far more complex than mere on and off switches (47). Some of the nerve cells in the hypothalamus seem to be sensitive to changes in the food supply present in the blood stream, particularly the level of fatty compounds (48) and also the level of blood sugar. But the hypothalamus also responds to messages carried by nerve fibers from various parts of the alimentary canal and from the liver. The hunger drive is also affected by outside stimuli—such "incentive objects" as the smell

Eating on the run, as at this newsstand, is generally less satisfactory—and likely to be less in volume—than eating under relaxed circumstances and in company.

of food from a restaurant kitchen or the sight of pastries in a bakery window—and by our eating habits and the social relationships we have built around eating. (We tend to feel hungry around our usual dinner time regardless of our physiological condition, and we usually eat more when we are with family or friends than when we are alone.)

Hunger and body weight

The hunger drive is closely related to the fact that the body contains a large number of cells, scattered throughout, that are especially designed for the storage of fatty compounds. In evolutionary terms, survival of the species presumably depended on the ability of these cells to store up energy that would tide the body over the prolonged periods of starvation that human beings once experienced frequently (and still do in many places). Under ordinary circumstances, the hunger drive keeps these cells filled to an appropriate level with fatty compounds. But when the body lacks other sources of food and energy, the fat cells are emptied and their contents used as fuel. This raises the level of fatty compounds in the blood stream—a change that serves as one of the triggers for the hunger drive.

Since the amount of fat stored in the body largely determines a person's weight, it might be said that the hunger drive tends to keep our body weight at its ideal level (49). Ordinarily we eat enough to

maintain our reserve stores of fat and keep our weight from falling too low (50). But we stop short of consuming an excess of food that would become fat deposits and make us too heavy (51).

Even a slight change in food intake can have a drastic effect on weight. For example, adding as little as ten medium-sized potato chips a day to one's usual diet would result in a gain of about eleven pounds a year. Yet most of us stay at the same weight over long periods of time. One is reminded of the workings of a thermostat that manages, by turning a furnace on and off, to keep a building within a temperature range of one or two degrees.

In this connection, note the experiment illustrated in Figure 9-8. The animal in the experiment was fed

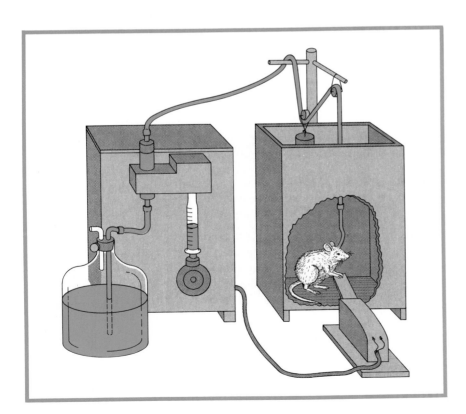

9-8
An animal that never eats— yet is properly fed

When the rat presses the bar, a squirt of liquid food is delivered directly to its stomach. It soon learns to press the bar just often enough to satisfy its hunger and maintain its normal intake of food (52).

artificially, with food delivered directly to the stomach. It never smelled, tasted, or swallowed the food. Nevertheless, it managed to maintain its body weight at the normal level. Indeed artificial feeding may have been an advantage in this respect—as will be seen in the following paragraphs about people who, despite the ordinarily fine-tuned workings of the hunger drive, become overweight.

Why do people get fat?

In the United States, it has been estimated, somewhere between a quarter and a third of all adults are at least 25 percent over their ideal weight—some by as much as 20 or 50 or even 100 pounds. The reason is a mystery that many psychologists have spent years trying to unravel.

In some cases, obesity seems to stem from metabolic disturbances. Instead of turning food into energy at the normal rate, the body stores an excessive amount of it as fat deposits. In most cases, however, obesity is simply the result of eating too much and exercising too little (53).

But why do people eat too much? Sometimes there seem to be emotional reasons. Clinical psychologists have found that many overweight patients overeat to relieve anxieties over competition, failure, rejection, or sexual performance. And some people eat simply as a matter of habit—regardless of whether their hunger drive signals the need for food—or have a strong preference for such high-calorie foods as butter, cheese, ice cream, pastries, and candy.

Studies have found that the eating patterns of fat people are unusual in several respects. For one thing, fat people tend to eat whenever they have the opportunity, even if they have already had a meal and would not normally be hungry. This was demonstrated in striking fashion in the experiment illustrated in Figure 9-9. In another experiment, in

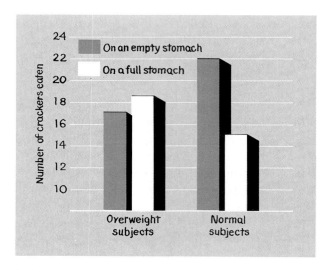

9-9 One clue to overeating
An experimenter worked with two groups of subjects, one group of normal weight and the other anywhere from 14 to 75 percent overweight. When the subjects arrived at the laboratory, having skipped the previous meal, half from each group were fed sandwiches, the other half nothing. They then took part in what they thought was an evaluation of the taste of five different kinds of cracker presented to them in separate bowls. They were told that they could eat as few or as many of the crackers as they wished in making their judgments. As the graph shows, the amount eaten by the subjects of normal weight was considerably lower if they had just eaten sandwiches. The overweight subjects, however, actually ate somewhat more on a full stomach than on an empty stomach. For a possible explanation of these results, see the text (54).

which clocks were manipulated to make the subjects think that dinner was being served later than usual, fat people ate more than their customary amount, though people of normal weight did not (55). Whenever overweight people sit down to a table, they tend to eat more and eat faster (56). They are particularly likely to eat a lot when the food tastes unusually good—and more likely than people of normal weight to be turned off by food that tastes bad (57).

In all these respects, the eating habits of overweight people closely resemble those of animals that have become fat after surgical destruction of part of the hypothalamus. Moreover, overweight people behave in a number of other ways very much like animals with damage to this part of the brain. They tend to be emotional and irritable (58, 59), to be more lethargic and less active than average (60), and to have less interest in sex (61).

It is possible that overweight people have some kind of brain abnormality affecting regions of the hypothalamus—something akin to the surgical destruction in experimental animals (62). Or it may be that the blood stream of overweight people carries some kind of chemical, produced by a quirk in the manner in which their alimentary canals and livers process food, that overstimulates the hypothalamus and thus creates more frequent and more intense hunger. Investigators are trying to learn whether such a substance exists—and if so, what it is and how it might be controlled (63).

Too many fat cells?

Another theory of obesity blames the cells designed for storage of fatty compounds. It has been found that at least some overweight people have an unusually large number of these cells in their body (64). In extreme cases, they may have fully three times as many as people of normal weight (65). The level of fatty compounds in their blood stream tends to be high at all times (66)—and the fat content of the blood, as has been mentioned, is one of the factors to which the hypothalamus is sensitive.

Thus overweight people, because of their excessive numbers of fat cells, may be more or less constantly hungry for reasons they cannot control by any act of will power. Their hunger may become particularly intense if they try to diet. Indeed it has been suggested that many fat people, because of the social pressure against obesity, are actually

underweight rather than overweight in terms of the requirements of their own bodies (67).

Why do some people have more fat cells than others? The answer seems to lie partly in heredity. Breeding experiments with animals show that some strains are more likely than others to produce fat offspring generation after generation (68). Similarly, overweight human parents tend to have overweight children.

Overeating in the period immediately after birth may also be a factor. Experiments with rats indicate that the number of fat cells in their bodies is increased by giving them excessive amounts of food during the first three weeks of life, after which overfeeding no longer has this effect. Similarly, the number of fat cells in the human body seems to be established during early childhood and to remain relatively constant from then on. Adults who go on

Does the tendency to be overweight run in families? The artist who produced this painting seems convinced that it does.

starvation diets show a decrease in the size of these cells, as their contents are drawn on for fuel, but no decrease in the number of cells (69). People who deliberately overeat to gain weight show an increase in the size of the cells but no increase in number (70). One approach to the obesity problem may be to urge mothers not to push babies to overeat during the early period when the number of fat cells is being established. But of course this approach comes too late for overweight people beyond the age of childhood, who continue to have their difficulties despite everything that has been learned thus far about the hunger drive.

Thirst

The thirst drive resembles the hunger drive in many respects. The common-sense observation—that we get thirsty when our mouths are dry—again turns out to be partially true. The drive does depend in part on messages carried to the brain from the mouth—as well as from the throat, which seems to signal how much water has passed through, and from the stomach, which signals whether it is empty or full (71). But again this is not the full explanation. A person may feel thirsty even when nerve fibers from the mouth and throat are under anesthesia, sending out no messages at all (72).

Again the hypothalamus plays an important part. A lack of water causes the cells of the body to become dehydrated, and certain nerve cells in the hypothalamus appear to be sensitive to this change. Moreover, a lack of water reduces the volume of blood flowing through the body, causing sensory receptors in the blood vessels and heart to send signals to the brain (73). The reduced volume of blood also causes the kidneys to produce a chemical that stimulates the hypothalamus (74).

Thus the thirst drive is triggered by various signs of imbalance in the body's water supply. Much as

in the case of hunger, the goal of the thirst drive is water, not the mere act of drinking. When the experiment that was illustrated in Figure 9-8 is changed, so that the animal receives water instead of food directly into the stomach, the animal soon learns to take in the normal amount of fluid even though it never drinks.

Other drives

The *sleep drive*, which plays an important part in the rhythm of our daily lives, was mentioned on pages 305–09 in the discussion of altered states of consciousness. This drive appears to be triggered by imbalances in brain chemistry, and possibly body chemistry as well, that build up while we are awake and active. When we sleep, we correct the chemical imbalances and wake up ready to function again at full efficiency. As in the case of hunger, it has been found that surgery on parts of the brain has drastic effects. Destruction of one area causes an animal to remain awake until it dies of exhaustion. Destruction of another area causes the animal to sleep almost constantly. But it is not clear whether this indicates that the brain contains an on switch and an off switch for sleep or whether the surgery merely interferes with a more complex circuitry that controls the drive.

The *temperature drive* is common to all warmblooded animals. In human beings its goal is to maintain the body's inner temperature at about 98.6° Fahrenheit (37° Centigrade). It appears to be controlled by cells in the brain that are sensitive to temperature changes. When stimulated by increased warmth, they send off messages that cause perspiration (which cools the body through evaporation) and that also cause more blood to move toward the surface of the body, where it loses heat more quickly. When stimulated by cooling, these brain cells induce shivering (the constriction of blood vessels in the skin) and increased

The sleep drive can be powerful enough to prevail even in the most uncomfortable circumstances, as on this park bench.

bodily activity and more heat production (75).

The *elimination drive* serves to rid the body of its waste products.

The *pain drive* leads us to avoid events that would damage our body. It accounts for such learned behavior as keeping our hands away from flames, being careful with sharp objects, and rest-

ing or swallowing medicine to relieve a headache.

To this list some scientists would add a *sex drive*. But sexual activity, though essential for survival of the species, is not essential for survival of the individual. Sex, and whether it is a drive or something else, is discussed at length in the postscript beginning on page 349.

Stimulus needs as a driving force

Drives are powerful forces. When they go unsatisfied, they may result in intense discomfort and eventually death. They have long been recognized and studied as primary sources for the energizing of behavior.

In recent years, psychologists have found that

our innate nature seems to demand certain other satisfactions. Food, water, sleep, and the other goals that satisfy the drives are not enough. In addition, we seem to have inborn tendencies to seek certain kinds of stimulation. We display what have come to be known as *stimulus needs*. There appear to be at least two kinds of stimulus needs; the *need for sensory stimulation* and the *need for stimulus variability*.

The need for sensory stimulation

One famous experiment that shows what happens to people who are deprived of sensory stimulation is illustrated in Figure 9-10. Volunteers remained in bed, with their senses of sight, hearing, and touch masked. Except during meal periods, they tasted and smelled nothing. In other words, activity of their senses was held to almost zero. Soon many of them found themselves unable to think logically. Their memories became disorganized. Sometimes they felt strangely happy. At other times they felt anxious or even panicky. Some of them began to develop symptoms associated with severe mental disturbance. They saw imaginary sights and heard imaginary sounds. The experience was so upsetting that nearly half of them had to beg off within forty-eight hours, even though they were being paid generously for each day they continued.

Other investigators, using similar techniques, have found less drastic effects. One study found that sensory deprivation may even produce some beneficial effects—for example, an increase in creative thinking and the discovery by heavy smokers that they can do without cigarettes when the usual incentive objects associated with smoking are removed (77). The conflicting results determined by different experimenters suggest that the expectations of subjects may play a part in the results. If subjects fear adverse consequences, perhaps they are more likely to experience distress.

At any rate, we do seem to have some kind of need for sensory stimulation if we are to continue functioning in a normal fashion. Why this should be true is not known. One possible answer lies in what has been discovered about the reticular activating

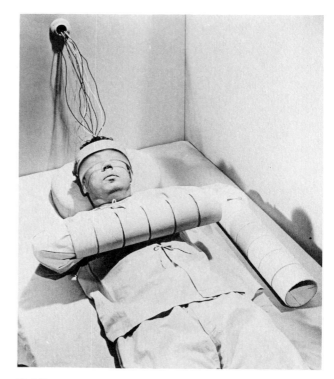

9-10 An experiment in sensory deprivation

This man is taking part in an experiment designed to show what happens when activity of the human senses is reduced as near as possible to zero. The eyeshade permits him to see nothing but a dim haze. The arm casts mask the sense of touch in his hands. The room is soundproofed, and he hears nothing but the soft hum of a fan. For what happens to him under these conditions, see the text. The wires at the top of the photo recorded his brain waves (76).

system of the brain (page 76). Nervous impulses from the sense organs pass through this system on their way to the sensory areas of the cerebral cortex, where they result in conscious sensations of sights and sounds. As they pass through, they seem to set off other impulses, which the reticular activating system sends to all parts of the cortex, keeping it in a state of activity and alertness. Without this barrage of impulses from the reticular acti-

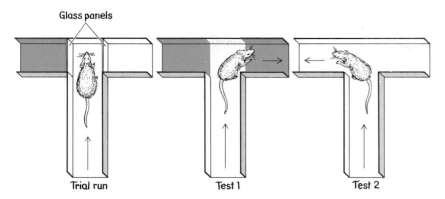

9-11 An animal's search for change

In the trial run a rat enters the T-maze at the bottom and is stopped by the glass panels at a point where it can see that the left arm is dark and the right arm is white. In test 1 the glass panels are removed and both arms are dark. The rat shows a strong tendency to enter the arm that was formerly white. If the trial run is followed by test 2, where both arms are white, the rat shows a strong tendency to enter the arm that was formerly dark. As the text explains, this behavior seems to be dictated by a preference for a change in stimulus (79).

vating system, it has been suggested, the cortex is handicapped (78).

The need for stimulus variability

As was stated in the chapter on perception, there is something inherently attractive and compelling about a *change* of stimulus. Indeed human beings seem to have an innate need for what is called *stimulus variability*. When we have the opportunity, we show an innate preference for a change in stimulation and tend to seek it out. This is also true of other organisms, as was demonstrated in the experiment illustrated in Figure 9-11. Even in this simple T-maze a rat shows a strong tendency to go to the arm that represents a change of stimulus— the dark arm that was originally white or the white arm that was originally dark.

The results of this experiment fit in with many other observations of animal and human behavior. Monkeys will learn to open a window, as in Figure 9-12, for the reward of seeing what is happening

9-12 The case of the curious monkey

The monkey, a prisoner in a dimly lit box, has learned to push open the window solely for the privilege of watching a toy train in operation for thirty seconds.

on the other side (80). Presented with the hooks and latches shown in Figure 9-13, a monkey will work hard to open them even though it has discovered that doing so leads nowhere. Human babies seem irresistibly attracted to rattles, toys hanging over the crib, and their own fingers (81). Adults gladly pay for the stimulus change represented by the lights flashing in a pinball game.

Stimulus variability and survival

The need for stimulus variability plays a useful role for the organism. Every stimulus change presents new information about the environment, and such information is often essential to successful adjustment and at times even survival. An organism with an inborn need for stimulus variability has a biological advantage over an organism without it.

One aspect of stimulus variability that deserves special mention is *stimulus complexity*. A young baby, to whom a toy rattle represents a strange and complicated stimulus, will play with it for a long time. An older infant will put it aside more quickly, and a schoolchild will not play with it at all. To a schoolchild a game of tag is endlessly fascinating, but a college student will settle for nothing less than football. To satisfy the organism's needs, the stimulus must have a certain amount of complexity. On the other hand, a stimulus that is too complex is not attractive. A child is more attracted to a nursery rhyme than to a Shakespeare sonnet.

These facts about stimulus complexity may remind you of Piaget's observations of the child's stages of intellectual development, which were discussed on pages 211–15. Piaget found that it is impossible to rush children from one stage to the next by trying to teach them the reasoning skills appropriate to the more advanced stage. At each level of development they can understand and profit from only such experiences and pieces of information as match what they already know—or that are just a little in advance of their existing

9-13 Why is this monkey working so hard?
Do the latches unlock anything? No. Does the monkey know this? Yes. Then why does the monkey bother to open the latches? For the answer, see the text.

information and skills. Similarly, all of us seek stimuli that are complex enough to intrigue us—but not so complex as to overwhelm and baffle us. It might be said that we have an innate curiosity—but only to the point where curiosity is rewarding rather than frustrating.

Emotions, drives, stimulus needs, and motives

All the matters mentioned in this chapter have a strong influence on behavior. We seek out events that arouse pleasant emotions (joy, love) and avoid events that arouse unpleasant emotions (distress, fear). The drives impel us toward such incentive objects as food. The stimulus needs give us a curiosity and a zest for variety in the sights and sounds with which we surround ourselves.

Thus all these matters, based at least in part on the ways in which our brains and bodies are programed by nature, have a bearing on the goals we seek in our day-to-day activities. They are closely related to the way we are motivated to behave, not only in our daily experiences but in our long-range planning. Indeed the line between emotions, drives, and stimulus needs, on the one hand, and motives, on the other hand, is difficult to draw. It is partly for the sake of convenience—rather than because of any clear-cut distinction—that psychologists separate the topics that have been discussed in this chapter from their studies of motives, which will be the subject of the next chapter.

(Summary begins on page 357.)

Postscript

Sexual feelings and behavior

There is one powerful force in human behavior that defies classification. Should sex be merely a subheading under the general topic of drives, like hunger and thirst? Perhaps—for among lower animals it has many of the characteristics of a drive. Should it have been discussed under emotions? Perhaps—for sexual passion is one of the most intense of all human feelings, and it is closely related to the emotion we call love.

If this were a book about lower animals, there would be less difficulty about classifying sex. Among nonhuman mammals, sex is almost as direct a drive as hunger, though less frequently triggered. Usually the female sex drive is quiescent, and over long stretches of time the female is not sexually attractive to the male of her species. At regularly recurring periods, however, the ovaries release hormones that activate a sex control mechanism centered in the hypothalamus of the brain. During these periods, which vary in frequency and length from species to species, the female seeks sexual contacts and engages in the kind of courtship and copulation characteristic of the species. The female's readiness is apparent from such clues as odors, vocal signals (the sex "calls" of cats), or changes in the color and size of the genitals. These cues in turn prompt the male to initiate sexual behavior.

Sex in many animals also resembles a drive in that the behavior that satisfies it is largely unlearned. Even when rats are raised in total isolation, with no opportunity to learn about the anatomy of the opposite sex or about the species' characteristic sexual behavior, they usually copulate like other rats at the first opportunity. Farther up the evolutionary scale, however, some learning seems necessary. Male and female monkeys raised in isolation do not ordinarily know how to behave toward each other at the first meeting (82).

Among human beings, sex bears only slight resemblance to a drive. True, sexual activity is most frequent during the years when the concentration of sex hormones in the blood stream is highest, from puberty into the middle years. But men and women of all ages can have the desire and ability to engage in sexual activity. The female's desires are not significantly dependent on her monthly hormone cycles. Nor is her sexual attractiveness to the male. Some people seek out sexual contacts frequently, without any particular stimulation by glandular cycles or external cues. Others never engage in sexual activity, even in the most provocative situations.

Human sexual behavior clearly does not depend on some "sex center" in the brain that operates like an on-off switch. Rather, it seems to result from a combination of many nervous pathways ranging all the way from the spinal cord to the cerebral cortex (83). Some of these pathways may be programed by heredity. Others have doubtless been created by experience and learning. Some are influenced by the activity of the sex glands in complex ways that have thus far defied analysis (84). Others may not depend on glandular activity at all.

Sexual behavior is influenced by a whole array of desires and preferences that all of us begin to learn in childhood and may continue to revise throughout our lives. It is molded by our personalities, moral standards, and social relationships—the ways in which we have learned to regard our parents and brothers and sisters, to establish friendships, and to view marriage and some of the problems that occur in marriage. Some people, indeed, value sexual experiences less for the physical gratification they provide than as acts of communication, friendship, or even hostility. (Many rapists seem to be motivated less by sexual passion than by a hatred of the opposite sex.) The emotion of love, though often associated with sexual desire, may be felt just as strongly in nonsexual situations—as toward a child, a parent, or a close friend.

The sexual revolution

At the beginning of this century, a team of scientists visiting our planet from outer space might have had trouble guessing how Americans produced their babies. They would have found little mention of sex in our newspapers or magazines. They would have found nothing taught about sex in the schools, even medical schools. For an indication that Americans engaged in sexual behavior, they would have had to look to the nation's laws—where they would have found only that Americans were supposed to be carted off to jail immediately if they entered into adultery, sex before marriage, or such "unnatural acts" as oral sex.

These days, visitors from outer space would get a far different impression. The United States in recent decades has gone through a widely publicized "sexual revolution" that has produced, among other things, an almost total freedom to discuss and write about sex. Indeed today's novels and movies often make it appear that Americans are programed by nature to spend most of their time engaging in sexual activity or preparing for it. The visiting scientists would be forced to wonder not how Americans reproduce—but how they manage to find time to do anything else.

Brand-new attitudes, same old behavior

The sexual revolution has created sharp shifts in public opinion. As recently as the 1960s, for example, polls showed that a considerable majority

The emotion of love is molded by a host of desires, preferences, and attitudes that all of us began to learn in early childhood.

of Americans believed sex before marriage was wrong. But a Gallup poll found that this attitude had turned around completely by 1973. By that time a majority of people, even counting those older and more conservative, had decided that sex before marriage is not necessarily immoral.

Some of the pioneers in the birth control movement went to jail for their beliefs. Now information is available in almost any library. The various methods of birth control are used by about 68 percent of married couples in the child-bearing years (85) and by most people who engage in sex outside marriage—although many young people remain ignorant of effective techniques and the number of illegitimate births among teenagers has risen sharply since the 1960s (86). Attitudes toward such practices as oral sex, for which some married couples went to prison only a few decades ago, have be-

come much more permissive. Most people are no longer horrified when a literary figure or popular musician, male or female, admits to homosexual activity.

Despite all the open discussion of sex and the changes in public attitudes, however, the sexual revolution seems to have had less effect on actual behavior than is generally supposed. For one thing, the United States of the past was by no means so sexless and proper as it pretended to be. The stringent old laws were seldom enforced—which was just as well, for there would never have been enough prisons to hold all the millions of women and the estimated 95 percent of men who broke them (87). And today's Americans are not nearly so preoccupied with sex as our literature and films suggest. In many ways people think, feel, and behave about sex just as they have always done. The pendulum of society's attitudes moves back and forth between strictness and permissiveness. It has done so throughout history from one period to the next and from one society to another. But what sex means to individuals, and the way individuals behave sexually, does not change nearly so much.

Individual differences: the forgotten message of the Kinsey reports

Many serious students of behavior, in fact, have concluded that the sexual revolution may have created as many problems as it has solved—and may have produced no net gain at all in human sexual fulfillment. One reason is that the new freedom to discuss sex has spawned a whole new profession whose members deluge the nation with what they claim are the secrets of sexual happiness. Like the authors of books guaranteed to make you lose twenty pounds in twenty days, they present advice that seldom works and for most people may actu-

Psychology and Society

The latest "scientific survey" on sex: How scientific is it?

Hardly a month passes without some magazine or book publisher coming out with what is advertised as the last word in sexual information—a brand-new, comprehensive, thoroughly scientific study of exactly how Americans feel and act. The statistics look impressive. Thousands of people took part in the survey. It turned out that exactly 51.6 percent of them are given to Behavior A, 22.9 percent Behavior B, and so on down the line to a mere 0.4 percent who indulge in Behavior G.

Sounds impressive. In actual fact, however, most of the highly publicized "sex surveys" have no scientific validity at all. They do not follow any of the rules carefully designed by psychologists for accurate sampling in public opinion polls (pages 16–17). Magazines often survey only their own readers—who are a small and special group interested in the subject matter and viewpoint of that particular publication. Many book authors, untrained in psychology, mail out thousands of questionnaires but have to base their statistics on the relatively few who bother to answer (because the questions tickle their own particular fancy). One of the best-selling sex surveys of recent years, *The Hite Report,* was guilty on both counts. The author sent out 100,000 questionnaires but received only 3,019

replies—many of them from people who learned about the survey in two specialized publications read by only a fraction of 1 percent of Americans. The sexual preferences tabulated in *The Hite Report* may hold for the 3,019 women who answered the questionnaire, but they tell nothing about American women in general.

Even the most serious sex researchers have problems. It is difficult to find a representative sample of people who will discuss their attitudes and behavior candidly and truthfully. It is difficult to know what to ask and how to phrase the questions to avoid influencing the responses. Kinsey, for all his painstaking efforts to be scientific, conceded that his own results were only "approximations of the fact," though he felt that they were "probably fair approximations" (88). Most of his popular imitators claim more but deliver much less. The latest so-called scientific survey may be interesting reading and may introduce you to some new viewpoints held by some people somewhere—but it is probably inaccurate in its statistics and certainly worthless as personal guidance. Perhaps it should be labeled, somewhat like a package of cigarettes, with a warning that it might be injurious to your mental health.

ally be harmful. Most of the sexual discussion found in popular magazines and books is written by people who have never attempted any scientific study of the facts. Even surveys of opinion and behavior

are often misleading, as discussed in the above box on Psychology and Society.

Much of the advice and alleged fact-finding with which the nation is bombarded is based on the assumption that sex is the most urgent goal of human life for all people at all times—an assumption that seems to sell magazines and books but goes counter to the most important single finding of serious sex investigators. This is the fact that there seems to be a wider range of individual differences in sexual appetite, capacity, and preferences than in almost any other human trait.

For the best information on sexual characteristics, we are indebted to the Kinsey reports. Although Alfred Kinsey's books on male and female sexual behavior were written a generation ago, they remain the most solid surveys ever made, based on studies of more than 5,000 men and nearly 8,000 women—many of whom reported behaving in ways that Kinsey himself, who was stern and somewhat prissy by today's standards, at first found shocking.

Kinsey's greatest contribution, though it has been ignored by many of today's popular writers, was the discovery that individual differences in sexual behavior are truly amazing. For men in their twenties and early thirties, Kinsey found that the median number of orgasms was two a week.* But at the lowest extreme he found men who never had an orgasm. At the other extreme he found men who were having as many as four a day or more, day in and day out (89).

Among women the individual differences were even greater. Kinsey found some women who had never in their lives experienced sexual excitement of any kind. He also found women who had been married for many years but had experienced only one or two orgasms in their lives. At the other extreme, he found women whose sexual desires were so frequent and intense that they could be satisfied only by masturbation—in some cases as

many as thirty or more times a week, with numerous orgasms on each occasion (90).

Sex and nature-nurture

What causes these enormous differences? The answer is a matter of dispute—another aspect of the nature-nurture argument. And, as usual, there is a good deal to be said on both sides.

Nurture, in the form of learned attitudes toward sex, certainly plays a part. Growing up in a home where sex is thought of as "dirty"—spoken of only in terms of the evils of masturbation and the horror of venereal diseases—tends to produce inhibitions that can curtail behavior and responsiveness and perhaps reduce capacity as well. The general attitude of society also has an effect. For example, many generations of females were doubtless influenced by the old notion that a "good" woman was supposed to find sex repugnant and engage in it if at all only as a concession to the "animal nature" of her husband. Among women who were born before the turn of the century and grew up when this idea was still widely accepted, Kinsey found that about a third of them never experienced orgasm in the first year of marriage and about a fifth of them were still having no orgasms in the tenth year of marriage (91). Among women born in this century, these figures have steadily declined as society has become more permissive.

Many sex researchers have concluded that our varying sexual capacities also depend on the fact that we inherit different patterns of glandular activity, sensitivity of the nervous system, and other physical characteristics that contribute to sexuality. It has been found that men who enter puberty early—showing the typical change of voice and rapid growth in height as early as the age of eleven—tend to have the most insistent sexual appetites

---

*The median is the midway point. Half the men reported two or more a week, the other half two or fewer.

Is sex overemphasized?

Has the sexual revolution solved our nation's sex problems, or has it created new ones? Many psychologists have concluded that the revolution has done both. They welcome today's liberation from old taboos and guilts—but they fear that our present society may be creating new conflicts and anxieties by overemphasizing sex. The problem has been described by Paul Gebhard, who is Kinsey's successor as director of the Institute for Sex Research, in these terms:

> We at the Institute were once happy to see the pendulum swing in the direction of greater permissiveness. When we started our work in the 1940s there was far too much repression and hypocrisy. The old idea that sex was "dirty" was a very harmful thing. But now we worry that the pendulum has swung too far. There is a lot of difference between freedom to enjoy sex, which is what we have always favored, and a *command* to enjoy sex, which is what society often seems to be imposing today.
>
> It's an unfortunate thing to give people the idea—as much of today's propaganda does—that they should be ready, able, and eager to have sex any time of the day or night, with anybody they happen to meet. True, *some* people can do that—but most of us can't. To the extent that today's atmosphere puts a burden on people to display a constant sexuality—or pretend to display it—the atmosphere is just as harmful in its own way as the old taboos (96).

A number of new problems, presumably resulting from the sexual revolution, have been observed by therapists and sex counselors. Among men, there has been a considerable increase in "performance anxiety," or a fear of failure that sometimes makes males unable to perform at all. Among women, it has been found that many feel cheated—or somehow inadequate—because they do not find sex as interesting or ecstatic as advertised in the magazines and movies. Moreover, both men and women who are persuaded to jump on the sexual bandwagon—by trying to behave as the magazines say everyone else is behaving—sometimes find the experience psychologically damaging. John Messenger, an anthropologist who has studied sexual behavior in many cultures, has concluded that today's society puts far too much pressure on individuals to act in ways that may be foreign to their own personalities and desires:

> I myself like to think that sex should be enjoyed for the sheer magnificence of it—that this is what sex is all about. But sex can be magnificent only when you engage in it in your own way and at your own choosing—as much or as little of it as you please, and according to your own tastes and preferences. All the solid research on sex ever done shows that no two people are alike in how they feel about sex, how much capacity they have for it, or what they like and don't like. The kind of sex behavior that is successful for one person can be absolutely devastating for another person, and vice versa. But much of the popular writing totally ignores this fact (97).

(92). Presumably their high level of sexuality, like their early onset of puberty, can be largely attributed to inborn factors.

Living with the differences

To some extent, levels of sexuality are subject to change. Kinsey found one woman, for example, who spent twenty-eight years of marriage without an orgasm, then began experiencing sexual climax for the first time. This is probably an example of how childhood training and society's taboos can inhibit sexual response, and of how a person can break out of the inhibitions. Masters and Johnson, a well-known team of sex investigators and therapists, have reported frequent success in helping men who thought they were impotent and women who were unable to reach orgasm (93).

In general, however, most aspects of sexuality seem to be well-established by the time of adolescence and to persist throughout life. This is particularly true of sexual capacity. Most men and women have their own pattern of desire and ability for orgasm. They are physically incapable of exceeding this rate of activity, except perhaps for brief periods, and are likely to be physically or psychologically uncomfortable with a lower rate.

The individual differences, however, seem to have very little effect on fulfillment. The research institute founded by Kinsey has found that frequency of sexual relations has scant relation to happiness in marriage. If the partners have similar desires, they can be as happy having sex once a month as every night of the week (94). Moreover, fulfillment does not appear to depend on preferences in expressions of sexuality. It has been found that couples who enter into sex with shyness and reserve are just as happy as those who take the uninhibited approach recommended by most of today's sex manuals (95). Many researchers worry, however, that the sexual revolution may have made it difficult for people to understand and accept their own individual patterns of feelings and behavior, as discussed in the box on Psychology and Society on the opposite page.

Sex and youth: a "lonely and . . . silent experience"

Young people in particular face a difficult task in trying to determine their sexual identities at the very time they are facing all the other problems of entering adulthood. Despite today's more permissive atmosphere, the task is still surrounded by confusion and self-doubt. One group of investigators who have made many studies of the sexual behavior of young people have concluded: "Coping with sexual development remains a lonely and overly silent experience" (98).

For many young people, the introduction to sexual intercourse is not nearly so glorious as they were led to believe. One striking bit of evidence comes from a survey made in Denmark, a nation that has been very permissive toward premarital sexual relations for a long time. You might suppose that sex would come natural in Denmark if anywhere. But only 26 percent of the men and women in the study reported that their first sexual experience was satisfactory. About 20 percent recalled it with mixed emotions, and all the rest, a majority of 54 percent, had negative feelings (99). Note these comments:

By women
It was definitely no experience. Neither I nor my partner got an orgasm.
I was curious and excited but it was horrible.
I was disappointed, pessimistic.

By men

Very awkward. Everything went wrong.

It was a great disappointment. An enormous failure. I was afraid of the next time and did not make new attempts for the following two years.

However, an unhappy introduction to sex did not by any means prove fatal to these young Danes. At the time they were interviewed, when their average age was twenty-three, all but a few were either married or had established some satisfactory relationship. The study indicates that it is probably as unrealistic to expect glorious success in one's first attempts at sex as in one's first attempts at playing the piano. Indeed not all of us will ever in our lives attain the kind of glorious, mind-boggling success described in the sex manuals—any more than all of us will ever be invited to play piano concertos with a symphony orchestra.

Even among college students who are living together, sexual problems are not unusual. One study of such relationships found that 70 percent were troubled by the fact that one partner had a higher interest in sex than the other, or that the times when they felt an interest did not match. In nearly two-thirds of the relationships, the woman was troubled by failure to reach orgasm as often as she would have liked (100).

Communication: the "absolute cornerstone"

Most serious researchers agree that establishing a satisfactory sexual relationship is an immensely complicated task that takes time and effort. Above all else, most believe, it requires honest and unabashed communication about the partners' desires and preferences.

Masters and Johnson have termed open discussion of sexual likes and dislikes the "absolute cornerstone" of a successful relationship (101). Indeed their treatment of sexually unsuccessful couples

In any relationship, the give and take of communication is the key and the cornerstone.

centers on the exchange of information, through gestures as well as words. Paul Gebhard says, "The chief stumbling block to sexual fulfillment is the fact that couples don't talk enough about their feelings. Even couples who have been married for twenty years—and know each other's preferences in food, reading, and music like the backs of their hands—often hesitate to tell each other what they like, dislike, or view with indifference in sexual matters" (102).

Unfortunately, open communication about sexual preferences is difficult for most people. It violates the popular belief that sexual performance is a natural gift and that everybody should automatically be "good in bed" without the need for any instruction, indeed even without giving the matter any thought. Or the idea that techniques picked up from a sex manual are sure to be effective with any partner under any circumstances, which is also untrue. The individual differences in tastes and responses are far too great to permit any magic formula for success. Moreover, many people find that too much attention to technique turns sex from a spontaneous expression of love into a mechanical performance that they find unsatisfactory or even distasteful (103).

The evidence seems to indicate that every sexual relationship is unique, bringing together two partners who are themselves unique. Most researchers believe that the partners have to learn by themselves how to make the relationship work—and that this learning process depends mostly on the give and take of communication.

Summary

1 Emotions are always accompanied by bodily changes. The body may be stirred up or toned down.

2 Many of the bodily changes in emotion are controlled by the autonomic nervous system and the endocrine glands. These changes include: a) heart rate, b) blood pressure, c) blood circulation, d) the composition of the blood, e) activity of the digestive organs, f) metabolic rate, g) breathing, h) salivation, i) sweating, j) goose flesh, and k) pupil size.

3 Other bodily changes in emotion are controlled by the striped muscles of movement. These changes include: a) muscular tension, b) trembling, c) eye blinking and other nervous movements, d) vocal expressions of emotion, and e) facial expressions.

4 One theory holds that every basic emotion represents in part a characteristic pattern of facial expression programed by heredity.

5 Pupil size generally increases when a person experiences interest or pleasure.

6 The *James-Lange theory* held that emotions occur when a stimulus in the environment sets off physiological changes. Feedback from these changes, sent to the brain from the body's sensory nerves, is then perceived as emotion. We do not tremble because we are afraid, but feel afraid because we are trembling.

7 The *Cannon-Bard theory* maintained that emotions occur when a stimulus in the environment sets off patterns of nervous activity in the hypothalamus. These patterns were considered to have two simultaneous effects: a) they are sent to the autonomic nervous system, where they trigger the bodily changes of emotion; and b) they are sent to the cerebral cortex, where they cause perception of emotion.

8 Today's cognitive psychologists regard emotions as composed of many complex factors. These include: a) information about events in the environment, delivered to the cerebral cortex by the sense organs; b) the brain's storehouse of information, which helps appraise and interpret new events; c) patterns of nervous activity in

the hypothalamus and the rest of the brain's limbic system, which trigger the autonomic nervous system into producing bodily changes; and d) feedback from the bodily changes.

9 The cognitive view agrees with James-Lange that feedback of physiological changes is important—and with Cannon-Bard that activity of the hypothalamus plays a part. But it holds that neither theory is the full explanation. What really determines emotions is the cognitive activity resulting from the stimulus that has produced the bodily changes and the entire environmental situation in which it occurs. This cognitive activity shows wide individual differences because of prior experience and learning.

10 Inborn factors that help create individual differences in emotional experience include: a) sensitivity of the autonomic nervous system, and b) the size and activity of the endocrine glands.

11 A *drive* is a pattern of brain activity resulting from physiological imbalances that threaten homeostasis. The drives include *hunger, thirst, breathing, sleep, temperature, elimination,* and *pain.*

12 The *hunger drive* depends on: a) nerve cells in the hypothalamus that are sensitive to changes in the food supply contained in the blood stream, and b) information sent to the hypothalamus from the alimentary canal and liver. The hunger drive is also affected by *incentive objects* in the environment (the sight or smell of food) and by eating habits and social relationships built around eating.

13 Although the hunger drive operates to keep most people at normal weight, more than one-fourth of American adults are at least 25 percent overweight. Possible explanations of obesity include: a) metabolic disturbances; b) overeating to relieve anxiety; c) an unknown chemical in the blood stream, caused by abnormalities in the way the alimentary canal and liver process food; and d) an excess of the bodily cells that store fatty compounds.

14 The *thirst drive* depends on: a) nerve cells in the hypothalamus that are sensitive to dehydration, b) signals sent to the brain from the heart and blood vessels when the volume of blood is lowered by lack of water, and c) stimulation of the hypothalamus by a chemical produced by the kidneys.

15 Closely allied to the drives are *stimulus needs*—or the organism's tendency to seek certain kinds of stimulation.

16 There are two stimulus needs: a) the *need for sensory stimulation,* and b) the *need for stimulus variability.*

Postscript

17 In animals, sex is clearly a drive. In human beings, sexual behavior depends largely on learned desires and preferences.

18 The "sexual revolution" has made public attitudes toward sex more permissive but has had less effect on actual behavior.

19 The Kinsey findings show that there is a wider range of individual differences in sexual appetite, capacity, and preferences than in almost any other human trait.

20 The individual differences are believed by many investigators to depend in part on nature—that is, inherited patterns of glandular activity, sensitivity of the nervous system, and other physical traits. They also depend on nurture (learning).

21 Though patterns of sexuality are to some extent subject to change, most of them seem to be established by adolescence and to persist throughout life.

22 The frequency and nature of sexual activity seem to have little effect on fulfillment, as long as both partners have similar desires.

23 For young people, trying to establish sexual identity has been called "a lonely and overly silent experience." First sexual experiences are often unsatisfactory.

24 Establishing a satisfactory sexual relationship takes time and effort. Honest and unabashed communication about the partners' desires and preferences, though difficult for many people, appears to be the key.

Important terms

Cannon-Bard theory	James-Lange theory
drive	pain drive
elimination drive	sleep drive
emotion	stimulus complexity
emotional stress	stimulus needs
fat cells	stimulus variability
hunger drive	temperature drive
incentive object	thirst drive

Recommended readings

Arnold, M. B., ed. *Feelings and emotions.* New York: Academic Press, 1970.

Balagura, S. *Hunger: a biopsychological analysis.* New York: Basic Books, 1973.

Darwin, C. *The expression of emotion in man and animals.* New York: AMS Press, 1972.

Izard, C. E. *Human emotions.* New York: Plenum, 1977.

Malmo, R. B. *On emotions, needs, and our archaic brain.* New York: Holt, Rinehart, and Winston, 1975.

Serban, G., ed. *Psychopathology of human adaptation.* New York: Plenum, 1976.

Stein, D. G., and Rosen, J. J. *Motivation and emotion.* New York: Macmillan, 1974.

Strongman, K. T. *The psychology of emotion,* 2d ed. New York: Wiley, 1978.

Outline

Chapter ten
Motives, frustration, and conflict
(with a postscript on sex roles and conflicts)

Everybody knows a Mr. A. He spends long hours studying. His favorite campus spot is the library. He is at the top of all his classes and makes nothing but A's. His goal is to get into one of the nation's best law schools—and eventually, as he has confided to some of his friends, to serve on the Supreme Court. Everybody agrees that Mr. A has one driving motive in life: to be a smashing success.

Maybe. But there is another possible explanation. Perhaps Mr. A is not ambitious at all. His real preference, if only he felt free to follow it, is to take life easy, move to some nice spot with a good surf, become a beach bum, and let the future take care of itself. But Mr. A has one motive that overrides all others: to please his parents. It is his parents who relish the straight-A college record and the thought of a brilliant law career for their son.

Or consider Ms. B. She is working hard to learn the obscure language of a South American jungle tribe and at the same time to become expert in paramedical techniques and public sanitation. She plans to devote her life to living with this tribe and helping them conquer disease and poverty. Everyone marvels at her selfless devotion to the cause of less fortunate people.

Is Ms. B really motivated by a burning desire to help others? Perhaps. But, on the other hand, her motive may be to exercise the power over others that would go along with being a sort of goddess to a backward tribe.

Then there are Ms. C and Mr. D, two happy-go-lucky free spirits who never seem to give a thought to the future. They barely squeak by in their classes. For whatever they do, from turning in their assignments to showing up at parties, they are usually late. They seem to have no plans beyond enjoying the next half hour. Everybody agrees that they have absolutely no ambition at all.

Again, maybe. But in fact Ms. C may have a

strong motive to achieve success, and Mr. D may have a strong motive for power over others. Both of them, however, have decided that they can never attain these goals (because of the learned help-lessness that was described on pages 112–18 or for other reasons that will be mentioned later in the chapter). Ms. C and Mr. D quit trying to satisfy their motives, and are just drifting along.

The goals of success and friendship

The examples just cited show how difficult it can be to judge motives from behavior. Though guessing other people's motives is a popular pastime, it is often futile. At times it is even difficult to be sure of our own motives. Yet motives, though hard to pin down or to study scientifically, seem to control much human behavior and are one of psychology's basic concerns.

A number of the early psychologists believed that motives could be fully explained in terms of inherited characteristics. These psychologists were impressed by the instinctive behavior displayed by many animals—for example, the way a spider spins its web and the way salmon migrate from river to ocean and back to the river to spawn. Since we human beings are also a form of animal life, why not assume that we too behave in accordance with instincts? The pioneer American psychologist William James theorized that there were no less than seventeen powerful human instincts: imitation, rivalry, pugnacity, sympathy, hunting, fear, acquisi-tiveness, constructiveness (the urge to build), play, curiosity, sociability, shyness, secretiveness, cleanli-ness, jealousy, love, and mother love (1).

It is now known that human beings have few if any instincts. Certainly we do not exhibit any elabo-rate built-in patterns of behavior, determined by the inherited wiring of the nervous system, like the web-spinning behavior of spiders or the nest-build-ing behavior of birds. Human habitations are a great deal more varied and flexible in design (see Figure 10-1). Yet there obviously are some forces within the human personality that initiate, energize, direct, and organize behavior. The drives and stimu-lus needs that were discussed in the preceding chapter often serve as such forces—but there are also others, such as the seventeen urges that James thought of as instincts. These forces are now called motives. Most psychologists define a motive as a desire to reach a goal that has value for the individual.

In studying motives, psychologists ask these questions: Why do certain goals (success, power, friendship, helping others) have so much value that we will devote vast amounts of effort and planning to reach them? And why do goals vary so greatly from person to person?

Most psychologists would agree that our goals and motives are determined in part by our biologi-cal characteristics and in part by learning. There is considerable disagreement, however, as to how these two factors operate and which is more im-portant. In other words, the nature-nurture argu-ment crops up once again.

Some psychologists believe that motives are based mostly on the biological demands of the drives and stimulus needs. The hunger drive, for

10-1 Instinctive versus learned home building
Built-in instincts lead lower animals like the oriole and spider to build the characteristic homes of their species. Human habitations are dictated not by inherited wiring of the nervous system but by convenience and imagination.

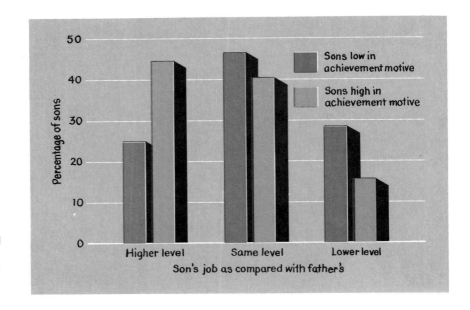

10-2
The achievement motive and rising in society

If you have a strong achievement motive, are you likely to wind up in a better job than your father's? The bars show the results of a study of fathers and sons, described in the text, that indicates you are about three times more likely to wind up at a higher level than at a lower level. If you are low in achievement motive, however, you are more likely to wind up at a lower than at a higher level (6).

example, might lead to attempts to attain success and power, thus making sure the drive will never go unsatisfied. Other psychologists believe that motives are cognitive processes that depend mostly on learning. Their view is based in part on the widespread individual differences that have been found in motivation. They hold that each of us, as a result of our individual life experiences and patterns of thinking, comes to value certain goals above others. Even in the same family, one brother may exhibit a strong tendency to be dependent on other people, another brother to be hostile to authority, a sister to achieve success in school and career. Certainly motives vary considerably from culture to culture. For the ancient Greeks, a strong motive was to achieve moderation in all things, especially in displaying emotion. For the Romans, it was to seem thoughtful and serious. For the Buddhists in classical India and China, it was to be without desire. Prominent in our own society are motives to attain success and friendship.

A happy pupil, holding proof that she has reached a goal dictated by her achievement motive.

The achievement motive

The desire to succeed—to perform well at all kinds of tasks and in a career—is called the *achievement motive*. People with a strong achievement motive work hard at everything they tackle and generally manage to make the most of their talents. When people who score high on tests designed to measure the achievement motive are matched with people of equal ability but lower in achievement motive, they do better on the average at many kinds of mathematical and verbal tasks (2) and other intellectual problems (3). They make better grades in high school (4) and in college (5). In their life work, they are more likely to rise above their family origins and move upward in society. Figure 10-2 illustrates a study in which men whose fathers all had middle-level jobs were divided into two groups, one that scored high and the other low on tests of achievement motive. As the graph shows, far more of the men high in achievement motive had risen to jobs above their father's level—and far fewer were in jobs below their father's level.

One reason people high in achievement motive are more successful in their careers appears to be that they are realistic about their abilities and the chances they are willing to take. They prefer jobs in which they have a reasonable chance of success and can obtain reasonable rewards. People low in achievement motive, on the other hand, are more inclined either to settle for an easier but low-paying job or to make a grandiose stab at a high-level job that is beyond their capacities (7). A study made in Germany showed that the achievement motive affects even the risks taken in driving an automobile. The study found that drivers high in achievement motive tend to commit only minor traffic offenses that represent calculated risks, such as illegal parking. Drivers low in achievement motive get into trouble for driving either too slowly or recklessly (8).

The strength of the achievement motive is clearly apparent in the determined faces of these runners.

Why do some of us develop a stronger desire for achievement than others? There are many reasons, relating to our experiences in home and school, what we read and see on television, the people we come to admire (and therefore try to imitate) or dislike. Our estimate of our own abilities, which may be accurate or distorted, also plays a part.

One study indicates that the way our parents treated us in childhood may be a crucial factor. A

10-3
Early training and the achievement motive

Do parents who encourage young children to be independent also encourage the achievement motive? So it would appear from these results of a study, described in the text, of the ages at which mothers demanded 20 forms of independent behavior. The mothers of sons who turned out high in achievement motive made about as many demands at the age of 2 as the mothers of sons low in achievement motive made at the age of 4—and about as many by the age of 5 as the other mothers by the age of 7 (9).

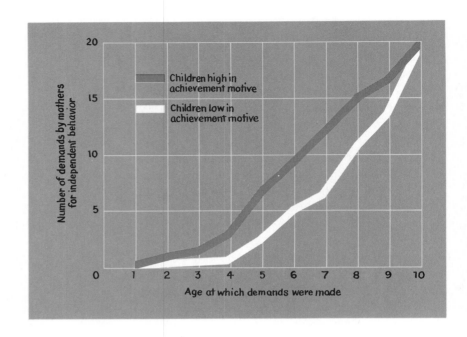

group of boys was divided into those who scored high and those who scored low for achievement motive. Their mothers were then asked at what ages they had demanded that the boys start to show signs of independence—that is, go to bed by themselves, entertain themselves, stay in the house alone, make their own friends, do well in school without help, and later earn their own spending money and choose their own clothes. Questions were asked about twenty such forms of independent behavior. As Figure 10-3 shows, all the mothers had made the twenty demands by the time their sons were 10 years old. But the boys who turned out to be high in achievement motive were urged to be independent at much earlier ages than the others. Encouraging independence in early childhood seems to strengthen the achievement motive—and parents who are overprotective seem to discourage it.

The power motive

The desire to be in a position of control—to be the boss, to give orders, to command respect and obedience—is called the *power motive*. At first glance, it may seem very much like the achievement motive. But the achievement motive is directed toward performing well at whatever one undertakes. The power motive, on the other hand, has less to do with good performance than with being top dog. Studies of American presidents have shown that those who had a strong power motive (as judged from their speeches) tended to take strong and decisive actions and had a great impact on our society—but were not necessarily good presidents who made important and constructive contributions (10).

It has been found that college students who have a strong power motive tend to be officers in campus organizations, serve on student-faculty committees, and work for the school newspaper and radio station. They like to have name plates, credit cards, and possessions associated with prestige, such as tape recorders, television sets, and framed pictures. They are quick to take up new fashion trends—for example, the move toward mustaches and beards that began on campuses in the 1970s (11). Both on the campus and in later life, men high in power motive tend to do considerable drinking (12) and to be reckless when they gamble (13).

In men, a strong power motive often seems to interfere with establishing satisfactory relationships with the opposite sex. A study of college students who were going together found that men who were high in power motive tended to be less satisfied than other men with the arrangement, and so did their partners. Moreover, these couples were much more likely to break up (14). When men high in power motive do marry, they seem to prefer sub-missive wives (15), and their marriages are less likely to be successful (16).

In a complex society such as ours, the power motive doubtless serves a useful purpose. Somebody has to run the government, the corporations, and all the other organizations that are essential to the functioning of an industrial nation. Moreover, though people who aspire to positions of power may pay a price in their personal relationships, they seem to find many satisfactions. Among the United States presidents of this century, it appears that those highest in power motive were the ones who enjoyed the job the most (17). But the power motive probably also directs the behavior of dictators, gang leaders, and the builders of fraudulent financial empires.

Avoidance of power

Some people, instead of seeking power, seem strongly motivated to avoid it, as if they feared

Students at work on a campus newspaper: Does the power motive dictate their presence on the staff?

rather than admired it. They shun situations in which their actions can be controlled by other people, and they do not like to exercise control themselves. The motive to avoid power is especially likely to occur among men who were the youngest members of a large family—perhaps because of early experiences in which they felt pushed around by older and more powerful brothers and sisters.

People who fear power and are motivated to avoid it try very hard to preserve their independence from authority. In college, they dislike anything that smacks of regimentation—such as large lecture classes and required courses of study. They would rather be graded on a paper they have prepared on their own than on an examination (18). A study of college women who had this attitude toward power showed that they were more likely than other students to leave the campus before graduation, by either transferring to another school or sometimes dropping out altogether (19).

People with a strong motive to avoid power are not very interested in such possessions as stereo sets and automobiles. When they do have material possessions, they are quick to lend them to others. If they own cars, they are more likely than other people to have an accident—almost as if to show their lack of concern. They tend to be close-mouthed about their own affairs, even to the point of lying if necessary to preserve their privacy. They shun careers in which they would have power over others and gravitate toward jobs in which they can help others, such as teaching (20).

The affiliation motive

The desire to be around other people is the *affiliation motive.* All of us grow up with this motive, which

These spare-time athletes appear to be motivated far more by affiliation than by achievement.

makes us first seek close attachments with our parents and later establish friendly relationships with others. The strength of the motive, however, varies widely. Some people maintain close ties with their parents all their lives and are extremely sociable in general. They are "joiners" who always like to be in a group and prefer to work in jobs where they cooperate with and have the help of others. Other people prefer to spend their time alone and to be on their own in their work. Some display the affiliation motive so seldom that they appear to be loners who care very little for human companionship.

To at least some extent, however, the affiliation motive appears to operate in everyone. It is particularly noticeable in people who are experiencing unpleasant emotions, for there seems to be considerable truth in the adage that "misery loves company." This fact was demonstrated by an experiment in which university women were asked to visit a psychology laboratory. When they arrived, they found a frightening piece of apparatus awaiting them and were told it was designed to deliver severe electrical shocks. After having been made anxious about the nature of the experiment, they were told that they had their choice of waiting their turn alone or in company. Fully 63 percent preferred company, with most of the rest saying they did not care one way or the other. In a control group of women who had not been made anxious about the experiment, the number who preferred company while waiting was only 33 percent (21).

In jobs that call for a group effort, it has been found that people high in affiliation motive would rather be with their friends even when they could work with strangers who were more competent and could offer more help. They are more pleased by signs that their group is getting along well emotionally than by its accomplishments. There is some evidence that students with a strong affiliation motive make better grades in classes where everyone

Clinging to mother: a clear example of the dependency motive at work.

is friendly and the instructor takes a personal interest and calls students by name (22), although this seems to be far more true of men than of women.

The dependency motive

Closely allied to the desire for affiliation is the *dependency motive*, which also appears to exist in all of us. The dependency motive probably stems from our experiences as babies, when we are completely dependent on our parents. They give us food, drink, warmth, comfort, and relief from pain. This tendency to rely on others—at least at times and for certain things—never leaves us. We continue to have a strong urge to depend on others to organize our lives, set up our schedules, help us with our work, comfort us, and give us support and pleasure. Like affiliation, the dependency motive is especially prominent in troubling situations. Hospital patients, for example, often have mixed feelings. Despite their illness and worry, they may enjoy the opportunity to be dependent on their physicians and nurses.

Behavior that stems from the dependency motive has been found to be more common among women than men. But this is because our society, at least until recently, has considered dependency to be appropriate, feminine, and rather attractive in women. The motive itself is probably equally strong in men—but they are less likely to display it because society has frowned on dependent behavior on the part of males. Often the motive is gratified by men in subtle ways. They may take their problems to the teacher or to the boss (though usually under the guise of being logical rather than emotional). Or they may tend to rely on columnists and television commentators for an interpretation of world events—and to give enthusiastic allegiance to political leaders with strong personalities.

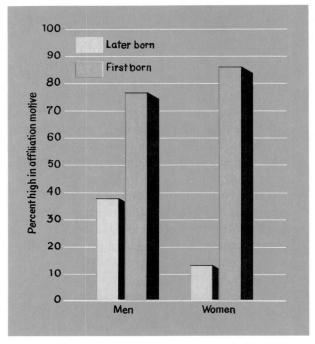

10-4 The affiliation motive: highest among first-borns

The bars show the percentages of males and females, from children to older people, who made high scores on a test measuring the affiliation motive. Note the wide discrepancy between first-born children and others (23).

Birth order and the motives for success and friendship

Were you the first-born in your family—or did you come along later? This may seem an odd question to ask in a discussion of motives, but it is more relevant than it may appear. First-born children are considerably more likely than others to have a strong motive for affiliation. In the study illustrated in Figure 10-4, for example, males and females ranging in age from eleven to sixty-two took tests designed to measure the affiliation motive. Men who were the first-born in their families (or only children) were found to be about twice as likely as other men to make high scores. First-born women were about six times more likely than others to show a strong affiliation motive.

Similar findings have been reported for the achievement motive. Indeed the motive has inspired many first-borns to become outstandingly successful. Any list of prominent people—eminent scholars, people listed in *Who's Who*, even presidents of the United States—contains an unusually high proportion of first-borns. The well-known peo-

Margaret Mead

Pablo Picasso

Jane Fonda

Muhammad Ali

Indira Gandhi

Winston Churchill

10-5
Besides success, what do these people have in common?
All these people, whose careers would indicate a high level of achievement motive, share another attribute. What? For the answer, see the text.

ple whose photos are shown in Figure 10-5 all were first-born children.

A possible explanation is that parents appear to treat a first-born child differently from later children. Mothers devote more time to the first-born, are more protective, take a greater part in the child's activities, interfere more, and are more extreme with both praise and criticism (24). Thus the first-born child is thrust from the start into an adult world and expected to conform to adult standards (25). Later children receive less attention and guidance from their parents and are more influenced by their relations with other children.

First-born children, again perhaps because of their early close interactions with their parents, have been found to be more trusting of authority than later-born children (26). First-born men, though not women, have a strong tendency to conform to social pressures (27). Moreover, just as the youngest child in the family seems to fear and shun power, first-borns often rate high in the motive to attain power. There seems to be some truth in an observation made by the psychoanalyst Alfred Adler, who once described the first-born child as a "power-hungry conservative" (28). There are of course many exceptions to these generalities.

Some other powerful motives

The motives that have just been discussed—achievement, power, affiliation, and dependency—are the easiest to study and have received the most attention from psychologists. There are other motives, however, that seem to influence all of us, sometimes very strongly.

The motive for certainty

Even very young children display a strong *motive for certainty*—that is, a desire to feel at home in their world, to know where they stand, to avoid the discomfort of unfamiliar and surprising events. They clearly enjoy the certainty represented by their own bed, their own toys, the presence of familiar people and objects in their environment. As they grow a little older, they like to have rules set for their conduct; they like the certainty of knowing what they are permitted to do and what they are not permitted to do. The prospect of uncertainty—sleeping in a strange house, being taken care of by a strange baby sitter, going to school for the first time—is likely to upset them.

Adults too tend to be motivated toward the known and away from the unknown. For some, such as explorers and astronauts, other motives prove stronger. In general, however, the desire for certainty operates strongly in most of us at most times. We like to feel that we know how our relatives and friends will act toward us, what is likely to happen tomorrow in the classroom or on the job, and where and how we will be living next year.

In some people, the motive for certainty is so strong that they seem to avoid any kind of change, even when the price of inaction is very high. You undoubtedly know people who continue to work in jobs they hate, or who persist in marriages they have long since decided are hopeless. Apparently they would rather stay with the known, no matter how unpleasant, than face the unknown. For most of us, however, the desire for certainty operates to keep our lives on an even keel. It takes three forms:

1 We like to think that we can predict what will happen next—that is, that future events will be orderly and foreseeable.
2 When unusual events surprise us, we like to understand them and relate them in some way to previous experiences.
3 We seek consistency among the various beliefs we hold and between our beliefs and our behavior.

The motive to live up to standards

All of us, as we grow up, begin to set rules for our own behavior. Through learning what society values and through identification with our parents and other adults, we acquire inner standards of many kinds. We also acquire a strong *motive to live up to our standards*. Most people want to be attractive, responsible, friendly, skillful, generous, honest, and fair. Some, because of a different early environment, have standards that call for them to be domineering, tough, and rebellious.

Our standards form what is called our *ego ideal* —our notion of how, if we were perfect, we would always think and act. Many of us acquire such high standards that we cannot possibly live up to all of them at all times. In fact the motive to live up to inner standards often requires us to suppress other powerful motives. Our standards may tell us that we should not take food from another person even

A basketball coach finds it impossible to restrain the hostility motive.

if we are hungry, that we should be kind even to people toward whom we feel hostile, that we should play fair no matter how much we want to win. As a result, we often feel shame and guilt, over our thoughts if not actually our conduct. In popular terms, our conscience hurts. The pangs of conscience when we fail to meet our standards can be painful indeed. This is why people who commit crimes sometimes behave in such a way that they are almost sure to be caught. Apparently they prefer punishment by imprisonment to the self-punishment that results from a serious failure to live up to inner standards.

The hostility motive

Though most of us do not like to admit it, all of us have a *hostility motive*. Evidence first appears in children at about the age of two. Up to then, all they seem to want from other people is their presence and the stimulation, help, and approval they provide. But at this stage, children begin to want something else from others. They want—at times—to see other people display signs of worry, fears of discomfort, actual pain. Later they may hope that misfortune will befall others and that they will have the gratification of knowing about it.

Some scientists regard hostility as a biological trait that makes aggression as inevitable for human beings as fighting over territory is for baboons and other animals (29). Others, probably a majority, believe that the hostility motive is learned and that it stems from the fact that children cannot have everything they want. Some of their desires are bound to be frustrated by the rules of society and by the conflicting desires of other people. They cannot always eat when they want to. They have to learn to control their drive for elimination except when they are in the bathroom. They cannot have the toy that another child owns and is playing with. Their mothers cannot always cater to their whims. Other children, bigger than they are, push them around.

Aggression resulting from hostility may take such forms as argumentativeness, sarcasm, physical and mental cruelty, and fighting. Yet, while all people are motivated at some time by hostility, not everyone displays aggression. Boys and men are more inclined to aggressive behavior than girls and women, for our society has traditionally approved of a certain amount of aggression in males, but has discouraged it in females. The social environment—especially the attitudes toward violence held by parents and by the community as a whole—seems to be a strong influence. Researchers recently studied a town in Mexico where violence was generally approved and admired. In this town violent incidents were very common. In another town public opinion disapproved of violence. In this town

Psychology and Society

Violence, movies, and television

During your lifetime, in the hours you have spent watching movies and television, how many acts of violence have you witnessed? How many fist fights, beatings, stabbings, shootings, gang wars, and rapes?

Even for the most casual moviegoer and television-watcher, the number would be staggering. One clue comes from a study of cartoon shows for children that appeared on television in the mid-1970s. Each hour of these cartoons, it was found, contained an average of 21.5 violent actions (37). And these were just kiddie shows, not adult fare like *The Godfather*.

Does violence on television and in the movies help account for the increased violence revealed by today's crime statistics? Some psychologists doubt that incidents seen on the screen have any real effect on behavior (38). Indeed some maintain that watching make-believe scenes of violence may have a cathartic effect—that is, it may enable viewers to release pent-up aggressive urges and therefore relieve any pressure to act (39).

There is considerable evidence, however, that violence shown on the screen often encourages real-life aggression. Some of the effects represent a subtle change of attitude. For example, one study found that people who watch a great deal of television tend to become distrustful of others and afraid of being victims of crime. They often try to protect themselves with extra locks on their doors, guard dogs, and guns (40). At the same time, they seem to become hardened to violence and less likely to be emotionally upset by real-life incidents of aggression (41). It might be said that they begin to take violence for granted, as a standard part of human behavior.

violent incidents were rare (30). Researchers have also found numerous small societies, for example in isolated parts of New Guinea and the Philippine Islands, where aggressive behavior is almost unknown (31).

There is considerable evidence that aggressive behavior is most likely to occur among people who, for whatever reason, happen to be in a high state of arousal. Experiments have shown that aggression seems to be encouraged by the use of alcohol (32) and by the discomfort of being exposed to loud noise (33) or working in an overheated room

(34)—even by the physical arousal created by brisk exercise (35). Some psychologists have suggested that the high level of violence in our society can be explained at least in part by the fast pace of modern life and the noise and crowding that occur in our cities (36).

It has also been established that aggression is encouraged by watching other people behave aggressively—that is, through the kind of observation learning that was illustrated on page 123 with the photographs of children attacking a doll with a hammer after watching a movie of an adult doing

Some more direct effects have also been observed. One group of experimenters arranged for preschool children to spend part of each day watching television programs that had been carefully selected so that one group saw violent cartoons and the other group cartoons that were free of violence. Those who saw the violent programs became more aggressive in their behavior during the course of the experiment, while the others did not (42). Another study followed a group of children from the time they were nine years old until they were nineteen. Boys who preferred violent television shows when they were nine turned out to behave much more aggressively at nineteen than other boys—though this was not true of the girls (43). On the other hand, aggressive behavior seems to decrease in children who watch television shows in which the characters solve their problems constructively, without resorting to violence (44).

Studies have also shown that adults tend to behave more aggressively after watching films that show aggressive acts (45). Moreover, a number of violent crimes appear to be real-life imitations of television or movie stories (46). Professional criminals sometimes learn new techniques from watching crimes on the screen (47).

The weight of evidence is that the effects of violence in the movies and television are at least suspect—and, in the opinion of many psychologists, clearly damaging. Should the display of violence be stopped? This is an issue that society must decide. It is surrounded by many arguments pro and con about censorship and even freedom of the press—for news reports of actual crimes are often followed by a sharp rise in similar types of crime, as after the first hijacking of an airplane in 1967 (48).

this. Experiments on imitation of aggression raise the issue of how our society has been affected by all the violence depicted in the movies and on television, as discussed in the box on Psychology and Society at the top of these pages.

The motive for self-actualization

A good deal of human history seems to revolve around the motive for hostility (leading to acts of violence, revenge, and war) and the motive for power (which has produced such despots as Hitler and Stalin). But should history lead us to take a pessimistic view of human nature? Among those who think otherwise are the humanistic psychologists (page 32)—who believe that the most powerful motivating force in human beings is the aspiration toward benevolent and spiritual goals. The humanists' view of human motivation is called the *theory of self-actualization*, which holds that people will always pursue the highest and most idealistic aims unless their development is warped by a malevolent social environment.

The theory was formulated by Abraham Maslow, one of the leading humanists. Maslow believed that human beings are innately inclined to seek beauty, goodness, truth, and the fullest possible development of their own unique potentialities for perfection and creativity. Human motives, he theorized, take the form shown in Figure 10-6. The physiological motives at the bottom of the pyramid are the most urgent. People must satisfy their hunger and thirst drives before they can undertake the search for safety, which is the next step upward. And only in a safe and stable society can they then begin to seek the higher goals to which human nature aspires.

The goal at the very top of the pyramid, self-actualization, is a sort of all-encompassing self-fulfillment. Self-actualizing people have satisfied their search for such esthetic pleasures as order, symmetry, and beauty. They accept themselves and others and the realities of existence, and they rejoice in the experience of living. Self-actualizers are spontaneous and creative and have a keen sense of humor. They have made the most of their abilities and have become all they are capable of

becoming (49). All this, to Maslow, represented the goal toward which all human beings by their very nature are motivated—though deprivation and social pressures may prevent some of them from ever reaching this ideal level of development. Some of the people Maslow regarded as having attained the top of his pyramid are shown in Figure 10-7.

One study indicates that people who seem to be self-actualizing are likely to be free from tendencies to be neurotic (50)—in other words, that self-actualization and what is often called "mental health" go hand in hand. But in general Maslow's theory does not lend itself to experimental proof or disproof. It must be taken largely on faith. To many psychologists the theory has the intuitive ring of truth. To others it seems too optimistic.

Unconscious motives

Another idea that has influenced many psychologists holds that human activities are often a response to *unconscious motives*—that is, to wishes and desires that we are not aware of, that in fact

10-6

Maslow's pyramid of motives
Maslow's theory holds that human motives take the form of this pyramid. Once the *physiological motives* at the bottom have been satisfied, human beings are freed to pursue the *safety motives*—and so on up the higher levels. For the meaning of the *self-actualization motive* that is at the very top, see the text.

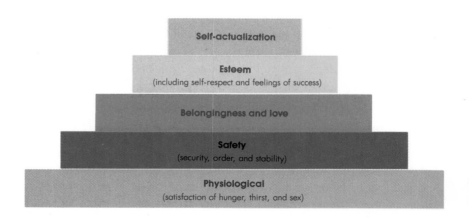

Self-actualization

Esteem
(including self-respect and feelings of success)

Belongingness and love

Safety
(security, order, and stability)

Physiological
(satisfaction of hunger, thirst, and sex)

we might vehemently deny, but that influence our behavior nonetheless, sometimes to a striking degree. The idea of unconscious motives was first proposed by Sigmund Freud and is part of his psychoanalytic theory of personality and the way it develops, which will be discussed in Chapter 12.

Freud's suggestion raises some very thorny psychological problems, among them the question of how a desire that is unconscious can operate to produce relevant behavior. But his idea does seem to explain some aspects of human behavior that would otherwise be baffling.

One example of what appears to be an unconscious motive is the phenomenon known as post-hypnotic suggestion. While subjects are under hypnosis, they may be told that after they awaken from the trance they will go and raise a window the first time the hypnotist coughs—even though they will not remember having received this instruction. Later the hypnotist coughs, and, sure enough, the subjects do open a window. If asked why, they say that the room was getting stuffy or that they felt faint. They have no suspicion that the real reason was to comply with the hypnotist's demand.

Other examples are all around us. A mother may seem to believe in all sincerity that she has the most generous, affectionate, and even self-sacrificing motives toward her daughter. Yet an unprejudiced observer might say that the mother's real motives are to dominate the daughter, keep her from marrying, and hold on to her as a servant. A man may earnestly deny that he has any hostile motives. Yet we may see that he performs many subtle acts of aggression against his wife, his children, and his business associates. A person may feel genuinely motivated to go to the dentist or to keep a date with a friend, yet conveniently "forget" the appointment.

Although the notion of unconscious motives is

Albert Schweitzer

Eleanor Roosevelt

Helen Keller

Albert Einstein

10-7 Some famous self-actualizers
These are some of the people whom Maslow regarded as having reached the very peak of human motivation.

puzzling, many psychologists agree that it is valid, including some who reject other aspects of Freud's theories. Accepting the idea leads to a rather startling conclusion: If motives can affect behavior even though they are completely unconscious, then we will often find it as difficult to analyze our own motives as to know the motives of others.

How-and when-motives affect behavior

One reason we are not very good at analyzing the motives of other people is that motives may not necessarily result in any behavior at all. For one thing, they may be thwarted by outside events—the circumstances of our lives—over which we have no control. The key here is *opportunity*—for we cannot fulfill any of our desires unless we have a chance to try. The achievement motive is often the victim of lack of opportunity. For example, a young woman wants very badly to have a professional career—but for lack of money she cannot get the necessary education. A young man wants very badly to work in advertising—but cannot find any advertising firm that will hire him.

Lack of opportunity may also thwart the affiliation motive. Young people eager for the companionship of the opposite sex may live in a community where young men greatly outnumber young women, or vice versa. For older people, the lack of opportunity is caused by the fact that women live much longer than men. Among Americans who are forty-five or older, there are nearly six million more women than men (51).

In other cases, motives are never gratified for reasons that lie within the self. Ms. C, mentioned at the start of the chapter, had a strong desire for achievement yet never showed any sign of striving for success—though she did not lack opportunity. Mr. D had a strong motive for power yet merely went on his happy-go-lucky way, never trying to attain a position of power. Psychologists have found so many discrepancies between motivation and behavior that their approach has changed greatly in recent years. At one time most of them were interested in classifying, defining, and measuring motives. Now most of them are concerned with the ways in which people act or do not act on their motives—in other words, with all the factors that determine whether we try to satisfy them, how hard we try, and how we go about seeking satisfaction. These factors, in which there is a wide range of individual differences, are the subject of the rest of the chapter.

Motive hierarchies and targets

All of us seem to have motives for achievement, power (or avoidance of power), affiliation, dependency, certainty, living up to standards, hostility, and (if we accept Maslow's theory) self-actualization. But there are great differences in the strengths of these desires. Each of us has built up a highly individual *hierarchy of motives* in which some have a top priority, while others are much less urgent. And of course the strength of a motive—the position it occupies in the hierarchy—plays a considerable part in determining how hard, if at all, we try to satisfy it (52). Some of us have such a strong affiliation motive that we are willing to ignore a weaker desire for achievement to avoid making our friends jealous. On the other hand, some of us are so intent on achievement or power that we are willing to sacrifice the friendships dictated by a weaker affiliation motive.

Our hierarchy of motives does not operate in a vacuum. It changes from time to time with the situation of the moment. No matter how high the affiliation motive may be in the hierarchy, none of us is invariably eager for affiliation at all times and with all people. (Indeed most of us know people with

"Did you hear about poor Walston?
He was consumed by ambition."
Drawing by Fradan; © 1975 The New Yorker Magazine, Inc.

whom we would not care to affiliate under any circumstances.) Nor are we always inclined to satisfy our motives for achievement or hostility, however strong they may be in general.

To a great extent, our desires of the moment depend on what psychologists call our *motive targets*—that is, the people to whom our various motives are directed. For example, a man may have strong motives for achievement toward his business associates, for power toward the members of his political club, for affiliation toward his parents, and for dependency toward his wife. His desires will change during the course of the day as he moves from one relationship to another. The motive targets, as well as the hierarchy, help determine which motive will prevail.

The effect of incentive value

As was mentioned in the last chapter, the hunger drive can be triggered by such incentive objects as the smell of food from a restaurant kitchen or the sight of pastries in a bakery window. In a somewhat similar way, motives are also triggered by incentives in the environment.

For example, a college woman goes home at the end of the day with no particular plans for the evening. A friend calls and suggests they go to an 8 P.M. tryout for parts in a school play. Going to the tryout is a potential incentive to act on any one of a number of motives—for achievement, say, or for affiliation. Whether the student responds eagerly or turns down the suggestion will depend in large part on how much *incentive value* trying out for a play holds for her.

The incentive value of any event or object varies considerably from one person to another. Two students may have equally strong desires for achievement, but one student's motive may center on getting good grades, the other's on finishing school as quickly as possible and starting on a job. As incentives for the affiliation motive, one student may place great value on joining a certain campus organization, while another may not value that organization at all.

Gauging your chances of success

Another factor that affects our decision to act or not to act on our motives is how much chance we have to get what we want. We are not likely to try very hard, if at all, unless we have a reasonable expectation of success. The college woman invited to try out for the campus play will probably turn down the suggestion if she believes that she has absolutely no chance—even though she places a high incentive value on getting a part. A male student may be highly motivated to call up a woman he has met in one of his classes, and he may place a high incentive value on going out with her. But if he feels shy and awkward around women and considers himself unattractive and uninteresting, he will probably take no action.

In gauging our chances of success, we try to

make a realistic appraisal of the situation. We may decide not to try out for a campus play because we have never had any acting experience. We may abandon any thought of a career in accounting because we always have trouble in math courses. But often we are influenced not so much by the facts as by our self-image—our own perception of ourselves and our abilities. Some people have an exaggerated opinion of their talents and are inclined to try anything (a tendency that may bring them one disappointment after another). On the other hand, people who have acquired learned helplessness always tend to be pessimistic about their chances, whatever the situation. They may be capable of far more success—at fulfilling their motives for achievement, affiliation, and other goals—than they themselves believe. They give up without really trying.

Expectancy of success and locus of control

Closely related to learned helplessness is another phenomenon that has been studied in recent years by many psychologists interested in the relationships between motives and behavior (53). This is the matter of whether we believe that we are in control of our own lives or at the mercy of outside events. It has been found that some people assume their chances of success depend largely on *internal factors*—their own abilities and efforts. Others feel that success depends more on *external factors*—sheer luck and the inherent difficulty of attaining whatever goal they seek (54).

The psychological term for this phenomenon is *locus of control*. (*Locus* is the Latin word for *place*). People who assume that the locus of control is internal tend to take responsibility for their own actions and to try hard to implement their motives. They also seem to feel that other people create their own successes and failures—and they are reluctant to give money or help to those who are in trouble (55). They are not easily influenced by the opinions of other people and are careful though not timid in the risks they are willing to take (56).

People who assume that the locus of control is external are less likely to strive for the goals dictated by their motives. They tend to rely on luck—and to be sympathetic to others who are in trouble, whom they regard as "down on their luck." They are readily influenced by the opinions of others (57) and inclined to be reckless. When they do succeed—in the classroom, a job, or marriage—they are less likely to take credit for their success than to consider themselves blessed by circumstances, or to decide that whatever they did right must have been pretty easy. All of these are of course general tendencies. None of us believes totally in external control or internal control.

Long-range plans, too much motivation, and running scared

All the factors just mentioned help determine how hard we try to implement a motive, if indeed we try at all. Moreover, our behavior at any given moment also depends on our long-range thinking about our goals. If the college woman invited to the tryout aspires to become a professional actress—or if she seeks a long-term affiliation with a group of theater people—she is much more likely to act than if she regards the experience as just a momentary diversion. Psychology's findings about the relationship of motives to behavior have been summarized in the theory that our actions in any situation are influenced by the following interplay of forces (58):

1 *The strength of our motive* (as determined by our hierarchy of motives and the target to which we are directing our actions)
2 *The way we perceive our chances of success* (influ-

enced by our attitude toward locus of control and any feelings of learned helplessness we may have acquired)

3 *The incentive value* of what we are doing or could be doing at the moment

4 *The relationship of present to future actions*—in other words, our judgments about the possibilities to which our behavior may lead, especially the incentive value of these future actions and the way we perceive our chances of future success

An interesting sidelight is the finding that a very high level of motivation does not always help attain a goal. On the contrary, a motive can be so strong as to be self-defeating (59). We may be so intent on the goal, so eager to attain it, that we lose our perspective and our performance suffers. This is often true of people who have a strong affiliation motive and want very badly to be liked. You have probably known people who tried so hard to win your friendship that their constant attentions, favors, and flattery became a nuisance.

It has also been found that attempts to implement a motive are often hampered by the fear of failure. This is especially true of the achievement motive. An example might be a college man who has long-range plans to become a lawyer. He takes a crucial examination that has great incentive value because he must meet the admission standards of the law school he wants to attend. His fear of failure may make him "run scared" and perform far below his capabilities.

Fear of failure at a varsity swim meet

The effect of fear of failure on the affiliation motive was demonstrated in an unusual experiment with the varsity swim teams at three universities. The members of the teams, men and women, were tested for motivation and divided into two groups. One had a high level of affiliation motive and a low fear of social rejection. The other group had a weaker affiliation motive and a greater fear of rejection. Later all the swimmers took part in a joint meet. Individual winners were determined by the time they made when swimming alone against the clock. There was also competition among groups of three swimming the course together, with their average time determining the winning trio.

The results were striking. On the average, the swimmers who were high in affiliation motive and low in fear of rejection swam more than 1.5 seconds faster in a group than when they were alone—as if the desire to win approval from their teammates spurred them to greater effort. The swimmers higher in fear of rejection did just the opposite. They were more than 1.5 seconds slower when swimming in a group—as if they did not want to outshine the other two members (60). (The differences in performance were considerably greater for men, incidentally, than for women—a fact that may or may not indicate some sex differences in the way motives operate.) The experiment has some interesting implications for psychology-minded athletic coaches seeking improved performance in team and individual sports.

Frustration and conflict

Motives that rank near the top of the hierarchy can be powerful forces in directing behavior, not only at any given moment but over a lifetime. Indeed two of the most important aspects of human personality and adjustment are these: 1) To what extent are our strongest motives gratified—and to what extent do they go unfulfilled? 2) If we fail to fulfill our motives, in what manner and how successfully do we cope with the failure?

It is inevitable, given the nature of human aspirations and human society, that most of us will never gratify all our motives. We are almost bound to encounter what psychologists call *frustration*. This is one of life's most unpleasant experiences and can have extremely unfortunate results—for frustration is a frequent cause of the anxiety and abnormal behavior that will be discussed in the next chapter.

Sources of frustration

Psychologists define frustration as *the blocking of motive satisfaction by some kind of obstacle*. On a very simple level, our motive to get somewhere on time may be blocked—therefore frustrated—by a flat tire. On a more complex level, any one of a number of obstacles may frustrate our motives to be actors, athletes, or successful in our relations with people we like.

In popular usage, the term *frustration* refers to the unpleasant feelings that result from the blocking of motive satisfaction—that is, the feelings we experience when something interferes with our wishes, hopes, plans, and expectations. But these feelings, which are really emotional responses to frustration, take so many forms that they cannot be described scientifically. They may range from mild surprise to murderous rage, from confusion to disappointment to anger to depression to apathy.

Frustration is a universal experience. Our environment is full of events that often seem especially designed to keep us from fulfilling our wishes. Even our own body and personality make frustration inevitable. The possible sources of frustration are usually broken down into four—but note how many possibilities exist in each category:

1 *Physical obstacles*—such as a drought that frustrates a farmer's attempts to produce a good crop. Or a broken alarm clock, traffic jam, or flat tire that prevents us from getting to class on time.

2 *Social circumstances*—such as a refusal by another person to return our affection, social barriers against minority groups, or problems of society that frustrate our motive for certainty by raising the threat of economic dislocation or war.

3 *Personal shortcomings*—such as when we want to be musicians but find that we are tone deaf, or aspire to be Olympic champions but lack the physical equipment. None of us is as talented as we would like.

4 *Conflicts between motives*—for example, want-

Too much work and too little time: a case of utter frustration.

ing to leave college for a year to try painting, but also wanting to please one's parents by remaining in school.

Frustration and the eye of the beholder

What kinds of physical obstacles, social circumstances, personal shortcomings, and conflicts are likely to be most frustrating? The answer is that frustration is entirely relative. It all depends on the situation.

A classic experiment was performed by observing the conduct of children aged two to five in a playroom equipped only with "half toys," such as a telephone without a transmitter and an ironing board without an iron. Despite the missing parts, the children played quite happily—until a dividing screen was removed and they saw much better toys in the other half of the room. Then, when a wire barrier was placed between them and the "whole toys," most of them showed signs of extreme frustration (61).

As the experiment showed, "half toys" are fun to play with if there is nothing better at hand. When better toys lie just beyond reach, the "half toys" are no longer good enough. Adult frustrations are equally relative. A man may be perfectly happy with his old used car until his neighbor buys a new model. A woman may be perfectly happy with her job until her friend in the next office gets a promotion. Many people who are successful and well liked suffer pangs of frustration because a brother or sister is even more successful and popular.

There are wide individual differences in the ability to tolerate frustration. This has been found true even among young children (62). Among adults, the evidence is all around us. You doubtless know men and women who carry on in normal fashion and even appear relatively cheerful despite serious physical handicaps or tragic disappointments. You

probably know others who are reduced to tears or temper tantrums if the breakfast bacon is too crisp.

Conflicts as a source of frustration

The most common of the four sources of frustration is conflict—which psychologists define as *the simultaneous arousal of two or more incompatible motives, resulting in unpleasant emotions.* The phrase "unpleasant emotions" is an essential part of the definition. A person whose motives are in genuine conflict experiences anxiety, uncertainty, and the feeling of being torn and distressed. This is why conflict is a potential threat to normal behavior.

One type of conflict occurs between the motive to live up to inner standards and some other motive. For example, most children acquire a desire to live up to a standard that calls for them to be obedient and respectful to their parents. Yet at times they may be motivated by hostility and want to strike out against their parents. Even though they do not actually commit any hostile act, the desire itself may produce shame or guilt. Adolescents and adults often experience similar conflict over what would happen to their self-respect and their image in society if they struck out angrily against a teacher or boss. Some are troubled by a conflict between an inner standard calling for independence and toughness and the motive to show signs of dependency or affection.

Another type of conflict occurs when two motives for different and incompatible goals are aroused at the same time. The achievement and affiliation motives are especially likely to pull in opposite directions. An example that you may have experienced is this: It is the night before an examination. The achievement motive, in the form of a desire for a good grade, pulls you in the direction of locking yourself in your room and studying. But friends call and suggest going to a party. The affiliation motive now pulls strongly in the opposite direction. Only one of the two motives can be satisfied. An agonizing decision must be made.

To complicate the problem, the decision is likely to cause anxiety no matter which way you turn. If you decide to study, you risk anxiety over losing the goal of being with your friends—and perhaps over the possibility that their regard for you may suffer. If you decide instead to go out with your friends, you risk anxiety over your grade—and perhaps also over the possibility of rejection by your teachers or parents.

Life is full of conflicts over pairs of goals that cannot both be attained. Shall I marry now (and lose my chance for other social experiences with the opposite sex) or wait (and risk losing the person I think I love)? Shall I try for a well-paying but difficult job (and risk failure) or settle for a more modest job (and give up the idea of being rich)? Shall I spend everything I earn (and risk my future security) or save some of it (and miss out on things I want to buy now)? Shall I live in a city or in the country? Shall I have a small family or a large one? The list of conflicts could be expanded almost indefinitely.

Approach and avoidance conflicts

Our conflicts are seldom simple. Indeed they are often so complex that we have trouble understanding them, much less coping with them. To help recognize the complexity, it is useful to note that some of our motives incline us to *approach* a desirable goal (as does the motive for achievement), while others make us seek to *avoid* something unpleasant (like the shame and guilt that result from failure to live up to our standards). Psychologists noted many years ago that these two desires to approach the good and avoid the bad can result in a truly bewildering array of conflicts (63), all

To move nearer or to run away? Two children caught in an approach-avoidance conflict.

falling in general into the four following classes:

1 An *approach-approach conflict* takes place between two motives that both make us want to approach desirable goals. However, we cannot reach both goals, for attaining one of them means giving up the other. We cannot simultaneously satisfy the motive to watch the late movie on television and the motive to get a good night's sleep. We cannot simultaneously roam around the world and settle down in a career. Thus we are often torn between alternatives—each of which would be thoroughly pleasant except for our regret over losing the other.

2 An *avoidance-avoidance conflict* occurs between two motives that make us want to avoid two alternatives that are both *unpleasant*. For example, you are too keyed up over tomorrow's examination to get to sleep. You would like to avoid the unpleasantness of tossing and turning in bed, and you could do so by taking a sleeping pill. But you would also like to avoid the grogginess you will

suffer tomorrow if you do take the sleeping pill.

3 An *approach-avoidance conflict* occurs when fulfilling a motive will have both pleasant and unpleasant consequences. For young people, the thought of getting married often creates an approach-avoidance conflict. Being married has many attractions—but it also means added responsibilities and loss of freedom.

4 A *double approach-avoidance conflict,* the most complex and unfortunately the most common type of all, takes place when we are torn between two goals that will both have pleasant and unpleasant consequences. A college woman from a small community wants to become a certified public accountant. But she knows that the best opportunities in this field exist in large cities, and she is worried about the crowded and impersonal aspects of big-city life. Now she falls in love with a classmate who

plans to go into business with his father, who runs a small-town automobile agency. She wants very much to marry this man and she likes the idea of living with him in a small community. But she knows that this community will give her very little opportunity for her chosen career as an accountant. Which way shall she turn?

To the double approach-avoidance conflict—so common in life—there is never a fully satisfactory solution. Whichever goal we choose, we are likely to feel at times that we made the wrong decision. Indeed making the decision can be so difficult that sometimes we are inclined to throw up our hands and abandon both goals. The various ways in which people cope with conflict—normal and abnormal—are the subject of the next chapter.

(Summary begins on page 397.)

Postscript

Sex roles and conflicts

One conflict worthy of special note arises from the mixed motives and inner standards that most of us have about how men are expected to behave (simply because they are male) and how women are expected to behave (simply because they are female). Recently this conflict has produced a great deal of debate over such issues as the women's liberation movement and the equal rights amendment—with some women and men vigorously in favor and others bitterly opposed. It has caused disagreements between husbands and wives over such matters as whether the wife shall work (and if

so whether her career should be considered as important as the husband's) and how to divide the housekeeping chores. It has also produced internal conflicts and self-doubts for members of both sexes—who, confused about the part they are supposed to play in modern society, sometimes hardly know how to regard themselves or each other.

Throughout history it has been assumed that men and women differ in important ways—almost as if they were members of two separate species (64). Men have been expected to act "masculine" and women to act "feminine." What these two words meant was never spelled out, but until recently everyone had a pretty good idea. Before reading on, stop to take the test offered in Figure 10-8, put together by a social psychologist to measure how people rate according to conventional standards of masculinity and femininity. What the score tells you will be explained in the next few paragraphs.

What it means to be masculine or feminine

The test is based on the fact that most people see far more contrasts than similarities between a typical man and a typical woman. In one study, for example, a group was asked to rate men on a scale ranging from "not at all aggressive" to "very aggressive," from "very illogical" to "very logical," and so on through a long list of personality traits. Then the subjects were asked to rate women on the same scale. Both male and female subjects agreed to a remarkable extent that men are generally aggressive, independent, dominant, competitive, logical, direct, adventurous, self-confident, and ambitious. Women were described as almost exactly the opposite—unaggressive, dependent, submissive, not competitive, illogical, sneaky, timid, lacking in self-confidence, and unambitious. Men were described as close-mouthed and women as talkative, men as rough and women as gentle, men as sloppy in their habits and women as neat. The subjects agreed that men do not usually enjoy art and literature and cannot easily express any tender feelings, but that women do like art and literature and find it easy to express their feelings (66).

The test in Figure 10-8 measures many of the traits generally considered to distinguish between men and women. Most men would make high minus scores on the test, most women high plus scores. But this would be true chiefly among older people and the less educated. Younger people, especially the college-trained, seem to be chang-

ing. When the test was given to students at Stanford University, where it originated, only half the males scored as masculine, likewise half the females as feminine. About 15 percent of both sexes wound up on the "wrong" side of the dividing point; these men had plus or feminine scores, the women minus or masculine scores. The other 35 percent fell in the gray area between + 1 and − 1.

This 35 percent was classified as androgynous—a word derived from a combination of the Greek andros, for man, and gyne, for woman. The androgynous students, both male and female, had some of the personality traits considered characteristic of men and some considered characteristic of women. In some situations they acted in typically masculine ways, in others in feminine ways.

The large number of students who scored in the androgynous range (as you may also have done—or as surely some of your classmates did) raises some interesting questions. Are men and women really as different as has always been assumed? Do our different bodies destine us to have different motives, emotions, interests, and personalities? Or do we behave differently (when we do) because somehow we have been taught to be different?

You're X-X (or X-Y) and stuck with it

The whole matter of masculinity versus femininity boils down to another aspect of the nature-nurture controversy that has been mentioned so frequently in the book. To start with the argument that nature may be the key factor, it must be pointed out that without question the workings of heredity have arranged for males and females to be different not only in their sexual apparatus but in every cell of their bodies. As was explained in the discussion of heredity on pages 37–38, all the cells in a woman's body contain an X-X pair of chromosomes, while all

1. self-reliant
2. yielding
3. helpful
4. defends own beliefs
5. cheerful
6. moody
7. independent
8. shy
9. conscientious
10. athletic
11. affectionate
12. theatrical
13. assertive
14. flatterable
15. happy
16. strong personality
17. loyal
18. unpredictable
19. forceful
20. feminine
21. reliable
22. analytical
23. sympathetic
24. jealous
25. has leadership abilities
26. sensitive to the needs of others
27. truthful
28. will take risks
29. understanding
30. secretive
31. makes decisions easily
32. compassionate
33. sincere
34. self-sufficient
35. eager to soothe hurt feelings
36. conceited
37. dominant
38. soft spoken
39. likable
40. masculine
41. warm
42. solemn
43. willing to take a stand
44. tender
45. friendly
46. aggressive
47. gullible
48. inefficient
49. acts as a leader
50. childlike
51. adaptable
52. individualistic
53. does not use harsh language
54. unsystematic
55. competitive
56. loves children
57. tactful
58. ambitious
59. gentle
60. conventional

10-8 Are you masculine, feminine, or both?

Write down next to each item a number from 1 to 7 indicating how strongly you display that particular trait. On the first item, for example, put down a 1 if you believe that you are never or almost never self-reliant, a 7 if you believe that you are always or almost always self-reliant, or some other number in between to indicate how far you lean in the direction of self-reliance or lack of it. When you finish rating yourself on all sixty items, see the footnote on page 389 for scoring instructions (65).

Which is male and which is female? An example of androgyny in physical appearance.

the cells in a man's body contain an X-Y pair.

In some species the two chromosome pairs create startling physical differences. The male red-winged blackbird, for example, is a solid shiny black except for the bright red and yellow-edged patches on his wings. His mate is not black at all. She is brown, with no wing patches but a heavily striped breast. Looking at the two of them you have to wonder how they ever manage to figure out that nature intended for them to get together. But among human beings there are no such pronounced differences in appearance. Except for their sex organs, boy babies and girl babies look very much alike. If they are wearing as much as a diaper it is impossible to tell them apart. When adult males and females are dressed alike in jeans and shirts, with hair the same length, it can be difficult at first glance to tell which is which.

The chromosome pairings do, however, produce an invisible but important difference resulting from the hormone output of the sex glands. As was explained on page 68, the male glands produce large amounts of androgens, the female glands large amounts of estrogen. Do the androgens make you act masculine? Or estrogen make you act feminine? The two hormones do seem to have some effects, starting even before birth. All fertilized eggs start out to grow into females. In the case of X-Y eggs, the Y-chromosome then orders a flood of androgen—and this androgen bath triggers the development of the male sex organs (67). Thus, in the early stages of pregnancy, Y-chromosome produces androgen produces male.

Many scientists believe that the two hormones may also affect the developing brain. Androgen may program the circuits of the brain into a tendency to operate in ways distinctively masculine, estrogen in ways typically feminine. Experiments with animals have shown that changing the balance of the two hormones, before or just after birth, can make male monkeys and rats grow up acting like females and females grow up acting like males (68). With human beings, a study was made of some young women who had been subjected to the influence of androgen before birth as an unexpected side effect of a new drug taken by their mothers. As a group these young women were more masculine than feminine in many respects. As children they were tomboys. They shunned dolls and preferred to play baseball and football. In adolescence they were not very interested in boys and felt uncomfortable acting as baby-sitters. They had doubts about marriage and motherhood (69).

But nature doesn't do it all

All in all, it seems quite probable that nature creates some inborn tendencies. But there is ample proof that heredity alone does not necessarily push men toward being independent and aggressive, nor women toward being passive and submissive. Whatever the effects of our X-X or X-Y chromosome pairs, our hormones, and the possible early programing of our brains, it has been found that the effects are by no means final and irreversible (70).

The evidence started piling up years ago when an anthropologist, Margaret Mead, reported the strange—to us—behavior of three tribes with whom she had lived in the wilds of the South Pacific island of New Guinea. The men and women in these tribes, biologically the same as the rest of humanity, had notions of masculinity and femininity far different from those that have prevailed in our society and most others.

In Tribe No. 1, both men and women were aggressive and violent. They were headhunters and cannibals. The women—perhaps because pregnancy interfered with their normal warlike habits—disliked having and caring for their children, especially the girl babies. In Tribe No. 2, both men and women were what we would call highly feminine. Both sexes shunned aggression. Both were gentle, kind, passive, and warmly emotional. Both took care of and nurtured the children.

In Tribe No. 3, the members of one sex spent all their time applying cosmetics, gossiping, pouting, engaging in emotional outbursts, and taking care of the children. Members of the other sex had clean-shaven heads, scorned any makeup or ornamentation, were active and domineering, and provided most of the tribe's food and other necessities. But the last sentence describes how the women behaved. The preceding sentence, about a fondness for cosmetics and emotional outbursts, describes the men (71).

Some boy-girls and girl-boys

In our own society some dramatic evidence comes from a study made by researchers at the Johns Hopkins University of a group of *hermaphrodites*—people born, through a quirk of nature, with some of the outward sexual characteristics of the male but also with some characteristics of the female. Until recently, when it was learned how to distinguish X and Y chromosomes under a microscope, there was no way to know for sure whether hermaphrodites were biologically male or female. Their parents and physicians could only guess. If they guessed male, then usually the inappropriate female characteristics were surgically removed and the baby was brought up as a boy. If they guessed female, the male traces were removed and the baby was brought up as a girl.

The Johns Hopkins researchers found a number of people who had been born as hermaphrodites and gave them the chromosome test. It turned out that some who had been reared as boys had the X-Y combination and were therefore indeed biologically males—but others had the X-X combination and were actually females. Similarly some reared as girls were indeed X-X and female—but others had the X-Y combination and were actually males. As far as behavior was concerned, however, the chromosomes did not seem to matter. Those who had been brought up as boys acted masculine, whether they were X-Y or X-X. Those brought up as girls acted feminine, even if they were X-Y and

biologically male. If you had met any of these people socially or at work, you would never have guessed that there was anything unusual about their sexual identity (72).

Learning to act masculine or feminine

All in all the evidence seems to show that, despite any inborn tendencies, nurture is the crucial influence. We learn to act masculine or feminine through a process called *sex typing* that occurs throughout the world. Every society assigns different roles to men and women and expects them to behave in different ways and to have different duties, interests, and standing in the community. As the New Guinea example shows, the assigned roles may vary considerably from one society to another. But whatever the particular customs, men are expected to act like men and women like women. They are taught to do so from birth.

A group of psychologists once interviewed parents on the first day of their newborn babies' lives. Half the babies were boys, the other half girls. Tests at the hospital where they were born showed that, as a group, the boys and girls were remarkably alike in every measurable trait. They could not be told apart by appearance, muscle tone, reflexes, or even size. Yet the parents of the boys believed that their babies were outstandingly strong, firm, hardy, alert, and well-coordinated. The parents of the girls described their babies as more delicate, more finely featured, softer, and less inclined to pay attention (73). The psychologists who made the study concluded that the physical and psychological characteristics of babies are mostly "in the eye of the beholder"—and it so happens that the eyes of most beholders look at males and females very differently, not just in the cradle but throughout life.

Parents treat their offspring in many different ways depending on the sex. When cooing to a

To score the test in Figure 10-8, first add up the numbers you have placed next to items 1, 4, 7, 10, 13, 16, 19, 22, 25, 28, 31, 34, 37, 40, 43, 46, 49, 52, 55, and 58. Divide the total by 20. The result is your masculinity score. Next add up the numbers next to items 2, 5, 8, 11, 14, 17, 20, 23, 26, 29, 32, 35, 38, 41, 44, 47, 50, 53, 56, and 59. Divide the total by 20. The result is your femininity score. Now subtract the masculinity score from the femininity score—and divide the result, which may be plus or minus, by 2.3. You now have your final score, which can be interpreted as follows: Over +2, traditionally feminine in tastes and behavior. Between +1 and +2, "near feminine." Between +1 and −1, mixed or androgynous (for the meaning of which see the text). Between −1 and −2, "near masculine." A minus figure greater than −2, traditionally masculine in tastes and behavior.

baby in a crib they use one tone of voice toward a girl, a different one toward a boy. Fathers playing with the baby are cautiously gentle toward a girl, more roughhouse toward a boy (74). Mothers in general feed boys more than girls, even on the first day of life (75). They dress the two sexes differently—even in the case of twins of opposite sex (76). They look at a baby girl more often and talk to her more frequently (77).

How parents encourage sex typing without knowing it

Even parents who say they believe in treating the two sexes in the same way make distinctions. Some convincing evidence comes from an experiment with young and theoretically liberated mothers. All these women claimed that boys and girls were alike and should be treated alike. Indeed almost all of them said that they encouraged their girls to be rough-and-tumble and their boys to play with dolls. But their conduct showed otherwise.

Half the mothers were introduced to a 6-month-old baby named Adam and were observed while playing with him in a room that contained a train (typically a male toy), a doll (typically female), and a toy fish (neuter). These mothers usually handed Adam the train.

The other half were observed while playing with a 6-month-old named Beth. These mothers usually handed Beth the doll—and afterward some of them remarked what a sweet and uncomplaining little girl she was. Actually, as you may have guessed, there was only one baby. (It happened to be a boy.) But 6-month-olds look so much alike that none of the mothers caught on. They gave "Adam" the traditional treatment for a boy, "Beth" the traditional treatment for a girl (78).

Thus we start being sex-typed while still in the cradle. As one study put it: "Wittingly or unwittingly, parents encourage and reinforce sex-appropriate behavior, and little boys and girls respond to parental encouragement and reward. So little boys learn to be independent, active, and aggressive; their sisters to be dependent and passive" (79).

Pressure from television, books, and schools

Television shows designed for children proclaim the same message: males are the world's movers and shakers, females their meek subordinates. A study of children's programs and the accompanying commercials showed that about three-fourths of all the characters on the screen were male, only one-fourth female. Little boys usually played football, went camping, and played with toy cars and construction sets. Little girls usually played at cooking and keeping house (80).

In children's picture books girls are generally portrayed as passive and doll-like, winning attention and praise only for their attractiveness, working mostly at tasks designed to please and help their brothers and fathers. Boys, on the other hand, are mostly shown as adventuresome, admired for their skill and achievements, and engaging in all kinds of acts requiring independence and self-reliance (81).

Teachers in nursery schools have been found to follow the same pattern. They talk more to boys, give them more individual help and instruction, and reward them more frequently for their accomplishments (82). In one way or another, often through open praise, they encourage boys to be independent and aggressive, to defend themselves in fights, and in general to be "brave little men." But the girls are praised mostly for their appearance, especially when they wear nice dresses and look feminine (83). Teachers, like parents, often are unaware that they treat the two sexes differently (84).

In kindergartens and elementary schools, teachers usually encourage boys to play a dominant role in the classroom and girls to take a back seat (85). They expect boys to be noisy and often troublesome, but girls to be quiet and well-behaved (86). When they assign chores, they ask boys to stack books and move furniture, girls to serve fruit juice and cookies (87).

Getting the message early

Of course some parents are more likely than others to mold their offspring into the traditional roles of masculinity and femininity (88). There are also differences in schools—and in various communities, social classes, and ethnic and racial groups. For example, the early training of black girls seems to encourage considerably more independence than the early training of white girls (89).

But by and large children have been brought up to believe that women should be pretty and preferably slim, while men should be tall and strong. Women should be passive, nonaggressive, and submissive toward men, while men should be active, aggressive, and dominant. The message sinks in very early. When offered a choice, girls as young as three and four display their femininity in the kinds of toys they select—the customary dolls, toy stoves, and dish sets. Boys shun such toys and prefer guns, trucks, and cowboy suits (90). Thus from the beginning society has switched your development onto one track if you are female, an altogether different track if you are male. The collisions to which this can lead—especially today when the old masculine-feminine traditions are being questioned—will be described in the following sections.

The built-in problems of being female

Until recently in human history it probably was to everyone's advantage for males to act masculine and females to act feminine. In the primitive societies in which humanity lived for countless generations, in fact, survival depended on a division of labor between the sexes. The women, bearing and nursing one child after another, could not roam far from home. Their chief job was as mothers and homemakers. The men were free to range far and wide hunting for animals to provide food. Moreover the men, being physically stronger, protected the home against wild beasts and unfriendly strangers. The tradition was established early and served a purpose. Women were dependent. Men were dominant (91).

Some social scientists believe that society still operates more smoothly when the sexes specialize in different roles—the male as breadwinner and link between the family and the outside world, the female as the source of affection and support within the family (92). Many observers, however, have concluded that there is no longer any need in our modern society for men to be masculine and women to be feminine. They point out that physical strength is no longer important. There are very few jobs in the industrial system that cannot be performed as well by a woman as by a man. In a world of nuclear weapons, aggressiveness of the kind that can lead to warfare is disastrous. The population explosion has turned large families into

Who says a woman can't do a man's job?

today's world they do cause trouble and conflict for both sexes. To see how this happens, we can start with the problems the roles create for women.

Putting women down

History tells us that women have never shared equally in society's esteem, praise, privileges, and rewards. In one way or another they were treated as the inferior sex in ancient Egypt, Greece, and Rome—and, on our own continent, by the Indians (93). In fact sexual discrimination may have been the first form of social inequality (94), practiced before people ever thought of discriminating against one another on the basis of race or social class. The division of labor between the sexes has varied from society to society—but, no matter how the jobs were split up, those assigned to men have always been considered more important (95).

The female inferiority complex

Many females grow up with a sort of built-in inferiority complex. By the time they get to kindergarten many of them have already decided that their fathers are more intelligent than their mothers (96)—an indication of how they feel about the two sexes in general. By high-school age their inferiority complex is in full flower. A study made in Baltimore found that girls were much more inclined than boys to be self-conscious, worry about their appearance, have a low opinion of themselves, and wish they could have been members of the opposite sex (97). This was more evident among white girls than among black girls—possibly because black girls are encouraged to be more independent.

By the time women reach college age many are

a liability instead of an asset—and women, in this age of birth control, have fewer children and more years to live after the last of them has gone to school or left home. Because they are not necessarily immobilized by children and are free to enter the work force, they are no longer dependent on men to support them.

You may reject this argument and prefer to believe that the masculine and feminine roles do serve a purpose. But there can be little doubt that in thoroughly down on themselves. In one study students were asked to predict their grades for the following term. The women were considerably less optimistic than the men—though in this particular group, as it turned out, the women actually did somewhat better (98). In general college women seem to have less hope for the future, in later life as well as in classes, than men (99).

Like most victims of an inferiority complex, women tend to have an external locus of control and believe that their fate is determined more by luck than by their own efforts. Some evidence comes from a recent study of their gambling preferences, in which observers watched what happened at booths at a county fair where customers had a chance to win prizes. It was found that a large majority of men preferred to try games of skill, such as tossing rings. Women, on the other hand, preferred games of sheer chance, such as bingo (100).

Suppressing the achievement motive

Perhaps the greatest problem of all for women results from the fact that they are encouraged to give full expression to their motives for affiliation and dependency—but are under pressure to suppress their motives for achievement and hostility. It is not considered feminine to be too successful, especially at the tasks and jobs that have been regarded as for men only. It is certainly not feminine to be competitive and aggressive. And here is where women find themselves in a bind.

In the past it was common for women, even the most capable ones, to conceal their intelligence, abandon any interest in such masculine subjects as mathematics and science, and either shun a career or settle for such a traditionally feminine job as nursing. Moreover they accepted the idea of being second-class citizens, bound to defer and cater to the male of the species. Many women still do this. But such behavior discourages a woman from becoming a self-reliant person, living by her own inner desires rather than by what society seems to expect and want. Indeed it has been suggested that the traditional standards for femininity call for a "compliant, dependent, self-effacing personality" that is likely to be accompanied by "neurotic needs and vulnerabilities" (101). One psychoanalyst has pointed out that many women are so crippled that they are afraid to assert themselves, be spontaneous, or try such new experiences as flying or driving an automobile (102).

The housewife's conflict

Of course many women genuinely prefer to be housewives and full-time mothers (103). They are not self-effacing or neurotic at all. They simply would rather take care of a house and bring up their children than perform work of other kinds. They find that being a housewife-mother provides ample satisfaction for their achievement motives and the most gratifying kind of self-fulfillment.

A sociologist who made a large-scale study of housewives in the Chicago area found that many of them regarded their roles as "self-expressive and creative"—a chance to build a richer and more varied way of life than they could attain in most jobs available in the business world. They enjoyed the freedom and challenge of being their own bosses. They saw their relationships with their husbands as a matter not of domination and submission but of developing a deep intimacy "suited to the unique needs of both personalities." They found motherhood to be a stimulating challenge demanding skill, creativity, and leadership (104).

It should be noted, however, that even the happy housewife is likely to experience conflict in today's

A determined advocate of women's liberation.

world. So much has been written about the rebellion of modern women against the traditional feminine role that a woman who accepts any part of the role is almost bound to experience self-doubts. Perhaps she does not really enjoy being a housewife and mother. Perhaps she can never be as self-fulfilled as women who prefer careers to homemaking. She may even, by failing to take a more active part in the rebellion, be a traitor to her sex.

She finds herself pulled in opposite directions—one by a tradition that seems also to gratify her own most basic desires, the other by today's emphasis on casting off the old feminine shackles.

The liberated woman's conflict

What about the women who are most dedicated to the ideas of liberation—those who have rebelled most sharply against traditional standards of femininity, who deplore the thought of devoting their lives to taking care of a house, a husband, and children, who want full independence both financially and psychologically? They too feel the pull of tradition. Brought up to be feminine, they developed inner standards calling for them to suppress the motives for achievement and hostility. These ingrained standards are hard to shake. Even the attempt to do so is likely to produce anxiety.

Thus even the most liberated women are likely to wonder at times if they would be more fulfilled if they became full-time housekeepers and mothers. They may also worry about how society in general—and men in particular—will react if they persist in being ambitious and competitive. This was shown in a recent study at a women's college in New Jersey that places strong emphasis on courses and issues related to the liberation movement. It was found that a considerable majority of the women at this school believed that a wife's career was as important as the husband's and that both should contribute equally to the family's finances. The majority wanted to work all their lives, wanted their husbands to share in the housekeeping, and rejected the idea that "the most important thing for a woman is to be a good wife and mother." But they also felt that men would not want to marry a woman who held such liberated views. Since most of them wanted marriage and children besides a career, they were caught in a conflict and "probably experiencing considerable anxiety about their futures" (105).

Such anxiety seems to be justified—for relationships between men and women are currently surrounded by considerable doubt. A growing number of women—especially the young and college-educated—are rebelling against their sex typing and determined to express their achievement motives by having careers. But many men still think of marriage in terms of the traditional masculine and feminine roles. A survey of college men made in the early 1970s showed that more than half of them wanted their wives to abandon their jobs either immediately upon marriage (13 percent) or as soon as a child was born (41 percent). Another 42 percent expected their wives to stay home and take care of the children at least through the early years. Only 4 percent were willing to have their wives pursue a career continuously (106).

The built-in problems of being male

Sex typing clearly creates conflicts for women in our society. Less well publicized is the fact that sex typing also creates conflicts for men. It is not easy to be as masculine as society has urged men to be. Nor is it easy to rebel against the masculine role—which for most men is as deeply ingrained an inner standard as femininity is for most women.

There is even more pressure on boys to be masculine than on girls to be feminine. Most families urge boys to be "little men" even before they have any idea what it means to be a man. They are constantly warned not to act like girls, not to cry, not to be "sissies." Most people have always considered it worse for a boy to be a sissy than for a girl to be a tomboy—and a recent study shows that this opinion is still generally held by today's college students, both male and female (107). The problem this creates for young male children has been summed up in these words:

> The little boy is asked to do something which is not clearly defined for him, based on reasons he cannot possibly appreciate, and enforced with threats, punishment, and anger by those who are close to him. . . . Anxiety frequently expresses itself in over-straining to be masculine, in virtual panic at being caught doing anything traditionally defined as feminine (108).

Suppressing the affiliation and dependency motives

The male conflict between motives is exactly the opposite of the female conflict. Boys and men are encouraged—often overencouraged—to express their motives for achievement and hostility. They are expected to welcome every opportunity to leap into competition. But they are expected to suppress their motives for affiliation and dependency and to suppress or at least conceal their emotions, especially any tender or vulnerable feelings. They have to keep a stiff upper lip—avoiding any show of fear or grief—even in the face of the most drastic kind of disappointment or tragedy.

Who says a man has no place in a beauty shop?

throughout life. At different ages and in different environments, the requirements vary. Boys may have to prove themselves by being athletic or by being tough, men by making a lot of money or by being a man's man in whatever way this is defined by their associates. But the burden of proof is always present—and the burden is heavier than most people think:

> It is a strain for women to have to act weaker, more dependent and submissive, and less competent than they really are, but it's probably a greater strain to have to act tougher, stronger, more dominant, and more competent than one really feels inside. It is also a strain to have one's masculine status constantly dependent on success at work and providing well for a family of dependents (111).

The struggle to play the masculine role can be fraught with anxieties. The motives for affiliation and dependency are universal. So are the emotions that accompany them. Society's demand to suppress them is in effect a demand to "transcend your humanity." And efforts to do so can never completely succeed: "Since it is impossible to program out all emotions, even the most extreme he-man can only approximate" the masculine ideal (109). Thus every man—aware of the stirrings of the softer and weaker emotions he tries so dutifully to hide—is bound to worry about his own masculinity.

The burden of being superior

While women grow up with a tendency toward built-in inferiority complexes, men are sex-typed into thinking of themselves as superior. For all the secret self-doubts they may have, they have been taught that they are the better of the two sexes, destined by birth to be lord and master. This has its obvious advantages—yet it too can be a burden. Robert Seidenberg, a psychoanalyst, has made these observations:

The male burden of proof

Girls and women are considered feminine unless they display overwhelming evidence to the contrary—but boys and men have to win the right to be called masculine. They have to *prove* their masculinity; they have to face and succeed in all kinds of "financial, intellectual, sexual, and physical tests" (110). The testing process starts early and continues

> It is quite probable that men become victims of their own advantages. An unearned superiority is thrust on them. This places a constant burden of proof upon them which causes distortions of character and personality which are tragic to behold. The man is placed, often through no need or desire of his own, in a position of proving why he, of two people, should automatically be the standard bearer of the family. Often, to prove his doubtful superiority, he must resort to pseudo self-enhancement such as uncalled-for bravery, cunning, tricks, and outmoded feats of cour-

age. . . . Men ultimately suffer the corruption of un-earned victories and ascendancy. Their personalities become warped by the myth of their own dominance and superiority (112).

And how is a man supposed to act toward a woman who is obviously as intelligent and well-educated as he is—perhaps even more so? A survey of Ivy League seniors showed that many of them felt extremely uncomfortable in such a situation. About 30 percent conceded that they had felt intellectually insecure or under strain. Some had simply decided to avoid such women. ("If a girl knows more than I do, I resent her." "I enjoy talking to more intelligent girls, but I have no desire for a deep relationship with them. I guess I still believe that the man should be more intelligent.") Others

had mixed feelings. They wanted intellectual companionship with women but found it threatening. One of them admitted that it made him feel "nervous and humble" (113).

It is perhaps as difficult to be automatically typed as superior as to be automatically typed as inferior. Men as well as women suffer anxieties over the way they are sex typed to perform—which may be totally at odds with their own motives and emotions, not to mention their physical strength and other capabilities. The traditional standards of masculinity and femininity may still serve a purpose or may have become obsolete—but as long as they continue to influence human behavior they will cause inner conflicts for both sexes, as well as some open conflicts between them.

Summary

1 A motive is *a desire to reach a goal that has value for the individual.*
2 Some psychologists believe that motives are based largely on drives and stimulus needs (for example, that the hunger drive might lead to attempts to attain success and power, thus making sure the drive will never go unsatisfied).
3 Other psychologists believe that motives are cognitive processes that depend mostly on learning.
4 Among important motives are desires for *achievement, power, affiliation, dependency, certainty, living up to inner standards,* and *hostility.*
5 Humanistic psychologists believe that human beings also have a *motive for self-actualization*—that is, to pursue the highest and most idealistic aims, rejoice in the experience of living, and make the most of their abilities.
6 Many psychologists agree with Freud's belief that we also have *unconscious motives* that influence our behavior even though we are unaware of them.
7 All of us seem to possess all the human motives, but to a widely varying degree. An individual pattern of motives, from strongest to weakest, is a *hierarchy of motives.*
8 The strength of a motive at any given moment depends on the presence of *motive targets,* or the people to whom the various motives are directed.

9 Often a motive cannot be fulfilled because of lack of opportunity. In particular, we may never have the opportunity to gratify all our desires for achievement.

10 Other factors that help determine whether we will try to fulfill a motive include: a) the strength of the motive (determined by the motive hierarchy and motive targets), b) the way we perceive our chances of success, c) the *incentive value* of any action we might take, and d) the relationship of present to future actions (our judgment of long-term consequences).

11 Our perception of our chances of success depends in part on *locus of control*—or whether we believe success depends on *internal factors* (our own abilities and efforts) or *external factors* (such as luck).

12 *Frustration* is the *blocking of motive satisfaction by some kind of obstacle.* The obstacles may be: a) *physical obstacles,* b) *social circumstances,* c) *personal shortcomings,* or d) *conflict.*

13 A *conflict* is the *simultaneous arousal of two or more incompatible motives, resulting in unpleasant emotions.*

14 Types of conflict are: a) *approach-approach* (seeking two desirable goals), b) *avoidance-avoidance* (seeking to prevent two undesirable alternatives), c) *approach-avoidance* (over a goal that will have both pleasant and unpleasant aspects), and d) *double approach-avoidance* (when we are torn between two goals that both have some desirable and some undesirable aspects).

Postscript

15 All societies expect men to be masculine and women to be feminine. Our society has traditionally defined masculine as being aggressive, independent, and dominant, feminine as being unaggressive, dependent, and submissive.

16 Differences in behavior between the two sexes may depend in part on the effects of the different hormones produced by the sex glands, including possible early programing of the brain.

17 Most differences in behavior appear to be the result of *sex typing,* or learning what society expects of males and females.

18 Sex typing begins at birth and is promoted by children's television, books, and schools.

19 The feminine role into which women are sex typed calls for what has been called a "compliant, dependent, self-effacing personality." As a result, many women acquire an inferiority complex and belief in external locus of control.

20 The masculine role into which men are sex typed calls for suppression of the affiliation and dependency motives and for constant proof of superiority.

21 The traditional standards of masculinity and femininity cause inner conflicts for both sexes and open conflicts between them.

Important terms

achievement motive
affiliation motive
aggression
approach-approach conflict
approach-avoidance conflict
avoidance-avoidance
  conflict
certainty motive
conflict
dependency motive
double approach-avoidance
  conflict

frustration
hostility motive
incentive value
inner standards
locus of control
motive hierarchy
motive targets
motive to live up to
   standards
power motive
self-actualization
unconscious motives

Postscript

androgynous
feminine

masculine
sex typing

Recommended readings

Atkinson, J. W., and Raynor, J. O. *Motivation and achievement.* New York: Halsted, 1974.

Bandura, A. *Aggression: a social learning analysis.* Englewood Cliffs, N.J.: Prentice-Hall, 1973.

Bandura, A. *Social learning theory.* Englewood Cliffs, N.J.: Prentice-Hall, 1977.

Bolles, R. C. *Theory of motivation,* 2d ed. New York: Harper & Row, 1975.

Lefcourt, H. M. *Locus of control.* Hillsdale, N.J.: Erlbaum, 1976.

Maslow, A. H., ed. *Motivation and personality,* 2d ed. New York: Harper & Row, 1970.

McClelland, D. C. *Power: the inner experience.* New York: Halsted, 1975.

Money, J., and Ehrhardt, A. A. *Man and woman, boy and girl.* Baltimore: The Johns Hopkins University Press, 1972.

Montagu, A., ed. *Learning non-aggression: the experience of non-literate societies.* New York: Oxford University Press, 1978.

Weiner, B. *Achievement motive and attribution theory.* Morristown, N.J.: General Learning Press, 1974.

Weiner, B., ed. *Cognitive views of human motivation.* New York: Academic Press, 1974.

Winter, D. G. *The power motive.* New York: Free Press, 1973.

Part six
Human
personality:
normal
and abnormal

Everybody analyzes it, has an opinion about it, and talks about it. In the course of a single day you may hear a half dozen comments like these:

She certainly has a pleasant personality.
I guess he's all right, but he doesn't have much personality.
My new roommate has such a disagreeable personality she's getting me down.
He wants to be a politician, but he just doesn't have the personality for it.

The human personality is infinitely varied and endlessly fascinating. Even our own personality intrigues and sometimes baffles us. We ask ourselves: Is my personality too aggressive? Is my personality basically shy and timid? Do people think of me as good-humored or sour? How normal am I?

This new section of the book describes what psychology knows about the origin and complexities of personality. The discussion follows naturally from the preceding chapters, for our personalities depend in large part on the emotions that life's events tend to arouse in us and on the motives that characteristically influence and guide our behavior. There are people with exuberant personalities who appear to be constantly experiencing the emotion of joy, people with quarrelsome personalities who appear to be constantly experiencing anger, and people with gloomy and frightened personalities who appear to be constantly experiencing fear and guilt. There are "strong" personalities who are highly motivated toward achievement and independence and "weak" personalities who are highly motivated toward dependence and submission.

Two other topics covered in the preceding section, emotional wear and tear and frustration of motives or conflicts between motives, are also powerful forces in molding personality. Life being what it is, these unpleasant experiences are an inevitable part of human existence. Our personality—and indeed the whole question of whether we will behave in manners generally considered normal or abnormal—depends in large part on how many of life's events we regard as emotionally upsetting or frustrating and how well we have learned to cope with the physical and psychological consequences. Some of us, as will be seen, manage to reconcile ourselves to the most disappointing and painful experiences. Others, in far less trying circumstances, lapse into physical illness or into psychological disorders.

Personality also depends on many other factors. Some of them appear to be inherited, like the structure of the nervous system and the glands. (Some psychologists, as you will see, even believe that there is an inherited genetic defect that gives some people a tendency to display at least mild symptoms of the mental illness called schizophrenia, if not the disturbance in its most full-blown and crippling form.) Other factors appear to be the result of learning and all the other psychological processes that have been discussed in preceding chapters.

Chapter 11 deals with the sources and effects of the unpleasant psychological experiences called anxiety and of the troublesome physical conditions called stress, which often accompany frustration and conflict. It also discusses the various strategies—sometimes successful, sometimes doomed to failure—that people develop to counteract them. It explains the difference between normal and abnormal behavior, and, in a postscript, lists some of the classifications of abnormal symptoms from mildly neurotic to cripplingly psychotic.

Chapter 12 describes various theories of what constitutes personality and of how it develops for better or for worse, as well as the therapies psychologists have devised for treating personality disorders. The message of the two chapters is that the rich and variegated fabric of human personality is woven from many strands—not only our emotions and motives but our perceptions, our characteristic ways of learning and thinking about the world, and some additional factors that have not been previously mentioned in the book. The fabric is delicate, yet it is remarkably resistant to the strains life places on it—and psychology can sometimes mend the damage that does occur.

Outline

Chapter eleven

Anxiety, stress, and coping

(with a postscript on classifications of abnormal behavior)

Do you remember the first day you arrived on campus—a stranger in an unfamiliar environment? Or worked at a new job, among people you had never seen before? Or were about to take a test that might or might not get you into the college of your choice? Or went to a doctor's office with symptoms that might prove serious?

If so, you doubtless remember how you felt. How would you describe it? Were you worried? Tense? "Jumpy"? All these terms are attempts to label what psychologists call *anxiety*—an emotion that has far-reaching effects on human personality and behavior.

Can you recall occasions when the pressures and strains of life seemed almost too much for you? Perhaps the end of a school term, when you had to rush to finish a paper, study for your exams, and at the same time look for a summer job? Or when you were beset by an accumulation of housekeeping chores or financial problems? Or torn by a conflict between motives? Did you experience some distressing physical symptoms—a racing heart, shortness of breath, trembling hands, a queasy stomach, a headache? If so, you were experiencing what psychologists call *stress,* the body's reactions to outside pressures. When the strains of life become too severe and overwhelming, the stress they cause may take the form of physical illness and even death.

The psychological experience of anxiety and the physiological states of stress are two powerful influences on human behavior. Life being what it is, we cannot avoid them. We are bound to encounter them many times in the natural course of events. To keep our behavior and our bodily well-being within normal bounds—and face life with reasonable optimism and zest—we have to learn to cope with them. If we seriously fail to cope, we may get physically sick or lapse into abnormal behavior by displaying the symptoms called *neuroses* or even the more serious forms of mental disturbance called *psychoses* (popularly known as insanity). Neuroses and psychoses are complex phenomena that can spring from many sources, but their causes always seem to include some form of intense or prolonged anxiety and stress.

Anxiety and its effect on behavior

Anxiety can be defined as *a vague, unpleasant feeling accompanied by a premonition that something undesirable is about to happen.* The feeling is closely related to the emotion of fear. Indeed it is very difficult to draw a sharp dividing line. The only difference is that usually fear is a reaction to a specific stimulus and has a "right now" quality about it. (We see a snake, know exactly what we are afraid of, and recognize that we are afraid right here and now.) Anxiety ordinarily does not have an obvious cause and is not so much concerned with the here and now as with some future unpleasantness. (When we arrive on a new campus or a new

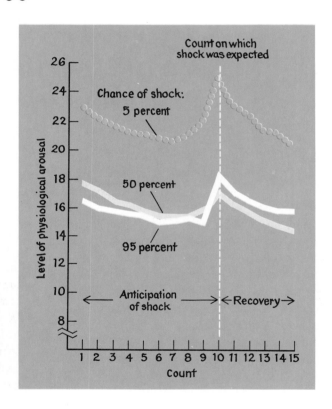

11-1 An experiment with surprising results
Subjects who had only a 5 percent chance of receiving a shock at the count of ten showed more physiological arousal—hence presumably more anxiety—than subjects who had a 50 percent chance or a 95 percent chance. For an explanation of this unexpected result, see the text. (The measure of physiological arousal shown here is electrical conductivity of the skin, affected by activity of the sweat glands.)

Harsh words in the family: They will probably be followed by anxiety experienced by all the family members for different reasons.

job, we have no idea what lies in store for us or why we should worry about it.)

The vagueness of anxiety makes it particularly difficult to handle. We usually cannot explain why we feel as we do or what it is that we fear may happen. Yet, for some unexplained reason, we find ourselves in the grip of the most uncomfortable of emotions. Our feelings can be intensely painful or can become chronic like a dull toothache, interfering over long periods with our sleep, appetite, and moods. The word *jumpy*, often applied to the feelings, is especially apt—for people plagued by anxiety are likely to have a lower threshold for other kinds of emotional response. They may be irritable and quickly moved to anger, and they may also overreact to pleasurable stimuli. They tend to have wide swings of mood and their behavior is often unpredictable.

Some anxiety-provoking situations

Although the causes of anxiety are difficult to pinpoint, there appear to be four situations in which it is most likely to occur:

1. We have conflicting motives. (Such as wanting to dedicate our life to helping others, yet at the same time wanting to make a lot of money.)
2. We experience a conflict between our behavior and an inner standard. (As when we do something we believe to be wrong.)
3. We encounter some unusual event that we cannot immediately understand and adjust to. (For example, when arriving on a new campus, not knowing what kind of behavior is expected.)
4. We are faced with events whose outcome is unpredictable. (For example, the score we will make on an important test.)

In all these cases, the emotion of anxiety is clearly related to motives. In situations 1 and 2, it is produced by a conflict between motives or between a motive and an inner standard. In situations 3 and 4, it is produced by frustration of the motive for certainty. Any situation that is clouded with uncertainty—not knowing what will happen, not knowing what is expected, not knowing the best course of action—has a built-in potential for creating anxiety.

Uncertainty as a source of anxiety

The most striking demonstration of how uncertainty leads to anxiety comes from an experiment that had totally unexpected and at first glance mysterious results. The subjects, all college men, were asked to listen to a voice counting to fifteen. At the count of ten, they were told, they might receive an electric shock. Whether or not this would happen depended on the draw of one card from a pack of twenty, which was shown to them. For one group, the deck contained only one shock card and nineteen no-shock cards—so that these subjects knew their chances of shock were only one in twenty, or 5 percent. For the second group, the chances were 50 percent. For the third group, the chances were 95 percent.

As the counting began, measurements were made of the subjects' physiological arousal, which presumably indicated the amount of anxiety they experienced. Common sense suggested that the group with the 50 percent chance of shock would show the most anxiety. The 5 percent group would feel relatively safe, and the 95 percent group would consider themselves almost certain to receive a shock and would be reconciled to it. Even the experimenters expected this result. To their amazement, however, the 5 percent group showed by far the most anxiety, as illustrated in Figure 11-1.

Why should this have happened? The answer lies in the comments of the 50 percent group. These subjects said they decided that their chances of getting a shock were high enough to lead them to

A class in relaxation training designed to relieve feelings of anxiety.

expect it—thus reducing the uncertainty—and merely to hope they would be spared. Thus they felt very much like the subjects in the 95 percent group, who were almost sure to get a shock. The subjects in the 5 percent group, on the other hand, experienced much more uncertainty. They felt that their chances of getting a shock were so low that they could not expect and reconcile themselves to it. Yet neither could they dismiss the possibility. It was this greater uncertainty that made them experience the greatest anxiety of all (1).

General and specific anxiety

Many studies have been made of anxiety and its effects. One finding is that some people seem to display anxiety in many of the situations they face. They feel anxious regardless of whether they are in their classroom or job, taking part in a social event, picking up the telephone, shopping, or even starting a vacation. They worry about many things and

have a vague uneasiness about all future events. Such people are victims of *general anxiety*. Others display only *specific anxiety* in some particular situation but not at other times (2). One well-known example is stagefright, which strikes many people who are otherwise generally free of anxiety. A type of specific anxiety often found among college students has to do with taking tests. *Test anxiety*, as it is called, is so common that it has been one of the most widely studied of all forms. Investigators have found that it can be relieved—and performance on tests can often be improved—by such measures as relaxation training and practice at concentrating on the test itself rather than on one's inner feelings (3).

Both general and specific anxiety seem to feed on themselves. The victim, having become anxious, is painfully aware of the signs of emotional arousal (increased heart rate, butterflies in the stomach)—and the very awareness increases the amount of anxiety. Relaxation training presumably counteracts this vicious circle. A recent experiment showed that even such a simple device as deliberately controlling one's breathing, to half the normal rate, can significantly lower some of the physiological signs of anxiety and the feelings of anxiety as well (4).

Anxiety is also relieved by alcohol and by such tranquilizers as Valium and Librium, presumably because these drugs reduce the activity of the brain's neurotransmitter noradrenalin (pages 56–58). But researchers point out that the relief is obtained at a price. Any anti-anxiety drug reduces the ability to cope realistically with the environment by meeting changes and challenges (5).

The effect of anxiety on learning and grades

Of particular interest to college students is the influence of anxiety on the ability to learn and on grades. Does it promote learning by increasing the desire to learn? Or does it interfere with learning?

Attempts to answer these questions—or any others about the effects of anxiety—are handicapped by the fact that levels of anxiety are difficult to measure. To classify people as high, medium, or low, psychologists have to rely mostly on questionnaires in which subjects are asked to describe their own feelings or report forms of behavior that would seem to indicate anxiety. These self-ratings are not necessarily objective, and it is impossible to assign a numerical anxiety quotient that would be nearly so accurate as an intelligence quotient. Most studies therefore content themselves with trying to compare one group of subjects who seem to show clear signs of a very high level with another group whose questionnaires and conduct seem to indicate a very low level.

Insofar as the facts can be determined, it appears that anxiety has a number of effects. People high in anxiety—either general or test anxiety—do better than others at simple learning tasks but more

poorly than others at difficult learning tasks (6, 7, 8). Presumably their anxiety impairs the intense concentration required for the learning of complicated materials. People high in anxiety seem to do particularly badly at learning when someone is watching them. Their performance at even simple learning tasks usually goes down sharply in the presence of an observer, while people low in anxiety do just about as well when watched as when alone (9).

How does anxiety affect actual performance in college? This question was explored by an investigator who selected one group of male students who appeared to be relatively high in anxiety and another group relatively low in anxiety. He examined their College Board scores, as an indication of their ability, and their actual grades in college. He found that students with the lowest levels of scholastic ability made approximately the same grades regardless of whether they were high or low in anxiety. So did students with the highest levels of scholastic ability. But at the in-between levels of ability—where, of course, most students fall—the students who were low in anxiety made significantly better grades than did the anxious students. Full results of the study appear in Figure 11-2 on page 410.

A follow-up study was made with anxious freshmen who were making such low grades that they were in danger of flunking out of college. One group of these freshmen took an active part in a counseling program in which they received advice about their problems in college, methods of study, campus life in general, and their relations with professors—advice that presumably would reduce their anxiety about the college situation. Another group, matched as closely as possible for College Board scores, type of high school attended, and other factors that influence performance in college, did not receive counseling. From midterm to the end of the first semester the counseled group made an average improvement of more than half a grade point. The group that was not counseled improved by less than a tenth of a grade point (11). Anxiety about the college situation appears to be a frequent—though perhaps correctable—cause of failure in college.

Since many of us live under crowded and noisy conditions that may be conducive to anxiety, it is useful to inquire into the effect that noise may have on college work and other forms of learning. The answer seems to be that noise in itself does not usually create problems. We may find it distracting at first but usually adapt to it rather quickly. However, our own emotional reactions to the noise may cause difficulties, especially when we are working on extremely difficult tasks. Experiments have shown that learners are most affected by noise when: 1) they believe that others taking part in the same study are not being subjected to as much noise, 2) they have no control over the noise, and 3) the noise occurs at unpredictable intervals (12). The last two factors, of course, are further examples of anxiety caused by uncertainty.

Anxiety and risk taking

One characteristic that influences the way people live their lives is the amount of risk they are willing to take. Some people are very conservative and hate to go out on a limb. Others seem to be born gamblers who take all kinds of chances. There appears to be a strong relationship between this refusal or readiness to take risks and anxiety.

An experiment that demonstrates this fact is illustrated in Figure 11-3. Note that subjects who appeared to be relatively free from anxiety tended to scorn the "sure thing" in the game that was used in the experiment. They made very few throws from the close distances where they were almost certain to succeed but would receive only a low score. They also tended to avoid the high risk of gambling that they could score from the longest distances, where they would have received the highest scores. Subjects who appeared to be relatively high in test anxiety made many more shots from the short distances and also "went for broke" more often by trying from the longest distances.

11-2
Anxiety and performance in college

The bars show the average grades made by high-anxiety and low-anxiety students of different levels of scholastic ability as indicated by their College Board scores. Note the pronounced differences found between the two groups at the middle ranges of scholastic ability (10).

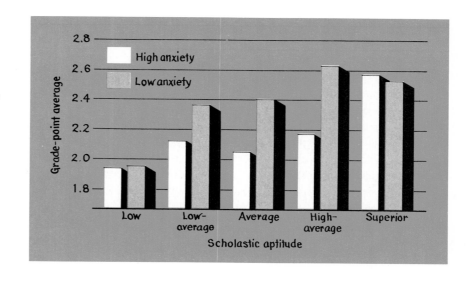

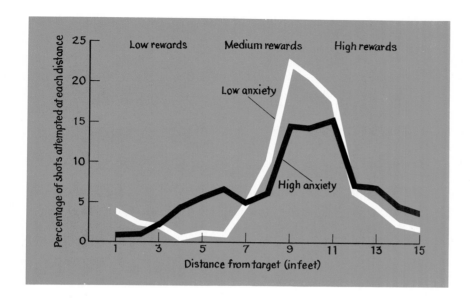

11-3
Anxiety, conservatism, and "going for broke"
Two groups of subjects played an experimental game in which they tossed rings at a peg, trying from any distance they chose. They were told that for ringing the peg from close distances they would receive low scores, from middle distances middle scores, and from far distances very high scores. Note that subjects who had been found low in anxiety chose a strategy of intermediate risks. Those who had been found high in anxiety tended to be either very conservative or to go for broke (13).

The experiment suggests that people who are highly anxious about success and failure tend to adopt either a very conservative or a very risky strategy in life situations. They are inclined to settle for the sure thing and thus avoid failure that would add to their anxiety, or else they tend to take the chances at which success is so unlikely that they can readily excuse their failure. You have probably observed people who take few chances in life, settle for jobs that seem beneath their abilities, and yet take an occasional flyer in a gambling casino or a risky investment. Less anxious people, on the other hand, seem to have enough confidence to take the middle-range risks that are most likely to lead to success in the long run.

Similarly, it has been observed that college students highly anxious about failure tend to leave examination rooms early (14), as if to avoid the further anxiety of continued effort. This behavior, of course, only increases the probability that they will actually experience the failure they find such a disturbing prospect.

The wear and tear of stress

To psychologists, as has been said, the term *stress* applies to the body's reactions to outside pressures—in other words, to the physiological wear and tear caused by attempting to adjust to events that cause emotional and other forms of arousal. In everyday language, of course, the word is also applied to the events themselves. The fact that many situations place a serious burden on the human organism has gained popular recognition in all the references made today to the "stress and strain" of modern life. Even people who have never taken a psychology course acknowledge that our society puts all of us under severe and often painful pressure caused by competition (for acceptance to college, grades, jobs, and promotions) and by social demands, worries about economic security and the possibility of war, crowded streets, and many similar concerns. People disillusioned with modern life often use the contemptuous term "rat race"—implying that existence has become a constant, mindless struggle for a prize of dubious value.

There is no question that modern life is stressful. Many events that are commonplace in our daily lives have been found to produce signs of stress even in lower animals. Exposure to noise—a standard feature of city life—raises the blood pressure of rats. Dogs that are raised in isolation and then suddenly introduced into a normal environment exhibit a long-lasting fear that makes them incapable of appropriate behavior (15). The human counterpart would be the abrupt shift of environment we experience when changing schools, jobs, or places of residence—or even the more general kinds of rapid change that have been occurring in technology, economics, and politics.

Whether life is really more difficult today than in the past, however, is dubious. Human beings have always been subject to conditions that cause stress. At one time the pressures came from fighting the elements and the animals and scrambling frantically for the next meal. And throughout history our ancestors were beset by pain, illness, and the danger of violent death. Today's sources of stress, though different, may be no more burdensome than those of the past—and indeed may actually be less so for many people. There is no way of knowing for sure.

Psychologists define stress as *the body's reaction to anything that threatens to damage the organism.* Stress can be caused by a disease germ, air and noise pollution, or the physical danger faced by a football player or a steeplejack. It can accompany any situation that produces anxiety, frustration, or conflict and therefore the physical wear and tear of intense or prolonged emotion. Thus stress depends not only on outside events but on our own feelings as we react to them. One person may experience severe stress over an event that leaves another person relatively calm.

Stress and the general adaptation syndrome

The damaging potential of stress, whatever its origin, has been dramatically demonstrated by Hans Selye, a biologist at the University of Montreal. Selye experimented with animals and exposed them to stressful physical conditions, such as the injection of poison in doses not quite strong enough to kill. The results, however, seem to be much the same as those produced in human beings by any form of external or internal pressure, including prolonged anxiety or other emotional tension.

Selye found that when an animal was injected with poison, its body automatically tried to defend itself. Most notably, its endocrine glands immediately sprang into action (as they also do in human emotional arousal). The adrenal glands in particular showed striking changes. They became enlarged and produced more adrenalin. They also discharged their stored-up supply of the hormones known as steroids, which make many contributions to the body's well-being. Because of this high level of activity of the adrenal glands, numerous physical changes occurred in the animals. For example, tissue was broken down into sugar to provide energy. The amount of salt normally found in the blood stream was sharply reduced.

After a few days of continued exposure to stress-producing conditions, the animals seemed to adapt. The adrenal glands returned to normal size and began to renew their supply of steroids. The salt level in the blood rose to normal or even higher.

Apparently the animals had adjusted to the situation and were perfectly normal.

Their recovery, however, was only temporary. After several weeks of continued pressure, the adrenal glands again became enlarged and lost their stores of steroids. The level of salt in the blood fell drastically. The kidneys, as a result of receiving an excess of hormones, underwent some complicated and damaging changes. Eventually the animals died, as if from exhaustion. They had been killed, so to speak, by an excess of the hormones they had produced in their own defense.

Another of Selye's important findings was that even during the period of apparent recovery, the animals were not so normal as they seemed. If a second source of stress was introduced during this period, the animals quickly died. In attempting to adapt to the original source of stress, apparently they had used their defenses to the maximum and were helpless against a new form of pressure (16).

To describe the sequence of events that takes place during prolonged stress—the initial shock or alarm, the recovery or resistance period, and at last exhaustion and death—Selye coined the phrase *general adaptation syndrome*. (To physicians the word *syndrome* means the entire pattern of symptoms and events that characterize the course of a disease.)

Psychosomatic illnesses

There are many indications that the general adaptation syndrome found in animals also occurs in human beings. It also appears that stress caused by frustration and conflict—indeed by any kind of prolonged emotional upset—can be just as drastic as the kind Selye produced by injecting poison. The physical results often take the form of *psychosomatic illnesses,* meaning bodily ailments that stem at least in part from mental and emotional causes. Dis-

eases that frequently seem to be psychosomatic include high blood pressure, heart attacks, stomach ulcers, diabetes, tuberculosis, multiple sclerosis, and possibly some forms of cancer (17)—as well as a host of minor illnesses including the common cold.

One study has suggested that perhaps all illnesses, not only those regarded as psychosomatic, usually are triggered by stress-producing situations. The study was made by compiling case histories of a group of patients suffering from a wide variety of physical ailments. It was found that all the patients had undergone some experience, shortly before the onset of the disease, that was psychologically distressing. (The experiences most frequently reported are listed in Figure 11-4.) The study suggests that under ordinary conditions our bodies are able to resist such external causes of illness as viruses and bacteria. It is when our usual

Emotional state believed to have triggered illness	Percentage of cases
Resentment or hostility	17
Frustration or rejection	13
Depression, hopelessness	13
Anxiety	13
Feelings of helplessness	12
Separation from a loved one	9
Stressful changes in life situation or threatening situation	9
Difficulties in relationship with therapist or experimenter	4
Miscellaneous	10

11-4 The emotional background of illness
Case histories of patients suffering from physical illnesses showed that all of them had recently experienced some type of stressful situation. The most common trigger for the illnesses was feelings of resentment or hostility (18).

Psychology and Society

Stress, illness, and the role of the physician

The relationships that have been found between stress and physical ailments shed considerable light on what was previously a medical mystery. Part of the puzzle centered on the fact that until recently there were only a few medicines or medical techniques that were physically effective in combating disease. Indeed some of the methods used in the past—such as drawing blood from an already weak patient by applying leeches—were actually harmful. Yet patients treated by the old methods often made spectacular recoveries. Even today, witch doctors in primitive societies cure many ailments as if by magic, as do faith healers in our own society.

Another part of the puzzle concerned that famous medical device called the placebo—a mere sugar pill, with no remedial value at all. Physicians have known for a long time that the number of people whose physical symptoms vanish after they take a placebo may be just as high as if real medicine had been prescribed. This phenomenon is called the *placebo effect*, and it causes great confusion in attempts to study the effectiveness of new drugs.

The key to the mystery now appears to be that any form of treatment comforts the patient, relieves stress, and thus helps the body mobilize its own defenses and throw off disease. The famous "bedside manner" of doctors in our great-grandparents' day may have been just as effective, in its own way, as today's techniques. Perhaps it would help today with the many people who complain that physicians—for all their blood tests, X-rays, and wonder drugs—often take an impersonal approach to illness that makes patients feel more like case histories than like suffering human beings.

---

defenses are weakened by stress that we are likely to get sick.

Can stress actually kill, as it killed Selye's animals? Some evidence that it can comes from a study of middle-aged men who died suddenly of heart attacks. Their backgrounds showed that four out of every five had been feeling depressed for periods ranging from a week to several months. (Depression, as will be seen later, is often a result of prolonged stress.) Just before the fatal attack, at least half of them had been in a situation likely to produce sudden and intense emotional arousal—in some cases an unusually heavy work load or other bustle of activity, in others circumstances creating a high level of anxiety or anger (19). It seems likely that stress was at least a contributing factor in their deaths. (The findings about psychosomatic illness are highly pertinent to the practice of medicine as discussed in the box on Psychology and Society at the top of the page.)

Who gets sick and who doesn't?— differences in stressful experiences

Everybody undergoes stressful experiences—yet not everybody comes down with a psychosomatic illness. Why? One reason seems to be that no two people have the same experiences, and that each experience has a sort of built-in potential for creating a certain level of stress, high or low. After studying the life experiences and medical records of large numbers of people, one group of investigators developed the Life Stress Scale shown in Figure 11-5, which assigns a numerical value to the amount of stress that adjusting to various new events seems to create. Note that these events include not only misfortunes but pleasurable happenings—such as getting married, achieving something outstanding, and even going on vacation or celebrating Christmas. Indeed getting married, assigned a figure of 50, was found fully half as stressful as the death of a husband or wife, which is at the top of the list with 100.

The likelihood of psychosomatic illness, the investigators concluded, is determined by the total number of stress units that occur within a single twelve-month period. When the number exceeded 200, more than half the people in the study developed health problems. Thus the scale indicates that a person is more likely than not to become sick if a single year's experiences include divorce (73 units), losing a job (47), a change in finances (38), the death of a close friend (37), and a change to a new kind of work (36). When the total exceeded 300, nearly 80 percent of subjects became ill.

Differences in resistance to stress

Although the Life Stress Scale serves as a guide to the potentially stressful effects of various experiences, critics regard it as too arbitrary to apply to all people under all circumstances (21). For one thing, any attempt to generalize about the stressful nature of events ignores the widespread individual differences in physical resistance to outside pressures. These individual differences are another reason some people get sick while others do not.

Experience	Stress units
Death of spouse	100
Divorce	73
Separation	65
Jail term	63
Death of close family member	63
Getting married	50
Being fired	47
Reconciliation in marriage	45
Retiring	45
Getting pregnant	40
Sex problems	39
New member in family	39
Change in finances	38
Death of close friend	37
Change to new kind of work	36
Change in work responsibilities	29
Trouble with in-laws	29
An outstanding achievement	28
Wife starts job or stops	26
Begin or end school	26
Trouble with boss	23
Change in work conditions	20
Move to new residence	20
Changing schools	20
Changing social activities	18
Vacation	13
Christmas holidays	12
Minor law violation	11

11-5 A scale of stress produced by various events
These are some of the figures in the Life Stress Scale, discussed in the text (20).

One study, for example, compared two groups of subjects, all of whom had been exposed to what appeared to be equal amounts of outside pressure (such as job difficulties, loss of a loved one, or financial problems). The group that developed illnesses of one kind or another turned out to have two characteristics: 1) a past history of some kind of bodily weakness, such as a vulnerable stomach or heart, and 2) a strong tendency to prolonged anxiety and worry. The group that did not get sick showed neither of these traits (22).

A recent study was made of executives of a Midwest utility company, all of whom had experienced various stressful situations, including transfer to a new job in a new city. An attempt was made to compare the personality traits of those who became ill and those who did not. Those who escaped illness turned out to have much more of what the researcher termed "hardiness." For one thing, they were more committed to themselves, their work, their families, and their social roles than were the illness-prone executives. They tended to have an internal locus of control (Chapter 10) and a sense of being responsible for their own destiny. They made vigorous attempts to face and solve their problems, in contrast to the more passive approach of the illness-prone (23).

Though this study indicates that active efforts to cope with stressful situations reduce the likelihood of illness, there is also evidence that too intense an effort can be harmful. In assessing the chances of suffering a heart attack, some investigators have found that the greatest risk is among people they have termed Type A. These people have an extremely high achievement motive and believe they can overcome any obstacle if only they try hard enough. They are ambitious and competitive and have a sense of urgency about getting their tasks done on time. They usually work to the limits of their endurance, and sometimes beyond it. When thwarted, they react with hostility and aggression. (This description, of course, fits many hard-driving and successful people, including numerous corporation executives.) The chances of suffering a heart attack are considerably less among Type B people—who are more easy-going and place less value on success (24).

High blood pressure and the power motive

One remarkable study indicates that high blood pressure—another potentially crippling psychosomatic illness—is closely related to the motive for power (Chapter 10). In this study, men in their early thirties were measured for motivation and for tendencies to gratify or inhibit their motives. Twenty years later, their patterns of blood pressure were measured. The study found that the early tests of motivation were remarkably accurate in predicting which of the subjects would have high blood pressure in later life. By far the greatest number of cases occurred among men who had been found, when in their thirties, to have a strong power motive that they tried to inhibit (25). Presumably the strong motivation, kept bottled up, produced frequent anger and thus chronic stress.

Selye's prescription for staying healthy

Selye believes that we all have our own individual pattern of resistance to damage by stress. The limits to what we can withstand are set by two factors. One is our general ability to adjust to stressful situations, or what Selye calls our "supply of adaptation energy." The other is the amount of wear and tear that the weakest part of the body can tolerate without succumbing to psychosomatic illness. (Some people have weak stomachs and are inclined to get ulcers. Some have heart structures that are susceptible to damage.)

The secret of a healthy and fulfilling life, according to Selye, is to live to the full extent of our capabilities—that is, to savor the excitement and emotionality of life but not to put undue strain on ourselves. The trick, he says, is to "determine our optimum speed of living, by trying various speeds and finding out which one is most agreeable" (26). If we find the pace damaging, we can pull back. If we thrive on it, we can venture a little further.

Selye believes that both the limiting factors in withstanding damage from stress—adaptation energy and the tolerance level of the weakest part of the body—are the result of heredity, determined by our genes. But this viewpoint may have been colored by his background in biology. Many psychologists hold that tolerance of distress also depends on nurture. They believe that we can learn to cope with anxiety and stress in a constructive way rather than letting them overwhelm and damage us (27). Some of the social issues raised by our knowledge of stress and psychosomatic illness are discussed in the box on page 418.

The psychological effects of stress

Along with the physical wear and tear of stress, notably including psychosomatic illness, go many psychological effects. Indeed the difference between normal behavior and abnormal behavior, which will be the topic of the rest of the chapter, seems to depend in large part on the amount of anxiety and stress that people experience.

The physical and psychological effects are sometimes difficult to separate. This is especially true in the case of *depression,* a common emotional disturbance that can range in severity from a mild neurosis to a crippling psychosis. One investigator has estimated that as many as thirty million Americans can expect to suffer from depression at some time in their lives (29). They may not even know what is wrong—for the milder form of depression does not necessarily cause them to feel unhappy or "blue." Nor do they necessarily appear depressed to their friends. But their depression can be detected by sensitive measurements of the activity of their facial muscles, through the method illustrated in Figure 11-6. When they are asked to think of a typical day in their life, the facial muscles tend to make tiny movements into a pattern indicating sadness—altogether different from the happy pattern

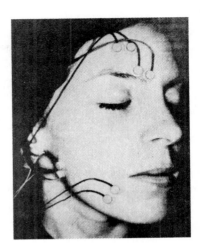

11-6 A depression-detecting device
Electrodes placed on the forehead and cheeks measure the activity of muscles responsible for facial expression and can detect changes not apparent to the eye. People suffering from depression show characteristic patterns of muscle activity, as explained in the text.

shown by nondepressed people when asked the same question (30). Mild states of depression typically result in feelings of unexplained fatigue and lack of enthusiasm. Their victims may have trouble getting any work done and may lose interest in activities that once gave them pleasure. Often they think they must be suffering from some disease, such as mononucleosis, that causes a lack of energy. Yet physical tests show nothing wrong.

There is considerable evidence that depression is related to brain chemistry. In particular, it seems to be associated with low levels of the neurotransmitter noradrenalin or with reduced effectiveness in the way this neurotransmitter operates at the brain's synapses (31). Animal experiments have shown that the amount of noradrenalin in the brain may decline substantially during stress (32).

A tendency toward depression, especially in its more extreme forms, appears to be at least partly

Psychology and Society
Unemployment, stress, and social policy

One of the fascinating aspects of psychosomatic diseases is the manner in which they may be related to upheavals in the social structure. What happens to the nation's health statistics when rapid inflation inflicts financial distress on great numbers of people? What are the effects of a severe recession that throws several million people out of work—and threatens countless others?

Attempts to measure the results are extremely difficult. Social changes occur constantly, and often many take place at the same time. There is no way to determine how much stress any one of them is likely to cause—especially since there are so many individual differences in what people find stressful and how well they can tolerate such events. Unemployment may be devastating to some people (especially if they have other stressful problems at the same time) but far less burdensome to others (especially if their life is going smoothly in other respects). Moreover, the statistics on how many people are unemployed in any given year are probably subject to considerable error.

Despite these difficulties, many social scientists are trying to explore the effects of social and economic problems. One study tried to examine what happened when government figures on the number of unemployed in the United States rose suddenly in 1970 from under 3 million to over 4 million, then stayed above the 4 million figure for the rest of the decade. The study found that by 1975 the number of deaths from heart and kidney diseases, both often psychosomatic, was nearly 3 percent higher than would otherwise have been expected. So was the total number of deaths in the nation. Admissions to state mental hospitals and suicides were higher by an even greater amount (28). The increases represented thousands of cases.

Do the figures represent cause and effect? We cannot be sure, but the study raises some provocative questions. Preventing unemployment and inflation, of course, is outside the realm of psychology. But what can psychology contribute in the way of making such social changes less stressful—or helping individuals cope with the stress?

---

the result of heredity (33). Apparently some people are born with a type of brain chemistry that is prone to low levels of noradrenalin and thus depression, just as other people are born with weak stomachs or weak hearts that are vulnerable to damage by stress. Women are more likely to suffer from depression than men, possibly because of biological factors, possibly for reasons related to the situations they find stressful and their learned reactions to stressful events (34).

At any rate depression is an emotional disturbance in which the physical and psychological aspects of stress appear closely intermingled. Many other psychological disturbances also seem to represent some form of failure to cope successfully with stressful experiences and their physical and emotional effects (35). If we have learned to handle stress and anxiety, our behavior remains within normal bounds. If not, we may slip across the line into abnormal behavior.

Successful coping and normal behavior

The photographs in Figure 11-7 show that even small children display different reactions to stressful situations. One child makes a strenuous effort to cope. Another quickly gives up.

Adults display an even wider range of differences. They may try to fight off the cause of the stress or throw up their hands. They may succeed in surmounting the stressful situation or they may fail. When they fail, as is sometimes inevitable, they may find a way of reconciling themselves to the situation—or, on the other hand, they may develop physical ailments or a crippling amount of anxiety, anger, or learned helplessness. To a considerable extent, all abnormal behavior is the result of unsuccessful coping. Some sort of maladjustment occurs between the individual and the environment (especially the social environment: family, friends, fellow workers, bosses, teachers). The individual experiences anxiety and stress and wants to relieve them—but does not know how (36).

Even in animal experiments, successful coping has been found an effective defense against stress. In one study, two groups of rats were subjected to the stress-producing stimulus of electric shocks. One group was permitted to learn a warning signal. In human terms, they discovered when the shock was coming and could prepare for it, and in the meantime they had nothing to fear. The other group received no warning at all. Though both groups were exposed to exactly the same number

11-7 To cope or not to cope?

These two 13-month-olds, photographed in a psychology laboratory, react in very different ways to a fence that separates them from mother and toys. The child at left makes an active effort to cope with the situation by first trying to climb the fence, then struggling to squeeze around it. The child at right sees no possible solution and bursts into tears.

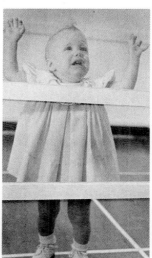
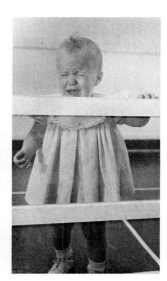

CROCK by Bill Rechin © Field Enterprises, Inc. 1979. Courtesy Field Newspaper Syndicate.

and intensity of shocks, the second group developed five times as many stomach ulcers as the other (37). A similar experiment produced a significant finding about levels of noradrenalin in the brain. Animals that had no way of predicting or preparing for the shock showed a decrease, as would be expected from what was said earlier about stress, noradrenalin, and depression. But the animals that could cope after a fashion, because they knew when the shock was coming and could relax in the meantime, actually showed an increase (38). It has been suggested that this experiment indicates "there may even be some psychological advantage from meeting and successfully coping with a manageable source of stress" (39).

Assertive coping:
1 Changing the environment

To constructive attempts to deal with anxiety and stress, psychologists often apply the term *assertive coping*. One form is a direct attempt to change the stressful situation. For example, let us say that we are experiencing frustration. One of our motives has been blocked. We feel bad about the situation. We may even suffer anger so intense that it amounts to rage and sets the stomach churning. Yet, if we can keep our wits about us, perhaps we can somehow manage to overcome the obstacle. We can face up to the difficulty and try to find some

way to overcome it. We can regard the situation as an exercise in problem solving and get busy seeking the answer.

Even a hungry animal, barred from getting food by a closed door, often tries to outwit its environment by gnawing through the barrier. A motorist frustrated by a flat tire can get busy changing it or try to find a phone and seek help. A student who wants to be an accountant but is weak in certain areas of mathematics can tackle these subjects and try to master them. Couples frustrated by a bad marriage can engage in assertive coping by going to a marriage counselor—or, if necessary, by ending the marriage.

Assertive coping with the environment consists in a meaningful attempt to change the situation in a constructive way that has a reasonable chance of success. The attempt may fail—but the effort itself seems to combat the damaging effects of stress.

2 Changing our own behavior

In many cases, the stress we suffer comes not so much from the environment as from our own behavior. Failure in college can result from inattention in class or insufficient study. Social unpopularity may reflect a grumpy, timid, or overaggressive approach to other people. (The way people's behavior toward us is largely determined by our own actions is one of the concerns of Chapter 14.)

Thus at times the only effective way to reduce stress is to change our own behavior. The couple who undertake marriage counseling will probably find that both partners have to make readjustments in the ways they act toward each other. Indeed people who seek counseling or therapy of any kind are in effect asking for help in changing their own behavior and attitudes.

3 Managing the internal wear and tear

Sometimes a stressful situation persists no matter how hard we try to change the environment or our own behavior. During severe economic recessions many people continue to suffer the strains of unemployment and lack of money no matter how hard they try or how far they travel in search of a job. Efforts to cope with the situation by changing their own behavior—such as training themselves for a new line of work—may fail. A person may also be helpless to do anything about such sources of stress as the illness of a family member or lack of talent for a chosen career.

In situations of genuine helplessness—not learned helplessness—there is just no escape from the source of stress. The only form assertive coping can take is an effort to control the effects. We must somehow keep the physical and emotional wear and tear within bounds, so that they do not destroy us physically or psychologically. There is no magic formula for this kind of coping, but many people have succeeded at it. Helen Keller (Chapter 7) was a conspicuous example. So are the hundreds of thousands of people who somehow kept their sanity and spirit in the concentration camps of the Second World War.

In talking about managing the internal effects, we are really discussing what is often called mental health. It is difficult even to define mental health, much less offer suggestions for attaining it. Perhaps it consists, as one psychologist has suggested, in harmony among physical well-being, effective functioning as a member of society, and a high level of personal morale (or sense of self-worth and self-reliance). Preserving mental health is possible even in the most difficult situations because the anxiety and stress we experience depend not so much on what the environment does to us as on the way we view ourselves and our relations to the environment (40). In exactly the same situation, a person with low self-esteem and an external locus of control suffers far more than a person with a positive self-image and an internal locus of control.

The normal personality

In attempting to define normal personality and normal behavior, psychologists for many years emphasized the word *adjustment*. Normal personality

A stressful situation indeed: How well, we can wonder, are the two motorists handling the internal wear and tear?

What it means to be normal: some comforting advice

Adding the term mental health to the English language—and its equivalent to languages around the world—has produced some unfortunate side effects. The term has often been misinterpreted and exaggerated, as have been the goals of Sigmund Freud and the newer schools of psychotherapy. Many people are intimidated by the concepts of mental health and the normal personality, which they see as demanding perfection beyond the reach of most ordinary mortals. They are vaguely dissatisfied because they worry that they—and life itself—should be far better than they are.

Actually, psychology's message to society is reassuring rather than frightening. Asked to describe the normal personality, most psychologists would probably agree on the following six points. Note especially the first of them.

1 Being normal does not mean being perfect. Everybody gets angry, has hostile thoughts, gets greedy at times, and does foolish things. Everybody encounters frustrations and conflicts and experiences anxiety and stress. Nobody can cope in a completely successful manner at all times. We can only do our best—which probably means to function more or less satisfactorily despite the inevitable problems of the human condition.

2 Normal people are realistic. They have learned not to expect perfection, either in themselves or in others. They are aware of their own limitations and accept the fact that other people also have limitations. Since they do not have unduly grandiose expectations, they are not surprised or overly ashamed or angry when they themselves fail or when others fail them.

3 Normal people can "roll with the punch." They may be unhappy at times over the state of the world or over personal disappointments, but they manage to live with these situations. They are flexible and can change their plans. They are confident of their ability to cope with whatever situations may arise—not necessarily as well as they would like, but at least after a fashion.

4 Normal people possess a certain amount of enthusiasm and spontaneity. They find things to do that give them pleasure, whether working productively or watching a sunset.

5 Normal people have a good deal of independence. They do not shift, like a weathervane, with every change in the wind, either in society as a whole or among their associates. They do not mind being alone. Indeed they enjoy a certain amount of privacy.

6 Normal people are capable of feeling and showing affection and of establishing close relationships with others—not necessarily many others, but a chosen few. They can love and be loved.

traits, it was generally believed, are those that help people adjust to the environment and to other people—in other words, to accept the realities of the physical world and of society and to behave in harmony with them. This description of the normal personality still persists to some extent. Indeed many colleges offer a course called the Psychology of Adjustment.

In recent years, however, many psychologists have come to believe that adjustment is too passive and negative a term, implying a self-effacing conformity to what other people are thinking and doing. Some have decided that adjustment, if taken to mean a more or less unquestioning acceptance of some aspects of society—such as mass killings in warfare and the spending of human resources on military equipment rather than on education—is itself abnormal (41).

Thus the emphasis has shifted. Growing numbers of psychologists now regard normal behavior not as mere adjustment but as an active effort to cope with the problems of life and achieve some kind of honest self-awareness, independence, and fulfillment. As was mentioned in Chapter 10, Maslow has suggested the term *self-actualization*. Other psychologists have defined normal people as those who maintain a stable sense of identity (42)—or who possess the inner freedom to make their own decisions rather than yielding to pressures from the environment and from other people (43). Some of the current thinking about being normal is summarized in the box on Psychology and Society.

Defense mechanisms and other questionable forms of coping

Besides assertive coping, people devise many other ways of trying to handle anxiety and stress. These other ways, by and large, are not nearly so effective. They may serve as stopgaps in an emergency. They may even be practiced over long periods, as a sort of life strategy, with some success and without serious damage. But they are questionable at best—and, when carried to extremes, they carry a serious risk. They lie in a sort of gray area between successful coping and downright failure to cope—or, in other words, between normal and abnormal behavior.

Prominent among them are certain devices, first described by Sigmund Freud, called *defense mechanisms*. Freud regarded these mechanisms as unconscious psychological processes, mental or symbolic, that people develop to relieve anxiety. Unlike assertive coping, they are not deliberate efforts to change the environment or one's own behavior or to deal realistically with anxiety and stress. Indeed all defense mechanisms are based to some degree on self-deception and distortion of reality. Yet everybody adopts some of them at one time or another. They are not necessarily harmful. But psychotic people often display them in exaggerated form.

Rationalization

One defense mechanism has been recognized ever since Aesop started the phrase sour grapes with his fable about the fox. (The fox, unable to reach an inviting cluster of grapes, consoled itself by deciding they would have been sour anyway.) Freud's name for this defense mechanism is *rationalization*—an attempt to deal with stressful situations by claiming that they never really occurred.

People often resort to rationalization to explain away their frustrations. A man, rejected by a woman, convinces himself that she was not nearly so attractive or interesting as he had supposed. A woman, turned down when applying for employment, convinces herself that the job was not really worth having.

People also use rationalization to reduce the anxiety caused by conflicts between motives and inner standards. A mother's real reason for keeping her daughter from dating may be jealousy, a motive of which her conscience disapproves. She rationalizes by claiming she is acting for the daughter's own good. A student cheats on an examination and rationalizes by claiming that everybody cheats.

Repression

Some people who suffer anxiety and stress over their motives simply try to banish the motives from their conscious thoughts—to the point where they seem to be totally unaware of their desires. This defense mechanism is called *repression*. People who at one time suffered severe anxiety and stress over sexual motives may repress these motives so thoroughly that they no longer seem to be aware of any sexual feelings or desires at all. Other people seem oblivious to the fact that they have any desires for dependency or hostility. Some cases of *amnesia,* or loss of memory, appear to be exaggerated forms of repression.

Sublimation

A motive that causes anxiety may also be transformed unconsciously into a different but related motive that is more acceptable to society and to oneself. This defense mechanism is known as *sublimation,* a process that enables a "shameful" motive to find expression in a more noble form. Freud believed that works of art are often the result of sublimation—that the Shakespeares and Michelangelos of the world may very well have channeled forbidden sexual urges into artistic creativity. Similarly, Freud believed that people may sublimate their urges toward cruelty into a socially approved desire to become surgeons, prosecuting attorneys, or even teachers with the power to discipline the young.

Identification

Another mechanism for relieving anxiety is to take on the virtues of some admired person or group that seems free of such anxiety. This process is called *identification.* An example would be a man, anxious about his own lack of courage, who identifies with a swashbuckling movie star or a group of mountain climbers so that he can believe he too possesses their daring. A woman anxious about her lack of social acceptance may identify with a popular roommate.

In a more complex form, identification may be established with a figure of authority who is resented and feared. Thus a young man may defend himself against the anxiety aroused by hostile feelings toward his boss by identifying with the boss. He may imitate the boss's mannerisms and express the same opinions, thus persuading himself that he possesses the same power. This type of identification may also be made with a group. Young people, anxious about their feelings of envy and hostility toward an exclusive clique, may identify with the group and adopt its standards. A study of prisoners in German concentration camps during the Second World War showed that many of them imitated the characteristics of the very guards from whose brutality they were suffering (44).

Reaction formation

People who display a trait to excess—that is, in an exaggerated form that hardly seems called for by the circumstances—may be using the defense mechanism called *reaction formation.* They are pretending to possess motives that are the exact opposite of the real motives that are causing their anxiety. For example, a man appears to be the soul

Who is identifying with whom? Could the father be relieving anxiety over the lost years of childhood?

of politeness. He is constantly holding doors for other people, saying "Yes, sir," and "Yes, ma'am," always smiling, agreeable, and apologetic for his mistakes. This exaggerated politeness and concern for others may simply be a defense mechanism he has adopted to conceal the fact that he has hostile motives and that his hostility is making him anxious. A woman who dresses in a provocative manner and is constantly flirting and telling risqué stories may be concealing her sexual inhibitions and fear of being unattractive.

Projection

The man who claims that everybody is dishonest and the woman who is convinced of the immorality of the younger generation may have reached their conclusions through honest examination of the evidence. On the other hand, they may be exhibiting

another defense mechanism called *projection,* in which people foist off or project onto other people motives or thoughts of their own that cause them anxiety. The man who talks too much about dishonesty may be concealing his own strong tendencies toward dishonesty. The woman who talks too much about the immorality of young people may be concealing her own strong sexual desires.

Projection often plays a part in disagreements between marriage partners. Many husbands complain that their wives are extravagant, although a disinterested observer can clearly see that it is the husband himself who is wasting money. Wives who are torn by sexual conflicts and urges toward infidelity may falsely accuse their husbands of having affairs. A marriage counselor who hears accusations by husband or wife of bad conduct or improper motives always looks for the possibility that the complaints represent projection rather than truth.

Projection is one of the most powerful and dangerous of the defense mechanisms. It works very effectively to reduce anxiety, but it does so at the risk of a completely distorted view of the truth about oneself and others. In its most exaggerated form it becomes the psychosis called *paranoia,* described in the chapter postscript.

The pro and con of defense mechanisms

The six defense mechanisms just discussed are the most common and easily recognizable. There are doubtless others. Indeed we human beings are remarkably ingenious at finding new ways to delude ourselves. In one way or another, we persuade ourselves that we did not really want the goals we cannot achieve, that our motives are completely admirable, that we are living up to our own and society's standards, and that our disappointments are somehow bearable.

Because anxiety and stress are so common, all of us use defense mechanisms from time to time—either those that have been mentioned or others of our own invention. Though these defense mechanisms are usually irrational, they often serve a useful purpose. They may help us through crises that would otherwise overwhelm and disable us. If nothing else, they may gain us time in which we can gather the strength, maturity, and knowledge needed to cope more realistically and constructively with our anxiety and stress. It is only in extreme cases that the use of defense mechanisms slips over into the realm of abnormal psychology.

Aggression as a response to anxiety and stress

There are other reactions to anxiety and stress that also lie near the borderline between normal and abnormal behavior. One of the most common is

Lonely in a crowd—an example of withdrawal.

Behind the obvious aggression lie some hidden sources of anxiety and stress at which we can only guess.

aggression, which is often produced by frustration. Children frustrated by other children who take their toys often get angry and strike out with their fists. Frustrated adults may kick at a tire that has gone flat, break an offending golf club, hit a tennis ball into the next county, or shout insults to a driver who has cut them off. This kind of behavior, aimed specifically at the source of the frustration, is called *direct aggression.*

When a direct attack on the source of frustration is impossible, people may display *displaced aggression* and vent their emotions on an innocent bystander. A man angry at a powerful and overdemanding boss goes home and behaves aggressively toward his wife and children. (In everyday language, he uses them as scapegoats.) A little girl angry at her parents takes out her aggression on a smaller child or on a pet. Scapegoating accounts for a great deal of the prejudice displayed against minority groups and foreigners. The prime example occurred when Hitler made the Jews scapegoats, blaming them for all the frustrations and conflicts that Germany was suffering in a time of economic and political tension.

Withdrawal and apathy

Some individuals react to difficult situations by *withdrawal*. To avoid further anxiety and stress, they shun close contacts with other people or any attempt to gratify their motives. We say of such people that they have "retreated into a shell" or that they have "quit trying." Rather than trying to cope assertively with their difficulties, they choose to escape by narrowing the horizons of their lives—often in drastic and self-limiting ways.

In similar fashion, some people display *apathy*. They are sad and listless, seem to lose all interest in what happens to them, and have a difficult time finding energy for the ordinary chores of life.

Regression

The experiment with the "half toys" described in Chapter 10—in which children aged two to five were frustrated by being separated by a barrier from desirable playthings—produced an interesting side effect. The children began to behave in a manner more appropriate to younger levels of development. Indeed they acted like children seventeen months younger, on the average, than their actual ages. This type of behavior—retreating toward activities that usually characterize a lower level of maturity—is called *regression*.

Displays of regression as a reaction to frustration and stress are common among children. A first-born child, upset by the arrival of a baby sister or brother, may go back to such forgotten habits as thumb sucking or may want to be fed from a bottle. Frustrated adults may regress to such childish behavior as weeping or throwing temper tantrums. People who are victims of extreme emotional disturbance sometimes display striking degrees of regression, as illustrated in Figure 11-8.

11-8

A case of regression

The girl at the left, a 17-year-old psychiatric patient, found the old photograph of herself in the center, taken when she was 5. She then cut her hair and made every attempt to look as she had at 5, as at the right (45).

The abnormal personality

Because so many forms of behavior lie in the gray area between what is normal and what is not, it is virtually impossible to make any absolute definition of the abnormal personality. Is it abnormal to believe in witches? It was not considered so by the American colonists. Is it abnormal for a young woman to faint from the excitement of attending a dance or the embarrassment of hearing profanity? It was not considered so in Victorian England. Is suicide abnormal? To most Americans, it may seem the ultimate in abnormality. Yet in the Far East a Buddhist priest who commits suicide as a form of political protest is regarded as exhibiting strength of character rather than abnormality.

From a statistical viewpoint, behavior can be called abnormal if it is uncommon and unusual—as popular terminology recognizes by referring to it as "odd." But this is not the whole story, for even unusual forms of behavior are not generally called abnormal unless they are regarded as undesirable by the particular society in which they occur. In our own society, the habit of working eighteen hours a day is probably rarer than heroin addiction. Yet an eighteen-hour work day is generally considered admirable or at least acceptable and is therefore called normal. Heroin addiction is considered undesirable and therefore called abnormal.

Since personal happiness is highly valued in the United States, being normal is generally equated with being happy. A trait or behavior is considered normal if it leads to happiness, at least much of the time, and abnormal if it leads to unhappiness. Though this criterion is widely accepted, there are some notable exceptions. Many people who commit vicious acts that could hardly be considered normal—such as wartime atrocities and mass murders in peacetime—seem to be perfectly happy.

In general, however, the working definition of abnormal behavior embraces the three points that have been mentioned. An abnormal personality trait or type of behavior is: 1) statistically unusual, 2) considered undesirable by most people, and 3) a source of unhappiness to the person who possesses or displays it. It must be admitted that the definition is not very satisfactory from a scientific point of view and would be rejected by many psychologists—chiefly on the ground that it sets up rigid standards that enable our society to stigmatize as abnormal anybody whose behavior is disliked or considered disruptive, whether or not that behavior can be judged abnormal by any scientific measure.

Stress and abnormal behavior

The relationship between stress and abnormal behavior has been clear ever since the time of Pavlov. In one experiment, Pavlov conditioned a dog to discriminate between a circle and an ellipse projected on a screen. The dog learned to salivate to the circle but not to the ellipse. Then the shape of the ellipse was changed gradually so that it became more and more like a circle. Even when the difference in appearance was very small, the dog still made the discrimination. But when the difference became too tiny for the dog to perceive and the discrimination became impossible, the dog began to behave strangely. At various times animals placed in this situation became restless, hostile, destructive, and apathetic, and they developed muscle tremors and tics (46).

Many other studies have shown that animals begin to exhibit abnormal behavior when they experience greater stress—caused by frustration or in other ways—than they can tolerate (47). The early experiments in learned helplessness (pages 112–18) are in a sense a demonstration of how the stressful effect of electric shocks, delivered regardless of what the animal does or does not try to do, produces neurotic behavior.

Learned helplessness in human beings is clearly the product of stressful situations and the acquired belief that the victim had no way of escaping. Perhaps an even clearer example is battle fatigue, or the breakdown sometimes suffered by soldiers—even those who have coped successfully with the difficulties of civilian life. The difference between normal and abnormal behavior always hinges on two factors: 1) the amount of stress and anxiety a person experiences and 2) the person's ability to handle this amount. Both factors, as will now be seen, are influenced by biological structure, psychological traits, and the environment.

Biological influences

As was stated in Chapter 9, there seem to be wide individual differences in glandular activity and sensitivity of the autonomic nervous system—perhaps also in the activity of the brain centers concerned with emotion. These individual differences may incline one person to be much more easily aroused and more intensely emotional than another. Thus some people, because of their inherited biological makeup, probably experience a great deal more emotional and physical wear and tear than others.

Certainly there is considerable evidence that heredity can contribute to tendencies toward the psychoses, which are the most severe forms of abnormal behavior (as described in a chapter postscript). Schizophrenia, for example, is more common among the close relatives of schizophrenics than among people whose family background shows no other cases (48). Studies also indicate that he-

reditary factors may produce tendencies toward manic-depressive psychosis (49) and perhaps toward other less extreme forms of abnormal behavior as well (50).

Psychological influences

Regardless of what kind of biological equipment we inherit, our acquired psychological traits also play a key role in determining how much anxiety and stress we are likely to experience and how much we can tolerate without lapsing into abnormal behavior. For example, if we acquire motives for achievement or power that we cannot gratify, or we have strong motives for affiliation and approval that are frustrated, we become extremely vulnerable. Particularly significant are our inner standards. An event that produces little or no anxiety in a person with relatively low standards of mastery and competence may produce almost unbearable anxiety in a person with higher standards. Clinical psychologists often see people who have suffered a crippling amount of anxiety and stress over violations of standards of sexual behavior, honesty, hostility, or dependency that would seem trivial to most of us.

Environmental influences

Also important is the environment to which we have been exposed from birth, especially the social experiences we have encountered. Some environments are much more likely than others to produce abnormal behavior. Statistical studies show that schizophrenia, for example, is most common among people living in the slums or near-slums of large cities (51). Perhaps this is because people forced to live in such an environment have a more stressful existence than people at more affluent levels of society. Or perhaps growing up in a slum environment reduces the individual's tolerance for stress and anxiety.

Environmental influences also help determine the particular kind of abnormal behavior a person is most likely to display. The culture of middle-class and upper-class America has traditionally maintained that individuals are personally responsible for what happens to them—and therefore people in this culture who fail to live up to inner standards of achievement and virtue are likely to suffer intense feelings of guilt or depression. Americans with a less affluent background are more likely to display symptoms generated by feelings of anger, bitterness, and suspicion.

To summarize, the chances that people will display abnormal behavior—and the particular kinds of abnormal behavior to which they are most prone—depend in part on the biological equipment they have inherited, in part on the psychological traits they have acquired, and in part on the environment in which they find themselves in childhood and adulthood. The three factors work together to make some people behave in a normal fashion and others to behave in ways that range from slightly neurotic to severely psychotic.

(Summary begins on page 437.)

Postscript

Classifications of abnormal behavior

Abnormal behavior takes many forms. Some deviations from the normal are so slight that they are popularly termed mere quirks—strange little habits like eccentricities in dress or speech. People who have somehow picked up such habits may seem a bit queer at times, but they are not seriously discomforted or prevented from functioning effectively. At the other extreme are the serious forms of mental disturbance that render their victims out of touch with reality and incapable of conducting the ordinary affairs of life. These drastic forms of abnormal behavior, called *psychoses,* are relatively rare. Yet, in a nation as large as the United States, it has been estimated that on any given day they afflict about a million people, two-thirds of whom are being treated in mental hospitals (52).

In a sort of twilight zone between normal behavior and the extreme abnormality of psychosis lie the conditions known as *neuroses* (or sometimes *psychoneuroses*). These are long-lasting emotional disturbances characterized by high levels of stress and anxiety. Their victims usually manage to get along in school, hold jobs, and conduct more or less successful family and social relationships. But their chronic feeling of being anxious and distressed interferes with their effectiveness and their zest for life. They are the people who are most likely to seek relief through psychotherapy. Estimates of how many people are neurotic vary widely. One study found that fully 30 percent of big-city residents were mildly to seriously neurotic (53). Other studies have placed the figure for the population as a whole as low as about 8 percent (54). Attempts to determine the number are handicapped by the difficulty of setting a dividing line between what is normal and what is not.

In a sense, every neurosis is unique. Each person experiences an individual pattern of stressful situations and responds to them in individual ways dictated by an individual set of biological, psychological, and environmental factors. Thus any attempt to classify the symptoms of neurosis has to be somewhat arbitrary. One classification system used by many psychotherapists includes the following.

Anxiety states

Anxiety, of course, is characteristic of most forms of abnormal behavior. But sometimes it is such an obvious and outstanding symptom that it constitutes what has been termed an *anxiety state*. Many neuroses fall into this category, which takes a number of forms. Two of the most common anxiety states are the following.

Anxiety reaction

The symptoms of an *anxiety reaction* are a chronic and relatively unfocused feeling of uneasiness and vague fear. People displaying anxiety reaction feel tense and jumpy, are afraid of other people, doubt their ability to study or work, and sometimes suffer from actual panic. They may experience such physical symptoms as palpitation of the heart, cold sweats, and dizziness. One man has described his feelings in these terms:

> I feel anxious and fearful most of the time; I keep expecting something to happen but I don't know what. It's not the same all the time. Sometimes I only feel bad—then suddenly for no reason it happens. My heart begins to pound so fast that I feel it's going to pop out. My hands get icy and I get a cold sweat all over my body. My forehead feels like it is covered with sharp needles. I feel like I won't be able to breathe and I begin panting and choking. It's terrible—so terrible. I can go along for a while without too much difficulty and then suddenly without any warning it happens (55).

Phobic reaction

Anxiety states sometimes become attached to a specific object or event. The victim is then said to be suffering from a *phobic reaction*—in other words, displaying an unreasonable fear. Two common phobias are *claustrophobia* (fear of confinement in small places, which makes some people unable to ride in elevators) and *acrophobia* (fear of high places, which affects some people when they have to climb to the top of a theater balcony). As was said on pages 91–94, phobias can be acquired through simple classical conditioning in childhood, as the child Albert acquired his fear of furry animals. But they can also develop in more complex ways and may be attached to any object at all. Some people are thrown into panic by a snake, an ambulance, or even a toy balloon.

Obsessive-compulsive reactions

Obsessions are thoughts that keep cropping up in a persistent and disturbing fashion. Some neurotics are obsessed with the idea that they have heart trouble or that they are going to die by a certain age. A common and mild form of obsession is the feeling of people starting out on a trip that they have left the door unlocked or the stove turned on.

Compulsions are irresistible urges to perform some act over and over again, such as washing one's hands dozens of times a day. The hostess who cannot bear to see a knife or fork out of line at the table and keeps emptying her guests' ash trays is exhibiting mild forms of compulsion. So is the businesswoman who cannot get any work done unless her papers are arranged in neat piles on her desk and she has a half dozen freshly sharpened pencils waiting all in a line. Or the child who steps on every crack in the sidewalk.

Obsessive-compulsive reactions seem to represent an attempt to substitute acceptable thoughts or actions for unacceptable desires that are causing conflict and anxiety. In particular, they may be an attempt to cover up feelings of hostility.

Hysteria

As used to describe neuroses, the word *hysteria* has a different meaning from the usual one. It refers specifically to the following two conditions.

Conversion reaction

This form of hysteria results in strange and often dramatic physical symptoms though nothing is physically wrong. People who display conversion reaction may suffer paralysis of the arms or legs and even blindness or deafness. They may lose all sensitivity in one part of the body. In one type of conversion reaction, called glove anesthesia, they lose all sensitivity in the hand, as if it were covered by a glove. They cannot feel a pinprick or even a severe cut anywhere from fingertips to wrist.

Dissociative reactions

People with dissociative reactions set themselves apart in some manner from the conflicts that are troubling them. One type of dissociative reaction is *amnesia,* or loss of memory. Another takes the rare form called *multiple personality*—in which the victims seem to be split into two or more completely different selves, representing aspects of their personality that they have been unable to integrate into a unity. (One of the selves may express the motive for affiliation by being kind and pleasant, while the other shows extreme hostility and aggres-

sion.) *Sleepwalking,* in which people move about and perform acts while asleep that they cannot remember after they wake up, is also a dissociative reaction.

Anxiety states, obsessive-compulsive reactions, and hysteria are not the only neuroses. There are many others. It might even be said that there are as many different neuroses, some of which defy classification, as there are neurotics. All are characterized by high levels of stress and anxiety lasting over a considerable period of time, but different individuals display different symptoms. Neuroses may be mild and cause little trouble, or they may be so severe as to verge on the psychotic.

Personality (or character) disorders

Some forms of abnormal behavior are difficult to classify. Unlike the neuroses, they are not clearly related to stress or anxiety. People who display them may not feel any particular discomfort, but they behave in ways that are often painful to the people around them. They seem to lack any desire—or perhaps ability—to act in ways that are socially acceptable. These forms of behavior are called *personality disorders,* or *character disorders.* The people who have acquired them seem to have some deficiency that makes them incapable of taking responsibility for the consequences of their own actions.

An extreme form of personality disorder is *psychopathic personality*. People with this type of personality seem to lack any normal conscience or sense of social responsibility and to have no feeling for other people. These psychopaths, as they are called, may seem on the surface to be quite charming, candid, and generous—but in truth they are selfish, ruthless, and addicted to lying. They have no love for anyone but themselves and take advantage of others without any feelings of guilt (56).

Indeed a total absence of anxiety of any kind is one of the outstanding characteristics of the psychopath—and of course a factor that makes psychopathic personality completely different from the neuroses.

Psychopaths are likely to be in and out of trouble all their lives, for they do not learn from experience and seem to have no desire to change. The word "psychopath" comes up frequently in court cases, for criminals who appear to experience no remorse for even the most cruel deeds are a good example of psychopathic personality in its most extreme form. Because of the social consequences that often occur, this abnormality is also known as *sociopathic personality* or *antisocial reaction*.

The causes remain a mystery. Some studies have indicated that psychopaths tend to have an autonomic nervous system that is especially insensitive and difficult to arouse (57). This biological characteristic might lead them to seek emotional excitement and at the same time to be oblivious to danger (such as the consequences of committing a serious crime). It also appears that some of them have come from families where they were overindulged as children and shielded from any experiences that might have produced frustration, anxiety, and stress (58). Psychopaths may be people who just "never grew up." They have retained a childish insistence on self-gratification and have failed to learn more mature and responsible ways of behaving.

Though psychopathic personality is the most spectacular form of personality disorder, it is by no means the only one. Among others are dependence on drugs, alcoholism, and some forms of immature or antisocial sexual behavior.

Types of psychosis

A psychosis can be defined as *any form of mental disturbance that is so severe as to make a person incapable of getting along in society*. Because more people are admitted to mental hospitals in the United States today than ever before, many people assume that the pressures of modern industrial civilization and city life have increased the danger of psychosis. However, the increased hospital admissions are due in large part to the fact that more people now live to an advanced age and therefore become subject to brain deterioration caused by poor circulation and other physical results of aging. Among younger people, there seems to have been little if any increase in psychosis. Indeed court records have shown that there were about as many commitments to mental hospitals, in proportion to population, in the relatively rural Massachusetts of the nineteenth century as in the highly industrialized Massachusetts of the twentieth century (59). The same types of mental disturbances found in the United States and other industrialized nations have also been observed in primitive societies throughout the world (60). The percentage of people who suffer from them appears to be much the same in all societies (61).

Organic and functional psychoses

In some cases the origins of psychosis are clearly physical. In *senile psychosis*, for example, some of the brain cells have been destroyed by such effects of aging as strokes, or hemorrhages of blood vessels in the brain. Psychoses caused by brain damage can also result from certain diseases, such as untreated syphilis of long standing, from excessive and prolonged use of alcohol and perhaps of other

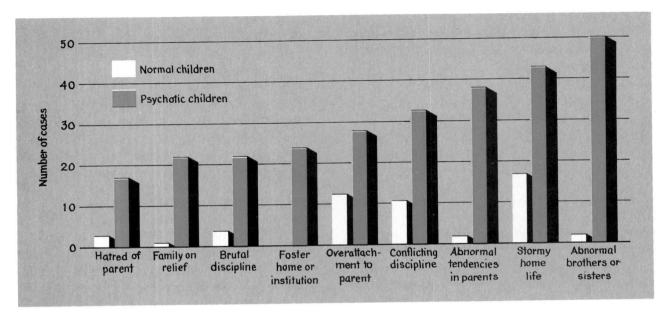

11-9
Normal and psychotic children: the differences in backgrounds
The bars show some of the more pronounced differences found in a study of the family backgrounds of a group of psychotic children as compared with a control group of normal children. Note that the bars labeled "abnormal tendencies in parents" and "abnormal brothers or sisters" point to hereditary factors, the others to environment (63).

drugs, and, though only rarely, from injuries to the head. All these are classified as *organic psychoses*.

In other cases, there is no clear-cut physiological explanation. No medical test shows anything physically wrong with the brain, but it simply does not seem to be functioning normally. These cases are therefore classified as *functional psychoses*. However, the distinction between organic and functional psychoses no longer seems to be as definite and useful as it once was. The evidence that a tendency toward psychosis can be inherited suggests that there may be some physical basis for most or all psychoses, even though the exact nature of the physical defects is not yet known. Some psychiatrists now believe that all psychoses are

caused by small, subtle chemical imbalances in the brain, especially in the amounts and effectiveness of the neurotransmitters. If so, they may some day be controllable through the use of new medications that will restore the proper chemical balance (62). The medicines called tranquilizers have already been found effective in relieving the symptoms of many patients and enabling them to return to a more or less normal life.

Even if all psychoses turn out to have some physical basis, however, psychological and environmental factors are undoubtedly important in determining which individuals will manage to overcome the tendency to psychosis and which will display psychotic behavior. As Figure 11-9 shows, the home and family backgrounds of people suffering from psychosis appear to be less favorable than average in many ways, including many that have no connection with heredity. The manner in which environment operates to encourage or discourage psychosis, however, is something of a mystery. Most people who grow up even in the worst homes do not become psychotic, whereas many people who come from the most privileged homes (or at least homes that appear on the surface to be privileged) do become psychotic. Perhaps there is an analogy here with the fact that some people become ill because of stress while others do not.

For reasons not understood, men appear to be more subject to psychosis than women. (The ratio of males to females among first admissions to mental hospitals is about four to three.) Married people are less likely to become psychotic than unmarried people, but this may be because people with psychotic tendencies are less likely to get married in the first place.

The three chief psychoses that have traditionally been classified as functional are : 1) *schizophrenia,* 2) *manic-depressive psychosis,* and 3) *paranoia.* The three require separate discussions.

Schizophrenia: the no. 1 crippler

Of all the psychoses, the most common is *schizophrenia,* which accounts for perhaps as many as 25 percent of first admissions to mental hospitals. It is particularly common among young adults in their twenties and occurs more often among men than among women. A survey sponsored by the World Health Organization in nine different countries showed therapists generally consider patients to be schizophrenic when they display the following behavior (64).

1 *Poor insight.*
2 *Incoherent speech* (often a spontaneous flow of conversation that cannot be understood).

3 *Delusions* (frequent and often extremely bizarre; schizophrenics may believe that they no longer exist or that their heads or arms are missing).
4 *Absence of emotion* (blank and expressionless face; little or no emotion shown in situations where a normal person would be upset or elated).
5 *Remoteness* (making it difficult for the therapist or others to establish any rapport).
6 *Worry about thoughts.* (Schizophrenics may seem to hear their own thoughts as if they were spoken aloud and could be heard by others. They may also feel that their thoughts are somehow being broadcast so that everyone knows about them.)

Although some or all of these symptoms are usually apparent in hospitalized patients, they occur in different forms and degrees of intensity. Some investigators have therefore concluded that schizophrenia is not just a single disturbance but many types that have been grouped together merely because they exhibit certain resemblances. If this is true, then it would seem futile to seek a common cause or common cure. Other investigators, however, believe that all the various forms of schizophrenia have a common basis, probably some hereditary defect. These investigators suggest that there is a *schizophrenia spectrum,* on which people with an inherited vulnerability range from a mere tendency to develop minor symptoms, through borderline behavior, and all the way to a display of the disturbance in its most severe and bizarre form (65).

The nature of the possible underlying defect is not known, but there are some clues. One study found that schizophrenics seem to have an abnormal pattern of metabolism that would affect the brain's neurotransmitters (66). It has also been noted that medication with amphetamines, which increase the amount of the neurotransmitter noradrenalin in the brain, seems to have some relation to the symptoms. When schizophrenic patients take amphetamines, their behavior becomes worse. And drug users who overdose on amphetamines may display symptoms that resemble schizophrenia (67).

It has also been found that schizophrenics show abnormal patterns of eye movements when they try to track a moving object, such as a swinging pendulum (68). Many of their close relatives, though not themselves victims of schizophrenia, display the same unusual tracking pattern (69), as if there were a family tendency to lack of coordination. These unusual patterns might indicate some defect in parts of the nervous system responsible for perception—which might in turn account for the fact that schizophrenics seem out of touch with reality as perceived by normal people. Even if some inherited defect is the basis for schizophrenia, however, the fact that not all people from the same family become schizophrenic points to the influence of environment, anxiety, and stress in determining whether the inborn tendency will actually affect behavior.

Manic-depressive psychosis

Depression has already been mentioned as one of the frequent psychological results of stress. In most cases, the symptoms are uncomfortable but not crippling. Sometimes, however, they are so incapacitating as to represent some form of the severe mental disturbance called *manic-depressive psychosis*.

As the name indicates, this psychosis is often characterized by extremes of mood, sometimes of wild swings from intense excitement to deep melancholy. In the manic phase, people suffering from manic-depressive psychosis tend to be talkative, restless, aggressive, boastful, uninhibited, and often destructive. In the depressive phase they may become so gloomy and hopeless that they refuse to eat. Some people who have this psychosis, indeed perhaps most, do not exhibit swings from one mood to the other but only one of the two phases, usually the depressive. Like milder forms of depression, manic-depressive psychosis is more common among women than among men (70). It is most likely to occur in middle adulthood.

Even without treatment, manic-depressive psychosis usually disappears—the manic phase ordinarily in about three months, the depressive phase in about nine. Its victims then return to normal, and about a quarter of them never have a second episode. In the other three-quarters the psychosis recurs, often several times.

Many investigators believe that the causes of the psychosis include both imbalances in brain chemistry, probably influenced at least in part by hereditary tendencies, and psychological factors. Often the symptoms occur after the loss of a loved one or after an event that causes a severe loss of social status or self-esteem. Other victims seem to have become so frustrated that they can no longer cope with their problems. They lapse into helplessness and find consolation in the fact that other people then give them the sympathy and attention that goes along with being sick (71). Some therapists believe that this cycle of events can best be broken through medical alteration of the brain chemistry, others that it can best be attacked through psychological therapy, still others that the two approaches should be combined.

The delusions of paranoia

The least common of the psychoses is *paranoia*, which is characterized by delusions that are spectacular and persistent. Some victims have delusions of grandeur and may believe that they are Stalin or Christ. Others have delusions of persecution and are convinced that other people are conspiring to kill them. The delusions of persecution are thought to be an extreme form of projection discussed earlier, in which those suffering from paranoia project onto the rest of the world their own hostile motives.

Summary

1 *Anxiety* is a vague, unpleasant feeling accompanied by a premonition that something undesirable is about to happen.

2 Anxiety is closely related to motives, especially conflicts between motives and frustration of the motive for certainty. Any situation clouded with uncertainty has a built-in potential for creating anxiety.

3 People who display anxiety in many different situations are victims of *general anxiety*. Those who display it in some particular situation but not at other times have *specific anxiety*. A specific type common among college students is *test anxiety*.

4 People high in anxiety do better than others at simple learning tasks but more poorly at difficult learning tasks. In college, anxiety does not seem to affect the grades of students of either highest or lowest learning ability. Among students of in-between ability, those with high anxiety make significantly lower grades than those with low anxiety.

5 In their approach to life, people high in anxiety tend either to be very conservative and avoid risks or to "go for broke." People low in anxiety tend toward the middle-range risks that are most likely to lead to success in the long run.

6 *Stress* is the body's reaction to anything that threatens to damage the organism—from a disease germ to intense and prolonged emotion.

7 The damaging potential of stress has been demonstrated by Hans Selye in experiments with animals subjected to small doses of poison. Selye found that the body automatically tries to defend itself in ways that include striking changes in activity of the endocrine glands, especially the adrenals. After a time the body seems to adapt and the glands return to normal. If the stressful conditions continue, however, the recovery proves to be only temporary and the animal dies—killed by an excess of hormones the body produced in its own defense. This sequence of events is called the *general adaptation syndrome*.

8 The bodily changes described by Selye also seem to occur in human beings, often as part of the stress caused by frustration, conflict, or any prolonged emotional upset. They often take the form of *psychosomatic illnesses,* meaning bodily ailments that stem at least in part from mental and emotional causes.

9 The psychological effects of stress include *depression*. This appears to be

associated with low levels or reduced effectiveness of the brain's supply of the neurotransmitter noradrenalin, which apparently can occur during stress.

10 *Assertive coping* is an effective defense against stress. It may take three forms: a) an attempt to change the environment and relieve the stressful situation, b) changing one's own behavior, or c) keeping the emotional and physical wear and tear within bounds.

11 Assertive coping is one key to *normal behavior,* which many psychologists define in terms of honest self-awareness, independence, fulfillment, a stable sense of identity, and inner freedom.

12 Among questionable forms of coping are the *defense mechanisms* described by Freud. These are unconscious psychological processes, mental or symbolic. They include: a) rationalization, b) repression, c) sublimation, d) identification, e) reaction formation, and f) projection.

13 Other questionable reactions to anxiety and stress include: a) direct aggression, b) displaced aggression, c) withdrawal or apathy, and d) regression.

14 *Abnormal behavior,* though difficult to define, is generally considered to be behavior that is: a) statistically unusual (and therefore "odd"), b) considered undesirable by most people, and c) a source of unhappiness to the person who displays it.

15 Abnormal behavior hinges on two factors: a) the amount of stress and anxiety a person experiences, and b) the person's ability to handle this amount.

16 The ability to handle stress and anxiety appears to be determined by: a) biological factors (such as glandular activity and sensitivity of the autonomic nervous system), b) psychological influences (such as motives and anxiety over failure to fulfill them), and c) environmental influences.

Postscript

17 *Neuroses* are forms of abnormal behavior that lie between normal behavior and the extreme abnormality of psychosis. They are frequently classified as: a) *anxiety states* (including *anxiety reaction* and *phobic reaction*), b) *obsessive-compulsive reactions,* and c) *hysteria* (including *conversion reaction* and *dissociative reactions*).

18 Some forms of abnormal behavior, difficult to classify, are called *personality disorders* (or *character disorders*). Unlike other forms, they are not clearly related to anxiety and stress. The people who display them seem to have some deficiency that makes them incapable of taking responsibility for their own actions. An extreme type is *psychopathic personality,* often found among criminals.

19 A *psychosis* is any form of mental disturbance so severe as to make a person incapable of getting along in society.

20 Psychoses have traditionally been classified as either: a) *organic* (caused by actual

damage to the brain, as in senility), or b) *functional* (having no apparent organic basis).

21 Three types of functional psychosis are: a) *schizophrenia,* b) *manic-depressive psychosis,* and c) *paranoia.*

Important terms

abnormal behavior
adjustment
amnesia
anxiety
apathy
assertive coping
coping
defense mechanism
depression
direct aggression
displaced aggression

general adaptation
  syndrome
general anxiety
identification
mental health
neurosis
normal behavior
placebo
projection
psychosis

psychosomatic illness
rationalization
reaction formation
regression
repression
specific anxiety
stress
sublimation
test anxiety
withdrawal

Postscript

acrophobia
anxiety reaction
anxiety state
claustrophobia
conversion reaction
dissociative reaction
functional psychosis
hysteria

manic-depressive psychosis
multiple personality
obsessive-compulsive
  reactions
organic psychosis
paranoia
personality (or character)
  disorder

psychopathic personality (or
  sociopathic personality or
  antisocial reaction)
schizophrenia
schizophrenia spectrum
sleepwalking

Recommended readings

Coleman, J. *Abnormal psychology and modern life,* 5th ed. New York: Scott, Foresman, 1976.

Dohrenwend, B. S., ed. *Stressful life events: their nature and effects.* New York: Wiley, 1974.

Gottesman, I. I., and Shields, J. *Schizophrenia and genetics: a twin study vantage point.* New York: Academic Press, 1972.

Serban, G., ed. *Psychopathology of human adaptation.* New York: Plenum, 1976.

Outline

Chapter twelve

Personality and psychotherapy

(with a postscript on personality tests)

If you sometimes have trouble understanding your own personality—or your friends'—take heart. You are not alone. The human personality is one of the most baffling of psychological phenomena, so complex that the English language has at least 18,000 words to describe the various traits that comprise it. These traits include the whole wide range of styles of thinking and using language, the gamut of emotions and motives, the innumerable forms of anxiety and stress and efforts to cope with them, normal and abnormal. To get some idea of the complexity, try rating yourself on one side or the other on the list of personality opposites in the box at the right.

Those ten traits can occur in any combination. You may fall at the left in all of them, at the right in all of them, or at the left in some and the right in others. Thus this short list alone can account for a great variety of individual personalities: 2 x 2 x 2 x 2 x 2 x 2 x 2 x 2 x 2 x 2, or 1,024. Moreover, you may not belong clearly at the left or the right but somewhere in between, again multiplying the possibili-

Motives	
ambitious, hard-working	or unambitious, lazy
independent	or dependent
friendly, a joiner	or unfriendly, a loner
like certainty	or prefer novelty, risk
Emotions	
high in anxiety	or low in anxiety
slow to anger	or hot-tempered
joyous	or gloomy
Cognitive styles	
thoughtful	or impulsive
down-to-earth	or dreamy, impractical
talkative, eloquent	or quiet, tongue-tied

ties. And these ten traits are just a small sample of all that exist. Small wonder that there are so many personalities in the world—and that personality is so difficult to understand and describe.

Personality theories

Since almost everything psychologists study is related in some way to human personality, it might be said that the entire science represents an attempt to create a comprehensive theory of personality—in other words, a set of general principles that will explain why people are alike in some ways and very different in others. But some psychologists have been especially interested in seeking these general principles. They have developed a number of theories that try to explain which personality traits are most important, the likeliest patterns of relationships among traits, the manner in which these patterns become established in individuals, and (at least by implication) how they can be changed. Personality theory has gone hand in hand with psychotherapy. Each of the main theories developed over the years has been accompanied by its own technique of treating people suffering from personality disturbances, as will be seen in a moment. First, however, we must define personality and explain what all personality theories try to accomplish.

A definition of personality

Personality can best be defined as the *total pattern of characteristic ways of thinking, feeling, and behaving that constitute the individual's distinctive method of relating to the environment*. There are four key words in the definition: 1) *characteristic*, 2) *distinctive*, 3) *relating*, and 4) *pattern*.

To be considered a part of personality, a way of thinking, feeling, or behaving must have some continuity over time and circumstance. It must be *characteristic* of the individual. We do not call a man bad tempered if he "blows up" only once in ten years. We say that a bad temper is part of his personality only if he shows it often and in many different circumstances.

The way of thinking, feeling, or behaving must also be *distinctive*—that is, it must distinguish the individual from other individuals. This eliminates such common American traits as eating with a knife and fork, placing adjectives before rather than after nouns, and carrying a driver's license—all of which are more or less the same for every American and do not distinguish one person from others.

A mass display of the positive personality trait of friendliness.

442

Though these first two elements are essential, they are not the whole story. For example, a woman might always wear a ring that is a family heirloom and the only one of its kind in the world. Wearing the ring is therefore both characteristic and distinctive. But this would hardly be considered part of her personality (unless perhaps she attached some deep significance to the ring, regarding it as a symbol of self-esteem and social acceptance). To be a part of personality, a trait must play a part in how a person goes about *relating* to the world, especially to other people. It is because of this element of relating that personality traits are often thought of as positive or negative. A positive trait, such as friendliness, helps the individual relate to people and events in a constructive manner. A negative characteristic, such as fear of social contacts, may produce anxiety, failure, and loneliness.

Of the multitude of possible personality traits, all of us possess some but not others. It is the particular *pattern* of characteristics we possess and display—the sum total and organization—that is the final element in the definition of personality.

The personality hierarchy

The various traits that make up the personality—all the characteristic and distinctive ways of relating to the environment—exist in a hierarchy from strong to weak. Some ways of thinking, feeling, and behaving are easily and frequently aroused. Others are less likely to occur. In a social situation, for example, there are many ways an individual can relate to the others in the group. The individual can be talkative or quiet, friendly or reserved, boastful or modest, bossy or acquiescent, more at ease with men or more at ease with women. One person may characteristically withdraw into the background, and we say that such a person is shy.

An example of a negative trait—fear of social contacts?

Another may characteristically display warmth and try to put the others at their ease, and we say that such a person is outgoing. Another may be talkative, boastful, and domineering, and we say that such a person is aggressive or "pushy." In each of the three individuals, certain responses are strong in the personality hierarchy and easily aroused.

Each person's hierarchy has a certain amount of permanence. The shy person behaves shyly under many circumstances, and the aggressive person has a consistent tendency to be boastful and domineering. However, the hierarchy may change considerably depending on the circumstances. A young woman who is aggressive around people her own age may behave shyly in the presence of older people. A man who is usually shy may have one close friend with whom he is completely at ease. All of us, no matter how friendly or reserved we may be, are likely to have a strong tendency to make friends if we have been isolated for a long time, such as after an illness or a stretch at a lonely job. After a round of parties, on the other hand, we are likely to want some solitude. The businessman who is ordinarily interested in his job and eager to talk about it may shun conversation when he gets home late at night after a hard day's work.

The three elements of personality theory

Many general theories of personality have been proposed over the years. They differ in many respects, but they all have three things in common (1):

1 Every theory is based on some fundamental viewpoint toward the basic quality of human nature. It assumes that there is a *core of personality* composed of tendencies and traits common to all of us. Different theories take different views of this common core, as will be seen, but all of them take for granted that it exists and is a force in shaping personality.

2 Every theory maintains that the tendencies and traits that make up the common core of personality are channeled in various different directions in different individuals by the process of *development*—all the experiences we encounter, from our childhood relationships with our parents throughout the rest of our life. Thus all theories agree that personality is the product of both nature (the common core that is part of our heritage) and nurture (the effect of individual development), though they do not necessarily agree on whether nature or nurture is more influential.

3 Every theory is concerned with what are called *peripheral traits*—that is, all the distinctive ways in which people relate to the environment. The peripheral traits are viewed as the inevitable result of the way individual development has acted on the common core of personality.

Freud's psychoanalytical theory

The most famous of all views of personality is Sigmund Freud's *psychoanalytical theory*. Freud's writings about personality development and the treatment of psychological disorders have been widely read and debated. Oddly, his method of treatment (*psychoanalysis*) has never attracted a large following. The American Psychoanalytic Association, to which most practitioners of psychoanalysis belong, has recently had only about 2,600 members (2). Nonetheless, his views have had a profound influence on many psychologists, including some who disagree with his therapy, and on literature, especially in the United States.

Anxiety, repression, and the unconscious mind

Some of Freud's ideas have already been prominently mentioned in preceding chapters. One was his concept of the defense mechanisms (Chapter 11) as a technique for relieving anxiety. Freud believed that anxiety is the central problem in mental disturbance, so painful an emotion that we will go to almost any length to get rid of it. He regarded the defense mechanisms as a method of eliminating from conscious awareness any motive or thought that threatens to cause anxiety.

Freud at work in his office in Vienna, about 1930, when he was still highly productive at the age of seventy-four.

The unconscious mind, composed in part of repressed motives and thoughts, was another of Freud's most influential concepts. He was the first to suggest the now widely held theory that the human mind and personality are like an iceberg, with only a small part visible and the rest submerged and concealed. All of us, he maintained, have many unconscious motives that we are never aware of but that nonetheless have a powerful influence on our behavior.

The details of Freudian theory are difficult to summarize. For one thing, he revised and enlarged on them throughout a prolific writing career that spanned four decades. Moreover, his followers have continued to make refinements, especially of the new ideas he developed late in life. The discussion here is confined to the basic principles (especially those that have had the greatest influence on psychologists) as they are now viewed by psychoanalytic theorists who regard themselves as classical Freudians.

Id and pleasure principle

A basic part of the human mind, according to psychoanalytical theory, is the unconscious *id*, made up of inborn, biologically determined forces that constantly struggle for gratification. One of these forces is the *libido*, consisting of sexual urges and such related desires as to be kept warm, well-fed, and comfortable. Another is an instinct toward aggression—an inborn urge to fight and dominate.

The id operates on what Freud called the *pleasure principle*, which insists on immediate and total gratification of all its demands. The libido seeks complete possession of everything desired and loved. The instinct for aggression wants to destroy everything that gets in the way. As we grow up, we learn to control the demands of the id, at least after a fashion. But the id remains active and powerful throughout life—a sort of beast within. It is the sole source of all the psychic energy put to use in thinking and behaving. Although it is unconscious and we are not aware of its workings, it continues to struggle to relieve all its tensions.

Ego and reality principle

The conscious part of the mind that develops as we grow up is called the *ego*. This is the "real" us as we like to think of ourself. The ego operates on the *reality principle*. It does our logical thinking and tries to help us get along in the world. Deriving its energy from the id, the ego perceives what is going on in the environment and undertakes behavior (such as finding food) necessary to satisfy the demands of the id. To the extent that the id's urges can be satisfied in some reasonable way, the ego permits them satisfaction. But when the urges threaten to get us rejected by society, the ego represses them or tries to provide substitutes that are socially acceptable. Freud held that artistic creativity, for example, represents a channeling of the libido's energy away from open sexual expression and into the production of paintings and literature—using the defense mechanism of sublimation discussed in Chapter 11.

Superego and Oedipus conflict

The ego, in its constant struggle to meet the irrational demands of the id in some rational way, has a strong but troublesome ally in the *superego*, the third part of the mind as conceived by Freud. In a sense the superego is our conscience, our sense of right and wrong. We acquire it in part by adopting the standards of behavior that we are taught by society from our earliest years. However, Freud's concept of the superego is a much stronger and more dynamic notion than the word "conscience" implies. Much like the id, the superego is mostly unconscious, exerting a far greater influence over our behavior than we realize. It is largely acquired as a result of the *Oedipus complex*.

According to psychoanalytical theory, all children between the ages of about two and a half and six are embroiled in a conflict of mingled affection and resentment toward their parents. The male child has learned that the outer world exists and that there are other people in it, and the id's demands for love and affection reach out insatiably toward the person he has been closest to —the mother. Although the child has only the haziest notion of sexual feelings, his libido drives him to possess his mother and to take the place of his father with her. But his anger against his father, the rival with whom he must share her, makes him fearful that his father will somehow retaliate. To further complicate matters, his demands for total love from his mother are of course frustrated. Thus he becomes overwhelmed with strong feelings of mingled love, anger, and fear toward both parents.

Resolving the Oedipus complex through identification?

This period of turmoil takes its name from the Greek legend in which Oedipus unwittingly killed his father and married his own mother and then, when he discovered what he had done, blinded himself as penance. Girls, according to Freudian theory, go through very similar torments in the years from two and a half to six, except that their libido centers on their father.

The Oedipus complex must somehow be resolved. This is accomplished through identification with the parents, especially the parent of the same sex. That is to say, we resolve our feelings of mingled love and hate for our parents by becoming like them, by convincing ourselves that we share their strength and authority and the affection they have for each other. Their moral judgments, or what we conceive to be their moral judgments, become our superego. This helps us hold down the drives of the id, which have caused us such intense discomfort during the Oedipal period. But, forever after, the superego tends to oppose the ego. As our parents once did, our superego punishes us or threatens to punish us for our transgressions. And, since the superego's standards are rigidly set in childhood, its notions of crime and guilt are likely to be illogical and unduly harsh.

In their own way, the demands of the superego are just as insatiable as the demands of the id. Its standards of right and wrong and its rules for punishment are far more rigid, relentless, and vengeful than anything in our conscious minds. Formed at a time when we were too young to distinguish between a bad wish and a bad deed, the superego may sternly disapprove of the merest thought of some transgression—which explains why some people who have never actually committed a bad deed still have strong feelings of guilt throughout life. (Freud's concept of the superego may remind you of something discussed in less dramatic terms in Chapter 11—the anxiety caused by conflicts between inner standards and motives.)

Superego versus ego versus id

The three parts of the mind are often in conflict, and Freud regarded conflict as the core of human personality. One result of the three-way struggle is anxiety, which is produced in the ego whenever the demands of the id threaten to create danger or when the superego threatens to impose disapproval or punishment. Anxiety arouses the ego to fight the impulses or thoughts that have created it. In one way or another—by using repression and

"Light on the id, heavy on the super-ego."
Drawing by Mahood; © 1974 The New Yorker Magazine, Inc.

the other defense mechanisms, by turning the mind's attention elsewhere, by gratifying some other impulse of the id—the ego defends itself against the threat posed by the id or the superego and gets rid of the anxiety.

In a sense the conscious ego is engaged in a constant struggle to satisfy the insatiable demands of the unconscious id without incurring the wrath and vengeance of the largely unconscious superego. To the extent that our behavior is controlled by the ego, it is realistic and socially acceptable. To the extent that it is governed by the passions of the id and the unrelenting disapproval of the superego, it tends to be maladjusted and neurotic.

If the ego is not strong enough to check the id's drives, a person is likely to be selfish, impulsive, and antisocial. But if the ego checks the id too severely, other problems may arise. Too much repression of the libidinal force can make a person incapable of enjoying a normal sex life or giving a normal amount of affection. Too much repression of aggression can seriously handicap a person in the give and take of competition. If the ego is not strong enough to check the superego, the result may be vague and unwarranted feelings of guilt and unworthiness, even an unconscious need for self-punishment. Thus it is the three-way conflict among ego, id, and superego, according to Freud, that often results in abnormal behavior.

Psychoanalysis: the therapy

The method of treatment developed by Freud was designed to dredge up into awareness the unconscious desires and conflicts that he considered the source of neurotic anxiety and guilt. The chief tool in psychoanalysis is *free association,* which often produces insights into hidden psychological processes. If you were to undertake psychoanalysis, you would be asked to lie on a couch, as relaxed as possible, and speak out every thought that occured to you—no matter how foolish it might seem, how obscene, or how insulting to the analyst. In this situation, as when drifting off to sleep, conscious control of mental processes is reduced to a minimum and unconscious forces become more apparent. The analyst would pay particular attention to occasions when your thoughts seemed to encounter what is called *resistance*—that is, when your train of thought seemed to be blocked by anxiety and repressions indicating unconscious conflicts. The analyst would also study your fantasies, slips of the tongue, and dreams in a search for clues to unconscious desires and conflicts. Freud believed that dreams, in particular, often reveal deeply hidden motives and conflicts, though in disguised ways that require painstaking psychoanalytic interpretation.

Another clue to the unconscious is what analysts call *transference.* Freud believed that in a sense none of us ever completely grows up. Neurotic people in particular tend to retain their childhood emotional attitudes toward such well-loved and much-hated persons as their parents and their brothers and sisters, and they often display or transfer these attitudes to the people they know as adults. If you were being analyzed, you might transfer many such attitudes to the analyst. At times you might display an overwhelming desire to please the analyst, as you once wanted to please your parents. At other times you might display resentment and hatred, even though the analyst had done nothing to provoke them.

Through your transferences, free associations, dreams, and reports of your everyday behavior, a pattern would gradually emerge of the unconscious problems that the analyst would say represented your real difficulties. The analyst would then interpret the problems and help you acquire insights into the unconscious processes and gain control over them. The goal in analysis is to strengthen the ego and provide what one analyst calls "freedom from the tyranny of the unconscious" (3).

In its classic form, psychoanalysis is a long process, requiring three to five visits a week for two to five years or more, and is therefore very expensive. In recent years, however, many analysts have attempted to shorten the treatment period. They have adopted various new and faster techniques for helping people achieve, if not full "freedom from the tyranny of the unconscious," at least enough insight to cope with their most serious problems.

Other schools of psychoanalytical theory: Jung and Adler

Freud was an important innovator who made many contributions to understanding the human personality. He was the first to recognize the role of the unconscious and the importance of anxiety and defenses against it. He also dispelled the myth, widely accepted before his time, that children do not have sexual urges or hostile impulses. He was a pioneer in recognizing the effect of childhood experiences on personality development.

His theory, however, has many critics. It is impossible to demonstrate the existence of an id, an ego, or a superego, which some psychologists regard as merely fancy terms for processes that have a simpler explanation (for example, conflicts between motives and inner standards). Some critics believe that Freud overemphasized the role of sexual motivation by generalizing from the conflicts of patients who had grown up during the repressive Victorian age. Even some of Freud's early disciples broke away from him and founded competing schools of psychoanalytical thought.

One Freudian who broke away was Carl Jung, inventor of the famous words *introvert* and *extrovert*. Introverts are people who tend to live with

Carl Jung

their own thoughts and to avoid socializing. Extroverts are people whose chief interest is in other people and the events around them. Jung felt that fulfillment of the human personality requires the expression of both introversion and extroversion— but that one tends to develop at the expense of the other, making people either too concerned with themselves or too preoccupied with external events.

Jung strongly believed that Freud had overestimated the importance of sexuality. He felt that the libido was far richer than Freud assumed—an all-encompassing life force that included deep-seated attitudes toward life and death, virtue and sin, and religion. Jung's theories place more emphasis than Freud's on the intellectual and especially the spiritual qualities of the human personality, less on the urges toward sex and aggression.

A key element in Jung's theories was the idea that human beings possess a *collective uncon-*

scious—an inheritance from all the events that have occurred in human history, and perhaps even in the days before humanity appeared and only lower animals roamed the world. In the collective unconscious lie traces of primitive humanity's fears and superstitions, the belief in magic, the search for gods. There also are memories of the great events in which humanity has participated—its disasters, its conquests and defeats, its happy and unhappy love affairs, its moving experiences with birth and death. Because of the collective unconscious, every person embodies in a sense the entire gamut of human experience. Jung believed that each of us, of whatever sex, possesses elements of both woman and man, mother and father, hero, prophet, sage, and magician.

To Jung, the collective unconscious was a significant part of the core of personality, a universal aspect of the human condition. It influences our behavior in ways that we can understand only dimly or not at all. It finds expression in the work of the artist and accounts for the strong emotions we sometimes feel, without knowing why, when we look at a great painting or statue. It crops up in our dreams, often giving them a strange and mystical quality that we find beautiful or frightening. This mystical aspect makes Jung's ideas difficult to grasp and impossible to test scientifically.

Another early disciple who rejected Freud's emphasis on sexuality was Alfred Adler, who proposed instead a theory that is as simple as Jung's is complicated. It was Adler who coined the term *inferiority complex,* which he regarded as the basis for most abnormal behavior. Adler believed that the core of personality is a universal human desire to be superior and to attain perfection. When this desire is thwarted, as it must often be, the result is feelings of inferiority that sometimes are crippling.

Some current trends in psychoanalysis

In recent years, new generations of psychoanalysts have added to and in some ways revised Freud's theories—as indeed he himself was constantly doing throughout his lifetime. These *neopsychoanalysts,* or new psychoanalysts, have tended to move away from Freud's emphasis on the id and its biologically determined instincts and toward greater concern with the ego and its attempts to deal with reality. One group, led by Heinz Hartmann, has concentrated on such ego processes as perception, attention, memory, and thinking. They regard the ego as an important force in itself rather than a mere mediator between the id and the superego (4).

Another group of neopsychoanalysts have turned their attention to cultural and social influences on personality, which were largely neglected

Jung would have called these people extroverts.

Erich Fromm

by Freud. One prominent member of this group is Erich Fromm, who has suggested that personality problems are caused by conflicts between the basic human needs and the demands of society. The core of personality, according to Fromm, is the desire to fulfill oneself as a human being—that is, to achieve a kind of unity with nature in the special way that is dictated by the human ability to think. Lower animals have no need to seek such unity, for they are simply a part of nature. They are not aware of any separation between themselves and their environment, including their fellow animals. But people must seek the unity through their own efforts; they must fulfill what Fromm regards as the five basic and unique human needs (listed in Figure 12-1).

It would be possible, Fromm believes, to create a society in which these needs could be harmoniously fulfilled. But no such society has ever existed. Therefore all of us tend to experience frustrations and personality problems. It is society, Fromm says, that

is "sick"—and it will remain so until people can relate to one another "lovingly" and "in bonds of brotherliness and solidarity," can transcend nature "by creating rather than by destroying," and can gain a sense of selfhood through their own individual powers "rather than by conformity" (6).

1 Relatedness	This need stems from the fact that human beings have lost the union with nature that other animals possess. It must be satisfied by human relationships based on productive love (which implies mutual care, responsibility, respect, and understanding).
2 Transcendence	The need to rise above one's animal nature and to become creative.
3 Rootedness	The need for a feeling of belonging, best satisfied by feelings of affiliation with all humanity.
4 Identity	The need to have a sense of personal identity, to be unique. It can be satisfied through creativity or through identification with another person or group.
5 A Frame of Orientation	The need for a stable and consistent way of perceiving the world and understanding its events.

12-1 Fromm's five basic human needs

The neopsychoanalytic theory of Erich Fromm holds that the core of human personality is the desire to fulfill these needs. Personality problems arise when the attempt to gratify them is frustrated (5).

Humanistic theories of personality

Much closer to Fromm than to Freud are the humanistic theories of personality. Indeed these theories assume a core of personality almost opposite to the Freudian assumption. Freud believed that the core was conflict, springing in large part from the ruthless and pleasure-seeking demands of the id. Humanistic theories, on the contrary, hold that human nature is basically good and that the core of personality is the desire to perfect our skills and find peace and happiness, rather than to fulfill urges toward sexuality and aggression. They stress the importance of Maslow's motive for self-actualization, which was discussed in Chapter 10. Their therapy is based on the belief that all people want to grow in positive ways and will do so if only they have the chance and the proper encouragement.

Rogers' "phenomenological self"

Among the prominent humanistic theorists is Carl Rogers, who stresses the importance of the self-image all of us carry around. This self-image, or *phenomenological self*, represents the way we perceive ourselves as functioning human beings. It consists of our judgments about our abilities, accomplishments, attractiveness, and relationships with other people. In part it is based on our own observations of our behavior and the reactions of other people. But it is also highly subjective, depending on our feelings about ourselves and the way we evaluate ourselves from good to bad.

Thus the phenomenological self does not necessarily correspond to reality. Many people who are considered successful and highly respected by others perceive themselves as unworthy failures. Nor does the phenomenological self necessarily

resemble the kind of person we would like to be. Neurotic people, in particular, often display striking differences when asked to describe first what they consider to be their real self, then the ideal self they wish they were (7).

To a considerable extent, our phenomenological self depends on the way we believe ourselves to be accepted and esteemed by other people. We need to feel approved if we are to lead meaningful lives in harmony with ourselves and with others, displaying a personality that is trusting, spontaneous, and flexible. We must grow up in a family and social environment that treat us with what Rogers calls *unconditional positive regard*. That is to say, we must be valued and trusted. Our opinions and behavior must be respected. We must be accepted and loved for what we are, even when we do things of which others may disapprove.

Unfortunately, few people grow up in such a completely favorable atmosphere. Most are treated with what Rogers calls *conditional positive regard*. Their families and later society at large respond warmly to only some of their thoughts and actions, disapprovingly to others. The "forbidden" thoughts and actions are likely to become a source of maladjustment.

The phenomenological self and neurosis

Maladjustment and abnormal behavior, in Rogers' view, are caused by people's failure to integrate all their experiences, desires, and feelings into their phenomenological image of self—a failure that often stems from conditional positive regard with its accompanying criticism and punishment. This idea can best be explained by an example. A young boy thinks of himself as being good and as being loved by his parents. However, he also feels hostility toward a younger brother, which he expresses one day by breaking his brother's toys. His parents punish him, and he now faces a crisis in integrating the experience into his image of self. He is forced to change his image in some way. What will he do?

All of us, says Rogers, try to perceive our experiences and to behave in a way that is consistent with our images of ourselves. When we are confronted with new experiences or new feelings that seem inconsistent with the image, we can take one of two courses.

1   We can recognize the new experiences or feelings, interpret them clearly, and somehow integrate them into our image of self. This is a healthy reaction. The boy just mentioned, for example, could under ideal circumstances decide that he does feel hostility toward his brother. This is something he must reckon with, but it does not make him "bad" or doom him to the scorn of his parents and society.

2   We can deny the experiences or feelings or interpret them in distorted fashion. Thus the boy may deny that he feels any hostility toward his brother and maintain that he broke the toys in retaliation for his brother's hostility (thus adopting the defense mechanism of projection). Or he may interpret the experience as proving that he is not a good boy but a bad boy, thus acquiring feelings of shame and guilt. He may decide that his parents do not love him and therefore feel rejected.

This second course of action is likely to cause trouble. Indeed Rogers believes that maladjustment represents an ever-widening gulf between phenomenological self-image and reality. Maladjusted people tend to regard any experience that is not consistent with their self-image as a threat. Their phenomenological self, as they conceive of it, does not match their true feelings and the actual nature of their experiences. Sometimes

Carl Rogers (with glasses) leading an encounter group.

they find ways of banishing the experience from their conscious thoughts. In any case they must set up more and more defenses against the truth, and more and more tension results.

Well-adjusted people, on the other hand, are those whose self-image is consistent with what they really think, feel, do, and experience—and who are willing to accept themself as they are. Instead of being rigid, their phenomenological self is flexible and changes constantly as new experiences occur.

Humanistic therapy

The method of therapy developed by Rogers, which is typical of humanistic therapy in general, is to provide an atmosphere of unconditional positive regard. The therapist displays great warmth and acceptance toward clients, thus creating a non-threatening situation in which they are free to explore all their thoughts and feelings, including those they have been unable to perceive clearly for fear of condemnation by other people or by their own consciences.

Originally Rogers refrained from expressing any reactions he might have toward the conduct of the people he treated. Later, however, he concluded that he should be more "genuine"—that is, should frankly describe his own feelings, including disapproval of some of the client's actions. But humanistic therapists are always careful to distinguish between criticism of an action and criticism of the person. The core of humanistic treatment is for the therapist to be genuinely understanding and empathetic at all times.

In the safety of this relationship with an understanding and accepting therapist, clients are expected to gradually acquire the ability to resolve their conflicts. The process, Rogers has said, takes three steps: 1) they begin to experience, understand, and accept feelings and desires (such as sexuality and hostility) that they had previously denied to consciousness; 2) they begin to understand the reasons behind their behavior; and 3) they begin to see ways in which they can undertake more positive forms of behavior. In a word, they learn to be themselves.

Many who hear about humanistic therapy for the first time ask the question: If all people were encouraged to be completely themselves, would the world not suddenly be filled with aggressive, brawling, muderous, sexually unrestrained, self-seeking egoists? Rogers answers with an unqualified no.

Social learning theories and behavior therapy

Humanistic theories hold that the core of personality is the urge to grow in a constructive way. Freud's psychoanalytic theory holds that the core is conflict. Another prominent group of theories take still another view. These are the *social learning theories,* which reject Freud's notion of the primitive drives of the id and do not necessarily take any stand at all on the question, so vital to the humanistic approach, of whether human nature is basically good or evil. Instead, the social learning theories regard personality as largely composed of habits—that is to say, of habitual ways of responding to the situations that arise in one's life. Beginning at birth, our experiences mold us in accordance with the principles of learning that were discussed in Part

Two of the book. Depending on what responses we have learned to display to events in the environment, we may either cope successfully or become helpless and neurotic.

Conditioning and cognitive learning

When social learning theories of personality were first formulated, most of psychology's knowledge of learning was confined to classical conditioning (pages 90–98) and operant conditioning (pages 98–108). Thus the theories originally stressed such phenomena as the ways in which unreasonable fears can be acquired through classical conditioning (pages 91–92) and the role of reinforcement in molding operant behavior. Considered especially important were the rewards and punishments provided first by the family and later by society in general. It was suggested that an individual moving through the cultural environment resembled a complicated version of a rat moving through a T-maze. We can predict the rat's behavior if we know in which arm of the T it has been rewarded with food and in which arm it has been punished by shock. Similarly, we could predict a human being's behavior if only we knew the full story of which of this person's actions had been rewarded by society and which had been punished (8).

Most social learning theorists today take a more cognitive view of the manner in which experience creates habitual forms of behavior. They agree that rewards and punishments influence learning, but they believe that factors inside the person—such as inner standards—are also important. One of the prominent members of this group, Albert Bandura, says:

> Humans [have] a capacity for self-direction. They do things that give rise to self-satisfaction and self-worth, and they refrain from behaving in ways that evoke self-punishment. . . . To ignore the influential role of covert self-reinforcement in the regulation of behavior is to disavow a uniquely human capacity (9).

> External consequences, influential as they often are, are not the sole determinants of human behavior. . . . People adopt certain standards of conduct and respond to their own actions in self-reinforcing or self-punishing ways. As a result behavior is regulated by the interplay of self-generated and external sources of influence (10).

Behavior therapy and relearning

Like social learning theories themselves, the therapies associated with them were originally based on

A birthday party—one of the rewards by which society molds behavior.

classical and operant conditioning. *Behavior therapy,* as first practiced by learning theorists, tried to eliminate whatever conditioned reflex or conditioned operant response was causing trouble—for example, an unreasonable fear produced by heights or confined spaces, or the habit of responding to certain situations with anxiety or anger. The behavior therapists made a direct attack on any such symptom of abnormal behavior by trying to break the old stimulus-response connection and substitute a more effective response. Among the techniques they developed and still use in many cases are the following.

Desensitization

A method often used to eliminate phobias is *desensitization,* which originally consisted of attempts to associate the stimulus that causes the fear with relaxation rather than with panic. If you sought relief from an unreasonable fear of snakes, for example, the therapist would ask you to relax as much as possible, then to imagine you were looking at a snake in a mildly fear-producing situation, such as from far away. If you could do this without losing your feeling of relaxation, you would then be asked to imagine a slightly more threatening sight of a snake—and so on until you could remain relaxed while imagining that you held a snake.

Actual relaxation, it has now been found, is not essential. Phobias can be desensitized and eliminated simply by imagining yourself in situations that have caused fear, in the presence of a therapist who encourages the process and praises improvement in the ability to respond calmly (11). Apparently just thinking about the fearful stimulus, in an atmosphere that offers support and promises relief, is enough to produce results.

Extinction

The method of *extinction* is a direct attempt to break a troublesome stimulus-response connection. In one case, it produced spectacular results with a 9-month-old boy who had somehow acquired the habit of vomiting shortly after every meal, weighed only twelve pounds, and was in danger of starving to death. An electrode was attached to his leg and shocks were administered whenever he began to vomit, continuing until he stopped. After a few experiences, the boy learned to stop vomiting as soon as the shock occurred, then soon quit altogether. After a few weeks he weighed sixteen pounds, was released from the hospital, and continued to gain weight at home, showing no sign of going back to the old habit (12).

The extinction of a response by pairing undesirable behavior with a disagreeable stimulus, such as a shock, is called *aversive conditioning*. The person under treatment learns to abandon the undesirable action in order to avoid the unpleasant consequences with which the therapist associates it. Aversive conditioning is always used with caution—or when nothing else seems possible, as in the case of the starving boy—but has proved effective in a number of situations, such as treating men who were sexually incapacitated by sadistic fantasies (13) or by transvestitism (14), which is the desire to dress in the clothing of the other sex.

Reinforcement

Behavior therapists also use a technique that is the direct opposite of aversive conditioning. Often they employ *reinforcement* of a positive kind as a reward for more effective and more desirable behavior. For example, one group of behavior therapists, dealing with disturbed adolescents who had never learned to talk well or to sit quietly at a school desk, treated them by withholding breakfast and lunch, then rewarding them with small amounts of food every time they showed any signs of constructive behavior. Given this kind of push toward acceptable behavior—with food as the reinforcement—the adolescents improved rapidly (15). The technique of reinforcement, as this example indicates, is the basis of behavior modification, which was discussed on pages 105–07. It is also used in the form of a token economy (pages 106–07), which has produced dramatic improvement in the behavior of mental hospital patients rewarded with tokens good for movies and other privileges.

New trends in behavior therapy: encouraging assertive coping

Some of the original practitioners of behavior therapy continue to believe that classical or operant conditioning produces the ineffective responses characteristic of most neurotics (16). Accordingly they rely on such techniques as desensitization, extinction, and reinforcement to change the responses. But most of today's behavior therapists, like the social learning theories on which their methods are based, have moved in a more cognitive direction. They now seek to change their clients' entire pattern of thinking about themselves, their problems, and the world around them. The new trend is to encourage assertive coping, along the lines discussed in the preceding chapter.

The difference between normal and neurotic behavior, according to the new school of behavior therapy, lies in a person's own convictions about ability or lack of ability to cope successfully with anxiety-producing or stressful situations. These convictions about "self-efficacy," as Bandura terms it, determine whether people will make any effort at all to cope, how hard they will try, and how long they will persist. Thus the key to therapy and behavior change is regarded as an enhanced regard for one's own self-efficacy. The key to this better feeling about oneself, in turn, is successful performance in situations that have previously caused anxiety or stress (17). The behavior therapist makes every effort to foster success, using any method that seems promising.

Learning to cope through observation and guided participation

One method now used by behavior therapists is based on *observation learning,* which was discussed on pages 122–23. Subjects with a phobia for snakes, for example, have been asked to watch a movie of other people approaching and eventually playing with a snake (see Figure 12-2). The subjects

12-2 Scenes from a movie that cures the fear of snakes
The photographs are stills from a motion picture that has successfully applied observation learning to the treatment of snake phobia, as described in the text.

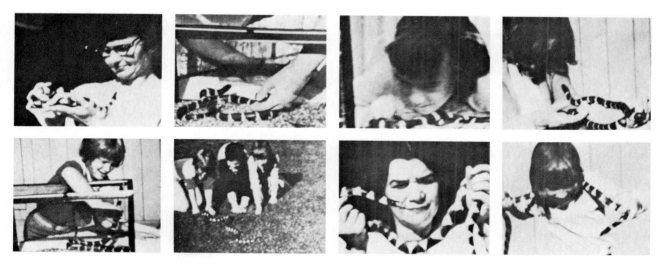

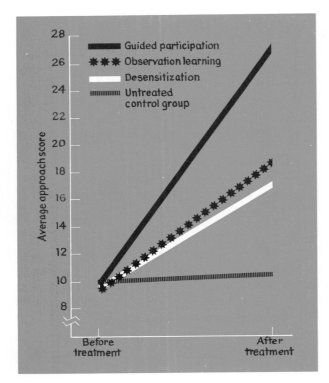

12-3 Snake phobia: different treatments, different results

Three groups of subjects suffering from snake phobia were treated through different techniques of behavior therapy: desensitization, observation learning (watching the movie illustrated in Figure 12-2), and guided participation in handling a snake. All three methods produced improvement, but in varying degrees (18). A score of zero meant that a subject could not even enter a room in which there was a snake. To achieve a perfect score of 29, subjects had to let a snake crawl over their lap while holding their hands passively at their sides.

can stop the movie and turn it back any time they begin to feel fearful. By eventually seeing the movie through to the end, they can observe that all the people shown, though perhaps frightened at first, were finally able to pick up a snake and even drape it around their neck—all without suffering any harm. If others could do this, why not the subjects?

The observation learning provided by the movie helps considerably to relieve the snake phobia, as can be seen in Figure 12-3. Even more effective, however, is the further step of watching a live model handle a snake, then joining the model—who again suffers no harm and indeed actually enjoys the experience—in playing with the snake. This *guided participation* in a previously anxiety-producing activity is another method used by behavior therapists.

In most attempts to enhance feelings of self-efficacy, therapists try to arrange real-life situations in which the client can practice assertive coping with successful results. People suffering from intense stage-fright have been treated effectively by guiding them step by step through the delivery of a make-believe speech (with the therapist the only audience), to brief comments made before just a few listeners (with the therapist again present to provide support and encouragement), to a full-scale address delivered in a large auditorium. People afraid to fly in airplanes have been taken by the therapist on inspection tours of a plane motionless on the ground during servicing, then on brief flights with the therapist alongside, then on longer flights—which finally they managed alone. One study evaluated the progress of people treated in this manner for severe phobias about public speaking, travel, shopping trips, heights, crowds, and other such matters. It was found that 80 percent got over their fears within a few days, though about half required some additional guidance and practice to make the cure permanent (19). Moreover, enhanced feelings of self-efficacy created by successful performance in one situation tend to improve the ability to cope with other situations as well (20).

Other therapies (including medical)

There are many other forms of psychotherapy, not all of them associated with personality theories. One estimate is that there are some 200 schools of thought about the treatment of people who are suffering from neurotic symptoms or who merely want to enrich their life— and as many as 10,000 specific techniques designed to help (21). There are also many forms of medical treatment, based chiefly on chemicals helpful in combating anxiety, depression, and the disoriented behavior and hallucinations of schizophrenia. These medicines all affect brain chemistry, chiefly by regulating the amount and effectiveness of the neurotransmitters.

Many forms of psychotherapy are very new, and their value has not yet been established. But it appears that the particular type of psychotherapy is less important than the personality and skill of the therapist and the establishment of a strong and trusting bond between therapist and client—as is explained in a box on Psychology and Society on page 460. Thus many therapists no longer limit themselves to any one method. Instead, they choose whichever technique seems most promising in each case. They may at times practice humanistic therapy, and at other times they may use behavioral therapy. Or they may combine the two— and perhaps supplement their treatment by referring the client to a physician for medical therapy.

Interactional therapies

Among the alternatives to psychoanalysis, humanistic therapy, and behavior therapy is a group of techniques called *interactional therapy*. These techniques emphasize the client's relationships with family, friends, schoolmates, fellow workers, and society as a whole. In general, interactional thera-

pists tell their clients: "In your relations with other people, you are now doing this and this and this. What you are doing is not working. Give it up for a while and try something else." Male homosexuals who are unhappy with their life style have been encouraged to stop associating with other homosexuals and seek out the company of women—a new interaction that sometimes results in a lasting switch to heterosexual behavior (23). Some clients are asked to play games in which they pretend to act like other people or to behave in extremely selfish or extremely generous ways, pointing the way to new types of interaction they have never tried before (24).

Among the interactional methods is *family therapy,* in which the therapist attacks an individual's problems by trying to change the behavior patterns of the entire family. Some therapists make videotapes of family interactions to help the members see why their behavior is unsuccessful and how it can be improved (25). An even broader approach is *community therapy,* in which the therapist seeks to set up new forms of interaction to replace existing patterns that are causing trouble between opposing groups, between public officials and citizens, and so on.

Group therapies

Group therapy is the treatment of several patients at the same time. It has been used by therapists of various schools of thought, including some psychoanalysts. The method is in part the child of necessity, for there are not enough trained therapists to treat all prospective clients individually. But it also seems to have genuine advantages with some clients. Joining a group may relieve the individual's

Psychology and Society

How well does psychotherapy work?

Especially in the United States, where psychotherapy has flourished more vigorously than anywhere else, it represents a large investment by society. It is impossible to estimate how many millions of hours have gone into the training of psychotherapists, the practice of various treatment methods, and research into new and better methods. Certainly people who undertake psychotherapy spend millions of dollars every year. Are the time and money a good investment? How well does psychotherapy work? How much does it contribute to society?

The results of therapy, unfortunately, are very difficult to assess. It is hard to determine whether a client has improved at all, much less to exactly what extent. Often different opinions are held by the therapist, the client, and outside observers such as the client's family and friends. Moreover, many people who display neurotic symptoms get over them eventually without any treatment at all.

One severe critic of psychotherapy is the British psychologist H. J. Eysenck, who became famous in the 1950s for a series of studies that led him to conclude therapy is no more helpful than the passage of time. But subsequent investigations have swayed most psychologists—including those who do not themselves practice therapy—to a very different conclusion. A recent survey of the best available evidence gathered over the years indicates that there can no longer be much doubt about the value of psychotherapy. Insofar as the results can be determined, it now appears that the average client probably shows greater improvement than about 75 percent of neurotic people are likely to experience without it (22).

Is one method of therapy better than another? The same survey found no real evidence that the type of treatment makes any difference. Therapists are about equally helpful regardless of their theoretical background or the techniques they use. Their personal qualities seem to be more important than their methods. They are most effective if they themselves are well adjusted, if they are experienced, and if they establish a warm and close relationship with the client. Men and women appear to be equally successful as therapists.

Do some clients have a better chance for improvement than others? It does not seem to matter whether the client is young or old, male or female. But the nature of the problem makes considerable difference. The less serious the disturbance, the greater the likelihood of improvement. Thus people with minor maladjustments of recent origin usually do better than people with severe and long-standing maladjustments. Neurotics are much more likely to benefit than psychotics. Cases of psychopathic personality (Chapter 11) are extremely resistant to treatment—perhaps because psychopaths do not experience the intense anxiety that most other disturbed people are eager to escape.

A desire to get rid of the neurotic behavior is one of the most important of all factors increasing the likelihood of success. Just as strong motivation for change is highly favorable, so is a willingness to work hard at eliminating the difficulties and a belief that the treatment will help. Clients do best when they trust and like the therapist and are convinced that the therapist understands their problems, sympathizes with them, and is going about the treatment in a way that promises relief.

A session in family therapy, led by the man at the rear.

anxieties by demonstrating that other people have the same problems. It also creates an interactional or social give-and-take that is impossible in a face-to-face session with a therapist. Some psychologists believe many clients show the greatest progress when treated through a combination of group and individual therapy (26).

In an *encounter group,* a number of people meet with the goal of shedding the masks they usually wear in public and presenting their true feelings. Encounters are usually led by a trained therapist, though sometimes they meet without a leader. The emphasis is on activities, games, and conversations that encourage members to interact with open displays of emotion, approval, criticism, affection, and hostility. The goal is to throw off the ordinary social restraints and explore what are often called "gut feelings." The assumption is much the same as in humanistic therapy—namely, that people will grow in a positive direction if freed of artificial barriers against perceiving their true self and interacting with others honestly and openly. The humanistic psychologist Carl Rogers has himself led numerous encounter groups.

Although encounter groups have been very popular in recent years, their effectiveness is controversial. Rogers considers them superior in some ways to his humanistic therapy as practiced on a one-to-one basis (27). Abraham Maslow, who devised the humanistic concept of self-actualization, concluded that encounter groups are highly useful in encouraging self-awareness and self-expression but can help relieve only minor difficulties, not serious neurotic problems (28). One study of the effects on some 200 college students who had taken part in encounter groups found that about a third changed for the better, a third were unchanged, and a third changed for the worse (29). The possibility of harm rather than improvement, it has been suggested, is especially great for people who have low self-esteem and cannot cope with group criticism (30).

Medical therapy

One highly controversial medical treatment for personality disorders is *psychosurgery,* in which parts of the brain are severed, removed, or destroyed. At one time many physicians regarded psychosurgery as the quickest and most effective solution for many severe disorders, including uncontrollable urges toward violence. But it was found that many patients, though improved in some ways, lapsed into a vegetablelike existence, unable to function effectively. The technique is seldom used today except as a last resort for patients who are hopelessly suicidal or who suffer from crippling forms of epilepsy (as in the case of the split-brain subjects described on pages 51–54).

In *electroshock therapy*, sometimes used to relieve severe depression, an electric current is passed through the head for a fraction of a second. New techniques make it possible to apply the shock to just one hemisphere of the brain (31). People treated in this manner go into a brief convulsion and then are unconscious for a time. When they wake up they are drowsy and somewhat confused, but advocates of electroshock believe that no permanent ill effects occur. The treatment seems to combat depression by producing a long-term increase in the amount of noradrenalin in the brain (32). As with psychosurgery, most psychologists shun the treatment except in extreme emergency.

Among the medications used to treat mental disorders are several that relieve the seizures of epilepsy—including a new drug called *valproate*, approved by the Food and Drug Administration in 1978. *Amphetamines* (page 313) are sometimes used to treat the abnormality called *hyperkinesis*, which affects about three million American children, making them overactive, irritable, and unable to concentrate. Although amphetamines ordinarily act as stimulants, they seem to have a calming effect on some hyperkinetic children.

Tranquilizers

The most widely used of all medications affecting the nervous system are the *tranquilizers*, which reduce the amount and effectiveness of the brain's neurotransmitters. Tranquilizers are especially valuable in relieving some of the symptoms of schizophrenic patients, such as hallucinations and delusions. They have greatly improved the atmosphere of mental hospitals by calming patients who were previously unmanageable. They have also enabled some patients, though by no means all, to return to a more or less normal life. In milder forms and doses, tranquilizers are frequently prescribed for people with less serious disturbances associated with anxiety and stress. Though they often serve as a crutch in times of crisis, their overuse may interfere with serious attempts to cope with the causes of anxiety and stress.

Antidepression drugs

Medications used to combat depression are known collectively as *psychic energizers*. Of the many types available, each works in a slightly different manner and may help some depressed people but not others. All seem to increase the brain's effective supply of noradrenalin and possibly other neurotransmitters (33). Also sometimes used in treating depression, especially when it is accompanied by swings toward manic states, are the salts of the metallic element *lithium*. This medication, taken regularly, prevents the ups and downs of mood in some people but not all. The way it works is not known.

All medical therapies are attempts to remedy the first of the factors mentioned in the preceding chapter as working together to produce abnormal behavior—biological, psychological, and environmental. Since the search for medications is still in its infancy, it seems likely that the future will bring many new drugs that relieve the biological causes of personality problems. It may even turn out that some disorders are primarily biological, in which case new medications may prove to be a specific cure. The great majority of psychologists, however, believe that most disorders spring from functional as well as biological causes and that psychotherapy should always accompany medical therapy.

The question of self-therapy

The techniques of medical therapy have to be prescribed and monitored by a physician. But what about psychotherapy? Can we serve as our own psychotherapists—solving our own problems and correcting any tendencies toward abnormal behavior? How helpful are all the popular books that suggest ways to better mental health and greater self-fulfillment?

These questions are not easy to answer. For one thing, advice on self-help techniques varies widely—from articles written by untrained people to carefully documented books in which serious therapists explain their theories and methods. The former are worthless and potentially harmful. The latter seem to help some readers but not others. One difficulty with all attempts at self-therapy is that they lack the support of a warm, close, and encouraging relationship with an understanding and sympathetic therapist—which is probably the most important ingredient of success.

All psychologists agree that sound knowledge about psychological processes encourages the development of normal, healthy, and effective personality. Thus everything in this course is potentially helpful. Some topics of particular value as signposts toward mental health are psychology's knowledge about the way unreasonable fears can be acquired through conditioning, learned helplessness and how it can be counteracted, emotions, motives, anxiety, stress, assertive coping with anxiety and stress, and the wellsprings of abnormal behavior, as well as the personality theories and methods of therapy described in this chapter. Also highly pertinent are many of the topics still to come —especially the manner in which personality develops and changes throughout life (Chapter 13) and the ways in which behavior is molded for better or for worse by relationships with other people (Chapter 14).

(Summary begins on page 467.)

Postscript

Tests of personality

If psychologists had a test that measured personality accurately and reliably, it would be one of their most valuable tools. Clinical psychologists could quickly analyze their clients' strengths and weaknessess, pinpoint sources of stress and anxiety, and determine the most effective way of helping in the struggle to cope. Guidance counselors would have a sure-fire guide to jobs and careers, for personality is a major factor in determining whether a person will be happy and successful as a salesperson, teacher, police officer, or accountant. Marriage counselors could quickly discover sources of friction and ways to relieve them—or spot couples so incompatible that the situation is hopeless. Research psychologists would have an invaluable aid in studying the conditions that foster or inhibit the flowering of personality.

Thus psychologists have spent a great deal of time, effort, and ingenuity on the creation of personality tests. Their goal, unfortunately, has been elusive. They have devised tests that are useful in many ways, but they have yet to find the perfect tests. Perhaps they never will. Personality is such a complex matter—the product of a tangled and endless weaving together of experiences beginning at birth, continuing throughout life, and unique for each individual—that the difficulties in measuring it are staggering.

All the personality tests now in use have some virtues but also many limitations. The tests fall into three classes: 1) *objective tests,* 2) *situational tests,* and 3) *projective tests.*

Objective tests

Many people have attempted to devise a measure of personality that meets the standard of objectivity considered ideal in any psychological test, as was discussed on page 235. They have come up with some *objective tests* whose scores are not seriously affected by the opinions or prejudices of the examiner. Since these tests are administered according to a standard procedure, the results should be the same regardless of who gives or scores them.

The most widely used objective test is the *Minnesota Multiphasic Personality Inventory,* or MMPI for short. The test is made up of nearly 600 statements like those shown in Figure 12-4. For each statement, subjects are asked to check whether or not it is true of their own behavior or to mark "cannot say." The method of scoring compares the individual subject's responses with those made in the past by large numbers of other people—especially with the scores made by people known to have such personality traits as tendencies to pessimism and depression, anxiety over health, emotional excitability,

12-4
**Some items
from a personality test**
The Minnesota Multiphasic Personality Test is made up of statements like these, which subjects are asked to mark true, false, or cannot say of their own behavior (34).

		Can't	
T	F	say	
☐	☐	☐	I have certainly had more than my share of things to worry about.
☐	☐	☐	I think that I feel more intensely than other people do.
☐	☐	☐	I have never done anything dangerous for the thrill of it.
☐	☐	☐	I think nearly everyone would tell a lie to keep out of trouble.
☐	☐	☐	I am happy most of the time.
☐	☐	☐	I tend to be on my guard with people who are somewhat more friendly than I had expected.
☐	☐	☐	My mother or father often made me obey even when I thought that it was unreasonable.
☐	☐	☐	I feel uneasy indoors.
☐	☐	☐	I refuse to play some games because I am not good at them.
☐	☐	☐	I find it hard to keep my mind on a task or job.

delinquency, or tendencies toward schizophrenia and paranoia.

Situational tests

In a *situational test,* the examiner observes the behavior of the subject in a situation deliberately created to bring out certain aspects of personality. For example, subjects might be asked to carry out some difficult mechanical task with the assistance of "helpers" who are in fact stooges and who behave in an uncooperative and insulting fashion (35). Or subjects might be put through what is called s stress interview, in which the people asking the questions are deliberately hostile and pretend to disbelieve the answers (36).

One weakness of these tests is that it is difficult to know whether the situation actually seems real to the subjects and whether their motivation and behavior are the same as in real life. Moreover, two different examiners watching a subject's behavior may reach different conclusions about it. Thus situational tests, though they may give valuable clues to personality traits, must be used and interpreted with caution.

Projective tests

The term *projection* was mentioned in the preceding chapter as a defense mechanism in which people attribute to others some of their own anxiety-causing motives. *Projective tests* of personality assume that a similar mental process can be observed and measured, even in people who are not using it as a defense mechanism, by providing conditions that encourage it. In the *Thematic Apperception Test,* or TAT for short, these conditions are created by asking the subject to make up stories

12-5 A projective test: What is happening here? What story does this picture tell? What led up to the situation? What is happening? How will events turn out? These are the questions asked in the Thematic Apperception Test, which uses drawings similar to this one. Try making up your own story before reading the discussion of the TAT in the text (37).

about pictures like the one in Figure 12-5, which you should examine before reading on.

The picture in Figure 12-5 is deliberately ambiguous. It could mean almost anything. Thus, in responding to it, you are likely to project some of your own personality traits. The story you make up may very well reveal something about your own motives, feelings, anxieties, and attitudes. Sometimes the amount of self-revelation is clear and dramatic, as in this story made up by one subject:

> The older woman represents evil and she is trying to persuade the younger one to leave her husband and run off and lead a life of fun and gaiety. The younger one is afraid to do it—afraid of what others will think, afraid she will regret the action. But the older one knows that she wants to leave and so she insists over and over again. I am not sure how it ends. Perhaps the younger woman turns and walks away and ignores the older woman.

The TAT technique has found its most widespread and successful use in measuring the strength of the achievement motive (38). A tendency to invent stories that contain frequent, intense elements of striving and ambition—or that on the contrary show little concern with success—appears to be a better measure of the achievement motive than the judgment of people who know the subjects well (39) or even the subjects' own assessment of their desire to achieve (40).

The *Rorschach Test* uses inkblots like the one shown in Figure 12-6. When subjects are asked what they see in the blots, they ordinarily mention twenty to forty things of which they are reminded. Their responses are scored for various characteristics that seem to reveal personality. For example, a tendency to respond to the blot as a whole may indicate that the subject thinks in terms of abstractions and generalities, while a tendency to pick out many minor details that most people ignore may indicate an overconcern for detail.

A number of other less formal projective techniques have been developed (42). In a *word association test,* the examiner calls out a word, such as "mother" or "bad" or "money," and the subject is asked to respond as quickly as possible with the first word that comes to mind. The examiner notes the nature of the associations that the test words

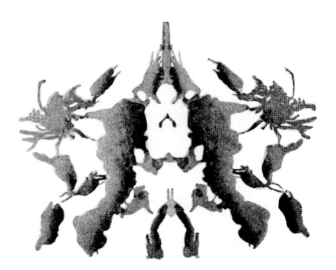

12-6 Another projective test: What do you see? This is an inkblot like those used in the Rorschach Test. Subjects are asked to examine it and report everything they see in it (41).

suggest and also the speed with which the subject responds. Any unusual delay in responding is taken to indicate that the test word arouses some kind of conflict. In a *draw-a-person test,* the subject is simply asked to draw a picture of a person on a blank paper. The sex of the drawing, its size, the facial expression, and other characteristics may contain personality clues. In a *sentence-completion test,* the examiner gives the subject a series of partially completed sentences such as the following:

> I sometimes feel . . . .
> When by myself . . . .
> When I was young . . . .

The subject is asked to complete the sentences with the first thoughts that come to mind. The responses, like the TAT stories, may suggest motives and conflicts.

Summary

1 *Personality* is the total pattern of characteristic ways of thinking, feeling, and behaving that constitute the individual's distinctive method of relating to the environment.

2 *Personality theories* are concerned with three aspects of human behavior. They assume: a) that there is some *core of personality* common to all human beings, b) that these common tendencies and characteristics of human beings are channeled in various directions by the process of *development*, and c) that the core of personality as modified by development makes each person a unique individual displaying a unique pattern of the *peripheral characteristics* that are generally known as personality.

3 Freud's *psychoanalytical theory* assumes that the core of personality is conflict—for example, conflicts between incompatible desires (many of which are unconscious) and between desires and fears of punishment for attempts to gratify them.

4 Psychoanalytical theory holds that the human mind has three parts or forces: a) the unconscious *id,* containing the person's instinctive drives toward sexuality (the *libido*) and aggression; b) the largely conscious *ego,* which is the person's contact with reality; and c) the largely unconscious *superego,* which punishes transgressions.

5 The superego is acquired largely as a result of the *Oedipus complex,* a conflict of mingled love and hate toward the parents that all children are assumed to undergo between the ages of two and a half and six. Children resolve the conflict by identifying with their parents and adopting what they consider to be their parents' moral judgments, which form the superego.

6 The central problem in mental disturbance, according to psychoanalytical theory, is anxiety—produced in the ego when the demands of the id threaten to create danger or when the superego threatens to impose disapproval or punishment.

7 *Psychoanalysis,* the method of therapy used by followers of Freud, is designed to dredge up into awareness the unconscious desires and conflicts that Freud considered the source of neurotic anxiety and guilt. It uses the technique of *free association* and examines *transference*, dreams, and slips of the tongue to provide insights and thus achieve "freedom from the tyranny of the unconscious."

8 Among the successors of Freud who have proposed variations of his theories are Jung, who introduced the concepts of *introvert* and *extrovert* and of a *collective unconscious;* Adler, who introduced the concept of *inferiority complex;* Hartmann, who has emphasized the role of such ego processes as perception, attention, and thinking in dealing with reality; and Fromm, who stresses the importance of cultural and social influences on personality.

9 *Humanistic theories* hold that the core of personality is a universal human urge to perfect our skills and find peace and happiness.

10 Rogers' humanistic theory stresses the self-image, or *phenomenological self,* which represents the way we see ourselves, our abilities, and our relationships with other people. Maladjustments occur when people fail to integrate all their experiences, desires, and feelings into the phenomenological self, which is therefore at odds with reality.

11 Rogers' therapy provides an atmosphere of *unconditional positive regard* in which clients are free to explore all their thoughts and feelings, including those they have been unable to perceive clearly for fear of condemnation by others or by their own consciences.

12 *Social learning theories* hold that the core of personality is the habitual ways we have learned to respond to events in the environment. The theories originally stressed classical and operant conditioning and reinforcement through rewards or punishments. Many of today's social learning theorists take a more cognitive view and emphasize inner standards, self-reinforcement, and self-punishment.

13 Behavior therapy regards personality disturbances as learned responses that can be changed through relearning. Its techniques include *desensitization, extinction* of undesired behavior (sometimes through *aversive conditioning*), *reinforcement* of more desirable behavior, *learning through observation,* and *guided participation* to help encourage assertive coping.

14 *Interactional therapies* concentrate on changing the disturbed individual's behavior toward other people. Some forms of this treatment are *family therapy* and *community therapy.*

15 *Group therapy* is the treatment of several patients at the same time. *Encounter groups* are one example.

16 Methods of *medical therapy* include: a) *psychosurgery,* b) *electroshock,* c) *tranquilizers,* and d) *antidepression medications.*

Postscript

17 There are three types of *personality tests:*
   a *Objective tests,* such as the Minnesota Multiphasic Personality Inventory (MMPI).
   b *Situational tests,* in which the examiner observes the behavior of the subject in a situation deliberately created to reveal some aspect of the subject's personality.
   c *Projective tests,* such as the Thematic Apperception Test and the Rorschach Test, in which subjects supposedly insert or project aspects of their own personality into the stories they make up about ambiguous pictures or into the kinds of objects they see in inkblots. Other more informal types of projective techniques include *word association, draw-a-person,* and *sentence completion tests.*

$$2.6$$

$$1 - 24$$

$$\frac{23}{12}$$

$$\frac{5}{12} \qquad \frac{6}{12} \qquad \frac{4}{12} \qquad \frac{1}{3} \qquad \frac{1}{2}$$

$$\frac{8}{12}$$

$$+1$$

Important terms

...oning	free association	phenomenological self
...py	group therapy	pleasure principle
...onscious	guided participation	psychic energizers
...erapy	humanistic therapy	psychoanalysis
...positive regard	id	psychoanalytical theory
...sonality	identification	psychosurgery
...ition	inferiority complex	reality principle
...ent	interactional therapy	reinforcement resistance
...erapy	introvert	social learning theories
	libido	superego
...ock	neopsychoanalysts	tranquilizers
...er group	observation learning	transference
...n	Oedipus complex	unconditional positive
...t	peripheral traits	regard
...erapy	personality	unconscious mind

Postscript

draw-a-person test	projective test	situational test
MMPI	Rorschach test	TAT
objective test	sentence-completion test	word association test

Recommended readings

Bandura, A. *Social learning theory*. Englewood Cliffs, N.J.: Prentice-Hall, 1976.

Brenner, C. *An elementary textbook of psychoanalysis,* rev. ed. New York: International Universities Press, 1974.

Freud, S. *New introductory lectures on psychoanalysis*. Ed. by Strachey, J. New York: Norton, 1965.

Hall, C. S., and Lindzey, G. *Theories of personality,* 3d ed. New York: Wiley, 1978.

Hersen, M., Eisler, R. M., and Miller, P. M., eds. *Progress in behavior modification*. New York: Academic Press, 1977.

Jung, C. G. *The basic writings of C. G. Jung*. New York: Random House, 1959.

Pervin, L. A., and Levenson, H. *Personality: theory assessment and research,* 2d ed. New York: Wiley, 1975.

Rogers, C. *On becoming a person: a therapist's view of psychotherapy*. Boston: Houghton Mifflin, 1970.

Yalom, I. D. *The theory and practice of group psychotherapy,* 2d ed. New York: Basic Books, 1975.

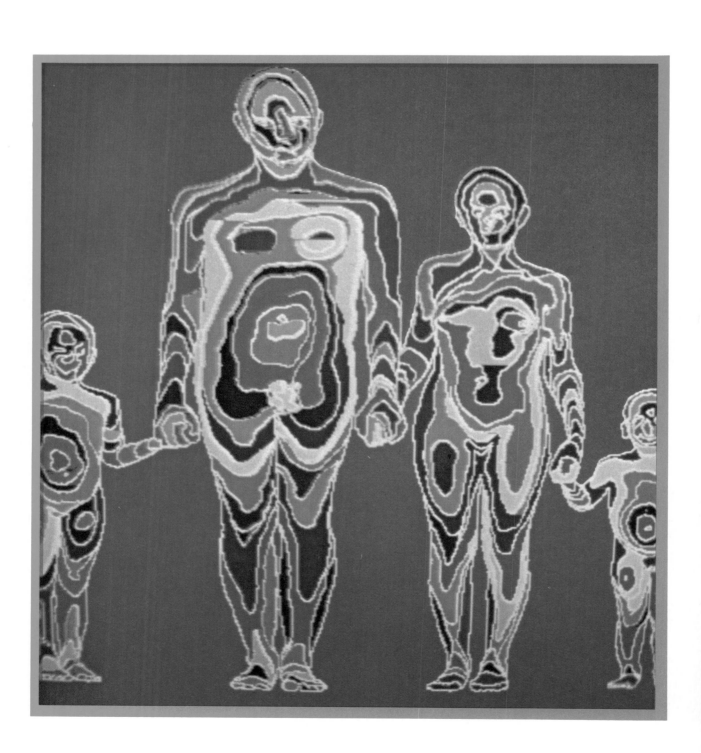

Part seven
Growing up
and living with
other people

The time has come, in this final section of the book, to examine in depth the nurture side of the nature-nurture argument. Previous chapters have described nurture rather loosely as the environment, as experience, or as the result of learning from experience. But what is it about our environment and experience that has the greatest influence on our thinking and behavior?

To some extent, we are influenced by the physical aspects of the environment. Eskimos, who live in the frozen North, develop different patterns of behavior—a whole different life style—from Polynesians on tropical islands. We modern Americans, living in an environment of such technological devices as automobiles, television, and computers, have a far different life style from the first settlers who hacked log cabins and little patches of farm land out of the wilderness. We have all kinds of new skills and techniques to learn. Our language is different, partly because of the addition of thousands of words for objects that did not exist a mere few hundred years ago. Our motives, though perhaps basically similar to those of our forebears, focus on previously unknown goals. Many new stimuli trigger our emotions and help mold our personalities.

But of all the environmental influences on our behavior, none is so powerful as the people around us. Long before the birth of psychology, this observation was familiar in literature. Four centuries ago, the poet John Donne wrote, "No man is an island." (In those prefeminist days, of course, *man* was still a synonym for *human being*.) Two centuries ago, Voltaire wrote, "God designed us to live in society." Modern psychology has reaffirmed these opinions—and begun to study all the many ways in which our behavior, our thinking, and our personality depend on our being members of society, in constant interaction with the other members.

Our dependence on others begins even before birth, for our size, physical health, and even intelligence are determined in part by how well our mothers took care of themselves during pregnancy. It continues throughout childhood, when our psychological development is molded by complex relationships with other people—at first our parents, later our schoolmates and teachers. It extends through our entire lifetime—for our behavior as adults has been found to depend on other people to an extent that might surprise even such astute observers as Donne and Voltaire.

Chapter 13 is devoted to *developmental psychology,* which is the study of how the way in which we grow up is dictated largely by the people in our environment. Chapter 14 discusses *social psychology,* which is the study of how we live with other people, how our behavior depends in large part on their behavior, and how theirs in turn depends on ours.

Outline

Chapter thirteen

Developmental psychology: from infant to adult

The influence of nature on our physical and psychological characteristics is exerted once and for all at the moment of union between the mother's egg cell and the father's sperm cell. The chromosomes and genes in these cells may tend to program our development along certain lines, as was described on pages 34–39. But from the moment of conception they can operate only as nurture thenceforth decrees by providing the environment in which the fertilized egg grows into a living baby and the baby into an adult.

Development is influenced by environment even in the womb. If the mother's diet during pregnancy lacks nutritional values and vitamins, the baby may never attain the IQ level that its genes might otherwise have made possible (1). Mothers who experience prolonged anxiety or anger during pregnancy may have babies who are of less than average size, overactive, and inclined to have digestive problems (2), as if they too had been subjected to damaging stress. Heavy drinking or smoking by the mother may harm the baby's health. Some babies, born to women who use narcotics, are themselves full-fledged addicts at birth.

Proper prenatal care, designed to give a newborn baby the best chance to thrive, is largely the province of physicians and nutritionists. But at birth a new set of influences begins to operate and to mold the baby's psychological traits. These influences are the domain of *developmental psychology*—which is chiefly devoted to study of the ways in which growing children gradually acquire all the patterns of behavior discussed in the book. These include the ways in which they perceive the world, learn, think, use language, experience emotions, and develop the motives, conflicts, and methods of coping with conflicts that will help determine their adult personalities.

For many reasons, developmental psychology is one of the most rapidly growing branches of the science. Numerous studies have shown that behavior patterns formed in childhood, though by no means permanently engraved on the personality, may incline adults to be dependent or independent, submissive or dominant, shy or friendly. Childhood experiences may serve to mold goals, philosophy of life, feelings about marriage, and behavior as parents. It is virtually impossible to understand adult behavior and the social problems it often creates without knowing something about developmental psychology. Moreover, developmental psychology can help parents understand individual children, find successful methods of rearing them, and handle the difficulties inherent in bringing them up.

Developmental psychology can help evaluate and improve the day-care centers now being established for the children of working mothers. It also shows promise of pointing a way to relieve the psychological difficulties that plague so many people in our society—such problems as alcoholism, drug addiction, criminal tendencies, suicidal depression, and schizophrenia. Once established as

a pattern of adult behavior, these problems are difficult to treat and eliminate. But clinical studies of disturbed adults and criminals indicate that their difficulties often began in childhood. Thus developmental psychology may suggest methods of preventing the difficulties or dealing with them more successfully in their early stages.

At one time the study of development was confined to the growing child. Now many psychologists view development as a process that continues throughout life, from cradle to grave. Even the most drastic handicaps caused by a deprived childhood, it has been found, can often be overcome in later life. The shy, withdrawn 7-year-old may blossom into a well-adjusted adult. The troubled adolescent may become a perfectly well-adjusted 30-year-old. Thus developmental psychology has expanded to the study not only of children but of adolescence, young adulthood, middle age, and old age—even the psychological events associated with the imminence of death.

Babies at birth: alike yet different

The human baby, though more helpless at birth than most other new-born organisms, is nonetheless a miraculous creation. From the moment the first breath is drawn, the baby is what has been called "a remarkably capable organism" (3). All normal babies are sensitive from birth to stimuli in their environments. They can see, hear, smell, and feel. Even babies a few hours old follow a moving object with their eyes (4). After a few days they can discriminate between the smell of their own mother's milk and the smell of milk from another mother (5).

Babies respond to stimuli with a wide range of inborn reflex behavior. When the sides of their mouths are tickled, they display the reflex illustrated

in Figure 13-1—the so-called rooting response that enables them to find food at the mother's breast. If the sole of the foot is gently pricked with a pin, they draw the foot away as shown in Figure 13-2—a reflex that enables them to escape from pain. If a bright light is flashed, they protect themselves by closing their eyelids.

Though all normal babies are aware of their environment and can react to the stimuli it presents, they differ in many ways in sensitivity and responses. They are alike yet different—in ways displayed so early that they almost surely represent inborn traits. To what extent are these inherited characteristics likely to persist and to what extent are they modified by nurture?

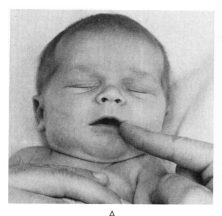 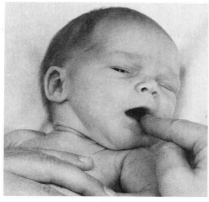 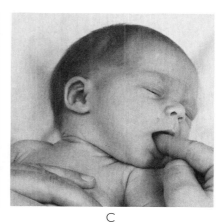

A B C

13-1 The newborn's rooting response
When the side of an infant's mouth is tickled (A), the reflex response is to turn the head toward the stimulus (B) and then try to suck the finger (C), as if it were a source of food.

13-2 Reflex escape from pain
When the sole of the infant's foot is touched by a sharp object, the reflex response is to pull the foot away from the offending stimulus.

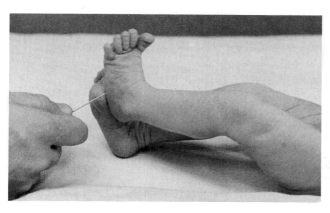 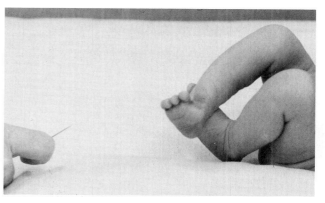

Differences in sensitivity and adaptation

Studies have shown wide individual differences in sensory threshold. With some babies, even the most gentle stroking of the skin produces a muscular reflex. Other babies do not respond unless the stroking is fairly firm. Some babies cry when exposed to sounds or light flashes of low intensity, others only when the intensity is much higher.

There are also differences in how rapidly babies display sensory adaptation and quit responding. When a sound loud enough to produce crying is repeated over a period of time, some babies get used to it very quickly. Others continue to show distress even at the thirtieth repetition (6). Similarly, some babies appear to become bored with a stimulus more quickly than others. If a series of pictures of the human face is projected on a screen above the crib, some infants pay close attention for a long time. Others soon stop looking, as if they had rapidly tired of the repetitive stimulus (7).

Differences in activity and irritability

Even in the very early days of life, some babies are much more active than others. They move their arms and legs with considerable force, tend to be restless when asleep, suck vigorously when nursing, and appear to have above-average appetites. As they get a little older, they tend to make loud noises when they babble, to bang their toys together, and to kick at the sides of their crib. Other babies are much more placid in these respects (8).

Another important difference among infants is in what might be called irritability. Some babies begin to fret, whine, or cry at the slightest provocation. Once they begin to fret, they often work themselves up into what looks like a temper tantrum and soon are bellowing at the top of their lungs. Other babies do not fret unless their discomfort or pain is intense. Even then, they may fret only for a half-minute or so and then stop, as if possessing some mechanism that inhibits the buildup of extreme upset (9).

Some pronounced differences have been found among babies of different ethnic backgrounds. If placed face down in their cribs, Caucasian infants immediately turn their heads to the side, whereas Chinese babies leave their face placidly buried in the sheets. An even more striking difference has been demonstrated by pressing a cloth briefly against the baby's nose. Caucasian and black babies try to fight off the cloth by turning away or

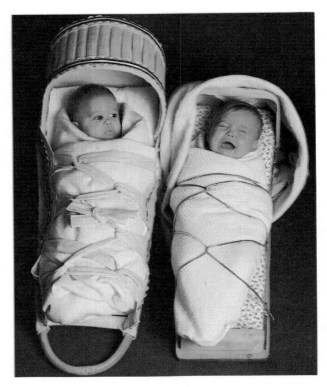

13-3 Happy Indian baby, unhappy Caucasian
These two infants have been placed on a cradle board, which Navaho Indian mothers have used for generations to carry their young. The Navaho baby is perfectly content. The Caucasian baby lodges a vigorous protest.

trying to dislodge it with their hands. Chinese babies simply accept the situation and start breathing through their mouths (10). A notable difference between Americans of Caucasian and Indian descent is illustrated in Figure 13-3.

Easy, slow-to-warm-up, and difficult babies

One group of investigators, after studying more than a hundred children from birth through elementary school, has concluded that most newborn

Americans fall into three distinct classes of temperament:

1 *Easy* children are generally cheerful. Their reactions to stimuli show a low to moderate intensity. They establish regular habits of eating and sleeping and are quick to adapt to new schedules, foods, and people.

2 *Slow-to-warm-up* children are less cheerful; indeed their mood seems slightly negative. Their responses are low in intensity. Their eating and sleeping habits vary and they tend to withdraw from their first exposure to a new experience. They take time to adjust to change.

3 *Difficult* children seem unfriendly and hard to please. They are given to unusually intense reactions, such as loud laughter, frequent loud crying, and temper tantrums. They show little regularity in eating and sleeping and are easily upset by new experiences.

A striking example of the difference between an easy and a difficult baby is shown in Figure 13-4. The photographs, which were made several years apart, are of an older sister and a younger brother —an indication that early differences in temperament do not necessarily reflect the parents' personalities or child-rearing methods. Regardless of

13-4 A contrast in infant temperament

Both these babies are three months old and are being offered a new kind of cereal for the first time. The girl at the top, an easy baby, eagerly accepts the new experience. The boy at the bottom, a difficult baby, fights it.

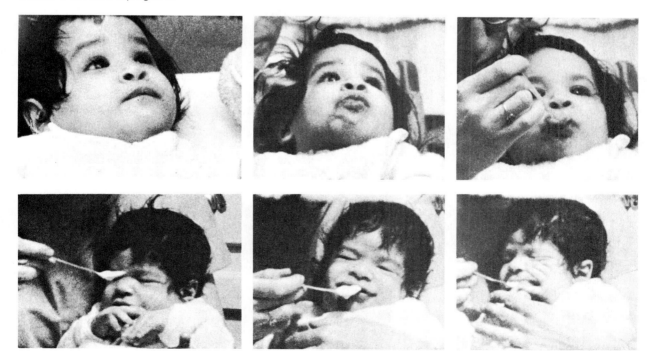

the parents' behavior or the general atmosphere of the home, about 40 percent of the children in the study were easy, 15 percent slow-to-warm-up, and 10 percent difficult. The remaining 35 percent showed a mixture of the three different kinds of temperament (11).

The investigators concluded that the three types require very different treatment during infancy and in the early years of school. Easy children thrive under almost any kind of treatment in early childhood—but, having adapted so well to the home environment, they may have trouble when their teacher and schoolmates make different demands. Slow-to-warm-up children require considerable patience. They do their best when encouraged to try new experiences but allowed to adapt at their own pace. Too much pressure heightens their natural inclination to withdraw.

Difficult children present a special problem. Because of their irregular habits, their resistance to adjustment, and their negative attitude, they are hard to live with—a trial to their parents and later their teachers. Attempts to force them to behave like other children may only make them more negative and difficult. Their parents must exercise exceptional understanding and tolerance to bring them around—slowly and gradually—to getting along with other individuals.

These findings about inborn differences in temperament, together with the other new knowledge about variations in sensitivity, activity, and irritability, are of great potential value to parents, the staffs of day-care centers, and teachers, especially in the early grades. The findings disprove the popular assumption that all young children are more or less alike and should behave as if cut from the same pattern. Developmental psychology has established that infants are individuals who require individual treatment if they are to develop to their maximum capability.

How long do early traits persist?

Though nature doubtless accounts for the differences observed in very young babies, nurture soon begins to take over. The traits a baby displays in the early weeks and months may persist for a time but do not necessarily constitute a lifelong blueprint. In the follow-up of easy, slow-to-warm-up, and difficult babies, it was found that they tended to show the same differences in personality at the age of two that they had shown in the cradle. But the pattern no longer existed by the time they were six to twelve (12).

Many studies have shown how rapidly change can occur in early childhood. One study explored such traits as irritability, readiness to smile, attentiveness, activity level, and vocal excitability. No significant relationship was found between the way babies scored on these psychological attributes before they were a year old and the way they scored at twenty-seven months. Indeed there were some spectacular reversals of behavior. One boy, as an infant, worried the investigators because he kept rocking his body and sucking on his forearm. By the time he was just a few months over two years old, his behavior was perfectly normal (13). A follow-up of the children, moreover, found no meaningful relationship between their 27-month-old behavior (in regard to irritability, attentiveness, activity level, and vocal excitability) and the scores they made at age ten on reading and intelligence tests (14). What such studies have to say about child-rearing methods is discussed in a box on Psychology and Society.

Effects of unfavorable environment: the neglected child

One topic that has always interested developmental psychologists is the effect of an extremely

Psychology and Society

Psychology's message to parents: optimism–and patience–often pay off

What conclusion can parents and prospective parents draw from the findings of developmental psychologists about the individual differences displayed by babies and the way these differences persist or vanish as years go by? What do the facts tell us about rearing our children?

The studies described in the text point to one message above all: It is very difficult to predict, from the way children behave in the early months or years, how they will behave even in the elementary school years, much less as adolescents or adults. This is hardly surprising, for development depends on many complex interactions between children and the people and events in their environment. We cannot know, at any given moment, what form these interactions will take in the months and years to come (15). Moreover, psychologists do not yet fully understand how different experiences mold development along different lines. The child's future, like life itself, defies attempts at prediction. All we can be sure of is that the years between infancy and adulthood will be full of unforeseen events—and that these events will often produce striking alterations in the patterns of temperament and behavior seen in the cradle (16).

Yet there is a natural tendency for parents to be wrapped up in the events of the moment—and to become discouraged and pessimistic if a child is difficult, irritable, overactive, or seemingly unable to pay attention. As a result they may treat the child with too little affection and sympathy, too much criticism and punishment. Out of such a relationship, the child may acquire the learned helplessness discussed in Chapter 3 as a serious handicap to progress in school, normal adjustment to life in general, and self-fulfillment.

The findings of developmental psychology suggest not pessimism but optimism about children and their potentialities. Difficult babies—boisterous, stubborn, and headstrong—often quiet down as they get older. Babies who seem restless and inattentive in the cradle often learn to concentrate and become star pupils in school. Even babies who seem anxious may turn out to be perfectly normal. If parents can remember that babies show a wide range of individual differences, need individual treatment, and thrive on warmth and love—and if they can tolerate behavior that at the moment may hardly be ideal—their patience will usually be rewarded.

unfavorable early environment. If children grow up in circumstances that seriously retard their progress, are they doomed to be ineffective and unhappy throughout life? Or do they have a chance to throw off their early handicaps? To put this another way: What chance does the neglected child have to develop into a normal adult?

Many of the first studies bearing on this problem produced pessimistic results. In the animal world, it was found that monkeys raised in isolation—a form of total neglect—grew up with many symptoms of maladjustment. They were unfriendly, aggressive, and sexually incompetent (17). Among human babies with a severely deprived childhood, many lasting effects of deprivation were observed (18). One investigator made a study of children who had spent the first three years of their life in the impersonal atmosphere of an orphanage, then had gone on to foster homes. Later these children were compared with a control group of children of the same age and sex who had been brought up from the very start in foster homes, where presumably they received more care and encouragement than is possible in an institution. Even after some years had passed, the orphanage children were found to be notably more aggressive, with strong tendencies to have temper tantrums, to kick and hit other children, and to lie, steal, and destroy property. They tended to be emotionally cold, isolated, and incapable of affectionate relationships (19).

There seems to be no doubt that deprivation seriously retards development. But other studies have indicated that the ill effects are often reversible. In a recent animal experiment, monkeys were isolated inside black boxes from birth until they were six months old. When they were permitted to leave the boxes, their behavior was decidedly abnormal. But they were then permitted to associate with other monkeys who had a normal social background. Within a few weeks the black-box monkeys began to improve and after six months they seemed almost completely normal (20).

Human subjects have also been found to display a remarkable ability to bounce back from the numbing effects of an unstimulating early environment. One study was made in an isolated Indian village in Guatemala, where babies are kept inside the family's windowless hut for most of the first year of life. (The tribe members believe that sunlight, air, and the stares of certain people cause illness in the young.) It was found that the babies, when they emerge from the hut, appear severely retarded by the standards of other societies. But they soon catch up in the development of physical skills, and by adolescence they do as well as most children on some tests of perception and memory (21).

Perhaps the most dramatic example of overcoming deprivation comes from Czechoslovakia, where a psychologist has reported the case of twin boys who spent most of the first six years of their lives under cruelly inhuman circumstances. They lived with a mentally subnormal father and an apparently psychopathic stepmother who totally excluded them from the family circle. They were never permitted outside the house but were kept in the cellar or in a small closet. None of the other children in the family was permitted to talk to them. Thus they grew up in almost total isolation except for their own company.

When the case was discovered, the twins looked more like 3-year-olds than 6-year-olds. They were barely able to walk or speak. They were so retarded, in fact, that it was impossible to test their intelligence. Yet, after they were moved to a favorable environment, they soon began to make progress. By the time they were 11, their IQs were about average and their social and emotional development also appeared to be normal (22).

A lot remains to be learned about the effects of early neglect and deprivation. The evidence to date, however, suggests these tentative conclusions: Human infants are extremely impressionable and their environment has a profound effect on their development from the moment they are born. A highly unfavorable environment can produce drastic damage. But infants often prove to be resilient and malleable, that is, capable of changing when circumstances change. Under the proper conditions for growth, early handicaps can sometimes be overcome.

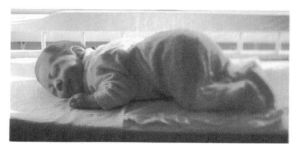
newborn

13-5 How the muscles of movement mature
As is explained on the following page, the process of maturation accounts for the increasing ability of babies to move around. Shown here are the progress from birth to walking alone and the average age at which each stage of development occurs.

3 months

6 months

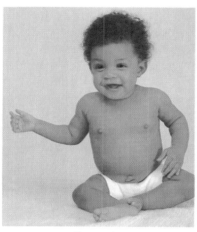
7 months

13 months

11 months

15 months

Physical and mental development

One of nature's most spectacular events is the growth of the helpless newborn baby into eager toddler (some time after the first birthday), experimenter with language (starting near the end of the second year), and eventually 6-year-old school-child, about to solve the mysteries of reading and writing. How many and varied are the accomplishments of those early years. How many new worlds are faced and conquered.

Part of this rapid early development is the result of *maturation*—the physical changes, taking place after birth, that continue the biological growth of the organism from fertilized egg cell to adult. Almost day by day, simply as the result of getting older, babies become capable of new feats of physical, perceptual, and mental skill.

Physical maturation

Even before birth, babies begin to use their muscles. Their movements can usually be felt in the womb in about the twentieth week of pregnancy. Newborn babies have all the muscle fibers they will ever possess, but the fibers still have a lot of growing to do. Eventually, at full maturity, the muscles will weigh about forty times as much as they weighed at birth. The muscles of posture, creeping, and standing must mature as shown in Figure 13-5 before the baby can walk alone, at around the age of fifteen months. The muscles of the hands and arms, as they mature, produce increased skill at reaching and grasping, as shown in Figure 13-6, on the following page.

The skeleton at birth is largely composed of cartilage, softer and more pliable than bone. This gradually hardens. The fibers of the nervous system grow and form additional synaptic connections to other fibers, and some of them develop protective sheaths that make them faster and more efficient conductors of nervous impulses. The brain, in particular, grows in size and weight—very rapidly during the first two years, then more slowly until growth is complete.

Much of the baby's remarkable progress in the early months of life reflects maturation of the body and the nervous system. Thus children all over the world, regardless of child-rearing practices, tend to display various skills at about the same age. They begin to smile at the sight of a human face at about four months, show vocal excitement to a new voice at nine months, search for a hidden object that they saw being covered by a piece of cloth at about twelve months. They begin to utter some of the basic sounds of language in the first few days of life—but they cannot really use speech until their brains have matured sufficiently at around eighteen months.

The process of maturation cannot be speeded up to any great extent. Indeed attempts to push children far beyond their level of maturation may be harmful (24). But environment does have some effect. Encouraging infants to perform skills—though without forcing them—is likely to produce the appearance of these skills at a somewhat earlier age. Infants whose parents talk to them a great deal may themselves begin speaking as early as the first birthday or shortly thereafter. Infants with less encouragement may not start until the age of two or even later. Skill at such cognitive tasks as remembering long lists of objects develops much earlier in societies that consider such activities important for young children than in societies that consider them unimportant.

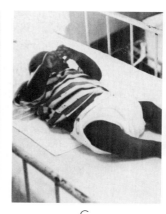
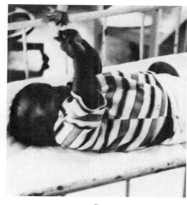

A   B   C   D

13-6 **First attempts at reaching**

Maturation produces rapid changes in what happens when a bright toy is held over a baby's crib. Very young babies (A), typically lying with head to one side, pay only slight attention. Later (B) they occasionally watch the hand that is extended in the same direction the head is turned. At about three and a half months (C) they no longer hold the head to the side and may clasp their hands together beneath the toy. Soon they begin to raise their clasped hands toward the object (D). This is the final stage before they actually reach for the object with an open hand and try to grasp it (23).

Intellectual development

The early years bring about marked advances in intellectual development—increased ability to remember past experiences, to make inferences, and to solve problems. Even at the age of three, children have remarkably good memories. In one experiment, 3-year-olds watched while five different toys were placed under five boxes of different shapes and colors. After the boxes had been hidden by a screen for a few seconds, the children were asked to find one of the toys—a doll, for example. Most of the 3-year-olds were able to remember which box covered the toy they were asked to find, indicating that they could keep track of five different objects without difficulty (25). And of course children at the age of three are only beginning to blossom intellectually. In terms of the Piaget theory of intellectual development that was discussed on pages 211–15, they have advanced only as far as the early part of the preoperational stage.

Many factors contribute to intellectual development. One is improvement in the process of perception. As children grow older, they begin to know what to search for in the environment and how to go about it. They develop strategies for seeking important information and ignoring irrelevant information. Their attention becomes more selective and they are able to maintain it over a longer time span. Their scanning of the environment becomes more systematic and orderly.

Progress in perceptual efficiency has been charted by recording children's eye movements, as

EYE MOVEMENTS:

The design to be scanned

Three-year-old

Six-year-old

 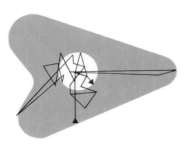 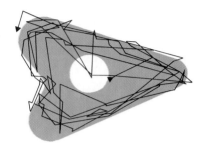

13-7 Progress in eye movements and scanning

When children were asked to study and remember the design at the left, a typical 3-year-old scanned the design with the simple eye movements shown at the center. A typical 6-year-old employed the much more elaborate and efficient scanning at the right (26).

shown in Figure 13-7. When 3-year-olds are asked to look at and remember an unfamiliar design, they do not yet know how to conduct an efficient search for information. They tend to keep their eyes fixed on parts of the design for a long time and may never get around to all the details. But 6-year-olds scan the entire design with rapid and extensive eye movements, paying particular attention to the contour line that determines its shape. Older children also become more adept at perceiving details (27)

and organizing them into meaningful patterns and entities.

Another important factor in intellectual development is a growing skill at understanding and using language, as was discussed on pages 180–86. In turn, adeptness with language facilitates the formation of concepts—which, as was discussed on pages 188–90, helps organize information into categories and facilitates the deep processing that creates long-lasting memory.

Personality development: birth to eighteen months

As with intellectual progress, the development of personality also seems to proceed in an orderly way, through a series of stages merging one into another. All the aspects of personality—emotions,

motives, and ways of coping with conflicts—begin to appear and undergo change. As children grow from the crib to the age where they can move about, then to the preschool age, and later into schoolchildren interacting closely with their class-mates and teachers, they enter into new and widening circles of influence. Their changing social experiences, going hand in hand with their intellectual development, mold their personalities in many different ways, for better or for worse.

The first stage of this process lasts from birth to about the age of eighteen months. During this period the infant has only limited social experiences, usually centering on one person who constitutes the greatest influence. Usually this person is the mother. It can, however, be someone else—the father, a grandparent, a babysitter, or a day-care teacher who takes care of the baby's first needs. Personality development depends to a large extent on the establishment of *attachment* to the person who constitutes the main source of interaction, comfort, and care.

The importance of attachment

Much psychological thinking about the very earliest development of attachment stems from a famous series of experiments by Harry F. Harlow, who took baby monkeys from their own mothers and placed them with doll-like objects that he called "surrogate mothers." As is shown in Figure 13-8, Harlow gave his baby monkeys two such surrogate mothers. One was made of wire, with a bottle and nipple from which the monkey received milk. The other was made of sponge rubber and terrycloth; it was an object to which the baby monkey could cling.

As the photographs show, the baby monkeys strongly preferred the terrycloth doll to the wire doll. Indeed they clung to the terrycloth mother even when feeding from the other. When a new

13-8 Baby monkey and surrogate mothers
The baby monkey has been taken from its own mother and placed with two surrogate mothers. Note how it clings to the terrycloth mother, even when feeding from the wire mother and especially when exploring a new and unfamiliar object that has been placed in the cage.

object was placed in the cage, they clung to the terrycloth mother while making their first hesitant and tentative attempts to discover what this strange and at first frightening object might be (28). Obviously there was something about the terrycloth surrogate that provided the baby monkey with what in human terms would be called comfort, protection, and a secure base from which it could explore new aspects of the environment.

In human infants during the first two years of life, attachment takes the form of a strong tendency to approach particular people, to be receptive to care from them, and to be least afraid when in their presence. Human babies, like monkeys, seem to be born with an innate tendency to become attached to the adults who care for them. They show a strong preference to approach the people who have served as continuous caretakers. This preference is particularly noticeable when they are bored, frightened, or in distress.

Attachment and exploration

The inborn tendency to attachment is a valuable asset in survival. It helps infants find nurturance and protection from distress and dangers, real or imagined. But if the tendency to remain closely attached to a parent persisted, children would never outgrow their dependency on their caretakers. To become self-sufficient, they must explore the environment, encounter new objects and new experiences, and learn how to cope with them.

Oddly, though attachment and exploration seem to be conflicting tendencies, they actually work hand in hand. Note in Figure 13-8 how the baby monkey engages in both activities at once—cautiously exploring a new object while clinging to its terrycloth surrogate mother. Human babies also seem to gather courage for exploration from their attachment to their mothers. In one experiment, babies just under a year old were placed in a strange room that contained a chair piled high with and surrounded by toys. When baby and mother were in the room together, the baby actively looked at the toys, approached them, and touched them. All this exploratory behavior dropped off, however, if a stranger was present or if the mother left the room (29).

The beginnings of anxiety

The experiment just described also produced results that point to another phase of development in the first eighteen months—namely, the first appearance of signs of anxiety. When the babies were left alone in the room, many of them very quickly began to cry, to make what appeared to be a rather frantic search for the mother, or to do both. They were exhibiting *separation anxiety,* which first appears among American babies around the age of eight months.

A possible explanation for separation anxiety is that the disappearance of the mother creates a strange and inexplicable situation that conflicts with the motive for certainty—which, as was discussed on page 372, is a very strong human motive. Since babies cannot understand or explain the disappearance of their mother, they become anxious. In an experiment that supports this conclusion, it was found that babies rarely cried if their mother left by way of a familiar exit, such as the doorway from the child's bedroom. Presumably this was an everyday event that the babies had assimilated into their experience. But they did cry if their mother disappeared in an unfamiliar way—for example, behind the door of a closet (30).

It might seem simpler to regard separation anxiety as reflecting the child's attachment to the caretaker, but this does not seem to be the case. Babies

13-9

A weird "stranger" and infant anxiety

The baby is reacting to the sight of the distorted mask—perhaps because it violates perceptual expectancies. At an earlier age, before learning what the human face is supposed to look like, the baby might have smiled instead of showing anxiety.

brought up at home, with their mother almost always around and with opportunities for attachment at a maximum, are no more likely to show separation anxiety than children who spend much of their time at day-care centers (31). American children reared by their mother display no more separation anxiety than children brought up in Israeli kibbutzim, where the mothers are absent for most of the day (32). Among children everywhere, regardless of child-rearing practices, separation anxiety begins at about eight months, seems most intense at thirteen to fifteen months, then gradually begins to disappear (33).

Even before separation anxiety becomes apparent, babies show what is called *stranger anxiety*.

They will usually smile if the mother shows her face above the crib. But if a stranger's face appears, they often show anxiety by turning away and perhaps breaking into tears. Again, the explanation may be that the appearance of the strange face creates uncertainty. The baby has acquired some sort of mental representation or perceptual expectation of the familiar face, which is violated by the unfamiliar face. Indeed behavior that seems to indicate stranger anxiety can sometimes be produced by showing the baby a distorted mask of the human face, as is shown in Figure 13-9. Among children everywhere, stranger anxiety first appears at about the age of seven months, increases to around the first birthday, then declines.

The first social demands: eighteen months through three years

The second important period in personality development, roughly from eighteen months through the third year, is dominated by children's first important experiences with the demands of society. When they leave the crib and begin walking about the house, they find innumerable objects that look like

toys provided for their own special delight but that in fact are expensive and fragile pieces of household equipment—or, like knives and electric light cords, are dangerous. For the first time, therefore, they encounter discipline. They discover that they can no longer do whatever they please. The rules of the home say that they must not destroy valuable property and must not get into dangerous situations. At the same time they encounter a rule of society holding that the elimination drive must be relieved only in the bathroom. They undergo that much-discussed process called toilet training.

The horizons of these children widen. They leave the self-centered environment of the crib and begin to take their place in the world of people, property, and property rights. Sometimes smoothly, sometimes with stormy difficulties, they begin to learn to become disciplined members of society.

Social demands and inner standards

In toilet training, children must learn *not* to do something—not to respond immediately to the bodily sensations that call for relief of the elimination drive. They must also learn *not* to respond to such external stimuli as the cupboard full of dishes that they would like to explore or the lamp that they would like to smash to the floor. In other words, they begin in this period to control and forgo forms of behavior that would ordinarily be their natural responses to internal or external stimuli.

The way they accomplish this difficult form of learning seems to depend chiefly on their relationship with the parent or other caretaker to whom they have formed an attachment. Their growing intellectual ability makes them aware of what the caretaker expects. If the relationship is a warm one, surrounded by mutual trust and pleasure, they seem to want to comply (34).

It is around the age of two that children first develop inner standards and the desire to live up to them, mentioned on pages 372–73 as one of the most powerful of motives. In one study, 2-year-olds watched someone play in a complicated manner—such as pretending to use toy kitchenware to cook a meal for a family—and then were told that it was

their turn to play with the toys. Many of them broke into tears or ran to their mother. Apparently they felt obligated to play with the toys in an equally sophisticated manner, yet they were unsure of their ability. This uncertainty over living up to a standard that was entirely self-imposed—since nobody taking part in the experiment suggested that they imitate the cooking—created anxiety and distress (35). The study indicates that children at the end of the second year have a remarkable understanding about their conduct and their abilities—and the way these may or may not live up to what other people seem to expect of them and to their own standards of doing the right thing. Younger children do not have these insights and standards and show no signs of distress when placed in the same situation.

The place of rewards and punishments

In learning to meet the social demands first encountered during the period from eighteen months to three years, rewards and punishments probably also play a part. Children are usually rewarded with praise and fondling when they are successful at toilet training or refrain from playing with a lamp after being told "No." And they may be punished, with disapproval if not physically, when they soil themselves, break something, or get into forbidden places. But the desire to live up to inner standards of proper conduct seems to appear even before children have learned to become anxious over possible punishment—and to have a stronger influence on behavior.

Punishment can actually upset the delicate balance between children's natural, constructive urge to explore the environment and the requirement of social discipline. This early period of life holds exciting possibilities for children and their self-image as active, competent, and increasingly self-sufficient human beings. By moving about in the world for

Psychology and Society

Being a good parent to the 2-year-old

Parents face a difficult problem with 2-year-olds. Certainly they must teach children to avoid danger. They must also try to curb any inclinations to let exploration turn into destruction. But there is a fine line to be drawn. At what point do constructive attempts to preserve children's safety and responsibility turn into harmful repression that may thwart normal development?

Psychology's findings about the inner standards of 2-year-olds emphasize the problem. As children grow increasingly conscious of themselves and their world, they spontaneously become aware of what is expected of them. They can distinguish between right and wrong. They become concerned over their ability to perform and the possibility of failure. They want to live up to their own standards of competence and goodness. The danger is that they may become overconcerned, overfearful, and inhibited. In Freudian terms, they may develop superegos so strong as to be crippling.

Some parents are overprotective of their 2- to 3-year-olds. They try to keep their children "tied to their apron strings" and object to any attempt by the children to undertake activities on their own. Other parents are too concerned with neatness

and order. They are upset when children make the slightest mess, get the least bit dirty, or merely touch a newly polished table. When parents are overprotective or overneat—and convey their concern either through punishment or in more subtle ways—children can acquire too much anxiety. Their fear of being disapproved of by their parents or violating their own rapidly shaping inner standards may generalize to all new objects or new activities. As a result they may develop strong inhibitions against trying anything new or challenging, including attempts to adjust to other people.

Parents who are more permissive during this difficult period, on the other hand, can set the stage for spontaneous, self-reliant, and effective behavior. Though they must stop their children at times, they do so only when absolutely necessary. They encourage attempts at anything new and constructive, such as drawing pictures or riding a tricycle. Thus their children learn that only some kinds of exploratory behavior are forbidden, not all. They discover that curiosity and attempts to operate on the environment are generally approved. They are likely to make a good start toward independence and self-confidence.

the first time, they acquire all kinds of fascinating information about the environment. By handling objects—and sometimes, unfortunately, destroying them—they learn that they have some power over the environment. They discover that they can roam about the world and perhaps rearrange it to their liking. They can reach for objects they want. They

can move objects around. They learn that they can satisfy many of their own desires. By reaching into the cookie jar, they can relieve hunger. By crawling under the coat a visitor has thrown on the sofa, they can find warmth. How parents can best aid in this exploration and discovery is discussed in a box on Psychology and Society.

The preschool years: four and five

By the time children are four, they begin to venture outside the home and play with other children. They may go to nursery school or kindergarten. This increasing social experience appears to be essential to normal development. Even monkeys, if raised solely in the company of the mother, with no opportunity to interact with other young monkeys, often turn out to be overfearful or overaggressive (36). As children move into broader social circles, they learn among other things that the world is made up of males and females, for whom society decrees different kinds of behavior. Boys begin to take on the characteristics that society considers appropriate to males, and girls to take on the characteristics considered appropriate to females. (This sex typing was discussed in the postscript to Chapter 10.)

Children of four and five become adept at using language and concepts. They continue to acquire

Why is the little girl unhappy? A problem in living up to inner standards?

inner standards and the urge to live up to them—and this process gives them their first feelings of guilt, representing that mysterious mechanism called conscience. Moreover, a new factor begins to influence their personalities. This is the period in which children begin to identify with their parents.

The identification process

Exactly what *identification* means and how it takes place are matters of debate. To psychoanalysts, it is a complex process involving the Oedipus complex and the superego, as was explained in Chapter 12. To many psychologists it means that children come to feel that they and their parents share a vital bond of similarity. Children bear the family name. They are often told that they look like their parents. Thus they consider themselves in many significant ways to be similar to their parents. Consequently they feel more secure, for they view their parents as stronger and more competent than themselves. They begin to imitate their parents' behavior to increase this similarity—and to share vicariously in the parents' strengths, virtues, skills, and triumphs.

Children with intelligent parents often come to think of themselves as intelligent. A boy whose father holds a job requiring physical strength usually begins to think of himself as being strong, and a girl with an attractive mother thinks of herself as being attractive. Unfortunately, children identify with their parents' faults as well as with their virtues, and it is not unusual for children to become aware of their parents' defects. They may see that their father is unable to hold a job and is the object of ridicule in the community or that their mother drinks

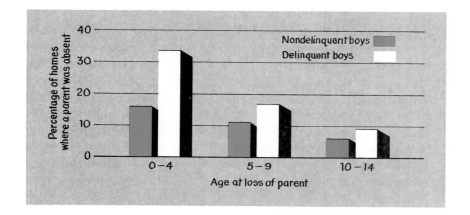

13-10
**Delinquency and loss
of a parent**

A study of the home backgrounds of delinquent boys, as compared with a matched control group of nondelinquent boys, found that considerably more of the delinquents had lost a parent through death, divorce, or other causes—particularly when they were very young (37).

too much and is unwelcome in the neighbors' houses. They may hear relatives criticize their parents. Or they may hear divorced parents bitterly criticize each other's conduct. Under such circumstances many children begin to believe that they too are unworthy, unlovable, hateful, stupid, lazy, or mean. Many children treated in guidance clinics for psychological problems exhibit identification with a "bad" parent.

Children may also be affected adversely by the loss of a parent. This is true when the loss occurs at any time in childhood, but especially when it happens before the end of the preschool years. As Figure 13-10 shows, a substantial number of delinquent boys come from homes in which a parent died or was absent for other reasons, with the percentage of delinquency greatest among the boys who were youngest when the absence began. Of the many ways in which the death of a parent or divorce can hamper a child's development, one is interference with the normal workings of the identification process.

Children and their peers: six to ten

The social influences that begin in the preschool years expand dramatically when children enter elementary school. Suddenly they come into close contact with large numbers of their peers—boys and girls of the same age with whom they share work and play. They spend much of their time with new teachers. They have to prove their competence at school tasks and at skills admired by fellow pupils. Although the home continues to be important in development, outside factors begin to play an increasingly influential role.

The classroom: success or failure?

In the world that children enter at six there is a new adult—the teacher—whose discipline they must conform to and whose acceptance they must court. Ordinarily the teacher is a woman, like the mother, and children's behavior toward their mother can be generalized toward her. But boys who are identifying with their father and rebelling against their mother often have trouble in the early grades. They may be less fearful of rejection by the teacher and therefore more reluctant to accept her influence. They typically get lower marks and cause more disciplinary problems than do girls.

The teacher usually plays a dual role in pupils' development. First, she teaches the intellectual skills appropriate to our society. Second, and perhaps even more important to personality development, she tries to encourage a motive for intellectual mastery. It is in the early years of school that children crystallize their inner standards of intellectual mastery and begin to feel anxiety if they do not live up to the standards. By the age of ten, largely because of the school experience, some children have developed an expectancy of success that is likely to bolster their self-confidence throughout life. Others have developed expectations and fears of failure—even the signs of learned helplessness.

Finding a place among peers

Besides adjusting to teachers and schoolwork, children must also learn to live with their schoolmates. And during the years from six to ten these peers have a particularly strong influence. There are three chief reasons.

1 Evaluation

It is mainly by comparing themselves with their classmates that children judge their own qualities. By the age of ten, they begin to lose some of their faith in the wisdom of adults. They seem to sense that their parents are either too full of praise for their virtues or too critical of their faults. They conclude that they can get a more realistic reading of their value from other children. For one thing, they can make direct comparisons. They can determine their rank among their classmates on such attributes as intelligence, strength, and skills of various kinds. For another thing, they believe that their classmates' opinions seem more objective, honest, and easily interpreted than their parents' judgments. They have no trouble determining whether other children regard them as competent and likeable or foolish and unpleasant.

2 Assignment of social role

It seems to be characteristic of human society, at least in our own culture, that every group has a leader, a close adviser to the leader, and a scapegoat on whom the group takes out its aggressions. Often there is also an individual who is looked up to as a source of wisdom, as well as one who acts as court jester, or clown. There may be a rebel and a psychotic. These roles, into which individuals naturally gravitate or are pushed by others, are found in groups of children as well as of adults. Once children have achieved or been assigned a role, they usually take it seriously, receive some kind of satisfaction from it, and assume more and more of the appropriate traits. The child who is a leader in the first grade, for example, is likely to develop many of the traits of skilled leadership. The class clown becomes increasingly buffoonlike.

3 Rebellion against the adult world

Most schoolchildren are to some degree rebellious against the adult world. (This has been especially true of boys, because sex typing has encouraged rebelliousness.) They are inclined to resent adult restrictions on the display of hostility and demands for cleanliness, order, and quiet. In the company of

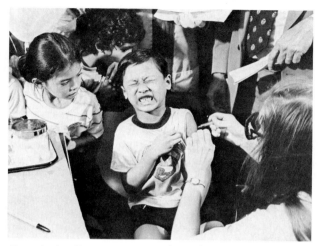
One of school's traumas: compulsory shots.

their peers, these young rebels can express their hostilities, make a mess, be noisy, and do all the other things that the adult world forbids. When they do so, they often receive the admiration of their classmates rather than disapproval.

The road to being dominant or submissive

One personality trait that is partially set by the end of the early school years is the tendency to be dominant or submissive in relations with other people. Children of ten who actively make suggestions to the group, try to influence and persuade others, and resist pressure from others often tend to remain dominant in their social relations. Children who are quiet and like to follow the lead of others may remain passive and submissive.

The tendency to be dominant or submissive is in part a function of group acceptance. Children who believe that they are admired by the group are likely to develop enhanced self-confidence and dominance over others. Children who do not consider themselves admired by the group are likely to develop feelings of inferiority and to be submissive. Physical attributes play an important part. The large, strong boy and the attractive girl are more likely to be dominant. The small, frail boy and the unattractive girl are likely to be submissive. Other factors are identification with a dominant or submissive parent and the kind of control exercised by the parents. Permissive parents tend to influence their children in the direction of dominance, while parents who restrict their children's activities tend to influence them in the direction of submissiveness.

New emphasis on inner standards

Although the motive to live up to inner standards appears by about the age of two, it plays a relatively minor part in behavior for some years. A preschool girl, for example, does not think of a kiss from her mother in terms of inner standards. She values the kiss for its own sake, because it satisfies the motive for affiliation and affection. By the time she is about eight, however, she takes a different view. She is likely to have developed an inner standard that says in effect, "I should be valued by my parents"—and she values a kiss as evidence that she is living up to this standard.

In general, it is in the early school years that the desire to live up to inner standards begins to take a top position in the hierarchy of motives. Three standards that become especially important are these:

1 Being valued by parents, teachers, and peers.
2 Mastering physical and mental skills.
3 Achieving harmony between thoughts and behavior. (Children develop a standard that calls for them to behave rationally and sensibly—and in a way that confirms their self-concept

and their identification with their parents and their other heroes.)

For children who have been sex-typed in the traditional manner, a fourth standard assumes prominence. These children want to behave in a manner appropriate to the sex typing—boys by exhibiting strength, independence, and athletic skills, girls by demonstrating social skills and suppressing any urges toward aggression.

The 10-year-old as a future adult

By the age of ten, children have made spectacular progress from their helpless days in the crib. Their body and nervous system have grown to near maturity. They are capable of many physical skills. Intellectually, they are well along in Piaget's stage of concrete operations and about to embark on the final stage of formal operations. Their personality has changed and blossomed. They now display many individual differences in personality—like those apparent in Figure 13-11.

In some ways, the 10-year-old child offers a reasonably accurate preview of the future adult. The trend of physical development and the pattern of mental processes have been established. Personality traits have emerged and may persist through adolescence and into adulthood, as indicated by the correlations shown in Figure 13-12. But note that the correlations are by no means perfect. Some are indeed very low. The child's personality is still subject to change—for development, though it proceeds rapidly and dramatically through the first ten years, does not end at that point. Adolescence and adulthood, as will now be seen, may switch development into entirely new channels.

13-11 Two sisters, two different personalities
The two young daughters of an astronaut exhibit very different reactions while watching their father on a space-walk broadcast over television. The girl at right stifles a yawn while her older sister casts a reproachful glance.

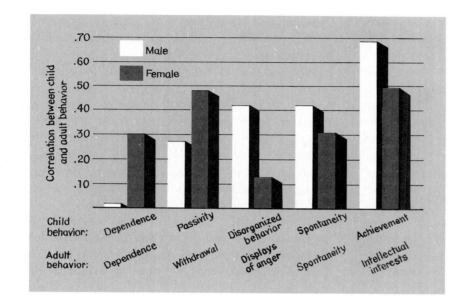

13-12
Some relationships between childhood traits and adult personality
The correlations were obtained by rating the behavior of children aged six to fourteen, then making ratings of the same subjects after they had become young adults. For males, note that dependence in childhood shows almost no correlation with dependence as an adult—but striving for achievement shows a high correlation. For females, disorganized behavior in childhood shows little correlation with displays of anger in adulthood—but striving for achievement shows a fairly high correlation (38).

Adolescence: fun or fury?

The question of whether adolescence is a joy or a burden has been pondered by many psychologists (as well as by many adolescents). The first American psychologist to become concerned with the problems of growing up concluded that adolescence was all in all a difficult time of life—a period of "storm and stress" (39). Many other psychologists agree. One study found that substantial numbers of people, looking back on their lives when they had reached the age of thirty, felt that their adolescent years were the time when they were most confused and their morale at its lowest ebb. They mentioned such difficulties as striving for recognition from peers of their own and the opposite sex, being under anxiety-producing pressures from their parents for scholastic and social achievement, and trying to establish their independence while still financially dependent on their parents (40).

Other psychologists, however, have reached different conclusions. Some studies have found that most adolescents, far from being in bitter rebellion, have a warm and mutually respectful relationship with their parents (41). And some investigators have concluded that most adolescents, far from being hopelessly confused and demoralized, are actually well adjusted (42). The conflicting evidence may reflect the vast range of individual differences—in both experiences and reactions to these experiences—that mark a period when all of us undergo rapid and intense growth, both physical and psychological.

The adolescent growth spurt

Adolescence is not so much a natural state of events as an invention of the modern industrial society. In simpler societies, even today in many parts of the world, the transition from childhood to full membership in the community is so smooth and imperceptible that it does not have a name. Children begin helping with the work of the community as soon as they can—and one day, without fuss, they quietly become self-sufficient and independent of their parents. They start rearing their own families and the cycle starts over again.

But the work of an industrial society requires a prolonged education. Most Americans remain in school at least until they are around eighteen. Many go to college until their early twenties. Some people who train for professions—for example, physicians—may not be able to earn a living until they are thirty. It is difficult to determine at exactly what point, in this extended preparation for full participation in society, the child becomes an adolescent and the adolescent becomes an adult.

Adolescence is usually defined as beginning with the onset of puberty—marked by menstruation in the female, the production of sperm in the male. This can occur at any time between the ages of eleven and eighteen, usually a year or two earlier in girls than in boys. The onset of puberty is almost invariably accompanied by rapid physical growth. A girl may suddenly grow three to five inches in height in a single year, a boy four to six inches. Along with the growth comes a change in physical proportions and strength. The girl begins to look like a woman, the boy like a man. All these changes are set into motion by increased activity of the pituitary gland, stimulating the sex glands (page 68) to produce large quantities of estrogen in the female and androgens in the male.

For boys, early puberty is a distinct advantage. These boys quickly become physically stronger and thus better athletes than classmates who are slower to mature. It has been found that they are more highly regarded by their peers (43) and by adults.

They tend to develop a great deal of self-confidence, social poise, and leadership abilities. Boys who are slow to show the growth spurt, on the other hand, continue to be treated as "little boys" while their bigger and more mature classmates are gaining this new respect. Sometimes they try to make up for their physical and social disadvantages by working too hard to attract attention. Sometimes they draw into a shell. Though they catch up later in physical development, they may continue as adults to be less confident, sociable, and enterprising, and more rebellious (44).

For girls, early puberty is a mixed blessing. It is awkward to look like an adult in a schoolroom full of children—especially to tower over the boys in the class. Moreover, early puberty makes a girl seem sexually provocative at a time when she is still unable psychologically to cope with such reactions

Developing a social identity: one of the many difficult tasks of adolescence.

(45). Later, however, girls who mature early seem to benefit. By the time they reach junior high school they seem to have a better opinion of themselves and better relations with both their classmates and their parents than girls who were late in starting puberty (46).

The search for identity

Adolescents typically begin to feel very grown-up and to crave independence. They seek to establish a sense of identity—that is, to think of themselves as possessing a distinct and unique character, of being people in their own right. But the search is surrounded by troublesome questions: *Who am I? What am I? What do I want to do with my life?*

Adolescents are concerned about the practical matter of choosing a career—a task complicated by the fact that today's society, though it seems to offer a bewildering number of possibilities, has few desirable positions open to young people. (The number of unemployed or underemployed has been greater in recent years for young people than for any other group.) They are also concerned about such intangible issues as moral values and religion. They are now well into Piaget's final stage of cognitive development—the stage of formal operations, as described on page 214—and can think in abstractions, form theories of what life is all about, and contemplate what society might be rather than what it seems to be. Often their thinking makes them critical of the values held by society and by their parents. Indeed the relationship between adolescents and parents is fraught with difficulties (but also rich in opportunities), as discussed in the box on Psychology and Society on page 500.

Studies of the mood of today's adolescents indicate that they tend to emphasize such values as love, friendship, privacy, tolerance, self-expression,

Playful yet serious: the first attempts to establish relationships with the opposite sex.

and self-fulfillment. Many are skeptical of the ethics and efficiency of government, business, and other social institutions. Some feel alienated from society—a fact that may help explain why such signs of psychological distress as delinquency, suicide, and adolescent pregnancies have increased in the last twenty years. Yet, despite the problems and the casualties, the majority of adolescents are at least reasonably well adjusted and confident about their future (51).

Sexual and moral development

One activity of overriding importance revolves around the first serious attempts to establish relationships with the opposite sex. Adolescents must try to establish their sexual identities at the same time they are coping with all the other difficulties of becoming adults. Society's sexual attitudes are more permissive today than in the past, as was

Psychology and Society

Adolescents and parents: enemies or friends?

Adolescents often complain that parents are impossible to live with. Parents complain that adolescents are impossible. Are they both right? Is this an inescapable fact of life?

Clashes are inevitable. Adolescents, in the midst of their struggle to establish identity, tend to be wrapped up in their own thoughts—preoccupied with their emerging view of the world, their behavior, and their appearance. They sometimes seem oblivious to anything else, including clocks, chores, and social amenities. Parents, as it happens, are often going through an identity crisis of their own. At the time their children are in adolescence, parents are at an age when some of them are inclined to feel that the world is closing in, shutting off the options of life style and career they had when younger (47).

The adolescent search for independence often takes the form of struggle against authority and discipline. To parents, surrendering authority often comes hard. After regarding daughters and sons as children for so many years, it is difficult to start treating them as adults. How can all the problems be made more bearable?

A great deal, it turns out, depends on the parents. Studies have shown that two kinds of parents aggravate the difficulties. The first insist that their word is law and that adolescents have no right to make any decisions. The second take a totally hands-off position—either because they do not really care or because they have exaggerated notions about the wisdom of letting children "do their own thing." In the first case, adolescents frequently display continued dependency, lack of confidence, and low self-esteem (48). In the second case, they may fail to develop a sense of responsibility for their own actions.

A recent study of high-school students and their mothers found that students who displayed the fewest behavior problems tended to have a very similar home background. Their mothers had a firm and fairly conservative set of values and clearly expressed their disapproval of using drugs, alcohol abuse, lying, and stealing. They enforced rules about doing homework and getting home at a set hour. But they also had a warm and affectionate relationship with the adolescents and offered them a good deal of independence and support (49). It appears that the best antidote to adolescent aches and pains is the opportunity to identify with and imitate parents who are not too strict, not too permissive—but reasonable, fair, respectful, and eager to show the road to adult responsibility and happiness (50).

discussed in the postscript to Chapter 9. But despite this more lenient atmosphere—or perhaps because of it—adolescents face many confusions and self-doubts. In the words of one group of investigators who have spent much time studying the sexual behavior of teenagers, "coping with sexual development remains a lonely and overly silent experience" (52).

Moral standards in general—not only of sexual but of other types of behavior as well—usually

Preconventional Level

Seven-year-old children are oriented to the consequences of their behavior.

Stage 1. Defer to the power of adults and obey rules to avoid trouble and punishment.

Stage 2. Seek to satisfy their own needs by behaving in a manner that will gain rewards and the return of favors.

Conventional Level

At around ten, children begin to become oriented to the expectations of others and to behave in a conventional fashion.

Stage 3. Want to be "good" in order to please and help others and thus receive approval.

Stage 4. Want to "do their duty" by respecting authority (parents, teachers, God) and maintaining the social order for its own sake.

Postconventional Level

Adolescents become oriented to more abstract moral values and their own consciences.

Stage 5. Think in terms of the rights of others; the general welfare of the community, and a duty to conform to the laws and standards established by the will of the majority. Behave in ways they believe would be respected by an impartial observer.

Stage 6. Consider not only the actual laws and rules of society but also their own self-chosen standards of justice and respect for human dignity. Behave in a way that will avoid condemnation by their own consciences.

13-13

Kohlberg's stage theory of moral development
Summarized in the table are the six stages in moral development found by Kohlberg. Among 7-year-olds, almost all moral judgments are made at the preconventional level. By sixteen, only a few are made at this level, and judgments made at the postconventional level become important (53, 54).

undergo rapid and often lasting change during adolescence. Though such standards appear much earlier, they are originally based mostly on a desire to obtain approval and avoid criticism. In adolescence, the standards take a new form— dictated not by mere self-interest but by principles.

The manner in which moral judgments develop has been studied extensively by Lawrence Kohlberg, who questioned boys seven years old through adolescence. Kohlberg presented his subjects with a number of hypothetical situations involving moral questions like these: If a man's wife is dying for lack of an expensive drug that he cannot afford, should he steal the drug? If a patient who is fatally ill and in great pain begs for a mercy killing, should the physician agree? By analyzing the answers and particularly the reasoning by which his subjects reached their answers, Kohlberg determined that moral judgments develop through a series of six stages, as shown in Figure 13-13. Children in the two stages of what he calls the preconventional level base their ideas of right and wrong largely on self-interest. They are concerned chiefly with avoiding punishment and gaining rewards.

Later, in the two stages of what he calls the conventional level, they become concerned about the approval of other people. Finally, in the two stages of the postconventional level, they become concerned with abstract moral values and the dictates of their own consciences.

Thus children's reasons for good behavior progress from sheer self-interest to a desire for the approval of others and finally to a concern for their own moral values and the approval of their own conscience. Apparently this stage-by-stage development takes place in other societies as well as our own. Kohlberg has found a similar progression among children in Mexico and Taiwan (55).

Development–and sometimes about-face–in adulthood

Though adolescence is in a sense the last step in the transformation of the infant into the adult, development does not end when we become old enough to vote, earn our own living, and marry if we wish. At eighteen, we have lived only about a quarter of today's average lifetime. If male, we can expect to live another fifty-two years; if female, another fifty-nine. We will face new crises and either solve or fail at them. We may still change spectacularly in many respects.

The long period from adolescence to old age brings about many physical alterations, as is shown in Figure 13-14. We may continue to look the same to ourselves, but not to our acquaintances. (Indeed people who attend a fortieth college reunion often have difficulty recognizing old

classmates.) At the same time we change on the inside. Personality patterns may become as unrecognizable as faces.

What becomes of the unhappy adolescent?

One of the most startling about-faces in personality has been observed among people who seemed badly maladjusted as adolescents. It has been found that even the most troubled adolescent—a failure in school, unsuccessful in social contacts, unpopular and despondent—may turn into a successful, happy, well-liked, and highly respected adult. In one study, 166 boys and girls were observed from shortly after birth until they were eigh-

26 years old

13-14 Adolescence to old age
The camera recorded these changes
as a woman progressed from 16 to
nearly 90 years old.

16 years old (top)

87 years old

47 years old

teen years old, then observed again at the age of thirty. As an example of the kind of change that some of them displayed between adolescence and adulthood note this finding:

[One subject]—a large, awkward, early-maturing girl who labored under the weight of her size and shyness, feeling that she was a great disappointment to her mother—worked hard for her B average to win approval and was a pedestrian, uninteresting child and adolescent. She had periods of depression, when she could see no point to living. Then, as a junior in college, she got excited over what she was learning (not just in grades to please her mother) and went on to get an advanced degree and to teach in college. Now she has taken time out to have and raise her children. . . . [She is] full of zest for living, married to an interesting, merry, and intelligent man she met in graduate school.

Similarly, a girl who was expelled from school at sixteen and a boy expelled at fifteen—for failing grades and misbehavior—were found to have developed into "wise, steady, understanding parents who appreciate the complexities of life and have both humor and compassion for the human race." An adolescent boy who could only be described as a "listless oddball" had turned into a successful architect and excellent husband and parent who called his adult life "exciting and satisfying." All told, just about half the subjects were living richer and more productive lives as adults than could have been predicted from their adolescent personalities (56).

Is trouble a blessing in disguise?

What causes such marked changes between adolescence and the age of thirty? One conclusion reached by the psychologists who conducted the study is that some people are just naturally "late bloomers." It takes them a long time—and often a change of environment that gets them away from their parents or even to a new community—to find themselves. Taking on a meaningful job may help. So may marriage and especially parenthood, with all its responsibilities and opportunities.

The authors of the study have also concluded that even the problems of a troubled adolescence may sometimes prove a blessing in disguise as the years go by. If adolescents go through a period of "painful, strain-producing, and confusing experiences" but manage to survive them, these experiences may in the long run produce greater insight and stability (57).

It is interesting to note that subjects in the study who seemed perfectly well adjusted in adolescence did not always turn out well as adults. About 20 percent of the subjects were found to have less fulfilling lives at thirty than would have been ex-

pected from the promise they showed at eighteen. Included in this group were a number of men and women whose early lives had been smooth, free from any severe strains, and marked by success in both school and social relations. At eighteen these subjects seemed well poised and self-confident. The boys tended to be much-admired leaders in athletics, the girls to be good-looking and socially skillful. Yet at thirty they were found to be "brittle, discontented, and puzzled." Perhaps too easy a childhood and adolescence, creating no need to face and overcome problems, can sometimes hinder future development.

Erikson's theory of psychosocial development

The idea that personality growth depends on facing and meeting crises is the basis of an influential theory proposed by Erik Erikson, a psychoanalyst who bases his conclusions on observations of people he has treated at all ages, some in childhood and others at various stages of adulthood. Erikson speaks in terms of *psychosocial development*. That is to say, he holds that development is a twofold process in which the psychological development of individuals (their personalities and views of themselves) proceeds hand in hand with the social relations they establish as they go through life. He has suggested that this development can be divided into eight stages, in each of which individuals face new social situations and encounter new problems (or "psychosocial crises"). They may emerge from the new experiences with greater maturity and richer personalities—or they may fail to cope successfully with the problems and their development may be warped or arrested.

Erikson's eight stages are shown in Figure 13-15. They begin with the child in the first year of life. At this stage the child's social relations are confined to the caretaker. Out of this relationship, Erikson be-

Stage	Crisis	Favorable outcome	Unfavorable outcome
Childhood			
First year of life	Trust versus mistrust	Faith in the environment and future events	Suspicion, fear of future events
Second year	Autonomy versus doubt	A sense of self-control and adequacy	Feelings of shame and self-doubt
Third through fifth years	Initiative versus guilt	Ability to be a "self-starter," to initiate one's own activities	A sense of guilt and inadequacy to be on one's own
Sixth year to puberty	Industry versus inferiority	Ability to learn how things work, to understand and organize	A sense of inferiority at understanding and organizing
Transition years			
Adolescence	Identity versus confusion	Seeing oneself as a unique and integrated person	Confusion over who and what one really is
Adulthood			
Early adulthood	Intimacy versus isolation	Ability to make commitments to others, to love	Inability to form affectionate relationships
Middle age	Generativity versus self-absorption	Concern for family and society in general	Concern only for self—one's own well-being and prosperity
Aging years	Integrity versus despair	A sense of integrity and fulfillment; willingness to face death	Dissatisfaction with life; despair over prospect of death

13-15

Erikson's stage theory of "psychosocial crises"

Erikson views the life cycle of development, from cradle to grave, as passing through eight stages. Each stage brings new social experiences and new crises—which, if surmounted successfully, lead to constant growth and a steadily enriched personality (58).

lieves, the child learns either to trust the social environment and what it will bring in the future or to be suspicious and fearful of others. In later stages the social environment widens and new psychosocial crises occur, again with outcomes that may be favorable or unfavorable.

Early adulthood, commitment, and marriage

Early adulthood demands many new adjustments. One entails choice of job and career, and often intense preoccupation with efforts to start up the promotional ladder. For women, these years may also require a decision as to whether to pursue a career, to marry and have children, or to do both.

Erikson believes that the really critical event, however, centers on moving into a relationship marked by intimacy, commitment, and love. For most of us, this means marriage—despite all the recent outpouring of books and magazine articles called *What's Killing Our Marriages?* and *Death of the Family.* Statistics show that between 90 and 95 percent of Americans get married sooner or later (59). Among the college-educated, the number is probably even higher. A survey of 2,500 students in the Boston area showed that 94 percent believed they would marry within ten years and 98 percent of them eventually (60).

It is true that far more marriages break up today than in the past. The divorce rate has quintupled since the early part of the century and doubled just since 1965 (61), to the point where more than two million Americans go through the divorce courts every year. But about four out of every five people who get divorced marry again (62), and second marriages seem to be remarkably successful. A survey made in Canada found that about 80 percent of husbands and wives described their remar-

Getting used to being a parent: one of the adjustments demanded in early adulthood.

riages as very satisfactory, 10 percent as satisfactory, and only 10 percent as unsatisfactory (63).

In one way or another, most people seem to cope with the crisis of early adulthood in a reasonably satisfactory manner. They form affectionate and nourishing relationships—in most cases with marriage partners, sometimes with close friends, and often with both. Most of them also commit themselves to children. A 1976 survey showed that about 90 percent of young adult women expected to become mothers (64).

Middle age and its responsibilities

The crisis of middle age, in Erikson's terms, centers on a conflict between "self-absorption" and "generativity." Self-absorption means a narrow concentration on one's own interests—especially in matters of getting ahead in life, making money, and enjoying material comforts. Generativity means a concern for others—partly for the psychological welfare of one's children, partly for humanity in general.

Ideally, Erikson believes, this crisis produces a wider outlook on the meaning of life—a sense of kinship with one's fellow human beings, with the ebb and flow of history, with nature itself. Old goals, especially selfish ones, may be abandoned. New satisfactions of the spirit may be found. People sometimes make radical changes in their life style. Men may switch careers—moving from a job they have held because of accident or habit, or for financial reasons, into something they have always wanted to do. Women who have spent their early years working as homemakers and mothers may take an outside job for the first time, thus encountering new problems but also finding new satisfactions. When the crisis of middle age is met successfully—and a quieter and deeper attitude toward the rhythm of life established—people are prepared to grow old with grace and contentment. The process of development, from its seeds in the newborn baby, has come full flower.

The problems and delights of aging

Old age, like adolescence, is an invention of modern technology. Until recently, the average life expectancy was only about fifty years. This is still true in parts of the world that have not yet caught up with today's advanced techniques of sanitation, nutrition, and medical science.

As recently as about a century ago, old people were a rarity. Typically, men died while they still had an unmarried child living at home. Women, because their genes incline them to greater longevity, lived a few years longer—but usually only until just after the last child married (65). Except for a small minority, the psychology of aging was not a matter for concern. Today, by contrast, there are about 25 million Americans who have passed what is generally considered the retirement age of sixty-five—and the problems and pleasures of the retirement years have become very much a part of psychological investigation.

To Erikson, the aging years represent a fork in the road that can lead either to a heart-warming sense of integrity or to feelings of despair. People who succeed in negotiating this crisis live out the final years of their lives with a sense of self-fulfillment and wisdom. They face the inevitability of death without fear or regret. Those who fail—often because they have not surmounted life's earlier crises—wind up embittered. They are dissatisfied with the way they have lived their lives. They regret what might have been. The prospect of dying fills them with despair.

Is it as bad as they say?

How many people find happiness in their aging years, and how many fail? Psychology's findings are contrary to what is generally assumed. Our society has been described as youth-oriented—and old age is often thought of as a period of decrepitude and dissatisfaction. One study showed that younger people assume that life will become less and less zestful with the passage of time, and they give the aging years the lowest rating of all for happiness and quality of life. But the study also showed that older people themselves tend on the average to give the period a much higher rating. They do not, as is commonly assumed, tend to "live in the past" (66).

There are problems, of course. Some people, after retiring, are plagued by financial difficulties. Some suffer from chronic illnesses. Many have to adjust to the loneliness caused by the death of a mate. Among people over sixty-five are about 1.3 million widowers and 6.8 million widows (67). But in one way or another, most people seem to cope with the problems. A study of men and women in their seventies found that three out of every four were satisfied with their lives. Most of these septuagenarians were still active, at least to the extent

Old age may bring not just what Erikson calls a sense of integrity but also a continuing zest for physical activity.

they found suitable to their physical endurance, and were not especially troubled by loneliness. Only a few showed signs of senility, which is mental impairment caused by brain damage that sometimes occurs with aging (68). In general, most people seem to find that the retirement years are not nearly so bad as they were led to expect—indeed full of pleasures that may differ in kind and intensity but are nonetheless as fulfilling as the joys of youth.

The psychology of dying

The chief reason for today's increased life expectancy is that science has conquered diseases such as pneumonia that formerly killed many people in the prime of life. Most deaths today result from chronic, long-lasting conditions such as cancer and ailments of the heart and circulatory system. Thus people are more likely to be aware that they are approaching the end of life—and must somehow reconcile themselves.

Psychologists have only recently begun to study the cognitive and emotional processes that occur with the knowledge that death is imminent. Their findings thus far are sparse and inconclusive. But the search goes on for information that may help ease this final episode and surround dying with a grace and dignity befitting the human spirit and the remarkable flow of events from cradle to grave.

Summary

1 *Developmental psychology* studies the ways in which children gradually acquire their patterns of thinking, emotions, motives, and other aspects of personality—and the ways in which these patterns may change in later life.
2 Babies at birth differ in: a) sensory thresholds and adaptation, b) activity and irritability, and c) temperament. Most appear to be easy children, some slow-to-warm-up, and some difficult.
3 Traits displayed in infancy often disappear by the time of elementary school.
4 Human infants are extremely impressionable. An unfavorable environment may produce drastic and sometimes long-lasting abnormalities. But infants are also resilient and malleable—capable of changing when circumstances change.
5 Physical development, including the acquisition of such skills as walking and talking, depends largely on the process of *maturation*—the physical changes, taking place after birth, that continue biological growth from fertilized egg cell to adult.
6 Personality development from birth to eighteen months is characterized by *attachment* to the mother or other caretaker. This period is marked by the appearance of *separation anxiety* and *stranger anxiety*.

7 The period from eighteen months through three years is characterized by children's first important experiences with the demands of society. Too much discipline or protection during this period may instill a crippling amount of anxiety and create lifelong inhibitions against trying anything new or challenging. The motive to live up to inner standards first appears at about the age of two.

8 The *preschool years,* four and five, are characterized by: a) the first notions of sex typing and conduct appropriate to males and females, b) the first feelings of guilt and conscience, and c) identification with the parents.

9 From six to ten, children come under the strong influence of their *peers*—that is, other children. Peers provide: a) evaluation, b) a social role, and c) an opportunity for rebellion against the adult world. During this period children acquire a tendency to be dominant or submissive and strong inner standards calling for: a) being valued by parents, teachers, and peers; b) mastering physical and mental skills; and c) achieving harmony between thoughts and behavior.

10 *Adolescence* is characterized physically by the sudden growth spurt that accompanies puberty. Psychologically, this may be a period of "storm and stress" —with much confusion over establishing independence and a sense of identity, striving for recognition, and being under anxiety-producing scholastic and social pressures. However, some studies have shown that most adolescents are well adjusted.

11 Moral standards—of sexual and other types of behavior—usually undergo rapid change during adolescence. Kohlberg has suggested that moral development occurs in six stages, in which children's reasons for good behavior progress from sheer self-interest to a desire for the approval of others and finally to a concern for their own values and the approval of their own consciences.

12 Continuing development in the years after adolescence often produces striking changes. Some of the most troubled and despondent adolescents turn out to lead happy and fulfilling lives as adults, while some untroubled and self-confident adolescents do not live up to their early promise.

13 One of the prominent proponents of the idea that development is a lifelong process is Erikson, who holds that *psychosocial development* (psychological changes occurring with changes in the social environment) proceeds in eight stages extending from infancy to old age.

14 According to Erikson, the critical event in early adulthood is moving into a relationship (usually marriage) marked by intimacy, commitment, and love. Middle adulthood brings a conflict between "self-absorption" (a narrow concentration on one's own interests) and "generativity" (a concern for others). Old age results in either integrity or despair.

$y^2 - 3y - 2 = 0$

A = 1
B = -3
C = -2

$\dfrac{-(-3) \pm \sqrt{-3^2 - 4(1)(-2)}}{2 \cdot 1}$

$\dfrac{+3 \pm \sqrt{9+8}}{2}$ $\dfrac{3 \pm \sqrt{17}}{2}$

$\dfrac{3 + \sqrt{17}}{2}$

$6x^2 + x - 1 = 0$

A = 6
B = 1
C = -1

$\dfrac{-1 \pm \sqrt{1^2 - 4(6)(-1)}}{}$ $\dfrac{-1 \pm \sqrt{1+24}}{}$

Important terms

attachment	maturation	sex typing
caretaker	moral development	slow-to-warm-up children
difficult children	psychosocial development	stranger anxiety
easy children	rooting response	surrogate mother
exploration	sense of identity	
identification	separation anxiety	

Recommended readings

Biehler, R. F. *Child development: an introduction.* Boston: Houghton Mifflin, 1976.

Conger, J. J. *Adolescence and youth: psychological development in a changing world,* 2d ed. New York: Harper & Row, 1977.

Dragastin, S. E., and Elder, G. H., eds. *Adolescence in the life cycle: psychological change and the social context.* New York: Halsted, 1975.

Erikson, E. H. *Childhood and society,* rev. ed. New York: Norton, 1964.

Jessor, R., and Jessor, S. L. *Problem behavior and psychosocial development: a longitudinal study of youth.* New York: Academic Press, 1977.

Kagan, J., Kearsley, R. B., and Zelago, P. R. *Infancy: its place in human development.* Cambridge, Mass.: Harvard University Press, 1978.

Kennedy, C. E. *Human development: the adult years and aging.* New York: Macmillan, 1978.

Mussen, P. H., Conger, J. J., and Kagan, J. *Child development and personality,* 4th ed. New York: Harper & Row, 1974.

Stone, J. L., Smith, H. T., and Murphy, L. B. *The competent infant.* New York: Basic Books, 1974.

Outline

Chapter fourteen

Social psychology
(with a postscript on aggression, altruism, and bystander apathy)

You are walking across the campus on a fine, sunny day. As you round a building, you come upon a group of students staring at a top-floor window. What will you do? Will you ignore them and walk right on? Will you, without breaking stride, glance up to see what has aroused their curiosity? Or will you stop and join them to find out what is going on?

What you are likely to do was demonstrated in an experiment in which psychologists set up a movie camera in an upper window of a New York City building and recorded the behavior of the people on the crowded street below. At a signal, a half-dozen confederates, mingling with the crowd, stopped and stared up at the camera. The film showed that most passersby found their example almost impossible to resist. Four out of five at least looked up. Though New Yorkers always seem to be in a hurry to get somewhere, about one in five actually stopped to join the group of starers. There

was nothing to see—but most passersby took a me-too attitude and looked anyway (1).

Even without any experimental manipulation, a city street offers some convincing evidence of the way other people influence our behavior. As you turn to the next page, note the street scenes in Figure 14-1. The photographs show that the way Americans look and dress has changed drastically from the year 1910 to the present. But in each photograph the people seem to be pretty much cut from the same pattern. Over the decades the street scene changes drastically. People wear hats in one period and abandon them in the next. Dresses go up and down from maxi to midi to mini and back again—or give way to slacks and pantsuits. Men switch from clean-shaven faces and crew cuts to beards and hair down to their shoulders. They shun jewelry or take to wearing it. But at any given moment in history, everybody looks pretty much like everybody else.

1910

Mid 1930s

1980

14-1
The American street scene:
then and now
How Americans look has changed
greatly over the years since 1910—yet,
no matter when the camera records
them, they all look more or less like
their contemporaries.

Society's influence and the process of socialization

At one time, psychology was chiefly interested in the individual. Most psychologists were content to separate the individual person from others, like a zoologist cutting one elephant out of the herd for tagging and measurement, and to study this person's behavior as revealed by experiments and test results. It was generally thought that traits observed in the laboratory gave a fair indication of how people would behave under any circumstances. Psychologists assumed that human personality patterns showed a great deal of consistency. Aggressive people would always tend to be aggressive, regardless of the situation. People who scored well on tests of manual dexterity would always be first-rate watchmakers, no matter where or with whom they worked.

Psychology was only a few decades old, however, when the influence of the social environment became apparent. As far back as 1898, a psychologist found that there can be vast differences between the way people perform on tests, taken in privacy, and their success at similar tasks when they are in company (2). Since this first experiment in what is now called *social psychology,* it has been established that human behavior and human personality are not necessarily consistent at all. It has been found, for example, that a child may be a chronic liar in one social situation (as around teachers) but not in a different social situation (as in the home). Or the child may consistently cheat in the classroom but never when playing with friends (3). Adults may be highly aggressive in some social situations but submissive in others. They may be generous around some people but selfish around others.

Human beings as social animals

Social psychology has been aptly defined as *the study of the manner in which the human being "thinks, feels, and behaves in social situations"* (4). To put this another way, social psychology is the study of how people influence and are influenced by other people, for much of our behavior is both a response and a stimulus to the behavior of others. What we do is determined at least in part—and often to a very great extent—by what other people are doing or what we think they expect us to do. At the same time, what we do helps determine what they do (5).

The individual in any kind of social situation—even in the company of just one other person—is like a football quarterback facing the other team's defensive unit. In deciding what play to attempt, the quarterback takes into account the defensive team's strengths and weaknesses and how it is lining up (or how he expects it to line up). In turn, what the defensive team does depends in large part on what it expects the quarterback to do—and, once the play is under way, on how he does it. The influence works both ways—on the football field and in life in general.

Living in a social setting

Other people are important to us because we human beings are social animals. We do not prowl the world alone or in the company of only a mate, as some other organisms do. Indeed we do not seem capable of existing in isolation. We need the company and help of other human beings to ac-

A scene in a city park, of one of society's shared experiences.

quire even such necessities as food, clothing, shelter, and protection against enemies. We can survive only by establishing some kind of *society*—which is the term applied to any group of people who occupy the same geographical area and cooperate in an accepted pattern of living together.

Ever since human beings appeared on earth they appear to have lived in societies, probably starting with the ancient cave communities. The people who live today in the most undeveloped parts of the world are banded together in some sort of society, like the tribes who occupy thatched huts in the jungles of South America. The people who live in a small rural town or in Chicago constitute a society. The United States itself is a society. Big or little, simple or complex, the society is a universal way of human life.

Learning society's ways

The society into which we are born begins to influence us almost from the moment of birth. As was explained in the preceding chapter, we develop from child to adult not in a vacuum but in close interaction with our parents, family, teachers, and schoolmates. From all these people, we learn the ways of our own society. We learn the English language. We learn how Americans speak, behave toward one another, and express or conceal their emotions. Later we learn what the people in our society believe and what they value. We learn the customs and laws that dictate a whole host of activities, from finding a mate to conducting a business deal.

This process is called *socialization*—the process by which children are integrated into the society through exposure to the actions and opinions of other members of the society. In many ways, children become creatures of their society, molded by its customs and rules (6). The sex typing discussed in the postscript to Chapter 10—the process of teaching males to be masculine and females to be feminine—is one aspect of socialization.

Cultures and subcultures

Every society has its own *culture*, or established way of life. The term culture embraces all the physical objects the society produces as part of its life style—its clothing, shelter, tools, and artistic creations. The term also includes the society's language, beliefs, political structure, family relationships, rules, and customary patterns of behavior. All these aspects of culture vary greatly around the world. The way of life in England calls for driving on the left side of the road, in the Orient for eating with chopsticks, in some countries for disregarding clocks and appointment times. There are societies where the women do all the work and the men devote themselves to ceremony and self-adornment (7). There are places where two friends would never dream of competing against each other in games or athletic contests (8). There are even places where cannibalism is approved.

Whatever the customs and rules may be, every society molds its children in accordance with its own culture. Socialization is a universal process. It is a form of learning that everyone undergoes—and that probably has a more pervasive and lasting effect than anything learned in school (although school also serves to socialize pupils).

In a society as complex as ours, not every child is socialized to follow the same customs and rules. Within our society there exist many *subcultures,* or ways of life that differ from one another in many important respects. Some of these subcultures exist partly because the nation has been settled over the years by people from many different parts of the world, bringing with them their own particular customs and values. Other subcultures have a religious basis. Still others depend on geographical and occupational considerations.

Children are socialized into far different patterns of behavior if they are born in a rural area than if they are born in a small city—and into still other patterns if they are born in a large city. They may grow up as members of subcultures as varied as a Zen commune, the world of music, the academic community, the business community, or the scientific community. The United States is a nation of many subcultures holding very different views on religion, politics, militarism, sexual behavior, the use of drugs, and life styles in general. In one way or another, however, socialization tends to shape people into the pattern of those with whom they have grown up.

The powerful urge to conformity

There are always rebels who resist the influence of socialization and break the rules. Sometimes their rebellion takes the destructive form of flouting laws designed for the protection of the society and its members. But rebellion may also produce progress. Without people who are willing to propose new ideas, a society might remain forever static, locked in a pattern set generations earlier. (Among the historical figures martyred by their society for daring to suggest changes in the culture were Socrates, Christ, Joan of Arc, and Galileo.)

Despite the exceptions, most people observe the customs and rules they have learned—and behave as they believe they are expected to behave. Indeed social psychologists have found that most human beings everywhere display a strong tendency to *conformity,* which is defined as the *yielding by individuals to pressures from the group in which they find themselves.* The group applying the pressure may be the society as a whole or any part of it, such as our family, friends, classmates, or business associates. It may even be made up of total strangers, such as the people sitting around us on a bus or in a theater.

14-2
A famous experiment in conformity

In this group of seven students brought together by psychologist Solomon Asch, No. 6 is the only real subject. All the others are in league with the experimenter. No. 6 believes he is engaging in a study of discrimination among lines such as those shown in Figures 14-3 and 14-4.

The incidents cited at the start of the chapter were harmless types of conformity. It is amusing but not very significant that all of us tend to gawk at a building when others are doing it—or that we follow the dictates of fashion in clothing, hair styles, and jewelry. Often, however, conformity has a much more profound effect on behavior.

The Asch experiment: agreeing that a wrong answer is right

One of the classic experiments on conformity was performed in the 1950s at Swarthmore College by Solomon Asch. It utilized the method illustrated in Figure 14-2, in which one real subject, who thought he was taking part in a study of perceptual discrimination, sat at a table with a group of confederates of the experimenter. The experimenter showed pairs of white cards with black lines of varying length, such as the lines shown in their relative sizes in Figures 14-3 and 14-4, and asked the group which of the lines in Figure 14-4 matched the test line.

For what the experimenter claimed were reasons of convenience, the people sitting around the table were asked to call out their judgments in order, beginning with the student at the experimenter's left. The real subject was always placed near the other end so that he would hear the judgments of

14-3 A test line in the conformity experiment

This was the relative size of one of the lines shown to subjects in the Asch experiment. They were asked which of the lines in Figure 14-4 matched it.

14-4 What line matches?

Which of these three lines, the Asch subjects were asked, matches the one shown in Figure 14-3? The correct answer is line 2. But the experimenter's six confederates around the table insisted unanimously that it was line 1—which is in fact the least like the test line.

several confederates before making his own. Sometimes the confederates gave the right answer, but on some trials they deliberately called out the wrong answer. On these trials 37 percent of the answers given by the real subjects who took part in

14-5

**An "independent" subject—
shaken but unyielding**

In the top photo, student 6 is making his first independent judgment, disagreeing with the group's otherwise unanimous but incorrect verdict. In the other photos his puzzlement and concern seem to increase until, preserving his independence despite the pressure from the group, he announces (bottom), "I have to call them as I see them."

the experiment were also incorrect. In other words, the subjects conformed with the group's wrong judgment much of the time.

Some of the subjects conformed on all trials, others on some but not all. Only one subject out of four remained completely independent and did not conform at any time. Even the subjects who showed independence, however, experienced various kinds of conflict and anxiety, as is readily apparent from the photographs of the subject in Figure 14-5. Some of their comments later were: "Despite everything, there was a lurking fear that in some way I did not

understand I might be wrong." "At times I had the feeling, to heck with it, I'll go along with the rest." "I felt disturbed, puzzled, separated, like an outcast from the rest." Thus the urge to conform—to go along with the group—was strong even among the most independent subjects (9).

**The Milgram experiment:
how to turn ordinary people into sadists**

Another experiment that produced even more dramatic results was performed by Stanley Milgram in a laboratory at Yale. Milgram selected eighty men of various ages and occupational backgrounds and asked them to take part in what he said was an important experiment in learning. Each subject was assigned to a group of four people—the other three of whom, unknown to the subject, were Milgram's assistants. One of the assistants was the "learner" in the make-believe experiment. The other two assistants and the subject were the "teachers," and their job was to instruct the "learner" by punishing him with an electric shock when he made an error. The subject was put at the controls that regulated the amount of shock (see Figure 14-6). Actually, no electricity was hooked up to the controls and no learning took place. The "learner" deliberately made errors and only pretended to feel pain when punished.

Of the eighty subjects, half were placed in a control group. These subjects were not subjected to any pressure to raise the shock levels and did not raise them very high. Thirty-four of these forty control subjects stopped at shock levels listed as "slight" or "moderate." Only six went above 120 volts. But it was a far different story with the other forty subjects. These forty were strongly urged by their fellow "teachers" to raise the amount of electricity higher and higher—and they did. Only six of them refused to go above 120 volts. The other thirty-four went right on, even though the "learner" at first shouted that the shocks were becoming painful and later began to groan and finally scream in pain. Seven of the subjects went up to what they thought was the maximum they could deliver—a "highly dangerous" shock of 450 volts. Many of the experimental subjects showed signs of doubt and distress about engaging in such a sadistic act, yet they conformed anyway to the pressures of their group (10).

A

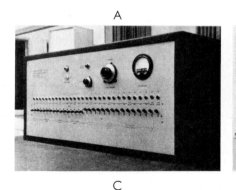

B

C

D

14-6

The Milgram experiment

Some scenes from a film on the Milgram experiment begin with the panel (A), which subjects believed to control the level of shock. In B, electrodes are attached to the wrists of a "learner." In C, a subject who will be at the control panel receives a sample shock of the kind he believes he will administer. In D, a subject breaks off the experiment after reaching as high a shock level as he is willing to administer.

(Copyright 1965 by Stanley Milgram. From the film *Obedience*, distributed by the New York University Film Library.)

Why we conform:
our dependence on our peers

Milgram's subjects were just ordinary people who presumably would never be guilty of cruelty under ordinary circumstances. The fact that they were willing to go to such outrageous lengths under group pressure is eloquent and even frightening proof of how strong is the human tendency to conform. The question, of course, is why do we have these tendencies? Why are they so powerful that they can sometimes make us behave in unexpected and almost unbelievable ways?

One reason seems to be that we depend on the people around us for many of our psychological satisfactions. It is pleasant to be an accepted, well-liked member of the group. It is highly unpleasant to be rejected by the group and perhaps even subjected to ridicule (11). Thus it is generally easier and more rewarding to conform. It can be very difficult to stand alone as a single dissenter.

Studies have shown, indeed, that unanimity within the group is the most powerful factor of all in producing conformity. If we are in a group where everybody agrees, we are under much stronger pressure to conform than if even one person expresses disagreement. This was demonstrated in an ingenious variation of the Asch experiment in which one of the confederates sitting around the table was a black and some of the actual subjects were known to be prejudiced against blacks. When the confederates were unanimous in the incorrect answers they gave, all the subjects showed the usual tendency to conform. But when the black confederate broke the unanimity of the group by giving the correct answer, the subjects were much less likely to conform (12). Even those who might have been expected to reject the black confederate's opinion seemed to welcome the excuse he gave them for breaking away from the others.

Four dress-alikes display one kind of conformity.

Conformity and the theory
of social comparison

Another reason for conformity is that the behavior of the people around us is often the only guide we have as to how we ourselves should behave. If you go to a party where you are the only stranger, how can you fit in? On a new campus, how are you expected to dress, behave in the classroom, and get along with your fellow students? Obviously, you have to look to the people around you for information. What they do is your only guide to what you are expected to do.

The human tendency to look to others for information has led to an important psychological concept called the *theory of social comparison*. The theory maintains that all of us feel the need to evaluate our own conduct, abilities, and opinions. Usually there is no objective and scientific way we can do this. Therefore we can only judge ourselves by comparing ourselves with other people—usually our friends or other people we believe to be similar to ourselves (13).

The more uncertain we are as to where we stand, it has been found, the more likely we are to make and rely on comparisons (14,15). This helps explain the results of the Milgram experiment. The subjects were in a highly uncertain situation. After all, they were taking part in a scientific experiment. And, if they were supposed to stop at a low level of electric shock, why did the controls on the machine go all the way up to 450 volts? They had no way of knowing what to think or how to behave—so they looked to the other "teachers," people who seemed to be just like themselves, for information. They compared their own opinions with the opinions of the others in the group. When the others proved to be so positive about raising the shock levels, who were they to argue otherwise?

Social comparisons and self-esteem

The theory of social comparison, besides explaining some of the facts about conformity, also bears in an important way on how our self-esteem—one might almost say our entire self-image—is affected by the people around us. We judge our abilities as well as our opinions, the theory holds, mostly by comparing ourselves with other people. We cannot state for sure, as a proven fact, that we are good students, good teachers, good athletes, or anything else. We have to try to decide how we rank in comparison with other people—notably our friends and other close associates. And we must also ask, "What do other people think of us?"

The opinions of other people play a far greater part in self-esteem than could ever be imagined by a person who has never been exposed to social psychology and its emphasis on social influences. For dramatic evidence, note this experiment and its surprising results:

The subjects were women attending high school or college. They were asked to try their hand at a

14-7

It's not true—but I believe it!

The graph illustrates the results of the experiment with high-school and college women discussed in the text. Subjects who were told they failed at a problem-solving task had a significantly lower opinion of their ability than subjects who were told they succeeded—even though they knew that the information about their performance had no relation to the facts.

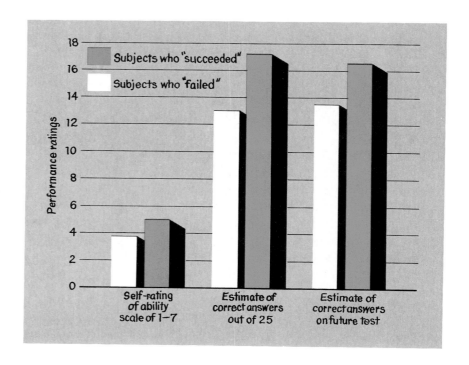

problem-solving task containing twenty-five items. After they had finished, the experimenters pretended to grade their attempts and then told them how they had scored. Actually, no grading was ever done. The experimenters simply decided arbitrarily to tell half the subjects that they had done badly, the other half that they had done very well.

This false information about performance was allowed to "sink in" for a time. Then the experimenters flatly admitted their deception. The women were told that their scores had never actually been compiled and that there was no truth at all in the information that they had done badly or well. Once the truth was out, the women were asked to rate their own ability at that kind of problem-solving, to estimate how many problems they had in fact solved correctly, and also to estimate how many they would solve correctly on a future trial.

As is shown in Figure 14-7, the results were startling. Apparently the women who had been told they did badly were never quite able to get over the loss of self-esteem they suffered—even though they knew that the unfavorable rating bore no relation to the facts and meant absolutely nothing. The women who had been told they did well, on the other hand, were much more confident—even though they too knew that the information was meaningless (16).

There could hardly be more convincing proof of the importance of the social comparison process. If our self-esteem and expectations of future performance depend so thoroughly on ratings by others that these ratings continue to affect us even after we are told they are false, then how can anyone doubt the importance of social influence in molding our thoughts and our lives?

Our attitudes toward life: how we acquire, cling to, and sometimes change them

Another important psychological characteristic we acquire largely through socialization is a set of very strong opinions and feelings that we think of as principles that guide our conduct. We grow up with what social psychologists call *attitudes* toward the people and situations we encounter. We have favorable or unfavorable attitudes toward members of ethnic groups, foreigners, rich people, poor people, males, females, homosexuals, children, teenagers, and old people. We have strong attitudes toward the nation's political parties, national defense, taxation, welfare, crime, unions, religion,

and all the other issues and institutions in society.

Attitudes represent far more than mere off-the-cuff opinions. They are deeply ingrained—as if constituting a basic part of our personality—and are powerful forces in directing our behavior. An attitude is defined as *an organized and enduring set of beliefs and feelings, predisposing us to behave in a certain way.* Note that by this definition an attitude is the combination of three essential factors: 1) a cognitive element (beliefs), 2) an emotional element (feelings), and 3) a behavioral element.

Thus a favorable attitude toward religion might

Panel 1: I'VE BEEN WONDERING ABOUT SOMETHING

Panel 2: I'VE BEEN WONDERING IF YOU EVER MET THAT CUTE LITTLE COYOTE THAT SPIKE TOLD YOU ABOUT...

Panel 3: I MET HER ALL RIGHT, AND SHE WAS THE CUTEST LITTLE THING I'VE EVER SEEN...BUT WE HAD STRONG RELIGIOUS DIFFERENCES...

Panel 4: SHE ATE BUNNIES!

© United Feature Syndicate 1975

include a belief about the existence of a higher power, emotional feelings of awe and humility connected with that belief, and a behavioral tendency to go to church, to respond favorably to the clergy, and to respond unfavorably to immoral or atheistic actions. A negative attitude toward the feminist movement would include a belief that a woman's place is in the home, feelings of attraction to passive women and distaste for militant women, and a tendency to seek out a dependent woman rather than a career woman as a wife.

It is chiefly the emotional component of an attitude that distinguishes it from a mere belief. A belief that the world is round has no emotional flavor. It is merely the cognitive acceptance of what is presumed to be a matter of fact. People who hold this belief are neither for nor against roundness—and in the unlikely event that science should suddenly discover that the world is shaped like a football, they would not hesitate to change their opinion. An attitude, because of its emotional overtones—because we are "for" or "against" whatever it is that the attitude concerns—is much more resistant to change. Since attitudes are so enduring, and since they influence so much of our behavior toward other people, social psychologists are particularly interested in the study of how we acquire them, usually cling to them, but sometimes change them.

Prejudices and stereotypes

Attitudes are not necessarily based on evidence. Some of them simply represent conformity to the social group. We have taken them over lock, stock, and barrel from the people around us—without ever looking at the evidence at all. Nor are they necessarily logical or consistent. Some psychologists have concluded, indeed, that the most remarkable thing about our attitudes is the amount of inconsistency we manage to tolerate (17).

For example, Mayor Smith is running for reelection. Mr. and Mrs. Jones, like their friends and neighbors, have a strongly favorable attitude toward Mayor Smith and the mayor's political party. But one day something rather upsetting occurs. The local newspaper publishes a strong and extremely persuasive editorial that describes in detail how Mayor Smith has failed to solve a number of urgent city problems. In fact the mayor has accepted graft as an inducement to permit gambling and to tolerate inferior performance on building contracts.

Will Mr. and Mrs. Jones change their attitude toward Mayor Smith? Not necessarily. Instead, they may do any one of several things. They may convince themselves that the newspaper is simply biased against the mayor. They may engage in a mental debate with the editorial, in which they disprove its allegations, at least to their own satisfaction. Or they may put the whole editorial right out of their mind and simply refuse to think about it. Our ingenuity at finding ways of maintaining our attitudes despite strong opposing arguments seems almost boundless.

Two kinds of attitudes that often fly in the face of fact are so common that social psychologists have given them special names:

1 A *prejudice* is an attitude that an individual maintains so stubbornly as to be virtually immune to any information or experiences that would disprove it. In our society, one of the most common prejudices is held by some whites against blacks and by some blacks against whites.

2 A *stereotype* is an attitude, shared by large numbers of people, that disregards individual differences and holds that all members of a certain group behave in the same manner. People are making judgments on the basis of stereotypes when they claim that all women are flighty or that all men are male chauvinists.

Prejudices and stereotypes affect many forms of human behavior. Even scientists are not always free of their influence. The best-trained scientists sometimes become so enamored of a particular theory that they refuse to abandon it even in the face of mounting proof that it is wrong. And in their personal relationships they may judge new acquaintances on the basis of stereotypes that make them suspicious of certain kinds of people who might prove highly congenial if only given a chance.

New experiences, new socialization, new attitudes

Attitudes in general are stubbornly resistant to change. We tend to cling to them like a child to its security blanket—and perhaps for some of the same reasons. Yet they are not entirely permanent

and unyielding. Sometimes the dyed-in-the-wool Republican switches to the Democratic party. Or a confirmed atheist joins the church—and a devout churchgoer drops out. Public opinion polls taken at intervals over recent decades have shown sharp changes in prevailing attitudes toward many institutions and issues—like the increased public acceptance of premarital sex mentioned in the postscript to Chapter 9.

One reason attitudes change is that the socialization process continues throughout life. In our early years, our parents are the chief instruments of socialization and we tend to adopt their attitudes as our own. Studies have shown, for example, that prejudices against minority groups are often passed along from parent to child (18). And a very large majority of children in elementary school have been found to favor the same political party as their parents (19). But as we grow older and are exposed to other socializing influences, the early influence of our parents begins to weaken. Although about 80 percent of elementary-school children prefer the same political party as their parents, one study found that the number drops to only about 55 percent among college students (20).

The freshman year in college is particularly likely to produce attitude change (21). Up to that time many students have lived in an environment where most people are quite alike in their attitudes. Then as freshmen they suddenly find themselves in the company of teachers and fellow students who hold attitudes they had not previously encountered. Students from a religious and politically conservative background may find themselves exposed to new attitudes of religious skepticism and political liberalism. Students whose family and friends have scoffed at literature and art may find themselves around people who admire Shakespeare and Rembrandt. These new socialization influences may have pronounced effects. Moreover, attitudes acquired in college tend to be long-lasting (22).

The college campus continues but changes the pattern of socialization.

Experiences that come after college can also have an effect. When we take a job we undergo a new kind of socialization. Each time we change jobs or get a promotion, each time we move to a new neighborhood or a new community, we come under new influences. We are also influenced by what we read and by what we see on television. The world changes and we change with it. Our attitudes can be compared to a house that undergoes frequent remodeling, expansion, and repainting over the years. In some ways the house never changes, yet it is never really the same.

Attitude change and the theory of cognitive dissonance

What kinds of new experiences and new information are most likely to produce attitude changes? One answer comes from proponents of what is called the *theory of cognitive dissonance*. This theory maintains that we have a strong urge to be consistent and rational in our thinking and to preserve agreement and harmony among our beliefs, feelings, and behavior—and therefore our attitudes. When there is a lack of consistency and harmony, we experience cognitive dissonance. We may manage to tolerate the inconsistency, as the Joneses did in the case of Mayor Smith. But cognitive dissonance tends to be highly uncomfortable, and we are strongly motivated to restore harmony by making some kind of adjustment in our beliefs, feelings, behavior, or all three. And changing any one of the three elements of an attitude may change the attitude itself.

In some cases, new factual information is enough to create cognitive dissonance and bring about a change in attitude. For example, many people who were once strongly opposed to birth control have been greatly influenced by all the factual information that has appeared in recent years about the population explosion and the danger of worldwide overcrowding. They once had the cognitive belief that a growing population is a good thing. This cognitive belief has now changed, and their attitude toward birth control has changed with it.

Events that alter the emotional component of an attitude may also create an inconsistency that calls for change. For an example, imagine what would happen if a man who had always regarded women as second-class citizens found himself in love with a woman who was an ardent feminist. Or consider an actual laboratory experiment in which college women underwent a deeply emotional experience related to cigarette smoking. The women, all heavy smokers, were asked to act out a scene in which the experimenter pretended to be a physician and they his patients. Each subject, visiting the "doctor," got bad news about a persistent cough from which she had been suffering; her X-rays had shown lung cancer; immediate surgery was required; before the operation she and the doctor would have to discuss the difficulty, pain, and risk. The experimenter tried to keep the scene as realistic as possible and to involve each subject emotionally to the greatest possible degree. As a result of the experience, almost all the women quit or drastically cut down on smoking. A follow-up eighteen months later found that they continued to show a significant change in their smoking habits (23).

Do attitudes change behavior— or vice versa?

It seems logical that a change in an attitude, caused by new beliefs or new emotional responses, should cause a change in behavior. Yet, strangely enough, the sequence of events is often exactly the opposite. In many cases, the change in behavior comes first—and this new behavior creates the change in attitude.

Many studies have shown that experimental manipulation of behavior can produce remarkable results. One such experiment concerned the highly controversial action of President Gerald Ford in extending a blanket pardon to his predecessor, Richard Nixon, for any crimes committed during the Watergate incident. College students who strongly opposed the pardon were asked to write essays taking the opposite view and justifying Ford's action. This simple act of writing an essay tended to create a more favorable attitude toward the pardon (24). A similar experiment was conducted with students who favored the legalization of marijuana.

After they were asked to write an essay opposing legalization, their attitudes tended to show considerable change (25).

In our everyday lives, new social situations often push us in the direction of changes in behavior, and these in turn often lead to changes in attitudes. This has been especially noticeable in recent years in the attitudes of whites toward blacks and of blacks toward whites. In general, it has been found that people who have attended school or worked with members of the other race hold more favorable attitudes, while those who have had no interracial contacts tend to feel less favorable (26). Undoubtedly the explanation is that new forms of behavior—that is, dealing with members of the other race, studying or working with them, and treating them as friendly companions—have produced attitude changes. The theory of cognitive dissonance maintains that the friendly behavior, when it conflicted with unfavorable beliefs and emotions, produced an imbalance that was remedied by a change in attitude.

Making a decision as a form of behavior change

One type of behavior likely to produce attitude change is the mere act of making a decision. In a classic experiment, a psychologist posing as a market researcher asked a woman to examine eight electrical appliances (a toaster, coffee maker, and so on) and rate them in terms of how attractive she found them. Once she had done this, the psychologist picked out two appliances that she liked equally well and asked her to choose one of them as a reward for helping in the study. Her choice was wrapped up and presented to her. Then she was asked to rate the eight appliances once more. This procedure was repeated with a number of different subjects—always with the same results.

Drawing by S. Gross;
© 1974 The New Yorker Magazine, Inc.

On the second rating, the women gave a higher mark than before to the appliance they had selected and received as a gift. But they gave a lower mark to the other appliance that had been offered to them—the one they had rejected (27). Once they had made their decision between the two appliances, they emphasized the good points of the one they had chosen and looked unfavorably on the one they had turned down.

People who buy an automobile often find themselves in a similar situation. In the advertisements and in the showrooms, a number of models look extremely attractive. But only one of them can be purchased. Once the decision has been made, automobile buyers behave very much like the women in the appliance study. One study showed that they tended to take pleasure in continuing to read ads for that particular model but avoided advertisements for other brands (28). They seemed to be looking for praise of their car, confirming the wisdom of their decision to buy it. They shunned any conflicting claims that might have raised doubts. In the case of both cars and appliances, dissonance theory would hold that choosing be-

tween attractive alternatives made these people uncomfortable. They relieved the dissonance by deciding that the alternative they chose was clearly superior, and they were determined to cling to this new attitude.

Attitude change and self-perception theory (or "Why did I do that?")

Many cases of attitude change can also be explained by another important concept in social psychology, called *self-perception theory*. This theory maintains that we try to discover the reasons for our own behavior when we find ourselves doing something that we cannot quite understand. We attempt to gain some perception of what it was about ourselves or the situation that made us act as we did (29).

Some examples you may have experienced are these: You are playing a friendly game of tennis, lose your temper, and throw your racket into the net—even though the outcome of the game means very little to you. Watching a telethon in behalf of a charity, you impulsively call the number shown on the screen and pledge a contribution much larger than you can really afford. You are puzzled. You are likely to ask yourself, "Why did I do that?"

When we do something that we cannot readily explain, our first impulse is to look for what social psychologists call *situational factors*—that is, to decide that we behaved as we did because circumstances pushed us in that direction. We are likely to decide that our loss of temper in the tennis game was the result of something our opponent or the spectators did. Our overgenerous contribution to charity was the result of the persuasiveness of the attractive telethon people.

This tendency to look for situational factors often serves as a handy excuse. If we get poor grades, we feel better if we can blame them on too heavy a course load, emotional stress over personal problems, or some other situational factor (30). Yet, strangely, we seem to look for situational factors even when we do something praiseworthy. If we stop on a highway to help an elderly couple change a tire, even when we are in a hurry, we are likely to explain our behavior by deciding that the couple looked very nice, unable to cope with their situation, and badly in need of help.

When we manage to find situational factors, we have no reason to question or change our attitudes. For example, if we decide that poor grades were caused by circumstances beyond our control, we do not have to worry about correcting a lackadaisical attitude toward study. Sometimes, however, we cannot find a situational explanation, no matter how hard we try. In such cases we are forced to decide that our behavior was prompted by *dispositional factors*—that is, our own attitudes. A change in attitude may well result (31).

At one time there was considerable argument between the dissonance theorists and the proponents of the self-perception theory. There seems to be a growing consensus, however, that both theories constitute valid explanations of attitude change. Dissonance theory seems to hold true in cases in which some conflict occurs among beliefs, feelings, and behavior. Self-perception theory seems to explain cases in which attitude change occurs without any such conflict (32).

When others try to change our attitudes: the art of persuasive communications

Up to this point, the discussion has been confined to attitude changes that occur more or less spontaneously, as the result of our own experiences and self-analysis. But all of us are under constant pressure from other people who are trying to persuade us to change. Politicians bombard us with speeches and press releases intended to foster favorable attitudes toward them and their party. Advertisers spend millions of dollars every year to try to create favorable attitudes toward their products. Many organizations work hard to win support for such causes as conservation, kindness to animals, and pollution control.

To social psychologists, all such attempts to change attitudes by transmitting information and making emotional appeals are known as *persuasive communications*. Because persuasive communications potentially have a great effect on our so-ciety and the behavior of individuals in that society, they have been studied in considerable depth.

Is anybody listening? If so, who?

Any attempt to influence the attitudes of large numbers of people faces many handicaps. For one thing, persuasive communications do not ordinarily reach very many people. A politician may make the most impassioned and convincing plea for support—yet his speech will be heard in person by only a few thousand people at most. Even if part of the speech is shown on television, it will still reach only a small proportion of Americans. One study indicates that only about one person in four watches national television news on any given evening (33). Moreover, those who do watch seem to pay only casual attention, for they remember very little of

Handing out a persuasive communication: Whom will it reach? What effect will it have?

what they have seen. A study found that viewers questioned later in the evening could recall only 6 percent of the news items they had seen (34). Newspaper accounts of a political speech reach and impress an even smaller audience, and editorials have a smaller readership still.

It has also been found that the audience likely to watch or read any appeal for attitude change—and to pay attention to it—is determined largely by a factor called *selective exposure*. This means that, by and large, persuasive communications reach only people who are already persuaded. The audience that turns out for a Democratic rally is overwhelmingly composed of confirmed Democrats. The people who read magazines favoring the conservation of natural resources are already dedicated to conservation. Since we all tend to associate with people we like and to read or listen to communications we find interesting, we are exposed mostly to people and communications we already agree with.

And who are you to tell me to change?

Let us now assume that a persuasive communication does succeed in reaching us, despite the handicaps. It argues for a viewpoint to which we are opposed. To adopt it, we will have to change an attitude. Will the persuasive communication actually persuade us?

Several factors help determine the answer. One of the most important is the matter of who is trying to persuade us—in other words, *the source of the communication*. Some sources are likely to have considerable influence. Others are less likely to convince us and may in fact only make us more opposed to what they are proposing.

The importance of the source was convincingly demonstrated in one of the very first experiments on the effectiveness of persuasive communications. Subjects in this study were asked to read a controversial argument on the development of an atomic energy project. Half the subjects were told that the argument had been written by a well-known atomic scientist. The other half were told that it came from the Soviet newspaper *Pravda*. As might be expected, there was a great deal more attitude change among subjects who believed that the scientist was the source (35).

Of great significance here is the *credibility of the source*. If the communication comes from someone whose knowledge or motives are suspect—in other words, from a source of low credibility—we tend to disregard it. If it comes from people who clearly know what they are talking about—in other words, from a source of high credibility—we are much more likely to accept it. The effectiveness is enhanced if the source seems to be fair, objective, and not particularly interested in wielding influence. A statement that Car X is superior is more impressive coming from a friend who understands mechanics than coming from a dealer who is trying to sell Car X.

What kinds of communications are most effective?

Just as the source influences effectiveness, so does the nature of the communication—that is, what kind of arguments it presents and how and when. In general, appeals to the emotions tend to be quite effective (36). One experimenter, dealing with actual voters in an actual election campaign, found that an appeal to vote for a candidate was considerably more successful when it was primarily emotional than when it was primarily logical (37). Appeals to fear are often particularly effective, as was shown by the experiment cited earlier in which women acted out the role of patients suffering from lung cancer. But sometimes the arousal of fear may backfire (38), presumably because the listener becomes so upset as to try to forget the whole matter.

The effectiveness of a communication addressed to an intelligent audience appears to be increased if it presents a fair rather than a one-sided argument, admitting that the other side also has its points (39). With a less intelligent audience, a one-sided argument may be more effective, perhaps because the listeners would be confused by hearing both sides (40). The one-sided argument also has a greater influence on an audience already leaning toward that side, while a fair argument is more likely to influence people leaning in the opposite direction (41).

The communication and the listener

A final factor that helps determine the effectiveness of a persuasive communication is the audience it reaches. Who is listening may be just as important as what is said and the source of the communication. For example, some people are much more easily persuaded than others. Indeed experiments have shown that people who tend to change their attitudes under one set of circumstances and in response to one kind of communication are also likely to change under different circumstances and in response to different kinds of communications (42). The crucial factor seems to be one's own opinion of oneself. People who are low in self-esteem tend to be much more easily persuaded than people who are high in self-esteem (43). Similarly, people who are anxious about social acceptance are more easily persuaded than those who have little anxiety (44).

In an odd way, the possibility that listeners will change their attitudes is also affected by their beliefs about the nature-nurture argument that has been mentioned so frequently throughout the book. This fact is so significant—especially as an influence that can discourage change for the better—that its implications are discussed in a box on Psychology and Society on page 532.

Change for the better: it is easier than most people think

One of the great barriers to progress—for both individuals and society as a whole—is the fact that many people take a pessimistic view of the nature-nurture argument. Although there is strong evidence that most human behavior is influenced just as much by environment and learning as by heredity—and often more so—many people still cling to the belief that human nature is determined at birth and resists any attempt to alter or improve it. This belief is evident in such familiar expressions as "People don't change," "That's just human nature," or "That kid was born to be bad." About themselves, people often say, "I can't help it; I'm just built that way," or "I was born unlucky."

The belief that human nature is largely inherited is a powerful deterrent to change in attitudes and behavior. In one experiment, university students were asked whether they thought the next five years might change their attitudes about some of their personality characteristics (such as whether they regarded themselves as trusting, curious, and so on) and toward various social issues (such as capital punishment and legalization of marijuana). It turned out that their answers depended largely on whether they thought their present attitudes were the result of nature or nurture (45). If they considered an attitude to be largely a matter of learning (as a majority did for being trusted or for favoring legalization of marijuana, they were significantly more likely to foresee possible change than if they regarded the attitude as something innate (as a majority did for the trait of curiosity).

The experiment suggests the hopeless position of an adolescent who decides that he was "born" to be a delinquent. He is likely to be totally unresponsive to any appeals to change his attitudes and behavior. If he could be convinced that his delinquency is the result of environmental influences, as it probably is, he would be much more receptive to the possibility of change.

Unfortunately our society has a way of implying that undesirable traits and attitudes are inborn and immutable. Many factors discussed earlier in the book contribute to pessimism about change for the better. One is the learned helplessness (pages 112–15) that many people acquire as the result of failure, punishment, and criticism. Another is the crippling effect of the conditional positive regard (pages 452–54) that Carl Rogers says families and society as a whole often display. In one way and another, many people become convinced that they are just naturally "dumb," or "awkward," or "bad." And accepting these labels as representing their inborn nature makes it unlikely that they will even consider change possible, much less try to achieve it.

Perhaps the greatest contribution of the social psychologists to human happiness and progress is the evidence they have accumulated about the influence of nurture in the form of the social environment. The findings indicate that attitudes and behavior are far more elastic than generally believed and that change for the better—in both human happiness and the way society functions—is always possible.

How we judge the behavior of others: attribution theory

We come now to an aspect of social psychology that has nothing to do with conformity, attitudes, or persuasive communications. Instead it deals with the way we judge the actions of other people—a process that deeply affects our lives because so much of our own behavior is a response to the behavior of others.

Suppose, for example, that you are standing in a group of people waiting for an elevator. The man next to you steps on your foot, causing you considerable pain. How will you react? The answer depends to a large extent on *why* you think the man hurt you. If he seems to be distressed and apologetic, you will probably assume that the incident was an accident and will laugh it off. If he seems to be hostile, you will doubtless be angry. In other words, you make a judgment. You decide that his stepping on your foot was either (1) an unfortunate accident, which he regrets, or (2) a deliberate attempt to hurt you. What you decide makes a tremendous difference in the way you then respond.

You are constantly engaged in making such judgments. An acquaintance pays you a compliment. If you decide that the acquaintance is sincere, you respond with pleasure. If you decide that the compliment is merely a hypocritical prelude to a request for a loan, you are turned off. You watch Mr. A, who aspires to the presidency, make a speech promising to cut government red tape, which is something you heartily favor. If you believe the candidate means what he says, you will probably vote for him. If you believe he is merely making an idle promise that he will forget the minute he is elected, you will not be impressed at all.

The way all of us make these decisions—and

tend to behave accordingly—is the basis of what is called *attribution theory*. The theory holds that we want to know *why* people act as they do. Self-perception theory, discussed earlier in the chapter, is one aspect of attribution theory—dealing with the way we try to understand our own behavior and personality. But we also try to attribute the behavior of other people to some underlying motive or other cause, so that we will know how to respond to their actions.

Why our judgment often fails: the fundamental attribution error

In a sense, attribution theory maintains that everybody behaves like an amateur psychologist, seeking to interpret behavior. (Like the psychoanalyst in the old joke who is greeted by an acquaintance with a "Good morning," and who then asks himself, "I wonder what he meant by that?") Unfortunately, this amateur psychology is often misguided. Many studies have shown that we have a strong tendency, when we judge others, to ignore the message of social psychology—namely, that behavior depends mostly on the situation. Instead, we tend to attribute other people's actions to deep-seated, consistent, and long-lasting personality traits.

For example, a waitress smiles at us and says she hopes we enjoy our meal. We conclude that she is warm and friendly, though her behavior may only reflect the fact that the boss has just warned her against being her natural surly self around customers. The man at the filling station scowls as he takes our money. We conclude that he is hostile and bad-tempered, though he may in fact merely have a headache. This tendency to attribute behavior to dispositional factors—rather than to aspects of the situation that may provide a far better explanation—is so powerful and widespread that it is called the *fundamental attribution error* (46).

Why we should fall into this error is difficult to explain, especially since it is so different from the way we judge our own behavior. As the earlier discussion of self-perception theory pointed out, we tend to attribute our own actions to situational factors rather than to our own personality traits. Yet in trying to interpret the actions of others we reverse ourselves and stress dispositional factors. Perhaps, as one investigator has suggested, thinking that we know what other people are really like gives us at least an illusion of being able to predict their behavior and is therefore comforting (47).

An attribution theorist's quiz game and its strange results

To demonstrate the fundamental attribution error, a group of psychologists devised an experiment that produced almost unbelievable results. The subjects participated as pairs in a laboratory quiz game. By lot, one member of each pair was assigned to make up the questions, the other to try to answer them. In front of both of them, the experimenters told the quiz maker to try to stump the quiz taker by posing questions that, though not impossible for someone possessing a great deal of general information, were difficult and challenging. Obviously, the situation was rigged in favor of the questioner, for everyone has acquired obscure pieces of information that another person could hardly be expected to know. The quiz maker could easily come up with questions that were almost sure to baffle the quiz taker. And this is exactly what happened. The quiz takers, by and large, did very badly in the game.

The strange thing was how the game affected the quiz takers' opinion of the quiz makers. Typically, they ignored the unfair circumstances and decided that the quiz makers were people who possessed knowledge far superior to their own. In other words, they proved to be victims of the fundamental attribution error—explaining the behavior of the quiz makers in dispositional rather than situational terms. So, likewise, did other subjects who watched the quiz game, even though they too knew how it favored the quiz maker (48).

Drawing inferences about the personalities of other people from their behavior—regardless of how much the situation might have affected that behavior—leads to many unwarranted assumptions by teachers about their students, by family members about other members of the family, probably even by psychotherapists and counselors about their clients (49). It helps explain why "con artists," who are often psychopaths adept at exuding a false charm (Chapter 11), find so many willing victims. It may pose a danger to our system of administering justice, as is explained in a box on Psychology and Society on the next page.

Compounding the error: guessing people's dispositions by guessing how they feel

The fundamental attribution error sometimes leads us to mistaken conclusions reached on the basis of mistaken impressions. For an example of how we may thus compound our errors, note this provocative experiment.

Psychologists made a videotape, without a sound track, of a college woman being interviewed. They then showed the videotape to two groups of male subjects. One group was told that the subject of the interview was sex, the other that the subject was politics. Afterward the subjects were asked to rate the woman on a scale of how

Psychology and Society

The fundamental attribution error and criminal justice

In a widely publicized news event of the 1970s, a newspaper heiress named Patty Hearst and some companions robbed a California bank. There was no question about her part in the holdup. The bank's security cameras recorded a moving picture of her brandishing a submachine gun.

When Hearst was found and put on trial, her lawyer made no attempt to deny the clear evidence of the cameras. Instead, he attributed her conduct to situational factors. Hearst had been kidnapped from her home by members of a radical activist group calling themselves the Symbionese Liberation Army. While being held for ransom, she was under harsh physical and mental pressure from her captors. Eventually she succumbed to this brain washing, as the defense called it, and joined the other SLA members in the robbery—an act she greatly regretted as soon as she was freed from the group's influence.

The jury rejected this defense, found Hearst guilty, and sentenced her to prison. The verdict was exactly what an attribution theorist would have predicted. From her behavior—the motion picture showing her with the gun—the jury made assumptions about her personality. They decided that she

was by disposition violent and dangerous, disregarding the possibility that she was merely an unfortunate victim of the situation.

Was justice done? The question is not easy to answer, for the case raises many thorny questions about whether a criminal act can ever be condoned and about an individual's duty to resist brain washing by violent companions. The verdict does, however, raise some doubt about our system of administering criminal justice.

Criminologists believe that a number of crimes—particularly assaults and sometimes murders—are committed only under intense provocation by people who would not ordinarily dream of doing such a thing. It is the situation, rather than their disposition, that triggers the action. But jury members and judges are just as likely as anyone else to fall into the fundamental attribution error. They are likely to infer a criminal disposition from a criminal act, regardless of the circumstances. Attribution theory suggests a nagging question about the possibility that otherwise law-abiding citizens, trapped into an uncharacteristic criminal act by some quirk of events, may be treated too harshly by our legal system.

nervous and anxious she seemed to be. Their ratings turned out to depend on what they had been told about the interview. If they thought the subject was sex, they found that the woman showed considerable anxiety. If they thought the subject was politics, they found that she showed

less anxiety. Thus exactly the same behavior—the same videotape of the same woman—created two very different impressions.

Next the two groups of subjects were asked to rate the woman's general tendency to be calm or flustered—in other words, her basic disposition.

The results followed the same pattern. Subjects who believed that the interview was about sex, and that it had flustered her, decided she was just naturally inclined to be apprehensive, nervous, and anxious. The other subjects did not (50).

In part, the experiment provided another demonstration of what was shown in the make-believe quiz game. The subjects jumped to the erroneous conclusion that acting flustered during a sex interview—a situation that might produce a certain amount of anxiety in almost everyone—indicated a disposition to be easily flustered in general. But the mistake was compounded by the fact that they only *thought* the woman acted flustered.

Why did this happen? We can assume that the subjects took the situation into account in judging the woman's behavior. They felt that a sex interview would naturally produce anxiety. Therefore they interpreted her behavior during the interview as showing anxiety. But in judging her general disposition, they fell into the fundamental attribution error and ignored situational factors. Thus they made a double error. They inferred her basic disposition from behavior that was itself only inferred. They made two guesses—either or both of which may have been totally wrong.

The everyday lesson of attribution theory

All of us are probably guilty at times of this compounded error. We watch person A being treated by person B in what we consider an abusive manner. Such treatment would make us angry—so we assume that A is angry. Then, on the basis of this assumption, we further assume that A tends to be hot-tempered in general. We watch person C making a fuss over person D. Such attention from C, whom we like very much, would greatly please us—so we assume that D is pleased. Then, on the basis of this assumption, we further assume that D is friendly and easily pleased in general. We could be dead wrong in thinking that A is angry or that D is pleased. And how they happen to feel in this particular situation does not necessarily reflect their basic disposition anyway.

The message of attribution theory, indeed, is that we have to be careful when we act as amateur psychologists analyzing the motives of other people. Fortunately, we often judge people correctly despite the difficulties. Studies have shown that even people untrained in social psychology usually look for consistency of behavior, rather than relying on a single and possibly uncharacteristic example. Most of us do not necessarily decide that a woman is witty simply because she makes one witty remark. Instead we wait for further evidence. If a man tells us he likes his job, we try to determine whether his words reflect his real opinion or merely the fact that his boss is listening. We also seek and consider the opinions of other people (which are often useful) as to whether the woman is witty and whether the man is sincere or just acting (51).

Interpersonal attraction: how we pick the people who influence us

Everything in the discussion thus far has stressed the ways in which our behavior is influenced by interactions with the people around us. Now we must ask: What factors determine which particular people will be around us? How do we come to be associated with one group rather than with another? Is it just sheer chance that dictates our acquaintanceships—or do we somehow make our own social environment?

Certainly chance plays a part. The family you happen to be born into determines the culture and subculture into which you are socialized, which in turn helps shape your attitudes. The neighborhood you happen to grow up in provides the playmates, classmates, and teachers who influence your childhood. Even in later life, you do not have full freedom of choice. Going to college because it is close to your home or offers you a scholarship can place you among students and instructors very different from those you might find on another campus. Taking a job puts you into close contact with co-workers who already happened to be there. Once you have your own home, the people next door move in or out without your permission.

Nevertheless, you do manage in college and afterward to choose many of the people with whom

you associate. You deliberately pick your close friends. You join groups you like and stay away from groups you find uncongenial. You spend a great deal of your time with companions of your own selection. Hence the importance of what social psychologists call *interpersonal attraction*—the manner in which we are attracted to certain people and repelled by others.

The chief finding about interpersonal attraction has been summed up in a single sentence: "We like those who reward us, and the more they reward us the better we like them" (52). But what do we find rewarding about other people—and why?

Similarity: "I like you because you remind me of myself"

One finding about interpersonal attraction bears out the adage: birds of a feather do indeed flock

In choosing our companions, are we birds of a feather?

together. All other things being equal, we tend to be attracted to people who are very much like us—or at least whom we perceive to be similar. The best demonstration was an experiment performed by a psychologist who arranged to operate a men's dormitory at a large university. The assignment of roommates was based on questionnaires and interviews about attitudes, interests, and tastes. Some roommates were put together because their replies showed them to be very similar, others because they were sharply different in many respects. As the term went on, it developed that roommates who were much alike usually got along well and became good friends. Those who were dissimilar did not like each other and did not become friends (53).

It has been found that the degree to which we find another person attractive shows a high correlation with the number of attitudes we share or think we share. Note the almost straight-line relationship illustrated in Figure 14-8.

Familiarity: "I like you because I know you"

Though social psychologists agree that birds of a feather flock together, they have disproved another adage. Familiarity does *not* breed contempt. Indeed the more familiar we are with other people—and the more chance we have to get used to them—the more likely we are to be attracted to them. One experiment, for example, brought together pairs of subjects who did not know each other. They did not speak but merely sat across from each other in the laboratory. Some pairs saw each other on only a few occasions, others as many as a dozen times. Afterward they were asked how much they liked each other. The more often they had been together—even in this casual fashion—the greater was the mutual attraction (55). Similar results have been obtained merely by exposing subjects to a photograph of another person, as is shown in Figure 14-9.

Other studies show that people are likely to be

14-8
The more similar the attitudes, the greater the attraction

The graph shows the results of an experiment in which college students were asked to rate a stranger on a scale of attractiveness. Their only information about the stranger came from reading a set of replies supposedly given to a questionnaire about attitudes toward politics and other issues. When the experimenter rigged the stranger's answers to indicate attitudes different from those of the subjects, the attractiveness rating was low. But it went up steadily as the percentage of shared attitudes seemed to increase, forming an almost perfect correlation (54).

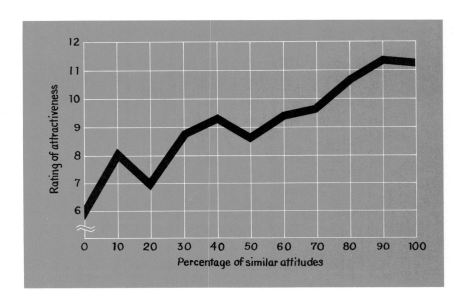

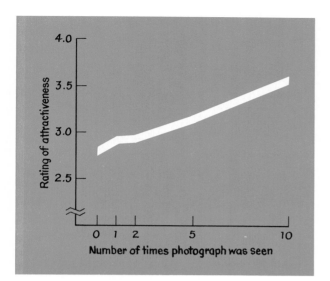

14-9 Even a photograph looks better the more often it is seen
The ratings of attractiveness were made by subjects asked to look at the photograph of another person. The lowest ratings were made by subjects who had never seen the photo before, the highest by subjects who had seen it most often (56).

most friendly with those who are familiar because they live next door in a college dormitory, an apartment building, or a row of houses (57). Even the mere prospect of becoming familiar seems to make other people more attractive. One study found that strangers introduced in a laboratory were more attracted to one another if told that they would work together in the future than if they thought they would probably never meet again (58).

"I like you because you like me—and are good (but not too good) at what you do"

Many studies have shown that we tend to be attracted to people who seem to be attracted to us

(59) or to hold a high opinion of us (60). We also tend to like people in whose company we have achieved satisfactions, as can be observed in the camaraderie that usually flourishes among members of a winning athletic team.

We seem to be especially attracted to people who at first do not seem to like us or to hold us in high regard, then later change their minds (61). Apparently there is a special reward—and thus a strong tendency toward attraction—in winning over a person who was at first critical.

In general, we also have a tendency to be attracted to people who are competent—who are good at what they do, whether it is singing, playing basketball, solving mathematical equations, or driving an automobile. Most of us, however, are

Victory on the athletic field: an example of liking people in whose company we have achieved satisfactions.

turned off by people who are *too* competent (62). Apparently we are uncomfortable around people who remind us of our own failings. We prefer them to have a few little weaknesses of their own.

Physical attractiveness: "I like you because I like your looks"

Most of us like to deny that physical appearance has anything to do with our judgments of other people. Beauty, we have been told, is only skin deep. And some of the greatest men and women in history have been physically unprepossessing or downright ugly. It seems unfair to like or dislike someone just because of facial features resulting from an accident of heredity. For more than a half-century psychologists have been asking college students what they value most in a person of the opposite sex, and physical attractiveness has always wound up near the bottom of the list (63).

In actual fact, however, physical attractiveness is more influential than most people care to admit. Even children judge one another on the basis of appearance. As early as the nursery school years, it has been found, the attractive boys are the most popular, the unattractive boys the least popular (64). Attractive children also receive preferential treatment from adults (65).

Many studies have demonstrated the ways in which adult relationships are influenced by physical attractiveness. In one study, college men were asked to rate the quality of an essay supposedly written by a college woman. When they believed that the writer was an unusually attractive woman, they gave the essay the highest marks. When they had no clues about her appearance, their marks fell in the middle range. When they believed she was unattractive, they gave the lowest marks (66).

Fortunately for those of us who have never won a beauty prize, female or male, opinions differ on what constitutes physical attractiveness. In one

What broke the ice? A mutual feeling of physical attractiveness?

study, subjects were asked to judge the attractiveness of a number of photographs of children, teenagers, and adults—and every one of the photos was ranked first by at least one of the subjects (67). There does, however, seem to be a sort of consensus. Fairly high correlations—though by no means perfect—have been found among the ratings made by different observers (68).

Why physical attractiveness counts: the matter of first impressions

Why is physical attractiveness so influential? One reason seems to be that it is immediately and obviously apparent. When we meet someone for the first time, we can only guess whether this person is similar to us in attitudes, interests, and tastes. We have no clear clues about competence and intelligence. We can see at a glance, however, how well the person meets our own ideas of attractiveness—and thus move toward acceptance or rejection.

As was explained in Chapter 8, first impressions strongly influence the way we perceive the world. Indeed perception was described as "the science of first impressions." Thus, when we meet new people, our initial reaction tends to have a lasting effect on how attractive we find them. If we like them, even just because of their physical appearance, we usually continue to like them—no matter if some of their subsequent behavior is objectionable. If we dislike them at the start, we are likely to continue to dislike them—even if their subsequent behavior is above reproach.

In one experiment, subjects first saw a stranger—actually a man who was an accomplice of the experimenter—in a laboratory waiting room. In his dealings with a secretary who was in charge of the waiting room, the stranger was at times extremely impolite, belligerent, and demanding. At other times, in the presence of other subjects, he was polite and pleasant. Later the subjects met the accomplice-stranger on three to twelve other occasions. As would be expected from what is known about the effect of familiarity, they liked the "pleasant" stranger better when they saw him twelve times than when they saw him only three times. But increased contact did not change their ratings of the "unpleasant" stranger (69). The effect of the bad first impression outweighed familiarity.

First impressions and implicit personality theory

Why are first impressions of other people so persistent? Social psychologists say the reason is that we carry around a working theory about people and their personalities. We have concluded that certain personality traits almost always go together. If for some reason we decide that a new acquaintance is "cold," for example, we automatically assume that this person will also tend to be irritable, humorless, unsociable, and self-centered. But if we perceive the new acquaintance as "warm," we expect this warmth to be accompanied by a good disposition, a sense of humor, friendliness, and generosity (70). This belief that personality traits come in clusters is called an *implicit personality theory*. All of us seem to hold such a theory, without being aware of it.

One trait that strongly influences implicit personality theory is physical appearance—for most of us believe that physically attractive people also have many other attractive qualities. In one study in which subjects were asked to judge the personality characteristics of people shown in photographs, the subjects read all kinds of virtues into photos of attractive people. They judged the attractive people, as compared with the unattractive ones, to be considerably more interesting, strong, sensitive, sociable, poised, modest, outgoing, and sexually responsive. This was true regardless of whether the judges were male or female (71).

The implicit personality theory that all of us seem to have developed leads us into error at times. For one thing, it is likely to make us think of other people as more consistent than they really are. Moreover, it can cause a chain reaction in which our theory changes our own behavior in a way that in turn changes the behavior of other people, as explained in a box on Psychology and Society on page 542. But implicit personality theory does help us categorize and deal with other people. Our theory has been acquired through experience and is probably right more often than it is wrong. Right or wrong, it is one of the tools we use in conducting the social relationships that—as everything in this chapter has emphasized—are such an important part of our lives.

(Summary begins on page 548.)

"If you don't expect to like me, I'll make very sure you don't"

Of all the many experiments in social psychology, one is particularly memorable for what it reveals about the workings of society, interpersonal relationships, and the secret of getting along with other people. Though simple in structure, the experiment produced results of remarkably subtle and intricate significance.

The subjects were college men. Each of them was merely asked to become acquainted over the telephone, in a ten-minute conversation, with a college woman he had never met. Before the call was made, the subject saw what he was told was a photograph of the woman. Actually the photograph was of someone else. Half the subjects saw the picture of a woman who had been judged particularly attractive by an independent panel. The other subjects saw the picture of a woman who had been judged physically unattractive.

As might be predicted from what has been said about the way people tend to infer personality characteristics from physical appearance, the subjects were strongly influenced by the photographs. When they were asked what they expected of their telephone acquaintances, those who thought they would be talking to an attractive woman said she would probably be sociable, poised, and humorous. Those who thought they would talk to an unattractive woman expected her to be unsociable, awkward, and uncomfortably serious.

Oddly enough, though the women to whom the men talked were not those shown in the photographs, they lived up to these expectations. Tapes of the telephone conversations showed that the women believed to be attractive actually did sound as if they were warm, charming, and humorous. The women believed to be unattractive sounded cold, clumsy, and humorless. How in the world can these results be explained?

Analysis of the tapes revealed the answer. The men were the cause. They *acted,* on the telephone, in line with their expectations. If they expected to like their telephone partner, they were eager and easy to respond to. If they did not expect to like their partner, they cast a pall over the conversation. Their own words inspired a chilly and stilted response (72).

The psychologists who conducted the experiment have called it a conspicuous example of a self-fulfilling prophecy. When you expect someone to be likable, your own friendly and accepting actions almost guarantee that this person will behave in a likable manner. When you expect to dislike someone, your own pessimistic and sour actions almost guarantee a cold and unsympathetic response. Either way, you help create the very behavior that you predicted. The experiment makes a point worth remembering in all social relationships: In everyday dealings with other people, it pays to be an optimist.

It is probably equally true that expecting other people to like us also tends to be a self-fulfilling prophecy. If we expect to be liked, we behave in a likable fashion. If we fear rejection, we tend to act tense, guarded, and not likable at all—and thus bring about the very thing we dreaded. The findings of social psychology indicate that people treat us not only as we treat them but also as we expect to be treated.

Postscript

Aggression, altruism, and bystander apathy

Many questions about social behavior continue to puzzle scientists. One of them has to do with the basic quality of human nature. Is it essentially "good," as the humanistic psychologists maintain (page 32)? Or is it essentially "evil," as crime statistics and history's records of war and cruelty might indicate? Is it perhaps even neutral—neither good nor evil but capable of being molded in either direction?

Perhaps we will never know the answer. The question may lend itself only to philosophical speculation, not to scientific proof. But science is learning more all the time about the way people sometimes treat each other with aggression and violence, sometimes with great kindness and generosity, and sometimes with thoughtless disdain.

Is aggression bred into our genes?

Some scientists, especially those in fields such as biology, have concluded that aggression is a part of our inheritance—indeed, as one of them describes it, "an essential part of the life-preserving organization of instincts" (73). They point out that human beings are just another form of animal life, and that the "law of the jungle" dictates that animals must often kill to survive.

Certainly aggression is common and apparently instinctive among lower animals. Even if a rat is raised in isolation—without any chance to observe and learn aggression from others—it will immediately show hostility toward any other rat that enters its cage. It uses the same aggressive tactics employed by other rats of its species (74).

Observations of fish in their natural environment have shown that certain males ordinarily attack only other males of the same species—presumably to protect their territories and their mates. But, if there are no other males of the species around, these fish will attack the males of other species. If there are no males of any kind available, the fish will attack females—and sometimes even kill their own mates. This behavior has been cited as proof that the fish has an instinct or drive for aggression so powerful that it has to find some outlet, even if this means violent destruction of the family (75).

Or is aggression learned?

Do these fish and rats, which seem obviously programed for violent behavior, tell us anything about human beings? Perhaps. But many psychologists—probably most of them—believe otherwise. They have concluded that human aggression, though it may have some relation to heredity, is largely the result of learning. Many experimental findings point in this direction. You may recall the photographs on page 123 showing how children tend to imitate an

Aggressive behavior: What are its wellsprings? What encourages or discourages it?

stimulus was applied, the monkey would attack other monkeys who ranked lower in the social hierarchy. But if the monkey was in the presence of others who ranked higher, it did not attack. Instead, it ran away. If even a monkey experiencing "brain control" modifies its aggressive behavior so drastically in accordance with the social situation, it seems only logical to many psychologists that social influences and learning must certainly affect human aggression.

There seems to be no way, at this stage of psychology's development, to say for sure whether violence is learned or is programed by heredity—or both. Whatever its origin, many scientists agree that it once had undoubted value in helping the human race survive but is obsolete and counterproductive in our present civilization. As one biologist states: "The need now is for a gentler, a more tolerant people than those who won . . . against the ice, the tiger, and the bear" (78).

Aggression's opposite: studies of altruism

For behavior that is the opposite of aggression—being kind, generous, and helpful to others—social psychologists use the word *altruism*. Cases of altruism are not reported in the newspapers so often as incidents of violence, but they take place with great frequency. People go to considerable trouble to help a sick neighbor, take in a family left homeless by a fire, and serve as volunteer firemen and hospital attendants. The amounts donated each year to charities are staggering.

As in the case of aggression, it can be argued that the behavior of lower animals points to a hereditary basis for altruism. Chimpanzees, for example, have been observed to share their food with another hungry chimpanzee in an adjoining cage—though they do so somewhat grudgingly (79). Many other animal studies have produced evidence of an altruistic concern for others (80).

adult who attacks a life-size doll—an indication that learning through observation can produce aggressive behavior. Similarly, it has been found that adults tend to behave more aggressively after watching a film showing acts of aggression (76)—or even after watching a football game with its violent bodily contact (77).

It has also been found that many aggressive people come from aggressive families and were punished severely for childhood misconduct. They may be imitating the behavior of their parents, even though it was once painful to them. Others seem somehow to have decided, from experience, that aggression serves in some way to bring social rewards. Having used it successfully on one occasion, they may adopt it as a way of life.

Even a monkey's display of aggression may depend greatly on learning and on the social situation. This fact has been observed in an animal that behaved aggressively in response to electrical stimulation through an electrode planted in the limbic system (pages 78–79) of the brain. When this

Some scientists maintain that altruism is an innate trait that has been passed along through the process of evolution. They point out that human beings have always had a better chance of survival when living with other people than when trying to make it alone. So it seems likely that those who were willing to cooperate with others had a better chance of surviving and passing along their characteristics to future generations (81). Again as in the case of aggression, it is impossible either to prove or disprove this theory.

Other psychologists believe the explanation lies not in heredity but in learning. They point out that there are wide individual differences in tendencies toward altruism. Studies have shown that the people most likely to be altruistic are those who have somehow come to feel a personal responsibility for others (82) and have learned to empathize (83)—that is, to feel the joys and pains of other people as if these emotions were their own. Having altruistic parents to imitate and identify with also plays a part. One study of boys who were regarded as generous found that they usually had fathers whom they perceived to be warm and helpful (84). Another study, looking into the backgrounds of a group devoted to promoting civil rights, found that the members were characterized by a close relationship with an altruistic parent—at least one and sometimes both (85). Whether altruism is or is not a basic and innate human trait, there seems to be no doubt that it can be at least encouraged or discouraged by learning and social influences.

Treating others with benign (or not so benign) neglect: bystander apathy

Closely related to studies of altruism and aggression is a line of investigation that was inspired by a well-publicized incident in New York City some years ago. A young woman named Kitty Genovese was murdered on the street one night in sight of thirty-eight neighbors who heard her cries and ran to their apartment windows. Although the assault went on for half an hour and many of the spectators watched for the entire time, no one called the police or took any other action. Why? Why do people sometimes help others who are in trouble but sometimes, as in the Genovese case, show a remarkable degree of what social psychologists term *bystander apathy*?

Experiments show that there is a close relationship between the number of people who witness an incident—such as the Genovese murder, a theft, a fire, or a call for help—and the likelihood that anyone will offer assistance. In a typical experiment, men students arriving at a psychology laboratory were asked to sit in a small waiting room until they could be interviewed. Some of the subjects waited alone, others in groups of three, and still others in groups of three that contained only one actual

Walking past a man who lies on a city street: a common case of bystander apathy.

14-10
The more spectators, the more apathy

How many students, sitting in the waiting room of a psychology laboratory, would report the presence of smoke that seemed to indicate a fire? The answer seems to depend on how many people are present. In group 1, there were three people in the room—one actual subject and two confederates of the experimenter who were instructed to ignore the smoke. In group 2, three actual subjects were waiting in company. In group 3—the only one in which a majority took action—the subject was alone in the room and presumably felt a greater sense of personal responsibility.

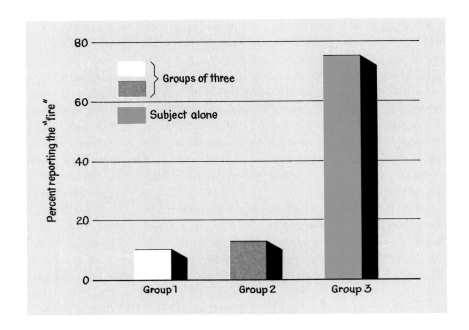

subject and two confederates of the experimenter. Soon smoke began to seep into the room through a ventilator in the wall. The smoke continued until someone took steps to report a fire, or, if no one made any move, for six minutes.

As Figure 14-10 shows, most of the subjects who were alone took action to report the smoke, usually very promptly. But when three subjects were waiting together, only 13 percent ever reported the smoke. Of the subjects who were sitting with the two confederates—who were instructed to pay no attention to the smoke—only 10 percent took action (86).

Kitty Genovese may have been a victim of the fact that, contrary to popular belief, there is no safety in numbers. Apparently a person who needs help is more likely to receive it if there is only one person around than if there are many. Several reasons have been suggested. First, the presence of others may relieve any single member of the group from feelings of personal responsibility. Second,

apparent indifference on the part of other spectators may cause the individual bystander to downgrade the seriousness of the situation. In some cases, bystander apathy may even represent a type of conformity. If a group of people seems to be ignoring the plight of a person in need, individual members may feel strong pressure to behave as the group is behaving.

Apathy, anonymity, and intimacy

Kitty Genovese may also have been a victim of the anonymity of big-city life. Studies have shown that people who need help are much more likely to receive it in a small town than in a city (87). In a large city, people can walk for blocks without meeting anyone they know. They are mere faces in the crowd. They do not have the intimate contacts with friends and neighbors that might produce offers of help.

Any increase in the degree of intimacy—even in just the matter of physical closeness—serves to reduce the tendency toward bystander apathy. Thus a person who collapses in the close confines of a subway car is much more likely to receive help than someone who collapses in the open spaces of a city street. This was demonstrated by investigators who fell to the floor of a New York subway car, as if suddenly stricken. When they were carrying a cane, as if they had a physical ailment, someone tried to help them in 95 percent of the cases. Even if they smelled of alcohol and carried a whisky bottle in a paper bag, indicating that they might merely have been drunk, someone went to their assistance half the time (88). The results were doubtless due to the fact that the bystanders—actually "by-sitters"—were in a face-to-face situation with the victims and in a confined space where they could not just ignore the incident and walk by.

You can't be a Good Samaritan if you're in a hurry

One experiment on bystander apathy was particularly ingenious. The subjects were men attending a theological seminary—people who might be expected to lend a helping hand to anyone in trouble. The subjects had volunteered to make a brief talk that would be recorded and distributed. When they arrived at the experimenter's office they received some printed material that was to be the basis of the talk. After studying it, they were directed to proceed to a recording studio in a nearby building. The route, as shown on a map given to each of them, took them through an alley in which they passed a confederate of the experimenter who was lying in a doorway, coughing and groaning as if in pain. The question, of course, was how many of them would stop to help the man in trouble—as did the subject shown in Figure 14-11.

The printed material that half the subjects studied was the story of the Good Samaritan, which, it seemed, might remind them of their duty to help others. The other half studied a discussion of job opportunities for seminary graduates, which, it was presumed, would have no effect one way or the other. In addition, an attempt was made to determine whether the men might be influenced by how much of a hurry they were in to reach the recording studio. Some of the men were told that they were early and should take their time, others that they were just about on schedule, and still others that they were late and should rush to the studio as fast as possible. In other words, a third of the subjects were put in what the experimenter deemed a "low hurry" situation, a third in an "intermediate hurry," and a third in a "high hurry" situation.

Which subjects offered to help the man in pain

14-11 A "Good Samaritan" offers help
One of the subjects in an experiment on bystander apathy stops to help a man lying in an alley doorway. Was he really a "Good Samaritan"—or did he just stop because he was in no special hurry to get anywhere? For the answer, see the text.

and which did not? It turned out that it made no difference whether the subjects had just read the Good Samaritan parable or the material on job opportunities. What did make a difference was whether or not they were in a hurry. Of the "low hurry" subjects, 63 percent offered help; of the "intermediate hurry" subjects, 45 percent; and of the "high hurry" subjects only 10 percent (89). The study suggests that it is difficult to be a Good Samaritan when you are in a hurry—an indication that the rush of big-city life, as well as the lack of intimacy, may contribute to bystander apathy.

Summary

1 *Social psychology* is the study of how human beings "think, feel, and behave in social situations"—or, in broader terms, the study of how people influence and are influenced by other people.

2 *Socialization* is the process through which children are integrated into the society through exposure to the actions and opinions of other members of the society.

3 *Conformity* is the yielding by individuals to pressures from the group in which they find themselves.

4 One reason for conformity is that we depend on the people around us for many of our psychological satisfactions and find it pleasant to be accepted and liked by the group.

5 Another explanation for conformity is offered by the *theory of social comparison*. The theory holds that we need to evaluate our own conduct, opinions, and abilities—and often can do so only by comparing ourselves with other people.

6 An *attitude* is an organized and enduring set of beliefs and feelings, predisposing us to behave in a certain way. Thus an attitude contains: a) a cognitive element (beliefs), b) an emotional element (feelings), and c) a behavioral element.

7 A *prejudice* is an attitude that an individual maintains so stubbornly as to be virtually immune to any information or experiences that would disprove it.

8 A *stereotype* is an attitude, shared by large numbers of people, that disregards individual differences and holds that all members of a certain group behave in the same manner.

9 One explanation for changes in attitudes is the *theory of cognitive dissonance*. The theory holds that we seek to preserve agreement and harmony among our beliefs, feelings, and behavior. When there is a lack of consistency—and cognitive dissonance occurs—we are strongly motivated to restore harmony by making an adjustment in our beliefs, feelings, behavior, or all three.

10 Another explanation for attitude change is *self-perception theory*. The theory holds that we often try to discover the reasons for our own behavior. Our first impulse is to seek *situational factors* (or circumstances that pushed us into acting as we did). If

we cannot find a situational explanation, we are forced to decide that our behavior was prompted by *dispositional factors*—that is, our own personality and attitudes. A change in attitude may result.

11 Attempts by other people to change our attitudes—by transmitting information or making emotional appeals—are called *persuasive communications*.

12 The effectiveness of persuasive communications is affected by *selective exposure*—the fact that most such communications reach only people who are already persuaded. It also depends on: a) the *source* of the communication, b) the *credibility* of the source, c) the nature of the communication, and d) the listener. Listeners who are low in self-esteem or anxious about social acceptance are more easily persuaded.

13 *Attribution theory* (of which self-perception theory is one aspect) holds that we want to know why people behave as they do. We usually attribute the behavior of other people to dispositional factors rather than situational factors. This tendency is so powerful and widespread that it is called the *fundamental attribution error*.

14 *Interpersonal attraction* is social psychology's term for the manner in which we are attracted to other people or repelled by them. The study of interpersonal attraction is important because it helps determine the people we choose to have around us and who therefore influence our attitudes and behavior.

15 In general, we are attracted to people who: a) are similar to us (especially in attitudes), b) are familiar to us, c) show that they like us, d) display competence (but not so much competence as to make us feel inferior), and e) are physically attractive.

16 *Implicit personality theory* is the term for the widespread human tendency to believe that certain personality traits always go together—for example, that a person who seems to be "warm" will also have a good disposition and a sense of humor.

Postscript

17 The question of whether human beings have an inborn tendency to display *aggression*—or whether aggression is the result of learning—is one of the unresolved issues in psychology.

18 The people most likely to display *altruism* (a tendency to be kind, generous, and helpful to others) are those who feel a personal responsibility for others and have learned to *empathize* (feel the joys and pains of others as if these emotions were their own).

19 *Bystander apathy* is a failure to assist another person who appears in need of help. Bystander apathy tends to be greatest when there are large numbers of other people around. It is encouraged by the anonymity, lack of intimacy, and rush of big-city life.

Important terms

attitude
attribution theory
cognitive dissonance
conformity
credibility of the source
culture
dispositional factors
fundamental attribution error
implicit personality theory
interpersonal attraction
persuasive communications

physical attractiveness
prejudice
selective exposure
self-perception theory
situational factors
social comparison theory
socialization
society
stereotype
subculture

Postscript

aggression
altruism

bystander apathy
empathize

Recommended readings

Aronson, E. *The social animal,* 2d ed. San Francisco: Freeman, 1976.

Bandura, A. *Social learning theory.* Englewood Cliffs, N.J.: Prentice-Hall, 1976

Bem, D. J. *Beliefs, attitudes, and human affairs.* Belmont, Calif.: Brooks-Cole, 1970.

Berkowitz, L., ed. *Advances in experimental social psychology,* Vol. 10. New York: Academic Press, 1977.

Berscheid, E., and Walster, E. C. *Interpersonal attraction,* 2d ed. Reading, Mass.: Addison-Wesley, 1978.

Buckhout, R., ed. *Toward social change: a handbook for those who will.* New York: Harper & Row, 1971.

Carlsmith, J. M., Ellsworth, P. C., and Aronson, E. *Methods of research in social psychology.* Reading, Mass.: Addison-Wesley, 1976.

Freedman, J. L., Carlsmith, J. M., and Sears, D. O. *Social psychology,* 3d ed. Englewood Cliffs, N.J.: Prentice-Hall, 1978.

Jones, E. E., et al. *Attribution: perceiving the causes of behavior.* Morristown, N.J.: General Learning Press, 1972.

Milgram, S. *Obedience to authority.* New York: Harper & Row, 1974.

Shaver, K. C. *An introduction to attribution process.* Cambridge, Mass.: Winthrop, 1975.

Zimbardo, P., Ebbeson, E. B., and Maslach, C. *Influencing attitudes and changing behavior,* 2d ed. Reading, Mass.: Addison-Wesley, 1977.

Statistical methods

The use of statistics as a tool in psychology began with Sir Francis Galton, an Englishman who did his most important work in the 1880s. Sir Francis was interested in individual differences—how people vary in height, weight, and such characteristics as color vision, sense of smell, hearing, and ability to judge weights. He was also interested in the workings of heredity. One of the questions that fascinated him was whether taller-than-average people tend to have taller-than-average children. Another was whether successful people tend to have successful children.

Since Galton's time, many investigators have pursued similar questions, such as: Do parents of above-average intelligence tend to have children of above-average intelligence? Do strict parents tend to produce children who are more or less aggressive than the children of lenient parents? Do people of high intelligence tend to be more or less neurotic than people of low intelligence?

To answer these questions, as Galton discovered, one must first make some accurate measurements. Galton himself devised a number of tests for such abilities as vision and hearing. Newer generations of psychologists have tried to perfect tests for intelligence and personality traits. But the results of the tests are meaningless unless they can be analyzed and compared in accordance with sound statistical practices.

Psychological statistics is the application of mathematical principles to the interpretation of the results obtained in psychological studies. It has been aptly called a "way of thinking" (1)—a problem-solving tool that enables us to summarize our knowledge of psychological events and make legitimate inferences from what we discover.

551

Probability and normal distribution

As an example of how we can profit from thinking in terms of statistical methods, suppose someone shows you two possible bridge hands. One is the bridge player's dream—thirteen spades. The other is a run-of-the-mill hand containing one ace, a few face cards, and many cards of no special value. The person who has put the hands together asks: "If you play bridge tonight, which of these hands are you less likely to pick up?"

Your first impulse would surely be to say, "The thirteen spades." When a bridge player gets such a hand, the newspapers report it as a great rarity. The player is likely to talk about it forever afterward. And, in all truth, a hand of thirteen spades is extremely rare. It occurs, as a statistician can quickly calculate, on an average of only once in about 159 billion deals.

But the other hand, whatever it is, is equally rare. The rules of statistical probability say that the chance of getting any particular combination of thirteen cards is only one in about 159 billion deals. The reason a hand of thirteen spades seems rarer than any other is that bridge players pay attention to it, while lumping all their mediocre hands together as if they were one and the same.

Think about the hand of thirteen spades in another way. Since it occurs only once in 159 billion deals, is it not a miracle that it should ever occur at all? No, it is not. It has been estimated that there are about 25 million bridge players in the United States. If each of them deals twenty times a week, that makes 26 billion deals a year. The statistical method tells us that we should expect a hand of thirteen spades to be dealt on the average of about once every six years.

Dreams and prophecies: why they often come true

The fact that we can expect a hand of thirteen spades to occur with some regularity explains some events in life that seem baffling to people who do not understand statistics. For example, every once in a while the newspapers report that someone shooting dice in Las Vegas has made twenty-eight passes (or winning throws) in a row. This seems almost impossible, and in fact the mathematical odds are more than 268,000,000 to 1 that it will not happen to anyone who picks up the dice. These are very high odds indeed. Yet, considering the large number

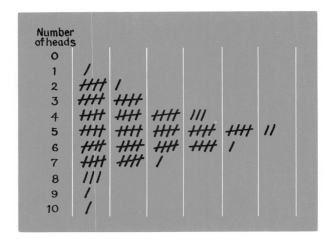

A-1 A tally of coin tosses

Ten coins were shaken in a cup and tossed on a table 100 times. This is a tally of the number of heads that appeared on each toss.

of people who step up to all the dice tables in Las Vegas, it is very likely that sooner or later someone will throw the twenty-eight passes.

The laws of probability also explain many of the coincidences that seem—to people unfamiliar with the laws—to represent the working of supernatural powers. A woman in Illinois dreams that her brother in California has died and the next morning gets a telephone call that he was killed in an accident. This may sound like an incredible case of mental telepathy, but the laws of probability offer a much simpler explanation. Most people dream frequently. Dreams of death are by no means rare. In the course of a year millions of people dream of the death of someone in the family. Sooner or later, one of the dreams is almost sure to coincide with an actual death.

Astrologers and other seers also profit from the rules of probability. If an astrologer keeps predicting that a catastrophe will occur, the forecast is bound to be right sooner or later, because the world is almost sure to have some kind of tragedy, from airplane accident to tornado, in any given period. And a prophet who makes a reputation by predicting the death of a world leader knows that there are many world leaders and that many of them are so advanced in age that their death would not be un-usual.

In a world as big as ours, all kinds of coincidences are likely to occur. The rules of statistics say that we should expect and not be surprised by them. Statistical analysis lets us view these coincidences for what they are and helps us recognize that they have no real significance.

What happens when you toss coins: a normal curve of distribution

One of the principles of probability, as Galton was the first to notice, has to do with the manner in which many things, including psychological traits, are distributed in the normal course of natural events. The principle can best be demonstrated by a simple experiment. Drop ten coins into a cup, shake them, throw them on a table, and count the number of heads. Do this a number of times, say 100. Your tally will almost surely turn out to be very much like the one shown in Figure A-1.

What you have come up with is a simple illustration of normal distribution. When you toss ten coins 100 times— a total of 1,000 tosses—you can expect 500 heads to come up, an average of five heads per toss. As the tally shows, this number came up most frequently. The two numbers on either side, four and six, were close seconds. The numbers farther away from five were increasingly infrequent. Ten came up only once, and zero did not come up at all. (Over a long period, both ten and zero would be expected to come up on an average of once in every 1,024 tosses.)

The tally shown in Figure A-1 can be converted into the bar graph shown in Figure A-2, which provides a more easily interpreted picture of what happened in the coin tossing. Note its shape—highest in the middle, then tapering off toward the extreme left and the extreme right. If a curve is drawn to connect the tops of the bars, we have a good example of the *normal curve of distribution* —which, as was explained in Chapter 1, is typical of the results generally found in all tests and measurements, of both physical and psychological traits. The curve for distribution of IQs, which was presented in Chapter 1, is repeated in Figure A-3. Note again that most people fall around the average of 100 and that only a few are found at the far extremes below 40 or above 160. The message of the curve is that in IQ (or height or weight or almost anything else) the people who are about average are in the majority—while some are as rare as those twenty-eight passes in a dice game.

Descriptive statistics

As a quick and convenient method of summarizing the characteristics of any group under study—as well as the distribution of these characteristics—psychologists use a technique called *descriptive statistics*. For example, suppose we draw up a new intelligence test and administer it to 10,000 college students. We wind up with 10,000 raw scores. To pass along what we have learned about the test, however, we need not quote every one of the 10,000 scores. Through the use of descriptive statistics we can summarize and condense. With just a few well-chosen

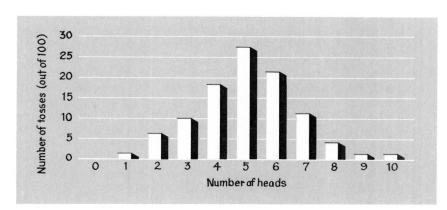

A-2

The tally in bar form

Here the tally of the coin-tossing experiment has been converted into a bar graph. Note the peak at the center and the rapid falling off toward each extreme.

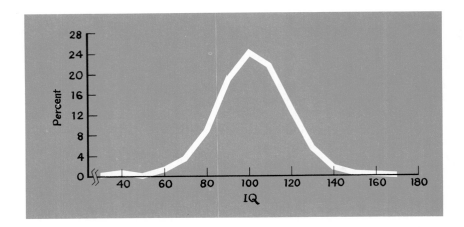

A-3

The normal curve of IQ distribution

The graph was constructed from IQs found in large-scale testing (2). Note that it looks very much like a line connecting the peaks of the bars in Figure A-2.

numbers, we can tell other people what they need to know in order to understand our results. Among the most commonly used forms of descriptive statistics are the following.

Number in group

Number in group is simply the total number of subjects we have studied. It is important because the chances of obtaining accurate results are greater if we study a large group than if we study only a small group. If we test only three people on our new intelligence test, we may happen to select three geniuses or three morons. A large sample is likely to be more representative of the population as a whole.

The statistical average (or mean)

Another useful piece of information is what in everyday language is called the *average*. For example, six students take an examination containing a hundred true-false questions and get test scores of 70, 74, 74, 76, 80, and 82. The average score—or in technical language, the *mean*—is the sum of the scores divided by the number of subjects who took the test. In other words, it is 456 divided by 6—or 76. Knowing that the mean is 76 tells us a great deal about the curve of distribution that could be drawn up from the scores. We know that the curve would

center on a figure of about 76—and that the majority of scores would be somewhere in this neighborhood.

Another measure of central tendency, or the point around which the scores tend to cluster, is the *median*. This is the halfway point that separates the lower 50 percent of scores from the higher 50 percent. In the example just given, the median would be 75, because half the scores fall below 75 and the other half fall above. The median is an especially useful figure when the data include a small number of exceptionally low or exceptionally high measurements. Let us say, for example, that the six scores on the true-false examination were 70, 74, 74, 76, 80, and 100. The one student who scored 100 brings up the mean score quite sharply, to 79. But note that 79 is hardly an "average" score, because only two of the six students scored that high. The median score, which remains at 75, is a better description of the data.

A third measure of central tendency is the *mode*—the measurement or score that applies to the greatest number of subjects. In the case of the true-false examination it would be 74, the only score made by as many as two of the students. The mode tells us where the highest point of the curve of distribution will be found. In a perfectly symmetrical normal curve the mode, the median, and the mean are the same. If the distribution is not symmetrical, but on the contrary tails off more sharply on the below-average side than on the above-average side, or vice versa (as often happens), it is useful to know all three of these figures.

Variability and standard deviation

Even when the normal curve is perfectly symmetrical, it may take different forms. Sometimes it is high and narrow. At other times it is shorter and wider. This depends on the *variability* of the measurements, which means the extent to which they differ from one another.

A crude way to describe the variability of scores made on a psychological test is simply to give the *range* of the scores—the highest minus the lowest. A much more sensitive description is provided by what is called the *standard deviation*, often abbreviated to *SD*. The standard deviation, which is computed from the data by a formula that will be explained later, is an especially useful tool because it indicates the proportion of scores or measurements that will be found under any part of the curve. As

Figure A-4 shows, the rule is that 34.13 percent of all the scores lie between the mean and a point 1 *SD* above the mean; 13.59 percent lie between 1 *SD* and 2 *SD*s above the mean; and 2.14 percent lie between 2 *SD*s and 3 *SD*s above the mean. Thus the *SD* gives a clear description of the variability of the measurements.

With intelligence quotients, for example, the mean is 100 and the *SD* is approximately 15. That is to say, an IQ one *SD* above the mean is 115. Armed with this knowledge alone, plus the general statistical rule illustrated in Figure A-4, we know that human intelligence tends to be distributed according to the figures in the following table:

IQ	Percentage of people
145 and over	0.14
130–144	2.14
115–129	13.59
100–114	34.13
85–99	34.13
70–84	13.59
55–69	2.14
under 55	0.14

The *SD* is also used to compute what are called *standard scores* or *z-scores*, which are often more meaningful than the raw scores made on a test. The z-score tells how many *SD*s a score is above or below the mean. It is obtained very simply by noting how many points a score is above or below the mean and then dividing by the *SD*. A z-score of 1 is one *SD* above the mean. A z-score of −1.5 is one-and-a-half *SD*s below the mean.

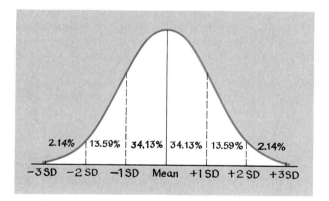

A-4 Using the SD to analyze data

In a normal curve of distribution, the standard deviation indicates how many measurements of scores will be found at various distances from the mean. As shown here, 34.13 percent of all measurements lie between the mean and 1 *SD* above the mean. Measurements that are between 1 *SD* and 2 *SD*s above the mean make up 13.59 percent of the total. Measurements between 2 *SD*s and 3 *SD*s above the mean make up 2.14 percent. The same percentages are found below the mean. Note that the figures do not quite add up to 100 percent. This is because 0.14 percent of measurements are found more than 3 *SD*s above the mean and another 0.14 percent are found more than 3 *SD*s below the mean. These various percentages hold for any normal distribution, although the size of the *SD* differs from one curve to another.

Percentiles

The meaning of *percentile* can best be explained by an example. A college man, a senior who wants to go on to graduate school, is asked to take the Graduate Record Examinations, which are nationally administered aptitude tests often used to screen applicants. He makes a score of 460 on the verbal test and 540 in mathematics. By themselves, these scores do not mean much either to him or to the faculty of the school he wants to attend. But records of other people's results on the test provide a means of comparing his scores with those of other college seniors. A score of 460 on the verbal test, the records show, lies on the 40th percentile for men. This means that 40 percent of all senior men who take the test make a lower score and 60 percent make higher scores. The 540 score in math lies on the 66th percentile for men. In other words, 66 percent of senior men make a lower score, and only 34 percent make higher scores. These percentile figures show the student and the school he hopes to attend how his ability compares with that of other prospective graduate students: he is well above average in mathematical ability (only a third of male college seniors make better scores) but below average in verbal aptitude.

Percentile ratings can be made for any kind of measurement, whether or not it falls into a normal pattern of distribution. A percentile rating of 99—or, to be more exact, 99.99—means that no one had a higher score. A percentile rating of 1—or, to be more exact, 0.01—is the lowest in the group.

Inferential statistics: the science of making generalizations

Descriptive statistics permits psychologists to summarize the findings of their studies and determine how one individual compares with the others. But psychologists need another tool to help them interpret and make generalizations from their studies. When psychologists study the behavior of a rat in a Skinner box, for example, they are not especially interested in how rapidly that particular animal demonstrates learning. Rather, their primary concern is to discover a general principle of behavior that says something about the learning processes of all rats—and, by implication, perhaps about the learning process in general. Psychologists studying the performance of a group of human subjects who memorize nonsense syllables—or who take part in an experiment on physical attractiveness—are not especially interested in those particular people. Their ultimate goal is to learn something about the behavior of people in general.

The mathematical tool they use is called *inferential statistics*—a set of techniques that enable them to make valid generalizations from their measurements of behavior.

Population and sample

Inferential statistics is important because science is interested in what is called the *population,* or sometimes the *universe*—that is to say, all people or all events in a particular category. But we cannot study or measure the entire population. We cannot give an intelligence test, for example, to every human being on the face of the earth. Even if we could, we still would not have reached the entire population, because many people would have died and many new people would have been born while we were conducting our test. We must settle for a *sample,* a group of convenient size taken from the population as a whole.

The rules of inferential statistics hold that we can make valid generalizations only if the sample we use is *representative* of the population we want to study. If we are seeking some general conclusions about the intelligence of the American population, we cannot use a sample made up entirely of college students or a sample made up of high-school dropouts. If we want to learn about political attitudes, we cannot poll only Republicans or people who live in big cities or people who belong to one church or one social class. Our sample must be representative of all kinds of Americans.

One way to ensure a representative sample is to choose it entirely at *random.* If each member of the total population has an absolutely equal chance of being studied—and if our sample is large enough—then it is very likely that the sample will represent all segments of the population. For example, the experimenter who wants to study the emotional behavior of rats in a laboratory cannot just reach into a cage and pull out the first dozen animals that are closest at hand. The very fact that they are close at hand may mean that they are tamer than the others and have a different emotional temperament. To achieve a more valid sampling, the experimenter might take the first rat, reject the second, take the third, reject the fourth, and so on. An investigator interested in student attitudes toward marijuana on a particular campus might draw up an alphabetical list of all students, then interview every tenth person on the list.

In the Gallup election polls, the random sampling starts with a list of the approximately 200,000 election districts and precincts in the nation. From this master list, about 300 districts are chosen at random. Then a map of each of the 300 districts is drawn up. On the map, one house is chosen as a starting point—again at random. Beginning at that point, and proceeding along a path drawn through the district, the pollsters collect interviews at each third residence or sometimes each fifth or twelfth residence, depending on the size of the sample they want (3).

Choosing valid control groups

The random technique of obtaining a representative sample is also standard procedure in selecting experimental and control groups. Ideally, every individual in the control group should be identical with a member of the experimental group. But this is of course impossible, because not even identical twins (who are too scarce anyway) are alike in every respect. To ensure as much similarity as possible between the experimental and control groups, subjects are usually assigned to one group or the other at random. Each individual who arrives at the laboratory has a 50-50 chance of being assigned to the experimental group and a 50-50 chance of being assigned to the control group.

Comparing two groups

For an example of how inferential statistics is used to compare two groups, such as an experimental group and a control group, let us imagine an experiment in which we try to determine whether physical health affects the learning ability of high-school students. We select an experimental group of sixteen representative, randomly chosen students who agree to take part in a rigorous health program. We arrange a supervised diet and exercise schedule, give them regular physical examinations, and promptly treat any illnesses or defects such as impaired vision or hearing. We also select a control group of sixteen similar students who do not receive any special treatment. At the end of a year, we find that the experimental group has a grade-point mean of 89, with a standard deviation of 3. The control group has a grade-point mean of 85, with a standard deviation of 4. Question: Is this difference of four points between the mean of the experimental group and the mean of the control group just a statistical accident? Or does it really mean that good health produces better grades?

Although four points may sound like a lot, the question is not easy to answer. The reason is that *any* two samples of sixteen people each, taken from the high-school population or any other population, are likely to have somewhat different means. Suppose we write the names of all the students in the high school (or in the city) on slips of paper and draw the slips from a hat. The grade-point mean for the first sixteen names we draw may be 85, for the next sixteen names 88, for the next sixteen names 87. If we pull twenty different samples of sixteen students each from the hat, we will find that the means vary from sample to sample, perhaps by as much as several points. So the question now becomes: Is the difference between the mean score of 89 for the experimental group and the mean score of 85 for the control group just an accidental result such as we might get by pulling samples from a hat? Or is it *statistically significant*—that is, does it indicate a real difference between our two groups?

Standard error of the mean

Helping answer the question is the fact that the means of randomly chosen samples, like raw measurements or scores themselves, tend to fall into a pattern of normal distribution. From our control group of sixteen with a grade-point mean of 85 and a standard deviation of 4, we can figure out the distribution of all the means we would be likely to get if we continued to pick samples of sixteen students at random, and we find that the curve looks like the one shown on the left in Figure A-5. We get the curve by using the formula (shown later) for the *standard error of the mean*. For the control group, the standard error of the mean turns out to be 1.0. For the experimental group, we get the curve shown at the right in Figure A-5. For this group the standard error of the mean turns out to be .75.

Having found the two curves, we can put them together as in Figure A-6, which shows a very high probability that there is a true difference between the grades of students who receive special medical care and the grades of students who do not. The possibility that the difference we found is merely a matter of chance is represented by the small area that lies beneath the extreme right-hand end of the control curve and the extreme left-hand end of the curve for the experimental group.

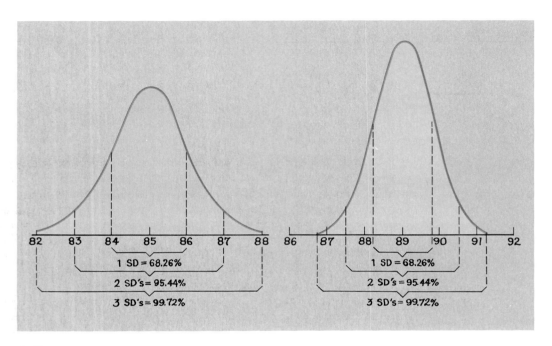

A-5 How means are distributed

These graphs show how the standard error of the mean of a sample is used to infer the true mean that would be found if the entire population could be measured. In the control group of high school students, at left, the mean is 85 and the standard error of the mean is 1.0. Thus we know that the chances are 68.26 percent that the true mean for the population lies between 84 and 86 (1 standard error above or below the mean of our sample), 95.44 percent that the true mean lies between 83 and 87 (2 standard errors above or below), and 99.72 percent that the true mean lies between 82 and 88 (3 standard errors above or below). In the experimental group, at right, the mean is 89 and the standard error of the mean is 0.75. Therefore the chances are 68.26 percent that the true mean of the experimental population would fall between 88.25 and 89.75; the chances are 95.44 percent that the mean would fall between 87.50 and 90.50; and they are 99.72 percent that the mean would fall between 86.75 and 91.25. Note how the two graphs use the same principle that was illustrated in Figure A-4.

Probability and significance

In actual statistical calculation the curves shown in Figures A-5 and A-6 need not be constructed. We can use the two means and the standard error of each mean to work out what is called *the standard error of the difference between two means.* We can then use this figure to work out the probability that the difference we found was due merely to chance. In the case of the hypothetical experiment we have been describing, the probability comes to less than .01.

It is an arbitrary rule of thumb in experimental work that a difference is considered *statistically significant* only when the probability that it might have been obtained by chance is .05 (5 chances in 100, or 1 chance in 20) or less than .05.

In reports on experiments that can be analyzed with this kind of inferential statistics, the probability figure is always given. You will frequently find the note

$$p \leq .05$$

This means that the difference would be found by chance

only 5 times or less out of 100 and is therefore statistically significant. In virtually all the experiments cited in this book, *p* was .05 or less.

The technique and significance of correlation

As was said in Chapter 1, *correlation* is a statistical tool used to examine two different measurements (such as the IQs of parents and the IQs of their children)—and to determine, from what would otherwise seem hopelessly jumbled numbers, what relationship if any exists between the two measurements.

Some correlations are *positive*. This means that the higher a person measures on scale *X* (for example, IQ) the higher that person is likely to measure on scale *Y* (for example, grades). Other correlations are *negative*. This means that a high score on scale *X* is likely to be accompanied by a low score on scale *Y*. For example, the frequency of premature births has been found to be negatively correlated with social class—meaning that there tends to be less prematurity among upper-income families than lower-income families. Negative correlations also exist between aggressive behavior in children and social class and between test anxiety and grades made in schools.

Scatter plots

A rough idea of the degree of correlation between two traits can be obtained by plotting each subject's score on scale *X* against the subject's score on scale *Y*. For each person, a dot is entered at a point corresponding to the scores on both scales, as shown in Figure A-7. The result is what is called a *scatter plot*. If the dots are scattered completely at random, we can see that the correlation is 0. If we should happen on one of those extremely rare cases where the dots form a perfectly straight line, running diagonally up or diagonally down, we know that we are dealing with a perfect correlation, either positive or negative. Most scatter diagrams fall somewhere in between. If a fairly narrow diagonal oval would enclose most of the dots, the correlation is rather high. If the oval must be fatter, the correlation is lower.

Correlation coefficients

A more precise measure of the relationship between scores on the *X*-scale and scores on the *Y*-scale can be obtained—without the need for constructing a scatter plot—by using various statistical formulas for calculating a *correlation coefficient*. (The formulas are presented later.) A correlation coefficient can range from 0 (no correlation at all) to +1 (a perfect positive correlation) or

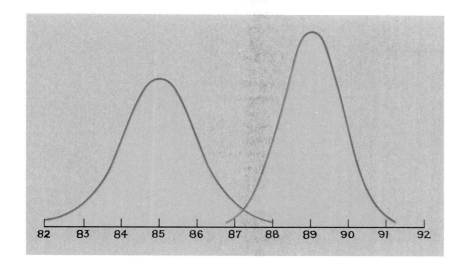

A-6
Is the difference between the means significant?
When we superimpose the curves shown in Figure A-5, we find that they have only the small gray area in common. This area represents the probability that the difference between the two means was due solely to chance. The probability that the difference is a real one is represented by the colored areas.

−1 (a perfect negative correlation). But correlations of +1 or −1 are very rare. Even such physical traits as height and weight, which would seem to go together in almost perfect proportion, do not reach a correlation of +1. Some typical correlations that have been found in various studies are the following:

Between IQ and college grades	.50
Between parents' IQs and child's IQ	.49
Between IQ and ability at pitch discrimination	.00
Between boys' height at age two and height at age eighteen	.60
Between boys' height at age ten and height at age eighteen	.88

Correlation and prediction

The correlation coefficients in the above table show that there is a considerable relationship between boys' height at age two and at age eighteen—and an even greater relationship between height at age ten and at age eighteen. Knowing that these relationships exist, we can make some predictions. We can say that a boy who is taller than average at two—or especially at ten—has a pretty good chance of also being taller than average at eighteen. Because of the .50 correlation coefficient between IQ and college grades, we can suggest that high-school seniors who make high scores on intelligence tests have a good chance of getting high grades in college, and that students with very low scores run the risk of failure.

It must always be kept in mind, however, that a coefficient of correlation is less accurate in making predictions than it sounds. Only when the correlation is very close to 1, as in the scatter plot that is shown at the right in Figure A-7, does every subject tend to show a close relationship between score on scale X and score on scale Y. Even in a correlation of .75, which sounds high, there is a considerable amount of scatter, representing subjects who scored relatively low on scale X but relatively high on scale Y, or vice versa. Since most correlations found in psychological studies are lower than .75, we must be quite tentative in making predictions.

Correlation, cause, and effect

Just knowing the degree of relationship implied by a correlation coefficient is often of value to psychologists. For example, it has been found that there is a positive correlation between strict discipline on the part of parents and the amount of aggressive behavior displayed by children. This fact has a number of implications for child-rearing practices and for developmental psychology.

Again, however, it is important not to exaggerate the degree of relationship expressed by a correlation coefficient. We cannot say that strict discipline always—or even usually—is accompanied by aggressive behavior. Moreover, we must avoid jumping to conclusions about cause and effect. Did the children become aggressive because the parents were strict, or were the parents strict because the children were aggressive? Is it possible that

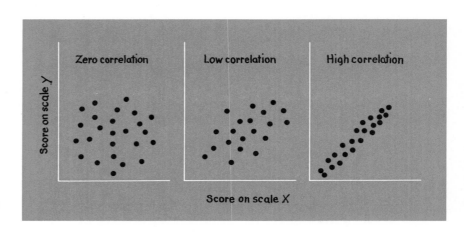

A-7

Scatter plots of correlations

For each subject, a dot has been placed at a point indicating both score on scale X and score on scale Y (4).

some third factor caused both the parents' strictness and the children's aggression? (For example, it may be that parents who are generally cold and rejecting of their children tend to be strict and that it is the coldness and rejection, rather than the strictness, that make the children aggressive.)

To avoid the danger of jumping to false conclusions on the basis of correlations, keep in mind that there is a very high correlation between the number of permanent teeth that have erupted through the schoolchild's gums and the child's raw scores for questions answered correctly on any kind of intelligence or aptitude test. But it would be foolish to conclude that more teeth make the child smarter or that better scores make more teeth appear. Increased maturity produces both the teeth and the higher scores.

The mathematical computations

The use of correlations and other descriptive and inferential statistics is not nearly so difficult as might be assumed. The mathematical knowledge required for these kinds of analysis is really not complicated at all. One need only be able to manipulate mathematical symbols, the most frequently used of which are explained in Figure A-8, and to apply the few basic formulas presented in Figure A-9.

The symbols and formulas are given at the start of this section on computations so that they can be found all in one place for future reference. They may seem rather difficult when shown all together in this fashion, but their application should be apparent from the examples that will be presented as we go along.

The kind of measurement that an investigator often wants to analyze is illustrated in Figure A-10. Here seventeen students have taken a psychological test and have made scores ranging from 60 to 97. The raw scores are a jumble of figures, from which we now want to determine the mean, the standard deviation, and the standard error of the mean.

The mean

The formula for computing the mean, as shown in Figure A-9, is

$$M = \frac{\Sigma X}{N}$$

N	Number of subjects from whom a measurement or score has been obtained
X	The numerical value of an individual score
Y	If each subject is measured on two scales, the numerical value of an individual score on the second scale
Σ	The Greek capital letter sigma, standing for "sum of"
ΣX	The sum of all the individual scores on scale X
M	The mean, which is the sum of the scores divided by the number of subjects
x	A deviation score; that is, the difference between an individual score and the mean for the group of which the individual is a member
y	A deviation score on the second scale, or Y-scale
SD	The standard deviation of the scores
SE_M	The standard error of the mean; also called the standard deviation of the mean
D_M	The difference between two means; for example, the difference between the mean (M) of scale X and the mean of scale Y
SE_{D_M}	The standard error of the difference between two means, used as a measure of whether the difference is significant
p	Probability, expressed in decimals ranging from .00 (no chance) through .50 (50-50 chance) to 1.00 (100 percent chance). A result is considered statistically significant when $p \leq .05$, meaning that there are only 5 chances in 100 (or fewer) that it was obtained by chance
r	Correlation coefficient obtained by the product-moment method
ρ	Correlation coefficient obtained by the rank-difference method
z	A standard score, expressed in number of SDs above or below the mean
C	Coefficient of contingency; type of correlation used to find relationships between events on a nominal scale

A-8 Some useful mathematical symbols
These are the symbols used in the statistical formulas discussed in this appendix.

1 For determining the mean:

$$M = \frac{\Sigma X}{N}$$

2 For determining a deviation score:

$$x = X - M$$

3 For determining the standard deviation:

$$SD = \sqrt{\frac{\Sigma x^2}{N - 1}}$$

4 For determining a z-score:

$$z = \frac{x}{SD}$$

5 For determining the standard error of the mean:

$$SE_M = \frac{SD}{\sqrt{N}}$$

6 For determining the difference between two means:

$$D_M = M_1 - M_2$$

7 For determining the standard error of the difference between two means:

$$SE_{D_M} = \sqrt{(SE_{M1})^2 + (SE_{M2})^2}$$

8 For determining the critical ratio:

$$\text{Critical ratio} = \frac{D_M}{SE_{D_M}}$$

9 For determining the coefficient of correlation by the product-moment method:

$$r = \frac{\Sigma xy}{(N - 1)SD_x SD_y}$$

10 For determining the coefficient of correlation by the rank-difference method:

$$\rho = 1 - \frac{6(\Sigma D^2)}{N(N^2 - 1)}$$

A-9 Some statistical formulas

These are some of the formulas most frequently used in psychological statistics. Their use is explained in the text and in the following figures.

1 78	**4** 74	**7** 92	**10** 74	**13** 70	**16** 82
2 97	**5** 80	**8** 72	**11** 85	**14** 84	**17** 78
3 60	**6** 77	**9** 79	**12** 68	**15** 76	

A-10 The raw material of statistical analysis: test scores of seventeen students

These raw scores, obtained by students on a psychological test, are analyzed in the text.

These symbols denote, as Figure A-8 shows, that the mean equals the sum of the individual scores divided by the number of subjects.

The way the formula is applied is illustrated in Figure A-11. The sum of the individual scores, which are shown in column one, is 1,326. The number of subjects is 17. Thus the mean is 1,326 divided by 17, or 78.

The standard deviation

The method of finding the standard deviation is also illustrated in Figure A-11. The formula for the standard deviation is

$$SD = \sqrt{\frac{\Sigma x^2}{N - 1}}$$

This means that we square each of the deviation scores, add up the total, and divide the total by the number of subjects minus 1. The square root of the figure thus obtained is the standard deviation.

The deviation scores shown in column two have been obtained by the formula $x = X - M$—that is, by subtracting the mean, which is 78, from each individual score. These figures in column two have then been squared to give the figures in column three. The sum of the x^2 figures is 1,224, and this figure divided by 16 (our $N - 1$) comes to 76.5. The standard deviation is the square root of 76.5 or 8.75.

The standard error of the mean

Finding the standard error of the mean for our group is extremely simple. The formula is

$$SE_M = \frac{SD}{\sqrt{N}}$$

Test scores (X)	Deviation scores (x)	Deviation scores squared (x^2)
78	0	0
97	+19	361
60	−18	324
74	− 4	16
80	+ 2	4
77	− 1	1
92	+14	196
72	− 6	36
79	+ 1	1
74	− 4	16
85	+ 7	49
68	−10	100
70	− 8	64
84	+ 6	36
76	− 2	4
82	+ 4	16
78	0	0
$\Sigma X = 1326$		$\Sigma x^2 = 1224$

$$M = \frac{\Sigma X}{N} = \frac{1326}{17} = 78$$

$$SD = \sqrt{\frac{\Sigma x^2}{N - 1}} = \sqrt{\frac{1224}{16}} = \sqrt{76.5} = 8.75$$

A-11 Computing the mean and SD
of the seventeen scores

Using the formulas in Figure A-9, we first compute the mean score (M) for the seventeen students, which comes out to 78. Once we have the mean, we can work out the standard deviation (SD). We start by obtaining the deviation scores ($x = X - M$), then squaring these deviaton scores to get x^2.

We have found that the SD of our sample is 8.75 and our N is 17. The formula yields

$$SE_M = \frac{8.75}{\sqrt{17}} = \frac{8.75}{4.12} = 2.12$$

Differences between groups

For an example of how to apply the formulas for analyzing differences between groups, let us return to the hypothetical experiment mentioned earlier. We had the school grades, you will recall, of an experimental group of sixteen students who took part in a health program; the mean was 89 and the standard deviation was 3. We also had the grades of a control group of sixteen students; the mean for this group was 85 and the standard deviation was 4.

The difference between the two means is easily computed from the formula

$$D_M = M_1 - M_2$$

which means that the difference between the means is the mean of the first group minus the mean of the second group—in this case, 89 minus 85, or 4. To know whether this difference is statistically significant, however, we must calculate the standard error of the difference between the two means. To do so, as Figure A-9 shows, we must use the fairly complex formula

$$SE_{D_M} = \sqrt{(SE_{M1})^2 + (SE_{M2})^2}$$

Our first step is to compute SE_{M1}, the standard error of the mean of our first or experimental group. We do so as shown earlier, this time with 3 as our standard deviation and 16 as our number of subjects.

$$SE_{M1} = \frac{SD}{\sqrt{N}} = \frac{3}{\sqrt{16}} = \frac{3}{4} = 0.75$$

We also compute SE_{M2}, the standard error of the mean of our second or control group, where the standard deviation is 4 and the number of subjects is 16.

$$SE_{M2} = \frac{SD}{\sqrt{N}} = \frac{4}{\sqrt{16}} = \frac{4}{4} = 1.00$$

Thus SE_{M1} is 0.75 and SE_{M2} is 1.00, and the standard error of the difference between the two means is computed as follows:

$$\begin{aligned} SE_{D_M} &= \sqrt{(SE_{M1})^2 + (SE_{M2})^2} \\ &= \sqrt{(0.75)^2 + (1)^2} \\ &= \sqrt{.5625 + 1} \\ &= \sqrt{1.5625} \\ &= 1.25 \end{aligned}$$

To complete our analysis of the difference between the two groups, we need one more statistical tool—the *critical ratio*. This is given by the formula

$$\text{Critical ratio} = \frac{D_M}{SE_{D_M}}$$

In the case of our hypothetical experiment we have found that D_M is 4 and that SE_{D_M} is 1.25. Thus

$$\text{Critical ratio} = \frac{4}{1.25} = 3.2$$

This critical ratio gives us a measure of the probability that our difference was due merely to chance. For reasons that mathematically minded students may be able to work out for themselves but that need not concern the rest of us, the magic numbers for the critical ratio are 1.96 and 2.57. If the critical ratio is as high as 1.96, then $p \leq .05$, and the difference is considered statistically significant. If the critical ratio is as high as 2.57, then $p \leq .01$, and the difference is considered highly significant. The critical ratio we found for our two groups, 3.2, is well over 2.57; thus we can have some confidence that the difference was not the result of chance.

Correlation coefficients

There are a number of ways of computing correlation coefficients, depending on the type of data that are being studied. The most frequently used is the *product-moment method,* which obtains a coefficient of correlation designated by the letter r for the relationship between two different measurements. The formula is

$$r = \frac{\Sigma xy}{(N-1)SD_x SD_y}$$

To use the formula we have to determine the amount by which each subject's score on scale X differs from the mean for all scores on scale X—in other words the value for x, the deviation score, which may be plus or minus. We must also determine the amount by which the subject's score on the second test, or scale Y, differs from the mean for all scores on scale Y—in other words, the value for y, which also may be plus or minus. We then multiply x by y for each subject and add the xy products for all the subjects in the sample. This gives us the top line, or numerator, of the formula. The bottom line, or denominator, is found by multiplying the number of subjects minus 1 ($N-1$) by the standard deviation of the scores

Subject	Test scores X	Test scores Y	Deviation scores x	Deviation scores y	Product of deviation scores (xy)
1	60	81	−12	+ 1	− 12
2	80	92	+ 8	+12	+ 96
3	70	76	− 2	− 4	+ 8
4	65	69	− 7	−11	+ 77
5	75	88	+ 3	+ 8	+ 24
6	85	96	+13	+16	+208
7	60	64	−12	−16	+192
8	75	75	+ 3	− 5	− 15
9	70	77	− 2	− 3	+ 6
10	80	82	+ 8	+ 2	+ 16
					$\Sigma xy = 600$

$N = 10$
For scale X, $M = 72$, and $SD_x = 8.56$
For scale Y, $M = 80$, and $SD_y = 9.98$

Thus

$$r = \frac{\Sigma xy}{(N-1)SD_x SD_y} = \frac{600}{(10-1) \times 8.56 \times 9.98}$$

$$= \frac{600}{768.9} = .78$$

A-12 **A product-moment correlation**
Shown here are the calculations required to determine the product-moment correlation between the scores made by ten subjects on two different tests, X and Y. First we compute the mean and *SD* for scales X and Y as was described in Figure A-11. Then we calculate each subject's deviation scores (x and y) for each scale and multiply them together to produce the product of the deviation scores (xy). Note that four subjects who scored above the mean on scale X also scored above the mean on scale Y (subjects 2, 5, 6, and 10). Four subjects who scored below the mean on scale X also scored below the mean on scale Y (subjects 3, 4, 7, and 9). Only two subjects (1 and 8) scored above the mean on one test and below the mean on the other. Thus multiplying the x deviations times the y deviations gives us eight positive products and two negative products. Σxy, the total of the positive products minus the negative products, comes to 600. The correlation coefficient works out to .78.

on the X-scale (SD_x) and then multiplying the product by the standard deviation of the scores on the Y-scale (SD_y). An example is shown in Figure A-12.

In some cases it is convenient to use the *rank-difference method,* which produces a different coefficient of correlation called ρ (the Greek letter *rho*), which is similar to but not exactly the same as r. The formula is

$$\rho = 1 - \frac{6(\Sigma D^2)}{N(N^2 - 1)}$$

The method of applying the formula is demonstrated in Figure A-13. Note that the D in the formula refers to the difference between a subject's rank on scale X—that is, whether first, second, third, or so on among all the subjects—and the subject's rank on scale Y. ΣD^2 is found by squaring each subject's difference in rank and adding to get the total for all subjects.

Contingency

One other frequently used type of correlation is known as the *coefficient of contingency,* symbolized by the letter C. This is used to find relationships between events that can be measured only on what is called a *nominal scale*—where all we can say about them is that they belong to certain groups. For example, we can set up a nominal scale on which all college students taking a humanities course are grouped in class 1, all taking engineering are grouped in class 2, and all taking a preparatory course for one of the professional schools such as law or medicine are grouped in class 3. We might set up another nominal scale on which we designate the students as males or females. If we then want to determine whether there is any relationship between a student's sex and the kind of college course the student is likely to take, we use the coefficient of contingency. Its meaning is roughly the same as that of any other coefficient of correlation.

Subject	Test scores X	Test scores Y	Rank X	Rank Y	Difference in rank (D)	Difference squared (D²)
1	60	81	9.5	5	−4.5	20.25
2	80	92	2.5	2	−0.5	0.25
3	70	76	6.5	7	+0.5	0.25
4	65	69	8.0	9	+1.0	1.00
5	75	88	4.5	3	−1.5	2.25
6	85	96	1.0	1	0.0	0.00
7	60	64	9.5	10	−0.5	0.25
8	75	75	4.5	8	−3.5	12.25
9	70	77	6.5	6	−0.5	0.25
10	80	82	2.5	4	+1.5	2.25

$\Sigma D^2 = 39.00$

$N = 10$
Thus

$$\rho = 1 - \frac{6(\Sigma D^2)}{N(N^2 - 1)} = 1 - \frac{6(39)}{10(10^2 - 1)}$$

$$= 1 - \frac{234}{990} = 1 - .24 = .76$$

A-13 Computing a rank-difference correlation

Here the same scores that were shown in Figure A-12 have been used to find the rank-difference correlation, which comes to .76—very close to the .78 found in Figure A-12 for the product-moment correlation. Note that here we disregard the individual scores on scale X and scale Y and use merely the rank of each score as compared with the others on the scale. Subjects 2 and 10 are tied for second place on the X scale. Their rank is therefore considered to be 2.5, halfway between second and third place.

Summary

1 *Psychological statistics* is the application of mathematical principles to the interpretation of results obtained in psychological studies.
2 The statistical method is of special importance as a *way of thinking*—reminding us that many events take place in accordance with the laws of probability and

that remarkable coincidences can often be explained as occurring by mere chance.
3 Many events in nature, including many human traits, fall into the pattern of the *normal curve of distribution*. In this curve, most such events or traits cluster around the average measurement, and the number then gets

smaller toward the lower and upper extremes.

4 *Descriptive statistics* provides a convenient method of summarizing scores and other psychological measurements. Important types of descriptive statistics are:

a The *number of subjects,* or N.

b Measures of central tendency, including the arithmetic average, or *mean* (total of all scores divided by N), *median* (point separating the lower half of scores from the upper half), and *mode* (most frequent score in the group).

c Index of *variability,* including *range* (obtained by subtracting the lowest score from the highest) and *standard deviation,* symbolized by *SD.* In a normal distribution, 34.13 percent of the scores lie between the mean and 1 *SD* above the mean, 13.59 percent between 1 *SD* and 2 *SDs* above the mean, and 2.14 percent between 2 *SDs* and 3 *SDs* above the mean, while 0.14 percent lie more than 3 *SDs* above the mean. The same pattern of distribution exists below the mean.

5 *Percentiles* are used to describe the position of an individual score in the total group. A measurement on the 75th percentile is larger than 75 percent of the measurements, or, to put it another way, 25 percent of measurements lie on or above the 75th percentile.

6 *Inferential statistics* is made up of procedures that allow us to make generalizations from measurements. It enables us to infer conclusions about a *population* or *universe,* which is the total of all possible cases in a particular category, by measuring a relatively small *sample.* To permit valid generalization, however, the sample must be *representative.* One way to ensure that the sample is representative is to choose it entirely at *random,* with each member of the population having an equal chance of being selected.

7 A set of findings is considered *statistically significant* when the probability that the findings might have been obtained by chance is only 5 in 100 or less. The figure is expressed mathematically as $p \leq .05$.

8 *Correlations* between two measurements—such as scores on two different tests—range from 0 (no relationship) to +1 (perfect positive relationship) or −1 (perfect negative relationship).

9 The symbols and formulas for the statistical analyses are shown in Figures A-8 and A-9.

Glossary

A

abnormal behavior Behavior that is statistically unusual, considered strange or undesirable by most people, and a source of unhappiness to the person who displays it.

abnormal psychology The study of mental and emotional disturbances and their treatment.

absolute threshold The minimum amount of stimulus energy to which a receptor will respond 50 percent of the time.

accommodation The process of changing one's cognitive view when new information dictates such a change; one of the processes emphasized in Piaget's theory of intellectual development.

achievement motive The desire for success.

achievement test A test that measures the individual's present level of either skill or knowledge.

acrophobia An abnormal fear of heights.

active processing The mental work performed by a listener in interpreting speech. The listener tries to recognize sounds, identify words, look for syntactic patterns, and search for semantic meaning.

acuity A scientific term for sharpness of vision.

adaptation The tendency of the sensory apparatus to adjust to any steady and continued level of stimulation and to stop responding.

addiction Physiological or psychological dependence on regular use of a drug.

adjustment Living in harmony with oneself and outside events.

adrenal glands A pair of endocrine glands, lying atop the kidneys.

adrenalin (*also called* **epinephrine**) A hormone secreted by the adrenal glands, associated with the bodily states of fear or "flight" situations.

aerial perspective A clue to distance perception; refers to the fact that distant objects appear less distinct and less brilliant in color than nearby objects.

afferent neuron A neuron that carries impulses from the sense organs toward the central nervous system.

affiliation motive The desire to be closely associated with other people.

afterimage The visual phenomenon produced by withdrawal of a stimulus. Withdrawal is followed briefly by a positive afterimage, then by a negative afterimage.

aggression A type of behavior arising from hostile motives; it takes such forms as argumentativeness and fighting.

agoraphobia Abnormal fear of being in open spaces.

all or none principle The fact that a neuron, if it fires at all, fires as intense an impluse as it can.

alpha waves A pattern of regular waves of seven to ten cycles per second characteristically found when the brain is at rest.

altered states of consciousness States of consciousness different from normal waking experience, such as those produced by sleep, hypnosis, or drugs.

altruism Behavior that is kind, generous, and helpful to others.

amnesia Loss of memory. It may be caused by physical injury or it may be a defense mechanism—an exaggerated form of repression.

amphetamine Any of a group of drugs that excite the central nervous system.

amplitude The characteristic of a sound wave that determines the loudness we hear.

androgens The male hormones, secreted by the testes.

androgynous Behaving in some ways society considers appropriate for females and in other ways considered appropriate for males.

antisocial reaction See **psychopathic personality.**

anxiety An emotion characterized by a vague fear or premonition that something undesirable is going to happen.

anxiety reaction A neurosis whose victims describe themselves as chronically uneasy for reasons they cannot explain; the anxiety is the outstanding symptom.

anxiety state A group of neuroses in which anxiety is a prominent symptom, including *anxiety reaction* and *phobic reaction.*

apathy A state of indifference in which people lose all interest in what happens to them.

apparent motion The perception of motion in stimuli that do not actually move, as in *stroboscopic motion* or the *phi phenomenon.*

applied psychology The application of psychological knowledge and principles to practical situations in school, industry, social situations, and treatment of abnormal behavior.

approach-approach conflict A conflict in which the aroused motives have two incompatible goals, both of which are desirable.

approach-avoidance conflict A conflict in which the individual has a single goal with both desirable and undesirable aspects, causing mixed feelings.

aptitude A capacity to learn or to perform, such as mechanical or musical aptitude; an inborn ability that exists and can be measured even though the individual has had no special training to develop the skills (such as at mechanical or musical tasks).

aptitude test A test that measures the individual's *capacity* to perform, not the present level of skill or knowledge.

assertive coping A constructive attempt to get rid of anxiety and stress in a meaningful way that has some chance of success.

assimilation The process of incorporating a new stimulus into one's existing cognitive view; one of the processes emphasized in Piaget's theory of intellectual development.

attachment The inborn tendency of babies to approach caretakers, to be receptive to their help and to be least afraid when in their presence.

attention The process of focusing perception on a single stimulus or limited range of stimuli.

attitude An organized and enduring set of beliefs and feelings toward some object or situation and a predisposition to behave toward it in a particular way.

attribution theory The theory that social behavior is often influenced by our attempts to attribute behavior to a motive or other cause.

autokinetic illusion The illusion of self-generated movement that a stationary object, such as a point of light seen in an otherwise dark room, sometimes creates.

autonomic nervous system A complicated nerve network that connects the central nervous system with the glands and the smooth muscles of the body.

aversive conditioning A type of behavior therapy that attempts to associate a behavioral symptom with punishment rather than with pleasure and reward.

avoidance-avoidance conflict A conflict in which there is simultaneous arousal of motives to avoid alternatives, both of which are undesirable.

axon The fiber of the neuron with end branches that transmit messages to other neurons or to muscles and glands; the "sending" portion of the neuron.

B

basilar membrane A piece of tissue dividing the cochlea more or less in half for its entire length. The organ of Corti, containing the hearing receptors, lies on this membrane.

behavior The activities of an organism, both overt, or observable (such as motor behavior), and covert, or hidden (such as thinking).

behavior genetics The study of how

human beings and other organisms inherit characteristics that affect behavior.

behavior modification The technique of changing the behavior, especially of disturbed people, by manipulating rewards and punishments.

behavior therapy A type of psychotherapy that concentrates on eliminating abnormal behavior, which is regarded as learned, through new forms of learning.

behaviorism A school of thought maintaining that psychologists should concentrate on the study of overt behavior rather than on "mental life" or consciousness.

binocular vision A clue to distance perception; refers to the fact that the two eyes, being about two and a half inches apart, receive slightly different images of any seen object.

biofeedback A method of achieving control of bodily and brain functions through the feedback of information about these functions.

blind spot The point at which the optic nerve exits from the eyeball, creating a small and mostly insensitive gap in the retina.

bodily movement The sense that keeps us informed of the position of our muscles and bones.

brain control A term for control of behavior through drugs or electrical stimulation of the brain.

breathing drive A biological drive aroused by physiological requirements for oxygen.

brightness One dimension of the visual stimulus; dependent on intensity.

brightness constancy The tendency to perceive objects to be of consistent brightness regardless of the amount of light they actually reflect under different conditions of illumination.

bystander apathy The tendency of people, especially under crowded conditions, to ignore others who need help or situations that call for action.

C

CAI See **computer-assisted instruction.**

Cannon-Bard theory A neurological theory of emotion holding that stimuli in the environment set off patterns of activity in the hypothalamus and thalamus; these patterns are then relayed both to the autonomic nervous system, where they trigger the bodily changes of emotion, and to the cerebral cortex, where they result in the feelings of emotion.

caretaker period The first eighteen months of life, during which babies' personality development depends chiefly on a close relationship with the mother or other caretaker.

case history An attempt to reconstruct a person's life to show how patterns of behavior have developed.

categories Logical groups into which materials can be lumped together; an aid to long-term memory.

cell body (of a neuron) The portion of a neuron containing its genes, as opposed to the fiber portion of the neuron.

central nervous sytem The spinal cord and the brain.

cerebellum The brain structure that controls body balance and helps coordinate bodily movements.

cerebral cortex The highest part of the brain, the surface of the cerebrum; a dense and highly interconnected mass of neurons.

cerebrum The large brain mass of which the cerebral cortex is the surface. It is divided into two separate halves called the left hemisphere and the right hemisphere.

certainty motive The desire to know where one stands and to be able to predict the course of events.

character disorder See **personality disorder.**

chromosome The mechanism of human heredity. There are twenty-three pairs of these tiny structures, forty-six in all, found in the fertilized egg cell and repeated through the process of division in every cell of the body.

chronological age A person's actual age in years and months; compared with mental age to produce IQ.

ciliary muscles The muscles that control the shape of the lens of the eye.

clairvoyance The supposed ability to perceive something that is not apparent to the sense organs; a form of extrasensory perception.

classical conditioning A type of learning process through which a response becomes attached to a conditioned (or previously neutral) stimulus.

claustrophobia Abnormal fear of being in enclosed places, such as elevators.

client A term used, in preference to "patient," by clinical psychologists to refer to the people they treat.

clinical psychology The branch of applied psychology concerned with the application of psychological knowledge to the treatment of personality problems and mental disorders.

closure The tendency to perceive an object in its entirety even when some details are missing.

clustering The organization of materials into groups, such as categories; an aid to long-term memory and retrieval.

cochlea A bony structure of the inner ear shaped like a snail's shell; contains the receptors for hearing.

codeine A narcotic drug derived from the poppy plant.

cognition All the mental processes entailed in thinking.

cognitive consonance Consistency and agreement among one's beliefs, feelings and behavior.

cognitive dissonance Lack of consistency among beliefs, feelings, and behavior. The theory of cognitive dissonance maintains that people are strongly motivated to relieve such dissonance, often by changing attitudes.

cognitive psychology A school of thought maintaining that the mind does not merely react to stimuli but actively processes the information it receives into new forms and categories.

collective unconscious In Jung's theory, a respository for the events of human history, superstitions, fears, etc., which influence all people.

color blindness A visual defect involving deficiency in color discrimination.

color constancy The tendency to perceive a familiar object as being of constant color, regardless of changes in illumination that alter its actual stimulus properties.

communication A general term for exchanges of information and feelings between two (or more) people. For its special meaning in social psychology, *see* **persuasive communications.**

community therapy A type of interactional therapy in which the therapist attempts to change conflicts and patterns of behavior through alteration of behavior in the community.

comparative psychology The study of processes common to several animal species, including man.

complementary hues Two hues that, when added one to the other, yield gray.

complexity The characteristic of a sound wave that determines the timbre we hear; caused by the number and strength of the overtones.

compulsion An irresistible urge to perform some act over and over again.

computer-assisted instruction (CAI) A method of programed instruction in which a computer is used as a teaching machine.

concept A mental grouping of objects or ideas on the basis of similarity.

conceptual intelligence The term used by Piaget to describe the developmental process after the age of two, in which the child increasingly uses concepts to organize the evidence of the senses and to engage in ever more complex thinking and problem solving.

concrete operations The term applied by Piaget to the stage of intellectual development (ages seven to eleven) when children can reason logically about objects they see but have yet to learn to deal with rules in the abstract.

conditional positive regard In Rogers' personality theory, the cause of maladjustments; approval of some but not all aspects of an individual's behavior.

conditioned operant Behavior learned through operant conditioning; a type of behavior with which the organism "operates" on its environment to obtain a desired result.

conditioned response A response that has become attached through learning to a conditioned (or previously neutral) stimulus; an example is the salivation by Pavlov's dog to the sound of the metronome.

conditioned stimulus In classical conditioning, a previously neutral stimulus (such as a sound) that through pairing with an unconditioned stimulus (such as food) acquires the ability to set off a response (such as salivation).

cones One of two types of receptors for vision located in the retina. The cones are receptors for color and are also sensitive to differences in light intensity resulting in sensations of black, white, and gray.

conflict The simultaneous arousal of two or more incompatible motives, resulting in unpleasant emotions.

conformity The yielding by an individual to pressures from another person or, more usually, from a group.

connecting neuron A neuron that is stimulated by another neuron and passes its message along to a third neuron.

conservation The principle that such qualities as mass, weight, and volume remain constant regardless of changes in appearance; learned by the child during Piaget's stage of concrete operations.

consolidation A process, requiring time, during which the memory trace becomes more resistant to extinction.

constant reinforcement Provision of

reinforcement for every desired response.

continuity The tendency to perceive continuous lines and patterns.

contour In perception, the dividing line between figure and ground.

control group A group used for comparison with an experimental group. The two groups must be alike in composition and must be observed under the same circumstances except for the one variable that is manipulated in the case of the experimental group.

conversion reaction A form of hysteria, sometimes causing paralysis, blindness, or deafness.

coping An attempt, constructive or destructive, to relieve anxiety and stress.

core of personality To personality theorists, the tendencies and characteristics common to all people.

cornea The transparent bulge in the outer layer of the eyeball through which light waves enter.

corpus callosum A large nerve tract that connects the left and right hemispheres of the cerebrum and enables the two hemispheres to cooperate and share in duties.

correlation The degree of relationship between two different factors; measured statistically by the correlation coefficient.

correlation coefficient A statistic that describes in numbers ranging from −1 to +1 the degree of relationship between two different factors.

counseling psychology The branch of psychology that concentrates on vocational guidance, assistance with marital problems, and advice in other situations regarded as less serious or deepseated than the behavioral problems usually treated by clinical psychologists.

creative thinking A highly imaginative and rare form of thinking in which the individual discovers new relationships and solutions to problems and may produce an invention or an artistic creation.

credibility of the source A factor in the effectiveness of a persuasive communication.

critical ratio A measure of the degree of difference between two groups.

culture The ways of a given society, including its customs, beliefs, values, and ideals.

curve of forgetting A graph plotting the course of forgetting.

D

decibel A measure of the amplitude of sound.

defense mechanism A process, generally believed to be unconscious, in which the individual maintains that a frustration or conflict and the resulting anxiety do not exist or have no importance.

delusion A false belief, such as imagining that one is already dead.

dendrite The part of the neuron, usually branched, that has the special function of being sensitive to stimuli and firing off a nervous impulse; the "receiving" portion of the neuron.

dendritic spines Outgrowths of a dendrite, capable of being stimulated by the axon of another neuron.

denial A defense mechanism, closely related to repression, in which the individual simply denies the existence of the events that have aroused anxiety.

dependency motive The desire to rely on others.

dependent variable A change in behavior that results from changes in the conditions that affect the organism—that is, from changes in an *independent variable*.

depressant A drug that reduces activity of the central nervous system.

depression The feeling of sadness and sometimes total apathy, often due to guilt or the inability to cope with one's problems; a result of frustration or conflict or possibly influenced by chemical imbalances in the brain.

descriptive statistics A quick and convenient method of summarizing measurements. Important figures in descriptive statistics are the number of subjects; measures of central tendency, including the mean, median, and mode; and measurements of variability, including range and standard deviation.

desensitization An attempt to eliminate phobias by associating the stimulus that has caused the fear with relaxation rather than with fearful behavior; a technique used in behavior therapy.

development In personality theory, the way the common core of human personality is channeled into individual patterns by learning and experience.

developmental psychology The study of changes that take place, physically and psychologically, beginning at birth and continuing throughout life.

difference threshold (*also called* **just noticeable difference** *or* **j.n.d.**) The smallest difference in intensity or quality of stimulation to which a sensory receptor will respond 50 percent of the time.

difficult children Those who seem to

display an inborn tendency to negative and stubborn behavior.

direct aggression Aggressive behavior focused directly on the obstacle that has caused frustration.

displaced aggression Aggressive behavior directed against an "innocent bystander" because the cause of frustration or conflict cannot itself be attacked.

dispositional factors Behavior-producing factors that represent lasting and consistent personality traits.

dissociative reaction A form of hysteria in which people undergo some form of loss of contact with reality; they dissociate themselves in some manner from the conflicts that are troubling them. Three forms are amnesia, multiple personality, and sleep walking.

dissonance theory A theory maintaining that inconsistencies among one's beliefs, feelings, and behavior create a state of cognitive dissonance that the individual then tries to relieve, often by changing an attitude.

DNA (deoxyribonucleic acid) The complex chemical of which genes are composed.

double approach-avoidance conflict A conflict aroused by motives toward two goals that both have their good points and their bad.

double blind An experimental technique in which neither the subjects nor the experimenter knows which subjects are in the control group and which are in the experimental group.

drive A psychological urge created by the body's demands for homeostasis.

drug abuse The use of drugs, especially heroin but also psychedelic drugs and others, without medical indication and to excess.

ductless gland See **endocrine gland.**

E

eardrum A membrane between the outer part of the auditory canal and the middle ear.

easy children Those who display an inborn tendency to be cheerful and adapt quickly.

EEG See **electroencephalograph.**

efferent neuron A neuron that carries impulses from the central nervous system toward the muscles or glands.

ego According to psychoanalytical theory of personality, the conscious, logical part of the mind that develops as we grow up and that is our operational contact with reality.

ego ideal Our notion of how we would always think and behave if we were as perfect as we would like to be.

electroencephalograph (EEG) A delicate instrument that measures the electrical activity of the brain.

electroshock A medical method of treating behavior disorders, especially depression, by passing an electric current through the patient's brain.

elimination drive A drive aroused by physiological requirements to get rid of the body's waste products.

emotion A feeling created by brain patterns accompanied by stirred-up or toned-down bodily changes.

emotional stress Wear and tear on the body created by the physical changes during emotional states.

empathy Understanding other people by putting yourself in their shoes and sharing their thoughts and feelings.

encoding A process in short-term memory that transforms information into the simplest and easiest form to handle.

encounter group A group of people who meet, usually under the leadership of a psychotherapist, with the goal of throwing off the masks they usually present in public and airing their true feelings.

endocrine gland (also called **ductless gland**) A gland that discharges chemical substances known as *hormones* directly into the blood stream, which then carries them to all parts of the body, resulting in many kinds of physiological changes.

engram Some kind of lasting trace or impression formed in living protoplasm by a stimulus; a deliberately vague term often used to describe the learning connection or memory trace.

environmental psychology Study of the effects of the physical environment on physical and psychological well-being.

epilepsy A form of brain malfunction that produces sudden mental blackouts and sometimes seizures or "fits."

epinephrine See **adrenalin.**

equilibrium The sense that gives us the information needed to keep us in balance and oriented to the force of gravity.

ESP See **extrasensory perception.**

estrogen The chief female hormone, secreted by the ovaries.

Eustachian tube A passage between the middle ear and the air chambers of the mouth and nose; it keeps the pressure on both sides of the eardrum constant.

existential psychology A school holding that our own attitudes toward events in our life are more important than the events themselves.

experiment A scientific method in which the experimenter makes a careful and rigidly controlled study of cause and effect, by manipulating an independent variable (or condition affecting the subject) and observing its effect on a dependent variable (or the subject's behavior in response to changes in the independent variable).

experimental group A group of subjects whose behavior is observed while the experimenter manipulates an independent variable.

exploration The baby's early attempts to examine new aspects of the environment.

extinction The disappearance of a conditioned response (or other learned behavior) when reinforcement is withdrawn.

extrasensory perception (ESP) Any of several forms of supposed ability to perceive stimuli through some means other than the sense organs.

extrovert An individual who dislikes solitude and prefers the company of other people.

F

family therapy A type of interactional therapy that attempts to change the patterns of behavior that various members of a family display toward one another.

fantasy Images; daydreams.

fat cells Cells scattered throughout the body that are designed for the storage of fatty compounds. An excess of such cells is believed to be a common cause of obesity.

feature detector A nerve cell that responds to special features of a stimulus reaching the sense organs—for example, to a horizontal line but not to a vertical line.

feedback In learning, information about how much progress is being made.

feminine The type of behavior society considers appropriate for females.

figure-ground In perception, the tendency to see an object as a figure set off from a neutral ground.

formal operations The term applied by Piaget to the stage of intellectual development (beginning at about age eleven or twelve) at which the child becomes capable of thinking in the abstract.

fovea The most sensitive part of the retina; contains only cones, which are packed together more tightly than anywhere else in the retina.

free association A tool of psychoanalysis in which patients, lying as relaxed as possible on a couch, are encouraged to let their mind wander where it will and to speak out every thought that occurs to them.

frequency The characteristic of a sound wave determining the tone or pitch that we hear; measured in number of cycles per second.

frustration The blocking of motive satisfaction by some kind of obstacle. (In popular usage, also the unpleasant feelings caused by the blocking of motive satisfaction.)

functional autonomy A principle holding that an activity that is originally a means to an end frequently acquires an independent function of its own and becomes an end in itself.

functional fixedness The tendency to think of an object in terms of its usual functions, not other possible functions; a common barrier to problem solving.

functional psychosis A psychosis having no apparent connection with any organic disturbance.

fundamental attribution error The common tendency to attribute the behavior of others to dispositional rather than situational factors.

G

galvanic skin reflex (GSR) A change in the electrical conductivity of the skin caused by activity of the sweat glands.

ganglion (*plural:* **ganglia**) A mass of nerve cells and synapses forming complex and multiple connections.

gene A tiny substance that is a molecule of *DNA*. The genes, grouped together into chromosomes, direct the growth of cells into specific parts of the body and account for inherited individual differences.

general adaptation syndrome A phrase coined by Selye for the sequence of events involved in prolonged stress; the initial shock or alarm, the recovery or resistance period, and at last exhaustion and death.

general anxiety The tendency to be anxious in many different kinds of situations.

general factor An intellectual ability posited by Thurstone as common to all the seven primary mental abilities.

Gestalt psychology A school of thought holding that all psychological phenomena must be studied as a whole (rather than broken down into parts) and in the context in which they occur.

gradient of texture A clue to distance perception; refers to the fact that nearby objects are seen more sharply and therefore appear grainier in texture than more distant objects.

grammar The rules of language for combining words into meaningful sentences.

group test A psychological test that can be given to many individuals at the same time.

group therapy A type of psychotherapy in which several patients are treated simultaneously.

GSR See **galvanic skin reflex.**

guided participation A technique used by behavior therapists for the practice of assertive coping.

H

hallucination An imaginary sensation, such as seeing nonexistent animals in the room or feeling bugs crawling under the skin.

hemispheres The two halves of the cerebrum and cerebral cortex. The left hemisphere appears to control language and logical thinking about details, the right hemisphere to be concerned with forms, patterns, and the "big picture."

Hering theory An early theory of color vision, holding that nervous messages must be paired as black-white, red-green, and blue-yellow; now believed to be generally true of the neurons from eye to cerebral cortex.

heroin A narcotic drug derived from the poppy plant.

heterosexuality Sexual attraction to members of the opposite sex.

hippocampus A part of the brain that appears essential to the transfer of information from short-term memory to long-term memory.

homeostasis An internal environment in which such bodily states as blood circulation, blood chemistry, breathing, digestion, temperature, and so on, are kept at optimal levels for survival of the living organism.

homosexuality Sexual attraction to members of the same sex.

hormones Substances produced by the endocrine glands and secreted into the blood stream; complicated chemicals that trigger and control many kinds of bodily activities and behavior.

hostility motive The desire to cause physical or psychological discomfort in others.

hue The sensation of color, determined by the length of the light wave.

human engineering A branch of applied psychology concerned with the design of equipment and machinery to fit the size, strength, and capabilities of the people who will use it.

humanistic psychology A school of thought especially interested in the qualities that distinguish human beings from other animals—such as desires for dignity, self-worth, and *self-actualization*.

humanistic therapy A form of psychotherapy based on the assumption that people will grow in a positive direction if only they have the chance.

hunger drive A biological drive caused by deprivation of food.

hyperkinesis A mental abnormality that makes children overactive, irritable, unable to concentrate, and "hard to handle."

hypnosis The act of inducing the hypnotic state, in which the subject is in a sort of dreamlike trance and highly susceptible to suggestions

from the hypnotist; sometimes used in psychotherapy.

hypochondriacal reaction An anxiety state in which the individual tends to excuse failures on the grounds of imaginary physical illness.

hypothalamus The portion of the brain that serves as a mediator between the brain and the body, helping control metabolism, sleep, hunger, thirst, body temperature, and sexual behavior, and that is also concerned with emotions.

hysteria A form of neurosis; includes *conversion reaction* and *dissociative reactions.*

I

id According to psychoanalytical theory, the unconscious part of the human mind comprising the individual's primitive instinctive forces toward sexuality (the *libido*) and aggression.

identification 1) A process in which children try to imitate the behavior of their parents or other "heroes." 2) In psychoanalytical theory, the process through which children resolve the Oedipus complex by absorbing their parents' characteristics into themselves. 3) As a defense mechanism, an attempt to relieve anxiety by becoming like another person or group.

illusion A perception that is a false interpretation of the actual stimuli.

illusory motion The perception of motion in an unchanging stimulus, such as in the *autokinetic illusion.*

imagery Forming a mental picture of events; an aid to long-term memory.

imitation See **learning through observation.**

implicit personality theory The assumption, held by most people, that certain personality traits are correlated with others—for example, that "warmth" of personality is accompanied by sociability and a good sense of humor.

incentive object A stimulus that arouses a drive or motive.

incentive value The particular desirability of any object or event that arouses a motive.

independence As used in social psychology, the tendency to make up one's own mind and decide on one's own behavior and thinking regardless of society's pressures.

independent variable A condition, affecting an experimental subject, that is controlled and varied by the experimenter, thus producing changes in the subject's behavior, called the *dependent variable*.

individual difference Any difference —as in physical size or strength, intelligence, sensory threshold, perceptions, emotions, personality, and so on—between the individual organism and other members of the species.

individual test A psychological test that is given by a trained examiner to one person at a time.

industrial psychology A branch of applied psychology, embracing the use of psychological knowledge in setting working hours and rest periods, improving relations between employer and employees, and so on.

inference A form of thinking; drawing logical conclusions from facts already known.

inferential statistics Statistics that are used to make generalizations from measurements.

inferiority complex A concept introduced by Adler to describe the condition of a person who for some reason has been unable to develop feelings of adequacy, independence, courage, and wholesome ambition.

information processing A description used by cognitive psychologists for the mental processes entailed in perception, learning, and thinking.

inhibition 1) The action of a neuron whose messages tend to stop another neuron from firing. 2) The suppression of behavior or emotional barriers to action, such as an inhibition against competitive or sexual activity.

inner ear The portion of the ear inward from the oval window; contains the cochlea, vestibule, and semicircular canals.

inner standards The principles we develop—and are motivated to live up to—of how we are supposed to behave.

insight 1) In problem solving, the sudden "flash of inspiration" that results in a successful solution (*compare* trial and error learning). 2) In psychotherapy, the discovery by the patient of psychological processes that have caused difficulties.

instinct An elaborate and inborn pattern of activity, occurring automatically and without prior learning in response to certain stimuli in the environment.

insulin A hormone, secreted by the pancreas, that burns up blood sugar to provide energy.

intellectualization A defense mechanism in which the individual tries to explain away anxiety by intellectually analyzing the situations that produce the unpleasant feelings and making them a matter of theory rather than of action.

intelligence The ability to profit from experience, to learn new pieces of information, and to adjust to new situations.

intelligence quotient (IQ) A numerical value assigned to an individual as a result of intelligence testing. The average intelligence quotient is set at 100.

intelligence test A test measuring the various factors that make up the capacity called intelligence. It measures chiefly the individual's ability to use acquired knowledge in a novel way.

intensity The strength of light waves, accounting for sensations of brightness.

interactional therapies Types of psychotherapy that concentrate on changing the individual's behavior toward other people.

interest test A test measuring the individual's interest or lack of interest in various kinds of amusements, literature, music, art, science, school subjects, social activities, kinds of people, and so on.

interference Failures of memory caused by the effect of old learning on new or new learning on old.

intermittent reinforcement See **partial reinforcement.**

interpersonal attraction A person's tendencies to like other people, largely determined by such factors as similarities in attitudes, interests, and personality.

interposition A clue to distance perception; refers to the fact that nearby objects interpose themselves between our eyes and more distant objects.

interpretation In perception, the meaning we attach to stimuli affecting the sense organs.

interview A scientific method in which the investigator obtains information through careful and objective questioning of the subject.

introspection Inward examination of a "mental life" or mental process that nobody but its possessor can see in operation.

introvert A term for people who tend to be preoccupied with their own thoughts and activities and to avoid social contact.

intuitive thought The term applied by Piaget to the stage of intellectual development (ages four to six) when the child is developing concepts that become more and more elaborate but are still based largely on the evidence of the senses.

IQ See **intelligence quotient.**

iris A circular arrangement of smooth muscles that contract and expand to make the pupil of the eye smaller in bright light and larger in dim light.

J

James-Lange theory of emotion A physiological theory holding that stimuli in the environment set off physiological changes in the individual, that the changes in turn stimulate sensory nerves inside the body, and that the messages of these sensory nerves are then perceived as emotion.

just noticeable difference (j.n.d.) See **difference threshold.**

L

latent learning Learning that takes place without reinforcement, almost as if by accident, then lies latent until reinforcement is provided.

learned helplessness A condition in which the organism has been subjected to punishment over which it has no control, leading to an impairment of the ability to learn or use old habits.

learning The process by which behavior becomes altered or attached to new stimuli.

learning by imitation See **learning through observation.**

learning sets Attitudes and strategies acquired in one learning situation and carried over to similar situations; "learning how to learn."

learning through modeling See **learning through observation.**

learning through observation (also called **learning through modeling, learning by imitation**) A type of learning in which the behavior of another organism is observed and imitated.

lens A transparent structure of the eye that changes shape to focus images sharply on the retina.

levels of processing A theory that long-term memory depends on how well we have analyzed and organized the material we learned.

libido According to psychoanalytic theory, a basic instinctual force in the individual, embracing sexual urges and such related desires as to be kept warm, well-fed, and happy.

lie detector A device designed to reveal whether a subject is telling the truth by measuring physiological changes, usually in heart rate, blood pressure, breathing, and galvanic skin reflex.

limbic system A set of interconnected pathways in the brain, including the hypothalamus, some primitive parts of the cerebrum that have to do with the sense of smell, eating and emotion, and other structures.

linear perspective A clue to distance perception; refers to the fact that parallel lines seem to draw closer together as they recede into the distance.

location constancy The tendency to perceive objects as being in their rightful and accustomed place and remaining there even when we move and their images therefore move across our eyes.

locus of control The belief that we are in control of our own life (inner locus) or at the mercy of outside events (external locus).

logical thinking An objective and disciplined form of thinking in which facts are carefully examined and conclusions consistent with the facts are reached.

long-term memory The permanent storehouse from which information can be retrieved under the proper circumstances.

loudness The hearing sensation determined by the amplitude of the sound wave.

LSD (lysergic acid diethylamide) A psychedelic drug.

M

made-up stories The organization of new materials by weaving them into narratives; an aid to long-term memory.

manic-depressive psychosis A functional psychosis characterized by extremes of mood, often by wild swings from intense excitement to deep melancholy.

marijuana The dried leaves and flowers of the hemp plant; a drug that affects different users in different ways, often interfering with short-term memory and concentration and producing feelings of elation.

masculine The type of behavior society considers appropriate for males.

maturation The physical changes, taking place after birth, that continue the biological development of the organism from fertilized egg cell to complete adult.

mean A measure of central tendency obtained by dividing the sum of all the measurements by the number of subjects measured.

measurement The assignment of numbers to traits, events, or subjects according to an orderly system.

median A measure of central tendency; the point separating the lower half of measurements from the upper half.

meditation A technique for producing an altered state of consciousness.

medulla The connection between the spinal cord and the brain; an important connecting link that is vital to life because it helps regulate heartbeat, blood pressure, and breathing.

memory trace The basis of a theory of remembering, holding that learning left some kind of trace in the nervous system that could be kept active through use but tended to fade away or become distorted through lack of practice.

mental age A person's age as measured by performance on an intelligence test; a person who scores as well as the average ten-year-old has a mental age of ten regardless of chronological age.

mental health A state of psychological well-being.

mentally gifted Having an IQ over 130.

mentally retarded Having an IQ below 70.

mental telepathy The supposed ability of one person to know what is going on in another person's mind; a form of extrasensory perception.

metabolism The bodily process that maintains life by turning food and oxygen into living tissue and energy.

middle ear The portion of the ear between the eardrum and the oval window of the inner ear; contains three bones that aid transmission of sound waves.

mnemonic device A form of memory aid in which memorized symbols provide organization for otherwise unrelated material.

mode A measure of central tendency; the measurement at which the greatest number of subjects fall.

modeling See **learning through observation.**

moral development The child's acquisition of standards of right and wrong, extensively studied by Kohlberg.

morpheme The smallest meaningful unit of language, made by combining *phonemes* into a prefix, word, or suffix.

morphine A narcotic drug derived from the poppy plant.

motion parallax A term describing the fact that when we move our heads, near objects move across our field of vision more rapidly than objects that are farther away.

motivated forgetting Forgetting because we want to forget.

motivation A general term referring to the forces regulating behavior that is undertaken because of drives, needs, or desires and is directed toward goals.

motive A desire for a goal or incentive object that has acquired value for the individual.

motive hierarchy The pattern of motive strength, from strongest to weakest.

motive targets The people to whom motives are directed. People may exhibit strong motives of affiliation toward a "target" such as their parents and of hostility toward other "targets."

multiple personality A dissociative reaction in which individuals seem to be split into two or more different selves, representing sides of their personality they cannot integrate into a unity.

muscle Fibers of tissue capable of producing motion by contraction and expansion. Three types are *striped muscles, smooth muscles,* and *heart muscles.*

muscle tension Contractions of a muscle; one of the bodily changes often observed in emotion.

myelin sheath A fatty sheath, white in appearance, that covers many neuron fibers and speeds the transmission of nervous impulses.

N

narcotic A term applied to a group of drugs that produce repose or sleep.

naturalistic observation A scientific method in which the investigator does not manipulate the situation and cannot control all the variables; the investigator tries to remain unseen or as inconspicuous as possible.

nature-nurture The argument over the relative importance of heredity and environment.

negative reinforcement Removing something the organism finds unpleasant, such as an electric shock or a loud noise.

negative transfer A process in which learning is made more difficult by interference from previous learning.

neopsychoanalysts The recent psychoanalytical theorists who have changed Freud's original ideas in various ways; "neo" means new.

nerve A group of neurons, small or very large in number, traveling together to or from the central nervous system; in appearance, a single large fiber that is in fact made up of many fibers.

nervous impulse A tiny charge of electricity passing from the dendrite end of the neuron to the end of the axon.

neuron The individual nerve cell; basic unit of the nervous system.

neurosis A form of emotional disturbance characterized by high levels of stress and anxiety over a period of time.

neurotic depression A form of neurosis in which the individual appears to be particularly sensitive to unhappy events; normal discouragement and grief are complicated and exaggerated by feelings of dejection, hopelessness, and guilt.

neurotransmitter A chemical released by one neuron that stimulates another neuron to fire; also sometimes inhibits the second neuron from firing.

nodes Booster stations along the axon of a neuron, helping speed transmission of the nervous impulse.

nonsense syllable A meaningless syllable, such as XYL or GEF, used in the study of learning.

noradrenalin One of the neurotransmitters. Also a hormone, secreted by the adrenal gland, that produces bodily changes associated with anger or "fight" situations.

norepinephrine See **noradrenalin.**

normal behavior Behavior that is relatively well adjusted, successful, and productive of happiness.

normal curve of distribution A bell-shaped curve that describes many events in nature; most cases cluster around the average, and the number declines approaching either the lower or the upper extreme.

obedience In social psychology, conformity to a figure of authority.

object constancy The tendency to perceive objects as constant and unchanging, even under varying conditions of illumination, distance, and position.

objective personality test A paper-and-pencil test administered and scored according to a standard procedure, giving results that are not affected by the opinions or prejudices of the examiner.

obsession A thought that keeps cropping up in a persistent and disturbing fashion.

obsessive-compulsive reactions A group of neuroses characterized by obsessions or compulsions.

Oedipus complex According to Freud, the conflict of mingled love and hate toward the parents that every child undergoes between the ages of two and a half and six.

operant avoidance Behavior, learned through operant conditioning, by which the organism attempts to avoid something unpleasant.

operant behavior Behavior that is not initially associated with or normally elicited by a specific stimulus.

operant conditioning The process by which, through learning, free operant behavior becomes attached to a specific stimulus.

operant escape Behavior, learned through operant conditioning, by which the organism seeks to escape something unpleasant.

opium A drug derived from the poppy plant, most commonly used in the United States in the form of heroin.

opponent-process theory (of color vision) A type of pattern theory maintaining that our visual sensation of color results from three types of cones plus nerve cells. Messages they pick up from the eye are sent along as signals paired as red-or-green, blue-or-yellow, and black-or-white.

ordinary sleep A state of the organism in which brain activity is different from that in the waking state and the muscles of the body are quite relaxed.

organ of Corti The collection of hair cells, lying on the basilar membrane, that are the receptors for hearing.

organic psychosis A psychosis caused by actual damage to the brain by disease or injury.

organism An individual animal, either human or subhuman.

organization In learning, a form of deep processing; an aid to long-term memory. In perception, the tendency to find a pattern in stimuli reaching the sense organs.

outer ear The visible portion of the ear; collects sound waves and directs them toward the hearing receptors.

oval window The membrane through which sound waves are transmitted from the bones of the middle ear to the cochlea.

ovaries Glands that, in addition to producing the female egg cells, secrete hormones that bring about bodily changes known as secondary female sex characteristics.

overlearning The process of continuing to practice at learning after bare mastery has been attained.

overlearning, law of The principle that overlearning increases the length of time the material will be remembered.

overt behavior Observable behavior, such as motor movements, speech, and signs of emotion such as laughing or weeping.

overtones The additional vibrations of a source of sound, at frequencies higher than the fundamental tone it produces; the overtones account for the complexity and timbre of the sound.

P

pain drive A biological drive aroused by unpleasant or noxious stimulation, usually resulting in behavior designed to escape the stimulus.

pancreas The endocrine gland that secretes insulin.

paradoxical sleep A state of the organism in which the brain's activity is similar to that in the waking state but the muscles are extremely relaxed; also known as REM sleep because it is accompanied by the rapid eye movements that characterize dreaming.

paranoia A functional psychosis characterized by delusions, sometimes of grandeur, sometimes of persecution.

parapsychology The study of psychological phenomena that cannot be explained in ordinary ways.

parasympathetic nervous system A division of the autonomic nervous system, composed of scattered ganglia that lie near the glands and muscles they affect. The parasympathetic system is most active in helping maintain heartbeat and

digestion under normal circumstances.

parathyroids A pair of endocrine glands, lying atop the larger thyroid gland, that regulate the balance of calcium and phosphorus in the body, an important factor in maintaining a normal state of excitability of the nervous system.

partial reinforcement Reinforcement provided on some but not all occasions.

participant observation A scientific method in which the investigator takes part in a social situation, encounter group, or the like in order to study the behavior of others.

pattern theory A theory of the operation of the sense organs; it holds that our sensations are the result of the entire pattern of nervous impulses sent to the brain by many "broadly tuned" sensory receptors that respond in different ways to different stimuli.

peers For any individual, other people of about the same age and standing in the community; equals.

percentile A statistical term used to describe the position of an individual score in the total group.

perception The process through which we become aware of our environment by organizing and interpreting the evidence of our senses.

perceptual constancy The tendency to perceive a stable and consistent world even though the stimuli that reach the senses are inconsistent and potentially confusing.

perceptual expectation The tendency to perceive what we expect to perceive; a special form of *set*.

performance Overt behavior; used as a measure of learning.

performance test An intelligence test or part of an intelligence test that

measures the individual's ability to perform such tasks as completing pictures, making designs, and assembling objects.

peripheral nervous system The outlying nerves of the body and the individual neurons that make up these nerves.

peripheral traits To personality theorists, the observable traits that spring from the core of personality as channeled by individual development.

persistence of set In problem solving, the tendency to continue to apply a certain hypothesis because it has worked in other situations, often at the expense of trying different and much more efficient hypotheses.

personality The total pattern of characteristic ways of thinking, feeling, and behaving that constitute the individual's distinctive method of relating to the environment.

personality disorder (*also called* **character disorder**) A type of psychological disturbance characterized by failure to acquire mature ways of coping with the problems of adult life.

personality test A test designed to measure the various characteristics that make up the individual's personality.

perspective A clue to distance perception; refers to the fact that three-dimensional objects can be delineated on a flat surface, such as the retina of the eye.

persuasive communications The transmission of information and appeals to emotion in an attempt to change another person's attitudes.

phenomenological self A concept proposed by Rogers in his theory of personality; one's uniquely perceived self-image, based on the evidence of one's senses but not necessarily corresponding to reality.

phi phenomenon Motion produced by a rapid succession of images that are actually stationary; the simplest form of *stroboscopic motion*.

phobic reaction An anxiety state characterized by unreasonable fears.

phonemes The building blocks of language; basic sounds that are combined into *morphemes* and words.

physical attractiveness A stronger influence than generally supposed on interpersonal attraction.

pitch The property of being high or low in tone, determined by the frequency (number of cycles per second) of the sound wave.

pituitary gland The master endocrine gland that secretes hormones controlling growth, causing sexual development at puberty, and also regulating other endocrine glands.

placebo A "sugar pill" that relieves illness through psychological suggestion, although it has no medical value.

pleasure principle According to psychoanalytical theory, the demand of the unconscious id for immediate and total satisfaction of all its demands.

pons A structure of neurons connecting the opposite sides of the cerebellum; it helps control breathing and is apparently the origin of the nervous impulses that cause rapid eye movements during dreaming.

population In statistics, the term for all people or all events in a particular category—such as all male college students in the United States.

positive reinforcement Encouraging desired behavior through reward.

positive transfer A process in which learning is made easier by something learned previously.

posthypnotic suggestion A suggestion made during hypnosis, urging the subject to undertake some kind of activity after the hypnotic trance ends.

power motive The desire to be in charge and control other people.

precognition The supposed ability to forecast events; a form of *extrasensory perception*.

preconceptual thought The term applied by Piaget to the stage of intellectual development (ages two and three) at which the child begins to use language to attach new meanings to stimuli in the environment and to use one stimulus as a symbol for another.

prejudice A deep-seated attitude that an individual maintains so stubbornly as to be uninfluenced by any information or experiences that might disprove it.

preoperational stage The term applied by Piaget to the period (ages two to seven) when the child's ability to use language begins to dominate intellectual development.

primary mental abilities According to Thurstone, the seven basic abilities that make up intelligence. They are verbal comprehension, word fluency, number, space, associative memory, perceptual speed, and general reasoning.

primary reinforcement Reinforcement provided by a stimulus that the organism finds inherently rewarding—usually stimuli that satisfy biological drives such as hunger or thirst.

proactive interference Interference by something learned in the past with the ability to remember new materials.

problem solving Thinking that is directed toward the solution of a problem.

programed learning A system of instruction in which the subject matter is broken down into very short steps, mastered one at a time before going on to the next.

projection A defense mechanism in which the individual hides anxiety-producing motives by accusing other people of having them.

projective personality test A test in which subjects are expected to project aspects of their own personality into ambiguous pictures or inkblots.

protoplasm The basic structure of living tissue, the "stuff of life."

prototype A model on which a concept is based; the ideal example of a category, to which other items included in the category bear a family relationship.

proximity In perception, one of the factors affecting organization.

psychedelic drugs Drugs, such as LSD, that often produce hallucinations and a sense of detachment from one's body.

psychiatrist A physician who has had special training in treating behavior disturbances.

psychic energizer Any of a number of drugs used to relieve depression by increasing brain activity.

psychoanalysis A type of psychotherapy developed by Freud, in which the chief tools are free association, study of dreams and slips of the tongue, and transference. Psychoanalysis attempts to give the patient insight into unconscious conflicts.

psychoanalyst A person, usually a physician, who practices psychoanalysis.

psychoanalytical theory of personality A theory originally formulated by Freud that emphasizes three parts of the personality: 1) the unconscious *id,* 2) the conscious *ego,* and 3) the largely unconscious *superego.*

psychokinesis (PK) The supposed ability of some people to influence physical events through exercise of the mind—for example, to make dice turn up as they wish.

psychological statistics The application of mathematical principles to the description and analysis of psychological measurements.

psychology The science that systematically studies and attempts to explain observable behavior and its relationship to the unseen mental processes that go on inside the organism and to external events in the environment.

psychopathic personality (*also called* **sociopathic personality** *or* **antisocial reaction**) A behavior disorder characterized by lack of conscience, a sense of social responsibility, or feeling for other people; also by selfishness, ruthlessness, and addiction to lying.

psychophysical methods Techniques of measuring how changes in the intensity or quality of a stimulus affect sensation.

psychosexual development The Freudian theory that psychological development goes through oral, anal, phallic, and genital stages.

psychosis The scientific name for the extreme form of mental disturbances often known as insanity. The mental disturbance is so severe as to make the individual incapable of getting along in society.

psychosocial development A term used by Erikson in his theory that psychological development goes hand in hand with changing social relations.

psychosomatic illness An illness in which the physical symptoms seem to have mental and emotional causes.

psychosurgery A controversial treatment for mental disturbance; cutting or destroying parts of the brain.

psychotherapy A technique used by clinical psychologists, psychiatrists, and psychoanalysts in which a person suffering from personality disorder or mental disturbance is treated by the application of psychological knowledge.

public opinion survey A scientific sampling of attitudes (for example, the Gallup poll).

pupil The opening in the iris that admits light waves into the eyeball.

pure science The seeking of knowledge for the sake of knowledge.

Q

questionnaire A scientific method similar to the interview but in which information is obtained through written questions.

R

random sample A statistical sample that has been obtained by chance methods that avoid any bias.

range A measurement of variability obtained by subtracting the lowest measurement from the highest.

rapid eye movement (REM) Small movements of a sleeper's eyes that occur during paradoxical sleep and dreaming.

rationalization A defense mechanism in which people maintain that a goal they were unable to attain was not desirable or that they acted out of "good" motives rather than "bad."

reaction formation A defense mechanism in which people behave as if their motives were the opposite of their real motives; often characterized by excessive display of a "good" trait such as politeness.

reality principle According to psychoanalytical theory, the principle on which the conscious ego operates as it tries to mediate between the demands of the unconscious id and the realities of the environment.

recall A way of measuring learning. Subjects are asked to repeat as much of what they have learned as they can.

receptor A specialized nerve ending of the senses, capable of responding to an environmental stimulus.

receptor site A spot on the cell body of a neuron that can be stimulated by the axon of another neuron.

recognition A way of measuring learning. Subjects are asked to recognize what they have learned—for example, by picking out the right answer in a multiple-choice test.

reflex An automatic and unthinking reaction to a stimulus by the organism. A reflex is inborn, not learned, and depends on inherited characteristics of the nervous system.

regression A retreat toward types of activity appropriate to a lower level of maturity; a result of anxiety and stress.

rehearsal Repeating information to keep it alive in short-term memory.

reinforcement In classical conditioning, the pairing of an unconditioned stimulus (such as food) with a conditioned stimulus (such as sound). (Here, the food is the reinforcement.) In general, the process of assisting learning by pairing desired behavior with something the organism finds rewarding.

relearning A sensitive method of measuring learning. Subjects are asked to relearn to perfection something they have learned and partially forgotten, and the time this takes is noted.

reliable test A test that gives consistent scores when the same individual is tested on different occasions.

REM See **rapid eye movement, paradoxical sleep.**

replicate To repeat an experiment at a different time with a different experimenter and different subjects but with the same results.

representative sample A statistical sample in which all parts of the population are represented.

repression A defense mechanism in which people suffering anxiety over motives seem to banish the motives from conscious thought, pushing them into the unconscious.

resistance In psychoanalysis, a blocking of the patient's thoughts by anxiety and repressions.

response A general term used to describe any kind of behavior produced by a stimulus.

reticular activating system A network of nerves in the brain stem and hypothalamus, serving as a way station for messages from the sense organs.

retina A small patch of tissue at the back of the eyeball; contains the nerve endings called rods and cones that are the receptors for vision.

retrieval The process of extracting information from long-term memory.

retroactive interference Partial or complete blacking out of old memories by new learning.

rods One of the two types of receptors for vision located in the retina. The rods are receptors for light intensity, resulting in sensations of black, white, and gray.

rooting response One of the infant's inborn reflexes; an aid to finding food.

S

sample A relatively small group whose measurements are used to infer facts about the population or universe. To permit valid generalization the sample must be representative and random.

saturation The amount of pure hue present in a color as compared to the amount of other light wave lengths mixed in; thus the complexity of the mixture of waves determines saturation.

scanning A process that takes place in short-term memory; the study of information that has arrived in sensory memory from the sense organs. Also the controlled movement of the eyes when the person is studying a stimulus.

scapegoating Blaming other people, often members of minority groups, for feelings of frustration or conflict of which they are not the cause.

schizophrenia A functional psychosis in which patients appear to lose contact with reality and live in a shell-like world of their own.

schizophrenia spectrum According to one theory, a group of symptoms ranging from very mild to extreme, to which people may have tendencies because of an inherited defect.

school psychology The application of psychological findings to methods of education.

secondary reinforcement Reinforcement provided by a stimulus that has acquired reward value through association with a primary reinforcing stimulus.

sedative A drug that reduces activity of the central nervous system.

selection In perception, the tendency to pay attention to only some of the stimuli that reach our senses.

selective exposure A term used by social psychologists to describe the fact that persuasive communications usually reach mostly people who already agree with them.

self-actualization Maslow's name for the human desire for self-fulfillment and harmony.

self-perception theory The theory that we often take the role of an outside observer trying to find the reasons for our own behavior.

semantics The meaning of the morphemes and words in language.

semicircular canals Three liquid-filled canals in the inner ear, containing receptors for the sense of equilibrium.

senile psychosis An organic psychosis caused by deterioration of the brain cells and other physiological changes due to aging.

sensorimotor stage The term applied by Piaget to the period of intellectual development during the first two years of life, when the child knows the world only in terms of sensory impressions and motor activities.

sensory adaptation The tendency of sensory receptors to adjust to a stimulus and stop responding after a time.

sensory memory A memory system of very brief duration, composed of lingering traces of information sent to the brain by the senses.

sensory-motor area A part of the brain's cortex serving as a control point for sensory impressions and motor movements of the body.

sensory register See **sensory memory.**

separation anxiety Fear of being separated from the caretaker; a form of anxiety that develops in the infant of about ten to eighteen months.

set A tendency to respond in a certain way; to be prepared or "set" so to respond.

sex drive A biological drive aroused by physiological requirements for sexual satisfaction.

sex typing The process through which society molds its members into its traditional patterns of femininity or masculinity.

shadowing The pattern of light and shadow on an object; often a clue to perception of three-dimensional quality.

shape constancy The tendency to perceive objects as retaining their shape regardless of the true nature of the image that reaches the eyes because of the viewing angle.

shaping The learning of complicated tasks through operant conditioning, in which complex actions are built up from simpler ones.

short-term memory A memory system in which information is held briefly, then either transferred to long-term memory or forgotten.

similarity In perception, one of the factors affecting organization.

single blind An experimental technique that keeps subjects in the dark as to whether they are in the control group or the experimental group.

situational factors Behavior-producing factors that depend on the situation of the moment, particularly the other people who are in the situation.

situational personality test A test in which the examiner observes the behavior of the subject in a situation deliberately created to reveal aspects of personality.

size constancy The tendency to perceive objects in their correct size regardless of the size of the actual image they cast on the eyes when near or far away.

sleep drive A biological drive aroused by the physiological requirements for sleep.

sleepwalking A form of dissociative reaction.

slow-to-warm-up children Those with an inborn tendency to need time to adjust to new situations.

smooth muscle A muscle of the internal organs, such as the stomach and intestines, or of the pupil of the eye, over which the individual ordinarily has no conscious control.

social behavior Actions taken in relation to another person or persons.

social class A subdivision of society characterized by the access it has or believes it has to power, determined in Western society largely by income and education.

social comparison theory The theory that often we can only evaluate our own abilities, opinions, and behavior by comparing ourselves with other people.

social learning theories of personality Theories maintaining that personality is made up of learned, habitual ways of responding to the environment.

social psychology The study of our behavior as members of society and the influence that the actions and attitudes of other people have on our behavior and thinking.

socialization The training of the young in the ways of the society.

society Any organized group of people, large or small.

sociopathic personality See **psychopathic personality.**

species-specific behavior A type of behavior toward which members of a species have an inborn tendency.

specific anxiety Being anxious in one particular situation although not in others.

spinal cord The thick cable of neurons connecting with the brain; a part of the central nervous system.

spontaneous recovery The tendency of a conditioned response that has undergone extinction to occur again after a rest period.

SQ3R system An efficient five-step study method (survey, question, read, recite, review).

S-R psychology See **stimulus-response psychology.**

standard deviation (SD) A statistical device for describing the variability of measurements.

standardized test A test that has been pretested on a large and representative sample so that one person's score can be compared with the scores of the population as a whole.

stereotype An attitude that disregards individual differences and holds that all people of a certain group behave in the same manner.

stereotyped behavior A tendency to repeat some action over and over again, almost as a ritual; a result of frustration.

stimulant A drug that increases activity of the central nervous system.

stimulus Any form of energy capable of exciting the nervous system.

stimulus complexity The relative level of simplicity or complexity possessed by a sensory stimulus. The organism apparently has stimulus needs for stimuli of a particular level of complexity found the most "comfortable."

stimulus discrimination The ability, acquired through learning, to make distinctions between stimuli that are similar but not exactly alike.

stimulus generalization The tendency of an organism that has learned to associate a stimulus with a certain kind of behavior to display this behavior toward stimuli that are similar though not exactly identical to the original stimulus.

stimulus need The tendency of an organism to seek certain kinds of stimulation. The tendency does not have the life-and-death urgency of a drive, nor is its goal as specific and clear-cut. Examples are the needs for stimulation, stimulus variability, and physical contact (or tactual comfort).

stimulus-response (S-R) psychology A school of thought that emphasizes study of the stimuli that produce behavioral responses, the rewards and punishments that help establish and maintain these responses, and the modification of behavior through changes in the pattern of rewards and punishments.

stimulus variability Change and variety in stimulation; believed to be one of the organism's inborn stimulus needs.

stranger anxiety Fear of unfamiliar faces, one of the first forms of anxiety that develops in the child at about eight months.

stress The bodily wear and tear caused by physical or psychological arousal by outside events.

stress interview A form of situational personality test in which the subject is asked deliberately hostile questions and the interviewers pretend to disbelieve the answers.

striped muscle A muscle of motor behavior, over which the individual ordinarily has conscious control.

stroboscopic motion Motion produced by a rapid succession of images that are actually stationary, as in motion pictures.

subculture A culture within a culture—that is, the ways of life followed by a group in a society that does not adhere to all the practices of the society as a whole.

sublimation A defense mechanism in which a forbidden motive is channeled toward a more acceptable goal, as when an artist directs sexual urges into the creation of paintings.

superego According to psychoanalytical theory, a largely unconscious part of the mind that threatens punishment for transgressions.

sympathetic nervous system A division of the autonomic nervous system, composed of long chains of ganglia lying along both sides of the spinal column. It activates the glands and smooth muscles of the body and helps prepare the organism for "fight" or "flight."

synapse A junction point between the axon of one neuron and the dendrite or cell body receptor site of another neuron.

synaptic cleft The tiny space between the axon of one neuron and the dendrite or receptor site of another neuron.

synaptic knob A swelling at the end of a dendrite; an important structure in the transmission of messages across the synapse.

synaptic vesicles Tiny sacs in the synaptic knob, containing neurotransmitters.

syndrome A medical term meaning the entire pattern of symptoms and events that characterize the course of a disease.

syntax The rules of language for sentence structure.

T

tabula rasa A "blank tablet"; a phrase used to describe the theory that the mind of a human baby is a "blank tablet" on which anything can be written through learning and experience.

tactual comfort Physical contact; one of the stimulus needs.

taste buds The receptors for the sense of taste; found on the tongue, at the back of the mouth, and in the throat.

teaching machine A device used in programed learning; the machine presents the program one step at a time and asks a question that the learner answers before going on to the next step.

temperature drive A biological drive aroused by physiological requirements that the body temperature be kept at a constant level (in human beings, around 98.6° Fahrenheit).

test A measurement of a sample of individual behavior. Ideally, a scientific test should be: 1) objective, 2) standardized, 3) reliable, and 4) valid.

test anxiety A form of specific anxiety common among students, centering on taking exams.

testes Glands that, in addition to producing the male sperm cells, secrete hormones that bring about secondary male sex characteristics, such as the growth of facial hair and change of voice.

thalamus The brain's major relay station, connecting the cerebrum with the lower structures of the brain and the spinal cord.

theory A statement of general principles that explains events observed in the past and predicts what will happen under a given set of circumstances in the future.

thinking The covert manipulation of images, symbols, and other mediational units, especially language, concepts, premises, and rules.

thirst drive A biological drive aroused by deprivation of water.

threshold The minimum amount of

stimulation or difference in stimulation to which a sensory receptor will respond 50 percent of the time.

thyroid gland An endocrine gland that regulates the rate of metabolism and affects the body's activity level.

tic The involuntary twitching of a muscle.

timbre The quality of a sound, determined by the number and strength of the overtones that contribute to the complexity of the sound wave.

tip of the tongue phenomenon A partially successful attempt at retrieval in which we cannot quite remember a word (for example) but seem to have it almost available or "on the tip of the tongue."

token economy An arbitrary economic system, often used in mental hospitals, in which patients are rewarded for good behavior with tokens that they can exchange like money for various privileges.

tranquilizer A drug that reduces anxiety and often eliminates the hallucinations and delusions of schizophrenics, apparently by slowing down the activity of the brain.

transfer of learning The effect of prior learning on new learning.

transference A psychoanalytic term for the tendency of the patient to transfer to other people (including the psychoanalyst) the emotional attitudes felt as a child toward such much loved and hated persons as parents and siblings.

tremor A shaking produced when two sets of muscles work against each other; one of the bodily changes observed in emotion.

trial and error learning A form of learning in which one response after another is tried and rejected as unsuitable, until at last a successful response is made.

U

unconditional positive regard The basis of Rogers' humanistic therapy; total acceptance of clients as people if not of all their behavior.

unconditioned response An automatic, unlearned reaction to a stimulus—such as the salivation of Pavlov's dog to food.

unconditioned stimulus A stimulus that is innately capable of causing a reflex action—such as the food that originally caused Pavlov's dog to respond with salivation.

unconscious mind In psychoanalytical theory, the bulk of the human mind, though we are not usually aware of it.

unconscious motives Desires of which we are unaware but which nonetheless influence our behavior.

V

valid test A test found to actually measure the characteristic that it is designed to measure.

variability In statistics, the amount of variation found in a group of measurements, described by the range and standard deviation.

variable A condition that is subject to change, especially in an experiment.

verbal test An intelligence test or part of an intelligence test that measures the individual's ability to deal with verbal symbols; it may include items measuring vocabulary, general comprehension, mathematical reasoning, ability to find similarities, and so on.

vestibule A chamber in the inner ear containing receptors for the sense of equilibrium.

visceral organs The internal organs, such as the stomach, intestines, liver, kidneys, and so on.

visual purple A light-sensitive substance associated with the rods of the retina.

vocational aptitude test A test that measures the ability to perform specialized skills required in various kinds of jobs.

vocational guidance The technique of helping a person select the right lifetime occupation, often through tests of aptitudes and interests.

W

wavelength The characteristic of light waves that determines hue.

Weber's Law The rule that the difference threshold, or just noticeable difference, is a fixed percentage of the original stimulus.

withdrawal A reaction in which people try to relieve feelings of frustration by withdrawing from the attempt to attain their goals.

X

X-chromosome One of the two chromosomes that determine sex; an X-X pairing produces a female, an X-Y pairing a male.

Y

Y-chromosome One of the two chromosomes that determine sex.

Young-Helmholtz theory A theory stating that, since the entire range of hues can be produced by combining red, green, and blue, there must be three kinds of cones differentially sensitive to these wave lengths.

References and Acknowledgments

**Chapter one
The aims and methods
of psychology**

1 See, for example, Skinner, B. F. *Beyond freedom and dignity*. New York: Knopf, 1971.

2 Jones, D. R. *Psychologists in mental health: 1966*. Washington, D.C.: National Institute of Mental Health. Public Health Service Publication, No. 1984, 1969.

3 Doob, A. N., and Gross, A. E. Status of frustrator as an inhibitor of horn-honking responses. *J Soc Psychol*, 1968, 76, 213–18.

4 Masters, W. H., and Johnson, V. E. *Human sexual response*. Boston: Little, Brown, 1966.

5 Kinsey, A. C., Pomeroy, W. B., and Martin, C. E. *Sexual behavior in the human male*. Philadelphia: Saunders, 1948.

6 Kinsey, A. C., et al. *Sexual behavior in the human female*. Philadelphia: Saunders, 1953.

7 Holden, C. Lie detectors. *Science*, 1975, 190, 359–62.

8 Terman, L. M., and Merrill, M. A. *Stanford-Binet intelligence scale: manual for the third revision, form L-M*, 1937. © 1973 by Houghton Mifflin Company. Reprinted by permission of the Houghton Mifflin Company. All rights reserved.

9 Jencks, C. *Inequality*. New York: Basic Books, 1972.

10 Kagan, J., and Moss, H. A. *Birth to maturity*. New York: Wiley, 1962.

11 Feldman, S. D. The presentation of shortness in everyday life—height and heightism in American society. Presented before a meeting of the American Sociological Association, 1971.

12 Wilson, P. R. Perceptual distortion of height as a function of ascribed academic status. *J Soc Psychol*, 1968, 74, 97–102.

13 Graziano, W., Brothern, T., and Berscheid, E. Height and attraction. *J Pers*, 1978, 46, 128–45.

14 Atkinson, R. C. Teaching children to read using a computer. *Am Psychol*, 1976, 29, 169–78.

15 Skinner, B. F. *Beyond freedom and dignity*. New York: Knopf, 1971.

16 Matson, F. W. Humanistic theory. *Hum*, March/April, 1971, 7–11.

17 Shapiro, J., et al. Isolation of pure *lac* operon DNA. *Nature* (London), 1969, 224, 768–74.

18 Heston, L. L. The genetics of schizophrenic and schizoid disease. *Science*, 1970, 167, 249–55.

19 Scarr, S. Social introversion-extraversion as a heritable response. *Child Develop*, 1969, 40, 823–32.

20 Williams, R. J. *Biochemical individuality.* New York: Wiley, 1956.

21 Hollingshead, A. B., and Redlich, F. C. *Social class and mental illness, a community study.* New York: Wiley, 1958.

22 Jencks, C. *Inequality.* New York: Basic Books, 1972.

Chapter two
Body and brain:
the physical underpinning
of psychology

1 Lewin, R. *The nervous system.* Garden City, N.Y.: Anchor Books, 1974.

2 Miller, N. E. From the brain to behavior. Invited lecture at XII Interamerican Congress of Psychology, Montevideo, Uruguay, March 30 to April 6, 1969.

3 Wolf-Heidegger, G. *Atlas of systematic human anatomy.* Basel, Switzerland: S. Karger, 1962.

4 Miller, N. E. From the brain to behavior. Invited lecture at XII Interamerican Congress of Psychology, Montevideo, Uruguay, March 30 to April 6, 1969.

5 Hubel, D. H. Vision and the brain. *Bull Acad Arts Sci,* 1978, *31,* 17–28.

6 Miller, N. E. From the brain to behavior. Inivited lecture at XII Interamerican Congress of Psychology, Montevideo, Uruguay, March 30 to April 6, 1969.

7 Snyder, S. H. Opiate receptors and internal opiates. *Sci Am,* 1977, *236,* 44–67.

8 Opiate-like substances in brain may hold clue to pain and mood. The New York *Times,* Oct. 2, 1977, p. 1.

9 Verhoeven, W.M.A., et al. Improvement of schizophrenic patients treated with [Des-Tyr^1]-γ-endorphin (DTγE). *Arch Gen Psych,* 1979, *36,* 294–98.

10 Levy, J., Trevarthen, C., and Sperry, R. W. Perception of bilateral chimeric figures following hemisphere deconnection. *Brain,* 1972, *95,* 61–78.

11 Drawings by a patient of Bogen, J. In Ornstein, R. The split and the whole brain. *Hum Nat,* 1978, *1,* 76–83. Bulletin of the Los Angeles Neurological Society, 1969, *34,* 73–105.

12 Galaburda, A. M., et al. Right-left asymmetries in the brain. *Science,* 1978, *199,* 852–56.

13 Geschwind, N. Personal communication, 1980.

14 Ornstein, R. The split and the whole brain. *Hum Nat,* 1978, *1,* 76–83.

15 Ornstein, R. As immediately above.

16 Gevins, A. S., et al. Electroencephalogram correlates of higher cortical functions. *Science,* 1979, *203,* 665–67.

17 Eccles, J. C. *The physiology of synapses.* New York: Academic Press, 1964.

18 National Science Foundation. To the heart of the brain. *Mosaic,* March-April, 1976, *7,* 28.

19 Lewin, R. *The nervous system.* Garden City, N.Y.: Anchor Books, 1974.

20 Nauta, W.J.H. Hypothalamic regulations of sleep in rats. *J Neur,* 1946, *9,* 285–316.

21 Leibowitz, S. F. Hypothalamic β-adrenergic "satiety" system antagonizes an α-adrenergic "hunger" system in the rat. *Nature,* 1970, *226,* 963–64. Also Leibowitz, S. F. Reciprocal hunger-relating circuits, involving alpha- and beta-adrenergic receptors located, respectively, in the ventromedial and lateral hypothalamus. *Pub Pro Nat Acad Sci,* 1970, *67,* 1063–70.

22 Valenstein, E. *Brain control.* New York: Wiley, 1973.

23 Sperry, R. W. Cerebral dominance in perception. In Young, F. A., and Lindsley, D. B., eds. *Early experience and visual information processing in perceptual and reading disorders.* Washington, D.C.: National Academy of Sciences, 1970, pp. 167–68.

24 Nathan, P. W., and Smith, M. C. Normal mentality associated with a maldeveloped rhinencephalon. *J Neuro NP,* 1950, *13,* 191–97.

25 Weiskrantz, L. Problems and progress in physiological psychology. *Brit J Psychol,* 1973, *64,* 511–20.

26 See, for example, Weiss, J. M., Glazer, H. I., and Pohorecky, L. A. Coping behavior and neurochemical changes. In Serban, G., and Kling, A., eds. *Animal models in human psychology.* New York: Plenum, 1976.

27 See, for example, Schildkraut, J. J. *Neuropsychopharmacology and the affective disorders.* Boston: Little, Brown, 1969.

28 Crosby, E., Humphrey, T., and Lauer, E. W. *Comparative anatomy of the nervous system.* New York: Macmillan, 1962. Based on the data in Figs. 337 and 339.

29 Funkenstein, D. H. The physi-

ology of fear and anger. *Sci Am*, 1955, *192*, 74–80.

30 Pfaffman, C. Gustatory nerve impulses in rat, cat, and rabbit. *J Neur*, 1955, *18*, 429–40.

31 Evans, C. L. *Starling's principles of human physiology*, 14th ed. Philadelphia: Lea & Febiger, 1945.

32 Globus, A., et al. Effects of differential experience on dendritic spine counts in rat cerebral cortex. *J Com PP*, 1973, *82*, 175–81. Copyright © 1973 by American Psychological Assocation; reprinted with permission.

33 Bennett, E. L., et al. Chemical and anatomical plasticity in the brain. *Science*, 1964, *146*, 610–19.

34 Schapiro, S., and Vukovich, K. R. Early experience effects upon cortical dendrites. *Science*, 1970, *167*, 292–94.

35 Lewis, E. R., Zeevi, Y. Y., and Everhart, T. E. Studying neural organization in *Aplysia* with the scanning electron microscope. *Science*, 1969, *165*, 1140–42. © 1969 by American Association for Advancement of Science.

36 Wolf-Heidegger, G. *Atlas of systematic human anatomy*. Basel, Switzerland: S. Karger, 1962.

37 Lewin, R. *The nervous system*. Garden City, N.Y.: Anchor Books, 1974.

38 Moruzzi, G., and Magoun, H. W. Brain stem reticular formation and activation of the EEG. *El Clin Neur*, 1949, *1*, 455–73.

39 Milner, B. The memory defect in bilateral hippocampal lesions. *Psych RR*, 1959, *11*, 43–52.

40 Riley, J. N., and Walker, D. W. Morphological alterations in hippocampus after long-term alcohol consumption in mice. *Science*, 1978, *201*, 646–48.

41 Scheibel, M. E., et al. Dendritic changes in aging human cortex. *Ex Neur*, 1975, *47*, 392–403.

42 See, for example, Diamond, M. C. The aging brain. *Am Sci*, 1978, *66*, 66–71.

43 Pribram, K. H. The neurophysiology of remembering. *Sci Am*, 1969, *220*, 73–86.

Chapter three
The basics of learning

1 Yerkes, R. M., and Morgulis, S. The methods of Pavlov in animal psychology. *Psych Bull*, 1909, *6*, 257–73.

2 Pavlov, I. P. *Conditioned reflexes*. London: Oxford University Press, 1927 [reprinted by Dover, New York, 1960].

3 Watson, J. B., and Rayner, R. Conditioned emotional reactions. *J Exp Psychol*, 1920, *3*, 1–14.

4 Harris, B. Whatever happened to little Albert? *Am Psychol*, 1979, *34*, 151–60.

5 Cooper, J. Deception and role-playing. *Am Psychol*, 1976, *31*, 605–10.

6 Forward, J., Canter, R., and Kirsch, N. Role-enactment and deception methodologies. *Am Psychol*, 1976, *31*, 595–604.

7 Sawrey, W. L., Conger, J. J., and Turrell, E. S. An experimental investigation of the role of psychological factors in the production of gastric ulcers of rats. *J Com PP*, 1956, *49*, 457–61.

8 Dekker, E., Pelser, H. E., and Groen, J. Conditioning as a cause of asthmatic attacks. *J Psych Res*, 1957, *2*, 97–108.

9 Jones, J. C. A laboratory study of fear. *Ped Sem*, 1924, *31*, 308–15.

10 Pavlov, I. P. *Conditioned reflexes*. London: Oxford University Press, 1927 [reprinted by Dover, New York, 1960].

11 Skinner, B. F. *The behavior of organisms*. New York: Appleton-Century-Crofts, 1938.

12 Verhave, T. The pigeon as a quality-control inspector. *Am Psychol*, 1966, *21*, 109–15.

13 From *The analysis of behavior* by James G. Holland and B. F. Skinner. Copyright © 1961 by McGraw-Hill, Inc. Used with permission of McGraw-Hill Book Company.

14 Neuringer, A. J. Superstitious key pecking after three peck-produced reinforcements. *J Exp An Beh*, 1970, *13*, 127–34.

15 Perin, C. T. A quantitative investigation of the delay of reinforcement gradient. *J Exp Psychol*, 1943, *32*, 37–51. Copyright 1943 by the American Psychological Association. Reprinted by permission.

16 Wickelgren, W. A. *Learning and memory*. Englewood Cliffs, N.J.: Prentice-Hall, 1977, p. 94.

17 See, for example, Robbins, D. Partial reinforcement. *Psych Bull*, 1971, *76*, 415–31.

18 Stolz, S. B., Wienckowski, L. A., and Brown, B. S. Behavior modification. *Am Psychol*, 1975, *30*, 1027–48.

19 Harris, F. R., et al. Effects of posi-

tive social reinforcement on re-gressed crawling of a nursery school child. In Ullmann, L., and Krasner, L., eds. *Case studies in behavior modification*. New York: Holt Rinehart and Winston, 1965.

20 O'Leary, K. D. Behavior modification in the classroom. *J App Behav Anal*, 1972, *5*, 505–11.

21 Baer, D. M. The control of developmental process. In Nesselroade, J. R., and Reese, H. W., eds. *Life-span developmental psychology*. New York: Academic Press, 1973.

22 Stolz, S. B., Wienckowski, L. A., and Brown, B. S. Behavior modification. *Am Psychol*, 1975, *30*, 1027–48.

23 Ayllon, T., and Azrin, N. H. *The token economy*. New York: Appleton-Century-Crofts, 1968. © 1968. Adapted by permission of Prentice-Hall, Inc. Englewood Cliffs, N.J.

24 O'Leary, K. D., and Drabman, R. Token reinforcement programs in the classroom. *Psych Bull*, 1971, *75*, 379–98.

25 Cohen, H. Study reported in *Beh T*, 1970, *1*, 2.

26 See, for example, Adler, C. S., and Adler, S. M. Biofeedback-psychotherapy for the treatment of headaches. *Headache*, 1976, *16*, 189–91.

27 See, for example, Kewman, D. G. *Voluntary control of digital skin temperature for treatment of migraine headaches*. Unpublished Ph.D. dissertation, University of Texas, 1977.

28 Miller, N. E. Biofeedback and vis-ceral learning. *An Rev Psych*, 1978, *29*, 373–404.

29 Bennetts, L. Biofeedback. New York *Times*, May 9, 1978, p. 32.

30 Patterson, G. R., Hops, H., and Weiss, R. L. Interpersonal skills training for couples in early stages of conflict. *J Marr Fam*, 1975, *37*, 295–303.

31 Solomon, R. L., Punishment. *Am Psychol*, 1964, *19*, 239–53.

32 Campbell, B. A., and Church, R. M., eds. *Punishment and aversive behavior*. New York: Appleton-Century-Crofts, 1969.

33 Miller, N. E. *Behavioral sciences report for overview cluster of the President's biomedical research panel*, 1975.

34 Munn, N. L., Fernald, L. D., Jr., and Fernald, P. S. *Introduction to psychology*, 2d ed. Boston: Houghton Mifflin, 1969.

35 Maier, S. F., Seligman, M.E.P., and Solomon, R. L. Pavlovian fear conditioning and learned helplessness. In Campbell, B. A., and Church, R. M., eds. *Punishment and aversive behavior*. New York: Appleton-Century-Crofts, 1969, pp. 299–342. By permission of Prentice-Hall, Inc. Englewood Cliffs, N.J.

36 Hiroto, D. S. Locus of control and learned helplessness. *J Exp Psychol*, 1974, *102*, 187–93.

37 See, for example, Tennen, H., and Eller, S. J. Attributional components of learned helplessness and facilitation. *J Pers Soc Psychol*, 1977, *35*, 265–71.

38 See, for example, Dweck, C. S., Goetz, T., and Strauss, N. *Sex differences in learned helplessness*. Unpublished manuscript, University of Illinois, 1977.

39 See, for example, Silberman, C. E. *Crisis in the classroom*. New York: Random House, 1970.

40 Hess, R. D., and Bear, R. M. *Early education*. Chicago: Aldine, 1968.

41 Coleman, J. S. *Equality of educational opportunity*. Washington, D.C.: U.S. Government Printing Office, 1966.

42 Strauss, J. S. Social and cultural influences on psychopathology. *An Rev Psychol*, 1979, *30*, 397–415.

43 See, for example, Coles, R. Like it is in the alley. In Kagan, J., Haith, M. M., and Caldwell, C., eds. *Psychology*. New York: Harcourt Brace Jovanovich, 1971, pp. 368–81.

44 Rosenhan, D. L. Effects of social class and race on responsiveness to approval and disapproval. *J Pers Soc Psychol*, 1966, *4*, 253–59.

45 See, for example, Depue, R. A., and Monroe, S. M. Learned helplessness in the perspective of the depressive disorders. *J Abn Psychol*, 1978, *87*, 3–20.

46 Garber, J., and Hollon, S. *Depression and the expectancy of success for self and for others*. Unpublished manuscript, University of Minnesota, 1977.

47 Rizley, R. Depression and distortion in the attribution of causality. *J Abn Psychol*, 1978, *87*, 32–48.

48 Abramson, L. Y., Seligman, M.E.P., and Teasdale, J. D. Learned helplessness in humans. *J Abn Psychol*, 1978, *87*, 49–74.

49 Abramson, L. Y., Seligman,

M.E.P., and Teasdale, J. D. As immediately above.

50 See, for example, Teasdale, J. D. Effects of real and recalled success on learned helplessness and depression. *J Abn Psychol*, 1978, *87*, 155–64.

51 Bandura, A., Jeffrey, R. W., and Gajdos, E. Generalizing change through self-directed perform-ance. *Beh Res Ther*, 1975, *13*, 141–52.

52 Miller, N. E. Studies of fear as an acquirable drive. I. Fear as moti-vation and fear-reduction as rein-forcement in the learning of new responses. *J Exp Psychol*, 1948, *38*, 89–101.

53 Miller, N. E., and Dollard, J. *So-cial learning and imitation*. New Haven, Conn.: Yale University Press, 1941.

54 Bandura, A. Behavior theory and the models of man. *Am Psychol*, 1974, *29*, 859–69.

55 Breland, K., and Breland, M. The misbehavior of organisms. *Am Psychol*, 1961, *61*, 681–84.

56 Garcia, J., and Koelling, R. Rela-tion of cue to consequence in avoidance learning. *Psychon Sci*, 1966, *4*, 123–24.

57 Rozin, P., and Kalat, J. W. Specific hungers and poisoning as adap-tive specializations of learning. *Psychol R*, 1971, *78*, 459–86.

58 Seligman, M.E.P. Phobias and preparedness. *Beh Ther*, 1971, *2*, 307–20.

59 Tolman, E. C., and Honzik, C. H. Introduction and removal of re-ward and maze performance in rats. *UC Pub Psychol*, 1930, *4*, 257–75. Originally published by the University of California Press; reprinted by permission of The Regents of the University of Cali-fornia.

60 Kimble, G. A. *Hilgard and Mar-quis' conditioning and learning*. New York: Appleton-Century-Crofts, 1961, pp. 73, 88–90.

61 MacFarlane, D. A. The role of kinethesis in maze learning. *UC Pub Psychol*, 1930, *4*, 277–305.

62 Wickelgren, W. A. *Learning and memory*. Englewood Cliffs, N.J.: Prentice-Hall, 1977, pp. 107–08.

63 See, for example, Lajoie, J., and Bindra, D. An interpretation of autoshaping and related phe-nomena in terms of stimulus-incentive contingencies alone. *Can J Psych / R Can Psych*, 1976, *30*, 157–73.

64 Bolles, R. C. Reinforcement, ex-pectancy, and learning. *Psychol R*, 1972, *79*, 394–409.

65 See, for example, Bolles, R. C. Re-inforcement, expectancy, and learning. *Psychol R*, 1972, *79*, 394–409.

66 See, for example, Bower, G. H. A selective review of organizational factors in memory. In Tulving, E., and Donaldson, W. *Organization of memory*. New York: Academic Press, 1972, pp. 93–137.

67 See, for example, Jenkins, J. J. Remember that old theory of memory? Well forget it! *Am Psy-chol*, 1974, *29*, 785–95.

68 John, E. R., et al. Observation learning in cats. *Science*, 1968, *159*, 1489–91.

69 Bandura, A. *Behavior theory and the models of man*. Presidential address presented at the meeting of the American Psychological Association, New Orleans, Au-gust 1974.

Chapter four
Memory and how to improve it

1 Adapted from Shiffrin, R. M., and Atkinson, R. C. Storage and re-trieval processes in long-term memory. *Psychol R*, 1969, *76*, 179–93. Copyright 1969 by the American Psychological Associa-tion. Reprinted by permission.

2 Sperling, G. The information available in brief visual presenta-tions. *Psych M*, 1960, *74*, (No. 11, Whole no. 498).

3 Peterson, L. R., and Peterson, M. J. Short-term retention of individ-ual items. *J Exp Psychol*, 1959, *58*, 193–98. Copyright 1959 by the American Psychological Associa-tion. Reprinted with permission.

4 Shiffrin, R. M., and Atkinson, R. C. Storage and retrieval processes in long-term memory. *Psychol R*, 1969, *76*, 179–93.

5 Miller, G. A. Language and psy-chology. In Lenneberg, E. H., ed. *New directions in the study of lan-guage*. Cambridge, Mass.: M.I.T. Press, 1964, pp. 89–107.

6 Bjork, R. A. Theoretical implica-tions of directed forgetting. In Melton, A. W., and Martin, E., eds. *Coding processes in human memory*. Washington, D.C.: V. H. Winston, 1972, pp. 217–35.

7 Miller, G. A. The magical number seven, plus or minus two. *Psychol R*, 1956, *63*, 81–96.

8 Sperling, G. Successive approximations to a model for short term memory. *Acta Psychol* (Amsterdam), 1967, *27*, 285–92.

9 Kintsch, W. *Learning, memory, and conceptual processes.* New York: Wiley, 1970.

10 Mandler, G. Organization and recognition. In Tulving, E., and Donaldson, W., eds. *Organization of memory.* New York: Academic Press, 1974.

11 Wickelgren, W. A. *Learning and memory.* Englewood Cliffs, N.J.: Prentice-Hall, 1977, pp. 2–4.

12 Patterson, M. M., Cegavske, C. F., and Thompson, R. F., Effectiveness of a classical conditioning paradigm on hind-limb flexor nerve response in immobilized spinal cats. *J Com PP*, 1973, *84*, 88–97.

13 Kandel, E. R. Nerve cells and behavior. *Sci Am*, 1970, *223*, 57–68.

14 Davis, K. L., et al. Physostigmine. *Science*, 1978, *201*, 272–74.

15 McGaugh, J. L., and Dawson, R. G. Modification of memory storage processes. *Beh Sci*, 1971, *16*, 45–63.

16 Goodwin, D. W., et al. Loss of short-term memory as a predictor of the alcoholic "blackout." *Nature*, 1970, *227*, 201–02.

17 Johnson, F. N. The effects of chlorpromazine on the decay and consolidation of short-term memory traces in mice. *Psychop*, 1969, *16*, 105–14.

18 Leukel, F. A comparison of the effects of ECS and anesthesia on acquisition of the maze habit. *J Com PP*, 1957, *50*, 300–06.

19 See, for example, Moore, R. Y.

Synaptogenesis and the morphology of learning and memory. In Rosenzweig, M. R., and Bennett, E. L., eds. *Neural mechanisms of learning and memory.* Cambridge, Mass.: M.I.T. Press, 1976.

20 Bennett, E. L., et al. Chemical and anatomical plasticity in the brain. *Science*, 1964, *146*, 610–19.

21 Greenough, W. T. Enduring brain effects of differential experience and training. In Rosenzweig, M. R., and Bennett, E. L., eds. *Neural mechanisms of learning and memory.* Cambridge, Mass.: M.I.T. Press, 1976.

22 Bennett, E. L., et al. Chemical and anatomical plasticity in the brain. *Science*, 1964, *146*, 610–19.

23 See, for example, Hyden, H. Biochemical and molecular aspects of learning and memory. *Pro Am Phil Soc*, 1967, *111*, 347–51.

24 Byrne, W. L., et al. Memory transfer. *Science*, 1966, *153*, 658.

25 See, for example, Wickelgren, W. A. *Learning and memory.* Englewood Cliffs, N.J.: Prentice-Hall, 1977, p. 7.

26 Ebbinghaus, H. *Memory.* New York: Columbia University, Teachers College, 1913 [reprinted by Dover, New York, 1964].

27 See, for example, Wickelgren, W. A. *Learning and memory.* Englewood Cliffs, N.J.: Prentice-Hall, 1977, pp. 368–69.

28 See, for example, Weiskrantz, L. Experimental studies of amnesia. In Whitty, C.W.M., and Zangwill, O. L., eds. *Amnesia.* London: Butterworths, 1966, pp. 1–35.

29 Kintsch, W. *Memory and cognition,*

2d ed. New York: Wiley, 1977, pp. 268–69.

30 Ebbinghaus, H. *Memory.* New York: Columbia University, Teachers College, 1913 [reprinted by Dover, New York, 1964].

31 Penfield, W. The interpretive cortex. *Science*, 1959, *129*, 1719–25.

32 Adapted from Underwood, B. J. Interference and forgetting. *Psychol R*, 1957, *64*, Fig. 1, p. 51. Copyright 1957 by the American Psychological Association. Reprinted with permission.

33 Wickens, D. D. Some characteristics of word encoding. *Mem Cog*, 1973, *1*, 485–90.

34 McGeoch, J. A., and McDonald, W. T. Meaningful relation and retroactive inhibition. *Am J Psychol*, 1931, *43*, 579–88. Reprinted by permission of the University of Illinois Press.

35 Tyler, R. W. Permanence of learning. *J Hi Ed*, IV (April 1933), Table I, p. 204.

36 Brown, R., and McNeill, D. The "tip of the tongue" phenomenon. *J Verb Learn*, 1966, *5*, 325–37.

37 Craik, F.I.M., and Lockhart, R. S. Levels of processing. *J Verb Learn*, 1972, *11*, 671–84.

38 Kintsch, W. *Memory and cognition,* 2d ed. New York: Wiley, 1977, pp. 229 and 236.

39 Wickelgren, W. A. *Learning and memory.* Englewood Cliffs, N.J.: Prentice-Hall, 1977, pp. 345–46.

40 See, for example, Craik, F.I.M., and Tulving, E. Depth of processing and the retention of words in episodic memory. *J Exp Psychol (Gen)*, 1975, *104*, 268–94.

41 See, for example, Meunier, G. F., Ritz, D., and Meunier, J. A. Rehearsal of individual items in short-term memory. *J Exp Psychol,* 1972. *95,* 465–67. Also Modigliani, V., and Seamon, J. G. Transfer of information from short- to long-term memory. *J Exp Psychol,* 1974, *102,* 768–72.

42 See, for example, Graf, R. C. Speed reading. *Psych T,* December 1973, 112–13.

43 Craik, F.I.M., and Tulving, E. Depth of processing and the retention of words in episodic memory. *J Exp Psychol (Gen),* 1975, *104,* 268–94, especially p. 292.

44 Clark, H. H., and Clark, E. V. *Psychology and language.* New York: Harcourt Brace Jovanovich, 1977, p. 153.

45 Bower, G. H. Improving memory. *Hum Nat,* 1978, *1,* 64–72.

46 Wickelgren, W. A. More on the long and short of memory. In Deutsch, D., and Deutsch, J. A., eds. *Short-term memory.* New York: Academic Press, 1975, pp. 65–72.

47 McGeoch, J. A. The influence of associative value upon the difficulty of nonsense-syllable lists. *J Genetic,* 1930, *37,* 421–26.

48 After Lyon, D. O. The relation of length of material to time taken for learning and the optimum distribution of time. *J Ed Psychol,* 1914, *5,* 1–9, 85–91, and 155–63.

49 Katona, G. *Organizing and memorizing.* New York: Columbia University Press, 1940.

50 Bower, G. H., et al. Hierarchical retrieval schemes in recall of categorized word lists. *J Verb Learn,* 1969, *8,* 323–43.

51 Adapted from Bower, G. H. Improving memory. *Hum Nat,* 1978, *1,* 64–72.

52 See, for example, Bower, G. H. Mental imagery and associative learning. In Gregg, L., ed. *Cognition in learning and memory.* New York: Wiley, 1972, pp. 51–88.

53 Bower, G. H., and Clark, M. C. Narrative stories as mediators for serial learning. *Psychon Sci,* 1969, *14,* 181–82.

54 Yates, F. A. *The art of memory.* Chicago: University of Chicago Press, 1966.

55 Adapted from Bower G. H. Improving memory. *Hum Nat,* 1978, *1,* 64–72.

56 Bugelski, B. R., Kidd, E., and Segmen, J. Image as a mediator in one-trial paired-associate learning. *J Exp Psychol,* 1968, *76,* 69–73.

57 Raugh, M. R., and Atkinson, R. C. A mnemonic method for the learning of a second-language vocabulary. *J Ed Psychol,* 1975, *67,* 1–16.

58 Gates, A. L. Recitation as a factor in memorizing. *Archives of Psychology,* New York, 1917, No. 40. By permission of the Trustees of Columbia University in the City of New York.

59 Kintsch, W. *Memory and cognition.* New York: Wiley, 1977, pp. 264–65.

60 Robinson, F. P. *Effective study,* rev. ed. New York: Harper & Row, 1961.

61 Harlow, H. F. The formation of learning sets. *Psychol R,* 1949, *56,* 51–65. Copyright 1949 by the American Psychological Association. Reprinted by permission.

62 Levinson, B., and Reese, H. W. Patterns of discrimination learning set in preschool children, fifth-graders, college freshmen, and the aged. *Mono Soc Res,* 1967, *32*(No. 7), 1–92.

63 Gagné, R. M. *The conditions of learning,* 3d ed. New York: Holt, Rinehart, and Winston, 1974.

64 James, W. *Principles of psychology,* Vol. I. New York: Dover, 1950, p. 662.

**Chapter five
Language and cognition**

1 Mussen, P. H., Conger, J. J., and Kagan, J. *Child development and personality,* 5th ed. New York: Harper & Row, 1979.

2 Brown, R. The first sentences of child and chimpanzee. In Brown, R., ed. *Psycholinguistics.* New York: Free Press, 1970, pp. 208–31.

3 Von Frisch, W. *Bees.* Ithaca, N.Y.: Cornell University Press, 1950.

4 Clark, H. H., and Clark, E. V. *Psychology and language.* New York: Harcourt Brace Jovanovich, 1977, p. 558.

5 Clark, H. H., and Clark, E. V. As immediately above, p. 515.

6 Vennemann, T. An explanation of drift. In Li, C. N., ed. *Word order and word order change.* Austin: University of Texas Press, 1975, pp. 269–305. Also Topics, subjects, and word order. In Anderson, J. M., and Jones, C., eds. *Historical linguistics I.* Amster-

dam: North-Holland, 1974, pp. 339–76.

7 Chomsky, N. *Aspects of the theory of syntax*. Cambridge: M.I.T. Press, 1965.

8 Clark, H. H., and Clark, E. V. *Psychology and language*. New York: Harcourt Brace Jovanovich, 1977, pp. 29 and 132.

9 Fromkin, V. *Speech errors as linguistic evidence*. The Hague: Mouton, 1973.

10 Clark, H. H., and Clark, E. V. *Psychology and language*. New York: Harcourt Brace Jovanovich, 1977, p. 292.

11 Pollack, I., and Pickett, J. M. Intelligibility of excerpts from fluent speech. *J Verb Learn*, 1964, *3*, 79–84.

12 Warren, R. M., and Warren, R. P. Auditory illusions and confusions. *Sci Am*, 1970, *223*, 30–36.

13 Clark, H. H., and Clark, E. V. *Psychology and language*. New York: Harcourt Brace Jovanovich, 1977, pp. 211–20.

14 Smith, M. E. An investigation of the development of the sentence and the extent of vocabulary in young children. *University of Iowa Studies in Child Welfare*, 1926, *3*(5).

15 Lenneberg, E. H. *Biological foundations of language*. New York: Wiley, 1967.

16 Atkinson, K., MacWhinny, B., and Stoel, C. An experiment on recognition of babbling. In *Papers and reports on child language development*. Stanford, Calif.: Stanford University Press, 1970.

17 Miller, G. A. *Language and communication*. New York: McGraw-Hill, 1951.

18 See, for example, Oyama, S. *A sensitive period for the acquisition of a second language*. Unpublished doctoral dissertation, Harvard University, 1973. For an interesting sidelight on acquiring regional accents, see Labov, W. *The study of nonstandard English*. Urbana, Ill.: National Council of Teachers of English, 1970.

19 de Villiers, J. G., and de Villiers, P. A. *Language acquisition*. Cambridge, Mass.: Harvard University Press, 1978, p. 210.

20 Farb, P. *Word play*. New York: Knopf, 1974.

21 Curtiss, S. *Genie*. New York: Academic Press, 1977.

22 Sachs, J. S., and Johnson, M. Language development in a hearing child of deaf parents. In von Raffler Engel, W., and LeBrun, Y., eds. *Baby talk and infant speech* (neolinguistics 5). Amsterdam: Swets and Zeitlinger, 1976, pp. 246–52.

23 Snow, C. E., et al. Mothers' speech in three social classes. *J Psychol Res*, 1976, *5*, 1–20.

24 Bruner, J. S. Learning the mother tongue. *Hum Nat*, 1978, *1*, 42–49.

25 After Brown, R., Cazden, C., and Bellugi-Klima, U. The child's grammar from I to III. In Hill, J. P., ed. *Minnesota symposia on child psychology*, Vol. 2. Minneapolis: University of Minnesota Press, 1969, p. 244.

26 de Villiers, J. G., and de Villiers, P. A. *Language acquisition*. Cambridge, Mass.: Harvard University Press, 1978, p. 278.

27 Brown, R., and Bellugi, U. Three processes in the child's acquisition of syntax. *Harvard Educational Review*, 1964, *34*, 133–51.

28 Bowerman, M. Learning the structure of causative verbs. *Papers and reports on child language development* (Stanford University), 1974, *8*, 142–78.

29 Brown, R. *A first language*. Cambridge, Mass.: Harvard University Press, 1973.

30 Slobin, D. I. *Psycholinguistics*. Glenview, Ill.: Scott, Foresman, 1971.

31 Slobin, D. I. Cognitive prerequisites for the acquisition of grammar. In Ferguson, C. A., and Slobin, D. I., eds. *Studies of child language development*. New York: Holt, Rinehart, and Winston, 1973, pp. 175–208.

32 Broen, P. The verbal environment of the language-learning child. *Mono Am Sp*, 1972, *17*.

33 Newport, E. L. Motherese. *Technical report no. 52, Center for Human Information Processing*. San Diego, Calif.: University of California, 1975.

34 Cross, T. G. Mothers' speech adjustments. In Ferguson, C., and Snow, C., eds. *Talking to children*. Cambridge, England: Cambridge University Press, 1977.

35 Clark, H. H., and Clark, E. V. *Psychology and language*. New York: Harcourt Brace Jovanovich, 1977, p. 327.

36 Vorster, J. Mothers' speech to children. *Publications of the Institute for General Linguistics*, No. 8. Amsterdam: University of Amsterdam, 1974.

37 Snow, C. E. Mothers' speech to children learning language. *Child Develop, 1972, 43,* 549–65.

38 Brown, R. *First language.* Cambridge, Mass.: Harvard University Press, 1973.

39 See, for example, Skinner, B. F. *Verbal behavior.* Englewood Cliffs, N.J.: Prentice-Hall, 1957.

40 de Villiers, J. G., and de Villiers, P. A. *Language acquisition.* Cambridge, Mass.: Harvard University Press, 1978, p. 272.

41 Chomsky, N. *Aspects of a theory of syntax.* Cambridge, Mass.: M.I.T. Press, 1965.

42 See, for example, Liebermann, P., Klatt, D. H., and Wilson, W. H. Vocal tract limitations on the vowel repertoires of Rhesus monkey and other non-human primates. *Science,* 1969, *164,* 1185–87.

43 Geschwind, N., and Levitsky, W. Human brain. *Science,* 1968, *161,* 186–87.

44 Kellogg, W. N., and Kellogg, L. A. *The ape and the child,* New York: McGraw-Hill, 1933. Also Hayes, K. *The ape in our house.* New York: Harper & Row, 1951.

45 Gardner, R. A., and Gardner, B. T. Communication with a young chimpanzee. In Chauvin, R., ed. *Edition du Centre National de la Recherche Scientific.* Paris: 1972.

46 Premack, A. J., and Premack, D. Teaching language to an ape. *Sci Am,* 1972, *227,* 92–99.

47 Premack, D. *Intelligence in ape and man.* Hillsdale, N.J.: Erlbaum, 1976.

48 Savage-Rumbaugh, E. S., Rumbaugh, D. M., and Boysen, S. Symbolic communication between two chimpanzees. *Science,* 1978, *201,* 641–44.

49 See, for example, Limber, J. Language in child and chimp? *Am Psychol,* 1977, *32,* 280–95.

50 Fodor, J. A., Bever, T. G., and Garrett, M. *The psychology of language.* New York: McGraw-Hill, 1974.

51 Clark, H. H., and Clark, E. V. *Psychology and language.* New York: Harcourt Brace Jovanovich, 1977, pp. 522–23.

52 Clark, H. H., and Clark, E. V. As immediately above, p. 558.

53 Bruner, J. S., Goodnow, J. J., and Austin, G. A. *A study of thinking.* New York: Wiley, 1956.

54 Fodor, J. A. *The language of thought.* New York: Crowell, 1975.

55 Bross, I.D.J. Language in cancer research. In Murphy, G. P., Pressman, D., and Mirand, E. S., eds. *Perspectives in cancer research and treatment.* New York: Liss, 1973, pp. 213–21.

56 Clark, H. H., and Clark, E. V. *Psychology and language.* New York: Harcourt Brace Jovanovich, 1977, p. 555.

57 Whorf, B. L. Science and linguistics. In Carroll, J. B., ed. *Language, thought, and reality.* Cambridge, Mass.: M.I.T. Press, 1956, pp. 207–19.

58 Kay, P. Synchronic variability and diachronic changes in basic color terms. *Lang Soc,* 1975, *4,* 257–70.

59 Clark, H. H., and Clark, E. V. *Psychology and language.* New York: Harcourt Brace Jovanovich, 1977, pp. 530–36.

60 Rosch, E. H. Human categorization. In Warren, E., ed. *Advances in cross-cultural psychology* (Vol. I). London: Academic Press, 1977.

61 Rosch, E. H. Natural categories. *Cog Psychol,* 1973, *4,* 328–50.

62 Zipf, G. K. *Human behavior and the principle of least effort.* Cambridge, Mass.: Addison-Wesley, 1949.

63 Clark, H. H., and Clark, E. V. *Psychology and language.* New York: Harcourt Brace Jovanovich, 1977, pp. 554–57.

64 Collins, A. M., and Quillian, M. R. How to make a language user. In Tulving, E., and Donaldson, W., eds. *Organization of memory.* New York: Academic Press, 1972.

65 Schank, R. C. Identifications of conceptualizations underlying natural language. In Schank, R. C., and Colby, K. M., eds. *Computer models of thought and language.* San Fransisco: Freeman, 1973, pp. 187–247.

66 Thorndike, E. L. *Animal intelligence.* New York: Macmillan, 1911.

67 Wason, P. C. Problem solving and reasoning. *Cog Psychol,* British Medical Bulletin, 1971, *27.*

68 Maier, N.R.F., and Burke, R. J. Response availability as a factor in the problem-solving performance of males and females. *J Pers Soc Psychol,* 1967, *5,* 304–10. Copyright 1967 by the American Psychological Association. Reprinted with permission.

69 Duncker, K. (trans. by Lees, L. S.).

On problem-solving. *P Mono,* 1945, *58*(No. 270).

70 Mackinnon, D. W. The personality of correlates of creativity. In Nielsen, G. S., ed. *Proceedings of the XIV International Congress of Applied Psychology, Copenhagen, 1961.* Copenhagen: Munksgaard, 1962, pp. 11–39.

71 Drawings are from Barron, F. The psychology of imagination. *Sci Am,* 1958. Reprinted with permission.

72 See, for example, Newell, A., and Simon, H. A. *Human problem solving.* Englewood Cliffs, N.J.: Prentice-Hall, 1972.

Chapter six
Intelligence: the problem of defining and measuring it

1 Thorndike, E. L., et al. Intelligence and its measurement: a symposium. *J Ed Psychol,* 1921, *12,* 123–47.

2 Zigler, E., and Trickett, P. K. IQ, social competence, and evaluation of early childhood intervention programs. *Am Psychol,* 1978, *33,* 789–98.

3 Holden, C. California court is forum for latest round in IQ debate. *Science,* 1978, *201,* 1106–09.

4 Wechsler, D. Intelligence defined and undefined. *Am Psychol,* 1975, *30,* 135–59.

5 Mussen, P. H., Conger, J. J., and Kagan, J. *Child development and personality,* 5th ed. New York: Harper & Row, 1979.

6 Thurstone, L. L., and Thurstone, T. G. Factorial studies of intelligence. *Psychometric Monographs,* Chicago: University of Chicago Press, 1941, No. 2.

7 Stevenson, H. W., Friedrichs, A. G., and Simpson, W. E. Interrelations and correlates over time in children's learning. *Child Develop,* 1970, *41,* 625–37. Also Stevenson, H. W., et al. Interrelations and correlates in children's learning and problem solving. *Mono Soc Res,* 1968, *33*(No. 7, Series no. 123).

8 Guilford, J. P. *The nature of human intelligence.* New York: McGraw-Hill, 1967.

9 Piaget, J. *The origins of intelligence in children.* New York: International Universities Press, 1952.

10 Stevenson, H. W., and Bitterman, M. E. The distance effect in the transposition of intermediate size by children. *Am J Psychol,* 1955, *68,* 274–79.

11 Goodnow, J. J., and Bethon, G. Piaget's tasks. *Child Develop,* 1966, *37,* 573–82.

12 Brown, R. W. *Social psychology.* New York: Free Press, 1965.

13 Cronbach, L. J. *Essentials of psychological testing.* New York: Harper, 1949.

14 Copyright (1967) by Harcourt Brace Jovanovich, Inc. Reproduced by special permission of the publisher.

15 Mussen, P. H., Conger, J. J., and Kagan, J. *Child development and personality,* 5th ed. New York: Harper & Row, 1979. See also Zigler, E., and Trickett, P. K. IQ, social competence, and evaluation of early childhood intervention programs. *Am Psychol,* 1978, *33,* 789–98.

16 See, for example, Wing, C. W., Jr., and Wallach, M. A. *College admissions and the psychology of talent.* New York: Holt, Rinehart, and Winston, 1971.

17 Bond, E. A. *Tenth-grade abilities and achievements.* New York: Columbia University Teachers College, 1940.

18 Conry, R., and Plant, W. T. WAIS and group test predictions of an academic success criterion. *Ed PM,* 1965, *25,* 493–500.

19 Matarazzo, J. D. *Wechsler's measurement and appraisal of adult intelligence,* 5th ed. Baltimore: Williams & Wilkins, 1972.

20 Harrell, T. W., and Harrell, M. S. Army general classification test scores for civilian occupations. *Ed PM,* 1945, *5,* 229–39.

21 Duncan, O. D., Featherman, D. L., and Duncan, B. *Socioeconomic background and achievement.* New York: Seminar Press, 1972.

22 Jensen, A. R. The heritability of intelligence. *Sat Eve Post,* 1972, *244,* 9.

23 McClelland, D. C. Testing for competence rather than for "intelligence." *Am Psychol,* 1973, *28,* 1–14.

24 Holland, J. L., and Richards, J. M., Jr. Academic and nonacademic performance. *J Ed Psychol,* 1965, *45,* 165–74.

25 Elton, C. F., and Shevel, L. R. *Who is tolerated? An analysis of achievement (Research report No. 31).* Iowa City: American College Testing Program, 1969.

26 Berg, I. *Education and jobs.* New York: Praeger, 1970.

27 Taylor, C., Smith, W. R., and

Ghiselin, B. The creative and other contributions of one sample of research scientists. In Taylor, C., and Barron, F., eds. *Scientific creativity*. New York: Wiley, 1963.

28 Wallach, M. A. Tests tell us little about talent. *Am Sci*, 1976, *64*, 57–63.

29 Jencks, C., et al. *Inequality*. New York: Basic Books, 1972.

30 Zigler, E., and Trickett, P. K. IQ, social competence, and evaluation of early childhood intervention programs. *Am Psychol*, 1978, *33*, 789–98.

31 Janke, L. L., and Havighurst, R. J. Relation between ability and social-status in a midwestern community. II. Sixteen-year-old boys and girls. *J Ed Psychol*, 1945, *36*, 499–509.

32 McNemar, Q. *The revision of the Stanford-Binet scale*. Boston: Houghton Mifflin, 1942.

33 Kennedy, W. A., Van de Riet, V., and White, J. C. A normative sample of intelligence and achievement of Negro elementary school children in the southeastern United States. *Mono Soc Res*, 1963, *28*(No. 6.).

34 Jensen, A. R. How much can we boost IQ and scholastic achievement? *Har Ed R*, 1969, *39*, 1–123.

35 Herzog, E., and Lewis, H. Children in poor families. *Am J Orthopsych*, 1970, *40*, 375–87.

36 Tiedman, D. V. *Righting the balance*. 2 vols. New York: College Entrance Examination Board, 1970.

37 Zigler, E., and Trickett, P. K. IQ, social competence, and evaluation of early childhood intervention programs. *Am Psychol*, 1978, *33*, 789–98.

38 Erlenmeyer-Kimling, L., and Jarvik, L. F. Genetics and intelligence. *Science*, 1963, *142*, 1477–79.

39 Jensen, A. R. How much can we boost IQ and scholastic achievement? *Har Ed R*, 1969, *39*, 1–123.

40 Kamin, L. *The science and politics of IQ*. Potomac, Md.: Erlbaum, 1974.

41 Stock, M. B., and Smythe, P. M. Does undernutrition during infancy inhibit brain growth and subsequent intellectual development? *Arch Dis Child*, 1963, *38*, 546–52.

42 Harrell, R. F., Woodyard, E., and Gates, A. I. *The effect of mothers' diet on the intelligence of the offspring*. New York: Teacher's College, Columbia Bureau of Publications, 1955.

43 Jensen, A. R. How much can we boost IQ and scholastic achievement? *Har Ed R*, 1969, *39*, 1–123.

44 Scarr, S., and Weinberg, R. A. IQ test performance of black children adopted by white families. *Am Psychol*, 1976, *31*, 726–39.

45 Jensen, A. R. The strange case of Dr. Jensen and Mr. Hyde. *Am Psychol*, 1974, *29*, 467–68.

46 Gottesman, I. I. Biogenetics of race and class. In Deutsch, M., Katz, I., and Jensen, A. B., eds. *Social class, race, and psychological development*. New York: Holt, Rinehart, and Winston, 1968, pp. 25–51.

47 Kagan, J. Inadequate evidence and illogical conclusions. *Har Ed R*, 1969, *39*, 274–77.

48 See, for example, Kennedy, W. A. A follow-up normative study of Negro intelligence and achievement. *Mono Soc Res*, 1969, *34*(No. 2).

49 Pearson, C. Intelligence of Honolulu preschool children in relation to parents' education. *Child Develop*, 1969, *40*, 647–50.

50 Wolf, R. M. The identification and measurement of environmental process variables related to intelligence. Unpublished Ph.D. dissertation, University of Chicago, 1963.

51 Belmont, L., and Marolla, F. A. Birth order, family size, and intelligence. *Science*, 1973, *182*, 1096–101.

52 Zajonc, R. B., and Markus, G. B. Birth order and intellectual development. *Psychol R*, 1975, *82*, 74–88.

53 Belmont, L., Stein, Z., and Zybert, P. Child spacing and birth order. *Science*, 1978, *202*, 995–96.

54 Chance, P. Race and IQ. *Psychol T*, 1975, *8*, 40–43.

55 Skeels, H. M. Adult status of children with contrasting early life experiences. *Mono Soc Res*, 1966, *31*(No. 3).

56 Sontag, L. W., Baker, C. T., and Nelson, V. L. Mental growth and personality development. *Mono Soc Res*, 1958, *23*(No. 2). By permission of the Society for Research in Child Development, Inc.

57 Owens, W. A., Jr. Age and mental abilities. *J Ed Psychol*, 1966, *57*, 311–25. Copyright 1966 by the American Psychological Association. Reprinted with permission.

58 Doyle, K. O. Theory and practice of ability testing in ancient Greece. *J Hist,* 1974, *10,* 202–12.

59 Elton, C. F., and Shevel, L. R. *Who is talented? An analysis of achievement.* Iowa City: American College Testing Program, 1969.

60 *Differential Aptitude Tests.* New York: Psychological Corp.

Chapter seven
The senses: our source of information

1 Bloom, W., and Fawcett, D. W. *A textbook of histology,* 9th ed. Philadelphia: Saunders, 1968.

2 Wald, G. The photochemical basis of rod vision. *J Op,* 1951, *41,* 949–56.

3 Liebman, P. Detection of color-vision pigments by single cell microphotometry—the method and its efficiency. Summarized in Riggs, L. A. Vertebrate color receptors. *Science,* 1965, *147,* 913.

4 De Valois, R. L. Neural processing of visual information. In Russell, R. W., ed. *Frontiers in physiological psychology.* New York: Academic Press, 1966, pp. 51–91.

5 Uttal, W. R. *The psychobiology of sensory coding.* New York: Harper & Row, 1973.

6 Pritchard, R. M. Stabilized images on the retina. *Sci Am,* 1961, *204,* 72–78.

7 Riggs, L. A., et al. The disappearance of steadily fixated visual test objects. *J Op,* 1953, *43,* 495–501.

8 Békésy, G. V. *Experiments in hearing.* New York: McGraw-Hill, 1960.

9 Wever, E. G. *Theory of hearing.* New York: Wiley, 1949.

10 Uttal, W. R. *The psychobiology of sensory coding.* New York: Harper & Row, 1973.

11 Dethier, V. C. Other tastes, other worlds. *Science,* 1978, *201,* 224–28.

12 Liebeskind, J. C., and Paul, L. A. Psychological and physiological mechanisms of pain. *An Rev Psychol,* 1977, *28,* 41–60.

13 De Valois, R. L., and Jacobs, G. H. Primate color vision. *Science,* 1968, *162,* 533–40.

14 De Valois, R. L. Neural processing of visual information. In Russell, R. W., ed. *Frontiers in physiological psychology.* New York: Academic Press, 1966, pp. 51–91.

15 Champanis, A., Garner, W. R., and Morgan, C. T. *Applied experimental psychology—human factors in engineering design.* New York: Wiley, 1949.

16 Champanis, A. *Man-machine engineering.* Belmont, Calif.: Wadsworth, 1965.

Chapter eight
Perception: the science of first impressions

1 Hochberg, J. *Perception,* 2d ed. Englewood Cliffs, N.J.: Prentice-Hall, 1978, p. 179.

2 Gibson, E. J. *Principles of perceptual learning and development.* New York: Appleton-Century-Crofts, 1969.

3 Hochberg, J. *Perception,* 2d ed. Englewood Cliffs, N.J.: Prentice-Hall, 1978, p. 2.

4 Argyle, M. *Bodily communication.* New York: International Universities Press, 1975.

5 Hochberg, J. *Perception,* 2d ed. Englewood Cliffs, N.J.: Prentice-Hall, 1978, Chapter 7, especially pp. 235 and 241.

6 Hochberg, J., and Galper, R. E. Attribution of intention as a function of physiognomy. *Mem Cog,* 1974, *2,* 39–42.

7 Hubel, D. H. The visual cortex of the brain. *Sci Am,* 1963, *209,* 54–62. Copyright © 1963 by Scientific American, Inc. All rights reserved.

8 Hubel, D. H., and Wiesel, T. N. Receptive fields and functional architecture in two non-striate visual areas (18 and 19) of the cat. *J Neur,* 1965, *28,* 229–89.

9 Whitfield, I. C., and Evans, E. F. Responses of auditory cortical neurons to stimuli of changing frequency. *J Neur,* 1965, *28,* 655–72.

10 Blakemore, C. Central visual processing. In Gazzaniga, M. S., and Blakemore, C., eds. *Handbook of psychobiology.* New York: Academic Press, 1975.

11 See, for example, McCullough, C. Color adaptation of edge-detectors in the human visual system. *Science,* 1965, *149,* 1115–16.

12 Sekuler, R., and Levinson, E. The perception of moving targets. *Sci Am,* 1977, *236,* 60–73.

13 Salapatek, P., and Kessen, W. Visual scanning of triangles by the human newborn.. *J Exp Child,* 1966, *3,* 155–67.

14 Hochberg, J. *Perception,* 2d ed. Englewood Cliffs, N.J.: Prentice-Hall, 1978, p. 5.

15 Treisman, A. M. Strategies and models of selective attention. *Psychol R,* 1969, *76,* 282–99.

16 Neisser, U., and Becklen, R. Selective looking. *Cog Psychol,* 1975, *7,* 480–94.

17 Postman, L., Bruner, B., and McGinnies, E. Personal values as selective factors in perception. *J Abn,* 1948, *43,* 142–54.

18 McClelland, D. C., and Liberman, A. M. The effect of need for achievement on recognition of need-related words. *J Pers,* 1949, *18,* 236–51.

19 Chase, W. G., and Simon, H. A. Perception in chess. *Cog Psychol,* 1973, *4,* 55–81.

20 Gibson, E. J., and Walk, R. D. The "visual cliff." *Sci Am,* 1960, *202,* 64–71.

21 Hochberg, J. *Perception,* 2d ed. Englewood Cliffs, N.J.: Prentice-Hall, 1978, p. 62.

22 From *Elements of psychology,* 2d ed., by David Krech and Richard S. Crutchfield. Copyright © 1969 by Alfred A. Knopf, Inc. Reprinted by permission of Alfred A. Knopf, Inc.

23 Gibson, J. J. *The perception of the visual world.* Boston: Houghton Mifflin, 1950. Adopted from Fig. 43, p. 95. Copyright © 1950, renewed 1978 by Houghton Mifflin. Used by permission.

24 *Experiments in optical illusion,* by Nelson F. Beeler and Franklin M. Branley. (Artist: Fred H. Lyon.) Copyright 1951 by Thomas Y. Crowell Co., New York, publishers.

25 Hochberg, J. *Perception,* 2d ed. Englewood Cliffs, N.J.: Prentice-Hall, 1978, p. 114.

26 Biederman, I. Perceiving real-world scenes. *Science,* 1972, *177,* 77–79.

27 Hochberg, J. *Perception,* 2d ed. Englewood Cliffs, N.J.: Prentice-Hall, 1978, pp. 182–83.

28 Bugelski, B. R., and Alampay, D. A. The role of frequency in developing perceptual sets. *Can J Psychol,* 1961, *15,* 205–11. Copyright 1961, Canadian Psychological Association. Reprinted by permission.

29 Fisher, G. Ambiguity of form. *Percep,* 1968, *4,* 189–92. Attneave, F. Multistability in perception. *Sci Am,* Dec. 1971, *225,* 6, 62–70. Drawings originated by Gerald Fisher.

30 McClelland, D. C., and Atkinson, J. W. The projective expression of needs. I. The effect of different intensities of the hunger drive on perception. *J Psych,* 1948, *25,* 205–22.

31 Soal, S. G., and Bateman, F. *Modern experiments in telepathy.* New Haven, Conn.: Yale University Press, 1954.

32 Rhine, J. B., and Pratt, J. G. *Parapsychology.* Springfield, Ill.: Thomas, 1957.

33 Ullmann, M., and Krippner, S. An experimental approach to dreams and telepathy. *Am J Psych,* 1970, *126,* 1282–89.

34 Krippner, S. *Experimentally induced effects in dreams and other altered conscious states.* 20th International Congress of Psychology, Tokyo, August, 1972.

35 Hansel, C.E.M. *ESP.* New York: Scribners, 1966.

36 Brier, R., and Tyminski, W. V. Psi application. In Rhine, J. B., ed. *Progress in parapsychology.* Durham, N.C.: Parapsychology Press, 1971.

37 Williams, H. L. The new biology of sleep. *J Psych Res,* 1971, *8,* 445–78.

38 See, for example, Hauri, P. Dreams in patients remitted from reactive depression. *J Abn Psychol,* 1976, *72,* 16–22. See also Gold, M. S., and Robertson, M. F. The day-night imagery paradox of selected psychotic children. *JAACP,* 1975, *14,* 132–41.

39 Winget, C., Kramer, M., and Whitman, R. Dreams and demography. *CPAJ,* 1972, *17,* 203–08.

40 Williams, H. L. The new biology of sleep. *J Psych Res,* 1971, *8,* 445–78.

41 Courtesy of Dr. William C. Dement. Prepared by Stanford University Medical Center, Sleep Disorder Clinic.

42 Berger, R. J. The sleep and dream cycle. In Kales, A., ed. *Sleep, physiology, and pathology.* Philadelphia: Lippincott, 1969, pp. 17–32.

43 Webb, W. B., and Cartwright, R. D. Sleep and dreams. *An Rev Psych,* 1978, *29,* 223–52.

44 Meddis, R., Pearson, A.J.D., and Langford, G. An extreme case of healthy insomnia. *EEG Clin,* 1973, *35,* 213–24.

45 Webb, W. B., and Friel, J. Sleep stage and personality characteristics of "natural" long and short sleepers. *Science,* 1971, *171,* 587–88.

46 See, for example, Hartmann, E. L. Sleep requirement. *Psychos Med,* 1973, *14,* 95–103.

47 Johnson, L. C., and MacLeod,

W. L. Sleep and wake behavior during gradual sleep reduction. *PMS*, 1973, *36*, 87–97.

48 Kripke, D. F., and Simons, R. N. Average sleep, insomnia, and sleeping pill use. *Sleep Res*, 1976, *5*, 110.

49 Kales, A., et al. Personality patterns in insomnia. *Arch Gen Psych*, 1976, *33*, 1128–34.

50 Kales, A., et al. Chronic hypnotic-drug use—ineffectiveness, drug-withdrawal insomnia, and dependence. *JAMA*, 1974, *227*, 513–17.

51 Lubin, A. et al. The effects of exercise, bedrest, and napping on performance decrement during 40 hours. *Psychophys*, 1976, *13*, 334–39.

52 Webb, W. B., and Cartwright, R. D. Sleep and dreams. *An Rev Psychol*, 1978, *29*, 223–52.

53 Pappenheimer, J. R. The sleep factor. *Sci Am*, 1976, *235*, 24–29.

54 See, for example, Hartmann, E. L. *The functions of sleep*. New Haven, Conn.: Yale University Press, 1973.

55 See, for example, Moruzzi, G. The sleep-waking cycle. In Adrian, R. H., et al., eds. *Reviews of Psychology 64*. Berlin: Springer-Verlag, 1972, pp. 2–165.

56 Kline, M. V. Personal communication.

57 Moss, C. S. *Hypnosis in perspective*. New York: Macmillan, 1965.

58 Hilgard, E. R., and Hilgard, J. R. *Hypnosis in the relief of pain*. Los Altos, Calif.: William Kaufmann, 1975.

59 Hilgard, E. R. *Hypnotic suggestibility*. New York: Harcourt Brace Jovanovich, 1965.

60 Hilgard, J. R. *Personality and hypnosis*. Chicago: University of Chicago Press, 1970.

61 Benson, H. *The relaxation response*. New York: William Morrow, 1975.

62 Ornstein, R. E. The techniques of meditation and their implications for modern psychology. In Naranjo, C., and Ornstein, R. E., eds. *On the psychology of meditation*. New York: Viking, 1971.

63 Deikman, A. J. Deautomatization and the mystic experience. In Ornstein, R. E., ed. *The nature of human consciousness*. San Francisco: Freeman, 1973, pp. 216–33.

64 Banquet, J. P. Spectral analysis of the EEG in meditation. *EEG Clin*, 1973, *35*, 143–51.

65 Wallace, R. K., and Benson, H. The physiology of meditation. *Sci Am*, 1972, *226*, 84–90.

66 Benson, H., and Wallace, R. K. Decreased drug abuse with transcendental meditation—a study of 1,862 subjects. In Zarafonetis, C. J., ed. *Drug abuse*. New York: Lea and Febiger, 1972.

67 Benson, H., Rosner, B. A., and Marzetta, B. R. Decreased systolic blood pressure in hypertensive subjects who practiced meditation. *J Clin In*, 1973, *52*, 8.

68 Orme-Johnson, D. W. Autonomic stability and transcendental meditation. *P Med*, 1973, *35*, 341–49.

69 Schwartz, G. E. *Pros and cons of meditation*. Presented to American Psychological Association, Montreal, 1973.

70 Otis, L. S. If well-integrated but anxious, try T.M. *Psych T*, 1974, *7*, 45–46.

71 Beary, J. F., and Benson, H. A simple psychophysiologic technique which elicits the hypometabolic changes of the relaxation response. *Psychos Med*, 1974, *36*, 115–20.

72 Abelson, H. C., and Fishburn, P. M. *Nonmedical use of psychoactive substances*. Princeton, N.J.: Response Analysis Corp., 1976.

73 Sjoberg, B. M., Jr., and Hollister, L. E. The effects of psychotomimetic drugs on primary suggestibility. *Psychop*, 1965, *8*, 251–62.

74 Marijuana shows signs of becoming youths' permanent recreational drug. *ISR Newsletter*, 1978, *6*, 5–6.

75 Clark, L. D., and Nakashima, E. N. Experimental studies of marihuana. *Am J Psych*, 1968, *125*, 379–84.

76 Hollister, L. E. Marihuana in man. *Science*, 1971, *172*, 21–29.

77 National Institute on Drug Abuse, *Marijuana and health*. Rockville, Md.: National Institute on Drug Abuse, 1977.

78 See, for example, Soueit, M. I. Hashish consumption in Egypt, with special reference to psychosocial aspects. *Bull Narcotics*, 1967, *19*(2), 1–12.

79 See, for example, Rubin, V., and Comitas, L. *Ganja in Jamaica*. The Hague: Mouton, 1975.

80 Barron, F., Jarvik, M., and Bunnell, S., Jr. The hallucinogenic drugs. In *Altered States of Awareness*. San Francisco: Freeman, 1972.

81 Brecher, E. M. *Licit and illicit drugs*. Boston: Little, Brown, 1972.

82 Kales, A., moderator. Drug dependency. University of California

at Los Angeles Interdepartmental Conference. *An In Med*, 1969, *70*, 591.

83 Aigner, T. G., and Balster, R. L. Choice behavior in rhesus monkeys. *Science*, 1978, *201*, 234–35.

84 Ciaramella, A. Personal communication, 1979.

Chapter nine
Emotions and drives

1 Laird, J. D. Self-attribution of emotion. *J Pers Soc Psychol*, 1974, *29*, 475–86.

2 Young, P. T. *Motivation and emotion*. New York: Wiley, 1961.

3 Shaffer, L. F. Fear and courage in aerial combat. *J Consult Psychol*, 1947, *11*, 137–43.

4 Elmadjian, F. Excretion and metabolism of epinephrin. *Pharm Rev*, 1959, *11*, 409–15.

5 Lacey, J. L., and Van Lehn, R. Differential emphasis in somatic response to stress. *Psychos Med*, 1952, *12*, 73–81. Also Lacey, J. L., Bateman, D. E., and Van Lehn, R. Autonomic response specificity. *Psychos Med*, 1953, *15*, 8–21.

6 Mandler, G. Emotion. In Brown, R., et al. *New directions in psychology*. New York: Holt, Rinehart, and Winston, 1962, pp. 267–343.

7 Izard, C. E. *Human emotions*. New York: Plenum, 1977, especially p. 96. See also Ekman, P., Friesen, W. V., and Ellsworth, P. C. *Emotion in the human face*. New York: Pergamon, 1972.

8 See, for example, Andrew, R. J. The origins of facial expressions. *Sci Am*, 1965, *213*, 88–94.

9 Ekman, P. Universals and cultural differences in facial expressions of emotion. In Cole, J. K., ed. *Nebraska symposium on motivation*, 1971, Vol. 19. Lincoln: University of Nebraska Press, 1971, pp. 207–83.

10 Sackheim, H. A., Gur, R. C., and Saucy, M. C. Emotions are expressed more intensely on the left side of the face. *Science*, 1978, *202*, 434–36.

11 See, for example, Gatz, A. J. *Manter's essentials of clinical neuroanatomy and neurophysiology*. Philadelphia: Davis, 1970. Also Peele, T. L. *The neuroanatomic basis for clinical neurology*. New York: McGraw-Hill, 1961.

12 Davidson, R. J., and Schwartz, G. E. Patterns of cerebral lateralization during cardiac biofeedback versus the self-regulation of emotion. *Psychophy*, 1976, *13*, 62–68.

13 Hess, E. H. Attitude and pupil size. *Sci Am*, 1965, *212*, 46–54.

14 Hess, E. H. The role of pupil size in communication. *Sci Am*, 1975, *233*, 110–19.

15 Ashear, J. B. Study cited in Hess, E. H. The role of pupil size in communication. *Sci Am*, 1975, *233*, 110–19.

16 Hess, E. H. The role of pupil size in communication. *Sci Am*, 1975, *233*, 110–19.

17 James, W. *Principles of psychology*. Vol. II. New York: Dover, 1950.

18 See, for example, Tomkins, S. S. *Affect, imagery, consciousness,*

Vol. I. The positive affects. New York: Springer, 1962.

19 Tyhurst, J. S. Individual reactions to community disaster. *Am J Psych*, 1951, *10*, 746–69.

20 Izard, C. E. *Human emotions*. New York: Plenum, 1977, especially pp. 12–13 and 18.

21 The automatic nature of emotional reactions is emphasized in Arnold, M. B. *Emotion and personality, Vol. I*. New York: Columbia University Press, 1960.

22 A more elaborate view of emotional appraisal is found in Lazarus, R. S., and Averill, J. R. Emotion and cognition. In Spielberger, C. D., ed. *Anxiety*. New York: Academic Press, 1972.

23 Schachter, S., and Singer, J. E. Cognitive, social and physiological determinants of emotional state. *Psychol R*, 1962, *69*, 379–99.

24 Maslach, C. The emotional consequences of arousal without reason. In Izard, C. E., ed. *Emotion, conflict, and defense*. New York: Plenum, 1978.

25 After Izard, C. E. *Human emotions*. New York: Plenum, 1977, especially pp. 85–97.

26 Izard, C. E. *Human emotions*. New York: Plenum, 1977.

27 Kagan, J. On emotion and its development. In Lewis, M., and Rosenblum, L. A., eds. *The development of affect*. New York: Plenum, 1978.

28 Opler, M. K. Cultural induction of stress. In Appley, M. H., and Trumbull, R., eds. *Psychological stress*. New York: Appleton-Century-Crofts, 1967, pp. 69–75.

29 Kagan, J. Discrepancy, temperament, and infant distress. In Lewis, M., and Rosenblum, L. A., eds. *The origins of fear.* New York: Wiley, 1974, pp. 229–48.

30 Gellhorn, E., and Miller, A. D. Methacholine and noradrenaline tests. *Arch Gen Psych,* 1961, *4,* 371–80.

31 Lacey, J. I., and Lacey, B. C. Verification and extension of the principle of autonomic response-stereotypy. *Am J Psychol,* 1958, *71,* 50–73.

32 Kagan, J. *Human psychological development.* New York: Scientific American, 1980.

33 Williams, R. J. *Biochemical individuality.* New York: Wiley, 1956.

34 Hohmann, G. W. Some effects of spinal cord lesions on experienced emotional feelings. *Psychophys,* 1966, *3,* 143–56.

35 Selye, H. Stress without distress. In Serban, G., ed. *Psychopathology of human adaptation.* New York: Plenum, 1976, p. 137.

36 Wickert, F. *Psychological research on problems of redistribution.* Washington, D.C.: Government Printing Office, 1947.

37 Ball, G. G. Vagotomy. *Science,* 1974, *184,* 484–85.

38 Morgan, C. T., and Morgan, J. D. Studies in hunger. II. The relation of gastric denervation and dietary sugar to the effect of insulin upon food-intake in the rat. *J Genetic,* 1940, *57,* 153–63.

39 Tsang, Y. C. Hunger motivation in gastrectomized rats. *J Com Psychol,* 1938, *26,* 1–17.

40 Wangensteen, O. H. and Carlson, A. J. Hunger sensations in a patient after total gastrectomy. *PSEBM,* 1931, *28,* 545–47.

41 Friedman, M. I., and Stricker, E. M., The physiological psychology of hunger, *Psychol R,* 1976, *83,* 409–31.

42 Anand, B. K., and Brobeck, J. R. Hypothalamic control of food intake in rat and cat. *Yale JBM,* 1951, *24,* 123–40.

43 Hetherington, A. W., and Ranson, W. W. Hypothalamic lesions and adiposity in the rat. *An Rec,* 1940, *78,* 149–72.

44 Valenstein, E. S., Cox, V. C., and Kakolewski, J. W. Re-examination of the role of the hypothalamus in emotion. *Psychol R,* 1970, *77,* 16–31.

45 Valenstein, E. S. *Brain control.* New York: Wiley, 1973, p. 88.

46 Valenstein, E. S. Stereotyped behavior and stress. In Serban, G., ed. *The psychopathology of human adaptation.* New York: Plenum, 1976, pp. 113–24.

47 Balagura, S. *Hunger.* New York: Basic Books, 1973.

48 Nisbett, R. E. Hunger, obesity, and the ventromedial hypothalamus. *Psychol R,* 1972, *79,* 433–53.

49 Stellar, E., and Corbit, J. B., eds. Neural control of motivated behavior. *NRPB, 11*(No. 4), Sept. 1973.

50 Nisbett, R. E. Hunger, obesity, and the ventromedial hypothalamus. *Psychol R,* 1972, *79,* 433–53.

51 Hervey, G. R. Regulation of energy balance. *Nature,* 1969, *222,* 629–31.

52 Epstein, A. N., and Teitelbaum, P. Regulation of food intake in the absence of taste, smell, and other oropharyngeal sensations. *J Com PP,* 1962, *55,* 155. Copyright 1962 by the American Psychological Association. Reprinted with permission.

53 Miller, N. E. *Behavioral sciences report for overview cluster of the President's biomedical research panel,* 1975.

54 Schachter, S. Some extraordinary facts about obese humans and rats. *Am Psychol,* 1971, *26,* 129–44. Copyright 1971 by the American Psychological Association. Reprinted with permission.

55 Schachter, S., and Gross, L. P. Manipulated time and eating behavior. *J Pers Soc Psychol,* 1968, *10,* 98–106.

56 Schachter, S. Some extraordinary facts about obese humans and rats. *Am Psychol,* 1971, *26,* 129–44.

57 Nisbett, R. E. Taste, deprivation, and weight determinants of eating behavior. *J Pers Soc Psychol,* 1968, *10,* 107–16.

58 Rodin, J. *Shock avoidance behavior in obese and normal subjects.* Unpublished manuscript, Yale University, 1972.

59 Rodin, J., Elman, D., and Schachter, S. *Emotionality and obesity.* Unpublished manuscript, Yale University, 1972.

60 Bullen, B. A., Reed, R. B., and Mayer, J. Physical activity of obese and nonobese girls appraised by motion picture sampling. *AJCN,* 1964, *14,* 211–23.

61 Nisbett, R. E., and Platt, J. Unpublished data referred to in Nisbett, R. E. Hunger, obesity, and the ventromedial hypothalamus. *Psychol R,* 1972, *79,* 433–53.

62 Schachter, S. Some extraordinary facts about obese humans and rats. *Am Psychol,* 1971, *26,* 129–44.

63 Miller, N. E. *Behavioral sciences report for overview cluster of the President's biomedical research panel,* 1975.

64 Björntorp, P. Disturbances in the regulation of food intake. *Adv Psychos Med,* 1972, *7,* 116–47.

65 Knittle, J. L., and Hirsch, J. Effect of early nutrition on the development of rat epididymal fat pads. *J Clin In,* 1968, *47,* 2091.

66 Björntorp, P., Bergman, H., and Varnauskas, E. Plasma free fatty acid turnover in obesity. *Acta Med Scan,* 1969, *185,* 351–56.

67 Nisbett, R. E. Hunger, obesity, and the ventromedial hypothalamus. *Psychol R,* 1972, *79,* 433–53.

68 Schemmel, R., Michelsen, O., and Gill, J. L. Dietary obesity in rats. *J Nut,* 1970, *100,* 1041–48.

69 Hirsch, J., and Knittle, J. L. Cellularity of obese and nonobese human adipose tissue. *Fed Pro,* 1970, *29,* 1516–21.

70 Sims, E. A., et al. Experimental obesity in man. *EMM,* 1968.

71 Blass, E. M., and Hall, W. G. Drinking termination. *Psychol R,* 1976, *83,* 356–74.

72 Cofer, C. N. *Motivation and emotion.* Glenview, Ill.: Scott, Foresman, 1972.

73 Epstein, A. N., Kissileff, H. R., and Stellar, E., eds. *The neuropsychology of thirst.* Washington, D.C.: Winston, 1973.

74 Epstein, A. N., Fitzsimons, J. T., and Simons, B. Drinking caused by the intercranial injection of angiotensin into the rat. *J Phys* (London), 1969, *200,* 98–100.

75 Miller, N. E. *From the brain to behavior.* Invited lecture at XII Interamerican Congress of Psychology, Montevideo, Uruguay, March 30 to April 6, 1969.

76 Bexton, W. H., Heron, W., and Scott, T. H. Effects of decreased variation in the sensory environment. *Can J Psych,* 1954, *8,* 70–76.

77 Suedfeld, P. The benefits of boredom. *Am Sci,* 1975, *63,* 60–69.

78 See, for example, Magoun, H. W. *The waking brain,* 2d ed. Springfield, Ill.: Thomas, 1963.

79 Dember, W. N. The new look in motivation. *Am Sci,* 1965, *53,* 409–27.

80 Butler, R. A. Discrimination learning by Rhesus monkeys to visual-exploration motivation. *J Com PP,* 1953, *46,* 95–98.

81 Mussen, P. H., Conger, J. J., and Kagan, J. *Child development and personality,* 4th ed. New York: Harper & Row, 1974.

82 Harlow, H. F., and Harlow, M. K. Social deprivation in monkeys. *Sci Am,* 1962, *207,* 136–46.

83 Whalen, R. E. Brain mechanisms controlling sexual behavior. In Beach, F. A., ed. *Human sexuality in four perspectives.* Baltimore: Johns Hopkins Press, 1976, pp. 215–46.

84 Beach, F. A. Hormonal control of sex-related behavior. In Beach, F. A., ed. *Human sexuality in four perspectives.* Baltimore: Johns Hopkins Press, 1976, pp. 247–67.

85 National Center for Health Statistics, *Contraceptive utilization in the United States: 1973 and 1976.* Advanced Data No. 36, 1978.

86 U.S. Bureau of the Census, *Perspectives on American fertility,* 1978, Series P-23, No. 70.

87 Kinsey, A. C., Pomeroy, W. B., and Martin, C. E. *Sexual behavior in the human male.* Philadelphia: Saunders, 1948, p. 392.

88 Kinsey, A. C., Pomeroy, W. B., and Martin, C. E. See immediately above, p. 153.

89 Kinsey, A. C., Pomeroy, W. B., and Martin, C. E. See above, pp. 195 and 198.

90 Kinsey, A. C., et al. *Sexual behavior in the human female.* Philadelphia: Saunders, 1953.

91 Kinsey, A. C., et al. See immediately above, p. 380.

92 Kinsey, A. C., Pomeroy, W. B., and Martin, C. E. *Sexual behavior in the human male.* Philadelphia: Saunders, 1948, pp. 306–07.

93 Masters, W. H., and Johnson, V. E. *Human sexual inadequacy.* Boston: Little, Brown, 1970.

94 Gebhard, P. H. Personal communication, 1979.

95 Vincent, C. E. Social and interpersonal sources of sympto-

matic frigidity. *Mar Fam L,* 1956, *18,* 355–60.

96 Gebhard, P. Personal communication, 1979.

97 Messenger, J. Personal communication, 1979.

98 Simon, W., Berger, A. S., and Gagnon, J. H. Beyond anxiety and fantasy. *JYA,* 1972, *1,* 203–22.

99 Hesselund, H. On some sociological sex differences. *J Sex Res,* 1971, *7,* 263–73.

100 Macklin, E. D. Heterosexual cohabitation among college students. *Fam Coord,* 1972, *21,* 463–72.

101 Masters, W. H., and Johnson, V. E. Personal communication.

102 Gebhard, P. H. Personal communication, 1979.

103 Vincent, C. E. Social and interpersonal sources of symptomatic frigidity. *Mar Fam L,* 1956, *18,* 355–60.

Chapter ten
Motives, frustration, and conflict

1 James, W. *Principles of psychology,* Vol II. New York: Dover, 1950.

2 Lowell, E. L. The effect of need for achievement on learning and speed of performance. *J Psychol,* 1952, *33,* 31–40.

3 French, E. G., and Thomas, F. H. The relation of achievement to problem-solving effectiveness. *J Abn,* 1958, *56,* 45–48.

4 Sadacca, R., Ricciuti, H. N., and Swanson, E. O. *Content analysis of achievement motivation protocols.* Princeton, N.J.: Educational Testing Service, 1956.

5 Morgan, H. H. *An analysis of certain structured and unstructured test results of achieving and non-achieving high ability college students.* Unpublished doctoral dissertation, University of Michigan, 1951.

6 Crockett, H. J. The achievement motive and differential occupational mobility in the United States. *Am Sociol R,* 1962, *27,* 191–204. By permission of the American Sociological Association.

7 Morris, J. L. Propensity for risk taking as a determinant of vocational choice. *J Pers Soc Psychol,* 1966, *3,* 328–35.

8 Hoyos, C. G. Motivationpsychologische Untersuchungen von Kraftfahrern mit dem TAT nach McClelland. *AGP,* 1965. Supp. No. 7.

9 Winterbottom, M. R. *The relation of childhood training in independence to achievement motivation.* Unpublished doctoral dissertation, University of Michigan, 1953. Summarized in McClelland, D. C., et al. *The achievement motive.* New York: Irvington Publishers, Inc., 1953. Adapted by permission.

10 Winter, D. G., and Stewart, A. J., The power motive. In London, H., and Exner, J. E., eds. *Dimensions of personality.* New York: Wiley, 1978, pp. 415–17.

11 Winter, D. G. *The power motive.* New York: Free Press, 1973.

12 See, for example, Brown, M. D. The effectiveness of the personality dimensions of dependency, power, and internal-external locus of control in differentiating among unremitted and remitted alcoholics and non-alcoholic controls. Unpublished doctoral dissertation, University of Windsor, 1975.

13 See, for example, McClelland, D. C., and Teague, G. Predicting risk preferences among power-related acts. *J Pers,* 1975, *43,* 266–85.

14 Stewart, A. J., and Rubin, Z. Power motivation in the dating couple. *J Pers Soc Psychol,* 1976, *34,* 305–09.

15 Winter, D. G., and Stewart, A. J. The power motive. In London, H., and Exner, J. E., eds. *Dimensions of personality.* New York: Wiley, 1978, p. 410.

16 McClelland, D. C., et al. *The drinking man.* New York: Free Press, 1972, p. 357.

17 Barber, J. D. *The presidential character.* Englewood Cliffs, N.J.: Prentice-Hall, 1972.

18 Winter, D. G. *The power motive.* New York: Free Press, 1973.

19 Stewart, A. J. *Longitudinal prediction from personality to life outcomes among college-educated women.* Unpublished doctoral dissertation, Harvard University, 1975.

20 Winter, D. G., and Stewart, A. J. The power motive. In London, H., and Exner, J. E., eds. *Dimensions of personality.* New York: Wiley, 1978, pp. 426–27.

21 Schachter, S. *Psychology of affiliation.* Stanford, Calif.: Stanford University Press, 1959.

22 Tschukitscheff, I. P. Über den Mechanismus der Hungerbewegungen des Magens. I. Einfluss des "satten" und "Hunger"-Blutes auf die periodische Tatigkeit des Magens. *AGP,* 1930, *223,* 251–64.

23 Dember, W. N. Birth order and need affiliation. *J Abn,* 1964, *68,* 555–57. Copyright 1964 by the American Psychological Association. Reprinted with permission.

24 Hilton, I. Differences in the behavior of mothers toward first- and later-born children. *J Pers Soc Psychol,* 1967, *7,* 282–90.

25 Feshbach, S. The dynamics and morality of violence and aggression. *Am Psychol,* 1971, *26,* 281–92.

26 Suedfeld, P. Sensory deprivation stress. *J Pers Soc Psychol,* 1969, *11,* 70–74.

27 Sampson, E. A., and Hancock, F. T. An examination of the relationship between ordinal position, personality, and conformity. *J Pers Soc Psychol,* 1967, *5,* 398–407.

28 Adler, A. Characteristics of the first, second, and third child. *Children,* 1928, *3,* 14–52.

29 Lorenz, K. *On aggression.* New York: Harcourt Brace Jovanovich, 1966.

30 Paddock, J., O'Neill, C. W., and Haver, W. *Faces of anti-violence.* International Society for Research on Aggression, Washington, D.C., Sept. 1978.

31 Bandura, A. *Aggression.* Englewood Cliffs, N.J.: Prentice-Hall, 1973.

32 Zeichner, A., and Pihl, R. O. Effects of alcohol and behavior contingencies on human aggression. *J Abn Psychol,* 1979, *88,* 153–61.

33 Geen, R. G., and O'Neal, E. C. Activation of cue-elicited aggression by general arousal. *J Pers Soc Psychol,* 1969, *11,* 289–92.

34 Baron, R. A., and Lawton, S. F. Environmental influences on aggression. *Psychon Sci,* 1972, *26,* 80–82.

35 Zillman, D., Katcher, A. H., and Milavsky, B. Excitation transfer from physical exercise to subsequent aggressive behavior. *JESP,* 1972, *8,* 247–59.

36 See, for example, Geen, R. G. *Personality.* St. Louis: Mosby, 1976.

37 Slaby, R. G., Quarforth, G. R., and McConnachie, G. A. Television violence and its sponsors. *J Com,* 1976, *26,* 88–96.

38 See, for example, Kaplan, R. M., and Singer, R. D. Television violence and viewer aggression. *J Soc Issues,* 1976, *32,* 35–70.

39 See, for example, Dollard, J., et al. *Frustration and aggression.* New Haven, Conn.: Yale University Press, 1939.

40 Gerbner, G., and Gross, L. The scary world of TV's heavy viewer. *Psych T,* 1976, *9,* 41–45.

41 Thomas, M. H., et al. Toleration of real life aggression as a function of exposure to television violence. *J Pers Soc Psychol,* 1977, *35,* 450–58.

42 Steuer, F. B., Applefield, J. M., and Smith, R. Televised aggression and the interpersonal aggression of preschool children. *J Exp Child,* 1971, *11,* 422–47.

43 Eron, L. D., et al. Does television violence cause aggression? *Am Psychol,* 1972, *27,* 253–63.

44 Leiffer, A. D., Gordon, N. J., and Graves, S. B. Children's television. *Har Ed R,* 1974, *44,* 213–45.

45 Hartmann, D. P. Influence of symbolically modeled instrumental aggression and pain cues on aggressive behavior. *J Pers Soc Psychol,* 1969, *11,* 280–88.

46 Mankiewicz, F., and Swerdlow, J. *Remote control.* New York: Quadrangle, 1977.

47 Hendrick, G. When television is a school for criminals. *TV Guide,* Jan. 29, 1977, pp. 4–10.

48 Bandura, A. *Aggression.* Englewood Cliffs, N.J.: Prentice-Hall, 1973.

49 Maslow, A. H. *Motivation and personality,* 2d ed. New York: Harper & Row, 1970.

50 Knapp, R. R. Relationship of a measure of self-actualization to neuroticism and extraversion. *J Consult Psychol,* 1965, *29,* 168–72.

51 U.S. Bureau of the Census. Current Population Reports, Series P-25, No. 519, 1974. Washington, D.C.: U.S. Government Printing Office, 1974.

52 Atkinson, J. W. The mainsprings of achievement oriented activity. In Atkinson, J. W., and Raynor, J. O., eds. *Motivation and achievement.* Washington, D.C.: V. H. Winston, 1974, pp. 13–42.

53 deCharms, R., and Muir, M. S. Motivation. *An Rev Psych,* 1978, *29,* 91–113.

54 Weiner, B. *Achievement motivation and attribution theory.* Morristown, N.J.: General Learning Press, 1974.

55 Phares, E. J., and Lamiell, J. T. Internal-external control, interpersonal judgments of others in need, and attribution of responsibility. *J Pers,* 1975, *43,* 23–38.

56 Strickland, B. R. Internal-external control of reinforcement. In Blass, T., ed. *Personality variables in social behavior.* Hillsdale, N.J.: Erlbaum, 1977.

57 Sherman, S. J. Internal-external control and its relationship to attitude change under different social influence techniques. *J Pers Soc Psychol,* 1973, *26,* 23–29.

58 Adapted from Atkinson, J. W., and Raynor, J. O. *Motivation and achievement.* Washington, D.C.: Winston, 1975.

59 Atkinson, J. W. Resistance and overmotivation in achievement-oriented activity. In Serban, G., ed. *Psychopathology of human adaptation. Proceedings of the Third International Symposium of the Kittay Scientific Foundation.* New York: Plenum Press, 1976.

60 Sorrentino, R. M., and Sheppard, B. H. Effects of affiliation-related motives on swimmers in individual versus group competition. *J Pers Soc Psychol,* 1978, *36,* 704–14.

61 Barker, R. G., Dembo, T., and Lewin, K. Frustration and regression. *University of Iowa Studies in Child Welfare,* 1941, *18*(No. 386).

62 Hutt, M. L. "Consecutive" and "adaptive" testing with the revised Stanford-Binet. *J Consult Psychol,* 1947, *11,* 93–103.

63 Lewin, K. *A dynamic theory of personality.* New York: McGraw-Hill, 1935.

64 See, for example, Tavris, C., and Offir, C. *The longest war.* New York: Harcourt Brace Jovanovich, 1977, pp. 2–3.

65 Adapted from Bem, S. L. The measurement of psychological androgyny. *J Consult Clin Psychol,* 1974, *42,* 155–62.

66 Broverman, I. K., et al. Sex-role stereotypes. *J Soc Issues,* 1972, *28,* 59–79.

67 Money, J., and Ehrhardt, A. A. *Man and woman, body and girl.* Batimore: Johns Hopkins University Press, 1972, pp. 24–37.

68 See, for example, Bardwick, J. M. *Psychology of women.* New York: Harper & Row, 1971, pp. 84–89.

69 Ehrhardt, A. A., and Baker, S. W. Fetal androgens, human central nervous differentiation, and behavior sex differences. In Friedman, R. C., Richart, R. M., and Van de Wiele, R. L., eds. *Sex differences in behavior.* New York: Wiley, 1973.

70 See, for example, Stoller, R. J. The bedrock of masculinity and femininity—bisexuality. *Arch Gen Psych,* 1972, *26,* 207–12.

71 Mead, M. *Sex and temperament in three primitive societies.* New York: Dell, 1935.

72 Money, J., and Ehrhardt, A. A. *Man and woman, boy and girl.* Baltimore: Johns Hopkins University Press, 1972, p. 18.

73 Rubin, J. Z., Provenzano, F. J., and Luria, Z. The eye of the beholder. *Am J Orthopsych,* 1974, *44,* 512–19.

74 Weitzman, L. J. Sex-role socialization. In Freeman, J., ed. *Women.* Palo Alto, Calif.: Mayfield, 1975, p. 108.

75 Lewis, M., and Als, H. *The contribution of the infant to the interaction with his mother.* Paper presented at the meetings of the Society for Research in Child Development, Denver, April 1975.

76 Brooks, J., and Lewis, M. Attachment behavior in thirteen-month-old, opposite-sex twins. *Child Develop,* 1974, *45,* 243–47.

77 Goldberg, S., and Lewis, M. Play behavior in the year-old infant. *Child Develop,* 1969, *40,* 21–30.

78 Will, J., Self, P., and Datan, N. Paper presented to the American Psychological Association, 1974.

79 Weitzman, L. J. Sex-role socialization. In Freeman, J., ed. *Women.* Palo Alto, Calif.: Mayfield, 1975, p. 109.

80 O'Kelly, C. G. Sexism in children's television. *Journalism Q,* 1974, *51,* 722–24.

81 Weitzman, L. J., et al. Sex role socialization in picture books for pre-school children. *Am J Sociol,* 1972, *77,* 1125–50.

82 Serbin, L. A., et al. A comparison of teacher response to the pre-academic and problem behavior of boys and girls. *Child Develop,* 1973, *44,* 796–804.

83 Joffe, C. Sex role socialization

and the nursery school. *J Marr Fam*, 1971, *33*, 467–75.

84 Serbin, L. A., and O'Leary, K. D. How nursery schools teach girls to shut up. *Psych T*, 1975, *9*, 56–58.

85 Baumrind, D. From each according to her ability. *School R*, 1972, *80*, 161–97.

86 Howe, F. Sexual stereotypes start early. *Sat R*, 1971, *54*, 76–82.

87 Pogrebin, L. C. Down with sexist unbringing. *Ms. Magazine*, Spring 1972, 18 et seq.

88 Weitzman, L. J. Sex-role socialization. In Freeman, J., ed. *Women*. Palo Alto, Calif.: Mayfield, 1975, pp. 118–19.

89 Ladner, J. A. *Tomorrow's tomorrow*. Garden City, N.Y.: Doubleday, 1971, pp. 120 et seq.

90 See, for example, Maccoby, E. E., and Jacklin, C. N. *The psychology of sex differences*. Stanford, Calif.: Stanford University Press, 1974, pp. 277–85.

91 See, for example, Robertson, I. *Sociology*. New York: Worth, 1977, p. 294.

92 See, for example, Parsons, T., and Bales, R. F. *Family, socialization, and interaction process*. Glencoe, Ill.: Free Press, 1953.

93 Tavris, C., and Offir, C. *The longest war*. New York: Harcourt Brace Jovanovich, 1977, pp. 16–18.

94 Robertson, I. *Sociology*. New York: Worth, 1977, p. 289.

95 Goode, W. J. *The family*. Englewood Cliffs, N.J.: Prentice-Hall, 1965, p. 70.

96 Ollison, L. *Socialization*. Unpublished study, San Diego State University, 1975.

97 Simons, R. G., and Rosenberg, F. Sex, sex roles, and self-image. *JYA*, 1975, *4*, 229–58.

98 Crandall, V. J. Sex differences in expectancy of intellectual and academic reinforcement. In Smith, C. P., ed. *Achievement-related motives in children*. New York: Russell Sage Foundation, 1969, pp. 11–45.

99 See, for example, Frieze, I. H. Women's expectations for and causal attributions of success and failure. In Mednick, M.T.S., Tangri, S. S., and Hoffman, L. W., eds. *Women and achievement*. New York: Halsted, 1975, pp. 158–71.

100 Deaux, K., White, L., and Farris, E. Skill versus luck. *J Pers Soc Psychol*, 1975, *32*, 629–36.

101 See, for example, Block, J., Von Der Lippe, A., and Block, J. H. Sex-role and socialization patterns. *J Consult Clin Psychol*, 1973, *41*, 321–41, especially p. 339.

102 Symonds, A. The liberated woman. *AJP*, 1974, *34*, 177–83.

103 See, for example, Gass, G. Z. Equitable marriage. *Fam Coord*, 1974, *23*, 369–72. Also Blake, J. The changing status of women in developed countries. *Sci Am*, 1974, *231*, 137–47.

104 Lopata, H. Z. *Occupation: housewife*. New York: Oxford University Press, 1972, pp. 35–36, 46, 74, 217, 219, 223, and 370–76.

105 Parelius, A. P. Emerging sex-role attitudes, expectations, and strains among college women. *J Marr Fam*, 1975, *37*, 146–53.

106 McMillin, M. R. Attitudes of college men toward career involvement of married women. *VGQ*, 1972, *21*, 8–11.

107 Feinman, S. Approval of cross-sex-role behavior. *Psychol Rept*, 1974, *35*, 643–48.

108 Hartley, R. E. Sex-role pressures and the socialization of the male child. *Psychol Rept*, 1959, *5*, 457–68.

109 Stevens, B. The sexually oppressed male. *Psychotherapy*, 1974, *11*, 16–21.

110 Stevens, B. The sexually oppressed male. See immediately above.

111 Skolnick, A., and Skolnick, J. H. *Intimacy, family, and society*. Boston: Little, Brown, 1974, p. 198.

112 Seidenberg, R. *Marriage in life and literature*. New York: Philosophical Library, 1970, pp. 281–302.

113 Komarovsky, M. Cultural contradictions and sex roles. *Am J Sociol*, 1973, *78*, 873–84.

Chapter eleven
Anxiety, stress, and coping

1 Epstein, S., and Roupenian, A. Heart rate and skin conductance during experimentally induced anxiety. *J Pers Soc Psychol*, 1970, *16*, 20–28. Copyright 1970 by the American Psychological Association. Reprinted with permission.

2 Spielberger, C. D. Anxiety as an emotional state. In Spielberger, C. D., ed. *Anxiety*. New York: Academic Press, 1971.

3 Wine, J. *Investigations of attentional interpretation of test anxiety.* Unpublished doctoral dissertation, University of Waterloo, Ont., 1971.

4 McCaul, K. D., Solomon, S., and Holmes, D. S. Effects of paced respiration and expectations on physiological and psychological responses to threat. *J Pers Soc Psychol,* 1979, *37,* 564–71.

5 Gray, J. A. Anxiety. *Hum Nat,* 1978, *1,* 38–45.

6 Taylor, J. A. The relationship of anxiety to the conditioned eyelid response. *J Exp Psychol,* 1951, *41,* 81–92.

7 Farber, I. E., and Spence, W. K. Complex learning and conditioning as a function of anxiety. *J Exp Psychol,* 1953, *45,* 120–25.

8 O'Neil, H. F., Jr., Spielberger, C. D., and Hansen, D. N. Effects of state anxiety and task difficulty on computer-assisted learning. *J Ed Psychol,* 1969, *60,* 343–50.

9 Ganzer, V. J. Effects of audience presence and test anxiety on learning and retention in a serial learning situation. *J Pers Soc Psychol,* 1968, *8,* 194–99.

10 Spielberger, C. D. The effects of manifest anxiety on the academic achievement of college students. *Mental Hygiene,* 1962, *46,* 420–26.

11 Spielberger, C. D., Denny, J. P., and Weitz, H. The effects of group counseling on the academic performance of anxious college freshmen. *J Counsel Psychol,* 1962, *9,* 195–204.

12 Glass, D. C., and Singer, J. E. *Urban stress.* New York: Academic Press, 1972.

13 Atkinson, J. W., et al. The achievement motive, goal setting, and probability preferences. *J Abn,* 1960, *60,* 27–37. Copyright 1960 by the American Psychological Association. Reprinted with permission.

14 Atkinson, J. W., and Litwin, G. H. Achievement motive and test anxiety conceived as motive to approach success and motive to avoid failure. *J Abn,* 1960, *60,* 53–62.

15 Fuller, J. L. Experimental deprivation and later behavior. *Science,* 1967, *158,* 1645–52.

16 Selye, H. *The stress of life.* New York: McGraw-Hill, 1956.

17 Miller, N. E. *Behavioral sciences report for the overview cluster of the President's biomedical research panel,* 1975.

18 Luborsky, L., Docherty, J. P., and Penick, S. Onset conditions for psychosomatic symptoms. *Psychos Med,* 1973, *35,* 187–201.

19 Greene, W. A., Goldstein, S., and Moss, A. J. Psychosocial aspects of sudden death. *Arch In Med,* 1972, *129,* 725–31.

20 Adapted from Holmes, T. H., and Rahe, R. H. The social readjustment rating scale. *J Psychos Res,* 1967, *11,* 213–18.

21 See, for example, Rabkin, J. G., and Struening, E. L. Life events, stress, and illness. *Science,* 1976, *194,* 1013–20.

22 Hinkle, L. E. The effect of exposure to culture change, social change, and change in interpersonal relationships on health. In Dohrenwend, B. S., ed. *Stressful life events.* New York: Wiley, 1974.

23 Kobasa, S. C. Stressful life events, personality and health. *J Pers Soc Psychol,* 1979, *37,* 1–11.

24 See, for example, Glass, D. C. Stress, behavior patterns, and coronary disease. *Am Sci,* 1977, *65,* 177–87.

25 McClelland, D. C. Inhibited power motive and high blood pressure in men. *J Abn Psychol,* 1979, *88,* 182–90.

26 Selye, H. Stress without distress. In Serban, G., ed. *Psychopathology of human adaptation.* New York: Plenum, 1976, especially p. 143.

27 See, for example, Miller, N. E. The role of learning in physiological response to stress. In Serban, G., ed. *Psychopathology of human adaptation.* New York: Plenum, 1976, especially p. 33.

28 Brenner, M. H. Personal stability and economic security. *Soc Pol,* 1977, *8,* 2–4.

29 Kline, N. S. *From sad to glad.* New York: Putnam's, 1974.

30 Schwartz, G. E., et al. *Facial expression and depression.* Paper read at annual meeting of the American Psychosomatic Society, Philadelphia, March 29, 1974.

31 Shildkraut, J. J. *Neuropsychopharmacology and the affective disorders.* Boston: Little, Brown, 1969.

32 See, for example, Weiss, J. M., Glazer, H. I., and Pohorecky, L. A. Coping behavior and neurochemical changes. In Serban, G., and Kling, A., eds. *Animal models in human psychobiology.* New York: Plenum, 1976.

33 Rosenthal, D. *Genetic theory and*

abnormal behavior. New York: McGraw-Hill, 1970.

34 Radloff, L. S., and Rae, D. S. Susceptibility and precipitating factors in depression. *J Abn Psychol*, 1979, *88*, 174–81.

35 Lazarus, R. S. The stress and coping paradigm. Paper delivered at the University of Washington conference on *The critical evaluation of behavioral paradigms for psychiatric science*, 1978.

36 Lazarus, R. S. See immediately above.

37 Weiss, J. M. Somatic effects of predictable and unpredictable shock. *Psychos Med*, 1970, *32*, 397–408.

38 Weiss, J. M., et al. Effects of acute and chronic exposure to stressors on avoidance behavior and brain norepinephrine. *Psychos Med*, 1975, *37*, 522–34.

39 Miller, N. E. The role of learning in physiological response to stress. In Serban, G., ed. *Psychopathology of human adaptation*. New York: Plenum, 1976.

40 Lazarus, R. S. The stress and coping paradigm. Paper delivered at the University of Washington conference on *The critical evaluation of behavioral paradigms for psychiatric science*, 1978.

41 See, for example, Laing, R. D. *The divided self*. Baltimore: Penguin, 1960.

42 Erikson, E. H. *Identity, youth, and crisis*. New York: Norton, 1968.

43 Bühler, C. Psychotherapy and the image of man. *Psychotherapy*, 1968, *5*, 89–94.

44 Bettelheim, B. Individual and mass behavior in extreme situations. *J Abn*, 1943, *38*, 417–52.

45 Masserman, J. H. *Principles of dynamic psychiatry*, 2d ed. Philadelphia: Saunders, 1961.

46 Pavlov, I. P. *Conditioned reflexes*. London: Oxford University Press, 1927 [reprinted by Dover, New York, 1960].

47 Masserman, J. H. *Behavior and neurosis*. Chicago: University of Chicago Press, 1943.

48 Rosenthal, D. Hereditary nature of schizophrenia. In Kety, S. S., and Matthysse, S., eds. Prospects for research in schizophrenia. *Neurosciences Research Program Bulletin*, 1972, *10*(4), pp. 397–403.

49 Reich, T., Clayton, P. J., and Winokur, G. Family history studies: V. The genetics of mania. *Am J Psych*, 1969, *125*, 64–75.

50 Gottesman, I. I. Beyond the fringe —personality and psychopathology. In Glass, D. C., ed. *Genetics*. New York: Rockefeller University Press and Russell Sage Foundation, 1968, pp. 59–68. Also Gottesman, I. I. Double talk for twins' mothers. (Review of A. Scheinfeld's *Twins and Supertwins*.) *Con Psych*, 1968, *13*, 518–20.

51 Hollingshead, A. B., and Redlich, F. C. *Social class and mental illness, a community study*. New York: Wiley, 1958.

52 Coleman, J. C. *Abnormal psychology and modern life*, 3d ed. Chicago: Scott, Foresman, 1964.

53 Srole, L., et al. *Mental health in the metropolis*. New York: McGraw-Hill, 1962.

54 Agras, W. S., Sylvester, D., and Oliveau, D. The epidemiology of common fears and phobias. *Comp Psych*, 1969, *10*, 151–56.

55 Denike, L. D., and Tiber, H. Neurotic behavior. In London, P., and Rosenhan, D., eds. *Foundations of abnormal psychology*. New York: Holt, Rinehart and Winston, 1968, pp. 345–90.

56 McCord, W., and McCord, I. *The psychopath*. Princeton, N.J.: Van Nostrand, 1964.

57 See, for example, Hare, R. D. *Psychopathy*. New York: Wiley, 1970.

58 See, for example, Maher, B. A. *Principles of psychotherapy*. New York: McGraw-Hill, 1966.

59 Goldhamer, H., and Marshall, A. W. *Psychosis and civilization*. New York: Free Press, 1953.

60 Benedict, P. K., and Jacks, I. Mental illness in primitive societies. *Psychiatry*, 1954, *17*, 389.

61 Murphy, J. M. Psychiatric labeling in cross-cultural perspective. *Science*, 1976, *191*, 1019–28.

62 Kline, N. S. Personal communication, 1970.

63 Yerbury, E. C., and Newell, N. Genetic and environmental factors in psychoses of children. *Am J Psych*, 1944, *100*, 599–605. Reprinted by permission of the University of Illinois Press.

64 Carpenter, W. T., Jr., Strauss, J. S., and Bartko, J. J. Flexible system for the diagnosis of schizophrenia. *Science*, 1973, *182*, 1275–78.

65 Reich, W. The schizophrenia spectrum. *JNMD*, 1976, *162*, 3–12.

66 Wyatt, R. J., et al. Reduced monoamine oxidase activity in

platelets. *Science,* 1974, *173,* 916–18.

67 Snyder, S. H., et al. Drugs, neurotransmitters, and schizophrenia. *Science,* 1974, *184,* 1243–53.

68 Holzman, P. S., Proctor, L. R., and Hughes, D. W. Eye tracking patterns in schizophrenia. *Science,* 1973, *181,* 179–81.

69 Holzman, P. S., et al. Eye tracking dysfunctions in schizophrenic patients and their relatives. *Arch Gen Psych,* 1974, *31,* 143–51.

70 Radloff, L. S., and Rae, D. S. Susceptibility and precipitating factors in depression. *J Abn Psychol,* 1979, *88,* 174–81.

71 Akiskal, H. S., and McKinney, W. T., Jr. Depressive disorders. *Science,* 1973, *182,* 20–29.

Chapter twelve
Personality and psychotherapy

1 Maddi, S. R. *Personality theories,* rev. ed. Homewood, Ill.: Dorsey Press, 1972.

2 Adams, V. Freud's work thrives as theory, not therapy. New York *Times,* Aug. 14, 1979, pp. C1–C6.

3 Kubie, L. S. *Practical and theoretical aspects of psychoanalysis.* New York: International Universities Press, 1950.

4 See, for example, Hartmann, H. Ego psychology and the problem of adaptation. In Rapaport, D., ed. *Organization and pathology of thought.* New York: Columbia University Press, 1951, pp. 362–93.

5 Based on Chapter 3, The human situation—the key to humanistic psychoanalysis, from *The sane society* by Erich Fromm. Copyright © 1955 by Erich Fromm. Reprinted by permission of Holt, Rinehart and Winston.

6 Fromm, E. *The sane society.* New York: Holt, Rinehart and Winston, 1955.

7 Butler, J. M., and Haigh, G. V. Changes in the relation between self-concepts and ideal concepts consequent upon client-centered counseling. In Rogers, C. R., and Dymond, R. F., eds. *Psychotherapy and personality change.* Chicago: University of Chicago Press, 1954, pp. 55–76.

8 Miller, N. E., and Dollard, J. *Social learning and imitation.* New Haven, Conn.: Yale University Press, 1941.

9 Bandura, A. *Behavior theory and the models of man.* Presidential address delivered before the American Psychological Association, New Orleans, August, 1974.

10 Bandura, A. Social learning perspective on behavior change. In Burton, A., ed. *What makes behavior change possible.* New York: Brunner/Mazel, 1976.

11 Wilkins, W. Desensitization. *Psych Bull,* 1971, *76,* 311–17.

12 Lang, P. J., and Melamed, B. G. Avoidance conditioning therapy of an infant with chronic ruminative vomiting. *J Abn Psychol,* 1969, *74,* 1–8.

13 Davison, G. C. Elimination of a sadistic fantasy by a client-controlled counterconditioning technique. *J Abn Psychol,* 1968, *73,* 84–90.

14 Marks, I. M. Aversion therapy. *BJMP,* 1968, *41,* 47–52.

15 Martin, M., et al. Programing behavior change and reintegration into school milieux of extreme adolescent deviates. *Beh Res Ther,* 1968, *6,* 371–83.

16 See, for example, Wolpe, J. *Theme and variations.* Elmsford, N.Y.: Pergamon, 1976, p. 29.

17 Bandura, A. Self-efficacy. *Psychol R,* 1977, *84,* 191–215.

18 Bandura, A., Blanchard, E. B., and Ritter, B. Relative efficacy of desensitization and modeling approaches for inducing behavioral, affective, and attitudinal changes. *J Pers Soc Psychol,* 1969, *13,* 173–99. Copyright 1969 by the American Psychological Association. Reprinted with permission.

19 Hardy, A. B. *Exposure therapy as a treatment for agoraphobia and anxiety.* Unpublished manuscript, Palo Alto, Calif., 1969.

20 Bandura, A., Jefferey, R. W., and Gajdos, E. Generalizing change through self-directed performance. *Beh Res Ther,* 1975, *13,* 141–52.

21 Havemann, E. Alternatives to analysis. In Derlega, V. J., and Janda, L. H., eds. *Personal adjustment.* Glenview, Ill.: Scott, Foresman, 1979.

22 Gomes-Schwartz, B., Hadley, S. W., and Strupp, H. H. Individual psychotherapy and behavior therapy. *An Rev Psych,* 1978, *29,* 435–71.

23 See, for example, Lamberd, W. G. The treatment of homosexuality as a monosymptomatic phobia. *Am J. Psych,* 1969, *126,* 94–100.

24 Zweben, J. E., and Miller, R. L.

The systems game. *Psychotherapy,* 1968, *5,* 73–76.

25 Bernal, M. E., et al. Behavior modification and the brat syndrome. *J Consult Clin Psychol,* 1968, *32,* 447–55.

26 See, for example, Luborsky, L., et al. Factors influencing the outcome of psychotherapy. *Psych Bull,* 1971, *75,* 145–61.

27 Rogers, C. Personal communication, 1969.

28 Maslow, A. Personal communication, 1969.

29 Lieberman, M. A., Yalom, I. D., and Miles, M. B. *Encounter groups.* New York: Basic Books, 1973.

30 Kirsch, M. A., and Glass, L. L. Psychiatric disturbances associated with Erhard Seminars Training. *Am J. Psych,* 1977, *134,* 1254–58.

31 Belensky, G. L. Presentation to a section of the Society of Neuroscience, Potomac, Md., 1976.

32 Kety, S. S., et al. A sustained effect of electroconvulsive shock on the turnover of norepinephrine in the central nervous system of the rat. *Pub Pro Nat Acad Sci,* 1967, *58,* 1249–54.

33 Janowsky, D. S., Khaled El-Yousef, M., and Davis, J. M. Acetylcholine and depression. *Psychos Med,* 1974, *36,* 248–57.

34 Reproduced by permission. Copyright 1943, renewed 1970 by the University of Minnesota. Published by The Psychological Corporation, New York, N.Y. All rights reserved.

35 U.S. Office of Strategic Services, Assessment Staff. *Assessment of men.* New York: Holt, Rinehart and Winston, 1948.

36 Mackinnon, D. W. Stress interview. In Jackson, D. N., and Messick, S., eds. *Problems in human assessment.* New York: McGraw-Hill, 1967, pp. 669–76.

37 Reprinted by permission of the publishers from Henry Alexander Murray, *Thematic Apperception Test.* Cambridge, Mass.: Harvard University Press; Copyright © 1943 by the President and Fellows of Harvard College; Copyright © 1971 by Henry A. Murray.

38 McClelland, D. C., Clark, R. A., and Lowell, E. L. *The achievement motive.* New York: Appleton-Century-Crofts, 1953.

39 French, E. G. Development of a measure of complex motivation. In Atkinson, J. W., ed. *Motives in fantasy, action, and society.* Princeton, N.J.: Van Nostrand, 1959.

40 DeCharms, R. C., et al. Behavioral correlates of directly measured achievement motivation. In McClelland, D.C., ed. *Studies in motivation.* New York: Appleton-Century-Crofts, 1955.

41 From *The Rorschach technique* by Bruno Klopfer and Helen H. Davidson, © 1962 by Harcourt Brace Jovanovich, Inc., and reproduced with their permission.

42 Garfield, S. L. *Clinical psychology.* Chicago: Aldine, 1974.

Chapter thirteen
Developmental psychology: from infant to adult

1 Harrell, R. F., Woodyard, E., and Gates, A. I. *The effect of mothers' diet on the intelligence of the offspring.* New York: Teacher's College, Columbia Bureau of Publications, 1955.

2 Sontag, L. W. War and the fetal-maternal relationship. *Mar Fam L,* 1944, *6,* 3–4.

3 Mussen, P. H., Conger, J. J., and Kagan, J. *Child development and personality,* 5th ed. New York: Harper & Row, 1978.

4 Gregg, C., Clifton, R. K., and Haith, M. M. A possible explanation for the frequent failure to find cardiac orienting in the newborn infant. *Develop Psychol,* 1976, *12,* 75–76.

5 Lipsitt, L. P. The study of sensory and learning processes in the newborn. *Symposium on neonatal neurology, Clinics in perinatology,* 1977, *4,* 163–86.

6 Bridger, W. N. Sensory habituation and discrimination in the human neonate. *Am J Psych,* 1961, *117,* 991–96.

7 Kagan, J. *Change and continuity in infancy.* New York: Wiley, 1971.

8 Irwin, O. C. The amount and nature of activities of newborn infants under constant external stimulating conditions during the first ten days of life. *G Psych Mono,* 1930, *8.* Also Wolff, P. H. Observations on newborn infants. *Psychos Med,* 1959, *21,* 110–18.

9 Kagan, J. Personality development. In Janis, I. L., ed. *Personality.* New York: Harcourt Brace Jovanovich, 1969.

10 Freedman, D. G. Ethnic differences in babies. *Hum Nat,* 1979, *2,* 36–43.

11 Thomas, A., Chess, S., and Birch,

H. G. The origin of personality. *Sci Am*, 1970, *223*, 106–07.

12 Thomas, A., and Chess, S. Development in middle childhood. *Sem Psych*, 1972, *4*, 331–41.

13 Kagan, J. *Change and continuity in infancy*. New York: Wiley, 1971.

14 Kagan, J., Lapidus, D. R., and Moore, M. Infant antecedents of cognitive functioning. *Child Develop*, 1978, *49*, 1005–23.

15 Horowitz, F. C. *Stability and instability in the newborn infant*. Paper presented at meeting of the Society for Research in Child Development, New Orleans, La., 1977.

16 Kagan, J. The form of early development. *Arch Gen Psych*, 1979. In press.

17 Harlow, H. F., and Harlow, M. K. Learning to love. *Am Sci*, 1966, *54*, 244–72.

18 Spitz, R. A. Hospitalism. In Eissler, R. S., et al., eds. *Psychoanalytic study of the child*. Vol. II. New York: International Universities Press, 1946.

19 Goldfarb, W. Effects of early institutional care on adolescent personality. *Am J Orthopsych*, 1944, *14*, 441–47.

20 Suomi, S. J., and Harlow, H. F. Social rehabilitation of isolate-reared monkeys. *Develop Psychol*, 1972, *6*, 487–96.

21 Kagan, J., and Klein, R. E. Cross-cultural perspectives on early development. *Am Psychol*, 1973, *28*, 947–61.

22 Koluchova, J. Severe deprivation in twins. *JCPP*, 1972, *13*, 107–14.

23 White, B. L., Castle, P., and Held, R. Observations on the development of visually directed reaching. *Child Develop*, 1964, *35*, 349–64.

24 McGraw, M. B. *The neuromuscular maturation of the human infant*. New York: Columbia University Press, 1943.

25 Kagan, J. The effect of day care on psychological development. *Progress report*, Harvard University, 1975.

26 Zinchenko, V. P., van Chzhi-Tsin, and Tarakonov, V. V. The formation and development of perceptual activity. *Sov PP*, 1963, *2*, 3–12. By permission of M. E. Sharpe, Inc. Publishers, White Plains, New York.

27 Gibson, E. J. *Principles of perceptual learning and development*. New York: Appleton-Century-Crofts, 1969.

28 Harlow, H. F. The development of affectional patterns in infant monkeys. In Foss, B. M., ed. *Determinants of infant behaviour*. London: Methuen, 1961, pp. 75–97.

29 Ainsworth, M.D.S., and Bell, S. M. Attachment, exploration, and separation. *Child Develop*, 1970, *41*, 49–68.

30 Littenberg, R., Tulkin, S., and Kagan, J. Cognitive components of separation anxiety. *Develop Psychol*, 1971, *4*, 387–88.

31 Kearsley, R. B., et al. Differences in separation protest between day care and home reared infants. *Pediatrics*, 1975, *55*, 171–75.

32 Maccoby, E. E., and Feld, S. S. Mother attachment and stranger reactions in the third year of life. *Mono Soc Res*, 1972, *37*, Serial No. 146.

33 Kagan, J. The form of early development. *Archives of General Psychiatry*, 1979. In press.

34 Maccoby, E. E. Personal communication, 1979.

35 Kagan, J. The form of early development. *Arch Gen Psych*, 1979. In press.

36 Suomi, S. J. Peers, play, and primary prevention in primates. *Proceedings of the Third Vermont Conference on the Primary Prevention of Psychopathology: Promoting Social Competence and Coping in Children*. Hanover, N.H.: University Press of New England, 1977.

37 Bowlby, J. Childhood mourning and its implications for psychiatry. Adapted from the *Am J Psych*, 1961, *118*, 481–98. Reprinted by permission of the University of Illinois Press.

38 Kagan, J., and Moss, H. A. *Birth to maturity*. New York: Wiley, 1962.

39 Hall, G. S. *Adolescence*. Vol. I. New York: Appleton, 1904.

40 Macfarlane, J. W. Perspectives on personality consistency and change from the guidance study. *Vita Humana*, 1964, *7*, 115–26.

41 Sorenson, R. C. *Adolescent sexuality in contemporary America*. New York: World, 1973.

42 See, for example, Offer, D. *The psychological world of the teenager*. New York: Basic Books, 1969.

43 Conger, J. J. *Adolescence and youth*, 2d ed. New York: Harper & Row, 1977.

44 Jones, M. C., and Bayley, N.

Physical maturity among boys as related to behavior. *J Ed Psychol*, 1950, *41*, 129–48.

45 Clausen, J. A. The social meaning of differential physical and sexual maturation. In Dragastin, S. E., and Elder, G. H., Jr., eds. *Life cycle.* New York: Wiley, 1975.

46 Weatherly, D. Self-perceived rate of physical maturation and personality in late adolescence. *Child Develop*, 1964, *35*, 1197–210.

47 Conger, J. J. *Adolescence and youth*, 2d ed. New York: Harper & Row, 1977.

48 Kandel, D. B., and Lesser, G. S. *Youth in two worlds.* San Francisco: Jossey-Bass, 1972.

49 Jessor, R., and Jessor, S. L. *Problem behavior and psychosocial development.* New York: Academic Press, 1977.

50 Mussen, P. H., Conger, J. J., and Kagan, J. *Child development and personality*, 5th ed. New York: Harper & Row, 1978.

51 Mussen, P. H., Conger, J. J., and Kagan, J. See immediately above.

52 Simon, W., Berger, A. S., and Gagnon, J. H. Beyond anxiety and fantasy. *JYA*, 1972, *1*, 203–22.

53 Based on Kohlberg, L. Moral and religious education and the public schools. In Sizer, T., ed. *Religion and public education.* Boston: Houghton Mifflin, 1967.

54 Kohlberg, L. The development of children's orientations toward a moral order. I. Sequence in the development of moral thought. *Vita Humana*, 1963, *6*, 11–33 (S. Karger, Basel, 1963).

55 Kholberg, L., and Kramer, R. Continuities and discontinuities in child and adult moral development. *Hum Dev*, 1969, *12*, 93–120.

56 Macfarlane, J. W. From infancy to adulthood. *Child Ed*, 1963, *39*, 336–42.

57 Macfarlane, J. W. Perspectives on personality consistency and change from the guidance study. *Vita Humana*, 1964, *7*, 115–26.

58 Adapted from *Childhood and Society*, 2d ed., by Erik H. Erikson, by permission of W. W. Norton & Company, Inc. Copyright © 1963, 1950 by W. W. Norton & Company, Inc.

59 See, for example, Glick, P. C. A demographer looks at American families. *J Marr Fam*, 1975, *37*, 15–26. Also Bane, M. J. *Here to stay.* New York: Basic Books, 1976, pp. 22–23 and 35.

60 Rubin, Z. *Liking and loving.* New York: Holt, Rinehart, and Winston, 1973, p. 160.

61 U.S. National Center for Health Statistics: *Vital Statistics of the United States*, 1978.

62 See, for example, Norton, A. J., and Glick, P. C. Marital instability. *J Soc Issues*, 1976, *32*, 5–20.

63 Schlesinger, B. Remarriage as family organization for divorced persons—a Canadian study. *JCFS*, 1970, *1*, 101–18.

64 U.S. Bureau of the Census, *Population characteristics*, Series P-20, No. 308, June 1977.

65 Bane, M. J. *Here to stay.* New York: Basic Books, 1976, p. 25.

66 Cameron, P. The generation gap. *Gerontologist*, 1972, *12*, 117–19.

67 U.S. Bureau of the Census, *Current population reports*, Series P-20, No. 323, 1977.

68 Neugarten, B. Grow old with me: the best is yet to be. *Psych T*, 1971, *97*, 45–49.

Chapter fourteen
Social psychology

1 Milgram, S., Bickman, L., and Berkowitz, L. Note on the drawing power of crowds of different size. *J Pers Soc Psychol*, 1969, *13*, 79–82.

2 Triplett, N. The dynamogenic factors in pace making and competition. *Am J Psychol*, 1898, *9*, 507–33.

3 Horowitz, E. L., and Horowitz, R. E. Development of social attitudes in children. *Sociometry*, 1938, *1*, 301–38.

4 Aronson, E. *The social animal.* San Francisco: Freeman, 1972.

5 Secord, P. F., and Backman, C. W. *Social psychology.* New York: McGraw-Hill, 1964.

6 Benedict, R. *Patterns of culture*, 2d ed. Boston: Houghton Mifflin, 1959.

7 Mead, M. *Sex and temperament.* New York: Morrow, 1935.

8 McGrath, J. W. *Social psychology.* New York: Holt, Rinehart, and Winston, 1964.

9 Asch, S. E. Studies of independence and submission to group pressure. I. A minority of one against a unanimous majority. *P Mono*, 1956, *70*(No. 416), Fig. 2, p. 7. Also Asch, S. E. Opinions and social pressure. *Sci Am*, 1955, *193*, 32. Copyright © 1955 by Scientific American, Inc. All rights reserved.

10 Milgram, S. Group pressure and action against a person. *J Abn,* 1964, *69,* 137–43.

11 Aronson, E. *The social animal.* San Francisco: Freeman, 1972.

12 Malof, M., and Lott, A. J. Ethnocentrism and the acceptance of Negro support in a group pressure situation. *J Abn,* 1962, *65,* 254–58.

13 Festinger, L. A theory of social comparison processes. *Hum Relat,* 1954, *7,* 117–40.

14 Gordon, C. Influence and social comparison as motives for affiliation. *JESP Supplement,* 1966, *1,* 55–65.

15 Radloff, R. *Opinion and affiliation.* Unpublished doctoral dissertation, University of Minnesota, 1959.

16 Ross, L., Lepper, M. R., and Hubbard, M. Perseverance in self-perception and social perception. Stanford, Calif.: Stanford University. *J Pers Soc Psychol,* 1975, *32,* 880–92. Copyright 1975 by the American Psychological Association. Reprinted by permission.

17 See, for example, Bem, D. J. *Beliefs, attitudes, and human affairs.* Belmont, Calif.: Brooks/Cole, 1970.

18 Horowitz, E. L., and Horowitz, R. E. Development of social attitudes in children. *Sociometry,* 1938, *1,* 301–38.

19 Hess, R., and Torney, J. *The development of political attitudes in children.* Chicago: Aldine, 1967.

20 Goldsen, R., et al. *What college students think.* Princeton, N.J.: Van Nostrand, 1960.

21 Freedman, J. L., Carlsmith, J. M., and Sears, D. O. *Social psychology.* Englewood Cliffs, N.J.: Prentice-Hall, 1970.

22 Newcomb, T. M. Persistence and regression of changed attitudes. *J Soc Issues,* 1963, *19,* 3–14.

23 Mann, L., and Janis, I. L. A follow-up study on the long-term effects of emotional role playing. *J Pers Soc Psychol,* 1968, *8,* 339–42.

24 Cooper, M., Zanna, M. P., and Taves, P. A. Arousal as a necessary condition for attitude change following induced compliance. *J Pers Soc Psychol,* 1978, *36,* 1101–06.

25 Fazio, R. H., Zanna, M. P., and Cooper, J. Dissonance and self-perception. *JESP,* 1977, *13,* 464–79.

26 Pettigrew, T. F. Racially separate or together? *J Soc Issues,* 1969, *25,* 43–69.

27 Brehm, J. Postdecision changes in the desirability of alternatives. *J Abn,* 1956, *52,* 384–89.

28 Ehrlich, D., et al. Postdecision exposure to relevant information. *J Abn,* 1957, *54,* 98–102.

29 Bem, D. J. Self-perception theory. In Berkowitz, L., ed. *Advances in experimental social psychology,* Vol VI. New York: Academic Press, 1972.

30 Jones, E. E., and Nisbett, R. E. The actor and the observer. In Jones, E. E., et al., eds. *Attribution.* Morristown, N.J.: General Learning Press, 1972.

31 Nisbett, R. E., and Valins, S. Perceiving the causes of one's own behavior. In Jones, E. E., et al., eds. *Attribution.* Morristown, N.J.: General Learning Press, 1972.

32 Fazio, R. H., Zanna, M. P., and Cooper, J. Dissonance and self-perception. *JESP,* 1977, *13,* 464–79.

33 Robinson, J. P. The audience for national TV news programs. *Pub Opinion Q,* 1971, *35,* 403–05.

34 Neuman, W. R. Patterns of recall among television news viewers. *Pub Opinion Q,* 1976, *40,* 115–23.

35 Hovland, C., and Weiss, W. The influence of source credibility. *Pub Opinion Q,* 1951, *15,* 635–50.

36 Weiss, W., and Fine, B. J. The effect of induced aggressiveness on opinion change. In Maccoby, E. E., Newcomb, T. M., and Hartley, E. L., eds. *Readings in social psychology,* 3d ed. New York: Holt, Rinehart and Winston, 1958, pp. 149–55.

37 Hartman, G. A field experiment on the comparative effectiveness of "emotional" and "rational" political leaflets in determining election results. *J Abn,* 1936, *31,* 336–52.

38 Janis, I. L., and Feshbach, S. Effects of fear-arousing communications. *J Abn,* 1953, *48,* 78–92.

39 Hovland, C. I., Lumsdaine, A. A., and Sheffield, F. C. *Experiments on mass communication.* Princeton, N.J.: Princeton University Press, 1949.

40 Aronson, E. *The social animal.* San Francisco: Freeman, 1972.

41 Hovland, C. I., Lumsdaine, A. A., and Sheffield, F. C. *Experiments on mass communication.* Princeton, N.J.: Princeton University Press, 1949.

42 Hovland, C. I., and Janis, I. L.,

eds. *Personality and persuasibility.* New Haven, Conn.: Yale University Press, 1959.

43 Cohen, A. R. Some implications of self-esteem for social influence. In Hovland, C. I., and Janis, I. L., eds. *Personality and persuasibility.* New Haven, Conn.: Yale University Press, 1959, pp. 102–20.

44 Sears, D. O. Social anxiety, opinion structure, and opinion change. *J Pers Soc Psychol,* 1967, *7,* 142–51.

45 Festinger, L. A. A theory of social comparison processes. *Hum Relat,* 1954, *7,* 117–40.

46 Ross, L. The intuitive psychologist and his shortcomings. In Berkowitz, L., ed. *Advances in experimental social psychology,* Vol. X. New York: Academic Press, 1977.

47 Jones, E. E. The rocky road from acts to dispositions. *Am Psychol,* 1979, *34,* 107–17.

48 Ross, L. D., Amabile, T. M., and Steinmetz, J. L. Social roles, social control, and biases in social-perception processes. *J Pers Soc Psychol,* 1977, *35,* 485–94.

49 Jones, E. E. The rocky road from acts to dispositions. *Am Psychol,* 1979, *34,* 107–17.

50 Snyder, M. L., and Frankel, A. Observer bias. *J Pers Soc Psychol,* 1976, *34,* 857–64.

51 Middlebrook, P. N. *Social psychology and modern life.* New York: Knopf, 1974.

52 Berscheid, E., and Walster, E. Physical attractiveness. In Berkowitz, L., ed. *Advances in experimental social psychology,* Vol. 7. New York: Academic Press, 1974.

53 Newcomb, T. M. *The acquaintance process.* New York: Holt, Rinehart and Winston, 1961.

54 Byrne, D. Attitudes and attraction. In Berkowitz, L., ed. *Advances in experimental social psychology,* Vol. IV. New York: Academic Press, 1969.

55 Freedman, J. L., Carlsmith, J. M., and Suomi, S. Unpublished study, 1967, cited in Freedman, J. L., Carlsmith, J. M., and Sears, D. O. *Social psychology.* Englewood Cliffs, N.J.: Prentice-Hall, 1970. p. 72.

56 Zajonc, R. B. Attitudinal effects of mere exposure. *J Pers Soc Psychol,* 1968, *8,* 18. Copyright 1968 by the American Psychological Association. Reprinted with permission.

57 See, for example, Festinger, L., Schachter, S., and Back, K. *Social pressures in informal groups.* New York: Harper & Row, 1950. Also Whyte, W. H., Jr. *The organization man.* New York: Simon & Schuster, 1956.

58 Darley, J. M., and Berscheid, E. Increased liking caused by anticipation of social contact. *Hum Relat,* 1967, *20,* 29–40.

59 See, for example, Tagiuri, R. Social preference and its perception. In Tagiuri, R., and Petrullo, L., eds. *Person perception and interpersonal behavior.* Stanford, Calif.: Stanford University Press, 1958, pp. 316–36.

60 See, for example, Worchel, P. *Self-enhancement and interpersonal attraction.* Paper read at the American Psychological Association, August, 1961. Also Deutsch, M., and Solomon, L. Reactions to evaluations by others as influenced by self evaluations. *Sociometry,* 1959, *22,* 93–112.

61 Aronson, E., and Linder, D. Gain and loss of esteem as determinants of interpersonal attractiveness. *JESP,* 1965, *1,* 156–71.

62 See, for example, Bales, R., and Slater, P. Role differentiation in small decision-making groups. In Parsons, T., and Bales, R., eds. *The family, socialization, and interaction process.* Glencoe, Ill.: Free Press, 1955.

63 See, for example, Tesser, A., and Brodie, M. A note on the evaluation of a "computer date." *Psychon Sci,* 1971, *23,* 300.

64 Dion, K. K., and Berscheid, E. *Physical attractiveness and social perception of peers in preschool children.* Unpublished research report, 1972.

65 See, for example, Dion, K. K. Physical attractiveness and evaluations of children's aggressions. *J Pers Soc Psychol,* 1972, *24,* 207–13.

66 Landy, D., and Sigall, H. Beauty is talent. *J Pers Soc Psychol,* 1974, *29,* 299–304.

67 Cross, J. F., and Cross, J. Age, sex, race, and the perception of facial beauty. *Develop Psychol,* 1971, *5,* 433–39.

68 See, for example, Murstein, B. I. Physical attractiveness and marital choice. *J Pers Soc Psychol,* 1972, *22,* 8–12.

69 Freedman, J. L., and Suomi, S. Unpublished study, 1967, cited in Freedman, J. L., Carlsmith, J. M., and Sears, D. O. *Social psychology.* Englewood Cliffs, N.J.: Prentice-Hall, 1970, pp. 72–73.

70 Kelley, H. H. The warm-cold variable in the first impressions of persons. *J Pers*, 1950, *18*, 431–39.

71 Dion, K. K., Berscheid, E., and Walster, E. What is beautiful is good. *J Pers Soc Psychol*, 1972, *24*, 285–90.

72 Snyder, M., Tanke, E. D., and Berscheid, E. Social perception and interpersonal behavior. *J Pers Soc Psychol*, 1977, *35*, 656–66.

73 Lorenz, K. *On aggression.* New York: Harcourt Brace Jovanovich, 1966.

74 Eibl-Eibesfeldt, I. Aggressive behavior and ritualized fighting in animals. In Masserman, J. H., ed. *Science and psychoanalysis, Vol. VI (Violence and war).* New York: Grune & Stratton, 1963.

75 Lorenz, K. *On aggression.* New York: Harcourt Brace Jovanovich, 1966.

76 Hartmann, D. P. Influence of symbolically modeled instrumental aggression and pain cues on aggressive behavior. *J Pers Soc Psychol*, 1969, *11*, 280–88.

77 Goldstein, J. H., and Arms, R. L. Effects of observing athletic contests on hostility. *Sociometry*, 1971, *34*, 83–90.

78 Eiseley, L., *The immense journey.* New York: Random House, 1946.

79 Nissen, H., and Crawford, M. A preliminary study of food-sharing behavior in young chimpanzees. *Journal of Comparative Psychology*, 1936, *22*, 283–419.

80 Hebb, D., and Thompson, W. The social significance of animal studies. In Lindzey, G., and Aronson, E., eds. *The handbook of social psychology, 2d ed., Vol 2 (Research methods).* Reading, Mass.: Addison-Wesley, 1968.

81 Campbell, D. Ethnocentrism and other altruistic motives. In Levine, D., ed. *Nebraska symposium on motivation, 1965.* Lincoln: University of Nebraska Press, 1965. For a sociobiologist's viewpoint, see Wilson, E. O. *On human nature.* Cambridge, Mass.: Harvard University Press, 1978.

82 Schwartz, S. Moral decision making and behavior. In Macauley, J., and Berkowitz, L., eds. *Altruism and helping behavior.* New York: Academic Press, 1970.

83 Aronfreed, J. The socialization of altruistic and sympathetic behavior. In Macauley, J., and Berkowitz, L., eds. *Altruism and helping behavior.* New York: Academic Press, 1970.

84 Rutherford, E., and Mussen, P. Generosity in nursery school boys. *Child Develop*, 1968, *39*, 755–65.

85 Rosenhan, D. The natural socialization of altruistic autonomy. In Macauley, J., and Berkowitz, L., eds. *Altruism and helping behavior.* New York: Academic Press, 1970.

86 Adapted from *The unresponsive bystander.* Bibb Latané and John M. Darley. Copyright © 1970 by Prentice-Hall, Inc. Used by permission of Prentice-Hall, Inc., Englewood Cliffs, N.J.

87 See, for example, Altman, D., et al. *Trust of the stranger in the city and the small town.* Unpublished research, Graduate Center, City University of New York, 1969.

88 Piliavin, I. M., Rodin, J., and Piliavin, J. A. Good Samaritanism: an underground phenomenon? *J Pers Soc Psychol*, 1969, *13*, 289–99.

89 Darley, J. M., and Batson, C. D. *From Jerusalem to Jericho.* Unpublished study, 1971.

Appendix

1 Hebb, D. O. *A textbook of psychology.* Philadelphia: Saunders, 1958.

2 Terman, L. M., and Merrill, M. A. *Stanford-Binet intelligence scale: manual for the third revision, form L-M*, 1937. Reprinted by permission of the Houghton Mifflin Company.

3 Gallup, G. *The sophisticated poll watcher's guide.* Princeton, N.J.: Princeton Opinion Press, 1972.

4 Ferguson, G. A. *Statistical analysis in psychology and education.* New York: McGraw-Hill, 1959. Copyright © 1959 by McGraw-Hill Book Company.

Picture Credits

Chapter one

Page	Source
6	J. Dauth, World Health Organization
7	Marcia Weinstein
8	Joel Gordon © 1979
11	Joel Gordon © 1979
12	Mimi Forsyth, Monkmeyer Press Photo
13	Plate 11, "The Consulting Room" from *Berggasse* 19: Sigmund Freud's Home and Offices, Vienna 1938, The Photographs of Edmund Engelman. Captions to the photographs © 1976 by Basis Books, Inc.; the photographs of Berggasse 19 © 1976 by Edmund Engelman. Used with permission.
14	Henri Cartier-Bresson, Magnum Photos
15	TL & TM: Joel Gordon © 1979 TR: Uzzle, Magnum Photos BL: Manheim, EPA Documerica BR: Rogers, Monkmeyer Press Photo
17	Mimi Forsyth, Monkmeyer Press Photo
18	Marcia Weinstein
19	Institute for Sex Research, Indiana University
20	UPI Compix
30	L: Culver Pictures R: Historical Pictures Service
31	L: Harvard University R: Culver Pictures
35	L: Courtesy of Dr. Landrum B. Shettles R: Dr. J. H. Tjio
36	Dr. Lorne MacHattie
37	Harvey Stein
39	Bill Hayward

Chapter two

Page	Source
47	Martin M. Rotker, Taurus Photos
51	Jason Lauré, Woodfin Camp & Associates
52	R. W. Sperry
53	Dr. Joseph Bogen, Roos Loss Medical Group Los Angeles, Ca.
54	Erik Arnesen
58	James Karales, Peter Arnold, Inc.
59	T: Martin M. Rotker, Taurus Photos B: Russ Kinne
63	Ginger Chih
64	Marcia Weinstein
66	Wide World Photos
67	Michael Weisbrot
72	UPI Compix
76	Harvey Stein
77	Joel Gordon © 1979
78	Joel Gordon © 1979
79	T: Arthur Leipzig B: UPI Compix

Chapter three

Page	Source
90	Animals, Animals, © Jerry Cooke
91	Janus Films
92	Sovfoto/Eastfoto
98	Raimondo Borea, Editorial Photocolor Archive
99	Will Rapport, Harvard University
100	H. S. Terrace
101	T: Monkmeyer Press Photo B: Elisabeth Weiland, Photo Researchers, Inc.
103	Wide World Photos
104	T: Michael Weisbrot B: Yerkes Regional Primate Research Center, Emory University
107	Lew Merrim, Monkmeyer Press Photo
109	Van Bucher, Photo Researchers, Inc.
111	Michael Weisbrot
114	Marcia Weinstein
123	T: Albert Bandura B: Ken Siegal

Chapter four

Page	Source
130	David Moskowitz
135	Ken Karp
141	Daniel S. Brody, Editorial Photocolor Archive
142	Dr. R. N. Haber & Dr. M. H. Erdelgi
147	Jim Amos, Photo Researchers, Inc.
151	Ken Karp
158	Marcia Weinstein
159	F. Harlow, University of Wisconsin Primate Lab
160	Mimi Forsyth, Monkmeyer Press Photo

Chapter five

Page	Source
172	© Marjorie Pickens 1979
174	Joel Gordon © 1979
176	Editorial Photocolor Archive
179	United Nations, M. Tzovaras
186	R. A. and B. T. Gardner
187	E. Sue Savage-Rumbaugh, Yerkes Regional Primate Research Center, Emory University
189	Dr. N. Pastore
193	Edahl, Editorial Photocolor Archive
194–95	Three Lions, Inc.
199	Harbrace Photo
200	Harbrace Photo

Chapter six

Page	Source
212	Michael Weisbrot
213	Marcia Weinstein
214	E. F. Bernstein, Black Star
216	Courtesy of Georgette & Geraldine Binet; *Time*, Paris Bureau
217	Copyright © 1971 by Houghton Mifflin Company. Reprinted by permission of Houghton Mifflin Company. All rights reserved.
219	Nancy Hays, Monkmeyer Press Photo
222	U.S. Signal Corps in the National Archive
227	David S. Strickler, Monkmeyer Press Photo
230	Erika Stone
233	Sybil Shackman, Monkmeyer Press Photo

Page	Source
237	Sepp Seitz, Woodfin Camp and Associates
244	Animals, Animals © Oxford Scientific Films

Chapter seven

Page	Source
247	Bettmann Archive
249	Harbrace Photo
255	T: NFL Properties, Inc. B: Edwin R. Lewis, Department of Electrical Engineering, Univ. of Ca., Berkeley
257	A. L. Yarbus
259	*Life* Science Library/Sound and Hearing Published by Time-Life Books, Inc.
261	Manfred Kage, Peter Arnold, Inc.
262	Joel Gordon © 1979
265	Russ Kinne, Photo Researchers, Inc.
270	Jasper Johns
271	American Optical Corp.
274	Ken Karp
275	James Maas, Cornell University

Chapter eight

Page	Source
286	AMNH
288	Harvey Stein
291	Julian E. Hochberg, *Perception*, 2d ed., © 1978, p. 196. Reprinted by permission of Prentice-Hall, Inc., Englewood Cliffs, New Jersey
296	William Vandivert
298	Michael Weisbrot
299	L: David Moskowitz R: Joel Gordon © 1979
300	David Moskowitz
301	Irving Biederman
313	Lawrence Fried, Magnum Photos

Chapter nine

Page	Source
324	Ron Fine, Uniphoto
325	L: Walter Chandoha R: David Moskowitz
326	Ken Karp
327	Wide World Photos

Page	Source
328	Ed Gallub
329	Sackeim, H. A., Gur, R. C., & Saucy, M. C. *Science*, 1978, 202, 434–36 with the permission of the American Association for the Advancement of Science.
330–31	Dr. Eckhard H. Hess
334	Owen Franken, Stock Boston
335	Andrew Sacks, Editorial Photocolor Archive
337	Cornell Capa, Magnum Photos
340	Ken Karp
343	Fernando Botero, *La Familia Pinzon*. Museum of Art, Rhode Island School of Design; Nancy Sayles Day Collection of Modern Latin American Art.
345	Carolyn Watson, Monkmeyer Press Photo
346	Bell Laboratories
347–48	Fred Sponholz
351	Michael Weisbrot
356	Joel Gordon © 1979

Chapter ten

Page	Source
363	TL: George E. Jones III, Photo Researchers, Inc. TR: Ron Willocks, Photo Researchers, Inc. BL: Marcia Weinstein BR: © Marjorie Pickens 1979
364	Doug Wilson, Black Star
365	Joe DiMaggio, Peter Arnold, Inc.
367	Mimi Forsyth, Monkmeyer Press Photo
368	Ginger Chih
369	© Marjorie Pickens 1979
371	TL: Pictoral Parade TM: René Burré, Magnum Photos TR: UPI Compix BL: UPI Compix BM: Pictorial Parade BR: Kaiser from Combine
373	UPI Compix
377	TL: Pictorial Parade TR: UN Photo BL: American Foundation for the Blind, Inc. BR: Crown Publishers

Page	Source
382	George Zimbel, Monkmeyer Press Photo
384	Ginger Chih
387	Joel Gordon © 1979
392	Joel Gordon © 1979
394	Harvey Stein
396	E. Natal, Rapho/Photo Researchers, Inc.

Chapter eleven

Page	Source
406	Rhoda Sidney, Leo de Wys
408	Ray Ellis, Photo Researchers, Inc.
417	Gary Schwartz, Ph.D., Harvard University
419	Dr. Michael Lewis
421	UPI Compix
425	Phoebe Dunn, DPI
426	L: Martin Rotker, Taurus Photos R: Ed Lettau, Photo Researchers, Inc.
427	J. H. Masserman

Chapter twelve

Page	Source
442–43	Jim Anderson, Woodfin Camp and Associates
445	Bettmann Archive
446	Ann Hagen Griffiths, DPI
449	Bettmann Archive
450	James Carroll, Editorial Photocolor Archive
451	E. Fromm
453	Ted Lau
455	Frank Siteman, Stock Boston
457	Albert Bandura
461	Linda Ferrer Rogers, Woodfin Camp and Associates

Chapter thirteen

Page	Source
477	H.F.R. Prechtl, 1977. The neurological examination of the full-term newborn infant. Second revised and enlarged edition. Heinemann, London. Clinics in Developmental Medicine, no. 63.
478	© Doris Pinney
479	Drs. Lillian & Edwin Robbins

Page	Source
483	All Erika Stone except
	BM: Kay Ellen Ziff
	BR: Michael Perlin
485	Dr. Burton L. White
487	Fred Sponholz
489	Jerome Kagan
492	Michael Weisbrot
495	Neal Boenzi, NYT Pictures
496	UPI Compix
498	Bernard Pierre Wolff, Magnum Photos
499	Paul S. Conklin, Monkmeyer Press Photo
503	Steven J. Kaiser
506	Ken Siegal
508	Joel Gordon © 1979

Part Opening Photos

Page	Source
xviii	One: Photo by: Joseph Marvullo
84	Two: Michael De Camp, The Image Bank
166	Three: DPI
242	Four: Pete Turner, The Image Bank
318	Five: Thomas Rampy, The Image Bank
400	Six: Nicholas Foster, The Image Bank
470	Seven: Dan McCoy, Black Star

Page	Source
	Chapter fourteen
514	T & M: Bettmann Archive
	B: Ken Karp
516	James Karales, Peter Arnold, Inc.
518–19	William Vandivert
520	Stanley Milgram
521	Joel Gordon © 1979
526	Erika Stone, Peter Arnold, Inc.
530	Martin A. Levick, Black Star
537	Richard Kalvar, Magnum Photos
539	Mitchell B. Reibel, Focus on Sports
540	Barbara Pfeffer, Peter Arnold, Inc.
544	Wide World Photos
545	Ivan Massar, Black Star
547	Dr. John Darbey

Abbreviations of periodicals cited, including short journal titles that were not abbreviated.

Acta Med Scan—Acta Medica Scandinavia

Acta Psychol—Acta Psychologica

Adv Psychos Med—Advances in Psychosomatic Medicine

AGP—Archiv für die Gesamte Psychologie

AJCN—American Journal of Clinical Nutrition

AJP—American Journal of Psychoanalysis

Am J Orthopsych—American Journal of Orthopsychiatry

Am J Psych—American Journal of Psychiatry

Am J Psychol—American Journal of Psychology

Am J Sociol—American Journal of Sociology

Am Psychol—American Psychologist

Am Sci—American Scientist

Am Sociol R—American Sociological Review

An In Med—Annals of Internal Medicine

An Rec—Anatomical Record

An Rev Psych—Annual Review of Psychology

Arch Dis Child—Archives of Disorders in Children

Arch Gen Psych—Archives of General Psychiatry

Arch In Med—Archives of Internal Medicine

Beh Res Ther—Behavior Research and Therapy

Beh Sci—Behavioral Science

Beh T—Behavior Today

Beh Ther—Behavior Therapy

Brain

Brit J Psychol—British Journal of Psychology

Bull Am Acad Arts Sci—Bulletin of the American Academy of Arts and Sciences

Bull Narcotics—Bulletin on Narcotics

Can J Psych—Canadian Journal of Psychology

Child Develop—Child Development

Child Ed—Child Education

Children

Cog Psychol—Cognitive Psychology

Comp Psych—Comprehensive Psychiatry

Con Psych—Contemporary Psychology

CPAJ—Canadian Psychiatric Association Journal

Develop Psychol—Developmental Psychology

Ed PM—Educational and Psychological Measurement

EEG Clin—EEG Clinical Neurophysiology

El Clin Neur—Electroencephalography and Clinical Neurophysiology

EMM—Exerpta Medica Monograph

Ex Neur—Experimental Neurology

Fam Coord—Family Coordinator

Fed Pro—Federal Proceedings

Gerontologist

G Psych Mono—Genetic Psychology Monographs

Har Ed R—Harvard Educational Review

Headache

Hum—The Humanist

Hum Nat—Human Nature

Hum Relat—Human Relations

ISR Newsletter

JAACP—Journal of the American Academy of Child Psychology

J Abn—Journal of Abnormal and Social Psychology

J Abn Psychol—Journal of Abnormal Psychology

JAMA—Journal of the American Medical Association

J App Behav Anal—Journal of Applied Behavior Analysis

JCCP—Journal of Child Psychology and Psychiatry

JCFS—Journal of Comparative Family Studies

J Clin In—Journal of Clinical Investigations

J Com—Journal of Communication

J Com PP—Journal of Comparative and Physiological Psychology

J Com Psychol—Journal of Comparative Psychology

J Consult Clin Psychol—Journal of Consulting and Clinical Psychology

J Consult Psychol—Journal of Consulting Psychology

J Counsel Psychol—Journal of Counseling Psychology

J Ed Psychol—Journal of Educational Psychology

JESP—Journal of Experimental Social Psychology

J Exp An Beh—Journal of the Experimental Analysis of Behavior

J Exp Child—Journal of Experimental Child Psychology

J Exp Psychol (Gen)—Journal of Experimental Psychology: General

J Exp Psychol (Hum Learn Mem)—Journal of Experimental Psychology: Human Learning and Memory

J Genetic—Journal of Genetic Psychology

J Hi Ed—Journal of Higher Education

J Hist—Journal of the History of the Behavioral Sciences

J Marr Fam—Journal of Marriage and the Family

J Neur—Journal of Neurophysiology

J Neur NP—Journal of Neurology, Neurosurgery, and Psychiatry

JNMD—Journal of Nervous and Mental Diseases

J Nut—Journal of Nutrition

J Op—Journal of the Optical Society of America

J Pers—Journal of Personality

J Pers Soc Psychol—Journal of Personality and Social Psychology

J Phys—Journal of Physiology

J Psych—Journal of Psychology

J Psych Res—Journal of Psychiatric Research

J Psychol Res—Journal of Psycholinguistic Research

J Psychos Res—Journal of Psychosomatic Research

J Sex Res—Journal of Sex Research

J Soc Issues—Journal of Social Issues

J Soc Psychol—Journal of Social Psychology

J Verb Learn—Journal of Verbal Learning and Verbal Behavior

JYA—Journal of Youth and Adolescence

Journalism Q—Journalism Quarterly

Lang Soc—Language in Society

Mar Fam L—Marriage and Family Living

Mem Cog—Memory and Cognition

Mental Hygiene

Mono Am Sp—Monographs of the American Speech and Hearing Association

Mono Soc Res—Monographs of the Society for Research in Child Development

Mosaic

Nature

NRPB—Neuroscience Research Program Bulletin

Pediatrics

Ped Sem—Pedagogical Seminary

Percep—Perception and Psychophysics

Pharm Rev—Pharmacological Reviews

P Mono—Psychological Monographs

PMS—Perceptual Motor Skills

Pro Am Phil Soc—Proceedings of the American Philosophical Society

PSEBM—Proceedings of the Society for Experimental Biology and Medicine

Psych Bull—Psychological Bulletin

Psychiatry

Psych M—Psychological Monographs

Psychol R—Psychological Review

Psychol Rept—Psychological Reports

Psychom Mono—Psychometric Monographs

Psychon Sci—Psychonomic Science

Psychop—Psychopharmacologia

Psychophys—Psychophysiology

Psych RR—Psychiatric Research Reports

Psychos Med—Psychosomatic Medicine

Psychotherapy

Psych T—Psychology Today

Pub Opinion Q—Public Opinion Quarterly

Pub Pro Nat Acad Sci—Publication of the Proceedings of the National Academy of Science

R Can Psych—Review of Canadian Psychology

Sat Eve Post—Saturday Evening Post

Sat R—Saturday Review

School R—School Review

Sci Am—Scientific American
Science
Sem Psych—Seminars in Psychiatry
Sleep Res—Sleep Research
Sociometry
Soc Pol—Social Policy

Sov PP—Soviet Psychology and Psychiatry

UC Pub Psych—University of California Publications in Psychology

VGQ—Vocational Guidance Quarterly
Vita Humana

Yale JBM—Yale Journal of Biology and Medicine

Name and reference index

This index lists all the studies cited in the book by page number and also shows the page on which full bibliographical data will be found in the list of References and Acknowledgments. Thus "Abelson and Fishburn (1976), *311, 600*" means that the study is cited on page 311 and that the full reference will be found on page 600. The fact that the *311* is in italics indicates that the study is cited in an illustration. Where a full name is given, as in "Adler, Alfred, 450," the individual is discussed in the text.

R

Rabkin and Struening (1976), 415, 608

Radloff (unpublished Ph.D. dissertation, 1959), 522, 614

Radloff and Rae (1979), 418, 436, 609, 610

Raugh and Atkinson (1975), 157, 593

Reich (1976), 435, 609

Reich, Clayton, and Winokur (1969), 429, 609

Rhine and Pratt (1957), 307, 599

Riggs, et al. (1953), 256, 598

Riley and Walker (1978), 78, 589

Rizley (1978), 115, 590

Robbins (1971), 105, 589

Robertson (1977), 391, 392, 607

Robinson, F. P. (1961), 158, 593

Robinson, J. P. (1971), 529, 614

Rodin (unpublished study, 1972), 343, 602

Rodin, Elman, and Schachter (unpublished study, 1972), 343, 602

Rogers, Carl, 452–54, 453, 461, 532

Rogers (personal communication, 1969), 461, 611

Rosch (1973), 192, 595

Rosch (1977), 192, 595

Rosenhan (1966), 117, 590

Rosenhan (1970), 545, 616

Rosenthal (1970), 418, 608–09

Rosenthal (1972), 429, 609

Ross (1977), 534, 615

Ross, Amabile, and Steinmetz (1977), 534, 615

Ross, Lepper, and Hubbard (1975), 523, 614

Rozin and Kalat (1971), 120, 591

Rubin, J. Z., Provenzano, and Luria (1974), 389, 606

Rubin, V., and Comitas (1975), 312, 600

Rubin, Z. (1973), 506, 613

Rutherford and Mussen (1968), 545, 616

S

Sachs and Johnson (1976), 181, 594

Sackheim, Gur, and Saucy (1978), 329, 601

Sadacca, Ricciuti, and Swanson (1956), 365, 604

Salapatek and Kessen (1966), 289, 598

Sampson and Hancock (1967), 371, 605

Savage-Rumbaugh, Rumbaugh, and Boysen (1978), 188, 595

Sawrey, Conger, and Turrell (1956), 94, 589

Scarr (1969), 39, 587

Scarr and Weinberg (1976), 228, 597

Schachter (1959), 369, 604

Schachter (1971), 342, 342, 343, 602, 603

Schachter and Gross (1968), 342, 602

Schachter and Singer (1962), 335, 601

Schank (1973), 194, 595

Schapiro and Vukovich (1970), 71, 589

Scheibel, et al. (1975), 78, 589

Schemmel, Michelsen, and Gill (1970), 343, 603

Schildkraut (1969), 58, 417, 588, 608

Schlesinger (1970), 506, 613

Schwartz (1970), 545, 616

Schwartz (unpublished study, 1973), 310, 600

Schwartz, et al. (1974), 417, 608

Sears (1967), 531, 615

Secord and Backman (1964), 515, 613

Seidenberg, Robert, 396–97

Seidenberg (1970), 397, 607

Sekuler and Levinson (1977), 288, 598

Seligman (1971), 120, 591

Selye, Hans, 412, 413, 416–17

Selye (1956), 413, 608

Selye (1976), 338, 602, 608

Serbin and O'Leary (1975), 390, 607

Serbin, et al. (1973), 390, 606

Shaffer (1947), 326, 601

Shapiro, et al. (1969), 36, 587

Sherman (1973), 380, 606

Shiffrin and Atkinson (1969), 131, 132, 591

Silberman (1970), 116, 590

Simon, Berger, and Gagnon (1972), 355, 604, 613

Simons and Rosenberg (1975), 392, 607

Sims, et al. (1968), 344, 603

Sjoberg and Hollister (1965), 312, 600

Skeels (1966), 231, 597

Skinner, B. F., 30–31, 31, 98–99, 101, 102

Skinner (1938), 99, 589

Skinner (1957), 185, 595

Skinner (1971), 11, 31, 587

Skolnick and Skolnick (1974), 396, 607

Slaby, Quarforth, and McConnachie (1976), 374, 605

Slobin (1971), 184, 594

Slobin (1973), 184, 594

Smith (1926), 180, 594

Snow (1972), 184, 595

Snow, et al. (1976), 181, 594

Snyder (1977), 50, 588

Subject index

(Page numbers in *italics* refer to illustrations.)